SIMON & SCHUSTER

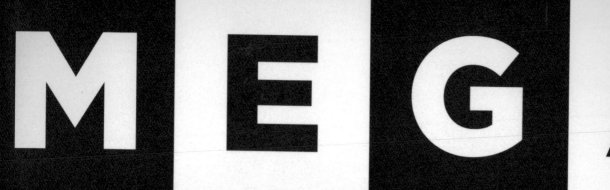

MEGA

CROSSWORD PUZZLE BOOK

#21

THE BIGGEST AND BEST SERIES FROM THE ORIGINAL CROSSWORD PUBLISHER

FEATURING
300
ALL-NEW
PUZZLES!

EASY-TO-USE
PERFORATED
PAGES

EDITED BY JOHN M. SAMSON

SIMON & SCHUSTER MEGA CROSSWORD PUZZLE BOOK

Series 21

300 never-before-published crosswords

Edited by John M. Samson

Gallery Books

New York   London   Toronto   Sydney   New Delhi

Gallery Books
An Imprint of Simon & Schuster, Inc.
1230 Avenue of the Americas
New York, NY 10020

First Gallery Books trade paperback edition September 2021

GALLERY BOOKS and colophon are registered trademarks of Simon & Schuster, Inc.

For information about special discounts for bulk purchases, please contact Simon & Schuster Special Sales at 1-866-506-1949 or business@simonandschuster.com.

The Simon & Schuster Speakers Bureau can bring authors to your live event. For more information or to book an event, contact the Simon & Schuster Speakers Bureau at 1-866-248-3049 or visit our website at www.simonspeakers.com.

Designed by Sam Bellotto Jr.

Manufactured in the United States of America

10 9 8 7 6 5 4 3 2 1

ISBN 978-1-9821-5700-5

COMPLETE ANSWERS WILL BE FOUND AT THE BACK.

FOREWORD

TITLE SEARCH by Harvey Estes

Each of the following sentences contains a one-word movie title spread across two or more words. The year of the movie appears in parenthesis.

 Example: I wonder if the extra lad dined with the other boys. (1992)
Answer: Extr**A LAD DIN**ed.

1. We told Sonja, "W.S. Gilbert is the best librettist." (1975)

2. The data in the memorandum bore no resemblance to truth. (2019)

3. When you get a little tipsy, choose a designated driver. (1960)

4. Dinner at Mama's was always a meal I enjoyed. (1979)

5. He's the introvert I goaded into coming to the party. (1958)

6. I have relatives in Idaho, Oklahoma, Maine, and Nevada. (1991)

7. Few zoos in Japan have a gator or a croc, Kyoto is the exception. (1976)

8. Do not brag and highlight your own accomplishments. (1982)

9. I come from Cuba bearing good news. (1995)

10. In days long gone, two RKOs were the theaters in our town. (1976)

11. The diva made ushers of her entourage. (1984)

The Margaret Award winner is THEATER IN THE ROUND by Elizabeth C. Gorski.

JOHN M. SAMSON

11 COMPLAIN, COMPLAIN by Jordan P. Conway

45 Down was also a pseudonym of Jonathan Swift.

ACROSS

1 Red-tag events
6 Monopoly square
10 Black belt's blow
14 Deal involving draft picks, maybe
15 Ritz-Carlton competitor
16 Where "you are," on a mall map
17 Short boot on the gridiron
19 2012 Ben Affleck thriller
20 Email saving
21 College football trophy
23 Basis for a civil suit
25 Straps on Santa's sleigh
26 Hidden stockpiles
30 Woodwind section member
33 Steer clear of
34 Victimizes, with "on"
35 2008 Soderbergh biopic
38 Lady's mate
39 "Heartbreak ___": Presley
40 Talk big
41 Rustic stopover
42 Prepare to advance on a fly ball
43 Flirt with
44 Novel postscript
46 Peanut, in Dixie
47 Composer Previn
49 Like breezeways
51 Left-leaning
54 Dress rehearsal
59 "Concord Sonata" composer
60 Chubby bird of the western plains
62 Borscht ingredient
63 Henrique of the NHL
64 Underdog win
65 Useful data, briefly
66 Identifies, slangily
67 Sown things

DOWN

1 "Not so fast!"
2 River through Pisa
3 Bonny girl
4 Change, as crossword clues
5 Feeling no pain
6 Suitless card
7 "What ___, chopped liver?"
8 Screen dimension unit
9 Facebook icon
10 Goes after
11 Shell-seeking crustacean
12 Hammond B-3, notably
13 Hacienda drudges of old
18 They may clash
22 Showy spring bloom
24 Resort island off Haiti
26 Left Coast state, informally
27 Scentini fragrance maker
28 March 17 fare
29 Kept under wraps
31 Smoke alarm sound
32 Elzie Segar's Olive
34 Miz Beaver's friend
36 Pull a fast one on, slangily
37 Still-life pitcher
39 Holbrook of "Into the Wild"
40 Boardroom VIP
42 Stadium seating level
43 Tru Kids, previously
45 Magician's utterance
46 Eldest of the Brady boys
47 Perp's cover story
48 David of "Separate Tables"
50 Tabloids twosomes
52 "Quickly," on memos
53 Put on, as cargo
55 Booze it up
56 Scammer's ploy
57 Like most garage sale goods
58 Court dividers
61 Practical joker's bit

Filled grid (handwritten):

Row 1: SALES | JAIL | CHOP
Row 2: TRADE | OMNI | HERE
Row 3: ONSIDEKICK | ARGO
Row 4: POSTAGE | HEISMAN
Row 5: TORP | REINS
Row 6: CACHES | OBOIST
Row 7: AVOID | PREYS | CHE
Row 8: LORD | HOTEL | CROW
Row 9: INN | TAGUP | TEASE
Row 10: EPILOG | GOOBER
Row 11: ANDRE | AIRY
Row 12: LIBERAL | TESTRUN
Row 13: IVES | SAGEGROUSE
Row 14: BEET | ADAM | UPSET
Row 15: INFO | PEGS | SEEDS

The answer to 61 Across may surprise you.

ACROSS

1 Gravy holders
6 Mixed-grill assortment
11 Country club figure
14 Be of the same mind
15 Lacking a tenant
16 Bunsen burner locale
17 Rockies–Andes line
19 Noon or midnight follower
20 "Moby-Dick," e.g.
21 Like a roughneck
23 Sinuous swimmer
24 Confession list
26 Word before pill or rally
29 Supply-side policies of the '80s
35 Starts the bidding
37 Laura of "Wild"
38 Leave off
39 Go it alone
40 Toddlers' taboos
41 Do some practice rounds
42 Blissful spot in Genesis
43 Chip-shot club
44 Farm machinery name
45 "Three's Company" pub
48 The Clintons studied it
49 Papal ceremony
50 SASE, e.g.
52 Baffling puzzle
55 Spanish veil
60 Fruit picker in 42 Across
61 Santa Fe resident
64 Shirt with a picture
65 Like city real estate, usually
66 In short supply
67 Put a stop to
68 Touches on
69 P's value in Scrabble

DOWN

1 Porters' burdens
2 Kid-lit meanie
3 Line of work
4 Flirt with, perhaps
5 Volleyball positions
6 Sierra Club founder
7 Be begrudging of
8 Thrilla in Manila winner
9 Danson of "Fargo"
10 Fuel in tins
11 What driftbreakers do
12 Currency in Cape Town
13 Comply with
18 Big name in pineapples
22 Diffuse slowly, as through a membrane
24 Pacific islands wrap
25 Roadside stopovers
26 Baffling puzzle
27 Lyric poem written in couplets
28 Co-owner of the Pequod
30 Really goes for
31 Salami choice
32 Drive forward
33 "Oh" R&B artist
34 Scatter, as confetti
36 Anonymous
40 Quill points
44 Crown maker
46 Latino pride organization
47 Passion Sunday's period
51 Easy job
52 Mayor Buttigieg
53 Cooking Channel fixture
54 Farm supply bagful
55 Get some face time with
56 Added stipulations
57 Deceitful sort
58 Liverpool's Penny ___
59 Penny-___
62 Rip off
63 Maned antelope

13 DOGGING IT by Michael Collins
63 Across is named after an English explorer.

ACROSS

1 Ungentlemanly sorts
5 Trumpet or guitar effect
9 Quid pro quo deals
14 Cookie deep-fried at fairs
15 McGregor in "American Pastoral"
16 Off limits
17 Canoe material
19 Knitwear synthetic
20 Head-butting beast
21 In need of salting
22 Caddies
24 Noncontiguous U.S. state
26 Guy, informally
27 Hermann who wrote "Siddhartha"
29 Beanery patrons
33 Inca Trail land
36 Hardy's "pure woman"
38 "Frasier" terrier
39 Provide a fake alibi for, say
40 Brief spat
42 Walk like an egret
43 Chekhov uncle
45 "Nothin' ___!" ("Forget it!")
46 Blood moon, to some
47 "Bewitched" witch
49 Prefix meaning "straight"
51 "I'm In" singer Keith
53 Tested the weight of
57 Valediction, e.g.
60 Suffix with auction
61 ___ broche (on a skewer)
62 Cafeteria stack
63 Ottawa Islands lo...
66 Co... victim
67 Sum... Olym...
68 Salt La... y ski reso...
69 Pedomet... u...
70 Pinta's sis... hi...
71 McJob train... often

DOWN

1 Hooded serpent
2 Sans serif typeface
3 Stuffed deli delicacy
4 Liberal arts maj.
5 Online media events
6 Touring, say
7 Domain of Mars
8 Joint in a shackle
9 One dropping a dime
10 Organization's basic structure
11 Far from inept
12 Lame, as excuses go
13 Three of the Brady Bunch
18 Do a nature walk
23 Getting up there
25 "Zip it!"
26 Bedeck with flowers
28 Tidbit for a titmouse
30 Cheese with a wax crust
31 Splash Mountain, e.g.
32 In the public eye
33 Apply blacktop to
34 Abba of Israel
35 Rip violently
37 Kool-Aid directions word
41 Where flotsam floats
44 Hauls
48 Core m... 'es, for short
50 Goat's an... sis, in sports
52 Ghostly pale
54 Pool hall fixt...
55 Please no end
56 Moshe of Israel
57 24-hr. cash sources
58 "Fiddlesticks!"
59 Have the backbone
60 Blissful spot
64 News agency initials since 1958
65 D.C. MLBer

14 "GOLLY!" by Jonathan H. Brill
We'll let you answer the question posed at 37 Across.

ACROSS

1 Hayride bundle
5 Amos Alonzo ____ Award
10 J. Edgar's agents
14 Muckraker Tarbell et al.
15 Arroz con ____
16 Viking letter
17 American crossover SUV
19 Sheepskin boots from Down Under
20 Balkan capital
21 Supermodel Sastre
23 "Beat it, buster!"
24 Isaac Asimov classic
25 Richard Gere title role
26 Toronto–Quebec dir.
27 Prefix for cue
28 Article in "El Sol"
30 More insolent
32 Elect to the Hall of Fame
36 Blade used only in water
37 "Have you figured out the theme yet?" response?
41 Fuss
42 Shrugs, e.g.
44 Red or green fruit
47 Chang of Ravenclaw
48 Fraulein's grandma
49 Brief moment
50 Word from the bleachers
52 Cursed
55 Toque, for one
56 ____ Oosh, Washington
58 Bo Diddley song covered by the Yardbirds
59 Sacha Baron Cohen persona
61 "Esquire" rival
63 Laughfest
64 In litigation
65 Barely makes
66 Stained Tiffany unit
67 Shorebirds
68 Energy efficient lights

DOWN

1 A good thing to hit
2 Looking up to
3 Native American sport
4 Foundation abbr.
5 Young herring
6 Rocky peak
7 Half a Basque game
8 Good witch of Oz
9 Dead duck
10 "Despicable Me" villain
11 Played to the audience
12 Fire vehicle
13 Empty ____
18 Ambient music pioneer
22 Narrow seaway
28 Wildcats of the NCAA
29 Horse sound
31 Language that gave us "guru"
33 Junker
34 Contract add-ons
35 Oympic skater Midori
36 Gives the go-ahead
38 Thomas A. Anderson's alias
39 Tyson's ring name
40 Put down
43 Melancholy
44 A flat alternative
45 Objects used as teaching aids
46 Movie director's cue
47 British bank draft
51 Inner turmoil
52 Taye on "Private Practice"
53 Doc bloc
54 Yiddish luck
57 Mideast bigwig
60 Former AT&T rival
62 Taylor of women's clothing

15 ADVICE FROM MISS MANNERS   by Jonathan H. Brill
... and that advice can be found at 38 Across.

ACROSS

1 Anna of "True Blood"
7 Testimonial gift
13 Transparency
16 Toshiro in "1941"
17 Pedantic
18 Prefix for cumulus
19 Modern fireplace fixture
21 Commotion
22 "No details, pls!"
24 French floors
26 "Sprechen ___ Deutsch?"
27 NFL Hall-of-Famer Dawson
29 "Baby, it's cold outside"
30 iPhone download
33 Calydonian boar huntress
36 Painter Modigliani
38 Advice from Miss Manners?
40 Muncie univ.
41 Exiles
42 Lead-in to how or body
43 Caddie's handout
45 Source of gluten
46 Thumbs-down votes
47 1970s acronym for a cohabitant
49 Photoshop file
50 Astigmatic view
52 Pope who wrote "Commentaries"
55 Anodized, e.g.
57 School spirit group
61 Come up with
62 Written laws
63 Nucelar physics units
64 Mary Jordan's "___ of Her Deal"

DOWN

1 Rorqual school
2 Bee prefix
3 Math proof trigram
4 Sushi eel
5 Peruvian of old
6 Aerialist savers
7 Late hrs.
8 Puppy's sib
9 Jackson 5 dos
10 College campus area
11 "Render ___ Caesar . . ."
12 Job-ad letters
14 Rogue character?
15 Sporran wearer
20 Yak
22 Renaissance man
23 With spite
25 Like the Dealey Plaza knoll
26 Bossa nova kin
27 Inters
28 Cyber-messages
30 Aftermarket options
31 Starbuck's ship
32 Facebook comments
34 "Bad" cholesterol
35 Compass doodle
37 Tennis center?
39 Inlaid flooring
44 Psychic power
47 Yeltsin's successor
48 "Loose" ship sinkers
49 Umbrage
50 Coleur in the French flag
51 Big Island flow of 2018
53 Dispute
54 Neck of land: Abbr.
55 Straightaway
56 Traffic cops?
58 Drama coach Hagen
59 FDR's wife
60 It ends in Nov.

16 "GET MOVING!" by Jim Holland
An alternate title can be found at 63 Across.

ACROSS

1 Bring in a tarpon, say
5 Cover story
10 Part of CD-ROM
14 "Dies ___" (hymn)
15 Enter forcefully
16 Couture magazine
17 Handy food storage items
19 Queens stadium
20 "Surfing the Zeitgeist" novelist
21 Legislative output
23 Type of matrix
26 Like Pierce's presidency
27 The agony of defeat
32 "Casino Royale" actress
33 Frescoist Andrea del ___
38 Chevy hybrid
39 ___ of time
42 Come around again
43 Beach Boys' "Catch ___"
45 Don't blink first
47 Catwalker
50 Frequently true
54 Where grass roots
55 Pilots' wear
57 Brought-back products
62 Ritual vestments
63 What rabbits are noted for/TITLE
66 Stir up
67 ___ nonsense
68 Not long
69 Ice Capades leap
70 "Question Mark Guy" of infomercials
71 "Terrible" stage

DOWN

1 Ortiz in "Fear the Walking Dead"
2 Like Northern Africa
3 Big name in auto parts
4 Where to buy a wrap
5 Semicircle
6 Kennel favorite
7 "___ restless as a willow . . ."
8 "Dumbo" setting
9 Nuts
10 Subdivide
11 Select
12 ___ ego
13 Belief in a "watchmaker God"
18 Command
22 Hardy heroine
24 Wordsworth works
25 Sheeran's "___ Team"
27 Hindu deity
28 Declare
29 Casa room
30 "Love It or List It" network
31 Presently showing
34 Four-part harmony section
35 Word in Crosby/Hope movie titles
36 Sped
37 Ampera, for one
40 Two-part
41 Eyelid woe
44 Sea eagles
46 Like brainiacs
48 Handy
49 Work on a score
50 "GWTW" family name
51 Cat of cartoons
52 Card ___
53 Ford fiasco
56 Retired NY jets
58 Manhattan river
59 Stern counterpart
60 Scoreless tie
61 1040 figs.
64 Shatner's sci-fi drug
65 "Full" sign

ACROSS

1 Horse for Lawrence
5 Couch potato
9 "Salud!"
14 Spy of a sort
15 Hawaiian coffee region
16 Draftsman's tool
17 Women's wear no longer in fashion?
19 "SNL" alum Cheri
20 Start of a case
21 DeLuise in "Wholly Moses"
22 "___ Gold" (Fonda film)
23 Insult, slangily
25 Old film dog
27 Hot liturgical garment?
32 Type of processor
36 Mauna___
37 Follow
38 Spoke hoarsely
40 Hack
41 Finished in a way
43 1773 Boston Harbor jetsam
44 Oil, in a way
46 Gets by hook or by crook
47 Wrigley Field climber
48 Web-footed shorebird
49 Informants no longer needed?
52 Rhames in "Dawn of the Dead"
54 Promoter of firearm safety
55 World Economic Forum host city
58 Preston powder room
61 Get around
65 To no ___ (in vain)
66 Presently popular writers?
68 Step daintily
69 Artsy-craftsy site
70 Spruce
71 Los Angeles couple
72 "On the ___ again . . ."
73 Moonwalker Cernan

DOWN

1 "Cornflake Girl" singer Tori
2 Defeat decisively
3 Edmonton loc.
4 Abutting
5 Do wedelns
6 Voldemort's title
7 Golden Rule word
8 Meter reader
9 Rainbow, for one
10 Obsolete ordinances?
11 Away from the wind
12 Withered
13 Shailene's "Divergent" role
18 Bella Swan portayer Stewart
24 "Finding Nemo" director
26 Attach in a way
27 ___ ease (restive)
28 Nary a soul
29 Contrail
30 Prefix for life or wife
31 Super Tuesday word
33 Ocular nerve
34 Superman portrayer
35 Launch times
39 One dismissing all doubts
42 Coifs
45 Popular spokesperson?
50 Less appealing
51 Stark ___ mad
53 New York pucksters, familiarly
55 Julie Andrews' title
56 Enterprise rival
57 HOV lane traffic
59 Aware of
60 Greek peak
62 "One clover, and ___ . . .": Dickinson
63 Brown VIP
64 Ferrara ducal family
67 Charisse in "Brigadoon"

18 CONFESSION OF AN ORACLE by Roland Huget
. . . and that oracle can be found at 51 Across.

ACROSS

1 California valley
5 Hobbits' home
10 Shoot up
14 Dumpster output
15 Scrabble pieces
16 "S.O.S." group
17 Composer Bartok
18 Elite squad
19 Swag
20 **Part 1 of quote**
23 Feedbag morsel
25 ____-Man
26 Caravan stops
27 **Part 2 of quote**
32 Not scratch resistant?
33 Lowly worker
34 Ho-hum
35 Ham it up
37 Asian cuisine
41 ___ Stic pen
42 Executive group
43 **Part 3 of quote**
47 Cut of meat
49 "Alice" waitress
50 Place to sweat
51 **Source of quote**
56 1998 Sarah McLachlan hit
57 Cathedral focal point
58 Blarney Castle's land
61 Land in "The King and I"
62 Puerto Rican harbor
63 Self-satisfied
64 URL starter
65 Charger
66 Utah lily

6 The latest, in gadgets
7 Holly genus
8 "Weed 'em and ___"?
9 Salinger girl
10 Snack dips
11 Wind player
12 Outranking
13 Motel postings
21 ___-daisy
22 New York is a proper one
23 Medical suffix
24 Pilot starter
28 Even if, briefly
29 Geological time span
30 However
31 Coffee, slangily
35 Caribou cousin
36 Wire part
37 Excessively
38 Punt stat
39 Ground troops
40 Footnote word
41 Blast furnace fuel
42 Lodge org.
43 Rodeo rope
44 Highway access
45 Rub out
46 Bruce Wayne's butler
47 Surge of seawater
48 Threw in the towel
52 Day care time-outs
53 Sop up
54 "Thinking Ahead" reader
55 Mrs. Dick Tracy
59 Weaver's work
60 Couch topic

DOWN

1 Noggin
2 Fruit drink
3 Blood sport, according to some
4 Show horse
5 2020 ___-home order

19 CROSS-COUNTRY RUN   by Roland Huget

16 Across is also the name of an Alfred Hitchcock thriller.

ACROSS

1 Fusion, for one
6 NYC sports radio station
10 Interview exam
14 Separate
15 Perry's lake
16 Double Dutch need
17 1998 Robin Williams role
19 "Yeah, right"
20 Give out, as jobs
21 Hotel units
22 Noah's second son
24 It aligns numbers on the screen
27 Spanish girlfriends
30 "___ to Watch Over Me"
31 Mideast peninsula
32 "Atlantic City" director
34 Metric meteorological unit
39 Thorns in the side
40 "Rubber Duckie" singer
42 Materializes
46 Mom's deflecting advice
47 Enamel, e.g.
50 Apteryx relative
51 Jousting tool
52 Bottom margin
55 Forever-day connector
56 Isthmus/TITLE
60 Line holder for a cast
61 Lotion additive
62 Literary twist
63 To be, to Jacques
64 Zoo staffers
65 Smooth transition in conversation

DOWN

1 Syrup source
2 MPH-rating org.
3 Uncover trends for marketing
4 Flight paths
5 High degrees
6 Serving of cake
7 Swiss denomination
8 "Fire!" preceder
9 Classic Nintendo game console
10 Colorful songbird
11 "Mr. ___" (1983 Styx hit)
12 Tarzan moniker
13 Leaves alone
18 Helps out
21 Pharaoh in Exodus
22 Dines on
23 In the thick of
25 British ___
26 Gangster's gal
28 Funny bit
29 Edwards or Vandenberg
32 Smart set
33 Top gun
35 Tombstone marshal
36 Rub the wrong way
37 Long shot
38 Burma's 1939 neighbor
41 URL ending
42 Shining brightly
43 "Daily" Metropolis paper
44 Mull over
45 A major one has four sharps
46 Small progress
48 "___ For You": Newton-John
49 Connection points
53 "Divergent" heroine
54 Land of poets
56 Little john

57 Stein filler
58 Maned antelope
59 Spud bud

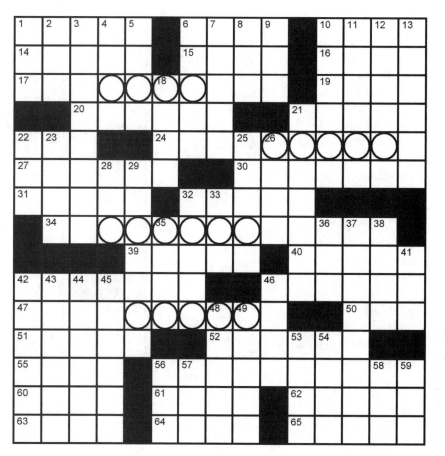

20 THEMELESS by Harvey Estes
Dumb joke alert for 1 and 45 Across!

ACROSS

1 45 Across, as a video blogger?
9 Took after
15 Conditionally released
16 Steal cattle
17 Like the Tacoma Dome
18 "Honey, ___": Shania Twain
19 McKellen of "Apt Pupil"
20 Radiator output
22 Scratched
23 They make you think
26 Press and more
29 To this day
30 Listing
32 Miss Universe, for one
37 "Garfield" cat
38 Bull sound
39 Takes to the station, e.g.
41 Begin, for example
42 Provo resident
44 Peru native
45 "Toy Story" toy
50 King who married Jezebel
51 By the book
52 BMOC, e.g.
55 Lake Erie port
57 Gives up
60 He made light work
61 Overdoes the criticism
62 Go back on one's word
63 Most unyielding

DOWN

1 Boo-Boo's buddy
2 ___-Day vitamins
3 Informed about
4 Tiny bit
5 Script ending
6 Start of a dance
7 Snob
8 Not long past
9 Where evidence is studied
10 Sound system noise
11 McCourt's "Angela's ___"
12 Keep the home fires burning
13 Dr. Hartman of "Family Guy"
14 Some Monopoly cards
21 Take it from me
23 Takes the bait
24 Ball game cancellation
25 Birthplace of Albert Camus
26 "Serpico" author
27 French I verb
28 Cartoon chipmunk
31 Not watched
33 Tufted-tail antelope
34 Trump impersonator Baldwin
35 Emeril's Big Easy restaurant
36 Jack or Diane, on "Black-ish"
40 Destiny
41 Be a resident of
43 "___ Heroes"
45 Caesar's mom
46 Part of URI
47 Monty Python alum
48 Having a lot to lose
49 Send to seventh heaven
52 Viva ___
53 They're kept in pens
54 "Do you want to hear a secret?"
56 Spot, for one
58 "All Things Considered" network
59 Ear irritator

21 THEMELESS by Harvey Estes

ABC and CNN used 14 Down as their theme for Hurricane Katrina coverage.

ACROSS

1 Truman Capote wore one
10 Madras mister
15 Gets used (to)
16 Out on a limb
17 "Not true!"
18 Say without thinking
19 Role model
20 Flippable top
21 Like favorite radio stations
22 Ceramic floor piece
24 Takeout option
25 "The Plague" novelist
28 Cotton alternative
30 Paramedic's skill
31 Thinks out loud
33 Spreadsheet entries
34 City near Tel Aviv
35 Cathedral nook
36 Instrument with hammers
38 Malone of "Stepmom"
39 Middle X, e.g.
40 Spiritual, e.g.
41 Like diner spoons?
43 ABBA drummer Brunkert
44 Shades
46 Moorehead on "Bewitched"
47 Buckles on
49 Sharp pain
51 Reel people
52 Honey holder
53 Davenport site
57 Riesling relative
58 Unkind kind of letter
60 Tenor role in "Porgy and Bess"
61 Scratch test giver
62 Long tales
63 Business worth

DOWN

1 Way to go
2 Dull discomfort
3 Cape Fear loc.
4 Remedy for wild pitches?
5 Ed.'s input
6 In the least
7 More religious than thou
8 During the course of
9 Half a fly
10 Angel in "Charlie's Angels"
11 "Home Improvement" star
12 Tidy up the place
13 As a reply
14 Goo Goo Dolls song of 2005
21 Shutterbug
23 British verb suffix
24 Printer's blue
25 Suit of armor ensignia
26 Blue Ridge Mountains locale
27 One cause of a Broadway bomb
29 Folk saying
32 Some flatware
37 Homes away from home
38 Denim leggings
40 Sound purchases?
42 Tried to get elected
45 Gone bad
48 Neighbor of Fiji
50 Totally befuddled
52 Barbershop sight
54 Ron Howard role
55 Wagon train's direction
56 Formicary residents
58 Bad review
59 "Grey's Anatomy" sets

ACROSS

1 Taciturn
11 Nightclub in a Manilow song
15 Congregation
16 "Yeah, right!"
17 Spruce
18 Dundee denizen
19 Barrier breaker of old
20 Without wasted words
21 River to the English Channel
22 Early Briton
23 Artist of a sort
25 Cool, once
28 "Let's get crackin'!"
29 Pig tail
30 Riders pull them
31 Turns over
32 Astronomical altar
33 One in your corner
34 Doctoral hurdle
35 Redding of notes
36 Like Leroy Brown
37 Scoreboard fixture
38 Helped the economy?
39 ___ Croix, Quebec
40 Take a chance
41 Furniture care brand
42 It helps circulation
44 Nile menace
45 Yawning, perhaps
46 Sarge's superior
48 Cone starter
51 "What's ___ for me?"
52 Campus gathering place
54 Diplomatic trait
55 Spoke well
56 Sommer of film
57 Mercury et al.

DOWN

1 Confesses, with "up"
2 Them, to us
3 Toga party venue
4 Mass. setting
5 Chat room "Like I care!"
6 With good judgment
7 Victor Vasarely's genre
8 Sales staff
9 Dairy powder
10 1040 digits
11 Sized up (the joint)
12 Behaved like some fans
13 At the forefront
14 Lingering sensation
21 "Brady Bunch" threesome
22 Rabbit fur
24 "Stupid me!"
25 Snacks
26 Having a connection
27 Offshore rig structure
28 Typewriter sound
31 Freezing depth
34 Lena of "Chocolat"
35 Drilling org.
37 Street acceptance, in slang
38 Alabama slammer ingredient
41 "Purple Rain" singer
43 Sporty Chevy, briefly
44 Change
47 Tedious task
48 Stuff to the gills
49 NY Met or LA Dodger
50 Discontinued GM line
52 "Oh! ___ Golden Slippers"
53 Old crone

23 THEMELESS by Marie Langley
29 Down comes from the setting of a footrace.

ACROSS

1 Obsessive need for news
10 Platter players
15 Yarn spinners
16 Range maker
17 Concern for one in the fast lane
18 Latin music
19 British fashion magazine
20 Long in the field of acting
22 Smooth-talking
23 Country renamed in 1939
25 Made swirls
27 Office squawk source
31 Browning piece
33 End of a Flintstone yell
34 Library volume
36 Union general at Gettysburg
37 Willingly
39 Barbershop band
41 Let go of
42 Adlai's 1956 slate mate
44 Polar bear prey
46 Cost-of-living stat
47 Go back over
49 Drew quickly
51 Like liters
53 "Gravity" singer Bareilles
54 Korean border river
55 Flag pin site
57 Persian ruler
61 "Ran" director Kurosawa
63 Tom Cruise facial feature
65 Keep getting
66 Reef explorer
67 Code subject
68 Use abbr. lang.

DOWN

1 Pt. of MIT
2 Mondavi Winery locale
3 Fingerboard ridge
4 Threat words
5 Dessert wine
6 Turns on
7 Easter prefix
8 Tehran's locale
9 Degree of easiness
10 Laughter syllables
11 Pictured mentally
12 Sole problem
13 Private 411
14 Jerry's car in "Seinfeld"
21 Spots on the TV screen
24 Drops off
26 Perignon, for one
27 Do-nothing
28 Vuvuzela, for one
29 Follow orders
30 Stable females
32 Neither hot nor cold
35 Relaxes in the tub
38 Regular newspaper columns
40 Affable
43 Belarus, prev.
45 Leaves high and dry
48 Fruit drink
50 Mint look-alike
52 Doomed
54 Barbecue area
56 Bonnet brim
58 Gad about
59 Cruising
60 Exec extra
62 "How cute!" exclamations
64 Be social

24 THEMELESS by Ben Gibbs
In 1988, 6 Down was inducted into the International Tennis Hall of Fame.

ACROSS

1 Shooting enthusiast
11 Dundee dweller
15 Verdi opera
16 Fine-tune
17 About a body in a belt
18 Sherman Hemsley sitcom
19 Datebook abbr.
20 Some hosp. workers
21 Mr. Big
23 Wrist injury, maybe
25 Left Bank artery
26 Feel dizzy
31 Radical '60s org.
32 Some football plays
35 Yellow hue
36 Carrier to Oslo
37 Big name in oil
38 Part of the Mass
39 Robust
40 Psyche segments
41 Congo tongue
42 Funny Milton
43 Funny Margaret
44 Charm
46 Purity unit
48 Silage
52 Dramatic success
55 Cologne article
56 Suffix with duct
57 2001 biopic about Murdoch
58 Kabuki, for one
61 Dietrich of "The Practice"
62 Washed with chemicals
63 High-strung
64 They make tracks

DOWN

1 Sled parts
2 Invites to the penthouse
3 Unmitigated
4 Italian prime
5 Hangs back
6 Tennis star Goolagong
7 Queens park name
8 Good, ironically, in slang
9 Place for Young men?
10 Unit of laughter
11 Slight variation
12 Communist Party official
13 Everybody
14 Vols or Titans
22 NEA or NRA
24 Venom source
27 Point of view
28 First extra inning
29 "My Cherie ___": Wonder
30 Howard of "American Graffiti"
32 Ability to ignore verbal attacks
33 Like Lucy
34 Putting in piles
38 Give the ax to
39 In custody
41 Old Testament character
42 What gentlemen prefer?
45 Where some wander far
47 Chemical analysis
49 Steak style
50 Animated Fudd
51 Makes out
53 Racetrack info
54 Get bent
55 A word from Pilate
59 Pahrump, Nevada's county
60 Hamelin critter

25 THEMELESS by Harvey Estes
The tiger also is now 17 Across.

ACROSS

1 The basic facts
11 In doubt
15 Not finished
16 Highly unusual
17 Like the Amur leopard
18 Pub round
19 Deducts from wages
20 In need of recharging
22 Permit
23 Snaky swimmers
26 Abstract sculpture
28 Part of the cardiac cycle
32 Key with one sharp
33 Monogamous partner count
34 Hulled wheat
36 Diet lunch
37 Greek treat
39 Caught sight of
41 Bubbly beverage
42 Rude folks
44 Petruchio, e.g.
46 "Oy" follower
47 Former building
49 Hose attachments
51 Whiteboard needs
53 Being broadcast
54 Direct deposit: Abbr.
55 I additions
57 Hopkins of "Gimme a Break!"
61 Irish lower house
63 Sworn out-of-court testimony
66 Behold, in Bologna
67 Maleficent motive
68 Staff symbol
69 Tide and others

DOWN

1 Extorted money from
2 Gambling city
3 Family-aid org.
4 Tomato supports
5 Sights in the western sky
6 "Star Trek: ___"
7 Drink suffix
8 Line to an outlet
9 Strike zone edge
10 Composed
11 SEP, e.g.
12 Porter's "Let's do it . . ." suggestion
13 Red Skelton's Freddie, for one
14 Old times
21 Blocks up
24 Chops (off)
25 Got some shut-eye
27 Jaundice
28 AKC registrant
29 Pushy
30 Plane stunts
31 Howe of sewers
35 Metronome speed
38 Eyes, to Shelley
40 Laura of "Recount"
43 Musher's vehicle
45 Snitch's activity
48 Ate into
50 "ER" actress Freeman
52 "King Tut" singer Martin
56 Kind of curl
58 Property right
59 Peak in les Alpes
60 Sugar bowl team?
62 Worldly fate
64 Fronton cheer
65 Richard Branson's title

26 CAKE MIX   by Patrick Jordan
"Scary group?" would be another clue for 17 Across.

ACROSS

1 Reveal indiscreetly
5 Capital on Africa's north coast
10 Like die-hard supporters
14 Count starter in Cologne
15 Soft palate dangler
16 "The Bachelor" bestowal
17 "Wannabe" group
19 Code-cracker Turing
20 Smash beyond repair
21 Sheltered, at sea
22 Picks up at the store
23 Celia Cruz music
25 Salt or sand particle
27 The Venus de Milo, e.g.
32 Sites with saunas
35 Chinese spiritual path
36 Powerless to move
37 Carried the day
38 Form-filling
41 Serpentine road section
42 Longhorn's gridiron rival
44 Get behind on bills
45 Hospital meal carrier
46 Shylock's demand
50 Grumpy's expression
51 Soil from a garden center
54 Instinctive sense, for short
56 West Coast wine valley
59 Ice skate securers
61 Locale of a garden snake?
62 Shower alternative
64 Tops for Bart Simpson
65 Ahead by a point
66 Madison Avenue award
67 Word before room or bet
68 Construction zone cone
69 Dropped into a mailbox

DOWN

1 Deserving the blue ribbon
2 Weight-loss surgeries, informally
3 "Sweet Love" singer Baker
4 Strands, as a sailboat
5 Snug bug's venue
6 Active footwear brand
7 1959 Oscar recipient Ives
8 Charge without evidence
9 Electrode firers
10 Relating to Riyadh's land
11 Peace Corps enlistee
12 Londoner's "Lordy!"
13 Bear lairs
18 Idina's "Frozen" role
24 Commedia dell'___
26 End in ___ (draw)
28 Reprimand to Rover
29 "You have a ___ nerve!"
30 Major or Minor preceder
31 Craft-shopping website
32 Give-and-take transaction
33 Springy sort of stick
34 High-grade burger meat
38 Update the motif
39 Cobbler's poker
40 Tangerine discard
43 Fragrant smoke
45 Preschool study
47 Confesses, colloquially
48 Elephant's ear description
49 UGG's underside
52 Delicatessen device
53 Take effect by degrees
54 Checks the background of
55 Problem-solving thought
57 It can be Olympic-sized
58 Latin word on cornerstones
60 Captured with a camera
63 USMC VIP

27 DRINKING SONGS by Patrick Jordan
A good one to solve during happy hour.

ACROSS

1 Some dietary taboos
6 Olympus resident
9 Abandon the beaten path
14 Dream interrupter
15 Brings out of danger
17 Like whack jobs
18 Educator Montessori
19 Oreo layer
20 Rest stops for caravans
21 Frankie Yankovic standard
24 Hair gel glob
25 Lords a-leaping count
26 Adjective for seawater
27 Within a crowd of
29 Sixth or horse follower
30 "That's my fault!"
34 Statistician's collection
35 Astounded state
36 Molded gold unit
37 Jimmy Buffett classic
43 Solution finder's shout
46 Ernie's scowling roomie
47 Display resentment
48 Slasher Freddy's street
49 1973 Eagles tune
53 Describe boastfully
54 Prince, to the king
55 "It's ___!" (delivery room phrase)
59 Chemical peel places
60 Conversation contribution
63 Work out by reasoning
65 Seafood platter sauce
67 Brine-cured spread
68 Introspective meditation
69 Traditional Irish ballad
73 Sandy sunning spot
74 Honored a passing flag
75 It's been aired before
77 Seder pancake
78 Sightseeing excursions
79 Far from long-winded
80 Salon clipping
81 Cryptology org.
82 Sprint winner's asset

DOWN

1 Skype necessity, for short
2 "Sweet home" state
3 Cheese-and-toast dish
4 Oscar winner Larson
5 Street savvy
6 Teri of "Dumb and Dumber"
7 Manager
8 Degrade in dignity
9 Pass out from rapture
10 Ben Stiller's "Tower Heist" costar
11 Insurance rate factor
12 Flooring installer's estimate
13 Tee-to-hole meas.
15 Create a digital image of
16 Gets a price for
22 Play the ponies
23 Crusty bakery item
24 Kind of joke
28 Solar Slew, to Cigar
29 Strikes sharply
31 Eyeball eagerly
32 Viewpoint sampling
33 Pipe or petunia part
35 Pearl Mosque locale
36 Currier's partner
38 Just slightly
39 Seminary subj.
40 "In case that fails . . ."
41 Chance to play
42 Pepe le Pew's pal
43 Dirt bike alternatives
44 Quite a quantity
45 Caribbean color
50 Frees, as a stubborn window
51 Like a loan shark
52 Knack for music
56 Eccentric
57 Excessive implementation
58 Kyoto coin
60 Drive up a wall
61 Mil. bomb experiment
62 Walter of Chicago Bears fame
63 Homer's head-slapping grunt
64 Applies, as muscle power
66 Campfire remnants
67 Fords of the '70s
69 Attire
70 Deem detestable
71 She directed Meg as Sally
72 Corporal's conveyance
73 Mayo-topped sandwich
76 Marge's mustached neighbor

28 BLOTTO by Victor Fleming
26 Across is also a type of craps bet.

ACROSS

1 Tick off
5 Makes a quick read of
10 Word with saw or off
13 Quattro competitor
14 Intensifies
15 Greek goddess of dining?
16 Made an ade
18 Kind of garden
19 Fine drivers?
20 Skin disorder
22 Did a deck job
23 "Pas de Deux" artist
24 Argues
26 Snowboard spin
30 Wipe out
31 Sinuous dance
32 Nabokov heroine
33 Early Scot
34 Doofuses
36 Jr.'s exam
37 Bout ender
38 "Aargh!"
39 Olympic swimmer Ledecky
40 Kleenex
42 Joshes
44 Papua language
45 "To reiterate . . ."
46 Revert
49 Minnie Pearl's hat dangler
52 Kerfuffle
53 Did cutting-edge maintenance?
55 Petting ___
56 Win back
57 Govt. agent
58 Boat that Naamah was on
59 "Headlines" rapper
60 Like the Mohave

DOWN

1 Sgt. superiors
2 Live ___ (indulge)
3 Made some salad bar bits
4 Prepare to pray, for some
5 Street savvy
6 Sgt. inferiors
7 "___ Am" (Alicia Keys album)
8 C and L, at times
9 Broad ranges
10 Bring down the house
11 Part of an agenda
12 Elizabeth in "Transamerica"
14 "Set Fire to the Rain" singer
17 Online meetup
21 British omega
23 Israeli leader Barak
24 Kind of perception
25 Swedish model Linder
27 Dillydallied
28 Daisy of "Dead Like Me"
29 Director of four Harry Potter films
31 In great demand
34 More dilapidated
35 Glaswegian miss
36 Waiting room group
38 Realm of Eris
39 Aptitude
41 Kipling python
42 Sub-par score
43 Like the tiger
46 Mideast strip
47 Gardenia or lilac
48 Library loan
49 Point on a graph
50 Off yonder
51 Moonwalker Cernan
54 JFK alternative

NO REPEATS   by Victor Fleming
Paul Valéry was a 12-time nominee for the Nobel Prize in Literature.

ACROSS
1 "12" cop
5 DOL division
9 Pin markers
14 Langston Hughes poem
15 Hopi neighbors
16 Cliff dwelling
17 Radio interference
19 Artery opener
20 **Paul Valéry quotation: Part I**
22 Take a course
23 Batman foe al Ghul
24 Draws a bead on
28 Paradise lost
30 Sphere beginning
32 Drama about Capote
33 Element from kernite
35 **Quotation: Part II**
37 Wine city near Turin
38 Held a racehorse back
39 ". . . ___ ye be judged"
40 **Quotation: Part III**
42 Shows shock
43 Chain of Hawaiian islands?
44 Nailed a final
45 Engine noise
46 DNA source
48 OPEC member
49 Pharmacy abbr.
52 **Quotation: Part IV**
56 Kaycee in "High School Musical"
59 Game that often ends in a tie
60 A Marx brother
61 Glass of "24"
62 Boat cover
63 Ovine sign
64 Tarot user
65 Samovars

DOWN
1 Cozy corner
2 Cathedral courts
3 Speedboat's wake
4 Part of COLA
5 Sprinted past
6 Hotel visits
7 Prefix for port
8 Shows curiosity
9 Prevailing mode
10 "I won't interfere"
11 "You ___ My Sunshine"
12 Boodles, for one
13 Ready to go
18 "Legend of the Guardians" owl
21 Emulated Clyde Beatty
25 Nashville instrument
26 Cropped up
27 School near Boston
29 Part of DIY
30 Didn't wait around
31 Stadium feature
33 Sobs
34 ___ Jackson (Ice Cube)
35 Conserve
36 Rob Roy led one
38 Quick summary
41 Hopi neighbors
42 St. Peter's sculpture
45 Congregation leader
47 "Fingers crossed . . ."
48 Henry, to Dorothy
50 Treat with contempt
51 Facebook friends
53 Spanish coins: Abbr.
54 Shamrock land
55 Teetotalers' org.
56 "All the Stars" singer
57 Thrice: Rx
58 Upstate NY school

30 63 ACROSS by Warren Houck
It may help to hyphenate the answer at 63 Across.

ACROSS

1 Barracks neckwear
8 Publicity blurb
13 Piano keys
14 Squalid dwelling
15 Birth place*
17 Golf green border
18 ___ segno
19 Merry melody
21 Prime number between CL and CC
22 "God Friended Me" network
25 Campaign missile
27 Deuce, for example
28 Dolt*
31 Experts
33 "Downton Abbey" maid
34 Le Carré spy Leamas
36 Six Flags attractions
37 Poe poem*
40 Flask inventor
43 Roughly handle
44 Hockey position
48 Hindu retreat
50 UPS union member*
52 Clanton at the O.K. Corral
53 Baseball club
55 Summer hrs.
56 Reddit Q&A
57 Non-PC salutation
59 New wave
61 Like Swiss cheese
63 Larva–to–adult transition
67 "Dreams From My Father" author
68 Iris rings
69 "Downton Abbey" daughter
70 Tissue cords

DOWN

1 Like a golf ball
2 Of a reproductive organ
3 First two words on a Monopoly space
4 Doughboy's defense
5 Demeanor
6 Halftrack's rnk.
7 Network name
8 Taxonomic division
9 Donnybrook
10 Egg-shaped
11 Well-deserved
12 "___ State" (Maryland)
16 Highlands hat
17 Wile E. Coyote's supplier
20 Thomas Hardy heroine
23 Building support
24 Beaver State capital
26 "Oh, snap!"
29 Nureyev, for one
30 Do an Orkin job
32 Slants
35 Like crossword puzzles
38 Kaffiyeh wearer
39 "Oh my!"
40 Toastmaster's spot
41 Edmonton football team
42 In accordance with
45 Language of Switzerland
46 Archenemies
47 Weimaraner's color
49 Warm-blooded animal
51 Highest pt. in the Beaver State
54 As well
58 Wild guess
60 "Oh, snap!"
62 Norway's largest city
64 "Who ___?" ("Les Miz" song)
65 Start for school?
66 Clara Cluck, for one

POMONA'S DOMAIN by Warren Houck
Frugivores will appreciate this theme.

ACROSS

1 Sunrise time
5 USA legal drama
10 Onstage crew
14 Oscar winner Kazan
15 Gordon's boss in "Gotham"
16 Helmet type
17 Nervous wreck*
19 Space
20 Red as ___
21 South Lawn parties
23 Twain's "___! I Feel Like a Woman"
24 Former Iraqi dictator
26 Easy victory*
28 Flightless fowl
29 Vegas opening
31 Fermenting fungus
32 ___ Nui (Easter Island)
34 Walkman successor
37 Rooftop fixture
38 Times of youthful innocence*
41 Oneonta campus
43 "Okey-dokey"
44 Rolaids rival
48 Go over like ___ balloon
50 Missile's wobble
52 Siesta
53 Rotational energy storer*
56 White whale
58 Hi-___ audio
59 Birds-and-bees class
61 Runner-up in a two-person race
62 Bear, to Brutus
64 Dazed*
66 Dom Pedro's wife
67 Van Halen brother

68 Pt. of NBA
69 Throw out
70 Early fly trap
71 Zoological wings

DOWN

1 Put-down artist
2 Iron Bowl team
3 Got smart
4 Birthday suit state
5 Ready to go
6 SOS responders
7 Esau's dad
8 Car named after an inventor
9 Disingenuous
10 Expert at IRS forms
11 Weather map balloon
12 B-2 feature
13 Part of TGIF
18 Footnote abbr.
22 Squalid
25 With voice or junk
27 Hourglass center
30 Fix Tabby
33 Good ___ (refurbished)
35 Shelley poem
36 "Saving Private Ryan" setting
39 Maids of India
40 Jezebel's husband
41 Port near Naples
42 James Joyce classic
45 Not everyday
46 Shade close to plum
47 Shimmer
49 More profound
51 Join metal to metal
53 Pomona's domain (and a theme hint)
54 Ooze
55 Pulls a bank job

57 "Golden Boy" heroine
60 XLIII x XIV
63 Balaam's reprover
65 Miss Prissy, for one

32 BODILY HARM   by Bonnie L. Gentry
Not to fear, these won't have you saying "Ouch!"

ACROSS
1 Stallone's commando
6 Winding routes
11 Valvoline competitor
14 Slower kind of mail
15 Talk Like a Pirate Day address
16 Sing-along syllable
17 Tots, slangily
19 Where the cookie crumbles, often
20 Taunt into action
21 Surprise supper
23 Wares: Abbr.
25 Blood: Comb. form
27 Hunch
28 Unlikely ballet dancer
29 Forceful cajolers
32 Two : company :: three : ___
34 Humidifier output
35 "Nobody doesn't like ___!"
38 Sang in Tyrol
42 Succotash beans
44 Words to no one in particular
45 Places for low-priority items
50 Suede surface
51 Twelve-grade school
52 Valuable deposit
53 Like a bad handshake
54 Purpose of cutting the budget
57 Tough phrase for TEFL students
59 "¡___ favor, señor!"
60 Heavy-metal fans
64 Moneypenny in "Skyfall"
65 Snowboarding bump
66 City in Crete, historically
67 ___ publica
68 Uppsala resident
69 Made a pot larger

DOWN
1 Gary Player's land: Abbr.
2 Bay State cape
3 Heads toward
4 "Nonsense!"
5 Cosmonaut Makarov
6 Stage name of Marshall Mathers
7 Took a chair
8 Say "brb" in a chat room
9 Eliel Saarinen's son
10 Part of BIOS
11 Memphis hospital
12 Bullet with a trail
13 South Pole wear
18 Quantum theory pioneer
22 Toronto bottle sizes
23 Some soft shoes, for short
24 Olympic swimmer Torres
26 "The Challenge" network
29 Wing it
30 What Snapchat had in 2017
31 Dr. Wells and Dr Pepper
33 Kind of cooler
36 80-pound bird
37 Babyhood
39 Witch hazel, for one
40 Dutch cheese burg
41 Johnny in "Finding Neverland"
43 Hostess ___ Balls
45 Surgeon summoner
46 Room recess
47 Routine tasks
48 Like dandelion greens
49 Hester Prynne's stigma
53 Boston hub
55 Current law?
56 Scary sound to a mouse
58 Machu Picchu resident
61 Wet firecracker
62 "Pioneer Woman" Drummond
63 Bummed

SWEEPS by Bonnie L. Gentry
Read 'em and sweep!

ACROSS

1 Pasture sounds
5 Numbers that never get smaller
9 Pharmacy weights
14 The good old days
15 "Godfather" henchman Brasi
16 Insistent retort
17 Sweeps
20 Fix some loose laces
21 Burton of "Star Trek: TNG"
22 Naval address
23 "Fables in Slang" author
24 Jack Swigert's alma mater
26 Not a copy: Abbr.
28 Sweeps
34 John of tennis
35 Dunhill in "11/22/63"
36 Phaser setting
39 "Anymore" singer Travis
42 "Fixing a ___": Beatles
43 Planet not in Holst's "The Planets"
45 Nina's mother in "Black Swan"
47 Sweeps
51 Turgenev's birth city
52 Chairman pro ___
53 "Shark Tank" network
56 Animus
59 B'nai ___
61 Clinique founder Lauder

63 Sweeps
66 Deer track
67 Bed of roses
68 "Up Where We Belong" is one
69 Place for a stickpin
70 Crockpot favorite
71 "A Bug's Life" princess

DOWN

1 Spandex
2 Marveled audibly
3 Blog contributor
4 Final Four game
5 Samuel Adams, for one
6 Makeup for Alice Cooper
7 McCartney's "___ Cor Meum"
8 Artillery discharges
9 Books with locks
10 Was a candidate
11 CIA mole Aldrich
12 Car sticker letters
13 Middling
18 "Shucks!"
19 Tombstone lawman
25 Cream purchase
27 Otto in the NFL Hall of Fame
29 "Say it ___, Joe!"
30 Pam in "Mars Attacks!"
31 "___ declare!"
32 Van Gogh painting
33 Wallace in "E.T."
36 Lock stitch
37 ___ Lung in "Kung Fu Panda"
38 Mausoleum vessel
40 "Sample a few"

41 Buster Brown's dog
44 Conductor von Karajan
46 Caravan transport
48 ___ libre (free verse)
49 A-listers
50 Dine downtown
54 Prince's "Raspberry ___"
55 Fronton basket
56 "___ most unusual day . . ."
57 Features of some jeans
58 Pdf form
60 What this isn't?
62 Bubbly drink
64 Excellent grade
65 Scant amount

ACROSS

1 Sorcerer
5 Get by
11 Public works project
14 "East of Eden" twin
15 Yom Kippur observer
16 First name in pharmaceuticals
17 Crowd-funded neighborhood cat shelter?*
19 One above a SPC
20 Freudian topic
21 Elusive one
22 Word with heat or meat
23 Aristophanes comedy, with "The"
25 Crowd-funded shoe-repair shop?*
30 To ___ (perfect)
31 Carpenter's tool
32 Willy Wonka creator Dahl
34 Girls of Spain
35 Suffix with lion
36 Crowd-funded auto junkyard?*
39 Do film work
42 Acapulco agreements
43 Shade of gray
47 Kind of soup
49 Israeli carrier
50 Crowd-funded volunteer agency?*
52 Classic Ford
53 Baltic port
54 Put down, slangily
56 Any ship
57 Had
58 Crowd-funding site
63 Rest room sign
64 Hosts
65 Ship part
66 Posed
67 Every twelve months
68 Paris airport

DOWN

1 Start a battle
2 "Thanks a lot" in Japan
3 Sail
4 Arboreal Tolkien creature
5 Aromatic spice
6 Reef ring
7 Easter preceder
8 "That Girl" girl
9 "Is that so!"
10 Goof
11 Expire
12 Andes animals
13 Turns whitish because of fungus
18 "You rang?"
22 MSRP poster
24 ___-mell
26 Sans sense
27 Smooths
28 Way to the top
29 Mexican coins
33 Secretaries
34 Boot camp reply
37 Tick off
38 Commoner
39 Indian Retreats
40 Spicy brew
41 Trig function
44 Red-carpet figure
45 Chapel Hill player
46 Like senior citizens
48 Nutritional abbr.
51 Bygone auto
52 Baggage checkers, briefly
55 Wee
58 Round Table knight
59 Rage
60 Nashville-based awards org.
61 White wine aperitif
62 Old MGM rival

60 ACROSS by Gary Larson
Take the answer to 60 Across literally.

ACROSS

1 Aromatic spice
6 Kitchen foil brand
11 Except
14 Positive pole
15 Poets
16 Letters after Chris Sununu's name
17 The Chacoan Peccary, e.g.
19 "Aladdin" prince
20 Wrongdoing
21 Long baths
22 It's known for its bell ringers
23 Stage solo
25 Clue suspect
28 Frames' inserts
30 Glosses over
31 Mystery writer's prize
32 Port-au-Prince is its capital
35 Brit. honor
36 Brown bag
39 Wane
42 Less than a fifth
43 Hawkeye
47 Bordeaux wine
49 Sometime in the future
50 NASA's milieu
54 Vino region
55 World's largest particle physics lab
56 Wear
58 Black gold
59 Simpson judge
60 Panhandler's request
63 Quick swim
64 Beauty parlor
65 Tweak
66 Summer on the Riviera

67 Church songs
68 Some Dodges

DOWN

1 Lot event
2 Not yet broadcast
3 Before noon
4 Suffix with sulf-
5 Capone's nemesis
6 "Fuzzy Wuzzy was ___"
7 Is without
8 To the point
9 Words of praise
10 Dummkopf
11 Applauded with shouts
12 Releases
13 "Really?"
18 Short dogs, for short
22 Hotshot
24 Rush job notation
26 Spanish pronoun
27 Keys on the piano
29 Rubber
32 Witch's work
33 Workmanship
34 Give or take
37 Quarries
38 Big Island coffee area
39 Environmental disaster
40 Small cobalt-colored bird
41 Utility belt item
44 Saw through

45 Immunity trigger
46 Carpenter's devices
48 Cartoon dog
49 Soldier of fortune, briefly
51 Sacred song
52 Table part
53 "No Country for Old Men" Oscar winners
57 Part of a comparison
60 "Quiet"
61 Wages
62 Tankard filler

A WALK IN THE PARK   by Mark McClain
41 Across was first available in 1987.

ACROSS

1 Half a faun
5 "___ girl!"
9 Wasn't oneself
14 Major or Minor lead-in
15 Decorative bedding item
16 Gather some wool
17 Leitmotif
19 Mattress brand
20 Satisfy
21 Carol, for one
23 Sub alternative
24 Big Bang theory alternative
27 Panamanian party
31 "I'm not impressed!"
32 Rebecca's firstborn
33 Off-white shade
37 Dog walker's need
41 PowerPoint's suite
44 Drained of color
45 Disturbance
46 Sandler in the movies
47 Itty-bitty
49 Daisy relatives
51 1974 "Mame" star
57 Soon, in verse
58 Social cold shoulder
59 Sanctuary divider
64 Barely enough
66 Metaphor for trouble
68 "That's someone ___ problem!"
69 Long division preposition
70 Percussion instrument
71 Old, in a hip way
72 Zap with a stun gun
73 Makes choices

DOWN

1 Periodontist's concern
2 Unwritten, in a way
3 Home to most Buddhists
4 Gas destination
5 Suffix of uncertainty
6 "We hold ___ truths . . ."
7 Nation ENE of Australia
8 Make changes to
9 Balaam's mount
10 Bat the breeze
11 Earth, in sci-fi lingo
12 Patronize, as a bistro
13 Hang loose
18 Midterm challenge
22 Rec center feature
25 Bills
26 Prefix for reliant or centered
27 Govt. disaster org.
28 Nile goddess
29 Pricing option
30 Shoo-in
34 Punched-in-the-gut sound
35 Patriots' org.
36 Greek letter
38 Hill worker
39 Battle reminder
40 Couturier's lines
42 Scott Turow bestseller
43 Mrs. Pickles in the comics
48 Ernie with a wedge
50 Barbecue joint side
51 Surgical light
52 Reunion attendee
53 Proceed aimlessly
54 Break an engagement
55 Lake ___ Vista, FL
56 Helps out with a heist
60 "Othello" conniver
61 Common sign word
62 Mardis Gras follower
63 Work units
65 Chinese menu general
67 Writer of weird tales

37 BIBLICAL FIGURES   by Mark McClain
A quartet of great significance.

ACROSS

1 Legendary lawman
5 Emulate a rat
9 Uncovered
14 Uninteresting
15 Unit pricing adverb
16 Accepted practice
17 1984 Eddie Murphy film
20 Embarrassing display
21 Petal supporter
22 Empath's gift
23 The O of NGO
25 Vet's workplace
27 Party event
36 Charles, to Elizabeth
37 "___ say more?"
38 Buddy-boy
39 Thief's take
41 Sits patiently
43 Depart by sea
44 Bitter-tasting
46 Play a banjo
48 1940s White House monogram
49 Frustrated channel surfer's cry
52 Suitable
53 Venerable toy store initials
54 Failing marks
57 Solemn pledges
61 Large chamber group
65 Misnamed agency in Orwell's "Nineteen Eighty-Four"
68 Cook Island native
69 Dumpster emanation
70 Novelist Ferber
71 Hitter's appearance
72 Legendary beast
73 Campus official

DOWN

1 Pulls back
2 One of the Baldwins
3 Pan's opposite
4 One with amazing talents
5 Dentifrice option
6 Equine negatives?
7 Back or head ending
8 Buggy driver's accessory
9 Sandra with an Oscar
10 Burro
11 Hialeah happening
12 Easily bruised things
13 Captain Sparrow's player
18 Aired again
19 Goof around
24 Became
26 Soul singer Redding
27 Quaint interjection
28 Raid target
29 Habituate (to)
30 Brewer's buy
31 Teddy Roosevelt's wife
32 Petrol measure
33 Site of Boise State's home games
34 Keats or Pindar
35 Nick in "Simpatico"
40 Turkish coin
42 Beachfront sound
45 Credit union transaction
47 Intended to say
50 MLB fan's datum
51 Tied securely
54 Austen classic
55 Official edict
56 Stuck-up sort
58 "Iliad" locale
59 Park in London
60 Woodstove accumulation
62 Subject in many paintings
63 Sicilian mount
64 Larger-life connector
66 Tax-deferred acct.
67 Part of TGIF

CHOICES by Pam Klawitter
Hundreds of films feature the works of 39 Across, including "Pretty Woman."

ACROSS

1 Upscale hotel amenities
5 Corp. money handlers
9 Fidel Castro's successor
13 "___ gonna happen!"
14 Cartoon pooch
15 Sheer linen fabric
16 He loved Lucy
17 Brooke Henderson's sponsor
18 Comes by honestly
19 Choices at the front door
22 Geronimo, notably
25 Wipe away
26 Choices in the checkout line
30 Baptism and marriage
31 Brand of mandarins
32 Common computer site
35 Mythical archer
36 Roulette bets
37 Carryall
38 Outmoded map letters
39 "Aida" composer
40 "File not found"
41 Choices at the Super Bowl
43 On purpose
45 Thorn in the side
46 Choices at the diner
50 Got up
51 Like a rock
52 Like Godiva
56 Ocean crosser
57 End of a threat

58 Source of energy
59 British rank
60 Big stinks
61 Knee

DOWN

1 Bummed
2 Key lime treat
3 Q&A part
4 Baseball features
5 Unoriginal one
6 Bank window letters
7 Plaint from the pen
8 Flower on Utah's flag
9 Find hysterically funny
10 End of a South American capital
11 Forearm bones
12 "___ we forget"
15 Falling-shapes game
20 Frat jacket letters
21 Total overhauls
22 Ranch holdings
23 Ark units
24 Fur baron
27 Fingering combo
28 They catch baddies by surprise
29 The river, in Spanish 101
32 Large-eyed primate
33 Reef formation
34 As such
36 "Rad!" in Dad's days
37 Curbside container
39 False front
40 Vermont, in Vichy

41 Admiral in a McCartney song
42 ___ scholar
43 2017 Cat 5 hurricane
44 WW2 investment
46 Like Reilly Opelka
47 Ostrichlike bird
48 Un-locked?
49 Sorta
53 Wolfed
54 Weasley of Gryffindor
55 Relative of 47 Down

CHUMP CHANGE   by Pam Klawitter
57 Across won an Academy Award at the very ceremony he was hosting.

ACROSS

1 Has an "oops" moment
5 "Star Wars" figure
9 Certain med. plans
13 Trick-taking card game
14 Google Play client
15 Land's end
16 Samberg of "Brooklyn Nine-Nine"
17 Tennis star Errani
18 Starbucks offering
19 La Sorbonne locale
22 Washday challenges
25 They support the choir
26 Changes in a heartbeat
30 Name in the cosmetics aisle
31 Some Grimm characters
32 Easy target
35 Squeaks (by)
36 Amazon transaction
37 Mascara target
38 Pen pal's afterthoughts, briefly
39 Whistling wind?
40 Like some pranks
41 Rye alternative
43 6 and Super 8
46 Anatolian capital
47 A lot that sounds like a little
51 In ___ (not yet born)
52 With the bow, in music
53 Leo's locks
57 David of "Separate Tables"
58 Part of a pirate's chant
59 Brewpub's offerings
60 Etcher's need
61 Bad way to run
62 Beltway ball club

DOWN

1 Historic chapter
2 Hermione's husband
3 Angler's purchase
4 Postcard silhouettes
5 Exactly like this
6 Morales of "NCIS: LA"
7 Laura or Bruce in the movies
8 "Green Zone" setting
9 Husky-voiced
10 Photo finish
11 Cuisinart rival
12 Mob attachments
15 Adjusters' concerns
20 Devil ___ Hatfield
21 "Paradise Lost" angel
22 Exorbitant
23 Mammoth features
24 Crafts in Cadiz
27 Still in bed
28 Colorful quartz
29 Less rainy
32 First decaf coffee
33 Former SAG president
34 Kingdom sections
36 Nightmarish address, briefly
37 Fate shines upon him
39 Steamboat pioneer
40 "The Last Jedi" hero
41 Took a close look
42 Inuit of film
43 Hawaiian "mountain"
44 Fiber ___ cable
45 Coin collector in Rome
48 "Divine Secrets of the ___ Sisterhood" (2002)
49 Dance with a queen
50 Hollow comeback
54 Carte lead-in
55 Shuttlecock stopper
56 Business end

ADDING A WING   by Fred Piscop
30 Across is known as the "Father of Electronic Music."

ACROSS

1 Column crossers
5 Publicist's concern
10 Made one's case
14 Planning session offering
15 Area served by LAX
16 One flavor in Sprite
17 In support of NFL exec Roger?
19 Sharing an ancestry
20 Spinning wheel's pedal
21 Ufologists' interests, briefly
23 Just sitting around
25 Stressed out
26 Curriculum segment
30 "Intégrales" composer
33 Jets' Super Bowl III win, e.g.
34 Puts the whammy on
35 Clown costume item
38 Smoke alarm sound
39 Gave a fig
40 Bit of "dinero"
41 Toss in
42 Leto of "American Psycho"
43 Modesto winery
44 "Star Wars Episode II" army
46 In a foul mood
47 Most of Iberia
49 Reveille's opposite
51 Breed of small hen
54 Civil War reenactments
59 Yemeni port
60 Angelic TV host Simon?
62 Item on a game rack
63 Cropped up
64 "Put your money away"
65 Shaker filler
66 Like a blowhard
67 Stash in the hold

DOWN

1 Geological fault
2 Nose wrinkler
3 "If I ___ you . . ."
4 Generations-spanning tale
5 Tristan's love
6 Catwalk strutter
7 Bandage brand
8 Young misses
9 "Enchanted" girl of kid-lit
10 Takes second
11 Resembling director Mike?
12 Bahrain bigwigs
13 Not exactly Mensa material
18 "To a . . ." writer
22 Beehive State natives
24 Hillary's conquest
26 Bay of Pigs locale
27 Essay page, for short
28 Actor Steve played for a sap?
29 Weight room unit
31 Dumped unceremoniously
32 Crimson or cerise
34 Jackrabbit, really
36 Resort locale, often
37 Hockey heavy
39 Recyclable item
40 BFF
42 "Woodstock" songwriter Mitchell
43 Hearty enjoyment
45 Finch family member
46 Kevin of "House of Cards"
47 Sings like Cab Calloway
48 Lecturers' platforms
50 Yawning chasm
52 Layered hairdo
53 Bar mitzvah highlight
55 "Terrible" phase
56 Advanced, as cash
57 Falsetto-voiced Muppet
58 Did in
61 LAPD part

41 AFTER U* by Fred Piscop
10 Down is the Hulk's relentless pursuer, a.k.a. Red Hulk.

ACROSS

1 Slumgullion
5 Float like an aroma
9 Rust Belt product
14 Words of approximation
15 Sunburn soother
16 Windy City hub
17 Get penalized in a board game*
19 Grand Canyon formation
20 Holiday preceder
21 Sleep cycle acronym
22 "The Faerie Queene" poet
24 Opposite of "sinister"
26 Father Time's facial feature
27 Bret who chronicled Roaring Camp
29 Turntable need
33 Remove a typo
36 Persian Gulf denizen
38 Be fearful of
39 Biblical shepherd
40 Key-related
42 Prank cigar sound
43 Mysterious Dickens character
45 Prefix meaning "ten"
46 Wild party
47 Fourteen-line poem
49 Palace resident
51 "No guts, no ___"
53 Holds back, as bad news
57 Hawaiian farewell song
60 ". . . ___ a lender be"
61 In spite of, for short
62 "Like a Rolling Stone" singer
63 Thanksgiving table vessel*
66 Exchange cross words
67 Highest-rated
68 Monotone lecturer, e.g.
69 Soft and crumbly
70 Within walking distance
71 Rejuvenating spots

DOWN

1 Repaired a boot
2 Discovered treasure
3 English county on the North Sea
4 Handwringer's feeling
5 Semiaquatic rodent
6 College endower, often
7 A proponent of
8 Like nail-biters
9 Dried out, with "up"
10 Nickname of Marvel's General Ross*
11 26 Down sign
12 Folies-Bergère costume designer
13 Lascivious look
18 Surveyor's measure
23 Give zero stars to
25 What lifers are in for*
26 Greasy spoon
28 Walked heavily
30 Letter starter
31 Lana of "Smallville"
32 Daringly innovative
33 Many Little League coaches
34 River of Aragón
35 Trotsky of the Red Army
37 Soy-based salad bit
41 Pauses on a journey
44 Kim of "NYPD Blue"
48 "___ big to fail"
50 Light as a feather
52 A sister of Cordelia
54 Scrooch down
55 Surname at Tara
56 Lecture jottings
57 Eden exile
58 Harp's ancestor
59 Bond girl Kurylenko
60 Auntie's mom
64 Eggs on a sushi roll
65 Big shot they're not

ALL WET   by Gary Larson
The Cartwright ranch was named after 35 Across.

ACROSS

1 Affected
6 Fruity cereal
10 Russian leader before 1917
14 Big bankruptcy of 2001
15 Choice
16 Telegram
17 Ski resort offering*
19 Poker player's declaration
20 Twitches
21 Ventilate
22 Cherish
23 Vitamin C source
24 S'more ingredient*
27 Kilt pattern
29 Finish off
30 Japan's JAL rival
31 Short piece
32 Mathematician Turing
34 Like some history
35 Tall North American pine*
38 Listening devices
41 Many ages
42 Thundering
46 UFC fighting style
47 Unruly crowd
48 Sew up
49 "The Last Picture Show" director*
53 TNT part
54 Take another stab at
55 Vein contents
56 Work out
57 Tony's cousin
58 Pricey vacation property (and a hint to clue* answers)

61 Purina competitor
62 Utopia
63 Monte Carlo wheel bet
64 Wranglers alternative
65 Yielded
66 More unusual

DOWN

1 Develop slowly
2 Central New York tribe
3 Glowing bullets
4 Turn's partner
5 Alabama island near Florida
6 Sumatran mammal
7 Surf sounds
8 Those with clout
9 Crosses out
10 Spin
11 Like
12 Four Corners state
13 Fresh start
18 Indian bread
22 Way to stand
24 Waldorf salad ingredient
25 Listens to
26 "Look ___ hands!"
28 Memorial Day solo
32 Spanish marinade
33 Spy novelist Deighton
34 Sculls
36 Very bright
37 Window part
38 Complicate
39 One-celled organisms
40 Music genre
43 One way to think
44 Set up

45 Bury again
47 Word of possibility
48 Computer giant
50 Toggery
51 Ballot caster
52 Cara of "Fame"
56 Push
58 Fly catcher
59 Brouhaha
60 Away

BORDER STATES by Gary Larson

17 Across is often referred to as a "poor man's Parmesan."

ACROSS

1 Baked ___
7 2013 Bruce Dern film
15 Tossed easily
16 More sudden
17 Pungent cheese
18 "Madam Secretary" star
19 ___ Paese cheese
20 Ukr., once
22 Source of gluten
23 "Frasier" character
24 Lincoln and Fortas
26 Takes steps
28 Storage space
29 Subcompact
30 Longoria of "Desperate Housewives"
31 1998 De Niro thriller
32 Seasoned
33 One year in a trunk
35 ___ cum laude
36 Make
38 Take a chance
40 Pen pal?
43 Reverse, e.g.
45 Prayer leader
49 Author of "The Divided Self"
50 Suffix for block
51 ___ contendere
52 S-shaped molding
53 Produce
55 Secluded valley
56 Yank's foe
57 W.C.
58 Established
61 2000 title role for Richard Gere
62 Persians, today
65 Fanning in "The Alienist"
67 Dilapidated
68 Big roll
69 2020 Liam Hemsworth film
70 Zane Grey novel

DOWN

1 "Mountain Music" band
2 Get trounced
3 Eisenhower's boyhood home
4 Govt. org. that aids entrepreneurs
5 They're tapped
6 Commotions
7 Turner of note
8 Movie critic Roger
9 Ass sounds
10 Wear the crown
11 Uncouth one
12 Putting away
13 "thirtysomething" actor
14 Beverage brand
21 Delirious
25 LP part
27 Let go
28 Relaxing in the tub
30 Go astray
31 Real estate ad abbr.
34 K through 12
37 Director Lee
39 Wrath
40 Esther Rolle role
41 More enthusiastic
42 Recline
44 Teacup handle
46 Ukraine neighbor
47 Warned
48 3-time Super Bowl MVP
53 Daytime serials
54 Michigan county or its seat
57 Security for a debt
59 Utopia
60 Yarn
63 Pro-Second Amendment grp.
64 Thoroughfares, for short
66 "The Wonder Years" nickname

44 FINAL COUNTS by Patrick Jordan
57 Across hosts the Heritage Golf Classic, a PGA Tour tournament.

ACROSS

1 Paris airport
5 Colonial essayist Thomas
10 Loco, to a Londoner
14 Chicken farm expense
15 Peggy of "Mad Men"
16 Geek Squad customer
17 Moment of a flare-up
19 Office cabinet insertion
20 Basset hound's dangler
21 Versatile vehicles, briefly
22 School fundraiser
24 Seemingly tireless type
26 Hired parker
27 Errol Flynn classic
32 Sweeten the deal with
35 Eggs on yeggs
36 Moo ___ shrimp
37 Green or greeting follower
38 Pulls out a pistol
39 Like Monday's child
40 CSI test substance
41 Out of the tether
42 Macbeth's cry to Macduff
43 Connecting concept
46 Some West Wing staffers
47 Sicilian spouter
51 Get-go
53 TV teacher Kotter
55 Pronoun for Nala
56 Working with gusto
57 South Carolina resort
60 Leave nonplussed
61 Flooring calculations
62 Bookmark menu entry
63 Outbuilding
64 Serves as a caretaker
65 Disney film with a light cycle race

DOWN

1 Put down, to a gangster
2 Baton race
3 Benefit from study
4 Gridiron gains, for short
5 Coke can feature
6 Hand cream substance
7 Horn-sporting goddess
8 Nantes negative
9 Contest hopefuls
10 Oblong camping bag
11 Staring with mouth agape . . .
12 Bring down a 13 Down
13 Branch location
18 Judge Doom's disguise
23 Priestly robes
25 Erosive chemical
26 Netflix customer
28 Prediction packs
29 Mortify
30 It flows past Louisville
31 Cowpoke's "Heck!"
32 Universal adapter letters
33 Paul of "12 Years a Slave"
34 Rewrite for the stage
38 "Been there, ___"
39 Vanish gradually
41 Abundant deposit
42 Approach dusk
44 Sprayed lightly
45 Make printed letters tactile
48 "All snug in ___ beds . . ."
49 "Peachy!"
50 "As You Like It" locale
51 Inelegant bunch
52 Bonneville Salt Flats site
53 Remote lowland
54 Nearly none
58 Crank's emotion
59 FDR's last veep

HEADWINDS by Patrick Jordan
2 Down was founded as a hobby by Pierre Omidyar in 1995.

CROSS

1 Film funnyman Rogen
5 Org. with a pet cause?
9 Key-changing guitar gadgets
14 Award for small-venue plays
15 Nile reptile, briefly
16 Take in a stray
17 Like roadside stand produce
19 "Fearless" star Perez
20 Sailor's "Certainly!"
21 Intense craving
22 Far from frazzled
23 Keyboard key
25 Driver ignoring the limit
26 LeBron James' position
29 Order from the throne
30 Granola bar ingredients
31 Angler's casting item
34 Winter Olympics arena
35 Sits alongside
37 ___ a soul (none)
38 Rainwater container
39 App-stopping command
40 Assertive personality variety
41 Insular outlook
44 Collusion, slangily
47 Got a rowboat going
48 Does some wheel-straightening
49 Kon-Tiki Museum site
50 Surgeon's charge
53 Trees have annual ones
54 "Medication" for a worrywart
56 Soup kitchen spoon
57 "A Little Night Music" heroine
58 ". . . as an estimate"
59 Financial report entry
60 Feeling sluggish
61 Suffix for six

DOWN

1 Dagwood's napping spot
2 Site once called AuctionWeb
3 It's out on a limb
4 Skirt edge
5 Back of a kitten's neck
6 "The trick is done!"
7 Dollar, at a dollar store
8 German gasp
9 College graduates' pursuits
10 Deemed irresistible
11 Mimicked a model
12 Voice a viewpoint
13 Work the helm
18 Play footsie, e.g.
22 Short-lived quarrels
24 Family-friendly expletive
25 Elite police unit
26 Job offer enhancer
27 Dopey dog of the funnies
28 Mail carrier's circuit
31 Machine gun description
32 Mega Stuf cookie
33 Cinematic Cannon
35 Em and Polly, for two
36 Bargain basement receptacles
37 Wall St. group since 1792
39 Corrugated metal hut
40 Austrian Alpine region
41 Two-position switch
42 Behind in the polls
43 Depression between hills
44 Caustic "Cheers" barmaid
45 Felon's false identity
46 Red deer females
49 Cry of dread
51 Apart from the rest
52 PayPal founder Musk
54 Diamond legend Ripken
55 Collection of antes

"QUIET DOWN!"   by Greg Johnson
35 Across is also the name of a 1983 pop hit by Billy Idol.

ACROSS
1 Batty
5 Old Bailey headwear
9 Go on the fritz
14 "Seeing your bet . . ."
15 "A likely story!"
16 City on the Tibetan Plateau
17 Kind of dish
19 Some pups
20 Therapeutic shriek
22 Seal group
23 Satie's "Sur ___ Lanterne"
24 Tongue jewelry
28 Banishes
32 "As I do"
34 ". . . ___ oxen free"
35 Dixie battle cry
37 Nucor's stock symbol
38 ___ in aardvark
40 Bug
41 Sigma follower
42 Chitchat
45 Hit-the-ground sound
46 Opens a sleeping bag
47 Lover of the arts
50 Troubadour tunes
51 Take in
53 Bawl
54 Aside
60 Karate schools
63 Citrus drink
64 Bakery product you can't buy
65 Hershey caramel candy
66 Erin Hamlin's sled
67 Just over three feet

68 Rival film of "A Bug's Life"
69 Got out of there fast

DOWN
1 Speech issue
2 Gooding of "Deadwood"
3 Chase rival
4 Not a good way to run
5 "Consider it done!"
6 Wading bird
7 Be sarcastic, say
8 Silver's NBA predecessor
9 Code word for "A"
10 "Syntactic Structures" author
11 Surcharge
12 Take advantage of
13 ___ de deux
18 Ho Chi Minh Trail locale
21 Angler with pots
25 Cut canines
26 One of two in Mötley Crüe
27 Trick
28 Emissary abroad
29 Bryn Mawr grad
30 Cheap
31 Bear up there
33 Kind
36 Item on an outdoor rack
38 Matterhorn, e.g.
39 Docked no longer
43 Lithe and nimble
44 In a bit
45 "Physician, heal ___"
48 Nose, in slang

49 Surveyor's math
52 Where Socrates shopped
55 Imperial autocrat
56 White on "Breaking Bad"
57 Beatles bassist
58 Microsoft browser
59 Oboe sliver
60 Broodmare
61 Miners dig it
62 Write hastily

FACILITIES   by Mark McClain
They're located right up front.

CROSS

1 Runs a pilot
5 "Boléro" composer
10 Drive-thru devices
14 Kasparov's castle
15 Green shade
16 Police emergency acronym
17 Trumpeter's gadget
18 Next ___ (emergency contact)
19 Some leafy greens
20 "The Bank Dick" is one
23 Throw a bone to
26 Long periods
27 Emergency signal
28 Sanctuary feature
31 Aromatherapy product
34 Sri Lankan export
37 Scored 100 (or 1)
38 Without a pause
39 Diez menos cuatro
40 Danson of "The Good Place"
41 "Merrie Melodies" sister series
43 Vice ___
44 Release, in a way
45 Court entry
47 Retro basketball move
49 Wild pansy
53 City planner's map
54 Odd and frightening
55 River to the Mississippi
59 Move very carefully
60 Dickens title opening
61 Racetrack surface
62 Mortarboard wearer
63 Four-time Australian Open winner
64 Senate position

DOWN

1 Aaron Rodgers' asset
2 Promissory note
3 Turn bad
4 Like shish kebabs
5 Dish sites
6 Allen in "Game of Thrones"
7 Minn. gridder, informally
8 Like Elphaba
9 ___-Lease Act
10 Request
11 Clemens nom de plume
12 Retail centers
13 Put restraints on
21 Normandy city
22 Dolittle's Sophie
23 G sharp equivalent
24 Take second at Belmont
25 Like some aprons
28 Rally site
29 Like the Texas star
30 Shipshape
32 Residential entrance
33 Genesis grandson
34 Back nine's first hole
35 Kid's song refrain
36 Balance sheet item
39 Solar phenomena
41 "Doctor Zhivago" director
42 Ballet wardrobe item
43 Let off steam
45 Frigid
46 Tibetan city
47 Amused look
48 Olympic blades
49 Digital image file
50 Thumbs-up votes
51 Ballerina's spring
52 Central Russian river
56 Shade
57 Brokerage acct. option
58 Frequently, in verse

48 DIMINUTIVITY I by Steven E. Atwood
Amusing wordplay by a Bay State puzzler.

ACROSS

1 Alcohol awareness org.
5 Justin Trudeau's sister
10 Casual day exclamation
14 Lyft rival
15 Nobelist writer Canetti
16 Guthrie of folk
17 Buffy Sainte-Marie, for one
18 Approaches
19 Score fewer points
20 Kid overacting in the school play?
22 Small serving of butter?
24 Splinter groups
26 "Hamlet" auth.
27 Little white lie?
30 Exxon, formerly
32 Some EMS calls
35 Shoot-___ (western)
36 One-inch putt
37 Hardship
38 A psychedelic
39 Part of a child's archery set?
41 Initiate an action
42 Had more points
43 SETI subject
44 "___ me" ("I approve")
45 Pen
46 Warble
47 Mildly amused reaction to an IM?
49 Theodore Cleaver, to Wally
51 Proved valid
53 Baby seabird?
55 Toy kitchen cookware?

59 Prefix for cure
60 Former Senator Hatch
62 Up to it
63 Extremities
64 Brewer Hall-of-Famer Robin
65 Dr. Dolittle's wife
66 Soul singer Marvin
67 "¡Hasta ___!"
68 Bygone monarch

DOWN

1 "___ obliged!"
2 "Doctor Sleep" heroine
3 Regard
4 Put on a costume
5 Red Jacket's tribe
6 Siren, e.g.
7 "World Factbook" compiler
8 Stringed instrument
9 Charles Guiteau, for one
10 Shire in "The Godfather"
11 Rob who caught Brady's passes
12 Rick's Café visitor
13 Adversary
21 iPhone no.
23 Skimpy swimwear
25 Sailor's bearings
27 Cuts down
28 "No more for me, thanks"
29 All friendly like
31 Form a cocoon
33 Call into question
34 "I gotta go"

36 Bob Bryan, to Mike
39 ___ metabolism
40 Elzie Segar character
44 Seasoned swabbie
47 Lend out
48 Suffix with ball
50 Mertens of tennis
52 Devil's Night activity
53 Rowlands in "The Notebook"
54 Short pants?
56 Stork relative
57 "Born Free" lioness
58 Blacken salmon
59 Cribbage pin
61 Paris street

DIMINUTIVITY II   by Steven E. Atwood

J.K. Rowling readers will know the answer to 55 Down.

ACROSS

1 Tried to touch base
5 Like humidors
9 Gig's 1,024
13 Great Lakes mnemonic
15 Computer company
16 Blue hue
17 Lissome
18 Chiang Mai native
19 Litter's littlest
20 Subcompact delivery vehicle?
22 Ten winks, maybe?
24 Sheffield loc.
25 Auntie of Patrick Dennis
27 Brewing ingredient
28 Nielsen number
30 Jive
33 Love seat go-with
36 Admit a member
38 Bleacher ___
39 Tiny corner store?
41 Weekend getaway?
43 "So that's what you're up to!"
44 Hyundai model
46 Comes by
47 Art Clokey character
49 Jackson in "Nasty Habits"
51 Novice gamer
53 Opera highlight
54 Friday, for one
57 Little chat room monitor?
59 Small musical group?
61 Rob in "Killing Kennedy"
62 Bear up there
64 Golf course rentals
65 Make out, at Hogwarts
66 Reluctant King of Israel
67 Host
68 Political commentator Perino
69 Web language
70 Geekazoid

DOWN

1 Slice thinly
2 Boston hub
3 Chatting online
4 Where salamis hang
5 Market research process
6 German exclamation
7 Cantankerous
8 Last king of Troy
9 Meghan who married a prince
10 Fair
11 Ben of "Treasure Island"
12 Watched Junior
14 Marge Simpson's sister
21 George Lopez, e.g.
23 Ron Reagan's sister
26 Terminus
28 Chinese zodiac animal
29 Hardly a super bowl
31 Food for wrens
32 FD personnel
33 Type of pollution
34 Diamond Head locale
35 Henceforth
37 Skulls
40 "All I Want for Christmas ___"
42 Golf major
45 ___ broche (skewered)
48 Hispanic grocery
50 Floss, for one
52 Pink wine
54 "Odyssey" enchantress
55 Hermione Granger's Patronus
56 Smiled for a selfie
57 Marisa's "My Cousin Vinny" role
58 QED middle
60 "Greenback Dollar" expletive
61 "Orange Sunshine"
63 Zero-___ game

#METWO   by Bonnie L. Gentry
The coin at 17 Across is sought after by collectors.

ACROSS

1 TSA agents' gear
6 Big Pharma division
11 LPGA member
14 Paintballer's cry
15 Cosmetics company
16 Poodle parlance
17 Winged Liberty Head coin
19 Falderal
20 Precollege exam
21 NASA's Continental cousin
22 Champagne grapes
24 It's picked in Kona
26 Workwear fabric
27 College sporting event with a queen
33 Punkah
34 Buddha's birthplace
35 Sooner city
36 Sit still, at sea
38 Brown URL suffix
39 Round gasket
40 "Let me get this straight . . ."
41 Brazil seaport
43 Suffix for malt
44 "Lighten up!"
48 "The Volga Boatmen" painter
49 JAG's White House successor
50 Williams of "Game of Thrones"
52 "No seats left"
54 Like the Nefud
58 Bavarian peak
59 Where "Lost" was once found
62 Took tea
63 Wrote "mispell," say
64 Hussar's weapon
65 Ian Holm's title
66 The ___ truth
67 Bombards with e-junk

DOWN

1 Pushover
2 "Circle of Treason" traitor
3 Drag-racing org.
4 Word from on high
5 Redman in "The Stand"
6 Drops of golden sun
7 Alan in "Flash of Genius"
8 Mariner's 2,025 yds.
9 Wet down
10 Batik step
11 Fire raiser
12 Anarchy
13 Checks one
18 Volleyballer Gabrielle
23 Benin's neighbor
25 Casino numbers game
26 Water down
27 Verse with 17 syllables
28 PFC
29 Time capsule words
30 "___, I'm Adam"
31 Belarus capital
32 Advantage
33 Pool clarifier
37 Voluminous volumes
39 Chili pot
42 Wide neckwear
45 Adrenaline injector
46 GMC truck
47 TripTik, notably
50 "Serpico" author
51 Choir voices
52 Hook's bosun
53 Trout nest
55 McEntire sitcom
56 Technicality
57 Some cable boxes
60 Vex
61 2020 SpaceX destination

58 ACROSS by Catherine Cetta and Bonnie L. Gentry
34 Down has a radius 1,700 times larger than the sun.

ACROSS

1 "Evan Almighty" boat
4 Miles from ___
11 Lush
14 Scot's dissent
15 Camden Yards MLBers
16 FDR power project
17 Wisdom awaiting awakening
19 L.L.Bean rival
20 Abbr. for a state or its capital
21 Low high tide
22 2019 Maren Morris album
23 "I Don't Care ___": Phil Collins
26 Coordinates
27 Demographic divide
31 Nine-digit ID issuer
32 Sputnik initials
33 Queen's label
34 Iditarod command
37 "You dig?"
39 Small songbird
40 Seattle–Des Moines heading
41 Bout ender
42 "One ___ time"
44 Sincere respect
48 Did sums
49 Bring together again
52 "Don't go!"
53 Mexican moolah
56 GI field meals
57 Tugboat task
58 Spring salad ingredients
61 Bedouin robe
62 Gawk
63 Windy City "L" operator
64 "The Last Jedi" heroine
65 Yoga class greeting
66 Your, of yore

DOWN

1 Jungian achetype
2 Arrested, slangily
3 "Breathless" sax player
4 Neither's partner
5 Address ending
6 Oscar Mayer product
7 Sharpen
8 Film director Kazan
9 Sign on for a second tour
10 Tee preceder
11 Part-time journalist
12 Surmounted
13 Nosedive
18 Tangle up (in)
22 MD for women
24 Carry-___ (some bags)
25 DC airport
26 Soak
28 One with a stage coach
29 Vintage film channel
30 Mastodon's era
34 UY Scuti, notably
35 Was but no longer is
36 Banish
38 Shiva forehead feature
39 "No surprises, please"
41 Rocker ___ Rock
43 St. Anthony's cross
45 Complete reversal
46 Wears away
47 Be in charge
50 Eric the Red's century
51 Literature class assignment
53 Falafel bread
54 Apt rhyme for cram
55 Italian evening
58 ISP option
59 Gangster gun
60 Waze way: Abbr.

52 ADDING ON   by Katherine Omak
An original theme by a veteran wordsmith.

ACROSS

1 Basis for a raise
6 Maze solution
10 Stare stupidly
14 "Humble" dwelling
15 Soother in saline wipes
16 Farsi speaker's land
17 Chicago, in the 1920s?
19 Khartoum's river
20 Sewing needle feature
21 NATO, e.g.
22 Cancel out
24 Chef's creation
25 "A ___ formality!"
26 Flavored like some dog treats
29 MP's quarry
33 Does a washday chore
34 Maidenform wares
35 Ship that sailed to Colchis
36 Coffee region of Hawaii
37 "The Elder" of Rome
38 The Harp constellation
39 Send via antenna
40 Brinker of kid-lit
41 Most Vassar grads
42 Wedding-dress trim
44 Group principles
45 Mudville complement
46 '60s talk show host Joe
47 "Seinfeld" gal
50 Do a recycling task
51 Stephanopoulos show, briefly
54 Alternative to Google or Yahoo!
55 An extra dollar in your paycheck?
58 This and that
59 Hurricane rescue op
60 Up to one's eyeballs
61 Huffy state
62 Meyers of late-night TV
63 Brother of Huey and Louie

DOWN

1 Disabling spray
2 uBid competitor
3 "Clue" clue
4 Bachelor's last words
5 Kegler's game
6 Tire puncture application
7 Much of the time
8 Haul to an impound lot
9 Big name in cognac
10 Rogers without Astaire?
11 Solo that may elicit a "Brava!"
12 "Leaves of Grass" poet Whitman
13 Replaceable joint
18 "No problemo"
23 Napoleon's palindrome center
24 When to air a telethon?
25 Has in mind
26 Theodore who played Tevye
27 Cinnabon stand come-on
28 Shaped like a typical volcano
29 Part of a Happy Meal
30 Response to "You wouldn't dare!"
31 Plumed wader
32 Horses with flecked coats
34 Noise from car horns
37 Distinct units of speech
41 Became inedible
43 Earn a blue ribbon
44 Rank amateur
46 Place for a rocking chair
47 Dwindles, as support
48 MGM beast
49 One in the "no" column
50 "Scram, cat!"
51 Nibble like a beaver
52 Calliope or Clio
53 Ghastly-looking
56 "___ been there"
57 Have a tab

AWARDS NIGHT   by Katherine Omak
Santa's scout would be another clue for 35 Across.

ACROSS

1 Command under "File"
6 Adriatic port
10 Boxing blow
14 Zellweger of "Jerry Maguire"
15 Urban uprising
16 Reason to use Febreze
17 "Lady Windermere's Fan" playwright
19 Man-eater of folklore
20 Got top billing
21 Issue forth
23 With a fresh approach
25 Fathered
26 Sniff out
30 Sold in the bleachers, say
33 Without peer
34 Gets stuck in mud
35 Shelf occupant of kid-lit
38 McNamara's ensemble
39 "Parade" composer Erik
40 Lab assistant of moviedom
41 Like some winks and grins
42 Did a haying job
43 Have a yen for
44 Brought up to speed
46 Said "no thanks"
47 Switch to another track
49 Box with headgear, perhaps
51 Sweet Sicilian wine
54 Put in place
59 Kitty starter
60 "Shameless" star
62 T-bone source
63 Sleek, in auto lingo
64 Fencer's maneuver
65 Shopper's aid
66 Impudent sort
67 Takes out, to gamers

DOWN

1 Favorable factors
2 Sit for a bit
3 Indigenous Peruvian
4 Within easy reach
5 Urban barbecue spot
6 Bouquet tosser
7 Feel feverish
8 Patronized Uber
9 Romantically linked pair
10 Canadian dollar, slangily
11 Painter of ballerinas
12 Special talent
13 Trapped like a cat, perhaps
18 Shoved off
22 Sets, as a price
24 Uses bleach on
26 Light touches
27 It doesn't fly on the Sabbath
28 "The Defiant Ones" star
29 Pull the plug on
31 Having little rainfall
32 Pint-sized
34 Landlocked African land
36 February 14 sentiment
37 Father of Pebbles
39 In a blue mood
40 Apr. addressee, for many
42 Letter before gamma
43 Haul away
45 Still in the out-box
46 It beats an ace high
47 Pint-sized
48 Vietnam city with a McCain memorial
50 Military mind game, for short
52 Places to graze
53 Cry of assent
55 One needing rehab, perhaps
56 Home to a small part of Egypt
57 ___ oil (varnish ingredient)
58 CPR pros
61 Radiologist's test, briefly

EXTRA LARGE   by Fred Piscop
Alternate clue for 42 Across: "Fiddler on the Roof" tailor.

ACROSS

1 Bistro order
5 Peace Nobelist from Egypt
10 Tough time for Caesar
14 Far from inept
15 College head, slangily
16 PBS series since 1974
17 Six ounces of Lite beer?
19 Annoying sort
20 How rules might be set
21 Thaw in the Cold War
23 Part of Goofy's outfit
25 Sacked out
26 Long-eared hound
30 Decline, as floodwaters
33 Take up or let out
34 Partygoer's souvenir
35 UNLV part
38 Tugboat sound
39 "Deathtrap" playwright
40 Lingerie item
41 Sushi roll option
42 "Psycho" setting
43 Name in English china
44 Electric train name
46 Having imperfections
47 Lavender or lilac
49 Part of a rural skyline
51 Get in touch
54 Queen of "Chicago"
59 "Free Willy" beast
60 Incense from a Christmas candle?
62 Heroic deed
63 Sun-baked brick
64 Prima donna's solo
65 Commuter's cost
66 Snagged with a lariat
67 Cobble or darn

DOWN

1 Hawaiian food fish, informally
2 "Voice of Israel" author
3 Tell-__ (some memoirs)
4 Didn't stick around
5 Upright relative
6 Van Gogh painted sunflowers here
7 Singer Lana ___ Rey
8 Dismissed summarily
9 Port of Phoenicia
10 Have in mind
11 Sad elephant call?
12 Clickable party notice
13 Full, and then some
18 Relocation pro
22 Arena level
24 Gulliver's exploits
26 Restrain, as breath
27 Lip balm additive
28 German bakery delivery vehicle?
29 Good to go
31 Like a supervillain
32 Pull a fast one on
34 Honor lavishly
36 Home caregiver
37 Risked getting pulled over
39 Chaney or Chaney Jr.
40 Place for rest cure
42 Eye-irritating bit
43 Vending machine features
45 Present from birth
46 Tongue-lashed
47 Mock, with "at"
48 Jazz pianist Chick
50 "Imagine that!"
52 Burn a bit
53 Chore list heading
55 Mosque leader
56 Word after a duffer's tee shot
57 Similar in nature
58 Mental aptitude
61 Cut back

ACROSS

1 Boats on the Thames
6 Did the crawl
10 Ming collectible
14 Guesstimate word
15 Met showstopper
16 Site that started as AuctionWeb
17 Big name in faucets
18 Two-tiered checker
19 Hereditary factor
20 Ballpark figure
23 A bridge seat
24 Recyclable item
25 Meet one's demise
29 Corn Belt natives
33 Lena of "Alias"
34 Blu-ray player button
36 Drill insert
37 Highly defensive attitude
41 "That's strange . . ."
42 State of uncertainty
43 Yemen's chief port
44 School for Torah study
46 Silversmith Paul
48 Packed away
49 Motown genre
51 Option for homeowners with wells
57 Blowgun missile
58 Totally jacked
59 Siding wood
61 Addict's torment
62 Where Perry "met the enemy"

63 Like a cheap speaker's sound
64 Garlic feature
65 Salutation starter
66 Pool table slab

DOWN

1 Inflate, as a résumé
2 Slangy prefix meaning "super"
3 Agnew's plea, briefly
4 "Fantasia" skirt
5 Places for troupes
6 Sushi bar libations
7 Place for a Fitbit
8 Ungrammatical contraction
9 It may involve a hat trick
10 Pig roast shunners
11 Be an accomplice to
12 All there
13 Art critic's asset
21 "A likely story!"
22 Largest of rays
25 N'awlins sandwich
26 Dodge artfully
27 Martini twists
28 Press coverage, informally
29 Numbers-drawing game
30 Bear patiently
31 Gunpowder component

32 "People" composer Jule
34 Thompson in "Love Actually"
35 Brother of Dubya
38 Social Register group
39 Dredged area, perhaps
40 Powder room
45 "Mad" Carroll character
46 Same old, same old
47 Sends to the Hill
49 Balkan capital
50 Seller's hope
51 One in custody
52 It survived Symplegades
53 "Be glad to!"

54 Creator of Felix and Oscar
55 Toon teacher Krabappel
56 Go bombastic
57 Daft Punk, for one
60 Nursery rhyme pocketful

26 ACROSS   by Gene Newman
26 Down is also the name of a street in central London.

ACROSS

1 Bean sprouts bean
5 Like Ulee's "gold"
10 Track part
14 Where more than half the world live
15 "Pagliacci" clown
16 African succulent
17 Giraffe*
19 Mother of Horus
20 Smoking restriction
21 Uppity sort
22 Bentley in "American Beauty"
23 Again, musically
24 Willingly*
26 What answers to clue* words are
31 Blaze
34 Shad product
35 Agitate
36 Togo's largest city
37 Make better
39 Admiral Zumwalt
40 Holy relic
41 "Rush" director Howard
42 Land on a lake
43 Surrounding*
47 ___ buco (veal dish)
48 "Totally awesome!"
49 Honolulu hue
52 Erudite
55 Male voice
57 Urn sound-alike
58 Shoemaker*
60 "Gem City" of Pennsylvania
61 Floridian horse center
62 Deal in
63 Letter opener
64 Rubber-base paint
65 Scraps

DOWN

1 Amazon parrot
2 Strunk & White subject
3 Capital of Gard
4 Iona College athlete
5 Like "Little Boy"
6 Plot hatched by Titus Oates
7 "Love comes ___ the eye": Yeats
8 "Londonderry ___"
9 Show assent
10 Endangered Amazon region
11 Further
12 Binary 10
13 For fear that
18 Cuba ___
21 Ply the needle
24 2016 Rooney Mara film
25 Like cupcakes
26 Holes 11–13 at Augusta National
27 Talking Stick, for one
28 Submarine base?
29 Smallest US coin
30 Tab holder
31 Cannes cop
32 Focal points
33 Cherubic deity
37 Divan's lack
38 "Got My ___ Working": Muddy Waters
42 Bangalore locale
44 Houston school
45 Bassinet
46 Shrek's candle
49 Copier powder
50 In regard to*
51 Grinds
52 Progeny
53 Mule's mom
54 Karita Mattila solo
55 Snip
56 Its logo is a smiling TV set
58 Mustard's rnk.
59 Mozart's "L'___ del Cairo"

WALK IT OFF by Gene Newman
Dinah Washington popularized the song at 56 Across.

ACROSS

1 Heavenly circle
5 League based in Cairo
9 Changes direction suddenly
14 "The check ___ the mail"
15 Retail complex
16 Like boxed candles
17 Complete a straight
18 Recognizing a scam
19 Ex-Yankee Martin
20 **Start of a quip**
23 Approval
24 Bishop's jurisdiction
25 Cousin of a fox
28 Just in case
30 Thunderbird degree
33 Double reeds
34 Trujillo locale
35 Any day now
36 **More of quip**
39 Film versions
40 Makes a pick
41 Summer sale sites
42 Digital token
43 Des Moines suburb
44 Most cunning
45 Some colas
46 Certify
47 **End of quip**
54 Sorta
55 Stem-to-branch angle
56 "What a Diff'rence ___ Makes"
57 Characteristic
58 Munsters' pet dragon
59 Fish served meunière
60 Fredo Corleone's brother
61 Pentagon plate
62 Protective order

DOWN

1 Platter player
2 "Don't you wish!"
3 Harry Potter's mom
4 Observers
5 Ethically neutral
6 Quaid in "Elvis"
7 Clef type
8 E-journal
9 Group within a group
10 Jim Bowie namesake
11 "First Lady of Song"
12 Droop from drought
13 Mud bath site?
21 Czarist order
22 Subject of debate
25 "Dubliners" author
26 Approximately
27 Well-mannered
28 "August: Osage County" playwright
29 Solar-flare measures
30 Patterned silk
31 He broke McGwire's homer record
32 Anxiety
34 Holy See overseer
35 Connecting flight?
37 Chinese menu claim
38 First nonelected president
43 Intellectual keenness
44 Elegantly slender
45 Cellist's need
46 Truism
47 Continental capital
48 Round bread of India
49 Drug that's smoked
50 2019 Beijing event
51 Simulacrum
52 Sabin's vaccine rival
53 Looks over
54 Milk buys: Abbr.

58 'S WONDERFUL   by Gary Larson
A humorous theme from this Washington wordsmith.

ACROSS

1 Unfreeze
5 Rose
10 Mop
14 Avowal
15 Kangaroo feature
16 Cover a lot of ground?
17 Cold, in Colombia
18 ___ fritz (not working)
19 Touched down
20 While supplies last?
23 Krazy ___ of the comics
24 Rice dish
25 Key material
27 Ledger listings
30 MRI alternative
33 Roadside restaurant
34 A fragrant tea
35 Duds
38 Brouhaha
39 Cloverleaf accesses
42 Skater Midori
43 Whimper
45 Put to sleep
46 Field measurements
48 Breath spray brand
50 Pickle brand
51 Sudden outburst
53 Take it easy
55 "Green Book" Oscar winner
56 Worn out specs?
62 Cherry variety
64 Wombs
65 "Vogue" rival
66 Pack a pack animal
67 Tender spots
68 Where the Clintons met
69 Vancouver gas brand
70 "Steppenwolf" author
71 McGregor in "Trainspotting"

DOWN

1 Vegetarian staple
2 Arthur Marx's instrument
3 Plugging away
4 "Yahoo!"
5 Thread holders
6 South Seas kingdom
7 Writer's block dilemma?
8 Cuatro y cuatro
9 Batted, exclusively
10 Bad Ems, for one
11 Haughty pose from a bit player?
12 Birdlike
13 First lady Ford
21 Dragster fuel
22 Blink of an eye
26 Snare
27 "Madam, I'm ___"
28 Fries, e.g.
29 Window treatment for an igloo?
31 Unlikely to bite
32 Wee drink
34 Alligator shoe?
36 Maine–Florida hwy.
37 Winter pear
40 Magic org.
41 Puerto Rican dance
44 2020 Super Bowl
47 Pretty marble
49 Refusals
50 Luggage piece
51 Valuable fur
52 Nom de guerre
54 Cruel sorts
57 Theater admonition
58 Western Indian
59 Deli salad
60 Scat queen Fitzgerald
61 Witnessed
63 Former GM division

ON THE RIGHT TRACK by Gary Larson

In 1986, 10 Down was asked to speak at CIA headquarters in Langley.

ACROSS

1 Old letter opener
9 TV role for Flockhart
15 In complete agreement
16 Informal
17 Place for a run?
18 Zen enlightenment
19 Monopolize
20 Wagers
22 Canon competitor
23 Place for a run?
27 Some are wild
28 Tan, Grant, and Adams
29 Eye-opener?
32 Tax type
33 Hamm with many goals
36 Place for a run?
41 Aliens, for short
42 Roll-call call
43 Puts on
44 Ides rebuke
46 Self-satisfied
48 Place for a run?
53 Bubbling on the stove
54 Country singer Axton
55 Announcer Hall
58 Prince's partner
60 Place for a run?
63 Ancient ascetic
64 Marking on a ship's hull
65 Handled
66 Recommended

DOWN

1 Morse T
2 Nevada county
3 Adjust
4 MLB positions: Abbr.
5 Sun god
6 2004 Will Smith film
7 Matures
8 Leaves alone
9 Ed.'s in-box filler
10 "The Sum of All Fears" author
11 Hand-dyed fabrics
12 Japanese mushroom
13 "Glee" actress Dianna
14 Bluffing
21 Sedate
24 Days of ___
25 Irish stew meat
26 1980s Dodge model
29 Mammy Yokum's grandson
30 Midback muscle, for short
31 Long-eared beast
32 Guileful
33 Hawaiian menu fish
34 Night spot
35 Spam, mostly
37 Not behind
38 Guffaw
39 Lago contents
40 Epiphany kings
44 Adrenaline injector
45 Knack
46 "Sophie's Choice" author
47 He has a Wild Ride at Disneyland
48 Superhero wear
49 Put down
50 Cursor mover
51 Chivalrous
52 Corps of Discovery explorer
56 Copenhagen citizen
57 Like batik
59 Hupmobile contemporary
61 Stir
62 Germany's NPR counterpart

60 FRONT TOOTH   by Jordan P. Conway
In 2010, 35 Down was inducted into the Country Music Hall of Fame.

ACROSS

1 Spewed obscenities
6 Risky venture, for short
10 Power trio instrument
14 Judge in the Bronx?
15 Type of flute
16 Russian river or range
17 Half-and-half half
19 Shea's successor
20 Doesn't need
21 Way to go
22 Hit the big time
24 Mascara spot
25 Overturns
26 Nylon developer
29 Not as loony
30 Going on, to Sherlock
31 Spice from nutmeg kernels
32 Apple Store buy
36 London lavs
37 Frugal sort
38 Barn topper
39 Ocracoke, for one
40 Gait slower than a canter
41 Seasonal mall worker
42 "Anticipation" singer Simon
44 Fill out, in a way
45 Ethiopia neighbor
48 Pull up stakes
49 Made smooth, in a way
50 Spreadsheet filler
51 Road trip expense
54 Chief Norse god
55 Nonverbal communication
58 Left-leaning GOPer
59 Lost fish of moviedom
60 Pacific island republic
61 Cry like a banshee
62 Romulus, to Remus
63 "Get Happy" composer Harold

DOWN

1 Pageant accessory
2 Trumpet effect
3 Seam yields
4 Caviar
5 Contest hopeful
6 Silverman in "Wreck-It Ralph"
7 Argued in court
8 LAX guesstimate
9 One without a title
10 Army enlistee
11 Disney mermaid
12 "Parade" composer Erik
13 Uses a letter opener on
18 Out-of-pocket amount
23 Jungle breast-beater
24 Unpredictable sort
25 Be silent, musically
26 Surrealist Salvador
27 Foo fighters
28 Where to play Marco Polo
29 "Stompin' at the ___": Goodman
31 Maples or Sokoloff
33 Emulate a hot dog?
34 Opening chip
35 "Big Bad John" singer
37 Harsh-sounding
41 Serengeti plain
43 Part of IPA
44 Pic, in ads
45 Utensil with short tines
46 Golden song
47 Penobscot's state
48 "Heart of Georgia" city
50 Moore who voiced Esmeralda
51 France, in Caesar's day
52 Square-mile fraction
53 Leave dumbfounded
56 Longbow wood
57 La Brea gunk

FRUIT FILLING   by Jordan P. Conway
53 Across sold for a record $53.9 million in 1987.

ACROSS

1 Hallmark buys
6 Petty squabble
10 Foundry by-product
14 Youngest-ever Oscar winner
15 Summon via intercom
16 Machu Picchu's land
17 Excerpt from a CNN journalist's speech?
20 Like doves
21 Grad-student projects
22 Hardy heroine
25 Like an oboe's sound
26 Nike competitor
31 "Black Swan" skirt
33 Type of anesthetic
34 Fish served "amandine"
35 Red, Black, and Yellow
39 "Criminal" singer's timepiece?
42 Hathaway of "The Intern"
43 Back up, as a file
44 Stradivari's mentor
45 Trim, as expenses
46 Port of Ukraine
47 Be indecisive
51 Prehistoric predator, briefly
53 Van Gogh painting
55 Least long-winded
61 Drink named after a comics character?
64 Org. opposed to fur farming
65 Pennsylvania port
66 Hustle or hornpipe
67 Leave rolling in the aisles
68 Highly prized
69 Vampire hunter's weapon

DOWN

1 Fugue finale
2 In a bit, to bards
3 Patronize Hertz
4 Salvador with a distinctive mustache
5 Whole boatload
6 Mushroom's genesis
7 Thumbs-down review
8 Whiskey bottle datum
9 Message with emojis, perhaps
10 Mall binge
11 Car dealer's offering
12 Flew like a javelin
13 Showing no fear
18 Yoga accessories
19 NO ___ TRAFFIC
23 Bottle sealer
24 2016 Tom Hanks film
26 Letter before Bravo
27 "Nothin' ___!" ("Forget it!")
28 Windows image
29 Caroline Wozniacki, for one
30 As performed by
32 Masters prop
34 Part of SUV
35 "___ to you, buddy!"
36 Pilots' guesses, briefly
37 Congressional creations
38 LaBeouf of "Disturbia"
40 Obama health initiative, initially
41 Spitball, e.g.
45 Ready for surgery
46 Bovines in paddies
47 They're hardly macho
48 Fish-tailed Disney character
49 Mountain climber's view
50 Bacon piece
52 Old anesthetic
54 Ranked player at Wimbledon
56 Cincinnati squad
57 "Shoo!"
58 Europe's most active volcano
59 Santa's burden
60 Only God can make one
62 YOU ___ HERE
63 Covert org. in "Argo"

PUB PASTIME   by Pam Klawitter
17 Across was first manufactured in the UK by Mackintosh's in 1937.

ACROSS

1 Alternative to Uber
4 Moving containers
8 Carried on a battle
13 Sleeping, perhaps
15 "Wake Me Up" singer Blacc
16 Gossip center?
17 Caramel-filled Hershey candy
18 Nathan of "The Producers"
19 Not together
20 Lyme disease symptom
23 Celery head
24 Gym shoe
28 Garlicky mayo
32 Accuse without proof
33 Meeting with a chairman
37 Skater Lipinski
38 Napkin edges?
39 Shipping lanes
42 Japanese IT giant
43 ABA members: Abbr.
45 Smallest Ivy League school
47 Jeweler's measures
50 Touring car
51 Newlyweds
53 Tropical patio
57 Pile on a sofa
61 Marisa of "Spider-Man: Homecoming"
64 Where losses are gains
65 Aussie gem
66 Fall bloom
67 Johnson of "Laugh-In"
68 "Arbitrage" star Richard
69 Ring-shaped cake
70 Coal stratum
71 Mount a diamond

DOWN

1 Keto no-no
2 Up partner
3 "Twilight" protagonist
4 Ale descriptor
5 "Ageless" beauty brand
6 Ready to eat
7 Fortune-tellers
8 Slimy character
9 It covers a lot
10 Cookie batch: Abbr.
11 Auction ending
12 Letters that spring you forward
14 Richie Rich's dog
21 Loses it on the roadway
22 De Armas in "Blade Runner 2049"
25 Neo in "The Matrix"
26 Snowy bird of marshes
27 Boxing stat
29 Tram contents
30 Laundry room pile
31 Midwest tribe
33 Bird features
34 Pub sign
35 Elroy's pup
36 Stable mom
40 From the first of Jan.
41 Size for a 48 Down
44 Lightly browned
46 Place for a bump?
48 Gym wear
49 It might be delivered on Sun.
52 Picnic cooler fill
54 Slangy turndowns
55 Cognizant of
56 Speck in the sea
58 Informant's wear
59 Animal-friendly letters
60 Line on a to-do list
61 Pub bill
62 Buckeyes' sch.
63 High pt.

FAIR AND BALANCED by Pam Klawitter

The phrase at 40 Across originated in 1970 on a poster promoting Earth Day.

ACROSS

1 Former St. Louis team
5 Shrek and Fiona
10 Jessica in "Fantastic Four"
14 Solemn column
15 Raptor's repast
16 Paint with a sponge
17 Doll utterance
18 2011 Seth Rogen comedy
20 StubHub printouts
22 SoHo studios
23 Newspaper sales data: Abbr.
24 Roof supports
26 Two for you, two for me
30 Vigor
31 Jacob's first wife
32 Goddess of plenty
35 Canadian singer Vannelli
36 Displayed disdain
38 "That makes sense"
39 Whoopi's "Ghost" role
40 "We have met the enemy and he is us" source
41 Mrs. Robert Kennedy
42 Coffee lightener
45 Curling stone material
49 Pain in the neck
50 Royally appropriate
51 Haifa residents
55 Knotted up
58 ___ fox terrier
59 Steak fish
60 Gulf State native
61 Prince Harry's alma mater
62 Flats in Philly: Abbr.
63 ___ Gorda, Florida
64 Tiny bit of progress

DOWN

1 Spanish Steps city
2 Like ___ out of hell
3 "La Bohème" heroine
4 Choppy, musically
5 Proposes
6 Program bug
7 They make the call
8 Superlative letters
9 A little short
10 Santiago send-off
11 Slangy guffaws
12 Montana mining town
13 It's deep
19 Five clubs, at times
21 Drug bust unit
24 Genealogy project
25 "___ my lips . . ."
26 Frozen waffles brand
27 Pound sterling
28 J. McCain's alma mater
29 A bit standoffish
32 DOL agency
33 Avenger Emma
34 Egoist's concern
36 Skiff or shell
37 Check out
38 Words that have a ring to them?
40 Citizens Bank Park team
41 David Rabe's "Visiting ___"
43 Part of AWOL
44 Where Aslan roams
45 Director Gerwig
46 Gun the engine
47 NCIS employee
48 They're often spoilers
51 Terrible ruler
52 Diet-friendly word
53 Dietary supplement
54 Email folder
56 Apex
57 Bird on Australia's coat of arms

64 "HOLD MY BEER!" by Patrick Jordan

Patrick's title sounds like a barroom brawl is about to take place.

ACROSS

1 Caldwell's "Tobacco ___"
5 "As a consequence . . ."
9 Fanny pack fastener
14 Rod between radials
15 Move as lava does
16 Appealing smell
17 Two-time Green Party candidate
19 Jerry Seinfeld's mom
20 "Chasing Pavements" singer
21 Exits dreamland
23 Head-turning shout
24 Eggo warmer
28 Feature of some shotguns
33 In an aimless manner
36 Lacking worldliness
37 Grateful Dead's Bob
38 Slender marsh plant
41 Adds cold cubes to
42 Rival of Max and Coco
44 Creosote quality
46 Tiffany lampshade
49 Upright shark fins
50 Short-term obsession
53 Its official bird is the cactus wren
57 Water bill basis
59 Recovered from a binge
60 Volatile situation
64 Not quite normal
65 Foil's cousin
66 Sarah Palin spoofer Fey
67 Library or tomato follower
68 Dinty Moore specialty
69 Music, macrame et al.

DOWN

1 High-ranking Hindu
2 Nitrous ___ (laughing gas)
3 Pinsetter's place
4 Big name in Round Rock
5 Pull-Ups wearer
6 Soil-working tool
7 Action film blaster
8 Capitol Hill assembly
9 Like much of northern Africa
10 The Magi made one
11 Zhivago, to Sharif
12 "That's the gospel truth!"
13 Reviews reproachfully
18 Determined to achieve
22 Item spun by Charlotte
25 Inning-ending calls
26 Possessing the skill
27 Devious types
28 "Is it too chancy for me?"
29 Claude in "Casablanca"
30 Risotto ingredient
31 Some festive nights
32 Reduction result
33 Shes that are shepherded
34 Composer's silent spot
35 "Let You Love Me" singer Ora
39 Coolidge Dam river
40 Carrier based near Tel Aviv
43 Prepare to cash
45 Magazine mailing
47 Geologist's billion years
48 Thick curtains
50 Hindu wonder worker
51 Realty office employee
52 "The Ballet Class" painter Edgar
53 Rush job letters
54 Guacamole tomato
55 Crayfish-eating wader
56 Keen enjoyment
58 Single Latina, for short
61 Take an alternative
62 Like leprechauns
63 It makes grass glisten

65 IMPAIRED VISIONARY   by Patrick Jordan

The source of the quote below ran for governor of Texas in 2006.

ACROSS

1 Lease term
5 Like spiderwebs
9 What Horner pulled out
13 Digital camera option
14 Made keener
16 Boxer's wear
17 Urge into action
18 Prepared to hear the anthem
19 Takes credit?
20 **Kinky Friedman's definition of an artist: Part 1**
22 Reduces to ribbons
24 Online gasp
25 Knockout liquid of yore
26 ICU workers
29 **Definition: Part 2**
34 Unanalyzed, as data
35 Initials before an alias
36 New car attraction
37 Fruitless fuss
38 **Definition: Part 3**
41 Ovid's 151
42 Ferocious eel
44 Alabama island near Florida
45 Ancestry.com discoveries
46 **Definition: Part 4**
50 Film crew's workplace
51 Mojave mounds
52 Creature in Petco's logo
54 Gamer icons

56 **Definition: Part 5**
60 Let off steam
61 Level-topped elevation
63 Emollient ingredient
64 Owl prey
65 Looks like
66 Unending change
67 Flexible Flyer
68 Bench press muscle, briefly
69 Shelter with stakes

DOWN

1 Mouths, slangily
2 Kosovo currency
3 Cyclotron particle
4 Beverly Hills drive
5 East China Sea port
6 Tiny skin opening
7 It features Draw Two cards
8 Snapple rival
9 Dolphins or Marlins, e.g.
10 F and G, on the Titanic
11 Cab alternative
12 Private dining area?
15 Passing
21 "Going there now," in a 59 Down
23 The items before us
26 Emmy category

27 Uranium mine gas
28 Ghillie Callum, for one
30 Approves
31 Delayed deliberating about
32 Skateboard stunt
33 Fire-starting stone
38 Serengeti scavenger
39 Neither Dem. nor Rep.
40 Gloomy to the max
43 Bumped up against
47 Cardamom and catnip
48 Sent out a press release

49 Curt refusals
53 Botanical transplant
54 Master-at-___
55 Rocky Mountain resort
56 WWW page code
57 Magazine with annual Style Awards
58 Grammar, to a grammarian
59 Galaxy message
62 Beavis' shirt of choice

ACROSS

1 "___ Zapata!" (Brando film)
5 "This is ___ confusing!"
10 Feds
14 Improve, hopefully
15 Boxer's stat
16 Classic theater name
17 2010 Dwayne Johnson title role
19 Shepherd's charges
20 Skateboard stunt
21 Work independently
23 Starter, perhaps
25 ___ time (ER stat)
26 Spring water?
32 Shining example
35 Meh
36 Like some blockades
37 Off-white hue
39 More nearly perfect
42 Paella essential
43 More recently released
45 Where Turkmenistan is
47 Took charge
48 Audi or BMW, e.g.
52 Appearance
53 Breakfast side
56 Invoke the 50-move rule in chess
61 Floating hazards
63 Nickel, for one
64 Annular deep-space nebula
66 Like some juries
67 Janitor's tool
68 Notable periods
69 Unnamed characters
70 Meddlesome sort
71 Job for a body shop

DOWN

1 Presidential thumbs-down
2 Figures in some ancient religions
3 Luthier's handiwork
4 Mother Goose's cat
5 Pound sound
6 Removable table part
7 Pride Rock abode
8 Hardware store array
9 "Sez who?"
10 "1917" setting
11 Like a manicured lawn
12 Suit
13 Wall St. facility
18 Sloppy piles
22 Big cat
24 Get rid of
27 Home of the NCAA's Cyclones
28 1971 Seuss character
29 Iniquitous
30 Iditarod event
31 Idatarod vehicle
32 Percussion instrument
33 Sword with a button
34 Bryn ___ College
38 Noted cliff-jumpers
40 Sixth of five?
41 Explosion, as of color
44 See 26 Across
46 Nose, to an oenophile
49 Within walking distance
50 Unaltered
51 Followed secretly
54 Primitive hunter's device
55 Titan's inter-division rival
56 Express agreement, in a way
57 Proper word
58 Eat in style
59 Party to, as a plot
60 Four-award acronym
62 GPS element
65 "Today" rival, briefly

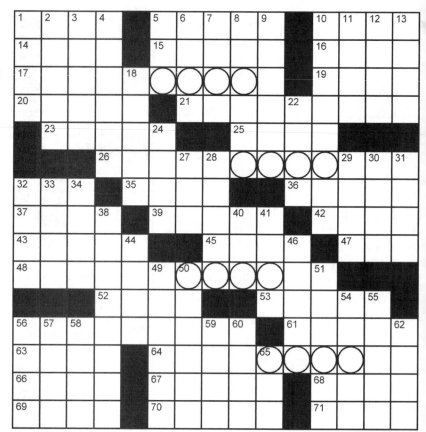

ACROSS

1 Oft-sprained joint
6 Drone delivery service
10 "___ the night before . . ."
14 Osprey's spot
15 "Omnia vincit ___"
16 Home of the Reds and Browns
17 ". . . ___ man with seven wives"
18 Corn syrup brand
19 Fitness centers
20 Retiring professor's swan song
23 Sound system
24 Descriptive term
28 Helpful pair
31 Exam room request
32 Ingolstadt interjection
35 Immortal screen idols
37 "Candida" playwright
39 Perjurer's tale
40 Stagger
41 It's used for wide-angle shots
46 Mme. of Spain
47 Philippine province
48 Historic canal
49 "Affirmative," in radio lingo
51 Shaving brush stuff
56 Alternative to an outright purchase
59 Avid enthusiasm
62 Affix
63 Santa ___ Park (racing venue)
64 High point
65 Nevada city on I-80
66 Made mention of
67 Explodes
68 Deli loaves
69 Hears in court

DOWN

1 Many Dickens characters
2 Send money
3 Woman in a Lead Belly song
4 Indian instrument
5 Floater in a cuppa
6 Boat's track
7 Apple product
8 180° from sur
9 Band follower
10 Unlike Humpty Dumpty
11 Tot's persistent question
12 Crest alternative
13 "Mamma Mia!" number
21 Centers of activity
22 Band of smugglers
25 Undies brand
26 Village leader
27 Green Palo Alto company
29 Fashion magazine
30 Expression in many emojis
32 Comparable to the proverbial fiddle
33 Bolivia neighbor
34 Sports
36 Villain's expression
38 Little gusts of wind
42 "The Time Machine" people
43 Cole of the James Gang
44 World's longest river
45 Caulk, essentially
50 Political event
52 Opera hero, usually
53 Caribbean nation
54 Lauder on the cosmetics aisle
55 Gets into a novel
57 Microwave, in slang
58 Corp. honchos
59 Microwave, in slang
60 Logical opening?
61 Current unit

68 ANTLERED TRIO by Fred Piscop
A nautical day begins and ends at 18 Across.

ACROSS
1 Police, slangily
5 Simplify (with "down")
9 Fixed a wingtip
14 "Gotcha"
15 Woodwind with a conical bore
16 Show conclusively
17 Worthy of a blue ribbon
18 Eight bells at sea, perhaps
19 Poe's "ungainly fowl"
20 Mosquito breeding area
23 Absorb, as a loss
24 Loaf choice
25 Facing the mound
29 Agra attire
32 Easy mark
36 "The Osbournes" wife
38 Iditarod Race racers
40 Flying Cloud automaker
41 Carolina Hurricanes, previously
44 Make a wrong turn
45 Arctic formation
46 Hypnotic state
47 Floored it
49 Las Vegas figures
51 Toes the line
52 Letters on a cruiser
54 Shade similar to ecru
56 Pail-passing team
63 Iditarod Race wear
64 Drought-plagued
65 James who played Sonny Corleone
67 Brains or beauty, say
68 Patronize Lyft
69 Cornell of Cornell University
70 Awning's offering
71 Tidbit for a titmouse
72 Muscle above a pec

DOWN
1 Stretch the truth
2 Makes a patsy of
3 Marmalade morsel
4 Z, on a frat house
5 Summer of disco
6 Wolfpack members
7 Orb seen in werewolf movies
8 Needing alignment
9 Deodorant type
10 Delivers a stemwinder
11 Realm of Eros
12 In all of history
13 Cub Scout group
21 Beat the rap
22 Brothers at Kitty Hawk
25 Grill residue
26 Twyla of choreography
27 Ballerina's rail
28 Wall hangings
30 Kicked in
31 Noisy squabble
33 Name meaning "peace"
34 Plea before sentencing
35 They're struck at shoots
37 Can't-miss
39 Pacific islands wrap
42 Beads holder on an abacus
43 Where Jekyll became Hyde
48 Managed to avoid
50 Take big steps
53 Go rollerblading
55 Came to the rescue of
56 Wild party
57 Celestial bear
58 Does some roadwork
59 Cheese with a moldy rind
60 Scored 100% on
61 Stunned state
62 Banjo player Scruggs
63 Sound systems, briefly
66 Natalie Cole's singing father

ANY WHICH WAY   by Fred Piscop

Van Gogh's "Portrait of Armand Roulin" can be viewed at 49 Down.

ACROSS

1 "Ricki and the ___" (2015)
6 Places for rubdowns
10 Assist feloniously
14 Orders from on high
15 Smart-mouthed
16 Defaulter's loss, for short
17 Jordan's capital
18 Seagoing apex predator
19 Abode in the wild
20 Pleaded for leniency
23 Reply to a captain
24 Pantyhose ruiner
25 Current unit
29 Dust Bowl's lack
31 Take steps
34 Porcine victim of Hercules
35 Cali NFLer
36 Use a Lawn-Boy
37 Risked future harm
41 Soccer chant word
42 Horses at stud
43 Ballet bend
44 Tiny bit
45 Offers further
46 What a nod signals
48 The big four-O, for e.g.
49 Uncommon sense
50 Captivated
58 Cruise stopover
59 Short-nosed dogs
60 Its pages aren't turned

62 Wood shaper's tool
63 Jigsaw starting piece
64 Shannon Airport's county
65 Peaty expanse
66 Gas in Vegas
67 Macho guys

DOWN

1 Big Pharma's overseer
2 Place for a swing
3 Tippy-top
4 Antlered ruminant
5 Airliner maintenance site
6 Name in English china
7 Postage stamp edge, for short
8 With the bow, in music
9 More spangled
10 "Get Happy" composer
11 Put up with
12 "Titanic," for one
13 Boris Johnson, politically
21 Shiva forehead feature
22 H.H. ___ (Saki)
25 Dominican VIP
26 Cash, informally
27 Trimmed expenses
28 Use "lie" for "lay"
29 Dollywood attractions
30 Invasive Argentine colonists

31 Walk casually
32 Clive or Kaepernick
33 Sound from an aviary
35 Comic-Con goer
38 Inedible orange
39 Up for grabs
40 Rival of FedEx
46 Silvery-gray shade
47 Best man's delivery
48 Change the fit of
49 Museum Folkwang site
50 Much blocked mail
51 Big stink
52 Spoonable pasta
53 How we enter the world

54 Frozen waffle brand
55 Letter before Baker
56 What buffalo do, in song
57 Made a rip in
61 "Baseball" documentarian Burns

APERTURES by Fred Piscop
7 Down is a prized fruit of Thailand.

ACROSS

1 Makes ecstatic
7 Not to be trusted
12 Deal involving interest
16 Ore of lead
17 Date-night option
18 Presque Isle's lake
19 New store sign
21 One of Monaco's 499
22 Timer grains
23 REO part
24 Cut deeply
26 Stanley Kowalski's cry
29 Like a bassoon's sound
30 34 Down's call
33 Touring, say
34 Shirking one's duties
37 Tennis star Ivanovic
38 It's good to break this
39 Phileas Fogg's portrayer (with 51-A)
40 Soda can feature
43 No longer edible
45 Hopping mad
46 Not subject to debate
47 Creme-filled snacks
48 Ramshackle dwelling
49 Beauty queens' wear
50 Gas station adjunct
51 See 39 Across
52 Tamerlane, for one
53 Type of jump or pole
54 Saw off, say
55 Nicki Minaj's genre
56 High dudgeon
57 Shoot the breeze
59 Shimmery fabric
60 Fawn
61 Lava, before an eruption
63 Capital of Taiwan
65 Refinery by-product
67 Deliberately avoid
68 Brief times, briefly
72 All-inclusive
73 Ichabod Crane's village
77 Ruffle the feathers of
78 "___ porridge hot . . ."
79 Lake near Syracuse
80 Scored 100 on
81 Gunpowder component
82 Insinuates

DOWN

1 Boy in "The Boxtrolls"
2 Zhivago's beloved
3 Computer scientist Turing
4 Works the bar
5 Tackle's neighbor
6 ___ Paulo, Brazil
7 Like durian
8 Civic automaker
9 Hertz rival
10 Noise pollution
11 Safe-cracking crook
12 Rental papers
13 Where the winds blow?
14 Ran on TV
15 Eligible for Medicaid, say
20 Opposite in nature
25 Unsuitable for farming
27 Finish-line banners
28 McGregor of "Star Wars" movies
30 Off-the-cushion shots
31 Inuit outerwear
32 Safari stop
34 "Nevermore" speaker
35 Three monkeys' avoidance
36 Prefix with life or wife
39 Salvage crew member
41 Display in the night sky
42 On the losing end
44 Trike rider
45 One in a tryst
46 Woody Herman's "___ Autumn"
48 Home to drones
49 Conical dwelling
51 Tuna trapper
52 Like a wrung-out towel
54 Laurel of slapstick
55 "___ Day People": Lightfoot
58 Left speechless
59 "Time After Time" singer
61 Stiller's comedy partner
62 Locale for a hope chest
63 This and that
64 Dot on a globe
66 "College GameDay" channel
67 Place in the Senate
69 Y-sporting collegians
70 Musical wrap
71 Police jacket letters
74 Maui memento
75 Harley, slangily
76 Ace's value, at times

BACK HAIR   by Fred Piscop
A supervillain in the DC universe is named 16 Across.

ACROSS

1 Shows signs of life
6 Knight's garb
10 Squirreled away
13 Firebug's misdeed
14 "Free Willy" creature
15 Rig for long hauls
16 Fairy-tale housebreaker
18 Brit's baby buggy
19 Increase the slope of
20 Larry Fine was a fine one
22 Stand in a gallery
25 South America's "backbone"
26 Place to haggle
30 Street talk
32 Kick to the curb
33 Capone facial feature
34 Observed warily
38 Sunroof option
39 Cut of beef
40 Castling in chess, e.g.
41 Baltic Sea feeder
42 Body-shaping surgery, for short
43 Bridge immortal Charles
44 Portray fury or fear, say
46 Like wasp nests
47 Low man in the choir
50 Arrange, as a blind date
52 Lake ___ (Mississippi River source)
54 Iris rings

59 Filleted flatfish
60 Combat-related trauma
63 Great burden
64 Payment at a booth
65 Love, Italian-style
66 "Game of Thrones" patriarch Stark
67 Without purpose
68 Pounded an Underwood

DOWN

1 Loses firmness
2 Gait slower than a canter
3 Archipelago unit
4 Teased mercilessly
5 Criticize snidely
6 Phobos and Deimos, to Mars
7 Javelin trajectory
8 "That's disgusting!"
9 Glaswegian gal
10 Infamous biblical king
11 .jpg or .gif file
12 Makeshift screwdrivers
15 Floor-cleaning tool
17 King of tragedy
21 Color similar to khaki
23 One on the lam
24 Vaquero's plain
26 Texas politico O'Rourke
27 Ardent, as a collector

28 Fan's reading, for short
29 Tragediennes
31 Couples-carrying craft
33 Uses a letter opener on
35 Olden times
36 In all of history
37 Declare untrue
39 Progressive Insurance gal
43 Eyes in awe
45 Soft shoe
46 Use a reverse stitch
47 Buffalo nickel creature
48 Do penance
49 Córdoba "cheers!"
51 Running total
53 ___ Spumante
55 "Goodness!"

56 Blue Angels stunt
57 Cropland segment
58 Program listing, for short
61 Bricklayer's burden
62 Pipe bend

52 ACROSS   by Bruce Key
Marilyn Monroe was the first 11 Down.

ACROSS

1 French textiles city
6 Tender strokes
10 Lasting emotional mark
14 "Later, gator!"
15 Nobelist Wiesel
16 Dinero unit
17 Luau or seder
18 Famed 15th-century caravel
19 Policy opponent
20 Skirt hoop of old*
23 "The Splendid Splinter" Williams
24 Neck-and-neck
25 Shockers in holsters
27 At the workplace, as training
31 Taxi device
32 Sergio of spaghetti westerns
33 About 10% of Muslims
35 Early Jesse Jackson hairdo
38 Part of a trap set
39 Eye twitch, e.g.
40 Emotional state
41 Not wonderful, but not woeful
42 Period after Mardi Gras
43 Share fifty-fifty
44 Savory jelly
46 Long look
47 Deadly sins, e.g.
49 Spreadsheet figures
51 Skeptic's laugh
52 What's found in clue* answers
58 Utterly spellbound
60 Mireille of "World War Z"
61 Mountain climber's tool
62 Nevada city on I-80
63 Baptism or initiation
64 Remove the stubble
65 Pre-op activity
66 Editor's "Leave it in"
67 Toast starter, often

DOWN

1 Guffaw, slangily
2 Germ for a patent
3 Bull artist
4 In need of GPS assistance
5 Lover of the arts
6 Tubular pasta
7 Set straight
8 "Proud Mary" singer Turner
9 "Lone Survivor" unit
10 Beauty treatment spot
11 "Playboy" feature*
12 Autumn blossom
13 PEDs
21 "___ been there"
22 Nosh on
26 Bosun, for one
27 Ransom E. of autodom
28 "I, Claudius" emperor
29 Tuba kin*
30 Nearest the center
31 Niagara Falls ambience
33 Blueprint bit, briefly
34 Seoul river
36 Act the gadabout
37 Baltic Sea feeder
39 Moves like an anaconda
43 Hookah filler
45 Lat's neighbor
46 Yukon SUV maker
47 Pitched too high
48 Chomping at the bit
49 Struck down, old-style
50 Jets' Super Bowl III win, e.g.
53 Tesla or newton
54 Arthritis symptom
55 Easily reached
56 Kicked in
57 They're splitsville
59 "Red state" org.

PATTERN SHOP by Katherine Omak

21 Across is also the name of the world's smallest shrew.

ACROSS

1 Asgard residents
5 Naja naja
10 Loaf end
14 Ill-fated Genesis brother
15 Bearer of the heavens, in myth
16 Shaft beneath a floorboard
17 Post–Civil War voting bloc
19 Steep-walled formation
20 River of the Carolinas
21 Language of ancient Italy
23 2002 British Open winner
25 Mr. Potato Head piece
26 Game fish with a sharp bill
33 Plumb crazy
35 Horn for Bird or Trane
36 River of Nantes
37 Perched on
38 Have faith in
41 Fail to name
42 Aegean region of old
44 "___ amuse you?"
45 Be too late for
46 Troubled history
50 "___ Got Rhythm"
51 Warbucks henchman (with "The")
52 Suitor's song
57 Battle-hardened
62 Like a superfan
63 Place for a John Hancock
65 Bread with hummus
66 Sign of welcome
67 Any day now
68 Close noisily
69 Campus bigwigs
70 All-star game side, at times

DOWN

1 React in shock
2 Bassoon's relative
3 Editorial strike-out
4 Eluded a baseman
5 Court docket
6 Ear-related prefix
7 Cobalt or navy
8 Informed on, with "out"
9 Guru's retreat
10 Smokehouse meats
11 "Suit"
12 "Frozen" snow queen
13 Not at all fatty
18 Woodland grazer
22 River to the Caspian Sea
24 Fight, but not for keeps
26 Tearoom treat
27 Issue to debate
28 Ooze, as charm
29 Boardinghouse units
30 Fisherman's maximum
31 Camera lens part
32 Cod fishermen's gear
33 Not of the clergy
34 "However," in tweets
39 Common mixer
40 Touts at tracks
43 Closely related
47 Stepped around
48 Newly decorated
49 Mocked, in a way
52 Robs of energy
53 The Dark Side
54 Pop singer Ora
55 Gouda alternative
56 James who sang "At Last"
58 BBQ side
59 Fork prong
60 Nephew of 14 Across
61 Evidence of a hailstone strike
64 First-down yardage

74 BY THE NUMBERS by Gary Larson
22 Across is definitely not a planet.

ACROSS

1 Work well together
5 Depended (on)
11 Rain-___ (Bubble gum brand)
14 Part of a pot
15 Soothsayer
16 Gym unit
17 Fifth-century Pope who was sainted
18 Emergency dialing
20 It's higher on the hwy.
21 Indian bread
22 Pluto, for one
23 Eject
26 Big name in rap
27 Italian bistro
28 Talked up?
29 Crossword snake
30 Annual Alaskan race
34 Convenience store chain
37 Pasta style
38 Pay dirt
41 Family members
44 Online cash-back offers
46 Moon of Uranus
47 Sidearm
50 Slick
51 Code word for A
52 Place to be put on
53 Even-steven
56 Orange cover
58 Poetic paean
59 Take in
60 Social slight
61 Very cool
62 Souped-up car
63 A dandruff shampoo

DOWN

1 Start to function?
2 Kind of list
3 Temporary measures
4 One dimension
5 Wood of the Rolling Stones
6 Gray and Moran
7 Maui neighbor
8 Mountaineer's tool
9 North Carolina university
10 TV room
11 Sullen
12 Poe poem
13 Began
19 Internet brokerage
23 Posting at JFK
24 Unimportant
25 Tyrolean calls
26 Took a shot, maybe
28 Radio button
31 Put ___ good word for
32 Gymnast's goal
33 Tankard filler
35 McFly's friend Doc Brown
36 Being aware of
39 Take
40 WNW's reverse
41 Crazy about
42 Frozen fries brand
43 Out of sorts
45 Something new
47 Bat an eye?
48 Submit
49 Dustin's role in "Midnight Cowboy"
51 Retro hairdo
54 Slangy affirmative
55 Since Jan. 1
57 Baseball stat

CENTER PIECE   by Gary Larson
The alternate title can be found at 35 Across.

ACROSS

1 Data-entry acronym
5 Lowlife
11 Coolers, for short
14 Whiff
15 Christmas, in the Vatican
16 Wolf or devil preceder
17 MP4, for one*
19 Favorite
20 Less sunny
21 Track event
22 Pat down
24 By its very nature*
26 "Hugs and kisses"
28 Jam ingredients
29 Indivisible
30 Temporary solution
35 Centrally located/TITLE
40 Bothered
41 Weep
43 Not so crazy
46 Keyboard bar
49 Like some drinkers*
54 "Zounds!"
55 Spout
56 Parlor game
58 1952 campaign nickname
59 Close race*
62 Ruby or Sandra
63 Blake's "Gossip Girl" role
64 Lavish affection (on)
65 Put the kibosh on
66 One who dotes, say
67 From square one

DOWN

1 Statehouse VIP
2 Despot Amin
3 Inborn
4 Ultimatum words
5 The skinny
6 Supermodel Campbell
7 Take off
8 Chair named for its designer
9 Mild cigar
10 Vietnamese festival
11 View
12 Orange snack
13 Scraps
18 Addams Family descriptive
21 "All in the Family" spinoff
22 V-8 Cafe owner in "Cars"
23 Rice-A-___
25 Go belly up
27 Lincoln and Fortas
31 Early hrs.
32 Zippo
33 Monogram of 58 Across
34 Tacks on
36 Robbery
37 WW1 spy Mata
38 Special time
39 Pebbles' pop
42 Longevity meas.
43 Pace
44 Stir
45 "___ to be alarmed"
47 Prefix with cab
48 To-do list
50 Itinerary, briefly
51 Complete, informally
52 Gourmand
53 Male bee
57 Way out there
59 Free PR
60 Sault ___ Marie
61 Hack

76 CAPITALIZATION by Richard Silvestri
Beatle fans should know the answer to 8 Down.

ACROSS

1 No longer a minor
6 Parts of overalls
10 Time to beware
14 Mountaineering tool
15 Erelong
16 Minimal change
17 Adidas founder Dassler
18 Final Four letters
19 Prefix with thermal
20 English auto tool?
22 State with certainty
23 Carnival locale
24 Yardwork equipment
26 Veto
30 Office machine
32 Egg-shaped
33 Group of islands
34 Turnpike tie-up
37 Type of type
38 In the air
39 Dreyfus Affair figure
40 Yellowstone sight
41 At ___ (confused)
42 "Borstal Boy" author
43 Barbaric
45 Really small
46 Horn, in Hull
48 Shot, for short
49 Seaside soarer
50 Wisconsin chap?
57 Goya's naked lady
58 Clickable image
59 River to the Seine
60 Fermi's study
61 Locked up
62 Lloyd Webber musical
63 Fermentation dregs
64 Newbie
65 Toledo title

DOWN

1 October birthstone
2 Pet name
3 Lots and lots
4 It's often panned
5 Put teeth into
6 Mandolin kin
7 Machu Picchu native
8 "Back in the U.S.S.R." airline
9 Indy 500 concert area
10 Cooling-off period?
11 Colorado lavatory?
12 Home of the Ewoks
13 Packs away
21 Something to pick
25 Sonic assault
26 Cattle catcher
27 Mean business?
28 Mississippi coffee?
29 LAX listing
30 Made a pick
31 Bumblers
33 Wooden shoe
35 Word of woe
36 More than a few
38 Chicken Little, for one
39 Snore symbol
41 Hail, to Caesar
42 Turns into
44 Starting squads
45 "My country" follower
46 Blood-related
47 Hold the floor
48 Former Ford
51 Sore all over
52 Cheerless
53 Approach to the altar
54 Put on a happy face
55 Golden Rule word
56 Time for a revolution

Don't be thinking baseball here.

ACROSS

1 State of matter
6 It's said with a sigh
10 Takes a curtain call
14 Find a caller
15 Pub projectile
16 Change the text
17 "Roots" Emmy winner
18 Making a crossing
19 Run in park
20 Actor drifting off?
22 Hester Prynne's mark
23 Gaggle formation
24 Came down in buckets
26 Alpine abode
30 Blade holder
32 Like some jackets
33 City in Deutschland
34 Thing in a thole
37 Apropos of
38 Sophisticated
39 Solstice time
40 Last Greek consonant
41 City on the Aar
42 Powerful ray
43 Took to the post office
45 Building beam
46 River to the Missouri
48 Have a bug
49 Put in the hold
50 What doting aquarium workers do?
57 Shave-haircut connection
58 Chamber group
59 Telecast component
60 Clanton and Turner
61 Carbon monoxide's lack
62 Noted name in fairy tales
63 Rolls roller
64 Cryptic character
65 Split to unite

DOWN

1 Ollie's partner
2 Ballpark figure expression
3 Bring the plane in
4 Frosted
5 Determined by deduction
6 Bit of wisdom
7 Eye protector
8 Geometric calculation
9 Mad rush
10 Middle East capital
11 Stranger dog?
12 Dorian Gray's creator
13 Home extension
21 Brooklyn basketballer
25 Feedbag morsel
26 Fans do it
27 Radiator sound
28 Opposed to a red dye?
29 Sign of summer
30 Roadside establishment
31 Give birth to
33 "By all means!"
35 Chip in a chip
36 Exit location, often
38 Picky person?
39 Glass vessel
41 Comic's routine
42 Odometer reading
44 Relaxed
45 Baseball great Hodges
46 Cornrow
47 Tall and lean
48 Be crazy about
51 Language of Pakistan
52 "Love Came to Me" singer
53 Roll up
54 Personal prefix
55 Lamebrain
56 Back from work

78 "NOW!" by Lee Taylor
The west end of Provo Canyon is found at 67 Across.

ACROSS

1 Fail miserably
5 South Bend team
10 LLC alias
13 Water pitcher
14 Secret stash
15 Ocean Spray prefix
16 Order to a loiterer?
18 Song ___ (Red River)
19 Antelope meat
20 Milky gemstone
21 Type of buddy
24 Above the timberline
26 Investment option
27 Curses or vows
32 Set of eight
33 Turns sharply
35 Braided Jewish bread
37 Order to a gas company?
41 Turned inside out
42 Former amateurs
44 Buddhist shrine
47 Glacial ridge
49 Greenpeace, for ex.
50 SNL specialty
52 College application part
54 Composer Hovhaness
55 Serial number?
60 Rice-A-___
61 Order for a watchmaker?
65 U-bolt cousin
66 Biblical hymn
67 Utah's "Family City USA"
68 Pack animal
69 Panache
70 Call from behind a counter

DOWN

1 Seek change
2 Oh homophone
3 Convened
4 "Well done!"
5 Clickable image
6 Anoushka Shankar's father
7 Cool treats
8 "Get lost!"
9 Tattoo dye
10 "Let it rest!"
11 Cream pie fruit
12 Went fishing
15 Order for the logging crew?
17 Short note
21 Show ___
22 Not a repro
23 Stuffing spice
25 Batch of laundry
28 Yearn (for)
29 Over yonder
30 Comes to a stop
31 Smooth and glossy
34 Order for the grape crushers?
36 Put on cargo
38 Super Bowl highlight
39 Cinerary vases
40 "I, Claudius" costume
43 Tofu source
44 Peloponnesian War winner
45 Raptor claws
46 Father of Prometheus
48 Start over
51 Kennel cries
53 "Dragonwyck" writer Anya
56 Cereal company
57 "My word!"
58 Move merchandise
59 Treater's words
62 Fury
63 Tex-___ cuisine
64 Ambulance attendant

IT'S ALL RELATIVE by Lee Taylor
The clue at 14 Across is correct, and a bit misleading.

ACROSS

1 Cannery row
5 "Get lost!"
10 Lovage, e.g.
14 Golden cookie
15 Siberian forest
16 Ham's word
17 Shoelace tie
19 Monument Valley feature
20 Like leftovers left too long
21 ATM bill
23 Winter affliction
24 "Leaving Las Vegas" actress
25 Chase baseballs
28 Twin town
34 Chestnut or almond
36 Arabian sailboats
37 F–J bridge
38 Parenthetical remark
39 "Uh-huh"
40 Dutch bloom
42 Hi-___ image
43 "Jersey Boys" role
45 Dorm disturbance
46 Germany, to Goethe
49 Cape ___ (cottages)
50 A&E segment
51 Unagi, at the sushi bar
53 Teensy-weensy
56 Peter Pan player, often
60 Yemen port city
61 What Roy boarded in "Close Encounters"
64 Call alternative
65 Word before child or city
66 Is under the weather
67 Bowlers and boaters
68 Loads cargo
69 Timbuktu's country

DOWN

1 Go for a run
2 JFK postings
3 Bring in the harvest
4 2014 Roma Downey film
5 Tablet accessory
6 Upside-down ___
7 Orange peel
8 Long ___
9 Broderick of "The Producers"
10 Domestic sci.
11 All tied up
12 Doctor's advice, often
13 Hee-haw
18 Nothing at all
22 German sausages
24 Make a visit
25 Wolf down
26 Book between Daniel and Joel
27 Preferred guests
29 Moments of bliss
30 Longtime Dolphins coach
31 Block house?
32 Alex Bregman's base
33 "Holy mackerel!"
35 Return to a former situation
41 J.M. Flagg's poster figure
44 Apollo's twin sister
47 Hangouts
48 Puts the kibosh on
52 Drop the ball
53 Trig or calc, e.g.
54 Think-tank product
55 Cashier's call
56 ___ cost (free)
57 Work on jerky
58 Branch of Islam
59 Spot for a houseplant
62 Que. neighbor
63 Trident-shaped Greek letter

80

BEFORE TAX*   by David Van Houten
Pitzhanger Manor is located in 22 Across.

ACROSS

1 Hand drum of India
6 Major productions
11 "Good Will Hunting" setting
14 Acoustic
15 Nearest capital to Gibraltar
16 Longoria in "Carlita's Secret"
17 Source of dirty money?*
19 Kurosawa film
20 Detroit union
21 Aid's partner
22 Walpole Park locale
24 Former Spanish coins
26 Packing
27 The Statue of Liberty was one*
31 Vergil's vagabond
34 "___ for Evidence": Grafton
35 "This is the life!"
36 Van Houten on "The Simpsons"
37 Sallow
38 Symphony finale, often
40 Line to Yankee Stadium
41 Boy in "The Lorax"
42 Incense burner
43 The press*
47 Used one's scull
48 Squirming
52 Page turner
54 Minnesota's state bird
55 One of Hawaii's Maunas
56 Totally
57 Easy street*
60 Green around the gills
61 Joie de ___
62 Mezzo Obraztsova
63 Nonclerical
64 Driveway sign
65 Hexagon's six

DOWN

1 Touch base again
2 Pervasive moods
3 Forehead features
4 Some solfège syllables
5 Language of NE France
6 Vintner Gallo
7 NATO or SEATO
8 Nigerian ethnic group
9 GoPro products
10 Like saunas
11 Acupuncture pathways
12 Croatian poet Gundulic
13 Sapidity
18 Reinforcement pieces
23 Tripod part
25 "Desire Under the Elms" son
26 Point after deuce
28 Manages
29 Cover a dice bet
30 Asgardian Marvel superhero
31 Arabic "A"
32 Current Spanish coin
33 "Of course!"
37 Turf intruder
38 Entourages
39 Blood type
41 "Kiss Me in ___": Streisand
42 Channing in "Hello, Dolly!"
44 16 1/2 feet
45 Apostolic number
46 BOGO deal
49 Used Elmer's
50 Michaels of "SNL"
51 "Get Yer ___ Out!" (Rolling Stones album)
52 Epitome of thinness
53 Scarlett O'Hara's daughter
54 Tribal history
58 B. Bailey's rank
59 CCV ÷ V

11 Down spent his entire playing career with the New York Knicks.

ACROSS

1 Feinted
6 Tusked animal
10 Poke fun at
14 Extant
15 Inventor's middle name
16 Cosecant reciprocal
17 Large-cent U.S. coin of yore*
19 Ultimatum end
20 Nolan Ryan, for nine years
21 Garage sale caveat
23 Cariou in "About Schmidt"
24 Miss America headquarters*
27 Dep. opposite
30 Mug marking
31 Stimulus check sender
32 Percolate
34 Spanish month
36 Fancy party
39 Capt. Merrill Stubing's boat*
42 Compact piano
43 Brynner in "Westworld"
44 Retained
45 Spoil
46 "How Dry I Am" syllable
48 Congo red, e.g.
49 Line 66° 34' north of the equator*
55 "Family Circus" creator Keane
56 ___ Scott v. Sandford
57 "Old MacDonald" sounds
60 "Shall Caesar send ___?": Shak.
62 Pricy property location (and a theme hint)
65 Email button
66 Vardalos and Long
67 Ledger page
68 Like Dave Chappelle's humor
69 "Enchanted" Levine heroine
70 Hogwarts professor Severus

DOWN

1 Courtney in "Insurgent"
2 Arm bone
3 Billy boys?
4 Musical set in Argentina
5 Deficiency
6 "Ugh!"
7 Olestra brand
8 "Belay!"
9 Bike spokes
10 Korea founder Ki ___
11 1970 NBA MVP
12 Map within a map
13 Diminutive
18 "Bet as much as you want!"
22 Descendant
25 "Be with you in ___!"
26 Pain in the neck
27 Deadly snakes
28 Bring in
29 Like a plane in a holding pattern
33 Burgundy grape
35 Operative
36 Menlo Park's valley
37 See from afar
38 Commune near Padua
40 Mephitic
41 German valley
47 Rocky ledges
49 Put to shame
50 Sore
51 Beldam
52 Filmmaker DeMille
53 Archetype
54 Notorious 2001 bankruptcy filer
58 Caffeine source
59 Cut short
61 Ice cream eponym
63 Butterfield in "Ender's Game"
64 Oft-stubbed digit

LOOK CLOSELY   by Brian E. Paquin
Can you find the things 37 Across in clue* answers?

ACROSS

1 Roman tribunal
5 Capital of Jordan
10 Diamond officials
14 Pearl Harbor's island
15 An Elon Musk company
16 Wordsmith Webster
17 Penn & Teller's forte*
19 Had on
20 Landscape feature
21 Made an aggressive poker bet
23 Semis
26 Spanish child
27 Hip-hop duo who wore their pants backward*
31 Incline
35 Lake, in Lyon
36 Franc replacement
37 Like things found in clue* answers
38 Parental ___
40 Nobelist physicist Enrico
42 Sale location, at times
43 Close with a knot
45 Ballet skirt
47 Affliction
48 Sign up, in Southampton
49 Mexican street food vendor*
51 Headless cabbage
53 Padded joint in hockey
54 Gangster known as "Scarface"
58 Sports summary

62 Maze material
63 Stuffed food item*
66 Brainchild
67 Belgian painter (1860–1949)
68 She, in Sherbrooke
69 Like Jeff Bezos' pockets
70 Peach pit
71 Einstein's second wife

DOWN

1 Hudson Yards developer
2 Courtroom promise
3 "___ she blows!"
4 Portends
5 Thrift machine
6 ___ culpa
7 RC honorific
8 "Space Jam" villains
9 Mother of pearl
10 Awkward
11 Cattle calls
12 Trim
13 She ___
18 Gocycle-GX, for one
22 U.S. standards org.
24 Brusque
25 Miffed
27 Donald Sutherland film
28 Arrested
29 More slippery
30 Kinda ___
32 Tribal eponym of Canada's capital
33 Madonna role of 1996
34 Wrapped up
37 Make a pass at
39 Caught some Z's

41 Fold, at the poker table
44 Tent part
46 Software customers
49 Apartment dweller
50 Giggly expression
52 Takes big strides
54 Litmus reddener
55 Vein in Mother Earth?
56 Manitoba Indian
57 Edmonton gas brand
59 Honeycomb unit
60 Tell-___ (celebrity memoirs)
61 "Guilty" or "not guilty"
64 Unit of coal
65 Beatitudes verb

83

52 ACROSS* by Brian E. Paquin
14 Across was ranked world No. 1 from 1986 until his retirement in 2005.

ACROSS

1 Gives off
6 Adventure
10 "Why don't we?"
14 Chess grandmaster Kasparov
15 Clicked image
16 Panache
17 Sight from Diamond Head
18 Daring exploit
19 Et ___ (and others)
20 Modern usury*
23 Fashionable Giorgio
26 Goes downhill
27 Dillydallying*
31 Happy as ___
32 Like Mr. Clean
33 Lets up
37 MLB scoreboard letters
38 Sidewalk events
39 Scrap of food
40 Flat-topped hill
42 Carol Burnett's alma mater
43 Narrow ridge
45 Key career choice?*
48 Comedy routine
51 Van Gogh flowers
52 Pre-calculator math exercise
56 Involved with
57 Fajita cousin
58 Capital of Korinthos?
62 ___ out (dispense)
63 Mistreats
64 Large sea duck
65 Leered at
66 Coin of Chile
67 Quaffed

DOWN

1 Amour-propre
2 Irish nickname
3 Outrage
4 "An American in Paris" song
5 United, for one
6 Omen
7 Dogfight winners
8 "Golly gee!"
9 Chasers for spicy foods?
10 Pipe problem
11 New York Harbor island
12 Contaminate
13 Obstacles
21 Insurance conglomerate
22 Perlman in "Hellboy"
23 Morning eye-opener
24 Valium drug company
25 Lille lasses: Abbr.
28 One way to be taken
29 Really annoys
30 Sparkle
34 Chess grandmaster Spassky
35 Salt water
36 Guy gatherings
38 Bite the bullet
41 Arranged in rows
43 Complied with a coxswain
44 Vanished into ___
46 Adrian Monk's condition
47 "Rocky ___" (1982)
48 Gooey, disgusting stuff
49 Gooey, sweet stuff
50 T-bill brother
53 Ming Dynasty item
54 Cool desserts
55 Just OK
59 What a kiss cam prompts
60 Coop
61 Covenant container

84 THEMELESS by Harvey Estes

29 Down is also the title of a Sylvester Stallone movie.

ACROSS

1 Fierce fish
10 "Vissi d'arte" singer
15 Drove off
16 Nut with a cap
17 Running event of eight feet?
18 Honeydew or cantaloupe
19 Must
20 Brit. word ref
22 Drinks like a cat
23 Riboflavin source
25 45 or 78
27 James in "The Green Mile"
31 Calculating
33 "Alice" star
34 Jumping the gun
36 Tigers of the SEC
37 High spot
38 Vocal cords, slangily
39 Bowlers, e.g.
40 Tel Aviv's nat.
41 Bedding
42 Brimless top
43 Sell to the end user
45 Tibetan monks' residence
47 1862 Tennessee battle site
49 Reinhart on "Riverdale"
50 "That makes sense"
51 Kluszewski of baseball
53 Nary a soul
57 Challenger's quest
59 Like safety glass
61 Gimlets and such
62 Watchful hours?
63 "Hop ___": Seuss
64 Saw

DOWN

1 Jersey home
2 Helm location
3 Get under one's skin
4 Concrete from a chute
5 Typical burg
6 King who sang "Jazzman"
7 "Key Largo" actress Hagen
8 Geometric art style
9 Like ___ in the headlights
10 Skye cap
11 Nocturnal wildcat
12 One cause of radio interference
13 Cotton-field sprayer
14 Beattie and Landers
21 Gives a hand to
24 Calvin of underwear
26 Call out
27 "___ de Lune"
28 Informal discussion
29 Too too
30 Carnation holder
32 Hot-blooded
35 Kidney-related
38 Flight plan filer
39 Waver
41 Rapper ___ Wayne
42 "Hogwash!"
44 Danny in "Do the Right Thing"
46 Dr. Evil's clone
48 Bails out
50 "Tell ___ the judge!"
52 Take a risk
54 Mayberry drunk
55 Disney clownfish
56 First eviction site
58 Crystal vision
60 "Good Will Hunting" setting

36 Down appeared in 27 Hollywood films.

CROSS

1 Cobbler fruit
6 Return fire
15 Put to rest
16 Like an Edward Hicks "kingdom"
17 "Sonnets to Orpheus" poet
18 When anxious people want it
19 French cathedral city
21 Certain
22 Lots to analyze
24 ___-Caps candy
25 Ran first
26 Soap-___-rope
27 Bottom lines
29 Tornado strengths
31 For night owls
33 Yours and mine
35 Twist arms
39 Proton site
40 Slyboots
42 Old Thailand
43 Cursive curlicue
45 "The Jackal" star Richard
46 Roman year
47 Battle of Britain heroes
49 C&W's McEntire
51 Small fry
52 WSW opposite
55 Eagle's perch
57 Borat's swimsuit
59 Granary with slats
62 Like Jaime Sommers
63 Return from the dead
65 Seder cracker
66 Alexander the Great's tutor
67 Sci-fi visitor
68 Big-top securer
69 Touches down

DOWN

1 Math curves
2 Drop
3 Swamp critter
4 Formed into clumps
5 Villains in "The Lion King"
6 Intelligence agent
7 Pay attention to
8 Desert refuges
9 Gas pump word
10 Fighting mad
11 Candy purchases
12 Choreographer Paula
13 Saint of Assisi
14 On edge, with "up"
20 Short pencils
23 In the midst of
28 Take the tiller
30 Drug lord in "Scarface"
32 Middle Eastern ruler
34 Seraglio
36 German shepherd of fame
37 Elevated to sainthood
38 ;–) and :–(
41 Greek restaurant menu item
44 Campaign targets
48 Drew a blank
50 Cracker type
52 Ostentatious display
53 Bête ___ (bane)
54 Watergate senator Sam
56 Cow catcher
58 Qantas mascot
60 Snug retreat
61 Swindle
64 Maiden name preceder

THEMELESS by Harvey Estes

At the 89th Academy Awards, 1 Across received six Oscars.

ACROSS

1 Damien Chazelle film
9 Deadly agents
15 Mars black, e.g.
16 Way
17 Like Fitbit products
18 Jipijapa hat
19 "Blondie" boy
20 One-time link
21 Fly by
22 Mark down drastically
24 Eastern bigwigs
26 Alias initials
27 Coin flips
29 USN rank
30 Tight-fitting
31 Some Motown music
33 Facility
34 Edison contemporary
38 Make new clothing from old
40 Dr. Alzheimer
41 Closet wood
43 Superabundance
44 Delt neighbor
45 Airport shed
50 "The Addams Family" cousin
51 Rhea's role on "Cheers"
53 Edwin in Reagan's cabinet
54 Sounds the hour
56 Off one's feed
58 Math subj.
59 Trojan War warrior
60 Mirabelle source
62 Result of ironing
63 Surfeits
64 Proven in beta
65 Visine doses

DOWN

1 Best, on the links
2 Danny of "Do the Right Thing"
3 Andes animals
4 Spanning
5 Hawaii's Mauna ___
6 "Dark Angel" star Jessica
7 Nick of "Hotel Rwanda"
8 Devised, with "up"
9 Gets narrower
10 Chart bubbles
11 Lawless character
12 All shook up
13 Blockhead
14 Coastal flier
23 Deli offerings
25 Preparing to bloom
28 ___ Quentin
30 Plane domain
32 Less naughty
33 "Beat it!"
34 Teller's specialty
35 With no parts missing
36 Comic bits, e.g.
37 Op. ___
39 Part of a tuba sound
42 Sun block?
44 Threw a Hail Mary
46 Undiluted fruit juice
47 Adjust for
48 Out for the night
49 School break
51 Leave off
52 Put to rest
55 Coconut flesh
57 Renaissance instrument
61 Prefix with night or day

THEMELESS by Harvey Estes

19 Across opens the 1999 film version of "Inherit the Wind."

CROSS

1 Content
8 Some stolen furniture?
15 Fan base
16 Quarterbacked
17 Article lengths
18 Trench of the western Pacific
19 Song about Bible Belt faith
21 Granada gents
22 Garfield's sidekick
26 PC core
27 Fescue, for one
32 Breaker box locale
36 Seasonal slider
37 Article of summer wear
38 Comment when you're stumped
42 Bother terribly
43 Instructive viewing
44 Some are "cat"
45 Science of light
48 Film about a July 4th beauty pageant
57 Getty of "The Golden Girls"
58 CN Tower site
59 Graffiti beards
60 Captivates
61 Pollination organs
62 Stands for

DOWN

1 "The Good Dinosaur" hero
2 Raise a sweat
3 Winged Foot hazard
4 State on the Seine
5 Auspices
6 Pastry filling
7 Condensed meaning
8 Big hit
9 Tracks
10 Polo on a screen
11 Military lockup
12 Morales of "My Family"
13 Paul in "12 Years a Slave"
14 Kind of dive
20 Gold chain style
22 Davis of "Do the Right Thing"
23 SkyMiles airline
24 Start of a legal conclusion
25 "High Flying, Adored" musical
27 Rival of 31 Down
28 Blabbed away
29 "Rise Up" singer Day
30 Little rascal
31 Tennis legend Monica
33 Gershwin title start
34 Funny Margaret
35 Cooking meas.
39 Sadden
40 Major addition
41 Thrown out
45 OPEC vessel
46 "Snow White" meanie
47 Clingy wrap
48 Bucks prefix
49 "Help ___ the way!"
50 ER imperative
51 Steph Curry's brother
52 Run off
53 "More" singer Perry
54 Gordian ___
55 To be, in Brittany
56 "The Hunger Games" director

37 DOWN   by Annemarie Brethauer
The clue at 16 Across refers to a Freddy Cannon song.

ACROSS

1 Old Yeller's yap
4 Heat to just below a boil
9 Moire-pattern painting
14 First Lady before Eleanor
15 Humorous Hardy
16 "Transistor Sister" item
17 Intl. student's class
18 Unlawful detention*
20 Place to put down roots?
22 Robert Morse monodrama
23 Homer's "On ___ Shore"
24 Badenov or Godunov
26 Some are gum
28 Org. cofounded by Jane Addams
30 Suffix with brew
32 Yore
33 Across the pond from Europe
36 He spent Tuesdays with Morrie
40 1040 agcy.
41 China setting*
43 Herb of grace
44 Sanctum sanctorum
46 Off-color
48 "Losing My Religion" band
50 Jellyfish Fields locale
51 "I do solemnly swear . . ." recitation
52 It's not cricket without one

56 Late-night bite
58 One chain by one furlong
59 Idiosyncrasy
61 Mounds of cottonwood fluff
64 "À votre santé"?*
67 Feel strange
68 "Star Wars" bobblehead, e.g.
69 Island now an Immigration Museum
70 Jamaican jam
71 Horseless rider?
72 "I Love a ___ Night"
73 "Don't take his advice," e.g.

DOWN

1 Guinness in "Doctor Zhivago"
2 New York's flower
3 Loudest volume*
4 Up to now
5 Samuel Richardson heroine
6 ___-nighter
7 Careen
8 "Nothing runs like a ___"
9 Ben of the Cars
10 Mai Tai accessory
11 "Rolling in the Deep" singer
12 Skateboard pad
13 Carries away
19 Vibe
21 Hooligan
25 Lava-lava, e.g.
27 Banded quartz
28 Three oceans touch it

29 SZA album
31 Patent preceders
34 Zimbalist on "77 Sunset Strip"
35 Brings peace of mind
37 B&B fare (and a theme hint)*
38 Show the door
39 Jersey fabric
42 Substitutes
45 Hall of fame
47 Activity centers
49 Number crunching
52 London counterpart of AMPAS
53 Very bitter
54 Like some scaredy-cats
55 Saltpeter
57 Pretentious
60 Wendy's drink

62 Pool party torch
63 Kind of 1990s fad bracelet
65 Brooke Baldwin's network
66 Will Smith film

WRITING TOOLS   by Jonathan H. Brill
A clever challenger from a Bay State puzzler.

CROSS

1 2010 Apple innovation
5 Flamethrower fuel
11 H.S. exams for college credit
14 Swing, as a mast
15 Mini-burger
16 Dodger great Hodges
17 Have- and what- followers
18 Roaring Fork realtor's listing
20 When DST begins
22 Morales of "Ozark"
23 Buckwheat's affirmative
24 Water balloon impact sound
26 Lends an ear
28 "Que pasa?"
31 Scull
32 Genesis creator
33 Highlands fishing spots
37 "The A-Team" character
38 Rival of Rafa and Roger
41 Bit of Fudd's laughter
42 Outdoes
45 Abu Dhabi dignitary
47 Bargain bin abbr.
48 Rod Laver Arena event
52 Bass lure
55 Rechargeable battery
56 Caribbean soft drink
57 Tooth's partner
60 Attach with needle and thread
62 "Nine" star
65 Part of TTFN
66 Zeta follower
67 When mammoths roamed
68 Jack-in-the- pulpit
69 Windburned
70 Merited
71 ___ majesté

DOWN

1 "___ Life Strange": Moody Blues
2 A sword after a beating?
3 Pep Boys stock-in-trade
4 Make seawater potable
5 POTUS foreign policy group
6 Shampoo additive
7 John Cena wins
8 Reference another website
9 Pope who crowned Charlemagne
10 3-D medical scan
11 Variety of chalcedony
12 Galileo, by birth
13 Classic toys often used on stairs
19 "Do ___ gentle into . . .": Dylan Thomas
21 Church service
25 "If/___" (2014 Broadway musical)
27 NBC skit show
28 Uterus
29 Back in the day
30 Patio stone
34 Flora Danica offering
35 Greek "Father of History"
36 Couch doctor
39 Doc bloc
40 Oast
43 Valentino's dance
44 Japanese flag symbol
46 "How the Other Half Lives" author
49 Nero's tutor
50 Glowing bullet
51 Perfume ingredient
52 "Ain't I a ___?": Bugs Bunny
53 Only signed Michelangelo work
54 Not a blood relative
58 Gulf of Oman land
59 Winter Olympics event
61 Identify
63 "Honey ___": Beatles
64 British omega

90 RACK 'EM UP by Patrick Jordan
Rudyard Kipling once nicknamed 25 Down "Hell's Basement."

ACROSS
1 Circus tent props
6 Render more readable
10 Nile serpents
14 Hatchling's sound
15 Rx label info
16 Trifling argument
17 Incriminating proof
19 Kind of loser or thumb
20 Is far from proud about
21 North in "The Shootist"
23 Calculated maneuvers
27 Caught a glimpse of
28 Notifications of danger
29 In need of Dramamine
30 Snack bar drinks
31 Smokehouse worker
32 Disco guy on "The Simpsons"
35 The 4077th on "M*A*S*H"
36 Wading pool wader
37 Hydrotherapy havens
38 Muscle above an ab
39 Buccaneer's bounty
40 Neat, at the bar
41 "Don't doubt my ability!"
43 Smoothie bar appliance
44 Act of contrition
46 Quaint villages
47 Rise from obscurity
48 Municipal planning division
49 Sound in a stairwell
50 Initial paint layer
56 Sonorous sound
57 Deep-bottomed bag
58 Quickly, to Shakespeare
59 Broadway constructions
60 Step in making Jell-O
61 Up in the clouds

DOWN
1 Acer desktops
2 Impedance unit
3 Sign that's Latin for "lion"
4 Cartoonish squeal
5 Scrooge's night visitors
6 Competitive superiorities
7 Kennel guests
8 Home of the NCAA's Cyclones
9 1970s bike
10 They're in black ink
11 Melanie C's nickname
12 "Gay" city of song
13 Paramount mount
18 Banana split bits
22 Wintry lawn coating
23 Take the gauge from E to F
24 Richard E. Byrd book
25 Southeast Alberta city
26 Incorrigible 36 Across
27 Inclined to irritability
29 Capital in the Andes
31 Settled on
33 Composer's "be silent"
34 Facebook clients
36 Notions
37 Ground
39 How it all began?
40 C, to Caesar
42 Christmas pageant tunes
43 Miss Marple
44 Marshmallow chicks
45 Quiz show questioner
46 Baseball walk-off
48 Baked pasta dish
51 "Claptrap!" in Cambridge
52 USN noncom
53 Clod
54 Emulate Pitt
55 "Miss Pym Disposes" novelist

SOLID-STATE   by Patrick Jordan

For eight seasons, 23 Across was a wide receiver with the Cincinnati Bengals.

CROSS

1 Patio zapper victim
4 Snowblower part
9 Picks performers
14 Teamwork impediment
15 Napoleon's penalty
16 Exceedingly
17 Frothy quaff
18 Horse traders drive this
20 Warhead deliverers
22 Told a state secret
23 Football analyst Collinsworth
24 Lawn-repairing roll
25 Alpine road segment
26 Considers irresistible
29 Photography session
31 Went along (with)
32 6, on the Beaufort Scale
36 Innovator's starting point
37 FLOTUS of 1933–45
38 Tongue-lolling comics dog
39 Unwavering bid
42 Plagiarized
43 Less speculative
44 Left in the fridge
45 Pete Alonso, for one
48 La Brea mastodon trapper
49 Bypass socially
50 Above the horizon
52 Dr. Eric Foreman on "House"
56 Cassette tape successor
58 Waikiki's ___ Wai Canal
59 Tennis score after deuce
60 Nick in "Hotel Rwanda"
61 Relocation vehicle
62 Proceeds along
63 Grove growths
64 Place for a patch

DOWN

1 Construction timber
2 Unsightly fruit?
3 Hits the road
4 Brought back to the crew
5 Shamrock-like plant
6 Monster truck features
7 Pioneer automaker Ransom
8 Soldier at Cold Harbor
9 Freed from (illness)
10 Growth in stagnant water
11 "Dracula" prop
12 Takes a crack at
13 Makes a shuffleboard slicker
19 Unlikely to mingle
21 Slasher film outbursts
24 Cook eggs in the oven
26 Scoffing phrase
27 Shortstop Gregorius
28 Baltic Sea tributary
29 Roundup critter
30 Like saddle shoes
32 Not as perilous
33 One with fervent fans
34 Christie's "Death on the ___"
35 Title page?
40 Emulates Joey Chestnut
41 Cameroon coin
42 Reporter's contacts
44 Dismissing all temptation
45 Squawking rainforest bird
46 Cause to crumble away
47 Disney's sassy meerkat
49 Request at a 29 Across
51 Idaho veggie
52 Cooked cabbage emanation
53 Lay down a lane
54 Chalk talk depiction
55 Far from foolhardy
57 "Claws" network

BACK STORY* by Roland Huget

The Himalayan cat is a crossbreed between a Persian and a 1 Down.

ACROSS

1 Bee's pollen pouch
4 Tablelands
9 Snouted ungulate
14 Not oneself
15 "You don't say!"
16 Make room on a drive
17 Object of a SETI search*
19 Supermarket section
20 Source of syrup
21 Deadly African snake
23 Chess champ Mikhail
24 No difference, in France
25 Phishing, for one*
27 High-ranking angel
29 Age that began in 1945
30 Ballpark fig.
31 Voodoo pin cushions
35 Splinter group
36 Plaything for Fido*
39 Cute Lucas creature
42 "Goodbye, Gabrielle"
43 Misfortune
46 Distance runners of yore
49 Site of a 1971 prison riot
51 Home seller's dream*
55 Termite predators
56 Rock concert need
57 Wyle and Beery
58 Sired, Biblically
59 Open Society founder George
61 Grade school crush*
63 Chain member
64 Host an event
65 Vietnam War Memorial designer
66 Affirmatives
67 Reaches across
68 Family man

DOWN

1 Blue-eyed cat
2 Young-and-old
3 Cut-and-paste graphics
4 Site with shafts
5 Cockney perdition
6 Slippery, in a way
7 Joanna Lumley sitcom
8 Terse note from teacher
9 Cause of a 1773 Boston revolt
10 "Entourage" agent
11 Crossword solving, say
12 Kind of architecture with minarets
13 Put back in office
18 First name in scat
22 Bandeau
25 Comrade of Mao
26 Optimistic
28 ASAP relative
32 Grassy stretch
33 Bucko
34 Schussboom
36 Timetable, for short
37 Duct issue
38 Tagged on the base path
39 Diplomat's posting
40 Nintendo controller, to gamers
41 Experienced hands
43 Take the top medal
44 Spencer in "The Help"
45 Canary Wharf area of London
47 Salon jobs
48 ___-Caps
50 Chinese weight unit
52 Is slack-jawed
53 Sound of a heavy hit
54 Adopt-a-pet org.
58 Tournament passes
60 Vein hope
62 Writers' org.

DOUBLE PLAY   by Roland Huget
". . . damn spot!"

CROSS

1 Big fishhook
5 ___-Ball (arcade game)
9 Take for one's own
14 First name in scat
15 Part of TTFN
16 Doubleday of baseball
17 It's not as the crow flies
20 Tex-___ cuisine
21 Very much
22 Van Gogh subjects
23 Oscar rebuff
24 Islands handouts
25 Heckle or Jeckle
28 Put a move on
32 Bushy dos
33 Like Cheerios
34 "Just kidding!"
35 Ted Turner's nickname
39 Hair package
40 Lab rat's course
41 Join forces
42 Iron Man, for Tony Stark
45 Manuscript doctor
46 Truth alternative
47 Harness racing pace
48 "What a thing to accuse me of!"
51 Test result
52 Tank content
55 Term used in an acceptance speech
58 Artist Édouard
59 Frankenstein's gofer
60 Pre-deal payment
61 Smart-alecky
62 All-purpose vehicles
63 Siamese greeting

DOWN

1 Lysol target
2 Lotion additive
3 Continual change
4 Simple cooler
5 Pigeon's roost, at times
6 Skewered serving
7 British boarding school
8 Word on perfume bottles
9 Stephen King's telekinetic teen
10 Wind player
11 Unwelcome burden
12 Apollo 12's Conrad
13 "___ bien!"
18 Sweet roll
19 Mod tee
23 OxiClean target
24 Woodworking tool
25 African serpent
26 On the wrong side (of)
27 Weightlifting sound
28 Passover cracker
29 Arctic first peoples
30 Framed words
31 Former anesthetic
33 Over 21
36 Mafioso code of honor
37 Game of nines
38 Pursuing the matter
43 Draws out
44 One-in-a-million, say
45 They can extend an inning
47 Southwest ski resort
48 Beliefs
49 Film rating org.
50 Female turkeys
51 High ranking NCO
52 No longer around
53 Camera setting
54 Dish made in a pot
56 Lucy of "Kill Bill"
57 Highlands hat

"IT'S ALL A FACADE"   by Pam Klawitter
Born in Canada, 16 Across became a naturalized U.S. citizen in 1998.

ACROSS
1 Crossword diagrams
6 Sailboat stopper
10 Beauty mark locale
14 Julianne of "The Hunger Games: Mockingjay"
15 Baseball family name
16 Trebek with all the answers
17 Justice Sotomayor
18 Try for $1.00 on "The Price Is Right"
19 Longish skirt
20 Troubling test results
23 Key fruit
24 Wide awake
25 Funny money
31 Jason Bateman hit on Netflix
32 Rubik with a cube
33 JFK alternative
36 Sticking places?
37 "Wicked" platform
39 Kind of drama "Elite" is
40 British isle
41 Ski-Doo product
42 Bestowal at a banquet
43 Bunch of nonsense
46 So long, mon frère
49 Red Sea resort
50 Discontinued Campbell's product
56 Liveliness
57 Romance novelist Roberts
58 Pyongyang locale
60 Country byway
61 "Yeah, right . . ."
62 Play backer
63 They're cracked in the kitchen
64 Tip the dealer
65 Bruin legend Cam

DOWN
1 Baseball execs
2 It's over your head
3 Home of the NCAA Gaels
4 Boring people?
5 Down with mal de mer
6 Friendly ghost
7 Chow chow
8 Newbery Medal winner Lowry
9 City bond, for short
10 Group in a tree
11 Still kicking
12 One who gives it up
13 Have a life
21 Down Under bird
22 It might be folded in a food truck
25 Front for front
26 Blue, in Bilbao
27 "Wide Awake" singer Perry
28 Willing associate
29 Bit of work
30 Raleigh–Richmond dir.
33 Show a bias
34 Richard of "Arbitrage"
35 Judge Hardy's son
37 ___-mo
38 KO count
39 Short odds at the track
41 Closed off
42 Like the North Slope
43 Sri Lankan teas
44 Miss a deadline
45 Welsh rabbit ingredient
46 Take a stroll
47 Hulk Hogan's headwear
48 Cake cover
51 School credit
52 Prefix for call
53 Arduous trip
54 Impulse
55 Rind
59 Gymnast Raisman

"STAY OUTTA MY LANE!" by Pam Klawitter
58 Across is located behind the Leaky Cauldron pub in London.

ACROSS

1 Support
6 Civic leader?
11 Preschool break
14 "Hamilton" number "___ Burr, Sir"
15 Hyland of "Modern Family"
16 Lines of tribute
17 Inning ender, at times
19 "Immediately!"
20 They may need to be filled
21 Sowing machines
23 Stringed sculpture
26 Like a bread knife
27 Vaudevillian Tanguay
28 Socialistic
30 Sapporo sport
31 Grandmas, to some
33 She explores with Boots
35 Olive Garden fare
38 Side at a picnic
39 Probes for
41 Stanford stats
42 Easy as ABC
44 Compete in a regatta
45 Corncrib filler
46 Duck genus
48 Bunch of toads
50 GPS suggestion: Abbr.
51 Log-in info
53 Horace Greeley's advice
55 Without worries
56 Super Bowl ticket word
57 ___-esprit (wit)
58 Where Hogwarts students shop
63 Verse opener
64 "Oklahoma!" aunt
65 Vaquero's range
66 "Animal Kingdom" network
67 Chat site admin
68 Some NCOs

DOWN

1 COVID-19 source
2 "Yay, team!"
3 D-backs on the scoreboard
4 Amazon's Rufus, memorably
5 Ultimate purpose
6 Grounded fliers
7 Rower's need
8 Bichon ___
9 Thieves, basically
10 Take heart
11 Not a scrap left over
12 Be very fond of
13 Flock seating
18 Camera settings
22 Insurance adjustor's concern
23 Brilliant bunch
24 Track shapes
25 It's found in a glass boat
26 Salon highlights
29 Warring parties
32 "Old Folks at Home" river
34 Allied by nature
36 Bakery treats
37 It's a plus
40 "Win With Willkie" is one
43 St. Patrick's Day events
47 Syracuse locale
49 Adds up to
51 Home of the Vols
52 Black Friday offerings
54 Fargo partner
55 Lie against
56 Hiker's snack
59 Prefix for thermal
60 Dillydally
61 Med. specialist
62 Greetings from Rocky

Alternate clue for 17 Across: One who doesn't take orders well.

ACROSS

1 Just okay
5 Sport coat material
10 Sing like Joe Cocker
14 "Back to you"
15 More on the mark
16 Bratty kid in "Blondie"
17 Food service elevator
19 Jack-o'-lantern output
20 "___ to believe . . ."
21 Prettifies at a patisserie
22 Big name in combines
23 Near, to bards
25 Board game randomizer
27 Stand in a bedroom
31 Ignited anew
32 Greedy monarch of myth
33 "Holy moly!"
36 Tip jar filler
37 Snake venom, e.g.
38 1941 Welles role
39 "Able ___ I . . ."
40 Tour de France gear
41 Where King marched
42 Crumb-collecting gadget
44 Like a leopard
47 Problems for divas
48 Shannon Airport's county
49 Subtle aroma, e.g.

51 Letter after upsilon
54 Tool in a golf bunker
55 Name in plastic containers
58 Beehive State tribesmen
59 Estuary
60 Spread measure
61 ___ sana in corpore sano
62 Afrikaners
63 Kickoff aids

DOWN

1 Designated driver's order
2 Fertility clinic cell
3 Florida State team
4 Scepter's mate
5 Facial hair, for short
6 Commodore Perry's lake
7 Wagon trail furrows
8 "Holy moly!"
9 Commit a faux pas
10 Monarch's stand-in
11 Wrench type
12 Gooey campfire snack
13 Lack during a blackout
18 English Channel isle
22 Coin-stamping tools
24 Suffix with sinus or senior
25 Simon Legree, notably
26 Drawing board creation

27 What the humble eat
28 Dunham of "Girls"
29 Like pastrami
30 One of Santa's team
33 Painting hanger's concern
34 "I'll get this one"
35 Don
37 Item on a game rack
38 Low-carb diet
40 Attack like Dracula
41 Rock candy, essentially
42 Cause of job burnout
43 Left Bank toppers
44 Rugby restart

45 Cover with tin, perhaps
46 Like many whiskey barrels
49 Fit for duty
50 Car-for-hire company
52 Add to the staff
53 "Et tu" day
55 BBQ morsel
56 Game with Skip cards
57 Yoga accessory

BEGINNINGS   by Fred Piscop
31 Across was a big hit for the Big Bopper.

ACROSS

1 Carbo-loading fare
6 Mexican resort, for short
10 Place for merit badges
14 Elia, to Lamb
15 Site with PowerSellers
16 Sailor's patron saint
17 ACDelco products
19 Musk of Tesla
20 Seaver in Cooperstown
21 Channel-clogging deposit
22 Two-thirds of YTD
24 Retro boot style
25 Got through to
26 "We need help!"
29 Aleut's wear
30 Turn away, as a gaze
31 "Chantilly ___"
32 Shower wall piece
36 Early bird's prize
37 18K gold vis-a-vis 14K
38 Ill-suited for farming
39 Frosty's makeup
40 Burl of "East of Eden"
41 Work like a dog
42 Month for pranks
44 ". . . but few are ___"
45 Avoided, as an issue
48 Utter bore
49 Greek yogurt option
50 Cartoon vamp Betty
51 Windy City rail inits.
54 Astronomical bear
55 Crop storage spot
58 Homer's order at Moe's
59 Green Gables girl
60 Bare minimum
61 Stuff to excess
62 Await a decision
63 BoSox rival

DOWN

1 Time traveler's destination
2 Brand for Fido
3 "The King and I" setting
4 La Brea pit substance
5 Invites to dinner, say
6 Pablo Casals' instrument
7 Border on
8 Carry-on, e.g.
9 Worker in beds
10 Burpee mailing
11 Deity prayed to in Mecca
12 Struck down, old-style
13 Placed an edge on
18 Big Bad Wolf's quarry
23 Official tree of several states
24 Biological weapon
25 Churchill Downs events
26 Fellers' tools
27 River near Rugby
28 ___ Beach, Fla.
29 Comic strip segment
31 Hopping mad
33 Rolled-over plans, perhaps
34 Like an "in concert" album
35 Shangri-La
37 Dangerous place to live
41 Having an hourglass figure
43 Bake sale org.
44 Holey, lightweight shoe
45 Gives the cold shoulder to
46 "M*A*S*H" land
47 Hawaii's place in an atlas
48 Fawned over, with "on"
50 Beethoven's birthplace
51 Kennedy family, notably
52 To-do list entry
53 Cultural pursuits
56 Binary code digit
57 Herd's milieu

98 GAME PIECES by Fred Piscop
10 Down is also the name of a Black Sabbath album.

ACROSS
1 Not as ruddy
6 Guide's offering
10 Nothing, in Pamplona
14 Take the podium
15 Plot division
16 Cyber-'zine
17 Londoner's crisp
19 Campaign poster word
20 Play for a patsy
21 Regrets deeply
22 Smelled skunky
24 Flawless
26 Fact fudger
27 Sound of relief
28 Break for a driver
32 Campaign poster word
35 "Sonic Dash" company
36 Ship to Colchis
37 Pucker-inducing
38 Basketball turnover
39 Texter's "carpe diem"
40 Nile predator, briefly
41 Starbucks size
42 Copperhead snake
43 Twitter symbols
45 Mahershala of "Green Book"
46 Practically forever
47 Settles from the bench
51 Added zip to
54 Winter road treatment
55 Love seat capacity
56 Show impatience on the road
57 "Blueberry Hill" singer
60 Fairy-tale opener
61 Paid newspaper notice
62 White sale purchase
63 Sorrowful drop
64 ___ avis (unusual sort)
65 They get results

DOWN
1 Infield fly
2 Left the sack
3 Informal goodbye
4 Olympus letter
5 Turn tail and run
6 "Don't play," in music
7 "Love Me, I'm a Liberal" singer
8 Sch. south of Providence
9 Payback of sorts
10 Persevere at all costs
11 In a frenzy
12 Timeline figure
13 Like centenarians
18 "That stings!"
23 Al Yankovic's "___ It"
25 "Jeopardy!" job
26 Copier paper size
28 Fiddle tunes
29 Trampled, with "on"
30 Eye lasciviously
31 Shabby, as excuses go
32 Carve in stone
33 Croft or Logan
34 Lover of Psyche
35 Males with racks
38 Put up with
42 Counting everything
44 Talon's place
45 1/1 song title word
47 Many a dreads wearer
48 "Goosebumps" author
49 Sports team honcho
50 Factory whistle times
51 Flu season protection
52 Dixie bread
53 Early Andean
54 Tend to the batter
58 Org. for advocates
59 "O Sole ___"

GEOMETRY COURSE   by Catherine Cetta
A progressive theme by a New England artist.

ACROSS

1 Beginning of a magical incantation
5 Toon robot dog
10 Wild party
14 Deadlocked
15 Backpack part
16 Sarah McLachlan hit
17 Sandwich shop option
18 Unapologetically blunt
20 Like argon
22 APR part
23 Grammy winner Mann
24 Blitzers at times
27 Make believe
28 Blood type group
29 Many Wisconsin farms
34 Utah canyon
36 Cupcake toppings
37 Antiquing "cheater"
40 Yarn bundle
42 "Scarborough Fair" herb
43 Shows again
45 "It's the Hard-___ Life"
47 "Big Sur" novelist
49 "Wha . . .?"
50 Sit-up targets
53 American purchase
56 Aquarium buildup
60 ___ 'easter
61 Holiday dinnerware
62 Airhead
65 "While you're ___ . . ."
66 Flu-ish feeling
67 Major Joppolo's post
68 Ire
69 Homies
70 Bonkers
71 Federal IDs

DOWN

1 "Mother Goose & Grimm" cat
2 Like the Borg, notably
3 College official
4 Place on a pedestal
5 African viper
6 Water main valve
7 Fool
8 Launched a Tweetstorm
9 Choose
10 "South Pacific" setting
11 Driver in "Marriage Story"
12 Part of SohCahToa
13 Cod relative
19 Having a high pH
21 Way up the hill
25 Unfathomable
26 Ballpark bummer
30 Play a longshot
31 "Barefoot Contessa" Garten
32 It possibly came first
33 Compass heading
34 Get-up-and-go
35 "Eeew, a mouse!"
37 Sacred chest
38 "___ whiz!"
39 Musician's gift
41 Intrinsic
44 Indian currency
46 Stylish
48 Horseshoe Falls locale
50 Husky relatives
51 Not harmful
52 Avers
54 Greet silently
55 Blackens on a grill
56 "I want it yesterday!"
57 Vare Trophy org.
58 Caesar's conquest
59 Service winners
63 Subway alternative
64 Bath boat, e.g.

"DO YOU READ ME?" by Katherine Omak

Fabergé launched 5 Across in 1964 and it is still available today.

ACROSS

1 Jared of "Suicide Squad"
5 Popular men's cologne
9 Motocross entrant
14 Mixed in with
15 "Titanic" heroine
16 Make blissful
17 John Lennon album
19 Aesopian finale
20 Land of the casbahs
21 Lanky, as a colt's legs
23 Get really ticked off
24 Binary digits
25 Big-eared brayer
27 Kept out of sight
28 Selling like hotcakes
31 Neowise, for one
35 Anagram of 15 Across
37 Constant annoyance
38 Listen to Mom, say
39 Musketeer cap feather
40 Black-and-white predator
41 Speck in one's eye
42 Sitar selection
43 W.C. Fields persona
44 Blossom visitor
45 Pre-Christmas lot buy
46 Its capital is Sydney: Abbr.
48 ___ rage (juicer's problem)
50 Pekoe packet
55 Places to worship
58 Sumner, for Sting
59 Serve a purpose to
60 Pioneering handheld device
62 Left Bank river
63 Resting on
64 FedExed, say
65 Faded to black
66 Clears after expenses
67 On pins and needles

DOWN

1 Priests with prayer wheels
2 Hirsch of "Lone Survivor"
3 Hint of color
4 More off-the-wall
5 Twisted tresses
6 Oblong tomato
7 Derive benefit from
8 Kinski title role of 1979
9 Send a tickler to
10 Sans escort
11 Riverboat gambler
12 List shortener, briefly
13 Have trust in, with "on"
18 "Awesome!"
22 Runway model's asset
26 Like rooftop panels
27 Muscle Beach denizen
29 "There ___ was a . . ."
30 Trickler on a cheek
31 Rooster's topper
32 Wind with a mournful tone
33 Lovely Rita, for one
34 Batter's asset
36 Persian export
37 Respond to an ump's bad call
39 What a rainbow flag symbolizes
43 Annoying sort
45 Like ravioli or Twinkies
47 Totally baffles
49 Offer a viewpoint
51 Ouzo flavoring
52 In bundles, as cotton
53 In the thick of
54 Oil baron J. Paul
55 Subdue with a shock
56 Not lopsided
57 Distance between wingtips
58 Arcade machine opening
61 Patronized Spago

IN THE BANK by Katherine Omak
67 Across is a popular ingredient in smoothies.

ACROSS

1 Barracks array
5 French military cap
9 Propelled, as a punt
14 App-launching symbol
15 Burl of "East of Eden"
16 Shed false tears, say
17 Military pullout
20 Like Dali's art
21 Not moving
22 Color like khaki
23 Floor exercise need
25 Satisfied sigh
28 Garage job using counterweights
35 ___ gin fizz
37 Sonic's game company
38 Squash variety
39 Grade schooler's adhesive
41 Black Halloween animal
42 Did a jackknife, say
43 "Let me clarify that . . ."
44 Checklist detail
46 Auditioner's CD
47 West Virginia resource
50 "Ben-Hur" novelist Wallace
51 Grid great Dawson
52 Steven Tyler's acting daughter
54 Turns outward
59 Region of Europe along the Oder
63 Broad appeal
66 Search blindly

67 "Superfood" berry
68 View as
69 Smart-alecky
70 Star in Lyra
71 Fateful March day

DOWN

1 Comic's routines
2 Color like khaki
3 One of a coupe's pair
4 Angry bull's sound
5 Service club since 1915
6 Demonic doings
7 Vet's visitor
8 "Sorta" suffix
9 Smart-alecky
10 Epps of "House"
11 Rob of "Code Black"
12 Expected landing hrs.
13 Muscle above a pec
18 Bog yield
19 Target of high-tech mining
23 Explosive measure
24 Winds down
25 Jelly in head cheese
26 Santa Anna siege site
27 Old Testament prophet
29 Food Network offering
30 Young Scot
31 Gastric juice, e.g.

32 Many a book club selection
33 Oreo filling
34 Bequeath funds to
36 Abbr. similar to etc.
40 An eligible receiver
45 Armed group
48 Disney's "Let It Go" singer
49 Item on a game rack
53 "Falstaff" composer
54 Dairy aisle offering
55 Gown designer Wang
56 Mireille of "The Catch"

57 Sales force, for short
58 Deuce beater
59 Negotiations hang-up
60 Bird feeder morsel
61 Words from a therapist
62 Some drive-thru features
64 WC
65 Curling surface

102 WAITING AT THE LIGHT   by Nicholas Machado
. . . while listening to the car radio.

ACROSS

1 "Brave New World" sedative
5 Do House work
10 Getz or Kenton
14 Gemma in "Captain Marvel"
15 Indian metropolis
16 Czar's car
17 Phony beginning
18 Superior group?
20 1970 Eric Clapton hit
22 Ned Flanders' son
23 Change of address, for some
24 First PGA Tour commissioner
27 Stipulations
29 "Bucking the tiger" game
33 Chicken ___ provençale
34 Fuddy-duddy
36 Like Shangri-la
38 1966 Beatles hit
41 Sunoco rating
42 Man or woman
43 NYC airport
44 Its flag has a beehive
45 Squealer's digs
46 Sporty auto, for short
48 Former frequent flier
50 "Silent Spring" killer
51 1967 Lemon Pipers hit
60 "Awesome!"
61 Tree of Knowledge locale
62 Hill dwellers
63 Plane
64 Too
65 Curative amount
66 Observers
67 Last team managed by Stengel

DOWN

1 Blackleg
2 "Not this time!"
3 Damon or Drudge
4 "Peer Gynt" dancer
5 Beaten by a nose
6 One of Bunyan's dogs
7 Hebrew letter
8 Bracelet danglers
9 Lab measure
10 Clambake salad
11 Luau torch
12 "You can say that again!"
13 Schnozzola
19 Mormons, initially
21 Charing Cross locale
24 Heron habitat
25 Send to the Hill
26 Valletta locale
27 Psychic parts
28 Wellspring
29 In favor
30 Not quite upright
31 Beatle with the beat
32 Mariana Trench locale
35 Be light, so to speak
36 Bird from a green egg
37 "Citizen Kane" estate
39 ___-di-dah
40 Shaver
45 Dash in "Mo' Money"
47 Field's partner
48 Kate McKinnon show
49 Elegance
50 Voodoo pin cushions
51 Last year's senior
52 City N of Carson City
53 Does brunch
54 "What ___ can I say?"
55 Displace
56 Great Trek trekker
57 Like some rumors
58 Cedar home?
59 Nephew of Cain

HETEROGRAMS by Nicholas Machado

... of which two fine examples can be found below.

CROSS

1 Cordon bleu
5 Keeps going
10 "Balderdash!"
14 Cupid's realm
15 Go on the fritz
16 Brain wave
17 Simon Says player
18 Florida citrus city
19 Stretch out
20 Study of fingerprints*
23 Seed
24 "___ De-Lovely"
25 Platypus origin
28 Part of CST.
29 Source of peat
31 Albee's art
33 Former tadpole
35 Skewer
39 What answers to clues* have
42 Site of Shah Jahan's tomb
43 With a wink and ___
44 "The Fox and the Crow" author
45 Director's word
46 Bird with a gray-blue neck
48 Switch ups?
49 La Réserve Genève, for one
51 Inventor of the Sudoku puzzle
53 In the public domain*
60 Rent
61 Beforehand
62 Put film in
63 "Boys for Pele" singer
64 Was all leers
65 Plebiscite
66 Lamarr in "Boom Town"

67 "Steppenwolf" author
68 Straw in the wind

DOWN

1 Sporting clothes?
2 Famous blue diamond
3 With who or whom
4 Italian-born physicist
5 "Tao Te Ching" author: Var.
6 Master of ledger domain?
7 Proscenium
8 Rock group Jethro ___
9 Fix Tabby
10 Like corkwood
11 Elba in "Cats"
12 Fair-hiring org.
13 Bromides
21 Opus Award org.
22 Dr. Dolittle's Gub-Gub
25 Dame Everage
26 Pirate's potable
27 "Oh, God!" star
29 Soaring birds
30 Elgar's "Coronation ___"
32 HBO's "Show ___ Hero"
34 Chief Whitehorse's tribe
35 ___ Anne de Beaupré
36 Durango coin
37 Retired Monopoly token
38 Cookbook abbrs.
40 ___ de toilette

41 Badger
45 Mushroom part
47 Stevenson misanthrope
49 Chowder fish
50 Poor verse
51 Lena Dunham series
52 Sudden outburst
53 Alta locale
54 Iditarod Trail terminus
55 Michelle of "Crazy Rich Asians"
56 Road hazard?
57 Microphone type
58 Like the White Rabbit
59 First lady's residence

TO A T by Richard Silvestri
The margarine at 9 Down has been around since 1937.

ACROSS

1 Red mark
5 Prefix for phone
9 Palermo pie
14 Natural emollient
15 Spoken
16 Moon of Uranus
17 Go up
18 Cicero's secretary
19 Turn away
20 Where the deer hunter's arrow landed?
23 Not vert.
24 Coventry clothiers
29 Undemocratic group?
32 Foam at the mouth
35 Hole in your shoe
36 La Scala highlights
38 Lively group?
40 "Peter Pan" pooch
41 Chance to spray?
44 John P. Marquand sleuth
45 Half, to start with
46 Girl in a Left Banke song
47 "The Tempest" king
49 The first video game
51 Professor's deg.
52 Makes a choice
54 Poetic eternity
56 Buchholz in the neighborhood?
62 Banded gemstone
66 Harbor alert
67 Wrapped up
68 "Haste makes waste," e.g.
69 Plot unit
70 Some vaccines
71 Wide in the waist
72 Integument
73 Wilson's predecessor

DOWN

1 "Star Trek" speed
2 Lamb by another name
3 Ledger entry
4 Canines that bite
5 Friend and foe of Godzilla
6 Iroquoian Indian
7 Dress
8 One way to read
9 Brand of margarine
10 Pique condition?
11 Vim and vigor
12 Snore symbol
13 Musketeer motto word
21 Human trunk
22 Coat of arms
25 Rigatoni relative
26 "The Graduate" heroine
27 Got a flat
28 Lingered on
29 Radiotherapy rays
30 Maryland's state bird
31 It may serve a duel purpose
33 Mane site
34 Walk with heavy steps
37 Put things right
39 Club combo
42 Passport need
43 Pressing person
48 Hatch a plot
50 Do some tidying
53 Mex. misses
55 Fowl pole?
57 Anklet
58 Doughnut shapes
59 Part of the eye
60 Toy ball material
61 "Doggone!"
62 First of a Latin threesome
63 Chew the fat
64 "Billions" billionaire
65 Carol contraction

STORE POSTING* by Gary Larson
Syracuse U. coach Jim Boeheim has employed the 63 Across for decades.

ACROSS

1 Naval cops
4 Ready to park one
9 Words of wisdom
14 Lyricist David
15 City in Spain
16 Laser printer powder
17 History
18 Mason, for one*
20 Walkway
22 Merry-go-round animal
23 Together
25 Grease gun's cousin
29 Pebble Beach rarity
30 Puts in stitches
33 Russian saint
34 Witchy laugh
37 Springfield bartender
38 Early bird's reward
39 ___ Kosh B'Gosh
40 Large wood screw*
43 Witness
44 Tart
46 Sushi ingredient
47 Some Ivy Leaguers
49 Comedian Love
50 "Tomb Raider" heroine
52 Wasn't colorfast
53 Sailor's patron
55 Black Sea republic
59 Frothy drink with tapioca balls
62 "Halt!"
63 Man-to-man alternative, on the court*
67 Part of TGIF
68 Worship
69 Be silent, in music
70 West in "Myra Breckinridge"
71 Royal pains
72 Phonograph needle
73 Start to save?

DOWN

1 Form
2 Polytheist
3 Bellagio bandit*
4 Keyboard key
5 Convex molding
6 Pickling juices
7 Smoothie fruit
8 Soapstone
9 Video game pioneer
10 On the ___ (in secret)*
11 At all
12 Go right
13 Go astray
19 In a lax way
21 Literary drudge
24 Pitch
26 Store posting (and theme hint)
27 Square (with)
28 Stars
31 Leftover bit
32 Serenade
34 Barbecue fuel
35 Fancy tie
36 Stud site
41 "The Gods ___-begging": Handel
42 Poi root
45 Cartoon office worker
48 Metallica drummer Ulrich
51 Bureau
54 Methods
56 Supporter of the arts?
57 Specks
58 Church recesses
60 Rears
61 Udder part
63 Stun
64 Words of praise
65 Votes against
66 Summer on the Riviera

CROSS TOWN   by Gary Larson
8 Down famously wrote his plays at a two-story loft in 11 Down.

ACROSS

1 "Fifty Shades Freed" heroine
4 AA, on Wall Street
9 Surfeits
14 Bagel topper
15 Variety of onion
16 Tin-lead alloy
17 Colorado research facility?
19 With lance in hand
20 Elba in "Cats"
21 Patricia in "Hud"
23 Took the bait
24 Musk of Tesla, Inc.
25 Oregon tax proposal?
28 Flips
30 Arm muscle
31 Wind dir.
32 Echo's voice
35 Track assignment
36 House pest in Nevada?
39 Golf coach Haney
42 Dark brown
43 Ol' Blue Eyes' monogram
46 Iroquois tribe
49 Humbly apologize
51 Connecticut moneymaker?
54 Words to Brutus
55 911 respondent
56 Harry Potter's Patronus
57 Pillow material
58 Dummies
60 Michigan deadbolt?
63 Peace goddess
64 Early Greek colony
65 Chef's phrase
66 What cowbirds don't build
67 Perfect
68 Hanoi holiday

DOWN

1 North African capital
2 Ramen soup strips
3 Guns N' Roses front man
4 Simians
5 Spy novelist Deighton
6 "Silent" prez
7 Monkey's uncle?
8 "Tiny Alice" playwright
9 Not as new
10 Down Under hrs.
11 Longtime home of 8 Down
12 Animate
13 Prepare for print
18 Sup
22 Doodlebug's dinner
25 Singer Fitzgerald
26 Computer operators
27 Showy flower
29 Race unit
33 Classic Jaguar
34 Rockies resort
36 Playlet
37 Italian car
38 Back muscle
39 Focused (on)
40 "Alice Doesn't Live Here ___" (1974)
41 Snuggles down
43 Suit perfectly
44 One is found in 43 Down
45 Performed poorly
47 Puts down
48 Do something
50 Sports page news
52 "Goodfellas" group
53 Cool place to live
57 Postponement
59 Fracking explosive
61 Publicity, slangily
62 2019 Miss America Franklin

61 ACROSS*   by Brian E. Paquin
"Eh, Cumpari!" was a #1 hit for 19 Across in 1953.

ACROSS

1 Piedmont wine center
5 Little white lie
8 First to stab Caesar
13 Tamer's work area
15 Pipework fasteners
17 "Homework counts for 20% of your final grade"?*
18 Courteous
19 Godfrey hiree/firee
21 Gummer in "Ricki and the Flash"
22 Painter's tool
25 Slate of coming-out girls?*
27 Dismal
28 Domain
30 Some tell-all authors
31 Finishes wrapping
33 Nautilus captain
35 Poor rep in the 'hood?*
41 Free electrons
42 Stingy
44 Speak like a sailor
48 Greek colonnades
51 Solemn promise
52 One not on the A-team?*
54 Axed
56 Typewriter type
57 Waugh's Brideshead, e.g.
59 Untangles
61 Going crazy (and a theme hint)
65 PGA golfer Brendan
66 Win from behind the bench
67 Bond foe Blofeld
68 School grp.
69 Kid's fort site

DOWN

1 Snowcapped peak
2 Chaplin's title
3 As well
4 Angered
5 Less biased
6 Snub
7 Honey bunch
8 Half pint
9 WMD of WW1
10 Comfort
11 High point in a story
12 Wardrobe
14 Thunder sound
16 Top tennis players
20 Sherlock's Irene
22 Platoon NCO
23 Maryland menu item
24 Seacrest's cohost
26 Watson in "The Circle"
29 "In conclusion . . ."
32 Poly ___
34 Unscripted?
36 Thorny bloom
37 Between, in Bordeaux
38 "Heaven forbid!"
39 Minimal high tide
40 Boarding site
43 Third degree
44 Smokey's no bear to them
45 Watching Stephen Colbert, e.g.
46 Splinter
47 Glossy fabric
49 Play charades
50 Soft drink brand since 1889
53 Emulates Tarzan
55 Relating to the ear
58 Trough fare
60 Ready to go
62 Needlefish
63 Mars discovery
64 Index omission

61 ACROSS   by Brian E. Paquin

The Tibetan name for 47 Across is Qomolangma ("Holy Mother").

ACROSS

1 Bob Dylan's "___ for You"
6 Drano ingredient
9 Like Daisy Fuentes
14 "Well done!"
15 Treaty of Rome group
16 Cue from a QB
17 PGA Tour $ ranking
19 Safecrackers
20 Tour de France winner Pantani
21 Apollo 17 mission artifact
23 Small crows
25 Bank jobs
26 Hog rider
31 High dudgeon
32 Toyota sports car
33 Finalize
37 Read over
39 Heavy impact sounds
41 Kiri Te Kanawa's title
42 The Duchess of York
44 Willow
46 Satellite navigation
47 Highest point on Earth
50 Least active
53 Dry, on a Spanish wine label
54 Part of a house inspection
57 Trajan's empire
60 Tuned in
61 Farthest from the center (and a theme hint)
64 Office communiqués
65 Raptors' org.
66 Stickhandles around
67 Raps on the wrist
68 Chew the fat
69 Oil spill

DOWN

1 Big Blue
2 Email header
3 Nursemaid
4 Go too far
5 Hot Wheels, e.g.
6 Hawaiian bridal wear
7 Reply to a schoolmarm
8 Ghostbusters' car
9 Feigned modesty
10 Like raw film
11 Counterfeit
12 Acute anxiety
13 Stick homes
18 Revealing, in a way
22 "___ get it!"
24 Draw off
26 Be off the mark
27 Quint's boat
28 Rip apart
29 Potpie part
30 The upstairs women of Downton Abbey
34 Union concern
35 Some plate cleaners
36 Buttinsky
38 Talk about seeing stars?
40 Harsh
43 Dolly Madison's parent
45 45 and 78
48 4x4, briefly
49 German general saluted by Churchill
50 Muslim leaders
51 Wooden rod
52 Woolly beast
55 Number
56 March wind?
58 Golfer Isao ___
59 Minute part of a minute, briefly
62 Forerunner of Diet Coke
63 Disapproving cluck

WINNERS by Victor Fleming
20 Across is known for being one of the longest hitters on the PGA Tour.

CROSS

1 Island near Key West
5 Canis lupis
9 Barn compartment
14 Rte. through Texas Canyon, AZ
15 Gem that symbolizes hope
16 Boat that's easily rocked
17 Layered haircut
18 Mind
19 Come up
20 2019 Safeway Open winner
23 "___ Bell to Answer" (1970 song)
24 Concert blaster
25 Finance grad
28 Gillette ___ II Plus
29 Is just right
31 TV golf analyst Azinger
32 Mineral in hemoglobin
34 Casual garment
36 "The Wizard of Oz" director
40 Cultural surroundings
41 Put faith in
42 Norse hub
43 Scholastic sports org.
45 Bollywood tune
49 More Spanish?
50 Smartphone forerunner
51 "Be honest!"
54 Athol Fugard character
56 "Red ___ for a Blue Lady"
59 Joan Crawford's last film
60 Spooky-sounding canal
61 Taurus neighbor
62 Stitch's pal
63 Ireland's ___ Féin
64 It might be acquired
65 Just managed, with "out"
66 Facebook links

DOWN

1 Pancho's amigo
2 Hammarskjöld's United Nations successor
3 BMW bike, to bikers
4 Bassett in "Malcolm X"
5 Tennyson's "The ___-Eaters"
6 Precedes a headliner
7 Judicial seat
8 Nothing new
9 Rogue
10 Infield cover
11 Folk singer DiFranco
12 Spanish article
13 The Phantom's creator Falk
21 Speak from memory
22 Dutch beer
25 Water pipe
26 Town
27 Cockpit abbr.
30 Red leader?
31 ___ Delta Theta
33 18-hole units
35 New ___ Beach, FL
36 Entrance requirement
37 Pandora's boxful
38 Corp. tech exec
39 Big part
40 Soccer ___
44 Angus and Ayrshire
46 Stationary
47 Attorney Allred
48 Under the weather
50 Like the sack dress
52 Burns/Denver film
53 Elysiums
54 Run into
55 "The Music of the Night" singer
56 "Pearls Before Swine" rodent
57 "R.I.P." singer Rita
58 "___ for Silence": Grafton

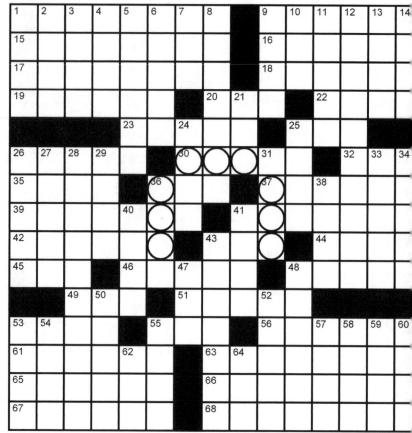

ACROSS

1 Joan in "Rebecca"
9 Klein of fashion
15 Samuel Gompers, for one
16 Mumford in "Fifty Shades of Grey"
17 Historic 30-second event of 10/26/1881
18 Mandate from on high
19 Cheer heard when Simone Biles performed
20 ___ v. Wade
22 Like expensive beef or fine Scotch
23 Give the once-over
25 "Bow, wow, wow, ___ Yale!"
26 They make hydrangeas blue
30 Alpha Centauri, for one
32 Delt neighbor
35 Norse trickster god
36 Yoga class need
37 Cantankerous
39 Persevere
41 Clothing lines?
42 Cut the mustard
43 Anonymous John
44 The Bee Gees, e.g.
45 Without exception
46 Station house
48 Rocky Mountain resort
49 "Natural" blackjack card
51 House near the White House
53 Rat Pack member, informally
55 Bookmarked spot
56 Space cloud
61 Texas team that switched leagues in 2013
63 Livery near the 17 Across
65 Word after dirty or strawberry
66 "My Way" lyricist
67 Felt
68 Puts in bold type

DOWN

1 Poisonous pufferfish
2 Burden or responsibility
3 ABBA ballerina
4 Bean curd
5 Ouzo flavorings
6 Coming-out announcement
7 "Ain't gonna happen"
8 Charge
9 Hand over
10 Rarebit ingredient
11 Townie
12 Lawman wounded in the 17 Across
13 "Amazing Grace" ending
14 Exigency
21 Select
24 "Voice of Israel" author
25 Makes a mess of things
26 Leader of the pack
27 Sea fan, for one
28 Outlaw who ran from the 17 Across
29 Floppy ___
31 Cream of the crop
33 Hammer in "The Lone Ranger"
34 Chicken company
36 Scintilla
38 Trawler gear
40 Camp
41 Scintilla
43 Sour cream amounts
47 Hipster beer, initially
48 Ring around the pupil
50 Cures beef
52 Become liable
53 Uses cotton balls
54 Homophone of I'll
55 eBay category
57 They were burned in the '60s
58 Cinerary vases
59 Michigan, for one
60 "Oy, vey!"
62 Ginsberg's "Plutonian ___"
64 "The Hunger Games" heroine

"PLAY BALL!" by Gene Newman
A humorous theme involving America's favorite pastime.

ACROSS

1 Chase baseballs
5 Murder victim in Genesis 4:8
9 Like a bull in the Vatican
14 Elton John musical
15 "¿Quién ___?"
16 Andean grazer
17 Cheek reddener
18 Evening in Bologna
19 Tiny Yokum's brother
20 Picket line sites?
23 Epithet
24 Oui antonym
25 Dragon parade holiday
26 Number of time zones in India
27 What Peeping Tom was?
33 Flower holder
34 Sault Ste. Marie school
35 Like haunted house visitors
38 "I Loves You, Porgy" singer
40 Detox nightmare
42 Diamond bag
43 Wampanoag chief
46 Graham of the gridiron
49 K–12 advisory org.
50 Rolaids spokesperson?
53 Stars and Bars org.
55 MAC college
56 Jack Horner's dessert
57 Zombie ingredient
58 Highlight of a flying trapeze act?
64 Round trip for Deimos
66 Onetime, at one time
67 2000 World Series venue
68 Rx ointment
69 "High Noon" hero Will
70 One of Nantucket's "Three Bricks"
71 Chariot horse
72 Seaweed gelatin
73 Where it's at

DOWN

1 Lip disservice
2 Blade handle
3 Purim month
4 Slackjawed
5 Approvals
6 "Diamonds and Rust" singer
7 Iberian river
8 Makeshift shelter
9 Hula-Hoop material
10 Garment for the Masses?
11 Trolley topper
12 "You're ___ one, Mr. Grinch . . ."
13 Like sumo wrestlers
21 Eyelid cosmetic
22 Comic screams
27 2016 World Series champions
28 "The Times They ___-Changin' ": Dylan
29 What you can't do to eggs
30 Leary's travel agent?
31 Not in stock
32 Apprehend
36 Sunrise locale, in Sonora
37 Precious
39 "___ walks in beauty . . .": Byron
41 Richard Petty sponsor
44 Unlike Supreme Court judges
45 Chevalier's theme song
47 Tout
48 Suffix for narc
51 California's motto
52 Knocks off
53 Army decoration
54 City of W India
59 What a climber clutches
60 J. Carter's alma mater
61 Tom yum kung eater
62 "___ la vie!"
63 Bad blood
65 "___ Gotta Be Me"

A SERIES TO REMEMBER by Gene Newman
"Thus with a kiss I die." —54 Across.

ACROSS

1 Kind of bake
5 Beanie's lack
9 Stengel who managed 20 Across
14 Coin once tossed in Trevi Fountain
15 Front-rank
16 Blazing
17 Son of Venus
18 Nuclear reactor parts
19 Soda stick-in
20 1956 World Series winners
23 Militant deity
24 Suffix for cabinet
25 Put down
28 McPlant's lack
30 School gp.
33 Cellar opening?
34 "Smallville" surname
35 Bed frame piece
36 1956 World Series losers
39 Aviation pioneer Sikorsky
40 To boot
41 Eliminate
42 L'Oréal hair product
43 La ___ Tar Pits
44 Coliseums
45 Blink of an eye
46 Panhandler?
47 What Don Larsen did on October 8, 1956
54 "Star-cross'd" lover
55 Reinhart on "Riverdale"
56 "Got it"
57 Smoke detector, e.g.
58 Apostle Paul, originally
59 Imaginative narrative
60 Pasta like ziti
61 Mrs. Einstein
62 "Three up, three down" results

DOWN

1 Reunion group
2 Plaster component
3 In alignment
4 "The Maltese Falcon" star
5 Refused entry
6 Carlsen's corner men
7 Brickyard 400 site
8 Arizona city
9 Dracula's bed
10 In pursuit of
11 Bold Ruler, to Secretariat
12 Stats for hurlers
13 Longbow wood
21 Vacuum brand
22 "Terrif!"
25 "___ as all outdoors"
26 Comic from Copenhagen
27 "___ and his money . . ."
28 Genius org.
29 Prefix for skeleton
30 Argue a case
31 Ankle bones
32 Befuddled
34 "American Sniper" sniper
35 Pottery decoration technique
37 Northern conifer
38 Frighten off
43 Morph into
44 Prince protégé ___ E.
45 Like taskmasters
46 Middling mark
47 Barbershop symbol
48 "___ old cowhand . . ."
49 "If all ___ fails . . ."
50 "Don't touch that ___!"
51 Isaac's firstborn
52 Stonehenge worshiper
53 Seattle couple
54 Nicki Minaj's genre

113 "TO GRANDMOTHER'S HOUSE WE GO"   by Stu Ockman
The path to her house begins at 4 Down.

ACROSS

1 Lively country dance
6 Lincoln or Madison
10 Porgy's gal
14 Source of oil
15 Muscle malady
16 Choir member
17 Windy City planetarium
18 Amalfi evening
19 Ft. Bragg locale
20 Fred Graham's "Kiss Me, Kate" role
22 "Don't judge a book by its cover," e.g.
23 Once, once
24 Wetland
25 PGA and LPGA event
26 "Give me a hint!"
27 Wrinkle, e.g.
28 Wise ones
31 Bow wood
32 H H H
33 Laurie in "The Hustler"
34 Academic URL suffix
35 Trolleys by the Thames
36 SpaceX CEO Musk
37 Rage
38 Lit up a room
39 Have a right to
41 Kind of line
42 Second course in a three-course meal
43 Sadie Hawkins Day catches
44 "Van Wilder" director Becker
48 Brown ermine
49 1947 Hope/Crosby film
51 Poker giveaway
52 T T T
53 Bring up
54 Litchi nut feature
55 RPI or MIT
56 "Die Fledermaus" maid
57 Like Victorian collars
58 Lyrical verses
59 New York team, familiarly

DOWN

1 Freak
2 Creek shrub
3 Merry melodies
4 Apparent
5 Titicaca locale
6 Kung Pao nut
7 Strand, in a way
8 "Comin' ___ the Rye"
9 Encouraging word
10 South-of-the-border highwayman
11 John Philip Sousa march
12 Nicki Minaj or Lady Gaga, e.g.
13 Muscle malady
21 Corp. bigwigs
22 Peer Gynt's mother
25 "Blecch!"
26 Pronoun for the QM2
27 Pac-12 team
28 Time before talkies
29 Like the Gospel of John
30 As a rule
31 Fruity drink
33 Obelisk base
34 Palindromic preposition
35 Café alternative
37 Secret follower?
38 Email command
40 Part of an IRA: Abbr.
41 Wild things
43 Shiner
44 2019 Presidents Cup captain
45 Mexican Oscar
46 Sock cotton
47 Big name in umbrellas
49 "Atlas Shrugged" author
50 Cuisine with lemongrass
52 Raul's uncle

114 THEMELESS by Harvey Estes
1 Down is also the title of a 1986 horror film.

ACROSS

1 Infield hit
5 Touch and then some
15 City near Tahoe
16 Without a break
17 Martian prefix
18 Tex-Mex condiment
19 Tear companion
20 Slippery one
21 Brought home
22 Greatest partner
24 Retired speedster
25 Catch in a trap
26 Faulkner title start
28 Cinematic Greek
33 California hrs.
34 Chinese island capital
37 Stretched tight
38 Sex appeal
41 Show up
42 "No lie!"
43 HBO alternative
44 Water servers
46 RSVP request
47 Checklist units
49 Wall Street option
51 Star chart
52 Bogged down
56 Wall St. group
58 ___ Hashanah
59 Steamboat of song
61 Initial stake
62 Tranquil tendency
63 Poetic negative
64 They've got the goods
65 Whitehall whitewall

DOWN

1 Cellar alternative
2 This minute
3 "Don't crowd in on me!"
4 Relatively cheesy
5 Diamond side
6 "Aren't ___ lucky one!"
7 Aspen rival
8 Immigrant's study: Abbr.
9 Homes for Babe and Porky
10 Mock
11 Imminent
12 Cause a jaw to drop
13 Behold, in old Rome
14 Outbuilding
23 Bristlelike part
24 Prolonged attacks
26 Draws a bead on
27 Give birth to
29 Giant with 511 homers
30 Have a bake sale, e.g.
31 Venomous pit viper
32 Ambiance
35 Smokin' Joe's opponent
36 Suffix with concert
39 Sea in Saint-Etienne
40 Poet Karlfeldt
45 Sudden bursts
48 Oppressive type
50 Unmitigated
51 Forward thinkers?
52 Fits of rage
53 "Blame It on the Bossa ___"
54 Genesis shepherd
55 Jeweler Lalique
56 Boxer's food
57 Look like
60 Alt-rock genre

115

THEMELESS   by Harvey Estes
54 Across is a phrase coined by Aristotle.

ACROSS

1 Reagan Era scandal
9 Short ___ (scant attention)
15 Dog that's 10–15 inches in length
17 Telethon quality
18 Masseurs work it out
19 Wisdom bit
20 Editorial cartoonist Rall
21 Admits, with "up"
22 "Cool!"
26 Stretched the truth
28 Morales of "My Family"
29 Fingers
35 Uncle Sam's lawyer
37 Separated at the joint
38 Japanese attack word
39 Resolute
40 Full of machismo
41 Whitewater enthusiast
45 Prefix for system
47 Notify of danger
48 Flowering tubers
54 Donkey or elephant, e.g.?
56 When to take a hike?
57 Richards of "Drop Dead Gorgeous"
58 Spooked

DOWN

1 "Da Doo Ron Ron" opening
2 Frosty covering
3 Prolific author
4 Trivia
5 High spirits
6 Expiate, with "for"
7 Used a fork
8 Bullpen stats
9 Site for three men in a tub
10 Entered the car, casually
11 Rodeo equipment
12 Cerebral output
13 Sideline pass
14 What poker players look for
16 Trains at a high level
21 Threw a big party for
22 "Coming of Age in Samoa" author
23 Sparkling vino
24 Hamelin menace
25 It takes a bow
26 Philippines island
27 "Summer Brave" playwright
29 Rack up
30 Cherished
31 Crumbly cheese
32 Spinach benefit
33 Father of Tiger Woods
34 Put in stitches
36 Leopard spots
40 Malcontent
41 Breakneck
42 Without equal
43 Many a con
44 "Lemon Tree" singer Lopez
45 Ostentatious display
46 "Bewitched" aunt
48 Adds to an email
49 Won't shut up
50 Pitcher's target
51 Jannings in "The Blue Angel"
52 It's "given" at birth
53 Coaster
55 Expert finish

116 LONG-WINDED GREETINGS by Taylor Warren Goff
What is your answer to the question posed at 59 Across?

ACROSS

1 Some prosecutors, briefly
5 PalmPilots, e.g.
9 Confident juggler's props
13 Trace or draw
14 Mass of grass
15 Mature
16 Greeting from a long-winded ghost
19 1948 Hitchcock film
20 President in "The Hunger Games"
21 "Deep Space Nine" changeling
22 Get ready
25 Temperature scale
27 Rodentia members
28 Tyson's trainer D'Amato
30 Shaq's sneakers, widthwise
31 Big name in home security
32 Scandalous gossip
33 Calf locale
35 Greeting from a long-winded cow
41 Cyclist Ullrich
42 Ga'Hoole birds
43 Perlman or Powlus
44 Eightfold prefix
47 Key below INS
48 Woodworking tool
49 ___ to go
52 Fools
54 Peruvian green sauce
55 Passing fancy
58 French bread
59 "How many O's are in this puzzle?" answer
64 2016 Paul Verhoeven film
65 Kermit the Frog's first home
66 Bath bottom?
67 Heroic act
68 Mideast capital
69 Uber rival

DOWN

1 Priestly vestment
2 Ronnie James of Black Sabbath
3 Cherub, in art
4 Nosy Parkers
5 Ramallah org.
6 Two and two together?
7 Idolatrous king of Judah
8 CIA employee, slangily
9 Freud's moderator
10 LP track
11 Treat
12 Gets weak at the knees
14 Arm-twisting
17 Greek wedding shout
18 Have student loans, say
22 Brit's baby buggy
23 Rolex rival
24 Austria's schilling successor
26 "The ___ Movie" (2014)
29 Rose
32 ___ double take
33 Stick candy
34 Orion's love
36 California art colony
37 Lost Generation poet Wilfred
38 Quotidian
39 Swampy substance
40 Canadian loonies
44 Pontificated
45 Sweet-talk
46 Musical triplet
48 Electric Mayhem Band drummer
50 Kennedy Ctr. musicians
51 Lip cosmetic
53 "Saturn" singer
56 Tall Corn State
57 Mournful cry
60 UK lexicon
61 German granny
62 Stamp on a bad check
63 "On the other hand . . ."

THEMELESS   by Elizabeth C. Gorski
Hint: The answer to 29 Across is not "toy train."

ACROSS

1 Assent to a yachtswoman
8 Soviet counterintelligence agency in 007 novels
14 Really dig
15 Level off
16 Kigali native
17 Kielbasa, e.g.
18 Place in the East Village
19 CEO's helpers
21 Cough up
22 "The Cloister and the Hearth" author
24 Fair-hiring acronym
26 Winter gutter barrier
29 American flyer
34 Zelmo of "M*A*S*H"
35 Na+ and Ca++
37 As a friend, in Arles
38 Invisible Woman's husband
41 Like Apple AirPods
42 Hammett dog
43 "A Bronx ___" (1993)
44 Junk mail addressee
46 Reacted to a punch
48 Bagel topper
49 14th-century Russian prince
51 indeed.com listing
54 Burrito meat
56 "Dancing With the Stars" judge Carrie Ann
60 Last Supper guest
62 Gym routine
64 Fiery cinnamon candies
65 Perplexed
66 Nasty looks
67 Red algae used in body scrubs

DOWN

1 Tourist city on the Jumna
2 Evergreens
3 South Dakota, to Pierre
4 Trivial point
5 Mitchell of NBC News
6 Loss leaders?
7 Single-celled organism
8 Christian in "Bobby"
9 The Taj Mahal et al.
10 Visitors from Messier 81
11 Run a header
12 Epic narrative
13 Black Panther Party cofounder
15 Letter addenda
20 Samwise Gamgee portrayer
23 "The Kite Runner" narrator
25 Element named after a physics Nobelist
26 Turkey's third-largest city
27 Michael of "Quills"
28 Aretha Franklin's "Someone ___ Eyes"
30 "Well, ___ that special?"
31 Present at birth
32 "Into the Wild" actor Hirsch
33 Sieved spuds
36 "It's the end ___ era"
39 Trauma center medic
40 Olympic skater Lipinski
45 Venerates
47 It's a puzzlement
50 Kiss and tell, e.g.
51 Jam-packed containers?
52 Receptive
53 Slalomist Miller
55 Hi-___ monitor
57 Childish retort to "Are not!"
58 Sunflower visitors
59 Joining words
61 "He said, ___ said"
63 Opposite width of AAA

118 CH-CH-CHANGES by Warren Houck
A shout-out to David Bowie for this title.

ACROSS

1 Zion National Park locale
5 Kalahari stopover
10 2000 Super Bowl winners
14 Sport with the largest field
15 Type of rope loop
16 "Don't bet ___!"
17 Container for a fly killer?
19 4,840 square yards
20 These, in Tours
21 Suffix for sermon
22 Earth colour
23 Boat measured in cubits
24 Institute for group education?
27 Bring about
29 Fitting
30 Four Monopoly properties: Abbr.
31 "The Cider House Rules" nurse
32 Check recipients
35 Quality gauge for cheap beer?
39 Hall-of-fame names
40 Smartly elegant
43 Cinerary vessel
46 Granola tidbit
47 Get by
49 Note from a young suitor?
53 Take in the sun
54 Barry Manilow hit
55 Ill. neighbor
56 Cheerios, e.g.
57 Texas Hold'em stake
58 Surprising exchange (and a theme hint)
61 Fateful March date
62 Boiled buckwheat
63 Ampule
64 Stick it out
65 Epsionage data
66 Proactiv target

DOWN

1 Swanky
2 Loomed large
3 Attu Islanders
4 On a winning streak
5 "___, buckle my shoe . . ."
6 Arterial trunk
7 Not pickled
8 "Looking for" in personals
9 Ultrasound determination
10 Flat bug
11 Leg of a relay race
12 Reflect
13 Toughens
18 It makes the grade
22 Square-dance group
25 Early Guatemalans
26 Blueprint stat
28 Cleveland Browns fan
32 Tanaka's target
33 Rudder locale
34 It's around a foot
36 Swift humor
37 Sharon in "Dreamgirls"
38 Campaign talk
41 Sarah Palin, by birth
42 Xbox One, for one
43 FedEx alternative
44 "Gorillas in the Mist" setting
45 French edict city
47 Tequila's cousin
48 Place de l'Étoile sight
50 That is, to Caesar
51 Dance of the '60s
52 Sabbath contribution
58 Snowmobile runner
59 Pallid
60 Foam used in kickboards

119 GLOBE THEATRE by Roland Huget
The source of the quote below can be found at 65 Across.

ACROSS

1 Lake predator
5 Sons of Anarchy rider
10 Some HDTVs
14 Beverage option
15 Stage commentary
16 Radius neighbor
17 **Part 1 of quote**
19 Former Georgia senator Sam
20 Finger-licking good
21 **Part 2 of quote**
23 Govt. securities
25 She, in Lisbon
26 Caprine comment
27 Pained expression
28 Defame
31 Munchkin
32 Some email attachments
34 Columbus sch.
35 USNS Comfort worker
37 **Part 3 of quote**
41 Performance site
44 Restroom, informally
45 Mexican years
49 Before, poetically
50 Puts down
54 Roman greeting
55 "Riddle-me-___"
56 MPH: Abbr.
57 Elon Musk company
59 **Part 4 of quote**
63 Apply
64 "Garfield" pooch
65 **Source of quote**
67 Noticed
68 Forest giraffe
69 Settled down
70 Slips up
71 Roman household gods
72 Christmas lights

DOWN

1 Road trip pause
2 Brom's Sleepy Hollow rival
3 Unwelcome lawn sign
4 Astronomer Hubble
5 Limbo prop
6 Nublar in "Jurassic Park"
7 "Trix are for ___!"
8 Prepared for publishing
9 Goodwill store transaction
10 Viking letter
11 Lang of "Rocky III"
12 Greenhouse section
13 Land of Enchantment capital
18 Pari-mutuel posting
22 Decorated, on a menu
24 Gin flavoring
29 Cerastes
30 Renders void
33 Disco guy of Springfield
36 NATO member
38 Villain
39 Jacuzzi sigh
40 Part of YSL
41 Long-winded
42 Kindle, for one
43 More destitute
46 Enterprise engine housing
47 Carried to extremes
48 Some string ensembles
51 "Chill!"
52 Revelation Mountains locale
53 Blow out
58 Kind of symmetry
60 Fresnel ___
61 Mufasa's brother
62 Scotch ___
66 "___ for Ricochet": Grafton

JUMPING THROUGH HOOPS by Mark McClain
Roundball wordplay at its finest.

ACROSS

1 Chin feature
6 Flower holders
10 Have a snack
14 Vietnamese hub
15 Soothing succulent
16 Public show
17 Immense, in verse
18 Costa ___
19 Have in abundance
20 Twenty second time-outs?
22 "The Quiet American" hero
23 Barbecue spice mix
24 Light-brown horses
26 Nonsense
31 Modernistic prefix
32 "Wonderfilled" treat
33 Soon, in sonnets
35 Put on the market
39 Brand name that means "stew"
40 Casual attire
42 Missouri neighbor
43 Old TV features
45 Equinox mo.
46 Not kosher
47 Inaudible roar
49 Least dense
51 Article supplement
55 1/5 an ABBA title
56 Yonkers Raceway gait
57 BIC pen cap, e.g.?
63 Go by Greyhound
64 Arduous trek
65 Listless feeling
66 Links org.
67 Radius neighbor
68 Lather, ___, repeat
69 1954 sci-fi classic
70 Sibilant hail
71 Spirited mount

DOWN

1 One in a white hat
2 Singer Cantrell
3 The Book of Mormon book
4 Blockhouse setting
5 Tone quality
6 Spartan
7 "East of Eden" director Kazan
8 Harbor sights
9 Add paprika, say
10 Concerns of "Deadliest Catch" captains?
11 Daisy's cousin
12 Period of time
13 Tract structures
21 Bucolic
25 Hupmobile rival
26 Flatware item
27 Port near Algiers
28 Ed Sheeran's "___ House"
29 Bob and Mike Bryan, notably?
30 Holds dear
34 Attacking, puppy-style
36 Tee shout
37 Mama llamas
38 Basic boat
41 German city
44 Shed a tear
48 Accepts eagerly
50 "Lucille" singer
51 Cocky walk
52 Hailing from Cork
53 Dart nameplate
54 Sushi bar array
58 Charged particles
59 Window ___ (A/C option)
60 Netflix series "___ with an E"
61 Clever scheme
62 Conked out

2 Down was written in reaction to the May 4, 1970 Kent State shootings.

ACROSS

1 Gaelic lake
5 Possessive pronoun
10 Some early PCs
14 Maritime greeting
15 Accept a check
16 Raise anchor
17 Timid sort
18 Acquire
19 Top flight
20 Casual denial
21 Golf bag items
22 Locality
23 Natural feeling
25 Kept clear of
27 Young fox
29 Book before Romans
32 Part of Caesar's boast
33 Scottish Arctic explorer
34 Covering less ground
36 Badgers
39 Mythical monster
41 Terse concession speech
42 "Auld Lang ___"
43 Task for an all-in-one device
44 Acronym for Melania
46 Starbucks cup
47 "Finding Nemo" locale
49 Twice-monthly tide
50 Ryder Cup side
51 Handle, in a way
54 They're on the books
56 On the up-and-up
57 "Moby-Dick" character
60 MLB box score figure
63 Get legitimately
64 Throat dangler
65 Cavern phenomenon
66 "The Rocky Horror Picture Show" hero
67 Lloyd in "Peyton Place"
68 Castro of Cuba
69 Small-screen award
70 Hit the bottle
71 Other than this

DOWN

1 Bowling surface
2 Neil Young protest song
3 Coder's creation
4 Bouncing off the walls
5 Dover tourist attractions
6 Sharpen
7 "The Raven" opener
8 "The Washington Post" composer
9 Slip up
10 Vicenza natives
11 Highlight of a visit to New York
12 Chop up
13 Celerity
22 Shortstop stats
24 Natural ___
26 Depository institution with no local branches
27 Subject of "The Founder"
28 Shakespearean villain
30 Crossing charge
31 Faint away
35 Spanish direction
37 African antelopes
38 Big name in arcade games
40 Glitzy display
45 Resort with baths
48 Spitchcock ingredient
51 Academy newbie
52 Break a peace treaty, say
53 Enjoy immensely
55 One of the five W's
58 Sinuous dance
59 Snape portrayer Rickman
61 Consequently
62 Dover fish
64 Sturm ___ Drang

122 BELT OVERHANGS   by Michael Collins
Shakira ("Hips Don't Lie") is a famous 58 Across.

ACROSS

1 Paparazzo's wares, for short
5 Multigenerational tale
9 Leave the sack
14 Apple on a desktop
15 Positive quality
16 Resort near Venezuela
17 "The Thin Man" role
18 Advice for the exhausted
19 Japanese noodle dish
20 Instinctive response
23 "Rocky III" costar
24 Hard as nails
25 Easter flower
27 Knocked flat
31 Bug bite consequence
34 Disheveled coif
37 Baseball stat
38 World's smallest republic
39 Litter box emanations
41 "___ you for real?"
42 Monologue deliverer
43 Bandleader's call
44 Places for mufflers
46 Of prime importance
47 Shakers, e.g.
48 "Scram!"
49 Hold in abomination
51 Cancel out
56 Twist the facts
58 Performer with finger cymbals
62 Alpha's opposite
64 BYOB part
65 Part of a ferry load, perhaps
66 Herb in pasta sauce
67 Eye rudely
68 Crushed underfoot, with "on"
69 Litter box emanation
70 Can't live without
71 With it, in a sense

DOWN

1 Worrisome engine noises
2 Folder's words
3 Brasserie handout
4 Aerial near-miss, e.g.
5 Garden hose attachment
6 Baldwin of "The Boss Baby"
7 Umbrella-inverting wind
8 Sparkling wine spot
9 "With parsley," on a 3-Down
10 Stat for a hurler
11 Torso-flattening surgery
12 App-based car service
13 Breathe like a dog
21 6 Down, among the Baldwins
22 Like centenarians
26 Neeson who voiced Aslan
28 Camera operator's device
29 "M*A*S*H" land
30 Like an alert dog's ears
32 Northern Plains tribe
33 Brother of Dewey and Louie
34 Hardness scale
35 Drooling dog of comics
36 Product similar to ricotta
38 AriZona competitor
40 Meter maid of song
45 Of a similar nature
48 Royal jelly maker
50 Lead-in to Little League
52 Pesky swarmers
53 Lexus competitor
54 Wyoming mountain range
55 Dwindle, as public favor
56 Slow-pitch pitches
57 Mosque leader
59 French home to Interpol
60 Stadium tier, perhaps
61 "Comfort and joy" season
63 Jazz great Evans

123 DIAMOND ANGLING by Michael Collins
A hybrid theme from two popular sports.

CROSS

1 Julian Lloyd Webber's instrument
6 ___ torch (patio light)
10 Criminal's flight
13 Hunter viewed by telescope
14 "Topaz" author Leon
15 Mets' field
16 Greg Maddux pitch
18 Any day now
19 Island near Barbuda
20 Showing mercy
22 Take a chance on
24 Machu Picchu's range
25 Loose-sleeved garment
29 President before Sadat
32 First-string squad
33 Left-hand column entry
34 Texter's "seems to me . . ."
37 ___ guy (reliable sort)
38 Barracks sites
39 Message from a sitcom sponsor
40 Well-put
41 On-the-sly meeting
42 Item on a game board
43 Like a buzzard's call
45 Gets wise with
46 Moved at a snail's pace
48 Marathon terminus
50 Prepares, as leftovers
53 Publicist's handout
58 Keynes subj.
59 Automatic out, at times
61 Simon & Garfunkel et al.
62 Like cobs and toms
63 Broadcaster
64 Mork's planet
65 Humble ones' lacks
66 "Uncle Tom's Cabin" novelist

DOWN

1 ___ Nostra
2 Andrews of "Dancing with the Stars"
3 Fuzz in a dryer trap
4 Trickster in Norse myth
5 About .035 ounces
6 Oktoberfest band horns
7 Golden-years income, briefly
8 Shut off, as an engine
9 Longtime home to Crusoe
10 Hard-hit shots
11 Observe Yom Kippur
12 Treats on some hotel pillows
15 Mutinied ship of literature
17 Totally botch
21 Thomas who skewered Tweed
23 Israel's parliament
25 Shankar's genre
26 On the pinnacle of
27 Be lifted for a reliever
28 Vientiane native
30 Assist in a felony
31 Sib's nickname
33 Fortnight's fourteen
35 Medieval war club
36 Homages in verse
38 "Turn up the heat!"
39 Woody Herman's "___ Autumn"
41 "Bye, old chap!"
42 Saffron-flavored dishes
44 Some tourneys
45 Germany's Graf von ___
46 Set of beliefs
47 Come back, as a dream
49 Horned zodiac symbol
51 Smartphone display
52 Monkey wrench
54 Reclue, as a crossword
55 Spheroid hairdo
56 Whacked, so to speak
57 Brontë heroine
60 Rapper ___ Rida

124 FINAL DENIALS   by Fred Piscop

Fred says he was watching "Dr. No" when this theme came to him.

ACROSS

1 Put-up job
5 Foiled candy
9 Paintball sound
14 Vegan's protein source
15 Chip-shot club
16 Old bomb of a car
17 Cross off the list
18 Landlocked African land
19 Have home cooking, say
20 Words to impatient shoppers
23 The calm within a storm
24 Liar's poker bill, usually
25 Judge to be
26 Pompous sort's attribute
27 Michael Jackson album
29 Part of a tire swing
32 Knicks great Patrick
35 Tuckered out
37 "Dear old" guy
38 Tentatively assign a job, perhaps
41 Tiny toymaker
42 Shaving mishaps
43 Ritzy country house
44 Socialite Sedgwick
46 "Thar ___ blows"
47 Eccentric's heir?
48 Carrier with blue and white jets
50 ___ Andreas Fault
51 Object of Indy's quest
54 Overtax, in a way
58 Pizza cuts, essentially
59 Word before life or estate
60 "La Bohème" heroine
61 Turn topsy-turvy
62 Reason for a small craft advisory
63 Serpents on Egyptian relics
64 Former fillies
65 Paris hub
66 See-through material

DOWN

1 Vermont ski spot
2 Warm and comfy
3 Not just smoldering
4 Remote button
5 Geisha's attire
6 At one's boiling point
7 Jam session highlight
8 Cut coupons
9 Play segment
10 Bedtime recitation
11 Fairly new car
12 Working diligently
13 Gymnast's ideal
21 Head, slangily
22 Patsy's "Ab Fab" friend
26 SASE, e.g.
27 Chelsea chap
28 Charitable offerings
30 Sandbox toy
31 "Hairspray" character Turnblad
32 Cousin of the saber
33 Join with a torch
34 One of four on a diamond
35 "The Apostle" author Sholem
36 Nine-day Catholic ritual
39 Strong thread
40 Tiny criticism
45 King Arthur's half-sister
47 Truce talk
49 Etchers' fluids
50 Hem and haw
51 Biscotto flavoring
52 Wins in a laugher
53 Potato-filled deli buy
54 Bear with a too-hard chair
55 2012 movie about a fake movie
56 Brown beef
57 Muslim holy man
58 Liquor in grog

125 "GOING DOWN!" by Fred Piscop
12 Down can be viewed at the Philadelpia Museum of Art.

CROSS

1 Whipped up
5 "The Spirit of '76" instrument
9 Soaks up the sun
14 Blows it
15 Line to the Holy Land
16 Hirsch of "Lone Survivor"
17 Not just occasionally
18 Tiny stream
19 Zellweger of "Cold Mountain"
20 Seized car
21 Prefix for ware
22 Brightened, with "up"
23 Soon, to a bard
24 Big commotion
25 Plugging away
26 Royal proclamation
28 Fish-fowl connector
30 Biblical boatwright
33 To this point
35 ". . . and I approve ___ message"
36 Bird in Wonderland
37 Explosive letters
38 Scarfs down
41 "China Beach" setting, briefly
42 "Draft Dodger Rag" singer
44 Basset hound's danglers
45 What this puzzle's title suggests
47 Hammer head
48 Kid-___ (TV for children)
49 Tag teams
50 Teased mercilessly
52 Paving crew need
54 Go from first to third grade, say
57 Lost-package inquiry
59 Solemn "Yes"
60 Green Gables girl
61 Gas tested for in homes
62 Cry from the flock
63 Heron's home
64 "Sorry, already have plans"
65 Cartoon skunk Le Pew
66 ___-do-well
67 Suttee piles
68 Cornerstone abbr.
69 Wine with a muscat flavor

DOWN

1 Stiller's longtime partner
2 "Get Happy" composer
3 Disappear from public view
4 Neighbor of Latvia
5 Pierre with a "last theorem"
6 Trojan War epic
7 Have serious money troubles
8 Pipe bend
9 Guardian Angel's hat
10 New World native
11 Act submissively
12 "Fish Magic" painter Paul
13 Progeny
22 Analyze grammatically
27 Melber of MSNBC
29 Some gallery hangings
31 An original sinner
32 Monticello, to Jefferson
33 Place to board
34 Second word of many limericks
35 Cuisine with green curry
39 "Over my dead body!"
40 Disco ___ of "The Simpsons"
43 Icy confection
46 Biblical cry of praise
49 Talked in a monotone
51 Auto body blemishes
53 More than just able
55 Map's closeup
56 Lab dish name
57 Cruise or safari
58 Not for the prudish
62 Jungle swinger

126

"STICK WITH IT!" by Harvey Estes
67 Across was a regular center square on "Hollywood Squares."

ACROSS

1 K. Janeway's rank
5 Oceanic ray
10 Muscovite, for one
14 Alan heard in "Toy Story 4"
15 Where the Ganges flows
16 Go to the edge of
17 "East of Eden" son
18 Drudges
19 Wheat ___
20 They're above corporals
23 Pacific island group
24 Top-shelf
25 "Would ___ to you?"
27 Hurled word
31 Australian Open arena
35 Gets dirty
36 Do an impression of
37 Animosity
40 Zion Williamson's org.
41 Supply with more weapons
44 Mariners' guide
47 Like a good listener
50 Left, on a liner
51 Chamber music instruments
53 Hibernians
57 "Star Trek" catchphrase (never spoken)
60 Navy commando
61 Play by Euripides
62 Stripped
63 Titicaca locale
64 Fencing blades
65 Vivacity
66 Up to speed
67 He was Uncle Arthur on "Bewitched"
68 Dr. Wells, for one

DOWN

1 Senior ___
2 It's from the heart
3 Kind of tournament
4 It's a wrap
5 Nurses a drink
6 Seriously involved
7 Put on a pedestal
8 Prickly sensation
9 "Not so hard"
10 "X-Men" villain
11 "A likely story!"
12 Junkyard dogs
13 Banking convenience
21 FDR's pooch
22 Center of revolution
26 OR hookups
28 Subtle clue
29 Isle near Corsica
30 Ruler of old
31 Avis adjective
32 German automaker
33 Big bargain
34 Pants problem
38 Maximum velocity
39 "Xanadu" band
42 Appraise again
43 Seriously impair
45 Dr. Foreman on "House"
46 Disco flashers
48 Afrika Korps commander
49 Friend of Snow White
52 Pulitzer poet W. H.
54 "Marcovaldo" author Calvino
55 Famous fiddle, for short
56 Laughing beast
57 English channel, informally
58 Rank below a marquess
59 Letter enc.
60 Place for jets?

THE MUSICIANS ARE THE MUSIC by Harvey Estes
The clue at 27 Down nearly stumped our test solvers.

CROSS

1 The RSV, e.g.
6 Babe in the stable
10 Ever so proper
14 Steel or pewter
15 Magazine founded by Guccione
16 Gambling city
17 Throw with oomph
18 Cable syst.
19 Morales of "My Family"
20 American pop/rock band/classic concerti
23 Brew topper
24 Early Web forum
25 Kidman of "Bombshell"
28 Per ___ spending
30 Ken of "Brothers & Sisters"
31 December package deliverer
32 Common correlative
35 No. 1 hit for 20 Across
39 Cruise site
40 Bathtub toys
41 "Nowhere Man" opening
42 Job listing?
44 Keeps at it
46 The way the cookie crumbles
48 Jewish scroll
49 Composer of 20 Across
54 Criminal plan
55 Fingertip protector
56 Despoil
58 Trim back
59 Bachelor ending
60 Rolex rival
61 Awash in admiration
62 Edible herring
63 Event in a ring

DOWN

1 "Foiled again!"
2 "___ the Music Speak": ABBA
3 Lacking pizazz
4 Eliot's "The ___ of J. Alfred Prufrock"
5 Sight to behold
6 Concentrate
7 Dorsey in "The Blind Side"
8 Hill builders
9 Meet the expectations of
10 Car radio button
11 Vibrations
12 Totally ridiculous
13 A wee bit wet
21 Dedicated poem
22 Like most people
25 Wealthy Londoners
26 "Would ___ to You?": Eurythmics
27 Churchill's home
28 Societal stratum
29 Added factors
31 Bridge triumph
33 Roughly
34 Phillippe of "Crash"
36 "Ghosts" playwright
37 Comic bits
38 2004 Jason Patric film
43 Chewed the scenery
44 G. Newsom, for one
45 Rhetorician
46 Iota follower
47 Non-blood relative
48 Like some shower floors
50 Scout recitation
51 Ars longa, ___ brevis
52 Subsided, with "down"
53 "Bus Stop" playwright
57 Eastern universal

ACROSS

1 French Revolution leader
6 Place for sweaters?
9 Cons
14 Coeur d'___, Idaho
15 "If I Ruled the World" rapper
16 "The Thinker" sculptor
17 Jack's ladder*
19 "Mona Lisa" feature
20 Publicity
21 Put up with
22 Wear well
23 Dog with a sad face*
27 Copycat
29 Green Mountain ___
30 "America" singer on Broadway
33 Playground sight
35 Spanish pronoun
38 Subject of an Easter song*
41 Holiday in Hue
42 Roof support
43 Line from the heart
44 Gazillions
45 Broadband alternative
46 "Foul Play" star*
51 Parisian ponds
55 Sitarist Shankar
56 Bedtime brew
58 Calculus calculations
60 Retrace one's steps/TITLE
61 Starbucks order
62 Rep: Abbr.
63 Falcon's home
64 Perfume base
65 "Affirmative!"
66 Diamond and Young

DOWN

1 "The Pirates of Penzance" heroine
2 Amazon assistant
3 Brings in
4 Gloss over?
5 Trueheart of "Dick Tracy"
6 Tie-up
7 Kind of diet
8 Query
9 LSAT takers
10 Music groups
11 "So long, mon frère"
12 Cultural center of Italy
13 Bergen dummy
18 Toothpaste holder
24 Newspaper section
25 Wonderland bird
26 Serengeti scavengers
28 Somewhat
30 On target
31 Previously named
32 Addams Family cousin
33 Pole position?
34 USMA grads
35 Locale of a small canal
36 Convene
37 Menu words
39 Lacoste logo
40 Like 1-800 calls
44 Do the Wright thing
45 Clobber
46 Desire
47 Fast runners
48 Happening
49 Toothless saw
50 Splinter groups
52 "Asteroids" maker
53 Filmmaker DeMille
54 "Land ___ alive!"
57 ___ impasse (stymied)
59 Military address
60 Howl at the moon

60 ACROSS   by Gary Larson
Will Smith and Naomi Scott also starred in the film at 28 Across.

ACROSS

1 Wrong
6 Mountaineer's worry
10 Sir's counterpart
14 Unbending
15 "The Real" cohost Love
16 Stickum
17 Acting class taught by actor James?
19 Whipped up
20 Securer of locks
22 Peace, in Russia
23 Word of warning
26 Bread locale in a Bengal bakery?
28 2019 Mena Massoud film
30 Sports facilities
31 Winner's cry
32 Speaker's spot
35 What's happening
36 Sad tale of a Swedish automaker?
39 Hard work
42 Stay away from
43 Blackberry, e.g.
46 Madagascar's ocean
48 Motor City
51 Attachment to a pagan idol?
54 Battle tactics
55 Wing
56 Rats
58 They may be drawn
60 Group think-about-drink sessions/TITLE
64 They're inflatable
65 Subsequently
66 Parting word
67 Unit of force
68 Gas brand in Canada
69 Perfume

DOWN

1 Semicircle
2 Actress Wasikowska
3 Grocery chain letters
4 Sailor or comedian
5 Camera memory chip
6 Aspersion
7 Heston's "El Cid" costar
8 Quick, in brand names
9 Passion paintings
10 Studio with a lion
11 Pie preference
12 Label for some TV jacks
13 Mongoose cousin
18 Frozen fries brand
21 Type in
23 Snare
24 First name in pharmaceuticals
25 Pallid
27 Shade of blue
29 Snatches
33 Give or take
34 Style of poker
36 Sully
37 Kaffiyeh wearers
38 Baby outfit
39 Maligned
40 Comparison
41 Bygone bookseller
43 Faddish disc of the 1990s
44 Stop running
45 @@@@
47 Jot down
49 Haberdashery item
50 Live
52 Wyle and Webster
53 Some stadium features
57 Jay on the Walk of Fame
59 Wind dir.
61 Palindromic diarist
62 Some appliances
63 Trial lawyer's advice

130 "HAPPY BIRTHDAY!" by Gary Larson
The title of the song at 17 Across is "Fun, Fun, Fun."

ACROSS

1 Dealt with
6 Amorphous mass
10 Hit the road
14 Thundering
15 Cork's country
16 Retin-A target
17 Ford in a Beach Boys song
18 Search
19 Progresso product
20 Give or take, in English class
23 Go downhill
26 Tibetan gazelle
27 Convent dweller
28 Wrath
29 Schlemiel
32 Take care of
34 "Who knew?"
37 Units of wisdom
38 Bottom dealer
40 "In Cold Blood" author
43 Film where Tom Hanks plays a cowboy
47 Hot spots
48 Dog that bit Almira Gulch
49 Word of support
50 Trading place
51 FYI cousin
53 Road safety items
56 Convention wannabe nominee
60 Western Indian
61 Be an accessory to
62 Hugo Award genre
66 "Livin' La Vida ___": Ricky Martin
67 Sports column?
68 Copier cartridge
69 Refuges
70 Postponement
71 Rice liquors

DOWN

1 Tabby
2 Ghostly form
3 Kona dish
4 O.K. Corral brothers
5 Big name in rap
6 Porgy's woman
7 Cooties
8 Juice source
9 Japanese box lunch
10 Zap
11 Walker's "Fast and Furious" role
12 Not the norm
13 Does penance
21 Withstand
22 Spuds
23 Top secret?
24 Spanish Main cargo
25 Striped official
30 Baggage tag for O'Hare
31 Trattoria sauce
33 Wholly absorbed
35 Religious figure
36 Daisy Buchanan's love
37 Bribe
39 Trendy
40 "The Godfather" director
41 Wiley Post, e.g.
42 1975 fad
44 Sweep
45 Pumpernickel source
46 Cry of success
48 Small-time
52 Warms up
54 Hungers (for)
55 Big name in aluminum
57 Earl Grey and Lady Grey
58 Clinton cabinet member
59 Online crafts market
63 Pen filler
64 Service charge
65 Form 1040 org.

LAST-PLACE STARTERS   by Gary Larson
The title explains itself at 60 Across.

CROSS

1 Yellow fruit
7 Mixture
14 Kind of instinct
15 Mob action
16 Strip mall
18 "Romanian Rhapsodies" composer
19 Thrust
21 Took to court
22 Tags
24 TV room
25 "The Waste Land" auth.
26 TiVo button
31 Comic Milton
33 Bulldog of New Haven
34 Theodor Geisel's pen name
37 Last circuit around the track
41 "If you ask me . . ."
43 Slur over
44 Car flap
49 Kind of order
50 Jeff Lynne's rock grp.
51 Recline
52 Units of resistance
53 Gets new actors for
58 Puts off
60 (Where those last-place starters can be found)
63 Upright
64 Red spot
65 Leaving little to the imagination
66 Beethoven's Opus 20

OWN

1 Pops
2 ___-Busch
3 Trailblazers
4 Pumped
5 Sounds in pounds
6 Witt in "Urban Legend"
7 Córdoba loc.
8 Riot spray
9 Iowa college town
10 Hosp. personnel
11 Ticket info
12 To-do list
13 "Moon River" lyricist
17 Auction bids
20 Put the kibosh on
21 Opposite of port: Abbr.
23 Sloppy digs
26 Long-running disputes
27 Terrif
28 Word of encouragement
29 Upset
30 Water source
32 Sci-fi princess
35 Telnet's successor
36 Wilt
38 Least heavy
39 Water, facetiously
40 Cribbage scorekeepers
42 Actor Brynner
44 Sun. talk
45 New West Pointers
46 Spot
47 Verdi opera
48 Spheres
52 Ready for drawing

54 Stadium in Queens
55 Playlet
56 Kind of support
57 Wish receiver
59 Peter Fonda title role
61 Vaping company
62 Got together

132

ACROSS

1 Big name in Baroque music
5 Sgt. Garcia's nemesis
10 Goes for
14 Site of the 1952 Winter Olympics
15 Wicker willow
16 Sans mixer
17 "Enough already!"*
19 Bahama ___ (rum drink)
20 CONTROL robot
21 KAOS agent, to CONTROL
23 Hammer or mallet, e.g.
26 Thermal starter
27 Marseille miss: Abbr.
30 Garnish request*
36 "Excuse me . . ."
37 Liechtenstein princess
38 Ballade closing stanza
39 Shania Twain song
40 Amaze
42 ICBM stopper
43 Sci-fi author Asimov
45 Melody
46 Genuflection joint
47 Door in a ship's floor*
49 Head set?
50 Wrath
51 Thick skin
53 At times, it's first
58 Word of surrender
62 Seltzer starter
63 Take up a collection/TITLE

66 "Yeah, sure!"
67 Noted spokescow
68 Spinoff group
69 MMA octagon
70 Big name in farm equipment
71 Shoe insert

DOWN

1 Each of two
2 Pale in the face
3 Happy and silent one?
4 Hard-to-find purchase
5 Animal house
6 Sugar suffix
7 Start the day
8 Constrain
9 Nicaraguan president
10 "Les Misérables" song
11 Carrots partner
12 Press down
13 Legal postponement
18 ___ gratias
22 Distributed
24 Dominates, on the playing field
25 Ray in "GoodFellas"
27 Hysterical
28 Tibet's "place of the gods"
29 "The Merry Widow" composer
31 Fly-fishing fish
32 Upper thigh
33 Donald's first lady
34 Abstemious
35 "It was the best of ___ . . ."
40 Winter squash
41 Radar's pop

44 Shake up
46 Most enthused
48 Piled up
52 "Obviously!"
53 Not of the clergy
54 Goya's "The Duchess of ___"
55 Keel extension
56 Tom or jack, e.g.
57 To be, in Latin class
59 "Dark Lady" singer
60 Shoestring
61 Novel ending
64 Topham Hatt's title
65 Half a laugh

59 ACROSS   by Brian E. Paquin
30 Down is also an expert crossword solver.

ACROSS

1 "Super Trouper" group
5 Jar Jar Binks actor Best
10 Headliner
14 Like Ivo Karlovic
15 Congo nomad
16 Gdansk native
17 Home of Keebler elves
18 Self-denying
20 Chosen ones
21 "It's cold outside!"
22 Maria Rainer's song
23 Makeup makeup
27 Inclines
28 Still to be achieved
29 Having two parts
31 Parked it
32 Looked after
34 "Nova" subj.
35 Nautical ropes
36 Espresso cup
39 Sales slips: Abbr.
42 Sgt's address
43 Make fizzy
47 Musical talent
48 Battery part
50 Firebug's crime
51 Interrogate with gusto
53 Blew to smithereens
55 Multitudes
57 "___ been fun!"
58 Bread machine?
59 Semiannual event/TITLE
62 "Later!"
63 New driver, often
64 Home of Little Havana
65 Parts of joules
66 Interjects
67 Calliope's cousin
68 For fear that

DOWN

1 Fictional Finch
2 Without exception
3 Sneeze response
4 Golden brew
5 Not together
6 Genetic mixture
7 Classic British roadsters
8 CPR practitioner
9 Tinted
10 Top of a steeple
11 "Piece of cake!"
12 Radcliffe College graduates
13 Puts up a fight
19 Embedded spy
21 Novelist Bao Lord
24 Sews back together
25 Protected care
26 Welfare org. since 1824
30 The vegetarian Simpson
33 Persian Gulf land
35 Country singer Clark
37 Apple gadget
38 Cloth connections
39 Gathering of yachts
40 Kept in stock
41 Did a hasty haircut
44 Fred in "Ghost Story"
45 Stiff labels?
46 Last in line
48 Baldwin of "30 Rock"
49 Mind bender
52 Property claims
54 Phoned for pizza
56 Average Joe
60 Kind of rifle
61 Harangue
62 Cartoon frame

COLLEGE TOUR by Wren Schultz
An original theme with a diagram featuring lateral symmetry.

ACROSS

1 Wedding ammo?
5 Grass clumps
10 John Wayne's nickname
14 Post-fall assurance
15 "Howdy, Hawaiian!"
16 Presque Isle lake
17 Third, for one
18 Frozen treats
19 Cooper's creation
20 What 37, 39, and 41 Across are?
23 Fat Tire, for one
24 Like a featherweight
25 National tree of India
28 Indian spice mix
32 Start of a backseat query
33 QB stats
35 Vinegar go-with
36 ___ Tai
37 Most common last name in the U.S.
39 With, in Würzburg
41 Chocolate
43 One of the South Park gang
44 ___ Arenas, Chile
46 31 Down, rightly
47 Doctor's determination
50 Mason's surveying partner
52 Dockers embellishment
55 ___ Rafael, CA
56 Archrivals
60 Citi Field stat
62 What 1, 5, and 10 Across represent?
65 Itch soother
66 Worry
67 Hope for
68 Jackalope, for one
69 Part of MS-DOS: Abbr.
70 Spread for bread

DOWN

1 Celery stick
2 Salah leader
3 Mozart's "___ fan tutte"
4 Just managed
5 Last
6 Peptic problem
7 Visitors, at home games
8 "Supergirl" network
9 Japanese fish dish
10 Mock mallards
11 Orenburg's river
12 X
13 "A mouse!!!"
21 Grim Reaper
22 Toothbrush brand
25 Sunbathe
26 Camp Swampy's org.
27 Astrophysicist deGrasse Tyson
29 Cookie maker of some acclaim
30 Croquet area
31 46 Across, wrongly
34 Full of oneself
35 Bart's bus driver
38 Regional event where people talk
40 Holiday ___
42 Defy gravity
44 ___ Bread restaurants
45 Angle
48 Skye in "XOXO"
49 "Casablanca" heroine
50 "Investor's Business ___"
51 Bullion bar
53 Windows font
54 Outback order
55 Smoke and mirrors
57 ___ sana in corpore sano
58 Almost too hip
59 Sleuth (out)
61 Krakauer's "___ the Wild"
63 Chuckle syllable
64 Derek Jeter's retired number

MOCKTAILS by Wren Schultz

11 Down was the first cartoon character to appear on a U.S. postage stamp.

ACROSS

1 Eastern crown
5 Sea turtle nesting site
10 1/16 cup: Abbr.
14 Tap-and-ride app
15 Perambulate
16 Word with hoop or skirt
17 Drink named after a Russian guy?
19 "Zoinks!"
20 First Family of 2001
21 Asks for more "Money"
23 Made soup, say
24 Drink named after a big brass?
27 Sung parts
29 April, so they say
30 Film
33 ___ before beauty
34 Brown pigment
35 "My man!"
36 III fathers?
37 Math proof trigram
38 D.C. baseballer
39 Tarsi
41 Peggy of song
42 Greene's "quiet American"
43 Use a cot
44 Muppet drummer
46 Drink named after a news anchor's short hairstyle?
48 Not just uni-
52 Working by itself
53 Beaming lights
54 "Both Sides Now" songwriter Mitchell
56 Drink named after a literary work?
58 Encourage
59 Banned refrigerant
60 Not a lick
61 Bout enders
62 Kierkegaard
63 What circles lack

DOWN

1 Cuban dance
2 "___ face!"
3 "Breaking Bad" cook
4 Data repository
5 Audi rivals
6 Email sign-off
7 "Generally . . ."
8 A-listers
9 Mongoose relative
10 HBO drama set in Baltimore
11 Toon on the Hollywood Walk of Fame
12 Suburb of Rabat
13 Launch site
18 Wine prefix
22 Spanish soldier-hero
24 Puts out a base stealer
25 Kidney related
26 Make jubilant
28 2006 Pixar film
30 Sport for young sluggers
31 Jack's golf rival
32 Location-based mobile game
34 Look
36 Member of 20 Across
37 Witty remark
40 Ones in Medicine Hat?
41 Not a thriller, for sure
42 Unidentified date
44 Maestro Toscanini
45 "Measure of ___": Clay Aiken
47 Trouser turnups
49 Elton John song
50 Political shift
51 Hebrides, e.g.
53 NFL Hall-of-Famer Swann
54 Stick (out)
55 "Mork and Mindy" planet
57 Muppet Elmo's friend

136 TURN! TURN TURN! by Fred Piscop
31 Down could be a clue for "Amazons."

ACROSS

1 Online conversation
5 Furbys, Pet Rocks et al.
9 Thefts on diamonds
14 Vesuvius emission
15 Lean against
16 In base eight
17 Tip jar filler
18 Voicemail prompt
19 Like smudge pots
20 Features of Shirley Temple's hairdo
23 Word after sewing or mess
24 Square on toast
25 Monarch before George I
26 Obedience school command
27 Bit of concert gear
29 Social climber
32 Sean of "Stranger Things"
35 Ghana's main port
37 Conductor's signal
38 The way up a lighthouse
41 ___ XING (street sign)
42 Give away a secret
43 Hot dog vendors' vehicles
44 Digitize, in a way
46 Mattress filler
47 Weather Channel graphic
48 Deal involving interest
50 In the doldrums
51 Roller on a dinner plate
54 Be left in suspense
58 Beauty's beloved
59 Iranian currency
60 Really liking
61 Enthusiastic reviewer
62 Cornfield unit
63 Dance lesson unit
64 Juvenile retort to "Ain't!"
65 One with ESP
66 Broadway title role of Terrence Mann

DOWN

1 Football scoreboard component
2 Where McCain was imprisoned
3 Ward off
4 To-do list entry
5 Wealthy campaign donor
6 Scrub a mission
7 Sahara formation
8 Burgoo or jambalaya
9 Ship's petty officer
10 Squirrel burials
11 Joyrider's ride
12 Has some grub
13 Like a fox, it's said
21 Backbone-related
22 Blue Grotto's isle
26 Title for Jagger
27 Deliverer of lines
28 Thom ___ (classic shoe name)
30 Kick out of office
31 They have a queen but no king
32 Nile serpents
33 Risky venture, for short
34 2004 Indian Ocean natural disaster
35 Italian bubbly
36 Pinball locale
39 Was off-center
40 Beanie or beret
45 Click and clack
47 "Resurrection" composer Gustav
49 Gerrit Cole, in 2019
50 It may be blank or icy
51 15th-century caravel
52 Key with an arrow
53 Take up, as a cause
54 Sign of remorse
55 Tax planners' suggestions
56 "Well done!"
57 Birthday child's secret
58 "Training" garment

WATERING HOLES by Fred Piscop
"Leaf cabbage" is another name of 34 Across.

CROSS

1 Brutus co-conspirator
6 Lake house
0 Email status
4 Orchestra tuners
5 Cookie in ice cream
6 Texter's "However . . ."
7 Source of books
0 In jeopardy
1 More reliable
2 Networkers' connections
4 "A-laying" birds
5 Urban stickball field
0 Alternative to plastic
3 Frost works
4 Crinkly green
5 "Snake eyes" value
8 Mark Twain novel, with "The"
2 Badminton barrier
3 Jared of "Panic Room"
4 Hole-in-one, usually
5 Signature at Appomattox
7 Year-by-year record
8 Conspiratorial group
1 Sales staffer, for short
3 Rack one's brains
6 Does away with
2 Where to get cheap stuff
4 Ronny Howard role
5 Causes of sudden death

66 Salami named for a city
67 Hardy lass
68 Vegging out
69 Unable to sit still

DOWN

1 Manilow song setting
2 Lie against
3 Weeps audibly
4 Beantown hoopster, for short
5 Home to most of Turkey
6 Leonard who wrote "Hallelujah"
7 "Break Your Heart Right Back" singer Grande, to fans
8 Department store department
9 Kelly's possum
10 Muskogee native, for example
11 Piano practice piece
12 Attendance count
13 "Are we ___ yet?"
18 "SNL" bit
19 Like a Brobdingnagian
23 Frying pan mishap
25 "Wheel of Fortune" option
26 Signal to start recording
27 Airbnb expense
28 Angsty music genre
29 "Cancel that" key

31 "Another thing . . ."
32 Shepherd's pie veggie
34 Place for a jeans patch
35 Keg party garb, perhaps
36 Place for a mural
37 Tributes in verse
39 Plumber's bend
40 Uncle on rice boxes
41 Hotfooted it
45 Target practice locales
46 Kazan with an honorary Oscar
47 Subjects of Darwinian theory

48 Explorer John or Sebastian
49 Visibly awestruck
50 Britain's Johnson
52 Take out
54 Often-baked pasta
55 Chisholm Trail city
57 Prefix for byte
58 Blood moon, to some
59 Let off steam
60 Mireille of "The Catch"
61 Hang around
63 ___ Paese cheese

ACROSS

1 Matzo serving
6 Give grub to
10 Rear, to a rear admiral
13 Unlike a zombie
14 Bulky hulks of folklore
16 Level out a fairway
17 America's tallest man-made monument
19 Tavern tipple
20 Allowed to mellow
21 Dog star
23 Wall decorator
27 Chooses to deal with
28 Irritate by rubbing
29 Having fewer furnishings
30 Stands in a queue
31 Light show shaft
35 2010 health law, briefly
36 Pummels with snowballs
37 2006 Verizon acquisition
38 Period permitted for a project
41 Personal hoard
43 Chilled grocery section
44 Whale's krill filter
45 Blast furnace output
48 Unemployed
49 Skillful speechifier
50 Neither awesome nor awful
51 Coke mixer
52 Traitorous internal group
58 Tree with an oval leaf
59 Sing Sing occupant
60 "Somewhere" director Coppola
61 Poseidon's dominion
62 Easily fooled folks
63 Tile layer's adhesive

DOWN

1 Chin-___ (gossip)
2 Attributing menu term
3 Dressmaker's concern
4 Original sinner
5 Sums on wanted posters
6 Hotel or theater area
7 Old-fashioned "Oh, wow!"
8 Cross an i or dot a t, e.g.
9 Says emphatically
10 Create a stockpile
11 Sheet folded into pages
12 Many a middle-schooler
15 Millennial Church member
18 1958 Pulitzer author James
22 Djokovic, for one
23 Probe in a feline way
24 Bead-based calculators
25 Trojan War ruler
26 Cure the munchies
27 Try a bite of
29 Like the Caribbean climate
31 Live partner
32 Quiz show conductor
33 Post-aerobics woes
34 Personal bearings
36 Clerical residences
39 Improve the readability of
40 Not nearby
41 It crosses a crossing last
42 Musketeers motto word
44 Thin-necked pear
45 Facial scrub targets
46 "Nobody's better than me!"
47 C, in Crete
48 "Flag" painter Jasper
50 Bus-boarding location
53 Kissimmee loc.
54 Remove with a hatchet
55 Sighting over Roswell
56 Betty Crocker boxful
57 Obstructionist's vote

THEMELESS by Harvey Estes

Original clues and a 26-Across diagram from a veteran wordsmith.

ACROSS

1 Vatican City soldier
1 Figure skater Katarina
5 Hogshead's home
6 Pertaining to most students
7 Fan
8 Guinness of "Star Wars"
9 Start a new day
0 Healthy ___ ox
1 Curling place
2 Popular cruise port
4 Musical event
6 Without restrictions
1 Eradicate
2 A wink and ___
3 Retired Monopoly token
5 Waffle topper
6 Eccentricity
7 Ticket to the World Series
9 Sitcom actress Meyers
0 Technical composition
2 Words before speak
3 Tennis player Smith
4 Equestrian activity
6 Fermented dairy food
8 Matt Dillon's job
0 Maiden name preceder
1 Fraternity letters
2 Driveway's end
5 Small handbill
9 Ref's call
0 Well-spoken
2 Hoosier Bayh

63 One noted for his trash talk?
64 End the defense
65 Drive nuts

DOWN

1 Free things
2 Wedding cake doll
3 "What's ___ for me?"
4 Came by
5 Opponent of Hannibal
6 Graphic prefix
7 Radius neighbor
8 Wistful word
9 Police car feature
10 Hummed
11 With little energy
12 Know-Nothing Party members?
13 Redford baseball film
14 Please
23 Ryan's "Sons of Anarchy" role
25 "___ Moi" ("Camelot" song)
26 Olympic pool measure?
27 First step
28 "The Right Stuff" et al.
29 White-tailed eagles
30 Forbidden acts
34 Int. peacekeeper
37 Phnom ___, Cambodia
38 This may be proper

41 Differ from the majority
43 Perfume tester
45 Sale locale
47 Sanctuary
49 Dr. Seuss environmentalist
53 Gillette razor product
54 Informal claim
56 "___ lineman for the county . . ."
57 Maine, to Monet
58 Magritte or Russo
61 Upper limit

140 THE LAST DANCE by Pam Klawitter
Argus Filch (49 Down) is the caretaker of Hogwarts School.

ACROSS
1 "It comes ___ surprise"
5 1983 Toto hit
11 Wai in "Tomorrow Never Dies"
14 Planking fish
15 "De Bello Gallico" author
16 Poem of dedication
17 Popular place on December 31st
19 Just out
20 Place to be
21 1974 CIA film spoof
22 Cleary's "Ramona the ___"
23 Trail mix morsel
25 Cineplex drinks
27 Lineman's workplace
32 Bonkers
33 Widely known
34 Stone in "La La Land"
38 ___-Grain cereal bars
41 Half a dozen for Jorge
42 Bulletin ___
44 God of love
46 Hitting coach's concern
51 Popular dip
52 Put on a pedestal
55 Rejuvenation resorts
57 P&L preparers
60 Verdi aria
61 Whole ___
62 Welcome respite at work
64 Pub quaff
65 One who's usually not revealed
66 Jazz singer Anderson
67 Calendar pgs.
68 Passes out
69 French salts

DOWN
1 Autumn bloomer
2 Hindu god
3 "Whatever you want!"
4 Denmark port
5 Temp. reducers
6 Website help pages
7 Take another tour
8 Mom's ultimate reason
9 "The Silent Spring" author
10 "We ___ the Champions"
11 Seeking company
12 Bad day for 15 Across
13 Eye source in "Macbeth"
18 Windless
22 Half a '60s pop group
24 Flasher on 17 Across
26 Mos in "Monster's Ball"
28 1994 David Spade comedy
29 Arthur Hailey novel
30 Memento of Maui
31 "GQ" staffers: Abbr.
34 "Cabaret" lyricist
35 Extinct cousin of the kiwi
36 Rubdowns
37 They're found in math class
39 Victoria Sta. arrivals
40 Tall Corn State
43 "Ground rule" hit: Abbr.
45 45 half
47 "___ as I Am" (2013 Claire Danes film)
48 Perky Peke, at times
49 Argus Filch's pet cat Mrs. ___
50 Lament
53 Cybercommerce
54 Fists, slangily
55 Empty pretense
56 Water sport
58 Full hairstyle
59 Chip off the old flock
62 Stars and Bars org.
63 Caltech degs.

141 QUENCH YOUR THIRST by Pam Klawitter
Al Pacino played 7 Down in the 2003 HBO miniseries.

CROSS

1 Sushi fish
5 Comment from a Brexit backer
1 MADD ad, for one
4 It might precede tat-tat
5 Hot, in a sense
6 Kanaka's wreath
7 Easy to reach
9 Kingklip
0 Umayyad Palace site
1 Prefix for biotic
2 Derby fish
3 Tet Offensive site
5 New York natives
7 Rams of Fort Collins
2 First family member
3 Craze
4 Not timely
8 Teapot feature
1 Tip follower
2 Things on a checklist
4 Elevator name
6 Olive branch, traditionally
1 Cultured gem
2 Prima ballerina
5 Scottish slope
7 First name in Gateway architecture
0 Skinny as ___
1 Sharer's word
2 "Old Mr. Boston" recipes/TITLE
4 2005 Prince hit
5 Antarctic penguin
6 Dagger of yore
7 Piggery
8 Board grooves
9 Smacker

DOWN

1 They're black and white and wet all over
2 Mallorca capital
3 Age that followed WW2
4 Makes an attempt at
5 New Deal org.
6 Blues singer James
7 "Angels in America" lawyer
8 Over the moon
9 Robert of "The Comedian"
10 Cessation
11 Enjoyable
12 Gets it
13 Is under the weather
18 Name on a B-29 of note
22 App trials
24 They're loaded in London
26 Ending for real
28 DDE's party
29 Distant, socially
30 Four-in-hand, e.g.
31 Incus locale
34 Word with stick
35 Lunched
36 Historic Boston event
37 Dais figure
39 Sun-dance dancer
40 Pirelli product
43 Gloucester sight
45 Instrument with two pardas
47 Tater Tots company
48 Showed off one's "guns"
49 Lacking a downside
50 Designer Versace
53 Facebook approvals
54 Somebody ___ problem
55 Head honcho
56 Reddish brown
58 Move, to Realtors
59 Comics canine
62 "Spy vs. Spy" magazine
63 Marais ___ Cygnes

142

THEMELESS by Rich Proulx

The answer to 20 Across is a bit of a spelling challenge.

ACROSS

1 What smoke detectors may trigger
12 Fall back
15 Volt or Bolt, e.g.
16 Yossarian's tentmate in "Catch 22"
17 Hawaii has two
18 Swell spot
19 Tooth protector
20 Polish bread
22 Jay Rivera's stage name
23 Mezzo-soprano Tatiana
25 Site to buy amphorae
28 "There is no i in ___"
29 Concert series
30 "Little Men" man
31 Hazy visions of a better place
34 As well
35 DIRECTV parent
36 Punk relative
37 "What the Butler ___": Orton
38 Corp. milestone
39 "Not recommended"
40 Peeping aid
42 NL East player
43 Slant
45 Slant
46 Communion responses
48 Bubble blowers
50 School org. founded in 1897
51 Spanish chess pawns
52 Chafes
56 Extremely soft, in music
57 Underground launch facility
60 "Light-Horse Harry" of 1776
61 Spokespersons
62 Sounds of delay
63 Perpetuity

DOWN

1 Own (up)
2 Homer's "On ___ Shore"
3 Waithe of "Ready Player One"
4 Ladderlike
5 "Miss Peaches" of jazz
6 Dome
7 Slant
8 Duffer's dream
9 TV brand
10 Hanukkah staple
11 "r u kidding?"
12 Hit the ground running
13 Timely question for a shop owner
14 The rank and file
21 Cereal bran
23 Bigelow product
24 Rides
25 Male trait
26 Obstacle to access
27 About to fall
28 Verne of Mini-Me fame
32 Self-destruction
33 Ground-nesting pollinators
41 Tricks
44 Pale
47 Surrealist André
49 Site of ASU
50 Tabloids
52 Marriage, e.g.
53 "Old age" adjective
54 Start of a Shakespeare play
55 Cares
58 Vicious of the Sex Pistols
59 TV home of Debbie Downer

143

THE BIG 5-O   by Fred Piscop
Fred constructed this one on his 50th birthday.

CROSS

1 Alley pickup
6 Pear discard
10 In need of a rubdown
14 On-fire feeling
15 Drooler of comics
16 Rock genre for Yes
17 Pinned figurine
19 Psyched up
20 Psychic's ability: Abbr.
21 Pass along on Facebook
22 Scott who created Dilbert
23 Hold for questioning
25 Cry of assent
26 "Hello!" musical (with "The")
32 Yarn shop buy
35 April 1 baby, e.g.
36 Obstacle to teamwork
37 Camper's setup
38 Like Caitlyn Jenner, for short
39 Item in a deck
40 Nuts-bolts connector
41 Prizefight venue
42 "Psycho" motel name
43 Intent gaze
46 Reddish brown
47 Factory-built home
51 Printer's proof, briefly
53 Glowing reviews
56 Hoopla
57 Need a rubdown
58 Canada's largest menagerie
60 "Jeopardy!" intro word
61 Biblical shepherd
62 Manage to avoid
63 "&" follower in company names
64 Cop's rounds
65 Does dock work

DOWN

1 Socked away
2 Everyday writing
3 Animal shelter's plea
4 Angler's need
5 Shoreline problem
6 Composer's closer
7 Olfactory stimulus
8 Steam up
9 Wriggly swimmer
10 James of "Boston Legal"
11 Sweetbread, e.g.
12 Clue board area
13 Dairy-aisle dozen
18 "Yikes!"
22 "A Sorta Fairytale" singer Tori
24 Not very much
25 Iowa straw poll city, once
27 Mrs. Pence
28 Bornean ape, briefly
29 Big exam
30 Legendary brute
31 Starts to snooze
32 Bambi, in adulthood
33 Number-picking game
34 Cause of a runner's high
38 Harness race pace
39 Soap unit
41 "Another thing . . ."
42 Detention center in a Behan title
44 Illegal coercion
45 Make the first bet
48 Threw for a loop
49 Be nuts about
50 Pair in an UGG box
51 Charlie Brown's "Blast it!"
52 Sonic rebound
53 Chorister's attire
54 Apartment listing datum
55 Chevy hybrid
58 Bar bill
59 In vitro cells

144 VARIABLE STARS by David Van Houten

55 Across is a satirical protest song against the Vietnam War draft.

ACROSS

1 Sphenoidal cavity
6 Carbonated cocktail
10 Dotty
14 "___ we all?"
15 ___ fixe
16 Lamb of literature
17 "Misery" star's Apple headphones?
19 Spare tire
20 Dr. Scholl's products
21 Swears (to)
23 Roundup rope
25 Baby's cry
26 Rocky crags
29 "Hearts Afire" star's line of blouses?
34 Diaphanous
36 Loblolly fruit
37 Avena sativa
38 Head of England?
39 Beguile
42 Soul seller
43 Coronado's quest
44 Squire-to-be
45 Attacked by jellyfish
47 "Rocky" star adds to the staff?
51 Heaviest fencing sword
52 Prefix for lateral
53 Movie music
55 "Alice's Restaurant" songwriter
59 "Almost there!"
63 Song for Christine Daaé
64 "Norma Rae" star worked on some nails?
66 Object of worship
67 Province
68 Undo errata
69 Air
70 Hardly a neatnik
71 "The defense ___!"

DOWN

1 H.H. Munro pen name
2 Armenia neighbor
3 Trawling equipment
4 Best in a joust
5 Hi-fi needles
6 Pamplona party
7 Mrs. McKinley
8 Epsilon follower
9 Martini garnish
10 Shellac
11 Elvis Presley hit
12 Car seen in "La Strada"
13 Notebook markers
18 Rafter
22 Twitter posts
24 Katniss Everdeen et al.
26 Kind of router bit
27 Wayne's costar in "The Quiet Man"
28 Beatles song
30 RV organization
31 Roadhouse
32 "Common Sense" author
33 Wells Fargo carrier
35 Patch up
40 Slangy denial
41 "Trolls World Tour" animation
46 Links reservation
48 Devour rapidly
49 Global food-safety org.
50 "Spider-Man" studio
54 Allude (to)
55 Pace or trot
56 Language of Pakistan
57 "A miss ___ good . . ."
58 British blue blood
60 Ryder Cup cheers
61 Guy
62 Racing-form data
65 Composer Ornstein

145

TREACHEROUS AREA by Adam Vincent
. . . and that area can be found at 65 Across.

CROSS

1 "Survivor" network
4 Tulsi Gabbard's birthplace
9 Ocean oases
4 Excuse
5 Shrimp net
6 Wet behind the ears
7 Motion sickness drug
9 Lumberjack
0 When magnolias bloom
1 Itinerary info
3 It turns singles into doubles
4 Perrier, for one
8 Strip joints?
1 West Point frosh
2 Sugarloaf Mountain site
3 Turntable speed
5 Vibes
9 Personal foul?
4 Crystal-lined rock
5 Used to be
6 Greek X
7 Funk
0 Quickly, in London
3 Grill a witness
7 Source of lobster coral
8 Chive relative
9 Private neckwear
3 "Pong" producer
5 Treacherous area
8 Hackneyed
9 Evidence
0 Degree from Wharton
1 More painful
2 Gets under control

73 "Gangnam Style" singer

DOWN

1 Musical finale
2 Pat baby on the back
3 Michelin ranking symbol
4 Lenin successor
5 Kind of wrestling
6 ___-tai
7 One with a manual
8 Pub fixture
9 How one might wake after a nightmare
10 Jazz instrument
11 The sky, for optimists
12 Dodge
13 Zorro's title
18 "Rent" role
22 Nothing but
25 Sushi seaweed
26 It's watched in sports bars
27 Be up against
28 Cliff rock
29 Teacher's helper
30 Artsy NYC neighborhood
34 Kitten sound
36 Census question
37 Masseuse's target
38 Slide after stopping
40 Chances
41 More paltry
42 Word spoken with a hat tip
43 Wine with a muscat flavor

48 Capital of Zaire?
49 Free (from)
51 Expresses disapproval
52 Prefix for cure
53 Shoots the breeze
54 Boasting old-school charm
55 Broadcasting
56 "Ran" director Kurosawa
60 Part-timer
61 Priestly outfits
62 Aussie greeting
64 Waze info: Abbr.
66 Nice name
67 "Help Wanted" ad abbr.

"ME TOO!" by Richard Silvestri
Alternate clue for 63 Across: What Guido d'Arezzo achieved?

ACROSS

1 Polish writing
5 Pottery fragment
10 Pointer's pronoun
14 Symbol of peace
15 Anouk in "La Dolce Vita"
16 Start of a choosing chant
17 Porky's water park ride?
19 One way to run
20 Legal conclusion?
21 Napa Valley vessel
22 Like moonstones
24 Second-rate
26 State with conviction
27 Coin honoring a royal?
33 Singer Lovato
36 [not my mistake]
37 Lethargy
38 "Casablanca" actor
40 Pendulum weight
42 Kind of spray
43 Out
45 Luftwaffe's WW2 foe
47 Corn concoction
48 Catchy Airbnb listing for a Left Coast home?
51 "Tu No ___ Para Mi": Fanny Lu
52 Goodyear product
56 Dilapidated dwelling
60 It sells, they say
61 Stamping machine
62 Not quite shut
63 Celebrity from wealth?
66 Big blow
67 Oklahoma tribe
68 "Dark Lady" singer
69 Bar on a car
70 Element #54
71 Buffalo Bill

DOWN

1 Henry Ford II's dad
2 Search for water
3 They make Brown green
4 Metric base
5 Jaunts through the jungle
6 Part of Excalibur
7 ___ Darya River
8 Do away with
9 Furthest underwater
10 Shade of blue
11 Sphere starter
12 In a while
13 Day-care denizen
18 For all time
23 Bad lighting?
25 Upright piano
26 Treaties
28 The point of writing?
29 Fell in folds
30 ___ facto
31 Mournful sound
32 Gardner of pulp fiction
33 Tie
34 Let up
35 Wire measures
39 Norton's workplace
41 Cry to Cratchit
44 Seeming contradiction
46 Plant bosses
49 State of rest
50 It's long in fashion
53 Neighbor of British Columbia
54 Prepared for a shot
55 Suspicious
56 Sitar tune
57 Trojan War hero
58 Hard to believe
59 Alder or elder
60 Utah's state flower
64 Did some roadwork
65 TV monitor?

CROSS

1 Stadium section
5 Millrose Games event
9 House publication
14 Make eyes at
15 Away from the wind
16 Antique shop item
17 Marine handyman's motto?
19 General direction
20 Work on the docks
21 Antitoxins
23 Partook of the cooking
24 Marshal Dillon portrayer
26 Spare tire
28 Religious pamphlet
30 Support
33 Isn't any longer
36 Bernie Taupin's forte
38 October birthstone
39 Super Bowl XXXIII MVP
41 Big flap
42 Inquirer's word
43 Bad to the bone
44 Mystery writer Cross
46 Classic Jaguar
47 Breakfast choice
49 Smelling a rat
51 Old anesthetic
53 Barbershop sharpeners
56 Not in operation
58 In the center of
60 Scotto of opera
62 Coe or Cram
64 Two AL teams?
66 Employed
67 Tale on a grand scale
68 List shortener
69 College books
70 Conclude the defense
71 It may be going

DOWN

1 Have a restless night
2 "___ Kick Out Of You"
3 Gantry of fiction
4 Preacher's directive
5 Venture to mention
6 TV alien
7 Twice tres
8 Put a spell on
9 Pump number
10 Robot play
11 Big top?
12 Nonstandard negative
13 Central point
18 Either "Bird Dog" singer
22 Takes the wrong way?
25 "Hit the road!"
27 "This can't be good"
29 Kind of basin
31 Innocent mischief
32 Head for the hills
33 Queen Anne's lace, e.g.
34 Peace Nobelist Myrdal
35 Change of Odysseus' crew on Aeaea?
37 Traffic markers
40 Came down to earth
42 Rabbit home
44 Opening remark?
45 Take away
48 Wall Street units
50 Over there
52 Stage platform
54 Elbows on the table
55 Brown ermine
56 Forget to include
57 Hunky-dory
59 Birdbrain
61 Connection for big wheels
63 Ultimate ending
65 Greek letters

148

SWAY BACK   by Gary Larson
In 1968, 21 Across shared the first interracial kiss in American TV history.

ACROSS
1 Online party notice
6 Cries of surprise
10 MLB's oldest team
14 Burdened
15 Footway
16 Et ___ (and others)
17 Revise a bill
18 Backyard pendulum*
20 Hot tubs
21 Enterprise captain
22 Till bill
23 Site of an annual ball drop*
27 Rite answer?
28 High dudgeon
29 Melted glace
30 Boot camp reply
32 Hockey face-off spot*
36 Dodge of the 1980s
37 Mockumentary rock band*
40 Where Mets once met
43 Summer Olympics event
47 Ford model
50 "Wheel of Fortune" request
51 Bambi's aunt
52 Be off
53 When collegians descend on Florida*
57 A Gabor
58 Flair
59 Can't take
60 Donna Summer hit (and a hint to clue* answers)
63 Wished (for)
64 Border lake
65 Canine command
66 Year's record
67 Time to attack
68 Give an edge to
69 Apprehensive

DOWN
1 Adaptable
2 Lily Munster, e.g.
3 Think-tank guys
4 It may be present
5 Purpose
6 Suitable
7 Japanese verse form
8 Skylit lobbies
9 Fortified wine
10 Disagreeably chilly
11 Arrogant attitude
12 Ate at home
13 Gentlemen of Verona
19 "I Wish" rapper ___-Lo
24 Trickle down
25 Madras dress
26 One of five
31 Jr. candidate
33 Ruler opposed by the Bolsheviks
34 Elevator cage
35 González in the 2000 headlines
38 Orange drink mix
39 Get from ___ (progress)
40 Made tough
41 JFK's alma mater
42 "1984" superstate
44 TV chef Wong
45 Running rampant
46 How streakers streak
48 No longer mint
49 Make waves
54 Totaled, as bar tab
55 Ancient Andean
56 German wine valley
61 Miss Pym's creator
62 London landmark
63 Mate

TRADE NAMES by Gary Larson
Although famous for his writings, Mark Twain was also the first 40 Across.

ACROSS

1 "___ the torpedoes!": Farragut
5 "S.O.S." group
9 Traitor
14 Send off
15 NFL quarterback Derek
16 She met Humpty Dumpty
17 ROD
19 "Me and Bobby ___"
20 Prov. on Hudson Bay
21 Lets alone
23 Some Prado hangings
25 SUE
29 Jump
32 Salt
33 In the style of
34 Schuss
36 Toon bartender Szyslak
38 Greensward
40 JOSH
43 Revlon rival
44 Undivided
45 East ender
46 Grogshop fare
47 Plural suffix
49 Like deposition testimony
51 GRACE
54 Monotheistic doctrine
58 Orwellian state
61 Brazilian hot spot
62 Bounce
65 OSCAR
67 Retreats
68 Morlock victim
69 Band known for its red plastic hats
70 Not those
71 "Baseball Tonight" channel
72 Biblical starting point

DOWN

1 Get the mist off
2 Acid in proteins
3 Tearing up
4 Mathematics degree?
5 Plot unit
6 The Crimson Tide, familiarly
7 La Scala cheer
8 Will of "Arrested Development"
9 Lavish party
10 Worrier's worry
11 Like
12 High card
13 Find out
18 Besides
22 Speech problem
24 Skirt type
26 Rock bottom
27 Online finance company
28 Open wide
30 Juju and mojo
31 Music genre
34 Russian vodka brand
35 Silkwood of "Silkwood"
37 Prefix with sphere
39 "Die Fledermaus" maid
40 French Open, for one
41 Dogpatch gal
42 Lennon's lady
48 Fixed charge
50 First person
52 Objects of worship
53 Stirs
55 Ticked off
56 It doesn't hold water
57 Fool
59 Alka-Seltzer sound
60 "Sounds good to me!"
62 Minerva McGonagall's Patronus
63 Mary Kay of cosmetics
64 Popular bread
66 Citrus quaff

150 A FEW POINTERS   by Lee Taylor
"The trouble with law is lawyers." —25 Across

ACROSS

1 Sharp insight
7 "Hey you?"
11 Stately shade tree
14 Blood cell source
15 Tribe that makes kachina dolls
16 ___ tai cocktail
17 Place side by side
18 "So sad!"
19 Surveillance org.
20 Burgoo or goulash
21 Bug-squashing sound
23 Manor laborer
24 Sharpen, as skills
25 John Scopes' attorney
27 Sink feature
29 ___ Paulo
30 Airline to Tokyo
33 Tippy top
34 Many a Trump message, formerly
38 Pale lager
40 Worship
42 Europe's highest peak
43 Petri dish contents
44 Value-added ___
45 Unit of resistance
47 Gives in
49 1979 Wings song
53 Jazz singer James
57 Nighttime call
58 "Peer Gynt" composer
59 "Nessun Dorma" is one
60 Corn unit
61 "Let Us Now Praise Famous Men" author
62 Novel by Sinclair Lewis
64 TV spots
65 Pole or Serb
66 Geronimo was one
67 Change the locks
68 Seahawks coach Carroll
69 Jerked

DOWN

1 Make blush
2 Admit, slangily
3 Let the sheep out
4 Spoke Siamese?
5 Type widths
6 Close shave
7 Roman combat formation
8 Green energy option
9 Sudden outpourings
10 Frank McCourt memoir
11 Show host
12 Surfer Hamilton
13 "Rosemary's Baby" star
22 Diligent tradesman
23 Grumpy expression
26 Mother Earth
28 Vaquero's workplace
30 "Dragnet" alert
31 Absolutely nothing
32 In the manner of
35 Break a fast
36 JFK posting
37 Western moniker
39 Quick drink from a hip flask
40 Top performance
41 Founding host of NBC's "Today"
43 Reach a goal
46 Hermione Granger, e.g.
48 Naval officer
49 Kansas City Chiefs stadium
50 Bootlicker
51 Ginny Weasley's Patronus
52 Exceeding all expectations
54 Treat counterpart
55 Church contribution
56 Oohed and ___
61 Cleopatra's pet
63 Place for a facial

FURNISH REFERENCES by Lee Taylor
Don't be misled by Lee's punny title!

CROSS

1 Waxing targets
6 Chanel and Austin
1 Gown counterpart
4 Group of eight
5 Jeweler's lens
6 ___ and the same
7 Nightclub gadabout
9 Game akin to Crazy Eights
20 Uncouth
21 Vitamin B3
23 Red train car
26 Big hits
27 Iron deficiency
28 "American Pastoral" novelist Roth
29 Longed
30 Head Start age group
31 Connecting point
34 And more of the same
35 Wound on a bobbin
38 Groom's attire
39 Chicago mayor Emanuel
41 Airline to Ben-Gurion
42 Likeness
44 It comes with age
46 Reviewer
47 Noggin toppers
49 Customers
50 Big sizes
51 Venomous African snake
52 Drive-thru machine
53 Omertà violator
58 New Jersey's Tappan ___ Bridge
59 Earth tone
60 Martial art with bamboo swords
61 Blow it
62 Hem or take in, e.g.
63 "In the Heart of the Sea" ship

DOWN

1 Droid
2 HDTV brand
3 NYC betting site
4 Word on a doormat
5 Olympics test for these
6 "Albert Nobbs" actress
7 "I'm such a klutz!"
8 Ryder or Stanley
9 Coffeehouse live show
10 Soap opera, e.g.
11 Binge watcher
12 Photographer Leibovitz
13 Day laborers
18 "Every saint ___ past . . .": Wilde
22 F ___ Frank
23 Escapade
24 Shark Bernardo's gal
25 Second-stringer
26 Beachcomber's find
28 Charity tourney
30 Sporty shirts
32 Refused to budge
33 CEOs
36 Statue base
37 Enduro wheels
40 Chinese dynasty
43 Desert delusions
45 Afternoon nap
46 Summer place
47 Mark a trail
48 Buffet patron
49 Less rosy
51 Sulk
54 No longer closeted
55 USN junior officer
56 Schiller's "___ to Joy"
57 Roman goddess of night

152 "GIVE ME A HAND!" by Lee Taylor

27 Down also starred in "Route 66" which ran from 1960 to 1964.

ACROSS

1 Telephone tone
5 Homo sapiens
10 Stately shade providers
14 Trendy berry
15 Battery terminal
16 Ancient France
17 Chicken tenders, e.g.
19 Subterfuge
20 Dusty storage room
21 Like a graveyard at night
22 Tuckered out
25 Bulletin board pin
28 Held in check
30 Pen points
31 Lady Gaga's "You ___"
32 Safe to consume
35 Existed
38 A punch in the mouth
41 Give the once-over
42 "That's enough!"
43 Glee Club member
44 Mozart's "___ fan tutte"
45 Deodorant type
47 Very close game
52 Menacing look
53 Moorehead in "Jane Eyre"
54 Loses ardor
56 Arp's genre
57 Chiromancer
62 Protagonist in "The Kite Runner"
63 Wide open
64 Alluring
65 Some jeans
66 Untrue
67 Major suffix

DOWN

1 Luftwaffe foe
2 Here, in French class
3 Photographer Goldin
4 Humongous
5 Rodgers' lyricist
6 Inept
7 Freeload
8 Hullabaloo
9 "Game of Thrones" patriarch Stark
10 White waders
11 First lady before Michelle
12 "That's ___ to my ears"
13 Glossy
18 Caesar's rebuke to Brutus
21 Subsided
22 "Thus ___ Zarathustra"
23 Pretty coin?
24 Provide with a quality
26 Open a castle door
27 Martin of "Adam-12"
29 Speaker of the House
33 Resign
34 Prefix meaning "equal"
35 "O Pioneers!" author Cather
36 SAG member
37 Was brilliant
39 Door handles
40 Secure hiding place
44 Wipes off
46 Give the once-over
47 2019 U.S. Open winner
48 Athlete's peak performance
49 Non-studio film
50 Dazzling success
51 Bruising defeats
55 Android operating system
57 Rotten review
58 In the past
59 Period
60 Business card abbr.
61 Source of gluten

CROSS

1 Port Said's canal
5 Giant Sequoia, e.g.
9 Grease someone's palm
14 Whistler's mother
15 Unicorn feature
16 Baseball's Hammerin' Hank
17 Laser focus
20 Sound systems
21 Fluffy hair products
22 Musical talent
23 Apollo 13 module
24 Oxymoronic card game
33 A, in German class
34 Cut the grass
35 Rook's board position
36 De la Garza of "Law & Order"
39 Julius Erving's nickname
41 Newhouse holdings
42 Roman army unit
44 Muesli ingredient
46 Helpful connections
47 Tall dessert order
51 Went underground
52 Neither here ___ there
53 Shows up
58 Readied windows for a storm
62 Major heart surgery
64 Loosen a knot
65 Jimmy Carter's middle name
66 Samara sources
67 Obstinate beasts
68 Rotunda feature
69 Breakaway group

DOWN

1 Lip disservice
2 Squad
3 Gender-specific suffix
4 Croatian capital
5 Math proposition
6 Becomes compost
7 Goof up
8 Cloisonné surface
9 Capital of Azerbaijan
10 2000 Super Bowl winners
11 Flower painted by Van Gogh
12 Dog treat
13 Puts to bed
18 Sharon in "Dreamgirls"
19 Stand-up guy
23 Less honorable path
24 Handed out
25 Exxon Valdez, e.g.
26 Eel, at the sushi bar
27 Piece of turf
28 Old Deuteronomy, for one
29 "___ you kidding me?"
30 Home of Bollywood
31 Freshen the stamp pad
32 Clean the slate
37 Quick drink
38 MSN rival
40 Raucous bird
43 Collarless coat
45 Well-founded
48 Spoke like Sylvester
49 Stringy
50 Party pancakes
53 Blue-green
54 Plays on words
55 Little touches
56 Warhol companion Sedgwick
57 Greek war god
58 John Adams served one
59 Cowgirl Evans
60 "Semper Fi" org.
61 "Hey you!"
63 Thai language

154 BROKEN SPIRIT* by Roger & Kathy Wienberg
The theme hint at 48 Down requires some thinking.

ACROSS

1 On the hook
7 British bozo
11 Baby food
14 Like the Oscars
15 Big city on the Big Island
16 Gardner in "The Naked Maja"
17 1980 Clint Eastwood film*
19 Short, briefly
20 Burn to remove fuzz
21 Irish New Age singer
22 Panoramic
23 David Rabe's "Visiting ___"
25 "The Man" Musial
27 It's about a 70-yard square
30 First light*
35 "Hogwash!"
36 Immoderate markup
37 Impudence
38 In plain sight
40 Book jacket bit
41 Reaction to a bad pun
42 Likewise
43 Wastes an opportunity
45 Yellowstone hrs.
46 Dessert similar to a cobbler*
48 Alpha follower
49 Film spool
50 Shakespearean royal
52 Slide
54 1997 Peter Fonda role
57 Religious observances
61 WW2 servicewoman
62 Rum-and-vodka drink*
64 Gulf state: Abbr.
65 Seniors' org.
66 Brand of cough drops
67 Solidify
68 Jack in Clancy novels
69 Most foxy

DOWN

1 Chocolate dogs
2 Crucifix letters
3 Shortly
4 Jumper cable?
5 Spiked
6 Jeff Lynne's grp.
7 Make less crowded
8 Machiavellian
9 "Let me find out"
10 Action figure
11 16 Across, for one
12 Zealous
13 Lackluster
18 Not overly taxing
22 Oreo part
24 "SNL" network
26 Salad bar utensil
27 Los Alamos project
28 Spelunker
29 Like questions with no answers
31 Ness of "The Untouchables"
32 Peter and Paul, but not Mary
33 Nautical "Halt!"
34 Busybody
36 Thing in a ring
39 Joined the crew
44 Storm center
47 DVD successor
48 Snifter contents (and a theme hint)
51 In a tangle
52 Gala giveaways
53 Curly cabbage
55 "Tomb Raider" heroine Croft
56 "First Take" network
58 ___-Ball (arcade game)
59 Between ones and hundreds
60 GPS part: Abbr.
62 "One for My Baby" setting
63 Chicago Fire org.

59 ACROSS   by Roger & Kathy Wienberg
Magic Johnson and Larry Bird were both 35 Across.

ACROSS
1 Flub
4 Take a breather
8 Home run, slangily
13 Barnyard sound
14 Foot part
15 Tea cart treats
17 Blow up in one's face*
19 Martial art
20 Stench
21 Cry of innocence
23 Bogged down
24 Kitchen gadget
26 Programme du bal*
28 Coast Guard rank
30 Take for a ride
31 Gaggle formation
32 Slave girl in "Turandot"
33 Core
34 Hammer end
35 Nontraditional NBA positions*
39 Grits ingredient
40 Fishing lure
41 Chicago–Detroit dir.
42 "Green Book" Oscar winner
43 Fenway team, for short
44 "Proceed with caution"
48 GE product*
52 Shrank
53 More aloof
54 Haiku, e.g.
56 Sky-search org.
57 Held to the mat
59 Publicity stunt group/TITLE
61 Eavesdropper
62 Academic gown
63 Indisposed
64 Thin cuts
65 Big gulp
66 Citrus drink

DOWN
1 Incorporate
2 Band aid
3 Ornate architectual style
4 Churchill's "so few"
5 Land of leprechauns
6 Fish-and-chips fish
7 Iota preceder
8 Disapproving sound
9 Savvy
10 Gin mixer
11 Made an impression?
12 Two-legged zebras
16 Without warning
18 Moscow complex
22 Sustain a loss
25 B-side to "Paperback Writer"
27 Haunted house decoration
29 Crackpot
33 Swine
34 Laundry cycle
35 Insurance contracts
36 Unedited
37 Refurbish
38 One way to start
39 Muslim bigwig
43 Thoroughfare
45 Cause of fatigue
46 Handed down (lore)
47 Fit for consumption
49 Painter Matisse
50 Spacious apartments
51 Further down
55 They who made a star trek
58 Rx writers
60 Droop

FLYING WITH CLASS by Michael Collins
41 Across is also the name of a 2019 Marc Anthony album.

ACROSS

1 Water-to-wine site
5 Spelunking buff
10 Dark German beer
14 The Bard's stream
15 Amazon Echo's assistant
16 Mideast gulf city
17 Palace protector
18 Lapidary's unit
19 2018 "Star Wars" film
20 Chicken/egg question
23 Comics shriek
24 Red Bull buy
25 Mercury and gallium, for two
29 Force to retreat in disorder
31 Alphabetically first mo.
34 Nuke event, briefly
35 "M*A*S*H" quarters
36 Astringent fruit
37 "None of your concern!"
40 Hatcher of "Lois & Clark"
41 Cartoon penguin
42 Terse response to "Why?"
43 Golf's "Big Easy"
44 Grumpy old man
45 Deadly sins, e.g.
46 Word after black or special
47 One of a schusser's pair
48 High number for a subcompact

56 Exceed 21 in blackjack
57 Derek of Cooperstown
58 Table extension
60 Cheese found in hors d'oeuvres
61 Innovative, as music
62 Mustachioed surrealist
63 Knighted Connery
64 Cunning stratagems
65 Shoot, but not lethally

DOWN

1 Tucker of "Modern Family"
2 Swear to be true
3 2014 Russell Crowe film
4 Naysayer
5 Hidden stockpiles
6 Shakespearean lament
7 Fashion designer Wang
8 Academic year finale, often
9 Occasional Fed issuances
10 Ewer's mate
11 Garlicky emanation
12 Cartoonists' creations, once
13 Yachter's speed unit
21 Boston hoopsters, for short
22 Butcher's trimmings
25 Lusterless finish
26 Mrs. Mertz on "I Love Lucy"

27 Sign of sorrow or joy
28 Sparkling wine, familiarly
29 Contradict in a debate
30 Difficult obligation
31 Pribilof Islands native
32 Rapper's entourage
33 Put back to 000
35 Blunder in print
36 Totally lose it
38 Saskatchewan city
39 Isolate in winter, perhaps
44 Laptop's "brain"
45 Women's golf attire

46 Again and again
47 Public to-do
48 Recedes from shore
49 100 percent
50 Home to many Russians
51 Strauss of denim
52 Footnote abbr.
53 Auto pioneer Ransom
54 Carnivore's craving
55 Manchurian border river
59 Bygone car adornment

GUNNING IT   by Michael Collins
11 Down is also the name of a 1990 hit by Ecuadorian rapper Gerardo.

ACROSS

1 Goblet feature
5 Automobile pioneer
9 Special Forces cap
14 Unveiling shout
15 Law office worker, briefly
16 Still in the game
17 Bird mummified by Egyptians
18 Big Band and others
19 Chopped finely
20 Alexa home-security feature
23 Developer's investment
24 Opposite of "paleo-"
25 Peach discards
26 Squirreled away
27 Shaving cream additive
29 "___ the Force, Luke"
32 Quaker in the wind
35 Burger tycoon Ray
36 Bear with a too-hard chair
37 Grocery store job
40 Mammoth feature
41 Show team spirit
42 Like an oboe's sound
43 Bummer for a QB
44 When cocks crow
45 Done with, with "of"
46 Well-kept
48 Short span, for short
49 Broadway's "Mamma ___!"
52 Hightailing it
56 Horned tempter
57 Skunk cabbage emanation
58 Spot for a roast
59 Lower in rank
60 Neuwirth of Broadway
61 Informant's wear
62 Turned visibly frightened
63 Direction in a Steinbeck title
64 Match components

DOWN

1 Revenuer's target
2 Social no-no
3 King's proclamation
4 Pandemic wear
5 Moved first in chess
6 Key in a Bogart movie
7 "Doggone it!"
8 Pageant entrant's wear
9 No-goodnik
10 "Middlemarch" novelist
11 Latino lady's man
12 On any occasion
13 Rafael Cruz, familiarly
21 How confident solvers solve
22 Pliocene or Miocene
26 "Doggone it!"
27 Laser gas
28 Drew the short straw
30 Floored it
31 Posing no challenge
32 Sparkling wine center
33 Shoot, but not lethally
34 Following birth
35 Have down cold
36 Implored on bended knee
38 Hopping mad
39 Jong who wrote "Fear of Flying"
44 Doggoned
45 Kick oneself for
47 Clear from a cache, say
48 Hoity-toity types
49 Cineplex attraction
50 Like 27 Down
51 Choreographer de Mille
52 ___ ghanouj (eggplant dish)
53 Brain part
54 Invention's origin
55 Temperature extremes
56 Maple yield

"LET'S MAKE SOME NOISE!" by Fred Piscop
1 Across received an Academy Award nomination for his role in that film.

ACROSS

1 Theodore in "The Defiant Ones"
6 Wilson in "Love Is Love Is Love"
10 Peelable tuber, informally
14 Zola who wrote "Nana"
15 "Almighty" Carell role
16 Bb or C#
17 Universe beginning (now universally accepted)
19 Sign to heed
20 Jazz jam highlight
21 Took charge of
22 Like Oscar Madison
24 Minuscule amount
26 Perched on
27 Reason to reboot
32 Like some kiwis
33 Particle for Bohr
34 Casual affirmative
37 Pay heed to
38 Richter scale event
40 Janet of the Clinton Cabinet
41 "To a . . ." poem
42 Muscles that "bounce," for short
43 Patches up
44 Hard shot in tennis
48 Lunchbox treat
49 Second tier of a stadium, perhaps
50 Evasive tactic
53 FEMA offering
54 Comfy shoes, for short
58 Like a tuned string
59 1990s period of overinvestment
62 Common clock-in hour
63 Nastase of tennis
64 Zellweger of "Chicago"
65 Haley who wrote "Roots"
66 Flea collar wearers
67 Fantasy league transaction

DOWN

1 Pimlico placements
2 Texter's "methinks"
3 Canal to the Baltic
4 Skateboarder's protection
5 Luau wear
6 Car buyer's incentive
7 Dr. Pavlov
8 Sun worshiper's goal
9 Wavelength measure
10 Is too nosy
11 Ceremonial splendor
12 The Miners of the NCAA
13 Refuse to grant
18 Rough stuff
23 Good earth
25 Fifth-century pillager
26 Doesn't just sit
27 Covert ops garb
28 "Metamorphoses" poet
29 Sal of "Exodus"
30 Merit reward
31 "Laughing" beast
35 They go deep at times
36 Richly furnished
38 Old name for Sri Lanka
39 Sound in an empty hallway
40 Think back on
42 Land bordering Lake Titicaca
43 "Chinese restaurant syndrome" additive
45 Whirlpool or tornado
46 Eatery in a Guthrie tune
47 Wonderland bird
50 Peak near Catania
51 Do exactly right
52 Shoreline formation
53 Plugging away
55 Chaplin of "Game of Thrones"
56 Like many college dorms
57 Mate on the Jolly Roger
60 "___ Buttermilk Sky"
61 Actor who said "I pity the fool!"

159 LONG AND HOLLOW by Fred Piscop
A novel theme from a noted wordmeister.

ACROSS

1 Layered mineral
5 Sound boosters
9 Fur magnate on the Titanic
14 Arabian Peninsula land
15 Gilbert of "The Conners"
16 Sharp uptick
17 Proverbial backbreaker
19 Skyscraper topper
20 Scotch pricing factor
21 Skimpy
22 Like a communicant's hands
23 Short time-out
25 Hunting garb
26 Hotel amenity
27 Bed quilt
31 At a rapid clip
34 Place to moor
35 Big stink
36 Stable newborn
37 Became visibly frightened
38 Frosty coating
39 Vegan protein source
40 Part of BTU
41 Homeschooler, often
42 Activist reverend Al
44 Windows forerunner
45 "Radiance" sculptor
46 Law and medicine, for two
50 Strikes, Biblical style
53 They're chained at the bank
54 Tabby's doc
55 Bagel shape
56 Item smoked ceremonially
58 Sun-baked brick
59 Make smooth
60 Big-eared leaper
61 "The Balcony" playwright
62 Said "nolo"
63 A party to

DOWN

1 Back biter
2 Public relations concern
3 Judicial agenda
4 Tiny soldier
5 Quick on the uptake
6 Seine feeder
7 Give an invocation
8 Tree surgeon's need
9 Take for granted
10 Therapeutic legwear
11 Reason to pack up and go
12 Brute
13 Exemplar of thinness
18 Variety, to life
22 Collapsed (with "in")
24 Old TV part
25 Want in the worst way
27 Powell of the Reagan cabinet
28 Jacquard invention
29 Cheese that's made backward?
30 British conservative
31 Vaudeville lineup
32 Playmate of Piglet
33 ___ Romeo
34 Craft for Pocahontas
37 Plays miniature golf
41 Code name?
43 Car radio button
44 Did the hucklebuck
46 Call a halt to
47 Perrier competitor
48 Duplicate, briefly
49 Dutch master Jan
50 Bambi, later on
51 The way it's done
52 Retired Monopoly token
53 Sound from Big Ben
56 Get-up-and-go
57 Honor society letter

FONT OF WISDOM   by Mark McClain
Paulette Goddard costarred in the film at 42 Across.

ACROSS

1 Like a nice spring day
5 Right in front of us
9 Goddess in the Louvre
13 Downwind
14 Home buyer's concern
15 Chimps and their ilk
16 Opera star
17 Military outfits
18 Toucan feature
19 After-hours delivery worker
22 Supermarket depts.
23 Main or Wall
24 Stately tree
26 Hocks
30 Loan contract info
33 Architectural style of 12th-century England
38 Sound of a crowd
40 Lack of musical talent
41 Rural structure
42 1936 Charlie Chaplin film
45 Came together
46 Illegal basketball move
47 Got hitched
49 The Cars lead guitarist
54 Softens, in a sense
58 "Saturday Evening Post" artist
61 Seedy fruits
62 Wedding reception tradition
63 Mercury project org.
64 Oft-fried veggie
65 Weasel cousin
66 Send forth
67 Spa treatment
68 Factor in admissions policy
69 Hair salon inventory

DOWN

1 Sloshed along the shore
2 Kicking partner?
3 Make merry
4 Bad guy
5 Installs, in an art gallery
6 Order from on high
7 Wind turbine element
8 Come after
9 Natural environments
10 Fencing form
11 ___ admiral
12 "Don't ___ me!"
14 Score for the Tigers
20 Capri, for one
21 Forced return, informally
25 "Death in Venice" author
27 Fleeting idea
28 River through Sudan
29 Glaswegian
30 Arsenal contents
31 Milne character
32 Swiss watchmaker
34 "Poppycock!"
35 Organic garland
36 Turkey Day tuber
37 Got taller
39 Change of direction
43 Copy paper purchase
44 Go after
48 Emerged
50 Stonewalled, in a way
51 Govt. obligation
52 Speak from a soapbox
53 Poked (around)
55 Disreputable
56 Bovine mascot
57 Adirondack chair parts
58 "Just do it" sloganeer
59 Fairy tale monster
60 NFL snapper
61 Fancy dresser

FOREGROUND NOISE   by Mark McClain

The tune of 42 Across is taken from Yale's "Boola Boola" fight song.

ACROSS

1 Start for brewery or management
6 "___ Will I Be Loved"
10 USMC E-2's
14 Concert worker
15 Improve
16 Lamb pseudonym
17 Colonial house exterior
20 Right under our noses
21 Big Apple subway org.
22 Contemplative state
23 Berry in a bowl
25 More than enough
26 Thomas Jefferson's private retreat
30 Sank a putt
31 Polk or Knox
32 Nutrition label word
35 Big name in casuals
36 Small hoppers
38 Blistex target
39 "Ben-Hur" author Wallace
40 King on Skull Island
41 Society for high-IQ folks
42 U. of Oklahoma fight song
45 ___ to grave
47 Purveyor of the 2x2x2 combo
48 Mountain lion
49 Biol. or geol.
50 Hodge-podge
54 Site of Wat Arun and Wat Pho
57 Case for small items
58 Trompe l'___ (art effect)
59 Love to bits
60 Ready to eat
61 Contrary nursery-rhyme girl
62 Skinflint

DOWN

1 Quite a bit of
2 Day sail destination
3 Trout relative
4 Struck from the books
5 Symbol of power
6 Start of a speculation
7 Folk dance
8 Patrick Mahomes target
9 They like to snuggle
10 Detail-oriented prig
11 Knapper's stone
12 Bengals' home, informally
13 Green hue
18 "Play Bridge" author Sharif
19 "___ my case!"
24 Dishonorable sort
25 Stimulate
26 Tiger's "Lefty" rival
27 Leak out slowly
28 Snow day implement
29 Qualified to vote, say
32 "The Last Jedi" hero
33 Cathedral recess
34 Russian dynast
36 Machine shop area
37 "I'm treating!"
38 First king of Belgium
40 Ektachrome company
41 Bovine comment
42 Handy storage item
43 In full measure
44 Branch of Islam
45 Tropical raccoon cousin
46 Incur, as debt
48 Trucker on the air
49 Start to awaken
51 Cambodia neighbor
52 Concerning
53 European border river
55 Hawaii's Mauna ___
56 "As ___" (Alicia Keys album)

162

FRIENDLY RELATIONS by Mark McClain
These relations are not in your immediate family.

ACROSS

1 Mess hall fare
5 Crooked handle?
10 "Peter Pan" reptile
14 Nike's swoosh, e.g.
15 Willing to take chances
16 Polynesian performance
17 Coin in Trevi Fountain
18 Light color
19 Curved-bill wader
20 Federal mortgagee
22 Bounty rival
23 Hauled into court
24 Forgeries
25 There are about 130 in a typical NFL game
28 Suburban home feature
30 Pioneer Web portal
31 Marvel's Thunderiders, originally
38 "Qué ___?" (slangy greeting)
40 Yuri Bashmet's instrument
41 Around-the-world toy
42 DVD authoring software tool
45 Ecru relative
46 Monthly outlay
47 Stupidly crazy
49 Worse than bad
52 Levelheaded
54 Ending for editor
55 Ranked item on Amazon
61 Add a bit of color to
62 Arabic god
63 "Star Trek" role
64 List shortener
65 "Your umbrella" of song
66 Enid resident
67 Bank (on)
68 Great Lakes acronym
69 Cherry Island's loch

DOWN

1 Staff sign
2 College credit unit
3 Folktale villain
4 Antipollution owl
5 "Cow school" athlete
6 Enticed
7 Agenda entry
8 Away from the shore
9 Get together
10 Knightly behavior
11 Cube eponym
12 Greek salad essential
13 Barrio structures
21 Do some housework
24 Opposing player
25 Bear with the hard chair
26 Laundry day unit
27 In addition
28 Spanish word for "stick"
29 5-Star General Bradley
32 Tied up
33 "It ___ Necessarily So"
34 Soft shoe, briefly
35 Scintilla
36 Ink jet color
37 Top-notch
39 All of a sudden
43 Symbol of slipperiness
44 German article
48 Gerald's veep
49 Blue alpine flower
50 Beatles album
51 Ultimate
52 No longer funny
53 Bonfire leftovers
55 Beer party
56 Muppet popular with tots
57 Trim partner
58 Last Supper guest
59 Yale supporters
60 Regrets

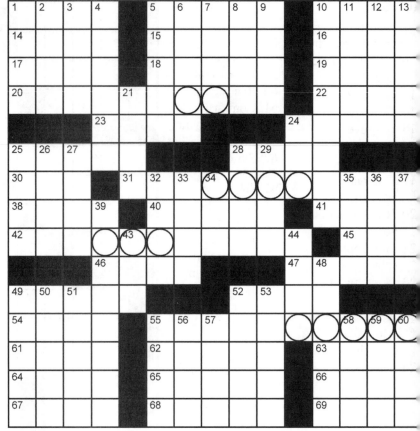

163 ALPHA MALES by Mark McClain
27 Across is a 1930 Ford Model A Sport coupe.

ACROSS

1 Shirt button
5 Substantial opening
10 Puts out feelers
14 "Rosamond" composer
15 State-run game
16 Gaffe
17 Flaky substance
18 So everyone can hear
19 Storage building
20 Corporate VIP
23 Day care attendee
24 According to
25 IRA option
27 Georgia Tech mascot
34 Showman Ziegfeld
37 Land east of Ireland
38 Wrap name
39 MLB Hall-of-Famer Aparicio
41 They glow in pits
43 Legendary beast
44 Arabic for "God"
46 Big joints
48 Ellipsis third
49 Ohio nickname
52 One who saves the day
53 Low joint
57 Sound of discovery
59 Tokyo–Kyoto rail line
64 Eye part
66 Flora and fauna
67 "I smell ___!"
68 Millions or phone starter
69 Fiji Water rival

70 "Tootsie" Oscar nominee Teri
71 Trebek on TV
72 Midterm admini- strations
73 Crafters' outlet

DOWN

1 Dance that originated in Bahia
2 Common jazz combos
3 Open
4 Costing more pounds
5 Geoduck, for one
6 Pocket problem
7 Elemental unit
8 Separated part
9 Like some art
10 Pompous sort
11 Moved like a viper
12 Eur. weight unit
13 Primer dog
21 Showdown word
22 Scraps
26 Server's item
28 Brit's slicker
29 Chap
30 Has a preference
31 Dot on a sailor's chart
32 Noted Roman historian
33 Type of fabric
34 Spare tire material
35 Humdinger
36 Service center offering
40 Japanese quaff

42 Vast amount
45 Sweet cicely, e.g.
47 Bit of info
50 "Absolutely!"
51 Anger, and then some
54 Gold spec
55 Unreliable sorts
56 Contestant
57 Helen's "Hitchcock" role
58 Obedience school lesson
60 "___ long and prosper" (Vulcan salute)
61 Maxwell of Bond films
62 Coup d'___
63 Earth tones
65 Charlie Parker's instrument

164

62 Across is considered the first Yuletide song to focus on Santa Claus.

ACROSS

1 "Coming through!"
10 Try to bite
15 Latitude or longitude, e.g.
17 Bare necessities
18 ___ de Mayo
19 Baynes of the NBA
20 When to give up?
21 Tanqueray and Sipsmith
23 Criticize severely
25 Water under the bridge
27 Somalian model
31 Garden spritzers
32 Pretentious
33 Small recorder
35 On the small side
36 Incessantly
37 Put a lid on
40 Bronx neighbor
41 Meet event
42 Tremulous tree
45 Schedule position
46 Dire sign
47 Beer, often
49 Pricing phrase
51 "Africa" singers
52 Sheriff Taylor's boy
56 Syrian president
59 Zeitgeist
62 Yuletide song with "click, click, click . . ."
63 Colombian coins
64 Superlative for filet mignon

DOWN

1 Job detail, briefly
2 "Beloved" writer Morrison
3 Stretch out
4 Insufficient quantity
5 Fluorescent bulb gas
6 VMI or VPI
7 Just a bit
8 Site for a bell
9 "And so . . ."
10 Minor gripe
11 Flowering
12 Check writers
13 This second
14 Agent cuts
16 Game rooms
22 Tennis player Gilles
24 London lad
25 Gaping chasm
26 Wolframite, for one
28 Weasel relatives
29 Elgort in "Baby Driver"
30 Safecracker's "soup"
34 ___ Rica
36 Survey choice, at times
37 Spot for a tent
38 Aviation hero
39 Stock holder
40 Binary choice
41 Chinese zodiac animal
42 Goes on the fritz
43 Quaint store
44 Barbecue sites
48 "Goodbye, Columbus" author
50 Bel ___ cheese
53 Langston Hughes, e.g.
54 "___ Walked Into My Life" ("Mame" tune)
55 Royal educator
57 "God" singer Tori
58 DOJ division?
60 Part of TGIF
61 1963 Martin Ritt film

THEMELESS by Harvey Estes

In 2011, 19 Across became the longest running sci-fi TV show in the U.S.

ACROSS

1 Phoenix origin
6 It was given by St. Nicholas
10 Pioneer automaker
14 Chardonnay source
16 Former Nair rival
17 Statutory considerations
18 Kipling's "Rikki-Tikki-___"
19 Lana Lang's hometown
20 Dreaded tsar
21 Mosquito-borne virus
22 At maturity's peak
24 Sulky pullers
28 Sound of rain
30 Course for an MBA
31 "Enquirer" couple
33 Balloon material
35 Earth pigment: Fr.
36 Djokovic rival
38 Baum canine
39 Earth, in sci-fi tales
41 Olympic swimmer Vollmer
42 Snake eyes, in dice
43 Based on reason
45 Ally in "The Breakfast Club"
47 Ball's studio
48 U-turn from NNW
49 Tombstone loc.
50 Golden-ager's euphoria?
57 Teen party
58 Purse
59 Passage in Latin
60 "Want to hear my plan?"
61 Highlands loch
62 Performs
63 Piped up

DOWN

1 Belter's tools
2 Noah's eldest son
3 YouTube comic Ryan
4 Collective abbr.
5 eBay user
6 Abrams on "Glee"
7 Pinky part
8 Hesse car company
9 Mirage setting
10 How a sneak thief sneaks
11 Honor Garbo's request?
12 Traumatized
13 Work period
15 Submits
23 End of a Descartes quote
24 Popular mulch
25 Put the 28-D to the metal
26 Strong acids, e.g.
27 Popular batteries
28 Floorboard item
29 Model from Mogadishu
32 "There!"
34 Apple-cheeked
37 Rodeo cowboy, at times
40 Feel far from fine
44 Canine tooth
46 Messenger with winged feet
47 "Mack the Knife" singer
48 Large and petite
51 Rubik of cube fame
52 Prime-time time, informally
53 Med. center
54 Absorbed by
55 Computer nerd
56 FDR's park

166

THEMELESS   by Harvey Estes
The first TV ad was during a game between 34 Across and 38 Across.

ACROSS

1 Starting from
5 Prefix for care
9 Top-notch
14 Twain's jumping frog
15 Like a stem-winder
17 Court doings
18 Aquinas College staff
19 Unlike free verse
21 Pop up
22 Wax producer
23 Folded fare
26 Awfully long time
27 Ford flub
29 Retreats across Russia
32 Sharp-tasting
34 Citizens Bank Park team
38 Ebbets Field team
40 Lake Nona locale
41 Using a few choice words
43 Tell fully
44 Sell to the end user
46 Resulted in
47 Ends of letters
50 Put a match to
52 Marilyn ___ Savant
53 Font option
56 Xfinity Series org.
58 Disco star
61 Hospital division
63 Unpaved way
64 Aftermath of stitches
65 Flunky responses
66 E.A. Robinson's Richard
67 Ward of "Sisters"

DOWN

1 Toothpaste box letters
2 Elsie, to Borden?
3 In a separate container, like dressing
4 Excoriate
5 Computer component
6 Undercut
7 Stage Magic, to Justify
8 "Lord, is ___?": Matt. 26:22
9 Ever so proper
10 Pilaf ingredient
11 Words of empathy
12 Chutney fruit
13 "Daily Planet" photojournalist
16 0.333333333
20 "The Miser" playwright
22 Sweat units
24 Spot for a computer
25 Cave ricochet
28 Award honoring Poe
30 Gene mutations
31 Chalkboard
33 Censorious
35 Ahead of time
36 Two-cents piece?
37 Arias, e.g.
39 Hose trouble
42 Card player's cry
45 One-dimensional
47 Young swine
48 Mall constituent
49 Long tales
51 Late for school
54 Nothing on the court
55 "Et tu" day
57 Emulate a sailor
59 Reactor licensor
60 Turtledove sound
62 La leader

THEMELESS by Harvey Estes

23 Across is also the title of a Netflix psychological thriller.

ACROSS

1 Come across as
11 Is unable
15 Bobby Vinton's "___ Polka"
16 Way out there
17 Mingle
18 Jazz singer James
19 Liberal follower
20 Lucci of soap fame
21 Ruhr refusal
22 Letters after CD
23 Pointer's cry
25 Campers
26 "Black Magic Woman" group
30 Veering off
32 Solidarity
33 Having teeth
34 Tempo phrase
35 May be seen now
36 Grazing ground
40 Refined
43 Morgan of "Glory"
44 Party person
45 iPod screen
46 Tack on
47 Opal's mo.
48 Eagerly expected
50 Range in Arkansas
52 Pine for
56 Flying toy
57 French Riviera resort
59 MBA subj.
60 Ten Forward lounge's ship
61 First name in baking
62 Crinkly suit material

DOWN

1 "Take a Chance on Me" group
2 House of Lords member
3 Gnat, for one
4 Son of Aphrodite
5 "The Bachelorette" network
6 Motives, in Marseilles
7 Major jolts
8 Basketball and baseball
9 Said "hold it!" concerning a order
10 1968 hit by the Turtles
11 Normandy city
12 Lingering sensation
13 Crèche scenes
14 Goes beyond
22 Issa in "Little"
24 Starbucks dispenser
26 Plant-based cleaning powder
27 Emperor penguin's home
28 Paper boss
29 Govt. security
31 Like the Tower of Pisa
37 Thurman in "The Avengers"
38 Radar antenna housings
39 49ers' paydirt
40 Less loquacious
41 They make fun
42 CT hrs.
49 Elizabeth in "Transamerica"
51 Upfront amount
52 Antidrug agent
53 Estrada of "CHiPS"
54 If that fails
55 Procrastinator's opposite
58 Smartphone "smarts"

168 ASSOCIATES by Patrick Jordan

28 Down is the highest volcano in Europe, and one of the most active.

ACROSS

1 "Born from Jets" automaker
5 Effortless victory
9 Listening eagerly
13 Undercarriage bar
14 Kashmir coin
15 Utter unwaveringly
16 Burnable bog brick
17 "Buy ___ the regular price get . . ."
18 No-hit sign
19 Phone annoyance
22 LAX screeners
24 Mountain formation periods
25 Like some oats
26 Kitchen-based course
28 Cologne article
29 Track support
32 In vitro fertility cells
35 Common platter shape
36 Coal or bargain holder
37 Moonwalker Bean
38 Erin's "Home Town" hubby
39 Breakfast meat
43 Imitate a cross cat
44 Brit's school exam
45 Test paper entry
48 Affect adversely
50 Sudan or Siam suffix
51 It may help fund a library
54 Paddington, for one
55 Art exhibit prop
56 Communicated phonetically
59 Demon descriptor
60 Sink a ball, in billiards
61 Excessively enthusiastic
62 Trust, with "on"
63 Camporee structure
64 Not risk insubordination

DOWN

1 Sugar shack need
2 Kindling creator's tool
3 Mobile native
4 Prerelease software version
5 Blab without a break
6 Removes the wrapper
7 Capable of cruelty
8 Czar after Catherine I
9 Noisy crib toy
10 Serve the needs of
11 Tea shop offering
12 Stock analyst's discovery
14 Absurdly ornate
20 Stag party?
21 Cold Stone Creamery item
22 Pound rhythmically
23 Italian wine option
27 Angular annex
28 Italian stratovolcano
30 Appear next to
31 Slam, slangily
32 "M*A*S*H" uniform hue
33 Windmill's wind catchers
34 A tripper may twist it
37 Pale brew
39 Chancy venture, informally
40 With the best ventilation
41 Render incomprehensible
42 Giggly Muppet monster
43 Forming a spiral pattern
45 Organic jewel material
46 Tres tripled
47 SpongeBob's pet Gary
48 Is dressed in
49 Issue a heads-up to
52 Unit on a treasure map
53 "Mission scrubbed"
57 It changes annually
58 Be a productive hen

169 HE'S REALLY GOING PLACES   by Pam Klawitter
The title explains itself at 51 Across.

ACROSS

1 Vegas opening
4 Put into words
8 Brief replies
13 Summer quenchers
15 "Garfield" waitress
16 Not secret
17 Runner's challenge
18 Yoga "therapy" animal
19 Sting operation
20 Super Bowl follower?
23 Tulsi Gabbard, for one
24 "Is Anybody Goin' to San ___?": Pride
28 Like Type B's
31 An expectant father, maybe
34 "Symphony in Black" artist
35 Tripod part
36 Swan genus
37 Frasier Crane's brother
39 Word with lymph
40 Elton's john
41 Leander's love
42 Isak Dinesen's love
43 Broadway's "Whoopi" was one
47 Prim and proper
48 Birthplace of Nicole Kidman
51 He's really going places
55 Low register
58 It's in the air
59 Elizabeth Reaser's "Twilight" role
60 Kind of mare
61 How LPs are reissued
62 "And Still" singer McEntire
63 Leaves speechless
64 Mackerel shark variety
65 Recipe amt.

DOWN

1 Garland's 1939 costar
2 "So long, amigo!"
3 1965 march site
4 Prepare to turn
5 One way to turn
6 Mosque figure
7 Match.com goal
8 "Never Be You" singer Cash
9 Modelesque
10 Old pro
11 MetLife rival, for short
12 It's the "Racer's Edge"
14 Big house
21 Black, in Bayonne
22 Goes on a Twitter tirade
25 Drip-dry fabric
26 Hard up
27 They might be rough
29 It might be thumped in the produce aisle
30 100 square meters
31 Preppy shirts
32 Unparalleled
33 Billed partner
37 Herculean labor site
38 401(k) alternative
39 Chopra or Enya
41 Drag racers
42 Swallow
44 IBM supercomputer
45 Cheap knockoffs
46 Bob or bun
49 "Ready?" response
50 Poetic feet
52 "Va-va-va-___!"
53 Turnblad in "Hairspray"
54 Low high tide
55 Daisy ammo
56 Louvre oeuvre
57 Trifling sum

170 63 ACROSS* by Gary Larson
In the Middle Ages, 21 Across was referred to as "white gold."

ACROSS

1 Troubles
8 Syringe amts.
11 Established
14 Before
15 Hamlin caveman
16 Spawn
17 Former Medellín Cartel leader*
18 Rick in "Ghostbusters"
20 Afflictions
21 Common condiment*
23 Electric dart shooter
26 First name in cosmetics
27 Undertaking*
32 Listening devices
33 Band aide
34 Curses
36 Continue
37 Down in the dumps
39 Transcript fig.
40 "Welcome" site
43 Subs
45 Commercial cost
47 Gawk at
50 Suspicious-looking*
52 "Spider-Man" director
54 Lindsay of "Mean Girls"
55 Preacher's summons to come forward*
58 Blackhearted
62 South American cowboy
63 Hemingway's Florida home/TITLE
66 It might be sticky
67 Sister or mother
68 Todd of Fleet Street
69 Operative
70 Program file extension
71 Longer

DOWN

1 Shoot
2 Around
3 Houston university
4 Perched
5 Heavenly body
6 Org. for Serena Williams
7 Post office machine
8 Search
9 Self-assurance
10 Wild time
11 Series of movements
12 More devilish
13 Preferences
19 Pack animals
22 Bone-dry
24 Develop
25 Catches, in a way
27 ___ of Good Feelings
28 Go-ahead
29 Smidgen
30 Hang loosely
31 Deanna Troi, for one
35 "Octomom" Suleman
38 Cry from Homer Simpson
40 Word of possibility
41 Dug into
42 Boy in "The Lorax"
43 Atlas, e.g.
44 Window feature
46 Pleased subscriber, often
47 Some toothbrushes
48 Big name in polling
49 Mass communication?
51 Down-to-earth
53 Worth in "Deathtrap"
56 Central point
57 First-class
59 Logician's diagram
60 "Got it!"
61 Astronomical dist.
64 Merino mother
65 Assent

CHINESE SOUP by Gary Larson
. . . and that soup can be found at 66 Across.

CROSS

1 Slip into
6 PC image file
9 Psychoanalysis pioneer
14 Eric Trump's mother
15 EMT destinations
16 Girl rescued by Don Juan
17 Pretty often
19 Unqualified
20 Forelimb bone
21 "Pay ___ mind"
22 Titter
23 Avoid cooked foods
25 Sang-froid
27 Words of desire
30 Like hectares
33 Verboten
36 Unaffectedness
38 Fizzy drink
39 System starter
40 Cheap, as housing
43 Neither partner
44 Logging tools
46 Scads
47 Triangular traffic sign
49 Mum
51 Sporty auto roofs
53 Remove
55 Grape juice brand
59 Like sweatpants
61 Pal
64 Half a court game
65 Kelly's former cohost
66 Chinese soup
68 Where the action is
69 Period
70 eHarmony meetup

71 Tricky
72 Mil. award
73 Opera singer Simon

DOWN

1 Provoke
2 Throat dangler
3 Tarnish
4 New York neighbor
5 Scottish refusal
6 Hanukkah coins
7 Wrinkle remover
8 Shutterbug's setting
9 1984 Heisman Trophy winner
10 Tries again
11 This or that
12 Peter Fonda title role
13 Challenge
18 Sony competitor
24 Roll call misser
26 Straw in the wind
28 Colorful salamander
29 Gypsy's deck
31 One on a pedestal
32 Wit
33 Hardy heroine
34 Smoothie fruit
35 Like many a saddle tramp
37 Dispatched
41 Some wild ones are sown
42 Sort
45 Overcasting a carpet, say
48 Vacation spots
50 Deny
52 Was in the red

54 Put in
56 Traction aid
57 Waste maker
58 Web spots
59 Thin nail
60 Sleekly designed
62 They're sometimes put on
63 Streetcar
67 Witness

172 PASSIVE VOICE   by Steven E. Atwood
1 Down is located in Siberia and is the world's largest freshwater lake.

ACROSS
1 Smithereen
4 Dance originated in Buenos Aires
9 Lowdown
13 Yucatán year
14 Like some kites
15 Intended
17 Not well
18 Fashion bigwig who's rolling in it?
20 Rochester film company
22 Author Fleming
23 Bird sound
24 Warwickshire river
25 Exert, as power
28 Dublin rock star
29 Uneaten piece of chicken?
31 Too much, in Tours
33 Racketeering statute
34 Nonverbal sounds
35 Believed gum was meant for blowing?
40 Unlocked?
41 "... ___ the whole thing!"
42 Enya's music
44 Convertible with the top down?
49 "___ have to do"
50 Goalie gloves
52 One-time "Sea of Islands"
53 Charge for service
54 HBO alternative
55 Genre of 22 Across
56 Committee head after a good meal?
61 Mark, as a box in a form
62 Trap using spring tension
63 "No Logo" author Klein
64 Full-screen closer
65 Stagger
66 "Capiche?"
67 "Quiet!"

DOWN
1 World's deepest lake
2 Romantically involved
3 Informed about
4 Assignment
5 "___ Maria"
6 Picker's object
7 Tribe of Israel
8 Amir of "Marlon"
9 "Heaven, ___ heaven ..."
10 Antiproton's chg.
11 Sea whip
12 Mano a mano
16 "Boots on the ground"
19 Road safety org.
21 Antenna sporter
25 Kristen in "Wonder Woman 1984"
26 Column measure
27 He spells "team" with an "I"
28 Type of transaction, for short
30 Twisted a wet towel
32 Lodge
35 Century's second decade
36 Cracked up over
37 Spoken
38 Thai coin
39 Great Basin natives
40 Takes a whiff
43 "Friends" baby
45 Music genre
46 Only antelopes born with horns
47 Clumsy
48 Quail
51 Hockey violation
54 Next
55 Fit of pique
57 Grand ___ vineyard
58 Actress Dawn Chong
59 Verbal gem
60 "What ___ bid?"

CROSS

1 Boston orchestra
5 Some are cocked
9 Lizzo's "___ Hurts"
14 Inspiration
15 Surmounted
16 Like ripped jeans
17 Eensy
18 Great initials for a bargain hunter
19 "The Godfather of Gangsta Rap"
20 2002 World Series player
23 To-do ___
24 Loquacious gift
25 Dallas-based airline: Abbr.
28 One way to stand
30 Foosball, by another name
34 Adams and Poehler
36 Draw even
37 Tesla, to SolarCity
38 Culturally aware, to a millennial
39 Work of admiration
41 2016 Rihanna album
42 Get ready, as a superhero
45 Knights of Orlando
47 They're peachy, but not keen
48 What a flip-flop lacks
51 Portable bed
52 [The nerve of some people . . .]
53 Support system?
54 It has three feet and cannot walk
56 Switch up the GPS (and the circled letters)
61 "Beauty and the Beast" sidekick
64 Takeout
65 Bloom of "Bloom County"
66 Backup strategy
67 Thus
68 "Hansel and Gretel" prop
69 Boxcars, on the Strip
70 Secretary
71 Film about John Reed

DOWN

1 Hummus holder
2 Thor's dad
3 Dramatic World Cup event
4 "Go introduce yourself!"
5 ___ for Humanity
6 Small matter
7 Attire for Tiberius
8 Scrub Daddy, for one
9 Emerald snake of rain forests
10 Actual
11 Snack brand since 1921
12 "I bet you can do it!"
13 Garden tool
21 Winter hrs. in Atlanta
22 [What?!]
25 Trip along Big Sur, e.g.
26 Attended
27 Whistler, for one
28 Bats around
29 Love affairs
31 Twitter blurb
32 Paved the way (to)
33 Losing dice throw
35 MacFarlane of "American Dad!"
40 "Il nome della rosa" author
43 Multi-port devices
44 Aqua ___ water
46 Diner employee
49 Huffed and puffed
50 Confucian path
55 Tittle-tattle
56 Cotton-candy holder
57 Blood and guts
58 Orphan in "The Boxtrolls"
59 Musher's transport
60 A dog's age
61 Vinyl albums
62 "Hostel" director Roth
63 Kind of modem

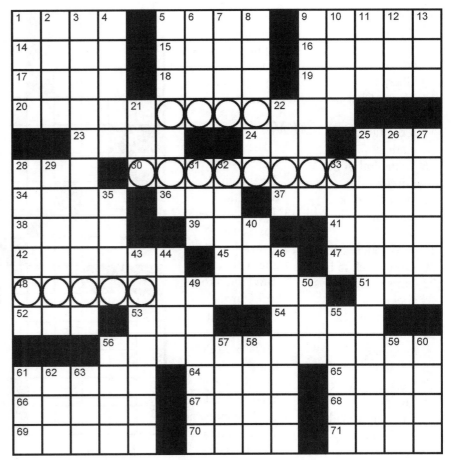

HEADWATERS   by Ted Williams
Caesar and Crassus were the other two members of 24 Across.

ACROSS

1 A real pain
5 Like the SoHo crowd
9 Sharp as ___
14 Lucky Charms charm
15 Common ___ math
16 Cathedral of San Lorenzo site
17 It can carry a tune, and then some
18 Folk jam session
20 Bring back to life
22 Nursery-rhyme pocketful
23 Turpitude
24 First Triumvirate member
25 All in the mind
27 Leisurely walk
28 Heliport
29 Licit, informally
31 Pitch perfectly
35 Axillary
37 Capital on the Willamette
39 Victory margin, maybe
40 Siegfried or Roy
42 "61*" subject
44 So yesterday
45 Gloomy Gus
47 Rubs the wrong way
49 Chris Kyle, e.g.
51 Frisk
52 Duplicated
53 Understood by a select few
57 Deceived
59 Singer Stansfield
60 Sleeping disorder
61 Wedge
62 B&B cousins

63 Covered with couch grass
64 Future litigator's exam
65 "A Bug's Life" princess

DOWN

1 "The Kite Runner" boy
2 Deal with difficulties
3 Landmark near Las Vegas
4 Escarole alternative
5 Brad Pitt's role in 7 Down
6 It's raised in anger
7 2004 Brad Pitt film
8 "I have not ___ begun . . .": Jones
9 Additional name
10 Flatware item
11 "It's the Hard Knock Life" musical
12 Island known for its hot dogs
13 Scrabble 5-pointers
19 Heroic verse
21 Chanel No. 5 holder
24 Etonian's dad
25 Maugham's "___ the Villa"
26 Pride Lands queen
27 Hairy
30 "Call of Duty" player
32 Clue for deer hunters
33 Martha's Vineyard, e.g.
34 Turner and Mack

36 Jogged the memory
38 Pinhead-size spy photo
41 Aerial tramway
43 Blast
46 Foot: Comb. form
48 Resort island of Florida
49 Slant
50 "___ Needs to Know": Shania Twain
52 Red Man plug
53 Squeaks (by)
54 Vaccines
55 "___ it a pity?"
56 Juan's house
58 Blue Jackets' org.

ROUGH STUFF by Ted Williams

J.K. Rowling readers will know the answer to 21 Down.

CROSS

1 Weather balloons, to some
5 Showed up
9 A little lower?
13 Phones
15 It's the top
16 Kind of hygiene
17 Purple flower
18 Joke part
20 Plains Indian
22 Get back
23 Miss Havisham, for one
26 Social standing
29 Clean plates
30 Landslide component
33 They're in the eyes of the beholders
34 In a noisy manner
37 Banana fiber
38 Miss-named
39 Periwinkle genus
40 Offered for sale
42 Incited to attack
43 Former frequent flyer
44 First lady
45 Fireplace tools
46 Hauls up on the carpet
48 Acting company
52 Masthead names
56 Record ranking/TITLE
59 Conspiracy group
60 Spanish for "stop"
61 Revlon rival
62 Nocturnal noise
63 Bright color
64 Barclays Center team
65 Scout's doing

DOWN

1 Where John Wooden coached
2 County wingding
3 Tabasco pot
4 Keystone Kops genre
5 Roaster rooster
6 Kwik-E-Mart guy
7 "It's Raining ___" (1982 hit)
8 Sweat it out?
9 Pistol handle?
10 "Toreador Song," e.g.
11 Tall and slender
12 Skedaddle
14 Shoulder blades
19 That girl
21 Speak Parseltongue
24 Leaves the Union
25 Empty semi's weight
26 Bombards with e-junk
27 Euphoniums
28 Separated
30 Chop finely
31 Stomach problem
32 Groups of two
35 Electronic systems on spacecraft
36 Harley support
38 River to the Gulf of Finland
41 Mideast capital: Var.
42 Floored it
46 Master of ledger-domain
47 Romeo and Juliet, e.g.
48 "Better you ___ me!"
49 Upset
50 David Rabe's "Good for ___"
51 Current
53 It's found among the reeds
54 Very unusual
55 Kane's Rosebud
57 Hail, to Caesar
58 Part of an email address

176 DIGITAL SEQUENCE by Roland Huget
31 Across was produced from 1970 to 2006.

ACROSS
1 Thailand, then
5 Bas-relief material
10 With, on le menu
14 Pre-Columbian Peruvian
15 Mork's language
16 Do the laundry
17 Memory stick
19 Massachusetts motto opener
20 Rio dances
21 That, in Tijuana
23 Proof letters
24 Pasture call
25 Vanguard S&P 500, for one
28 Ginza capital
29 Jacques in "Mon Oncle"
31 Toyota sports car
32 Supply's partner
34 Menu selector
35 "The Hobbit" setting
38 Long, as odds
40 "Hooray!"
41 Hubby's side of the story
44 Soaks up
45 Columbus inst.
48 Circular camera accessory
50 Felonious flames
52 Prefix for thermal
53 Word on perfume bottles
54 Workshop grippers
55 Pom-pom flowers
57 Friend of Robin Hood
60 Make ready for the OR
61 Mrs. Alexander Hamilton
62 Mother of Prometheus
63 Hospital fluids
64 Extend membership
65 Bucket of bolts

DOWN
1 Doesn't act to help
2 Take a breath
3 Keen insight
4 Venomous tree snake
5 Venus and Mercury
6 Drop the ball
7 Roof rack item
8 Built up a nest egg
9 "Be right there!"
10 Bowl over
11 Utterly defeat
12 Intrinsic nature
13 Wheel cheese
18 Emulated Casey
22 Guitar, to Clapton
25 Gran Paradiso locale
26 Early in the workday
27 Champagne glass
30 Intel rival
32 "Joltin' Joe" of baseball
33 Bus station
35 Funny bone, e.g.
36 Tablet download
37 Thrift shop business
38 Pipsqueaks
39 Downtime
42 Seine dot
43 Automatic caller
45 Absorb slowly
46 Mother on "The Golden Girls"
47 Open with a click
49 Skillful deceit
51 "Aladdin" tiger
54 Hammer part
56 Place to unwind
58 Pewter element
59 Taoism founder Lao-___

CROSS

1 King Louie, for one
4 Mural base
9 California missionary Junípero
14 Fleur-de-___
15 Worry-induced affliction
16 Affaire de coeur
17 Computer program fodder
19 Zeppelin, for one
20 Dr. Dre's buds
21 Blini ingredient
23 Back muscle, for short
24 First-rate
25 "Too Darn Hot" musical
27 "Amadeus" or "Gandhi"
29 Nike rival
30 ___-nighter
31 Pats on
35 Balance due
36 Pie chart alternatives
39 "The Sweetest Taboo" singer
42 SE Asian capital
43 New Haven Ivy Leaguer
46 Toolbox item
49 Underground tank
51 "You missed your chance"
55 Chalet feature
56 "Just kidding!"
57 Mower's track
58 Behind bars
59 Cause of hesitation
61 Reject, Tinder-style (and a theme hint)

63 Pastrami ___
64 More reasonable
65 Sturgeon delicacy
66 Pole tossed at Highland games
67 Instrument with pipes
68 Reliever's stat

DOWN

1 "Arabian Nights" hero
2 Natural disinfectant
3 Romance language
4 Courage
5 Ernest J. Keebler, for one
6 Hugo genre
7 Goes for money
8 Golden cookies
9 Like much of Bach's music
10 Rock subgenre
11 Wrapped meat dish
12 Charge drinks
13 Point of a "Draw me" challenge
18 School near the Rio Grande
22 Thurman in "The Avengers"
25 '80s Chrysler model
26 Rug rats
28 Mount in Crete
32 "Ick!"
33 Grille protector
34 Japanese honorific
36 Sugar source

37 Sit, in a studio
38 Hotfoot it
39 Spokesperson, slangily
40 Home of a Penn State campus
41 Bother
43 Hummel showcase
44 Find great satisfaction in
45 Summer beverage with lemon
47 List of players
48 Farm female
50 Bell sound
52 Wonder Woman's weapon
53 In serious conflict

54 "The Addams Family" hand
58 Large Hadron Collider org.
60 Tournament pass
62 Small legume

ACROSS

1 Lightning bursts
8 Hocked
14 Company shunner
15 Speed of sound
16 Goes along with
17 Ministers
18 Bar order
19 ___ heel
20 Some linemen, in the NFL
21 Menu fish
23 Play charades
24 "___ lovely time"
27 Gets up
30 Cone source
31 Qualms
33 Recall cause
35 Tavern round
36 A girl named Frank
37 Tripoli native
40 Boxer's 19 Across
44 NASA spacewalk
45 Used keyboards
47 Chopin opus
48 La ___ Jackson
50 Baseball great Slaughter
52 Wyo. neighbor
53 What Bismarck ruled with
56 Jimmy Carter's birthplace
59 Least
60 Fuel source
61 40% of all insects
62 Meet
63 Waugh's Brideshead, e.g.
64 Less muddled

DOWN

1 March in "Inherit the Wind"
2 South African monarchy
3 Bit of finger-pointing
4 Messy dresser
5 Pitch
6 "Sleepy John" of blues
7 French possessive
8 Footway
9 Broadway opener
10 Engulf
11 General insurance
12 Locally prevalent
13 Last course
15 Sprays an attacker
19 Got grounded?
22 Vein contents
25 Make-or-break date
26 Black key above G
28 Krabappel of "The Simpsons"
29 Be aware of
32 Start of a counting-out process
34 Slug suffix
36 Ray of "The Green Berets"
37 Beatles album
38 Many keys
39 Rifle weapon
40 Guy
41 Gin berry
42 DNA component
43 Man of many words
46 Problem children
49 "Hotel du Lac" author Brookner
51 Sewing kit item
54 Marker tip material
55 "That makes sense"
57 Diane in "Secretariat"
58 A, as in Edison
60 FDR program

"HOW DOES THAT GRAB YA?" by Harvey Estes
Mr. Jackson was the first 40 Across.

CROSS

1 "Pipe down!"
5 Skating competition
10 Agenda listing
14 Absorbed by
15 "Lead ___ into temptation . . ."
16 Disney lioness
17 See
20 As a result of this
21 German airship
22 Speak hesitantly
23 Caustic chemical
25 Tending (to)
26 Wise old saying
28 Nouveau ___
32 Stuff and nonsense
33 Phoenician trading center
34 Shaky
36 Carpe diem
39 Stuffed deli snacks
40 West Point mascot
43 "Grand Hotel" studio
46 Daisy relative
47 Chill out
48 Elton John's sign
50 Paul Anka's "___ Beso"
52 NY hrs.
53 De-suds
57 African fly
59 Crucial moment
61 Peace Nobelist Wiesel
62 Atahualpa, notably
63 Overmedicated
64 "Why don't we!"
65 Watering hole
66 Caledonian Canal loch

DOWN

1 Snooty
2 Not prepared
3 Franchise acquired by Disney in 2012
4 Stockings
5 Silly stuff
6 A firewood
7 Don Juan's mom
8 "La Dolce Vita" setting
9 Procedure part
10 Private
11 Man of the cloth?
12 Climatic scapegoat
13 Good drawer?
18 Not too bright
19 Tack on
24 Winemaker Gallo
27 Computer nerd
29 "Now ___ time . . ."
30 Hold together
31 Color gradations
34 Mossad weapons
35 Woman of rank
37 "Right away"
38 Winter season
41 Snags
42 Keeps going
43 Dadaist Duchamp
44 Auto front
45 Manhattan buyer
47 Salazar in "Alita: Battle Angel"
49 Colorado Park name

51 Knocks for a loop
54 Heartland state
55 Annapolis initials
56 Personal quirks
58 Town on the Thames
60 Mai ___ cocktail

180 LANGUAGE OF THE NETTERLANDS by Harvey Estes
Get it togetter now!

ACROSS

1 Figure skater Rippon
5 "There's gold in them ___ hills!"
9 Mild cheddar
14 All-night bash
15 Duffer's target
16 Orchestra section
17 Environs
18 Took the bus
19 Duke, to North Carolina
20 Falconry trainees?
23 Antenna site
24 Match a poker bet
25 Easy mark
27 Biographical bit
28 Slightly
31 Whiz
33 Like some gems
35 Eastern priest
36 Varsity outerwear?
40 Feeling, informally
41 Chopin's homeland
42 Words before lightly
45 NASDAQ cousin
46 Moo ___ pork
49 ___ Xer
50 Fleecy female
52 Rat out
54 Results of water bombs with filling nozzles?
58 "Carmen" composer
59 ___-da-fé
60 Tear channel
61 Castle of dance
62 One-armed bandit
63 Pining oread

64 Pointed
65 Boulevard liners
66 Go to market

DOWN

1 Domain of Lawrence
2 Venturesome
3 Strongly opposed
4 Daniel of "Ugly Betty"
5 Engine regulator
6 Filly's foot
7 Alan in "Bridge of Spies"
8 Coral communities
9 Cerebral surface
10 End note
11 Chair for a pair
12 2nd Amendment right
13 Fashion monogram
21 Very little
22 NBA shoe width
26 Type of meeting
29 Golden agers' org.
30 Mustard choice
32 Made a case
33 Road that led to Rome
34 Tyne of "Cagney & Lacey"
36 Ball of fire
37 David Balfour's uncle
38 Draw straws
39 Pay homage
40 Chill (out)
43 Small sofa
44 Run a tab
46 Sit lazily
47 Big shot
48 Pull the plug on
51 Degauss a tape
53 Mineral deposits
55 Half scores
56 Buyer of call options
57 Tiny bit of matter
58 Chomped into

FORMERLY   by Rich Proulx
"Once upon a time . . ."

CROSS

1 Went very fast
5 Nile wader
9 Sanskrit for "king"
14 Drunk
15 Dole's running mate in '96
16 "Wifey" author
17 Downward Dog, after going up?
20 Thick
21 First king of Israel
22 Larry King's former network
23 Unplug a dial-up modem to avoid a hack, e.g.?
27 4x4
30 "Jabberwocky" opener
31 Pampering place
32 Roti alternative
34 His or hers
36 What you are since starting this puzzle
40 Former animal shelter?
42 Harbors, no longer?
44 "Hannah and Her Sisters" Oscar winner
45 Three-card monte, for one
47 Boob tube ban
48 Some tennis serves
50 Somewhat
52 Shocking sound
53 Retired members of a campaign trail motorcade?
58 Thai language
59 Teri in "Young Frankenstein"
60 Its closest relative is a wombat
64 Former sassy observers?
68 Former Mexican president Enrique Peña ___
69 Hands that are the devil's tools
70 At the peak of
71 Test for minerals
72 Requirement
73 Opposite of doffs

DOWN

1 Evacuated
2 Sumptuous
3 Skip Bayless' former network
4 Question of identity
5 Tina Turner's ex
6 Night depositories
7 Standoff
8 Blowhole projection
9 Judge's stat
10 Spacebar neighbor
11 Power
12 Surrounded by
13 Youngman or Penny
18 Blue message
19 Some Nikons, for short
24 "Victory!"
25 Each
26 Claw
27 De novo
28 Preflight roll
29 Smoke a Juul
33 Response to a 49 Down
35 Endangered marine reptile
37 TV physician
38 Chanteuse James
39 Inform the host
41 "___ Reader"
43 Noel
46 Hack job?
49 USAF noncom
51 Hockey feint
53 "The Vampire Diaries" heroine
54 Line on a graph
55 Three ruled simultaneously in 1410
56 Played the butler
57 "How pathetic"
61 Regarding
62 Kings of ___ (rock band)
63 Nile biters
65 Letter after zeta
66 Cowboy Rogers
67 Homer's neighbor

182 "HOLD THE MAYO!" by Roger & Kathy Wienberg
The Gold Mask of Tutankhamun is displayed at 31 Down.

ACROSS
1 One of the Bee Gees
6 Trial figure
11 Stir-fry pan
14 Cockamamie
15 Spectrum Center, for one
16 Pappy Yokum's grandson
17 Thanksgiving breakfast side?
19 Yule fuel
20 Pumps, in a way
21 In a competent manner
22 Lollygags
24 Minute arachnid
26 Complex unit
28 Cool veggie?
33 Vamooses
34 Fix
35 Trifle
36 "Aquarius" musical
37 Fish chowder fish
38 Used a chute
39 One of the humanities
40 Jimi Hendrix hairstyle
42 Overly diluted
44 Keepsake fruit?
47 Zoo sights
48 Green light
49 Pilfer
51 Entrée go-with
53 "What a shame!"
57 Expert
58 Lunch order found in three answers
61 Summer drink
62 Drizzling
63 Pieterse of "Pretty Little Liars"
64 River bottom
65 Helps with a heist
66 Keyed in

DOWN
1 Lovely Beatles girl
2 Burden of proof
3 Wickiup covering
4 Calligraphy mishap
5 Jane Rochester, ___ Eyre
6 Prattle
7 Caspian Sea feeder
8 Like many cardboard boxes
9 Hawaiian game fish
10 Collided with
11 Juice source
12 Clarinet cousin
13 Oktoberfest buys
18 Rowdy of "Rawhide"
23 "Silent Spring" killer
25 "Think" sloganeer
27 Brit. reference
28 "It matters to me"
29 Poked holes in
30 Stable employee
31 Egyptian Museum site
32 Whirlpool
33 Bollywood's ___ Rukh Khan
37 Railroad support
38 Keep one's distance
40 Math branch
41 Thanos, to the Avengers
42 Roused
43 "Today I ___ man"
45 Music genre
46 Word before "special" on a menu
49 DNA collector
50 Like many missed field goals
52 Fails to be
54 Talk like Daffy Duck
55 Throb
56 Caviar source
59 Hunting dog
60 "Spring ahead" letters

56 ACROSS by Roger & Kathy Wienberg
"Tennis, anyone?"

CROSS

1 Poisonous shrub
6 Join forces
1 Swag ___
4 Studio sign
5 Complete reversal
6 Density symbol
7 Landmark near Waikiki Beach*
9 Thole insert
0 Bill dispenser
1 Math proof trigram
2 Slink past
4 Less doubtful
6 Cartoon chipmunk
7 Brothers Grimm fairy tale
1 Take off fast
3 Affirmatives
4 Father figure
5 Drop for a 10-count
6 Dollars, in slang
8 Top-notch
9 Printer's measures
0 Bar game
1 Astronomer Hubble
2 Fourteen Points president*
6 Onion cousin
7 Discharges
8 Unwelcome tidings
1 Vichy water
2 Tax refund sender
5 New Haven collegian
6 Be clamorous/ TITLE
9 Gout spot
0 Jimmies

61 Christopher in "Morning Glory"
62 2013 Joaquin Phoenix film
63 Cantankerous
64 Bakery staple

DOWN

1 Carbonated drink
2 Troop group
3 Sir's counterpart
4 Ready-fire connector
5 Game with hoops
6 Sloppy-track winner
7 Biblical verb suffix
8 Has remorse
9 Family patriarchs
10 Charms
11 Ramshackle
12 Pequod captain
13 Like "Saw" films
18 Super Soaker brand
23 Rubina in "Slumdog Millionaire"
24 "Amscray!"
25 I, pretentiously
27 G.I. Joe, e.g.
28 Masterpiece
29 Child's request
30 Idyllic place
31 Slant
32 Covert ops garb
36 Pots and pans
37 Nearly depleted
38 Brouhahas
40 Bump from a schedule
41 Sea inlet
43 Animal shelter

44 Song from "Nashville"
45 Teller of tall tales
48 "Little Women" woman
49 Natural balm
50 Glides across powder
52 Self-assembly retail giant
53 Accelerates
54 Editor's override
57 Ern's Kellogg's pal
58 Average mark

PROPER NAMES   by Ted Williams
The drink at 5 Down is mentioned in "The Raven."

ACROSS

1 Fabergé creations
5 Pusher chaser
9 Marsh plant
14 Govern
15 Famous last words
16 Render defenseless
17 What little things mean
18 Arnold the voyeur?
20 Immaculate
22 Take the money and run
23 Intended
24 Wander aimlessly
25 Wood decay
27 Strong point
28 Hallway runner
29 Cease and desist
31 Family auto, usually
35 Come up against
37 Maternally related
39 Unhealthy chest sound
40 Harass
42 Get the wrinkles out
43 Harper Valley gp.
44 Samuel of code fame
46 Elevenses vessel
49 Pan fish with a lousy name?
52 Vaughn of "The Break-Up"
53 Inside this
54 Landing area
57 Mean Greene?
59 Revered one
60 External
61 Masquerade ___
62 Western alliance
63 Dilapidated
64 Act like an ass
65 Flying pest

DOWN

1 Notable time periods
2 Bolt down
3 Van Sant the pessimist?
4 Quail dog
5 Drink of forgetfulness
6 1946 Bikini event
7 AAA suggestions
8 Sports trophy
9 Beach headwear
10 Conductor's coworker
11 Passé
12 Lefty in Cooperstown
13 Eurasian wheat
19 Hadrian's highway
21 Mekong Buddhist
24 Banner phrase
25 Uncolorful
26 Country bumpkin
27 Warning signal
30 Biscotto ingredient
32 Brown looking smart?
33 Saxophone range
34 Orderly
36 Modified to soften
38 Altogether
41 Edward Scissorhands' talent
45 Best man's concern
47 An inning has three
48 Pro tem
49 Complete confusion
50 Variety show
51 Alpine ridge
52 Oscar winner Davis
54 Not fully closed
55 Smidgeon
56 Web of intrigue
58 Subside

58 ACROSS* by Gary Larson
"Golden buttons" is another name for 8 Down.

CROSS

1 Highlands fishing spots
6 Jazz diva Jones
0 Gospel music award
4 Steer clear of
5 Indian bread
6 Delete a scene
7 Some stock-market activity*
9 "Winter Song" pianist
0 "La Bamba" singer Ritchie
1 Pan-fry
2 PC program
5 Donkey or elephant, e.g.?*
7 K through 12
9 Disney frame
0 Tales and such
1 "Common Sense" writer
4 Ventilate
7 HBO miniseries starring Frances McDormand*
1 Director Craven
2 Portions
3 Showy
4 Topham Hatt's title
5 Something to shuck
7 Nimble*
3 Trifle
4 Sackcloth and ___
5 Skillful
7 Wild plum
8 Moolah/TITLE
2 Try out
3 Vets' concerns
4 Boxing great Joe
5 They last flew in 2003

66 Commotions
67 Spanish 101 verb

DOWN

1 Solid-state light
2 Female gametes
3 Low island
4 Home theater component
5 Wrap
6 Bitter-___ (diehard)
7 Tarnish
8 Invasive yellow flower
9 Director Lee
10 Particular
11 Music hall
12 Prospect
13 Lucy's landlady
18 Word of woe
21 Curl one's lip
22 Shining
23 Working stiff
24 Romeo's rival
26 Unpopular spots
28 Patel in "Hotel Mumbai"
31 Trading place
32 Had a bite
33 Part of TGIF
34 Show flexibility
35 Far North abode
36 Set
38 Throws off
39 Notch made by a saw
40 Grocery chain letters
44 White-sale items
45 Working stiff
46 Unlike toadstools
47 Wears well
48 Keys

49 Hamlet's father, onstage
50 Rowed
51 Beethoven's "___ Joy"
52 Rapunzel feature
56 Town NNE of Santa Fe
58 Transcript fig.
59 Injured
60 Sportage maker
61 Ukr., once

THEATER DISTRICT*   by Roland Huget
Don't be thinking "jokers" at 51 Across.

ACROSS

1 "The Sound of Music" baroness
5 ___ voce (softly)
10 Yep's opposite
14 Come together
15 Built-up
16 Auction site
17 No difference, in France
18 Verse romance
19 Needing Tylenol
20 London's Great Exhibition of 1851 attraction*
23 Moves unsteadily
24 Fritter away
27 Four-door model
28 Mercury car division founder*
32 Hot shade
34 "Wag the Dog" ploy
35 "The Time Machine" people
36 Commuting option
39 Sleeveless woman's garment
42 Dead to the world
43 Jack Russell's dinner?
45 Golfer's concern
46 Stand in
48 Shaken glass orb*
51 Some wild cards
55 Benjamin, in slang
56 Uncharged particle
58 NASA program with a lunar landing*
62 Big blow
64 Heads-up
65 At hand
66 Part of UAE
67 Tyler Perry film persona
68 Memo starter
69 Absolut competitor
70 Transitional precip
71 Hardy heroine

DOWN

1 Kicks out
2 "Life Among the Lowly" lowlife
3 Had them rolling in the aisles
4 Elite athlete
5 Sweet additive
6 End of a threat
7 Recipe amt.
8 "Bye for now!"
9 First-year law student
10 Nestlé instant success?
11 "New World Symphony" highlight
12 Equal footing
13 Needle hole
21 Core belief
22 Leatherworking tool
25 Pants, in slang
26 Improve text
29 Nerd relative
30 Gained a lap
31 Youngest Greek god
33 Lackluster
36 Pear variety
37 Catering vessels
38 Heed the ref's whistle
40 Info on a dust jacket
41 Provide lodging for
44 Had great confidence in
47 "You can be certain!"
49 Pontiac muscle car
50 Trout amandine, e.g.
52 Garfield's girlfriend
53 Wisdom teeth
54 Saws wood, so to speak
57 Really bother
59 Copier issues
60 "Skywards" airline
61 Sign over
62 Krypton is one
63 Torah holder

187 TONGUE-TIED   by Roland Huget
"Dodger blue" would be another clue for 32 Across.

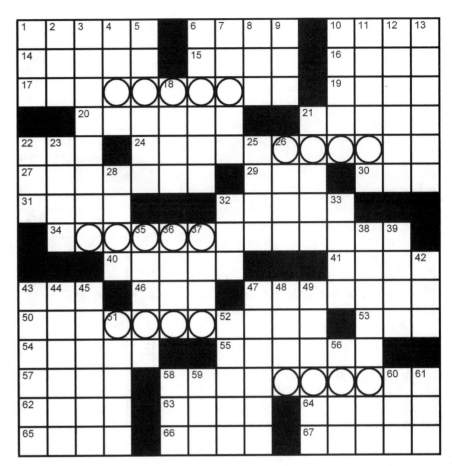

ACROSS

1 Tusked animals
6 Psyche's husband
10 Word with liquor or candy
14 Means to a proof
15 Red-tag event
16 Letter-shaped girder
17 Gary Larson strip
19 Speed along
20 Put down
21 Norwegian Bliss has 20
22 Like new recruits
24 Union demand?
27 Log-in requirements
29 Sturm ___ Drang
30 Messy abode
31 Grand Ole Opry tie
32 Cyan-blue
34 One-rate levy system
40 Bank card
41 Rep on the street
43 In the past
46 Feel poorly
47 Off the boat
50 Hush-hush
53 PC port
54 They're calling Danny Boy
55 Rocket "brakes"
57 School on the Thames
58 "Hasta la vista, pal!"
62 Squire in "Silas Marner"
63 Oscar Night stretch
64 Beneath the surface
65 Deuce topper
66 Cask dregs
67 Chinese zodiac animal

DOWN

1 Crunchy sandwich
2 Gasp of delight
3 Stayed young at heart
4 Widespread
5 Shrimp dish
6 Some exam answers
7 Like a Georgia night of song
8 Immemorial
9 Match the bet
10 Brought on board
11 Ancient calculator
12 Serving implement
13 Like Oscar Night attire
18 Try for a part
21 Hip-hop physician?
22 Barbecue spices
23 Beginning
25 Greek liqueur
26 E pluribus ___
28 Fork locale
32 Take steps
33 Mark on metal
35 "Waterworks"
36 Wader of 37 Down
37 World's longest river
38 Inflammatory
39 Millennials' parents
42 Ball belle
43 Side of things
44 Fender product
45 Stand against
47 Chocolate breakfast cereal
48 Court dividers
49 Narrow waterway
51 Tiny, informally
52 Type of wave or spree
56 Former sci-fi magazine
58 Any partner
59 Run out of juice
60 "Golly!"
61 Bruins superstar of yore

188 MOVERS by Fred Piscop
... but not shakers.

ACROSS

1 Catchall abbr.
5 Handle word
9 Jack who shunned fat
14 Cheese in puff pastries
15 Cookie often dunked
16 "School's Out" singer Cooper
17 Do a diner chore
19 Principal port of Iraq
20 Slippery swimmer
21 Canon camera
22 No-goodnik
24 Like formal wear
26 Three Dog Night's "loneliest number"
27 Twinkies maker, once
31 Bondsman's offering
35 Place to land
38 Hurricane rescue op
39 Voracious marine mammal
40 Competitor of Denny's
41 Biblical queen's land
42 "Author unknown"
43 Beef cut above the round
44 Balzac's "Le ___ Goriot"
45 Rifle range position
46 Innovation's origin
47 Recycled tire
49 Troy, NY sch.
51 Minnesota iron ore range
55 Mr. Met and Mrs. Met, e.g.
59 Cote call
60 Press for payment
61 Take out or let in
62 What AKC handlers do
65 Celery portion
66 Rank below marquess
67 Having the means
68 Tot's equine
69 "A Visit From St. Nicholas" opener
70 Vegetable in V8 juice

DOWN

1 Drew back
2 More on the mark
3 Numbered part of a market
4 Do-over at Wimbledon
5 N'awlins sandwiches
6 Bookmarked addresses, briefly
7 "Chi-Raq" director
8 Tax write-off
9 Polio vaccine pioneer Albert
10 Do some plank smoothing
11 Insurer's concern
12 Zoning area, perhaps
13 Sign of remorse
18 "The Hen and the Fox" fabulist
23 Puccini title heroine
25 Patronize UPS, say
28 [titter]
29 Chris of tennis fame
30 Sword with a curved blade
32 River to the Ligurian Sea
33 iPhone image
34 Sprinter's assignment
35 Voice of the Apple Watch
36 Sound of a mic drop
37 "Tosca" setting
41 Sailboat spar
45 Song of praise
48 In-box contents
50 Petunia's toon mate
52 Sun-baked brick
53 Valveless horn
54 Alaska, in some maps
55 Col. Potter's post
56 Glee club voice
57 Keypad symbol
58 Galley notation
59 Theda in "Cleopatra"
63 Not yet refined
64 Apply with a tissue, say

WINNING FORMULA   by Fred Piscop

The marble sculpture at 55 Across is permanently displayed at the Louvre.

ACROSS

1 Gondolier's milieu
6 Smokehouse meats
10 Tom Brady's former team
14 Italian fashion house
15 Now!
16 London essayist
17 1971 Elton John hit
18 Maltese monetary unit, once
19 Regrets deeply
20 Paris landmark
23 Barnum's Wild Man of ___
25 Brooding bird
26 Actress Vardalos
27 Andy's TV and radio pal
28 Cocoon occupant
31 Like a hedgehog
33 Did a 10K
34 Chaplin of "Game of Thrones"
35 Blossom visitor
36 Job seeker's fashion advice
42 UN financial agcy.
43 Brewery need
44 Go for the gold
45 Slow, on a score
48 Ratchet wheel part
49 Vaccine fluids
50 Dashboard gauge, for short
51 Merman's home
53 Chef who says "Bam!"
55 Nike of Samothrace
59 Bibliographer's abbr.
60 Forearm bone
61 Offer forbidden fruit to
64 A smattering of
65 Pear discard
66 How some popcorn is popped
67 Swing support, perhaps
68 Roulette bet
69 Like five-star hotels

DOWN

1 Radar's rank: Abbr.
2 "Some ___ born great . . ."
3 Site of German guns in a 1961 movie
4 Decks out
5 Jousting weapon
6 Saintly symbol
7 "Not gonna happen!"
8 McCartney's "dear" sheepdog of song
9 Alley pickup
10 Land liberated by San Martin
11 Many college benefactors
12 Men's jewelry item
13 Strut showily
21 Disembark, in a way
22 Pitcher plant's prey
23 Poet of yore
24 Congresswoman Ilhan
29 Colorful card game
30 Italian cheese city
32 Chest muscle, informally
34 Be absorbed slowly
35 Ballistics lab specimen
37 Command to a puppy
38 Tree surgeon's tool
39 John Q. Public
40 Apple Watch voice
41 Bit of wax on a letter
45 Most despicable
46 Paper lion?
47 Generic
48 Dog studier of note
49 Court sister of Venus
52 Draw out
54 Recurring theme
56 Sheer delight
57 Concerning, on a memo
58 D-Day city
62 Snapfish product, for short
63 "Give it a whirl!"

TRUCKIN' by Jordan P. Conway

33 Across has been nicknamed "The Venice of the East."

ACROSS

1 Food truck fare
6 ATM opening
10 Pilots with the right stuff
14 Appointer of Kagan
15 "I did it!"
16 Ready to serve
17 Hockey's "sin bin"
19 Ranch vacationer
20 Movie star's double
21 Approached peak flavor
23 Sierra Nevada products
25 Contest mail-in
26 Up-to-date
30 "Weird Al" song, e.g.
33 Umeda Sky Building site
34 Wedge with seafood
35 Like blue states: Abbr.
38 Zebra feature
39 Took measured steps
40 "Star Trek" navigator
41 Wordplay from Groucho
42 Johnson of the UK
43 Predatory felines
44 Lake near Syracuse, N.Y.
46 Horse with a mottled coat
47 Ate in style
49 Abode in the wild
51 Steeps, as tea leaves
54 Lake activity
59 Work at a copy desk
60 Clean energy source
62 Spare, e.g.
63 Cabal's contrivance
64 Overdo a part
65 Futurist of sorts
66 "Ain't happenin'!"
67 Stressed out

DOWN

1 Pajama halves
2 Provide a fake alibi for, e.g.
3 Water-to-wine site
4 Gulf sultanate
5 Zoe of "Avatar"
6 "People" composer Jule
7 Chem class
8 Sign of spoiled food
9 Hailer's holler
10 Figure in a sum
11 Trash collection site
12 Bitter-___ (die-hard)
13 In run-down shape
18 Loss-of-a-ball miscue
22 Working stiff
24 Featured menu offering
26 Blowout victory
27 "Hairy man" in Genesis
28 "1812 Overture" sounds
29 Barely make, with "out"
31 Iowa State's home

32 Abacus beads holder
34 Fat in pie crusts
36 Carrier to Ben-Gurion
37 Ponder silently
39 Luau bowlful
40 Have a late meal
42 Barracks array
43 Castle fortification
45 Like "it," in grammar
46 "New Look" designer
47 Counts calories
48 Not from a major studio
50 Let up, as rain
52 Channel for armchair jocks
53 Flight student's milestone
55 Like petting-zoo animals
56 Privy to
57 Clears after taxes
58 Euphoric feeling
61 Sever, with "off"

191 BOARD MEMBERS   by Jordan P. Conway
Don't expect to find a chairman sitting at this board.

CROSS

1 County happenings
6 Domesticated insects
10 Bit of hair gel
13 Like a diamond in the rough
14 Greased auto part
15 Paul in "The Good Earth"
16 Plum or peach, e.g.
18 Etcher's fluid
19 Midsize Nissan
20 Cher doesn't use one
22 Skip past
24 "Come here ___?"
25 More scratchy, as a voice
29 Avoid a pothole, say
31 24-book Greek epic
32 Scorpio's birthstone, perhaps
34 Prettifies, as a pastry
38 Meaty part of a lobster
39 Twist out of shape
40 YTD part
41 Song from a choir
42 Alaska gold rush town
43 Year-end mall temp
44 Zap with a Taser
46 Spends the night in
48 Buttonholes, essentially
51 Common burrito filler
52 Japanese writing system
55 Share on Facebook, say
60 Golden ___ (senior)
61 Transit clerk's workplace
63 Male gobblers
64 [see other side]
65 "Mr. Cub" Banks
66 Tricky road curve
67 Kate of "House of Cards"
68 Watery-eyed

DOWN

1 Act the mother hen
2 Start the pot
3 iPhone graphic
4 Litter castoff, perhaps
5 Dark chapter in MLB history (with 62-D)
6 Place to bend an elbow
7 Jump for joy
8 "On the Waterfront" director Kazan
9 Match components
10 Box office buy, slangily
11 "Pokémon" cartoon genre
12 U.S. vice president before Pence
15 Faithful servant
17 Partner of fortune
21 Bathwater tester
23 Affix, as a patch
25 Loaded with calories
26 Comrade-in-arms
27 "The King and I" setting
28 History Channel reality series
29 Electronic music pioneer Edgard
30 Pipe bend
33 Dawber of "Mork & Mindy"
35 Six-pack units
36 Singer James portrayed by Beyoncé
37 Concert ticket datum
39 Bearded African beast
43 Low-risk wager
45 "For shame!" sound
47 Gull-like bird
48 Stingray relative
49 Largest city of Nigeria
50 Agenda details
51 Patisserie worker
53 Quark's place
54 ___ Scotia lox
56 Sponge opening
57 Chaplin of "Game of Thrones"
58 Make homogeneous, perhaps
59 "___ went thataway!"
62 See 5 Down

192 IMPLANTS by Lee Taylor
. . . but not the medical kind.

ACROSS

1. Tree asp
6. Put away
10. Q-Tip
14. Reverent
15. Gyroscope part
16. Krakatoa outflow
17. Hula attire
19. Nearly new
20. Adirondacks activity
21. Life force in yoga
22. Threatening words
25. Clinton running mate
27. The Merry Pranksters' vehicle
28. Inquisition target
30. Loosens laces
32. Slang for "super"
33. Like the Nautilus
36. Trudges
38. English translation of "Elle"
39. Some boxing blows
43. Like Shangri-la
46. Yeats' homeland
47. Grow more grass
50. Tights type
52. Ingest
53. C___ crossword
56. Thick pieces
57. Candid
59. Hardly a green car
61. "Once more ___ the breach . . .": Shak.
62. Diminutive wedding attendant
66. The Bee ___
67. Deep sleep
68. Like "American Horror Story"
69. Whirlpool
70. Doubloon, for one
71. Statue garment

DOWN

1. Low no. for 59 Across
2. Bring to light
3. Extinct kiwi cousin
4. Amateurish
5. Give a boost
6. H.H. Munro
7. Downsizing phase
8. Where Spica is
9. VT time
10. Say "Yesh" to the breathalyzer
11. Sushi condiment
12. Pennsylvania, in Washington
13. Katniss Everdeen, for one
18. Yarn shop purchase
21. Type of colony Australia once was
22. Resistance measures
23. Rod attachment
24. Descartes' "therefore"
26. Friend of Katniss
29. Verge
31. Logger's nemesis
34. Major river in Thailand
35. Canadian flag feature
37. Del Frisco's menu item
40. Twain rafter
41. Himalayan adventure
42. Scene sites
44. Overdoes it
45. Métier
47. Safe haven
48. Brought home
49. Announced
51. Propped (up)
54. Nanook of the North abode
55. "The Impossible" actor Watts
58. Curious to a fault
60. One-time ugly duckling
62. Net neutrality org.
63. "This American Life" host Glass
64. Heavy sleeper
65. "Go Set a Watchman" author

193 DUCK, DUCK, GOOSE   by Lee Taylor

Nancy Sinatra famously wore 45 Across in a 1966 song video.

ACROSS

1 "The Music of the Night" lyricist
5 Stops dithering
9 Gucci rival
14 A long way off
15 Watchdog warning
16 Picture puzzle
17 Upbeat
18 1989 hip-hop hit
20 Inspiring slogan
22 Citizen living abroad
23 It leads to extra innings
24 More barren
26 University official
28 Himalayan pack animal
29 Antidrug message: "Just ___!"
31 Assent with a salute
35 Copped some z's
39 Small town
40 Block the flow
42 Prod into action
43 Slander
45 Fad footwear of the 1960s
47 Herbert Hoover, for one
49 Language spoken in Vientiane
50 Golf lesson topic
53 Lush with vegetation
57 Roofing material
58 Rascal
61 Joe Palooka, for one
62 1983 UB40 hit
65 Euro precursor in Padua
66 Roughly
67 Bath waters
68 Igneous rock builder
69 Live bait
70 Thanksgiving side
71 Iditarod vehicle

DOWN

1 Damages
2 Brewing
3 Dreads wearer
4 What to do if you don't succeed
5 Kimono sash
6 Indiana hoopster
7 "Jurassic Park" menace
8 Play hooky
9 Make believe
10 Yank's foe
11 Let up
12 Add voices to a film
13 Up until now
19 Ingrid's "Notorious" costar
21 "That works for me"
25 Scraped by, with "out"
27 Band with the 1998 hit "Iris"
29 "Plaza Suite" playwright
30 Cut ___ (boogie)
31 Washboard muscles
32 "That's tasty!"
33 Before, to Burns
34 Epic tale
36 San Diego attraction
37 Chow down
38 Dentist's deg.
41 Fenway Park's Pesky's ___
44 Satellite launchers
46 Sharp remark
48 Make one's way
50 Juice box attachment
51 Zumba alternative
52 Fervor
53 Sidewinder spit
54 The "A" in CAT scan
55 Chutzpah
56 Bald tire's lack
59 Out of town
60 Bounty alternative
63 Mojito ingredient
64 USNA grad

194

THEMELESS by Alyssa Brooke

48 Across is also the first African-American woman to join the LPGA tour.

ACROSS

1 Sudden halt
9 Bawdy
15 In solitude
16 Estevez of "Bobby"
17 Not kosher
18 Moon mission name
19 "___ yer old man!"
20 Far East cuisine
21 Put down
22 2004 Richard Gere film
24 Not more than
27 Infuriates
28 Tom's cry
29 Close examinations
32 Is in session
36 Skating legend
37 Sinbad's bird
38 King of Calais
39 Ukraine's "Mother of Cities"
41 "The Crucible" setting
43 Holler
44 Precollege education
46 "Beats me"
48 First African American to win a tennis major
53 Fail-safe
54 They hang from rims
55 Letter on a key
58 Frozen spike
59 Split
61 Higher up
62 Tire tool
63 Back streets
64 School session

DOWN

1 Roaster's spot
2 Salt's saint
3 Range in which the von Trapps sang
4 Patriotic org.
5 Slow movers
6 Formal headgear
7 Ryan of "Love Story"
8 Grave risk
9 Magazine patrons
10 Get in the way of
11 Plant material used for fuel
12 Type of wrench
13 Shade of purple
14 Half a shortbread cookie
22 Mother bear
23 Betray discomfort
24 Running wild
25 Garr in "Young Frankenstein"
26 Additional
30 Diet guru Jenny
31 "HuffPost" owner
33 It's pumped at the gym
34 Square setting
35 Minuteman's place
40 Buggy, e.g.
41 Salt cellars
42 Identify incorrectly
43 Ancient pillager
45 Gore or Stahl
47 Amount to take
48 "Hotel du Lac" author Brookner
49 Union chapter
50 Bird sound
51 Ancient tribe of Peru
52 Refute
55 Wear a long face
56 Extremely popular
57 Passage in Latin
60 Dorm VIPs

THEMELESS by Alyssa Brooke
The Big Dipper is another example of a 4 Down.

ACROSS

1 Best of the theater
5 '50s White House name
10 Sky sightings
14 Happy days, economically
16 Terse negative
17 Line of five feet
18 Let loose
19 In love with
20 Advances anew
22 Closes the defense, in court
24 Sally has two
25 Up and at 'em
28 One who goes on and on
32 Slangy refusals
33 Job dismissal
35 ___ kwon do
36 Drawing power of the San Diego Zoo?
39 TGIF part
40 One of TV's Jeffersons
41 Mine, to Maurice
42 Most impertinent
44 Hound's trail
45 Physical opening
46 Ireland's patron
49 Accepts reality
52 Regular
56 Club for Lydia Ko
57 Make a reel copy of
59 Madre's son
60 Point-blank
61 Root beer brand
62 Cut
63 Mechanic's ___

DOWN

1 Omar in "The Mod Squad"
2 Picked straws
3 Zilch
4 Orion's Belt, for one
5 Office slips
6 "Looks ___ everything"
7 "Good Will Hunting" setting
8 Roman legion's route
9 Brontë heroine
10 Develop
11 From here to eternity
12 2006 Sony animated film
13 Takes note
15 Devonshire dad
21 Potted plant place
23 Dire dilemmas
25 "Winter of Artifice" author Nin
26 Flagship of 1492
27 "Now!"
29 Halloween wear
30 Prince William's aunt
31 Let up
33 Sea peril
34 Stern radio rival
37 Wanted-poster name
38 Kind of maneuver
43 Dictator's aides
44 Custer's sword
47 Not that, and more
48 Trimmed back
49 Artifact, to an archaeologist
50 Intense desire
51 It may be spun
53 Singer Braxton
54 Twist an arm
55 Genesis setting
58 Punch sound

THEMELESS by Harvey Estes

George Harrison recorded a version of 60 Across for his "Dark Horse" album.

ACROSS

1 HBO political comedy series
5 Check the books
10 When curtains rise
14 Fallen from favor
16 Brest milk
17 Where your quarters may be located
18 "Woe ___!"
19 Eponymic Lauder perfume
20 Less forgiving
22 UFC octagon
25 Pioneering 1940s computer
26 Sonora snack
29 Alpo alternative
32 Malia's sister
34 Vivacity
35 Iced coffee drink
37 Bud
38 Quiet rebuke
41 Address book no.
42 Refuse receptacle
43 Russian Orthodox saint
44 Salon strokes
46 Oxen collar
47 NY Met or LA Dodger
48 "Many ___ has to fall, but . . ."
50 Plod through
52 Listing
55 "Air Music" composer
59 Go for a spin
60 Everly Brothers classic
63 Just so
64 Ancient Hebrew people
65 "Storms in Africa" singer
66 Lower oneself
67 Affectation

DOWN

1 Type of squad
2 Mireille of "World War Z"
3 Tighten text
4 Fir ball
5 Way back when
6 Net destination
7 Pops
8 "Rhyme Pays" rapper
9 Italian Riviera's Cinque ___
10 Ballerina Markova
11 Bewitch
12 "Spring ahead" event
13 Sinus, for one
15 Mr. Met's old home
21 Atlas legend, for example
23 Boxes with bows
24 Coarse
26 Dry runs
27 Detached feeling
28 Knock off
30 Island of SW Florida
31 Pipes up
33 Place for vows
36 Committee
39 Like some cold sprays
40 Ulan Bator locale
45 Coin of Cádiz
49 More than mad
51 Turgenev Museum site
52 Comedian Johnson
53 NASDAQ cousin
54 Hatcher in "Tomorrow Never Dies"
56 Indian flatbread
57 "___ so sorry"
58 Private dining area?
61 Take in, as big game
62 Kobe currency

THEMELESS by Harvey Estes

34 Across was first used in a 1963 game between 1 Across and 61 Across.

CROSS

1 West Point team
5 Come clean
0 Big ref.
4 Pinot ___
5 It's shocking
7 Popeye and Bluto, slangily
8 Proof of purchase
9 SEP, e.g.
0 Jeff Bridges had two in "Tron"
1 Country cousins
2 Lacey's TV partner
4 Drug dispensers
5 Lift, in a way
6 Anticrime acronym
9 Designer Saab
0 Poor group
3 OCS grads
4 Homer's second viewing, e.g.
7 Childcare writer LeShan
8 It may be double
9 Catches forty winks
1 Drum sites
2 Ancient tribe
6 Luncheonette lures
8 Discriminator of a kind
9 Crenshaw, e.g.
0 Choir ends
3 "The Recruit" org.
4 You can make it conversing
6 March 31st animal
7 Thumb your nose at
8 Teen fave
9 NBA team
0 Must, informally

61 Annapolis team

DOWN

1 Tomfoolery
2 Greet with loud laughter
3 Will-o'-the-wisp
4 2020 et al.
5 "Hot dog!"
6 Lament loudly
7 Cairo artery
8 Email links
9 Ora ___ nobis
10 Neglect
11 She sponsored Columbus
12 Property of racers
13 Eugene's ladder in "Tangled"
16 Beyoncé's wig in "Goldmember"
20 Tie in
23 Slangy refusals
24 Pampered, with "on"
26 Oscar de la ___
27 Bury
28 Toe woes
31 Barn roof spinners
32 Parsley units
34 Instigation invitation
35 He overthrew the Directory
36 "Lucky Number" singer Lovich
37 Porcelain glazes
40 Lab garments
43 Buzzing bug
44 "I, Robot" author
45 In a steadfast way

47 "___ is as good as a wink"
48 Prudential rival
50 Welk's upbeat
51 Cool off like a boxer
52 Inverness inhabitant
55 Holiday drink
56 Vietnam War Memorial designer

198 STRING THEORY by Mark McClain
. . . as detected by sensitive instruments.

ACROSS

1 Reading rental
5 Hailing from Haarlem
10 Go along with
14 Pricing option
15 Very, on a score
16 Crime boss
17 Cheddar spec
19 Annual sports award
20 The heavens
21 Metal polishing brand
23 Officially, but maybe not in real life
26 Legendary frontiersman
27 Thingy
28 Abject failure
29 Atlanta-based cable outlet
32 Aunt in "Oklahoma!"
33 Correspond
34 Otto I's realm: Abbr.
35 Related
36 Slimming schemes
37 Horn's sound
38 Sorority letter
39 Avis rival
40 Push off to the side
41 Big name in security
42 Powerful poker pair
43 Title for Jeanne d'Arc
44 Missed the boat
46 Stormy sound
47 Turn into cash
49 Homecoming group
50 Mideast line
51 Wildflower that thrives in forests
56 Kyrgyzstan locale
57 First name in cosmetics
58 Beehive, say
59 Nursery rhyme contrarian
60 Deteriorates
61 Flanged fastener

DOWN

1 Finder's ___
2 Loosey-goosey
3 Make a move
4 Like a machine screw
5 Scurried
6 Wedding party member
7 Autocrat of old
8 Corden's "Karaoke" vehicle
9 Trout stream wear
10 Frigate's milieu
11 Short-legged pet
12 Omar on-screen
13 Fluctuate wildly
18 Sans premium or discount
22 Cowpoke's accessory
23 "Freedom Trilogy" folk singer
24 Mutual fund descriptor
25 Issue in some industrial areas
26 Defensive football ploy
28 Plays the worrywart
30 "Agnes Grey" author
31 Irish ___ (hunting dog)
33 Really excited
36 Boxing Day month
37 Dissipates
39 Long-eared loser
40 Mecca native
43 Tonsorial jobs
45 Team race
46 Spam alternative
47 500 sheets
48 Snow Queen in "Frozen"
49 Fortitude
52 The Tigers of the SEC
53 MD's coworker
54 Univ. URL tag
55 Rug rat

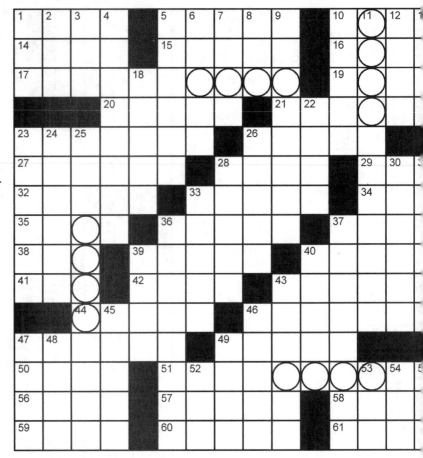

STUFFED SHELLS   by Mark McClain
. . . but not of the edible kind.

CROSS

1 Did the crawl
5 Principal Iraqi port
10 "Grand" baseball feat
14 "Firework" singer Perry
15 "Over the Rainbow" composer
16 Smaller version
17 #1 Google activity?
19 Off-road wheels
20 Hereditary bits
21 Boot part
22 IOU
23 Glasgow girl
26 "A ___ story!"
28 Barnes Ice Cap locale
33 Chiapas cheer
34 Nabisco wafer
35 Landform of caves and sinkholes
39 Many an eastern European
41 Saw features
43 Barnyard male
44 Chocolate alternative
46 Fruity soft drinks
48 Imaging test
49 Spread for scones
52 International document
55 Back part
56 Clear up
57 Center of San Jose
60 Eye clinic acronym
64 One in opposition
65 Gangland struggle for territory
68 Golf bag items
69 Wear away
70 Let up on
71 Shipped
72 Moroccan capital
73 Cannon in "Out to Sea"

DOWN

1 Propeller protector
2 Salary
3 Lots and lots
4 Rita Skeeter's column "Me, ___ & I"
5 Cheers, for one
6 Canine comment
7 Narrow opening
8 Truckee River city
9 Chancellor Merkel
10 Squarely (in the middle)
11 Like Pink
12 Heavy workbench item
13 Erroll Garner classic
18 Track star Bolt
24 Peevish mood
25 Mum
27 Etcher's need
28 Pear named after a Belgian
29 Pasta ___ Carbonara
30 North Carolina cape
31 Wintry precip
32 Beard softener
36 Capital on the Tiber
37 First name in desserts
38 Adjust sails
40 "American Idol" contestant
42 Go underground
45 Deli menu initialism
47 Do-to-do, to Verdi
50 Rolex ___ Perpetual
51 Not meant for kids
52 "___ all she wrote!"
53 Zellweger in "Judy"
54 "All gone," to a tot
58 Mysterious glow
59 "No ___!" ("Sure!")
61 "Jersey Boys" number
62 "Sing it, Sam" speaker
63 Intense
66 Rx watchdog
67 Patronize Circus Circus

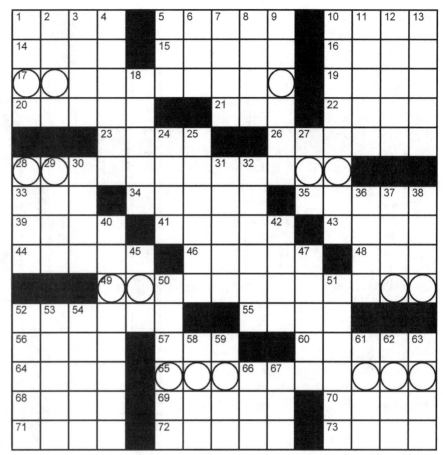

200 JOB SQUAD   by Gary Larson
37 Down once tricked Yoko Ono into paying $10,000 for a blade of grass.

ACROSS

1 Carson's Fern
4 Frigid
10 Doing business
14 Slip in a pot
15 FDR center
16 Cathedral center
17 Dim-witted server?
19 Second feature
20 Without a clue
21 De-rind
22 White House worker
23 Angry coach?
26 Stir
29 Gained a lap
30 Collectible frames
31 Littleneck
35 Mary Richards' friend
39 Make a doily
40 Exhausted officer?
42 Witchy woman
43 Muddle
45 Whip
46 Loathsome
47 Venomous snake
49 Pain reliever
51 Happy cowpoke?
57 Simians
58 Inspiration
59 USMCA predecessor
63 Observe Thanksgiving
64 Refined rodeo worker?
66 Extremities
67 Vocalist Kitt
68 Auction action
69 Twiggy digs
70 Revolt
71 Porky's place

DOWN

1 Verdi opera
2 Romp
3 Rolaids rival
4 Pop-up producer
5 Short-story award
6 Excerpts
7 Farewells
8 Unmoving
9 Kitchen gadgets
10 How verbal contracts are taken
11 "Going Rogue" author Sarah
12 Steer clear of
13 More modern
18 Bremen brewery
24 Years back
25 Senior org.
26 Takes steps
27 Withdraw gradually
28 Utah ski resort
32 Test site
33 Suffix for emir
34 Hosts
36 Where Lima is
37 Painter of limp watches
38 Seasoned
40 In use
41 However, in a tweet
44 Least true
46 Spreading fast online
48 Comparative shopper
50 Bic part
51 Willow Smith's brother
52 Think out loud
53 Imparts
54 Two-time loser to Ike
55 Draws nigh
56 Social stratum
60 Smart keys
61 Twerp
62 Panda of old cartoons
65 Moo ___ pork

FOUR-LEGGED FRIENDS* by Jonathan Brill
Can you find all six friends?

CROSS

1 Gets ready to drag
5 "Good to go"
11 Hotel amenity
14 Zeno's birthplace
15 San Francisco district*
16 Bronze
17 Taqueria take-out order*
19 Brazil parrot
20 Leading sportswear company
21 Unsaturated alcohol
23 Rockies range
24 UFC sport
27 Stalwart
28 Adam's apple locale
29 Professional charges
30 "How the Other Half Lives" author
31 All alone
35 Ending to hair or fish
36 They're found in clue* answers
39 Hitting stats
40 Municipal lawmakers
41 Soon, to Shakespeare
43 Comparison words
44 Swedish poet Karlfeldt
48 Rump, anatomically
50 Août's season
51 Part of an act
52 Right away
54 Transpire
55 Small bite
56 Jah worshiper*
60 Hardware store chain
61 Utter
62 Judith Shakespeare's mom
63 Sibilant sound
64 "Empress of Soul" Knight*
65 Like the irate golfer?

DOWN

1 Sales promotion
2 Gave the slip to
3 Cinéma ___ documentary
4 Like a derisive grin
5 New Testament book
6 Mekong River dweller
7 D-Day transport
8 Pou ___ (standing place)
9 Energy units
10 Gear part
11 Taking the lead?
12 Take-offs*
13 Psycho follower
18 Kinsler of baseball
22 Start to drum or plug
24 French art song
25 Most Grinchlike
26 Semitic love goddess
29 Fencing sword
32 RMN's VP
33 Saint or Muppet
34 RMN was his VP
36 Extremists
37 Uranium-238 and carbon-14
38 100 points, to a jeweler
39 Nuts or fruit*
42 Manchurian river
45 Kvetch
46 Mad
47 Lamented
49 Scrawny animal
51 NY bar overseer
53 Father of Tiger Woods
54 Young newts
57 Madrid Mrs.
58 Just a bit
59 "___ questions?"

202 IT'S ALL ABOUT PERSPECTIVE   by Wren Schultz
. . . and that perspective is centrally located.

ACROSS

1 J. Edgar Hoover Building tenant
4 Went down
8 Suffix for corpus
11 Web page section
13 Evil Queen's daughter in "Descendants"
14 Tie-in
16 Food ___
17 Turnpike stop
19 Chuck
20 Tampa Bay NFLer
21 Mauve, for one
22 Fido's find
23 Highest world capital city
25 Back in
26 Jammies, for some
28 Check out
30 Level, in Liverpool
31 You are, in Spanish class
32 Jayhawker's capital
34 Friction ___
36 Poker-faced
38 Where Elvis served for two years
40 Weekend warrior's cry
42 From a distance
45 Me ___ movement
46 With great perception
48 Silver-gray tree
50 Gary of "Point Break"
52 Expected
53 Kind of wonder "Take On Me" was

55 Stack the deck
56 Hidden valley
57 **Element of a perspective drawing (with 59-A)**
59 **See 57 Across**
60 Brio
61 Uniform
62 Designer Oscar de la ___
63 First in space?
64 They go by the script?
65 Email address suffix

DOWN

1 Like FDR's presidency
2 Ives in "East of Eden"
3 Pugsley Addams' cousin
4 Layout
5 Guacamole fruit
6 Nada
7 Food for 27 Down
8 Point-blank
9 Ray in "GoodFellas"
10 Walks in
11 Response to pollen
12 Robert Ludlum hero
15 Kanye's sister-in-law
18 Watering hole
20 Sang-Moon of the PGA
23 Puts on Angie's
24 Fly, as time
27 Sand dollars
29 Reef denizen
32 Ache

33 Sagal in "Sons of Anarchy"
35 Dolores Umbridge's Patronus
37 Fire starter
39 Observed shiva
41 Articulate
42 Looking down
43 Fireworks finish
44 Amphitheaters
46 Frat party item
47 "Did you hear . . .?" speaker
49 "___ for Homicide": Grafton
51 Protest placards
54 Joyce Carol Oates novel
56 Attendee

58 "___ been had!"
59 Quid ___ quo

THEMELESS   by Wren Schultz
Our test solvers had a good laugh at the clue for 19 Across.

CROSS

1 Lombardi Trophy sport
9 Mercedes-Benz sedan
15 High
16 Crisp out
17 Pedigree
18 Cash in
19 Nasal spray?
20 Battlefront?
21 Ballot marks
22 Miracle-___
23 Bartender's pull
25 Voice of Snerd
28 Angular measures
29 Rathskeller quaff
30 First name of a second lady
32 Absence of chaos
34 Prefix with watt
36 More modern
38 Duffer's hazard
39 Buffalo
41 Passover meal
43 End of creation?
44 "Pollyanna" author Porter
46 Doctor office fees
48 Breadwinners
49 Le mari de la reine
50 It cometh before the fall?
51 Turner of history
52 Like a puppy with a bow in its hair
55 Catch phrase?
57 Bottom of the corporate ladder
59 Place of power
60 "In the end . . ."
61 Email address symbol
62 "Game of Thrones" setting

DOWN

1 Groundhog Day mo.
2 Co-owners word
3 Frank
4 One side in an age-old dilemma
5 "Orca" star
6 Chandler citizen
7 Profession
8 Gamer's bane
9 Rant
10 "Ta-ta, old chap!"
11 Top
12 Sight of an ancient lighthouse
13 Retires comfortably?
14 Sylvia in "The Tamarind Seed"
20 Struck at the plate
23 Miller Park team
24 Like Granny Smiths
25 Porter's load
26 March Madness quarterfinals
27 Nonelected governors
31 Turn (to)
33 Tach readings
35 A of AFLAC
37 Army boots
40 Mining method
42 Potato offshoot
45 Make smarter
47 Capital on the Missouri
50 Falafel holder
52 Thé alternative
53 Rocket
54 Texter's "carpe diem"
56 You, to Yves
57 Gaping gullet
58 D.C. United org.

END RHYME by Lee Taylor

Vecturists have a definite solving edge at 28 Across.

ACROSS

1 Cathedral area
5 Sleek fur
10 Makes a selection
14 Put the whammy on
15 Papal court
16 Cut coupons
17 Pronto
18 Double curves
19 Escalator clause
20 Commuting option
21 Stick-in-the-mud
23 Bums around
25 Bags
26 Stand-up guy
28 What vecturists collect
31 Speechified
33 Feeble
34 Pipe material
37 Roasters spot
38 Ladder steps
40 River into the Caspian Sea
41 Nothing alternative
42 Like Death Valley
43 Washington city
45 Kigali is its capital
47 Like many dirt roads
48 1996 horror film
51 Greenland air base site
53 Pompous
56 Bibliography abbr.
59 Bacchanalia
60 Turn out
61 Tiny parasites
62 Cherokee or Wrangler
63 Set things right
64 Austen heroine
65 ___ Royale National Park
66 Double agents
67 "___ and ye shall find"

DOWN

1 Not quite closed
2 Tuscany tower town
3 Old-school missive
4 Daring adventures
5 Pooh-pooh
6 Venerable
7 Born and ___
8 Told a big one
9 "Piece of cake!"
10 Comes to pass
11 Walks doggedly
12 Squiggle in Spanish
13 Neuters
22 Dip a dougnut
24 Perfect serve
26 Musical ending
27 Kind of exam
29 Held the title to
30 Frat party feature
32 Superstar lineup
34 Period of concern for Nielsen
35 Femme fatale
36 Potter's need
39 Coffee dispenser
40 Strings at a luau
42 Win over
44 Monkey in Disney's "Aladdin"
45 Enter again
46 Bring into agreement
48 Japanese sliding screen
49 Reactor parts
50 Brightest star in Orion
52 Plugs hard
54 "You may be ___ something"
55 Fan favorite
57 Wile E. Coyote's supplier
58 White House concern

THE SOUND OF SILENCE*   by Lee Taylor
. . . and that sound can be found in clue* answers.

ACROSS

1 Digital clock toggle
5 Salary
8 Most senior
14 Harper Lee's "Go ___ Watchman"
15 Memorable time
16 Stadium employee
17 Backpack*
19 Doha resident
20 Outdo
21 Water filter brand
22 "___ got a feeling . . ."
23 Prefix with star or bucks
24 Clothes lines*
26 Damsel
28 Major artery
29 Math subj.
30 Try really hard
32 Festooned with tissue
36 Celebrity skewering
38 Maui crater
39 Little Italy fare
40 Dover's county
41 Charity fund-___
43 Grab a bite
44 "Smart" guy
46 Her looks could kill
48 Country on the Gulf of Aden*
51 Responded to a charge
52 Bane of banks
53 Detox symptom
54 Camera stands
57 Command from Picard
59 Aide-mémoire*
60 Pothead
61 Director Van Sant
62 Rookie
63 Silenus and Marsyas
64 K1 and K2: Abbr.
65 Diving duck

DOWN

1 Invites
2 Maître d's offering
3 Alpine grouse*
4 Like the human genome on April 14, 2003
5 Kulak
6 Curved paths
7 Himalayan beast of burden
8 Men's magazine
9 Memorized
10 "Can't Help Lovin' ___ Man"
11 Online business
12 Put food on the table
13 Gives it a go
18 Superlative for Nestor
21 Bears out
24 Beach facing Diamond Head
25 Karate training exercise
26 Former German capital?
27 ___ vera
31 Shows emotion, e.g.
33 Nom de plume*
34 JFK postings
35 Facts and figures
37 Rough guess
39 Not the main event
41 London news agency
42 Female monarch
45 Tenant
47 Eurostar terminals
48 This jumper can't jump
49 Coup d'etat group
50 Fort Knox bar
54 Bolt fastener
55 Ominous
56 Garbage boat
58 Even a little
59 "The Wizard of Oz" studio

METAMORPHOSIS by Roger & Kathy Wienberg

33 Across is also the name of a UK drink composed of cider and beer.

ACROSS

1 Neanderthal
4 Ditty syllable
7 It's played with a bow
12 About-face
15 Han Solo's son Kylo ___
16 NASA Deep Space Habitat capsule
17 Picnic running event
20 $ buying power
21 Fluffy wrap
22 Peak near Olympus
23 Crude transport
24 Fire starter?
25 Almond
27 Sign on
30 Deals with adversity
33 Cause of Cleopatra's demise
36 Big Board newbie
37 Surfing annoyance
39 Decimal base
40 End
42 Grand canyon
44 Not missing anything
45 Worldwide workers' gp.
46 Like a shrinking violet
47 Not suitable
51 Table spread
55 What Horton heard
56 Words often said to Santa
58 Complete metamorphoses

60 Christine Daaé's stage
61 Rihanna song "Te ___"
62 Caterpillar bristles
63 Black tea from India
64 Barker in "La Dolce Vita"
65 1040 ID

DOWN

1 Exceed
2 Dumas swashbuckler
3 Folds a flag
4 Eternal City fountain
5 Like Windsor Castle
6 Hidden motive
7 Brown's "The Da Vinci ___"
8 Slip
9 LLC center
10 Moves about from place to place
11 SSS designation
13 Identify with
14 Edifying org.
18 Scientologist Hubbard
19 Archimedes' cry
24 Alert for Friday
26 Chilled jelly garnish
28 Golf's ___ play
29 Desires
30 Mets field
31 Results of right-to-work laws
32 Providers of ocean views
33 Hotel amenity
34 Bolt partner
35 Simian

38 Welcome sight on flight boards
41 New Jersey cape
43 Disco dance
45 Phrase of agreement
48 Brazil seaport
49 Athlete's best effort
50 Street address alternative
52 Registers
53 "Aunt ___ Cope Book"
54 Colleague of Kent and Lane
55 Horse halter
56 Mosque prayer leader
57 MLB injury rosters
59 "R.I.P." singer Rita

THEMELESS by Brian E. Paquin
A wide-open challenger from a Canadian cruciverbalist.

ACROSS

1 "Spring ahead" hrs.
4 Challenging
8 Piles
13 Green org.
14 "Take ___ down memory lane"
16 Hogwarts student Macmillan
17 Encountered
18 Wily negotiator
20 Winter gutter barrier
22 Checkbox option
23 Eastern mister
24 Farm misters
25 Flaky
26 Extra
27 Has a bite
28 Type of wave
29 Rake parts
30 One eager to punch out
33 Mensch
36 Common CAPTCHA
38 Beauty or brains
41 Prospectors' finds
42 Thinker Descartes
43 Lecturer's lectern
44 A ___ apple
45 Gossip columnist Hopper
46 Pint in a pub
47 Grand Canyon St.
48 ___ up (neatens)
49 Sticky reminders
52 Before, to a bard
53 Do a bang-up job?
54 Flying pests
55 Mesh
56 Setbacks
57 Chop ___
58 J. Namath's 173

DOWN

1 Medium-sweet, in wine country
2 Diner deals
3 Ore-Ida nugget
4 Giggles
5 Elementary matter
6 School basics, initially
7 Ocean sunset locales, e.g.
8 ___ and now
9 Cold War ___
10 TV's "Sanford ___"
11 Justin Trudeau's father
12 Best-of-seven ___
15 Ideal score
19 "Mustn't do!"
21 Catches sight of
25 Internist's skill
26 Depicted exactly
28 Crawl through water
29 Yukon, e.g.: Abbr.
31 MLB pitcher nicknamed "Kitty"
32 German tennis star Tommy
34 Submissive
35 Was puzzled about
37 Silver services
38 Goes with the flow
39 Wild West hangout
40 Southern snooze
44 Dada creation
45 Kind of fit
47 Catches a bug
48 Head, in Le Havre
50 Office telephone game
51 College sweater letter

208 THEMELESS by Brian E. Paquin
28 Across is worth about a penny.

ACROSS
1 Big bomb
9 Shoulder warmers
15 Lou in "Pumping Iron"
16 Bluto's nemesis
17 Work as a turf accountant
18 Having a twist
19 "That squares things!"
21 TBS network
22 Potato tool
25 Churn up
26 Puts out (a runner)
27 Babylonian wind god
28 Hogwarts coin
29 Style of jazz
30 Chess pieces
31 Those who don't believe in spirits?
35 Meanie
37 Challenge
38 Medal of honor
40 Strive for
41 Trig. function
42 In this place
43 Sherilyn of "Twin Peaks"
44 Toil
46 Northwest European
47 Sweet cereal grass
48 Prokofiev's "___ and Lolly"
49 Forwards a Trump posting
51 "The Dark Knight" hero
53 In a guttural way
57 Pop up
58 Sensed instinctively
59 Measurement that is often squared
60 Lacking pizzazz

DOWN
1 Juvenile newt
2 Shell-game item
3 Miff
4 Worked on a boat
5 Roughage
6 Antiquing "cheater"
7 Social media discourse
8 Come up short
9 Salesman's pitch
10 Cornucopia
11 G.I. Jane's address
12 Got super excited about
13 Full of it
14 Faithful factions
20 Oscar-winning Brando role
22 "First Blood" hero
23 Flawless
24 Like Jordan almonds
26 Highway fee
28 "Felicity" star Russell
29 Treadless
31 A-1
32 Old wives' ___
33 Remorseful about
34 Shorthand pro
36 Big city haze
39 "Golly!"
43 Rock lobster?
44 One-edged sword
45 Ogden Nash animal
46 Twins share them
47 Swagger
49 Big name in pasta sauce
50 Victuals
52 CAT scan cousin
54 Season of nice weather in Nice
55 Renowned bandleader Brown
56 Passing stats

22 Down drove Ramona Hill to a 2020 Hambletonian win at the Meadowlands.

ACROSS

1 Reo maker
5 On one's uppers
9 Bastille Day's month
13 Fuel from a bog
14 It sailed past Charybdis
15 Bee-gotten
17 Heavy set?
19 Clark in "The Misfits"
20 Complete perfectly
21 Posting at JFK
23 Successor
24 Substance
26 Enrolled
28 Recoiled (from)
31 Construction worker
33 Vandals
34 Beatle hairstyle
35 Like some lawn mowers
38 Key near Ctrl
39 Dead set?
41 Zilch
42 They're bold
44 Order's partner
45 Headey on "Game of Thrones"
46 No. ___ (tourney favorite)
48 Relieved
49 "Feliz ___"
51 Trails off
53 Simians
54 Quick swim
56 Mischievous sort
60 "Our Gang" girl
62 Deep set?
64 Took steps
65 Yearn
66 Singer Fitzgerald
67 Canadian gas company
68 Big name in ice cream
69 Porn

DOWN

1 Newspaper page
2 Letterman's former rival
3 Wacky
4 Zany trio
5 Peace accords
6 Lucky strike
7 Hideous giant
8 Club roll
9 Spree
10 In the near future
11 Swing set?
12 Stiles student
16 Unlikely candidate for prom king
18 Surprise attack
22 Harness driver McCarthy
25 Norse thunder god
27 Not that
28 Spawning fish
29 Luau dance
30 Closed set?
32 High-tech watch
34 Israeli spy group
36 Niblick's number
37 Delighted
39 Reputation on the street
40 "The Sweetest Taboo" singer
43 Isolates
45 Glasgow girls
47 What toadstools aren't
48 "Voice of Israel" author
49 Zippo
50 Without delay
52 Jails a-sail
55 Push
57 Pre-storm status
58 Rights org.
59 Future JD's hurdle
61 Tumult
63 Whichever

OPTS IN*   by Jordan P. Conway
Pemaquid Point Lighthouse can be seen at 39 Across.

ACROSS

1 Dramatic dance
6 Time machine destination
10 Petty squabble
14 Buried Chipmunk item
15 Word in sale ads
16 Legal tender
17 Nassau is a popular one*
19 Bocelli solo
20 Game played in alleys
21 Six-pack component
23 Heads out
25 Public 10 Across
26 Some whiskey purchases
30 Give a push to
33 In total darkness
34 Muscleman's quality
35 Nonstick kitchen spray
38 B-school subj.
39 Bristol locale
40 Shirt named for a sport
41 Bar code?
42 Couldn't put up with
43 Gold or 16 Across
44 Miocene and Pliocene, for two
46 Stool pigeon
47 Scatter, as rose petals
49 "Later, gator!"
51 Removes from the throne
54 Holm of "All About Eve"
59 Arrow-shooting deity
60 Marilyn Monroe facial feature*
62 Bubbly wine
63 Huck Finn's craft
64 Dry-heat bath
65 Tax write-off
66 In days of old
67 Spotify offerings

DOWN

1 Arbitrator's skill
2 Pasture measure
3 Common or proper word
4 Golf club part
5 When first spotted
6 Desperado chasers
7 Colonial insect
8 Neat freak's opposite
9 Pound a Smith-Corona
10 Like hen's teeth
11 Alternative to UPS Ground*
12 Like many Russians
13 Macbeth's title
18 Mireille of "The Catch"
22 Channel for score updates
24 Most nimble
26 Pit stop intake
27 Machu Picchu native
28 Devo's headgear resembled these*
29 Pewter component
31 Kentucky politico Paul
32 Have yet to settle up
34 Bed ___ & Beyond
36 Stephen Baldwin's sib
37 Streetlight circler
39 Kind of apple or Apple
40 Tire pressure fig.
42 Cry of pain or laughter
43 Wall Street worker
45 Some fast-food sodas
46 Galley notation
47 Great buy
48 Sculpted body part
50 Intense, as pain
52 River of Aragon
53 Ex–press secretary Spicer
55 Birthright seller in Genesis
56 Created, as cotton candy
57 Soften, with "down"
58 JFK postings
61 NY Jets' org.

"IACTA ALEA EST" by Fred Piscop
. . . as Suetonius said to Caesar on January 10, 49 BCE.

ACROSS

1 First to strike Caesar
6 Take forcibly
11 Hieroglyphics critter
14 Ring-exchange locale
15 Boring tool
16 Cloak-and-dagger org.
17 Critical juncture
20 Fresh-mouthed
21 Unsettled issues
22 Was in awe of
23 Something to cast
26 "Peter Pan" dog
27 Parter of the Red Sea
30 Annapolis grad's rank
33 Insert into the lineup
34 "Masterpiece" airer
36 Showers with compliments
40 "Iacta alea est" (with 42-A)
42 See 40 Across
43 Like some jeans legs
45 Suffix in record books
46 NATO charter member
47 Newly invigorated
49 DuPont acrylic fiber
51 Raw bar morsel
54 Site of Mohammed's tomb
56 Books on tape, e.g.
59 Seek the hand of
60 Use an e-cig
64 Pass the 17 Across
67 Football filler
68 Praises to the skies
69 Fed the kitty
70 Homage in verse
71 Needing two seats, perhaps
72 Catches one's breath

DOWN

1 Al who created Li'l Abner
2 Salve ingredient
3 Show signs of awakening
4 "No way!"
5 Banksy's realm
6 Breakfast fare
7 Talks, talks, talks
8 Problem for a diva
9 Feudal drudge
10 Thing with growth rings
11 Lexus competitor
12 Mythical temptress
13 Bamboo eater
18 Fryer filler
19 Acid in red wine
24 Have high ambitions
25 Sugar meas.
27 Paperless pooch
28 Worker protection org.
29 Slip through a crack
31 It's under the cornea
32 "Beauty and the Beast" villain
35 BBC's nickname (with "The")
37 "Herzog" author Bellow
38 Calgary gas brand
39 "South Park" kid
41 Skin layer
44 ___ Perignon
45 Throw one's support behind
48 Takes the plunge again
50 Steep-sided valley
51 Chocolate source
52 Like many tabloid stories
53 Have a crush on
55 Poker pot note
57 Capital on a fjord
58 Poke with a pike
61 Gets off the fence
62 Participant in a slam
63 Doesn't go on forever
65 Paint swatch option
66 Happy hour hangout

212 CONCERTED EFFORT   by Mark McClain
. . . involving various instruments.

ACROSS

1 Bryn ___ College
5 One meaning of "S"
10 Canterbury locale
14 Melville's second novel
15 Yemeni metropolis
16 Spoonbill relative
17 Heralds of cold weather
19 Natalie Wood's sister
20 "Christine" hero
21 Speedy warship
23 Rest period
25 Haul around
26 Pentagon honchos
33 Waze info: Abbr.
35 Major appliance
36 America's Cup craft
37 Lead-in for motive or pilot
39 Project details, informally
41 Any of three "squares"
42 Performed abysmally
44 Do some work on a bush
46 17th Greek letter
47 Marionette attachments
50 MacGraw of "Love Story"
51 Apple Newton, initially
52 Razor asset
58 Bert's buddy
62 Pro-veganism org.
63 Car shoes press against these
65 Very dry

66 Jacob's wrestling opponent
67 Check before publication
68 Speck
69 Actress Portia de ___
70 Take care of

DOWN

1 Granny in "The Simpsons"
2 Latin love
3 Showing signs of use
4 Corkscrew pasta
5 Little Rock–Shreveport dir.
6 Downton Abbey worker
7 Green Gables lass
8 The Four ___ ('50s vocal group)
9 "And in conclusion . . ."
10 Weight unit in a Tesco store
11 "Buy it now" site
12 Supreme Court complement
13 Imperialist of yore
18 Gets over a troubled time
22 Red stone
24 Cherry discards
26 Got together
27 Baseball card company
28 Fend off
29 Come up again
30 Laptops from Taiwan
31 Ayatollah's predecessor
32 Normandy city

33 Wood file
34 Odile's black skirt
38 Prominently displayed
40 Hair salon sound
43 Certain seaweed
45 Wound down
48 Cravat clasp
49 Small attic
52 Mail app folder
53 Main character
54 Working hammer and tongs
55 Ian Fleming novel
56 Suppresses
57 Squeaks (by)
59 Like Michelangelo's "David"
60 "You can count on me!"
61 Cornerstone abbr.
64 Old Testament judge

213 CRYING INSIDE   by Mark McClain
Eddie Murphy first voiced 22 Across in 2001.

ACROSS

1 Aromatic tea
6 Baseball's "Sultan of Swat"
10 Party giver's request
14 Hot dog option
15 Home to most humans
16 Salon debris
17 "The" is our only one
20 Minerva McGonagall's Patronus
21 Anon partner
22 Shrek's friend
23 Urge to action
24 River between Indiana and Kentucky
25 Cause of a flight delay
29 Opening for "nail" or "nob"
32 How some reports are delivered
33 "Nothin' but ___!"
34 Ill humor
35 They can be pumped or bumped
36 ATP members
37 Org. for brainy sorts
38 Parlor designs, casually
39 Maple syrup source
40 Less of a people person
41 Mischievous, in a way
42 Evade the issue
44 Table leveler

45 Chess match result
46 "No more for me!"
49 Not in the office
50 Whiskey cask wood
53 Gray force
56 Coup d'___
57 Mideast prince
58 Office 365 app
59 Moist in the morning
60 Couple
61 Purchase alternative

DOWN

1 Grammy winners for "War Machine"
2 ___ butter (lip gloss additive)
3 Examine evidence
4 Mahbub in "Kim"
5 Necessary nutrients
6 Not for tots
7 Help-line caller
8 Hermana del padre
9 Steelworker's wear
10 Thick-skinned beast
11 Hacky ___
12 Downright awful
13 Capybara, to anacondas
18 Off-white
19 Exhausting labor
23 Assails with snowballs

24 Bakery sight
25 Trendy apartments
26 Typeface since 1982
27 Scrumptious
28 Like a klutz
29 Like most Indians
30 Elizabeth in "Godzilla"
31 Iris feature
34 Underlying
36 Contracted title
37 Slender marine carnivore
39 Spun out
40 Jeweler's weight unit
42 Drum brake part

43 Queen Elizabeth's uncle
44 Easy mark
46 Tea option
47 Tiny particle
48 Work on a bone
49 The "Toreador Song" is one
50 Dolphin cousin
51 City north of Des Moines
52 NASCAR's Petty
54 Australian coin bird
55 Long-handled chopper

214

UNSPECIFIED LOCATION   by Brian E. Paquin
66 Across is also the title of a 1963 Akira Kurosawa film.

ACROSS

1 "Open wide!"
6 Emerald ___
10 Used to be, formerly
14 Great Plains tribe
15 Norwegian king
16 Sty sound
17 All over
19 Mrs. Ned Flanders
20 Tarzan's friends
21 Consumed
22 Talk up
23 "My Gal ___"
25 Missouri's unofficial slogan
27 Thoroughly
33 AAA job
34 "___, With Love" (1967)
35 Noncleaning sponge
39 Quahog
41 Heavenly flareups
43 Mr. Ferrari
44 Vagabonds
46 More modern
48 Dieter's unit, briefly
49 In various places
52 Tijuana treat
55 "Softly ___ Leave You"
56 Knighted Guinness
57 Hunt down
61 Verne's mad mariner
65 Scotch mixer
66 Everywhere
68 Like a dime
69 Pale brown
70 Scrooge's one-time fiancée
71 Back talk
72 ___ out (scold)
73 2015 Stallone film

DOWN

1 Divan
2 Tout de suite, initially
3 Easily handled, asea
4 Rival of Sampras
5 Female lobster
6 Tall Corn State
7 Skirt feature
8 Take on cargo
9 Still
10 How some boxers fight
11 Dowager
12 Roman year
13 Blackhawk footwear
18 Conquistador Ponce ___
24 Home security brand
26 "Rattle and ___" (U2 album)
27 Tingle
28 Part of a plea
29 Clean the deck
30 In harmony
31 Big name in skin care
32 Weary in appearance
36 Back in the day
37 Baron
38 Pebble Beach target
40 Hudson Valley tribesmen
42 "Calendar Girl" singer
45 Ready to race
47 Some LSU linemen
50 To a degree
51 Obstruct
52 Observes Lent
53 Kauai greeting
54 Luke and Yoda, e.g.
58 Alternative to potatoes
59 Taj Mahal site
60 Buddy
62 "Legally Blonde" heroine
63 Beauty spot
64 Had debts
67 "The Blacklist" network

THEMELESS by Brian E. Paquin
Hint: The answer to either 28 or 29 Down is not "Little Joe."

ACROSS

1 Lighthouse fixture
8 More expansive
14 "To sum up . . ."
16 Camden Yards player
17 Playwright McNally
18 B-side of the Beatles "Help!"
19 With passion
21 Jen's "Hunger Games" role
22 Kind of milk that brings tears?
25 Greek promenade
26 Potato-chip brand
27 Rocker Rundgren
28 Regarding
29 "What?"
30 Patrol car alert
31 TVs, slangily
34 Rupture from overfilling
37 Summer headwear
38 Homer's addition to the English language
39 Mil. rank
40 Hamilton bills
41 Bubbly chocolate bar
42 Was acquainted with
44 Demond's "Sanford and Son" costar
45 Messed up
46 Feel strange
47 Pursuit of pleasure
49 Solar ___
51 Tesla cars lack these
55 Small of stature
56 Makes speechless
57 Lend a hand to
58 Bruises

DOWN

1 In fine fettle
2 ___ for the books
3 "I'm ticked!"
4 Presage
5 Obvious
6 Compost item
7 Required
8 "Tada!"
9 Ground force
10 "Toy Story" brat
11 Fell facedown
12 Bronco who wore #7
13 Doesn't own
15 Deteriorated badly
20 Fierce way to fight
22 Attempt
23 Internet ad
24 Hospital jewelry?
26 Elegance
28 One of the Cartwright brothers
29 One of the Cartwright brothers
31 Salerno loc.
32 Mandalay Bay action
33 Campfire treat
35 Winter blanket
36 Wearing footgear
41 Big name in Italian suits
42 Big name in Italian sportswear
43 McKinley's birthplace
44 Put back to zero
45 Guitarist "Sleepy" John
47 Ice-fishing shelters
48 Man, for one
50 Sundial hour
52 On-base club
53 Quiz whiz Jennings
54 Greeting from Kaa

216 THEMELESS by Harvey Estes
54 Across was our country's first known 23 Across.

ACROSS

1 Innocuous epithet
5 Prefix for America
9 Make a swap
14 McEntire sitcom
15 On ___ with (equal)
16 Quite a hit
17 SDI concern
18 Is unable
19 "The Wild Duck" playwright
20 "Screaming Eagles" soldiers
23 One who studies caves
24 Nemo's creator
25 A, e.g.
29 Title of respect
31 Greek salad cheese
33 Money set aside
34 Cops, slangily
36 Reagan was pres. of this
38 Coastal catch
39 Some navels
42 Freelancer's enc.
45 "Swan Lake" step
46 Becomes more frank
48 With the sound off
50 Storage unit on board
54 Louisiana Purchase president
57 Sister's attire
58 Area east of the Urals
59 Tempo-setting phrase
60 Crème de la crème
61 Lat. gender
62 Straight up, at the bar
63 Closet eaters?
64 Queens stadium
65 Volsteaders

DOWN

1 Faucet flaws
2 Postgame report
3 Make a long story short
4 Burrito cousin
5 343 meters per second
6 Ornamental shoulder pads
7 ___ Domingo
8 Brand of taco sauce
9 Ardent desires
10 Android science
11 Schoolyard retort
12 Difficult to fathom
13 Shore flock
21 "What's My Line" panelist
22 Bridgestone product
26 Sprayer from above
27 Kinks hit
28 Meadow moms
29 "Get lost!"
30 Take another tour
32 Remote batteries
35 Old Sturbridge Village artisan
37 Marlin, for instance
40 Will subjects
41 Litigates
43 Come up in a sub
44 Sermon ending
47 Kind of girl party
49 Brief trip
51 Badlands sights
52 "In your dreams!"
53 Board flaws
54 Gender-inclusive pronoun
55 Gabriel's aura
56 End note

INCONSTANT CONSONANTS   by Patrick Jordan
Can you guess the odd trait of the answer to 22 Across?

CROSS

1 Ladder parts
6 Greenhorn at West Point
11 Put in power
16 Skirt with a widespread hem
17 Aida, to Amneris
18 Arouse resentment in
19 Bluto's frequent expression
20 Kuwait and Qatar kingpins
21 Bright blue
22 Mariana Trench locale
25 Direct, as a dart
26 Gets a glance at
27 Tammany Tiger creator
28 Copious quantities
31 Bears do it
33 "What that person ordered"
34 Squad car occupant
37 **Odd trait of the answer at 22 Across: Part 1**
44 Avoid being noticed
46 Sports shoe company
47 Watts of "I Heart Huckabees"
48 "Here's another point . . ."
49 Money in the bank
52 Serving twin purposes
53 Heavy or sheet follower
55 Abstainer's amount
56 Stop hiding
58 **Odd trait: Part 2**
61 Dr. Ruth topic

62 "Let's try something ___"
63 Undercover 34 Across
65 Shape-slimming garment
68 More than occasionally
70 Still in the sack
74 Starting square
75 **Odd trait: Part 3**
79 Hootenanny instrument
82 Tossed dish
83 County in a Letts play
84 Spy-obtained info
85 Perform wearying labor
86 "2 Broke Girls" workplace
87 Literary adventurer Beau
88 Make a modification to
89 "___ Fell on Alabama"

DOWN

1 Speaks scratchily
2 Bones that parallel radii
3 Sibling's daughter
4 Layered type of rock
5 Medieval menial
6 Advanced algebra subj.
7 Wheels for the well-off
8 Vote out on "Big Brother"
9 Awaiting furnishings
10 Blonde "Frozen" queen
11 Spill-cleaning org.

12 Indie rocker Phair
13 Like a square's sides
14 "Treatise on Radioactivity" author
15 Forms swarms
23 Kin gained by marriage
24 Scriptural shipbuilder
29 Warning phenomenon
30 260 fortnights
32 Hiring fairness inits.
33 Doe's beau
34 Jumper cable feature
35 Former Houston gridder
36 Salsa alla genovese

38 Widespread ruination
39 Dorset Horn, e.g.
40 Charged for a late book
41 Whiskey-based drinks
42 Celeb's concern
43 Ovenware glass
45 Served as a pawnbroker
50 Oscar winner Hathaway
51 Body with six-year terms
54 Hang like a hound's tongue
57 Put a crack in, say
59 Got some good out of
60 Sequenced correctly

64 Keep tabs on Tabby
65 "___ or go home"
66 Laughably lame
67 Pays a flat fee
68 Common key in Chopin's works
69 "Make like a tree and ___!"
71 Safari leader
72 Itching to begin
73 ___-broom (woadwaxen)
76 Rae on "Insecure"
77 Nip-in-the-air season
78 Wordless approvals
80 Spa pulsator
81 "Terrific!" in Tabasco

218 NIRVANA by James Connolly
"I'll gladly pay you Tuesday . . ." —7 Across

ACROSS
1 Surgical garb
7 Popeye's fat friend
12 Radiator's sound
16 Up-and-comer
17 Left the recliner
18 Fail to mention
19 1946 Hope/Crosby movie
21 Olive Oyl's mother
22 Pixar dinosaur
23 Secluded valleys
24 Sire, biblically
25 Green lights
27 Stab, so to speak
28 Musical measure
30 "You" homophone
31 Buffalo skater
33 No-frills
35 Morse "T"
38 Eric Clapton song
43 On cloud nine
45 "You bet!"
46 Prefix meaning "billionth"
47 Gave a fig
48 Gourmet mushroom
50 Miserly Marner
51 Concert stage array
52 Airline ticket datum
53 Rope in
54 Happiness based on false hope
58 Wino's affliction
59 Gastric juice components
60 Kitty starters
62 Place for a rubdown
65 "The loneliest number"
66 Awful coffee
67 Befitting a monarch
71 Explorer John or Sebastian
73 ___ Major (Sirius's constellation)
75 "Vissi d'arte," e.g.
76 In need of irrigation
77 Result of a perfect union
80 Update, as décor
81 Blow away
82 Firebird
83 Lifeline reader
84 Toned down
85 Good-natured exchange

DOWN
1 Paint, in a way
2 Slopping the hogs, e.g.
3 Non-imaginary numbers
4 Cancels out
5 Spam sender
6 Skyline obscurer
7 Groundskeeper, at times
8 Twist from O. Henry
9 Swabs' tools
10 Pitchfork-shaped letter
11 "I'm in favor!"
12 Put to a whetstone
13 .gif or .tif file
14 Muscle-bone connector
15 Governor's domain
20 Prefix with violet
24 Runny cheese
26 Full, and then some
28 Old hat
29 Like an unswept fireplace
32 Certain twin
33 BMX ride
34 "Shut up!"
35 Brew that won't give you a buzz
36 San Antonio shrine
37 Oprah's production company
39 Somewhat, informally
40 Sound, as an argument
41 Pass into law
42 Rhinoplasty targets
44 Car named for an inventor
48 Victor at Gettysburg
49 Dory propellers
50 Villainous look
52 Turn in a game of dreidel
53 Guinness suffix
55 Speaker with a burr
56 Intimidated
57 Bollywood's home
61 Protect, as freshness
62 Painful reminders
63 "Gay" capital of song
64 Put up with
66 Indian corn
68 African bard
69 Theater path
70 Eye surgery tool
72 Ammonia attribute
73 Pack like sardines
74 Unkempt sort
77 A welcome sight?
78 Health org. since 1847
79 Auto grille cover

CAPPERS by James Connolly
46 Across is a popular bar mitzvah dance.

CROSS

1 Iraq's principal port
6 MLB team accused of sign-stealing
12 Mineralogists' studies
16 Fall bloom
17 Layers studied by geologists
18 Whimper like a baby
19 Make like a dreidel
21 "Put your money away"
22 Muscle-bone connector
23 Do perfectly
24 Rode the waves
26 Art Deco master
27 Lose luster
29 Bedtime ritual
30 Raring to go
32 Celestial shower type
35 Big name in bowling centers
38 Kind of A/V cable
39 Hoops squads
40 Airport pickup option
43 Coin flipper's phrase
45 Felt nostalgic
46 Dance done to "Hava Nagila"
47 Collective bargaining side
48 Instruments for Parker and Coltrane
49 Verb in two Commandments
50 Handy hints
51 Copy center supply
52 Like some fingerprints
53 Earth-friendly prefix
54 Kit Kat layer
55 Geisha's accessory
56 Sci-fi weapon output
57 Not unusual
59 Place for tiki torches
61 Name on fairway mowers
63 Italian port on the Adriatic
64 Degrees for execs
68 Roll call notation
70 Word after pack or gym
71 1951 Brando shout
73 Turnpike fee
74 Create a ruckus
77 Boosters at the Yale Bowl
78 ___ skiing (Olympics sport)
79 Sculpting medium
80 "The Sweetest Taboo" singer
81 Pre-euro Spanish coin
82 Watergate evidence

DOWN

1 Turkey recipe word
2 "___ our conversation . . ."
3 Time spent on duty
4 Hand down a verdict
5 He sang of Alice
6 Say "May I?"
7 Regular beau
8 Make an outline of
9 Post on Yelp
10 Ear-related prefix
11 Depletes gradually
12 Port of Portugal
13 Take shelter
14 Bull on a Glue-All bottle
15 In sorry shape
20 "Actually . . ."
25 Duct tape's many
28 Nabokov title heroine
31 March 17 slogan word
32 Any of the Seven Dwarfs
33 Holiday lead-ins
34 Bill's time-traveling pal of movies
35 Sharp-witted
36 In a tizzy
37 Go bananas
39 Handyman
41 Gladiator's milieu
42 Off one's rocker
44 Part of LAPD
45 Solar energy collector
46 On a winning streak
48 Cushiony seat
49 "Will you allow me?"
51 Topper with a pom-pom
52 A bit tardy
54 Brown songbird
55 Hardly within walking distance
58 Threat ender
59 Protection for an idea
60 Mafia's code of silence
61 Palm fruits
62 Virus named for an African river
63 Count of jazz
65 Softly hit fly
66 Without help
67 Holders of valuables
69 Mouse catcher
70 Lambastes verbally
72 Reason to cram
75 Brewpub brew
76 AriZona beverage

FACTORY VISITORS by Todd Gross
"So shines a good deed in a weary world." —Willy Wonka

ACROSS

1 Dance moves
6 Ferguson and Kilborn
12 Top card
15 Dave Garroway's show
16 Bank staff
18 Road occupant
19 Golden ticket holder
21 Coffee container
22 CBS series since 2003
23 Made like new
24 Money in Italy
26 Cracker topper
28 Golden ticket holder
30 Suffix for slogan or wagon
31 Alphabetical, for one
33 Frosted dessert
34 Harbor feature
35 Slide down
36 Put a stop to
39 Take place
42 Help a felon
45 Very well
48 Golden ticket holder
51 Deer horn
52 SPECTRE villain
53 Pester
54 Grant in "Plaza Suite"
55 Morning times
57 Go around and around
59 Dench in "Spectre"
61 Pick up the check
63 Long sandwich, for short
66 Golden ticket holder
70 Purify
72 Form of evidence
73 Two trios
75 Helper: Abbr.
76 Bathtub booze
77 Golden ticket holder . . . and final winner
80 Ryan of "Top Gun"
81 Blooper for LeBron
82 Congressman Hoyer
83 Sales pitches
84 Gets a C, say
85 Lucas Oil Stadium team

DOWN

1 Political position
2 "Well played!"
3 More controversial
4 Take a break
5 The S in CBS: Abbr.
6 Whodunit feature
7 Incorporate the latest updates
8 Bass player?
9 Wastrel
10 King clam
11 Full-house initials
12 Luxury vehicle brand
13 Holiday air
14 Iowa senator Joni
17 Give a lecture
20 At that spot
25 Work with
27 Uptown gala
29 Queeg's minesweeper
32 Not too bright
34 Clout
35 Use a phaser
36 "Spenser Confidential" director
37 Alan in "Flash of Genius"
38 "No, Mikhail"
39 Spoon-shaped
40 French film
41 ___ d'Azur
43 Tanning salon units
44 Musical acuity
46 Set on fire
47 "Misery" star
49 Kind of school
50 Hybrid tea
56 "Timecop" star
58 Second section
59 Dubya's brother
60 Central New York city
61 Silicon Valley cars
62 Install a new floor
63 Ebert's former partner
64 Like draft email
65 White and Grable
66 Molten rock
67 Short confession
68 Brooklyn's county
69 Win, lose, and draw
71 Ex post ___ (retroactively)
74 They can swim backward
78 Big bone
79 John Wayne's alma mater

ACROSS

1 Takes a meeting with
5 Summertime swarm
10 Tank engine of TV
16 Put swaddling clothes on
17 Energy or entry follower
18 Black out, in a way
19 2012 film with three Oscars
20 "Ben-Hur" venue
21 Code of silence
22 Dress pattern, properly?
25 Model builder's buy
26 Shower that slickens streets
27 Picnic shade source
28 "To Have and Have Not" hero
30 Tonsorial Depp role
33 Gives consent
35 British flag, properly?
41 Tiny degree
42 Bamboo piece
43 Cartography close-ups
47 "My heart skipped ___"
50 They make kitties grow
52 "Sunrise, Sunset" singer
53 Receive news about
55 1935 Kentucky Derby winner
57 WasteWise program org.
58 Misfit, properly?
62 End the conference
65 Beowulf's beverage
66 Gather the old gang again
67 Some happen in hammocks
71 Inactive periods
75 Kiltie's cap
76 Spectrum invoice, properly?
79 University of Illinois location
82 Stick for 62 Down
83 Periodic table stat
84 Charity offering
85 Gazpacho ingredient
86 Nip's pal
87 Bully's threat
88 Minds the bar
89 Lunging weapon

DOWN

1 1955 Kentucky Derby winner
2 Ron Weasley's owl
3 First manned moon lander
4 Had words with
5 Tickled pink
6 "I, Claudius" emperor
7 Keep from occurring
8 Four-part harmony voice
9 Pool table top
10 Home of Russell Sage College
11 Mini border
12 Idolizing verse
13 Like crooked cards
14 Getting things done
15 Nine have panhandles
23 Lots and lots
24 Iron's output
28 In insufficient supply
29 Undergoing angst
31 LP scratchers at clubs
32 Persian Gulf capital
34 Taoist's life force
35 "Industry" state
36 Japanese hot-pot dish
37 Brainy breakthrough
38 Pulitzer or Peabody, say
39 Brief claim of innocence
40 Starting lineup
44 Even once
45 Hunt and peck
46 Delta assignment
48 Insurance scam crime
49 Hat in "Ratatouille"
51 Ornamental pillowcase
54 Lassie's coat
56 Verb after you or they
59 Princess Elsa's sibling
60 Impudent boldness
61 Admire to an extreme
62 Maestro Toscanini
63 More highly valued
64 Mishmash
68 Monastery manager
69 Board smoother
70 Take effect over time
72 Displayed sudden glee
73 Jousting weapon
74 Smog component
76 Rick's place, for one
77 Croquet ball material
78 Rustic lodgings
80 Feel afflicted
81 A forerunner of GameCube: Abbr.

SNIGGLING   by Jim Leeds
Bigfoot fans will know the answer to 47 Down.

ACROSS

1 Mixes it up
6 Apple relative
10 Pops, to tots
15 Amp schlepper
16 Polaris bear
17 "1234" singer
18 Piaf's "La Vie ___"
19 Zodiac border
20 Steed's partner
21 Area near NYU
22 Like gift cards
25 Ryan's "Sons of Anarchy" role
26 Staggering dizzily
27 Clydesdale color
28 Kind of bore
30 Slip or trip
31 Treasure Island locale
34 Center of L.A.
36 Cast leader
37 Second sight
40 Put on the telly
41 Fiber food
43 Keyboard bar
46 Bow rub-on
50 Sweepstakes
52 "It's ___ unusual day . . ."
53 Tarnish
54 Get ready to drive
55 Least prevalent
57 Flash Gordon's love
58 Needed: Abbr.
60 You can drop into this
61 Each
63 Cause of glandular fever
67 Book by strategist Sun Tzu (with "The")
71 Droning beetle

72 Head start?
75 To this point
76 "Watchmen" network
77 Prepares to be knighted
79 Discussion
81 "You Make Me ___ Young"
82 Umeda Sky Building locale
84 Droid: Comb. form
85 Canadian Conservatives
87 Miami team, to fans
88 Maleficent
89 Position properly
90 Ducks behind bushes
91 Badger's den
92 "Na zdrowie!" is one

DOWN

1 Arizona desert
2 North Carolina moniker
3 Smart scale company
4 "___ for Ricochet": Grafton
5 Oozings
6 Brownish purple
7 Flare up
8 Much, to Mascagni
9 Some rafters shoot them
10 Award for an RAF ace
11 Tesla model
12 Put to rest, as a rumor
13 Have grand plans
14 Heinz Field team
15 Kidney artery

23 Swedish rug
24 Statistics
27 ___ Paese cheese
29 Wild retreats
32 Spa jets
33 Salt
35 Vain about
38 Cross home
39 Obsolete Spanish coin
41 Lunch favorite
42 Lobster coral
44 72, at Augusta
45 ACLU concern: Abbr.
47 Monster truck stunts
48 In the infirmary
49 "Science Guy" on PBS
51 "Stiffelio" is one
56 Ore-Ida nugget

59 Wilde remark
62 Kitty with no fur?
63 Former Big Apple mayor
64 Tiny tree
65 Former "Vogue" editor Diana
66 Takes a long look
68 Hearty bread
69 Missing
70 Hennery feature
73 Ham spice
74 Riding garb
78 "I Wish" rapper ___-Lo
80 GM green car
81 Arizona's Agua ___ River
83 Mule's sire
86 Italian gold

THE OLD SWITCHEROO   by Jim Leeds
13 Down holds 3 ounces and is used for espresso.

CROSS

1 "Singing Cowboy" Gene
6 Some Marine NCOs
11 Venomous snake
16 Hang
17 Places in the heart
18 Fountain of Rome
19 Marriage counselor's sphere?
21 Many a "Today" show sign
22 Having one sharp
23 Words to an old chap?
24 Converts to bone
26 Wishes undone
28 Barn door fastener
30 Siberian tent
31 Rob of "90210"
33 Calliope, e.g.
35 False
39 "High Hopes" insect
41 New York Times Co. v. United States, e.g.
43 Tracy and Hepburn, often
47 Fourth dimension
48 Minority medical student org.
49 French donkey
50 Tennis star Monfils
52 Adirondack retreat
54 Nipper
55 Seized item
57 Tenterhook
59 Relevant
61 Epithet for Anaïs Nin?
64 "Hamilton" star Phillipa
65 Instead (of)
66 Cold spell
68 New York cardinal
72 Source of light
74 Recipe directive
76 Genoese magistrate
77 Michael Jackson album
81 "The Man" singer Blacc
83 Muumuu go-with
84 Megan on "The Blacklist"
85 Ad slogan for Omaha Steaks?
88 Mensa locale
89 Forward payment
90 Deep-six
91 Hornpipe cousins
92 "The Deep" director
93 Knocks off

DOWN

1 Look up to
2 Father of the Titans
3 Walmart rival
4 Campus in Troy, NY
5 Himalayan mystery
6 Bowed greeting
7 Bypasses bedtime
8 Weimaraner warning
9 Jackson 5 member
10 Fresh
11 Eager
12 Vagrants
13 Shot size at Starbucks
14 Bacchanal cry
15 Edges
20 Hockey stick wood
25 "Baby Love" singers
27 NYSE membership
29 College prep exam
32 Fly in the ointment
34 Label of 77 Across
36 Utah peaks
37 Matt in "The Great Wall"
38 ___ Dogs (2012 "AGT" winners)
40 Waveless
42 "HuffPost," e.g.
43 "Money" singer ___ B
44 "Last ___ is a rotten egg!"
45 Petal support
46 Ex-Patriot Junior
51 Perjures
53 Urge on
56 KFC option
58 Fresnel ___
60 "___ Indigo"
62 Loudmouths?
63 "Wonder" singer Merchant
67 What drones lack
69 Vladimir Nabokov novel
70 TSA, for one
71 Stallion sounds
73 "Let ___ Again" (Sinatra song)
75 French Bourbon?
77 Lake Tahoe lift
78 Pocket problem
79 Learning method
80 Mother of Hera
82 Winds up
86 AED user
87 3280.8 ft.

"OOPS!"   by Richard Silvestri
"The Oil City" is the nickname of 24 Down.

ACROSS
1 Persian Gulf nation
6 Nobel, for one
11 British bishop's headdress
16 Man without a country
17 All in
18 George Jetson's son
19 River formation
20 Cronelike
21 Wimbledon winner Fraser
22 Fowl cars?
25 Dunderhead
28 Straight
29 PIN place
30 Louisville Sluggers
32 Tie the knot
33 Prefix for while
35 Piece of animation
38 Went after flies
40 Series segment
42 Wide mouth
43 Be a kvetch
46 Fail to mention
47 Touring company's slogan?
52 Audi alternative
53 Eat away at
54 Long-running NBC show
55 Home of Gallo Winery
57 Some zoo workers
61 Hydrocarbon suffix
62 House opening?
64 In the style of
65 Marquee name
66 Sounds of satisfaction
67 Clever comeback
70 Freudian topic
71 Carnival ride for jewelers?
75 Hitching post?
76 Calendar notation
77 Indian prince
82 Pizzeria order
83 Puerto Rican port
84 Get home safely?
85 Silly Soupy
86 True partner
87 Macaroni shape

DOWN
1 Proof sign-off
2 Lizzie Borden's weapon
3 Up to, poetically
4 PC key
5 Ring advantage
6 In need of laundering
7 Showed disomfort
8 Satie and Estrada
9 Take out
10 Tree of life location
11 Amahl's creator
12 End of the small intestine
13 Sting operation
14 Indiana, to Harrison
15 Seeing things
23 Redcoat general
24 Wyoming city
25 Six-pack makeup
26 Dust maker
27 Stock panic
31 Kind of gun
34 Monopoly payment
35 Finish
36 Emmy winner Falco
37 Reply to "Shall we?"
39 First prime
41 They're heard but not seen
43 Pursue with passion
44 Cabinet dept.
45 Wrath
47 A few
48 Second word of a fairy tale
49 Follow-up exam
50 Sci-fi film with a 2010 sequel
51 Malt ending
56 Fields of activity
57 Showed contempt for
58 Tombstone marshal
59 Syncopated song
60 Sellout sign
63 Noah of "The Daily Show"
64 Immediately
66 On the double
68 1985 Kate Nelligan film
69 Not windy
71 Colleen
72 ___ podrida (stew)
73 Gas or elec.
74 Oct- minus one
78 Every last bit
79 Triangular sail
80 Fuss
81 Cut down

PRECRASTINATION   by Richard Silvestri
"I don't know. I can't tell the future, I just work there." —The Doctor

CROSS

1 Bit of hardware
6 Climbing plant
11 Terra follower
16 Angry in the extreme
17 As ___ (usually)
18 Self-evident truth
19 Kidney-related
20 Kind of pneumonia
21 Fab Four name
22 **Start of a resolution by the Doctor**
25 Addled by age
26 Slapstick missile
27 Fermentable liquid
31 PC key
32 A winner breaks it
34 Former fast flier
37 Dodges
39 Calls into question
41 Take pleasure in
42 Genesis peak
46 MC alternative
47 **Middle of resolution**
50 Let go
51 Calculus calculations
52 A little off
54 Burton brew
56 Menu listing
57 Serpent tail?
58 Lofgren of the E Street Band
60 3.0, e.g.
62 Seasonal song ender
63 RR stop
64 Hound
67 **End of resolution**
74 Lake near Reno
75 Gives a darn
76 Make fun of
77 Subject of a watch
78 Concert site
79 Time for a shower?
80 "Flowers for Algernon" author
81 Item of value
82 Unqualified

DOWN

1 Voice of the iPhone
2 All hands on deck
3 Hindu princess
4 List shortener
5 "War of the Worlds" author
6 "La Bamba" singer
7 Hot
8 Like some pregnancies
9 Dry red wine
10 Protagonist
11 Traveling showmen
12 Rust, for one
13 Salon service
14 Burkina Faso neighbor
15 Word from a Latin lover?
23 Big bucks
24 Snobbish
27 Is no longer
28 Of a reproductive gland
29 Gear position
30 Figures of speech
33 Monroe's successor
34 Synopsis
35 Raise one's grade?
36 Cowpoke's nickname
38 Singing syllable
40 Puts on a coat
42 Disney mermaid
43 Backboard attachment
44 "Wheel of Fortune" purchase
45 Col.'s command
48 Big Ten team
49 Canterbury can
50 Justice Dept. division
53 Linus Van Pelt's shirt
55 National songs
56 Right on most maps
59 Topiary tool
60 "Bonanza" star
61 Volkswagen model
63 Beat the goalie
65 Dr. Kildare portrayer
66 Attack
67 Final check?
68 Sea call
69 Final Four initials
70 Seized vehicle
71 Kind of board
72 Home to billions
73 Give a hoot
74 Sound of disapproval

226 TAKE THE "A" TRAIN   by Lee Taylor
Daniel Webster and Franklin Pierce are both alumni of 15 Down.

ACROSS

1 "Matilda" author
5 Baking potatoes
12 Of sound mind
16 Face shape
17 Its capital is Asmara
18 Visa rival
19 "Nautilus" captain
20 Taking a stand against
21 Olfactory sensor
22 Kid with base behavior?
24 Cause of black lung disease
26 R&B quartet ___ Hill
27 Major conflict
28 Bert's "Sesame Street" buddy
29 Homer Simpson exclamation
32 Instagram uploads
35 Kitchen whisk
36 Ludicrous
38 Foot-long sandwich
39 "It's freezing!"
40 Major blunder
42 Grecian Formula target
47 Roman orator
48 Tony winner Hagen
49 ___ de Cologne
50 Farm measure
51 Dance of Dublin
53 Shakespeare noble
55 Smallest cont.
56 Gave the go-ahead
57 Left ventricle exit
58 Calyx leaves
62 Skeleton site?
64 Napier of "Home Town"
65 Montoya in "The Princess Bride"
66 Boy in a Johnny Cash song
67 Ballot marks
69 Act agreeable
71 Locale of slanted columns
76 Sign of things to come
77 "Day ___": Beatles
79 Pastel shade
80 Egghead
81 Inclined to look the other way
82 Talking Stick team
83 Designer Schiaparelli
84 Larger-than-life figures
85 Coach K

DOWN

1 Spanish lady's title
2 State with conviction
3 Soccer great Mia
4 Doc Brown portrayer
5 Mirror graffiti in "The Shining"
6 Fertilizer component
7 Recipe instruction
8 Pigpen
9 Evergreen shrubs
10 Pavarotti or Caruso
11 "Volsunga ___"
12 Justice O'Connor
13 Check number
14 Bella Swan's daughter
15 Andover's school rival
23 Succinct
25 Far from convinced
27 Virtual surfing spot
29 Ten, in Torino
30 Comparable (with)
31 Part of Hispaniola
33 In the current situation
34 Solzhenitsyn's prison
35 Coffee maker brand
37 Noncoms
39 Pigtails
41 French dip's dip
42 "Greed is good" speaker
43 Sacred glow
44 Bitter-tasting
45 Frothing at the mouth
46 Played again
52 Fire extinguisher gas
54 Like upscale communities
56 Bullfight cry
58 Gold medalist Biles
59 Cloisonne material
60 Cheapskates
61 Meeting plan
62 Stage manager's job
63 Puts forth effort
66 Rocky debris
68 Muscle contraction
70 "___ be all right"
71 Forthcoming
72 Hang in the balance
73 Here, in Havana
74 Engine buildup
75 Leisure
78 "National Velvet" horse

TAKE THE "O" TRAIN   by Lee Taylor

1 Down was Connie Francis' biggest hit and reached #1 in the UK Singles Chart.

CROSS

1 Bridge forerunner
6 Tippy tops
11 Rotating engine parts
15 Temporary tattoo ink
16 Go from first to second
17 Engrained behavior
18 Social event at Dunder Mifflin?
20 Cause to smile
21 Brief stay en route
22 Hindu god with an elephant trunk
24 "___ overboard!"
25 Page-turner, e.g.
27 Harry Potter, for one
31 "Not only . . ."
32 Classic soda brand
33 Damascene
35 Fonda in "9/11"
39 Sugar craving
41 Men of the hacienda
43 "Ich bin ___ Berliner": Kennedy
44 Ages and ages
45 Philip of "Kung Fu"
46 Satisfied sigh
47 Computer virus
49 Chekhov play
53 Big rig
54 Stir up
55 Hold to be
56 Start of a Christmas carol
59 Salinger or Soulé
61 ER procedure for a fractured ulna
64 Big racket
65 Yacht race
66 Like mortarboards
71 Gobsmacked
72 Pasternak's physician
75 Not in a million years
76 Chopin opus
77 Cornwall neighbor
78 Reined right
79 Like the VCR
80 VCR option

DOWN

1 "___ Sorry Now?"
2 Bulk
3 Useful facts
4 Scissors sound
5 City south of Seattle
6 Quaker in the woods?
7 Blacken a burger
8 ISS predecessor
9 Little newt
10 Hellishly dark
11 Nigeria neighbor
12 Treat badly
13 Collins on "Supernatural"
14 Place
17 Mr. Rogers portrayer
19 Northwestern U. site
23 Knee injury site
25 Pack it in
26 Four Corners corner
27 Beginnings
28 Upgrade the electrical
29 Wunderkind
30 Shake a leg
31 "Dude!"
34 Hither partner
36 Temporary wheels
37 More overcast
38 "Ain't That ___": Fats Domino
40 Coffee alternative
41 Meek
42 Part of SASE
45 Ice Bucket Challenge cause
48 Made a picture puzzle
49 Plastic ingredient
50 Like a buttinsky
51 Spielberg's shout
52 Gator tail
54 Put on display
57 "Ring of Bright Water" animal
58 Drunken IM message
60 Off the streets
61 Squeeze dry
62 Lyric soprano Fleming
63 "___ at the office"
64 Stupefied
66 Bay of Fundy wonder
67 At any time
68 Magma
69 Prima donna traits
70 Wrapped up
73 Hagen in "Key Largo"
74 Groovy track?

228 NASHVILLE CONNECTION   by Wren Schultz

A clever theme from a noted wordsmith and "Wheel of Fortune" winner.

ACROSS

1 Patch up
5 Abet, in a way
11 Landlocked SE Asian land
15 Like one who can take it
17 "Finding Nemo" hero
18 See 16 Down
19 Singer of 44/54 Across (with 20-A)
20 See 19 Across
21 Ragtop alternative
22 Word preceding torch or bar
23 SLOTUS (2001–2009)
24 It might replace "gee" or "haw"
25 Teen woe
27 Split decision?
29 Road crew supply
32 Takes in
34 It's on your list
35 It's crimped into the ferrule
37 Beginning of "the end"?
39 Regale again
44 Song referenced in clue* answers? (with 54-A)
46 Rat
47 "I Do" singer Loeb
48 Bakery whiff
50 Pub pull
51 Put atop
54 See 44 Across
57 Rarely seen Scot
58 Scottish John
59 With one's feet up, maybe
60 They're no secret at Victoria's Secret
62 CBer's "please reply"
64 General on a menu
65 Mad Hatter's creator
68 Cheese burg
70 Peace Nobelist Murad
71 Where to get dates
74 Hambletonian Stakes distance
77 Sportscaster Andrews
78 Celebrated
79 Bumbling
81 Excited
82 Seasonal stalactite
83 Excited
84 Paleontologist Geller*
85 Waitress Green*
86 Actor Tribbiani*

DOWN

1 NY Knicks' home
2 Californie, for example
3 Dragon Roll wrap
4 Ex-Bears coach Mike
5 Maple Leaf, for Canada
6 ___ a soul
7 Chess great Nimzowitsch
8 "Call Me" rockers
9 "Some ___ Hot" (1959)
10 Tennis center?
11 Cooler unit
12 In homeownership, it's above all
13 Climate change factor
14 Drains
16 Yucatán Mayan ruins site (with 18-A)
24 Mercutio's friend
26 Jerk
28 Skateboarding half-pipe ramp
29 Nonstick surface
30 Come to
31 Ups
33 Keep from burning, say
36 Willis Tower, formerly
38 Cajun chef Prudhomme
40 Many a Scorpio's birthstone
41 Trigger
42 Bedding
43 Start of a stadium cheer
45 Utter
46 Maxim
49 Kissing disease
52 Scales in the sky
53 Tesla model
55 Said "nolo"
56 City WNW of Cheyenne
58 Following Fatima's faith
61 Camel cousin
63 Pitcher, for one
65 Freighter load
66 "Bye, amigo!"
67 Olympic pentad
69 "Megatron" singer
70 Word with miss or beer
72 Where to find 57 Across
73 Equine hybrid
75 Ed Sheeran's "___ House"
76 Fencing equipment
78 Cone locale
80 Have a go

SECOND TO NONE   by Pam Klawitter
The first 30 Down–marked item ever scanned was a pack of Juicy Fruit gum.

ACROSS

1 The Munsters' car
7 Romanov royals
12 Depeche ___
16 Shell out
17 Poole, to Jekyll
18 Bridget's role on "Blue Bloods"
19 Granny Smith, to Grandpa Smith?
21 Banned insecticides
22 Perez in "Birds of Prey"
23 Jaffe or Barrett
24 Plan to lose
25 What Eric Clapton's band once was?
30 "Suits" network
33 Hindu Mr.
34 Sought a seat
35 Slippery swimmer
36 Okefenokee Swamp denizen
38 Williams of "Get Out"
42 Throws in
43 Mexicali meat
45 Bread-box size
47 Choice findings on the roadside?
52 Ike's Texas birthplace
53 Really aggravates
55 Girls' weekend getaways
58 Keynote speakers
61 Military standing
62 "___ a perfumed sea": Poe
63 Questionable factors
64 "___ for Outlaw": Grafton
66 Pronoun for Miss Piggy
67 Nicest of the Brady kids?
73 Vance on "NCIS"
74 Miner's quests
75 Stallone role
79 Sherilyn of "S.W.A.T."
80 Latest additon at the junkyard?
83 Muffin type
84 Sandbox retort
85 "Scat!"
86 Romantic destination
87 One about to be shot
88 Beginning stages

DOWN

1 Get wind of
2 Fair kin
3 Droid downloads
4 Smithsonian artifact
5 Scornful looks
6 Shogun's capital
7 Claire Dunphy, for one
8 Refuse consent
9 Shake like ___
10 Creator of Curious George
11 Abbr. on a business card
12 Doc on the front lines
13 Used Grubhub
14 Said the same
15 Winning trio
20 Hardly hale
24 Cub's home
26 Fireman's stat
27 Blog pest
28 Asian capital
29 Online urging
30 Lines at the checkout counter
31 It's found in bars
32 Cultural opening
37 How music was once stored
39 Tons of, slangily
40 Words before water or pursuit
41 "I ___ reason why . . ."
42 Fairy-tale ender
44 Squeeze out a win
46 Hunting vehicle
48 Type of switch
49 Lou Gehrig's base
50 Big test
51 Truckee River city
54 Go cross-country
55 Break down
56 Kitchen gadgets
57 London football club
59 Yank out of the bunk
60 Part of a Vegas nickname
63 Cyclotron bit
65 Fly barrier
68 British heavy weight
69 Has aspirations
70 Jagged-edged
71 Get behind
72 LOLs
76 Parcel (out)
77 Brandling, often
78 Makes a choice
79 Dillinger's nemesis
80 Dance specialty
81 Guadalajara gold
82 Premium cable channel

ACROSS

1 Gluck of the opera
5 Improvises some riffs
10 Charcoal drawing, e.g.
16 Canvassing type
18 Boot part
19 Resort of 3 Down
20 Earned, after expenses
21 O.T. book
22 1944 Philippines invasion site
23 Mellow
24 Bale contents
25 Skilled worker, briefly
27 Iraqis, e.g.
29 Man cave's forerunner
30 Get bigger
34 Baseball card stat
35 "Frozen" character
37 Long ago, long ago
38 Fossey, who engaged in gorilla welfare
39 "I Shot Andy Warhol" star Taylor
40 Curve shape
43 Eye tinters
45 Blow up
47 Point of interest
49 "The Crucible" town
51 Ralph of "The Waltons"
52 Cheers up
54 Threaten
56 Generic guy in "Dilbert"
57 Apple carrier
58 "House" actor Omar
60 Cosmonaut Gagarin
62 Family diagram
63 Southern Hemisphere constellation
64 Begins immediately
68 HST succeeded him
69 Just know
71 Cry of frustration
72 Olympic gymnast Raisman
73 Frequency meas.
74 Bust place
78 "___ declare!"
79 "Scent of a Woman" star
81 Holder of 21 merit badges
83 Bombastic speaker
84 "Save the Whales" group
85 Ariana Grande's dress size
86 Listerine victims
87 Lacking width and depth

DOWN

1 Lets in
2 Let out
3 Enclave of SE France
4 Gallery objects
5 Word after viva
6 Every 24 hours
7 Human being
8 Raft propeller
9 Sign of a Broadway hit
10 Prison on the Hudson River
11 Cap locale
12 NY hrs.
13 As far as humanly possible
14 Something to start over with
15 Delilah portrayer Lamarr
17 Mideastern hill
23 "Chiquitita" group
26 Rte. 66, e.g.
28 Gotten out of bed
29 River feature
31 Capital on the Oregon Trail
32 JFK info
33 Kauai garlands
36 Pitched in
38 Erasures
40 The best
41 Source of x-rays
42 Feline chicken?
44 Hong Kong harbor sight
46 Big-mouthed pitchers
48 Out-and-out
50 BLT topping
53 One place to spot whitecaps
55 Give a nod to, perhaps
59 Head honcho
61 Lance at court
64 Kind of counter
65 Cleveland resident
66 Bring on
67 Beeped
70 Catch in a trap
72 Price phrase
73 Gordian ___
75 Walken's "Joe Dirt" role
76 Lady birds
77 Mind reader's gift
80 "Lord, is ___?": Matt. 26:22
81 Sight in a T. rex nest
82 Corporate VIP

231 THEMELESS by Harvey Estes
Think "football" at 44 Down.

CROSS

1 "Dunno"
10 Dental compound
17 Best pair
18 Emerge
19 Yellow vessel of song
20 Ancient ascetic
21 City area, informally
22 Make piles
23 Tommy's gun
24 "Mazel ___!"
25 Join the army
27 Song for Scotto
29 Cover, in a way
31 Rod attachment
32 Inconsiderate
33 Clean energy type
34 Shot source
37 Boxer in "Cinderella Man"
39 Inside diameter
40 Ever so sincere
42 FBI guys
44 Pump product
47 Personal appearance
48 Ill-bred
50 NY winter hrs.
51 Spoke one's mind
53 Alexandra, e.g.
56 Ship that could talk
57 Really steamed up
59 "Arthur" Oscar winner
63 Toon with a blanket
65 Let out
67 Cafeteria list
68 Platform article
69 Boxing's Oscar ___ Hoya

70 Blarney attraction
72 Frequently, in literature
73 Naughty kids
75 Cold feet
77 Staff note
78 More like a thick fog
80 Where future attorneys study
82 Raptors play here
83 Kid's hideout
84 Vehicles with bells
85 Analyzed closely

DOWN

1 Publishers, e.g.
2 Open, for example
3 Water fountain
4 Bark beetle victim
5 Build up
6 Pack to the future?
7 Agitate
8 Kind of block
9 Ethnic ending
10 Cel material
11 Greater amount
12 Changes for the better
13 NASA craft
14 Solo
15 NAPA inventory
16 Hillary's conquest
23 Founder of Reprise Records
26 "I am a villain; yet ___": Shak.
28 Grill seasonings
30 Dressing gown
32 Nota ___ (note well)
35 Be specific about
36 City layouts
38 Hub-to-rim lines
41 Menu section
43 Trait bearer
44 Some kickers try to split them
45 Spring hoax victim
46 John Hancock
49 Primal impulse
52 This may be proper
54 Whiskered barker
55 Passed-hat contents
58 Seasoned vets
60 Leaves
61 Set free
62 Fought, in Folkestone
64 Aspen activity
66 Hunting trip
70 Beer truck freight
71 Prefix for type
74 SMU center: Abbr.
76 Mouflon mamas
79 Luau paste
80 Canadian corp.
81 In ___ signo vinces

232   A RIVER RUNS THROUGH IT   by Bonnie L. Gentry
. . . and through it and through it.

ACROSS

1 "None for me, thanks"
6 Like Noah's passengers
12 Kind of paint
16 Oscar-winning role for Sally
17 Responsibility for a groundskeeper
18 It's often added to a million
19 Risky to the max
22 No. on a periodic table
23 Is doubled?
24 Dutch artist known for optical illusions
25 2019 Miss America Franklin
26 Rarely seen item on casual Friday
27 Ref. that recently added "bigsie"
30 It may change with a promotion
31 Playing fast and loose
35 Homer Simpson's outburst
36 Prove to be mistaken
37 Junk, e.g.
40 Moved to a new home
44 Dyson product, briefly
46 "___ lighter note . . ."
47 "With this ring, ___ wed"
48 Fate of Ferdinand Marcos
50 "Would you look at that!"
52 Chairman of the Cultural Revolution
53 Resort amenity
55 Speakers at memorial services
57 Bassist John Such
59 Bucky Beaver's toothpaste
61 Tokyo-based IT company
62 They're banned in Hawaii
68 At full bubble
70 Support for Atletico Madrid
71 Peppery
72 Hail-fellow-well-___
73 Knock-down drag-outs
75 Night, to the Bard
76 Do some practice punching
77 Emulate Samson?
82 Once, it meant "once"
83 "Problem" singer Grande
84 Sinks in the muck
85 Root words?
86 Persisted with
87 Vehicles for winter trails

DOWN

1 Crib occupant
2 "The Merchant of Venice" heiress
3 Indian encountered by Columbus
4 Target of Internet filters
5 Mattress problem
6 "Stormy" bird
7 ". . . even ___ speak"
8 "Bring ___ pray you . . .": Shak.
9 Peter Pettigrew's disguise
10 Ordinal suffix
11 Shelley's "Modern Family" role
12 Takes a liking to
13 Entertaining laser displays
14 Doing a pirouette
15 ___ verte (green clay)
20 San Francisco street that crosses Ashbury
21 Wine made from the Moscato grape
26 Govt. securities
27 Subject for teacher's pet?
28 Snaky swimmer
29 Material of no consequence
32 Pierre's brilliant thought
33 Goat with recurved horns
34 It may be sun-brewed
38 When some tiebreakers are broken
39 Clemson helmet features
40 "Green Mansions" heroine
41 End-of-roster abbr.
42 Kiwi product
43 Approach excitedly
45 Convincing, as an argument
49 Big Island feast
51 Sounds from a sot
54 "___ for Peril": Grafton
56 Early even score
58 Law office visitors
60 Feel crummy
63 Shake ___ (get moving)
64 It's passed in pews
65 In need of refining
66 Like many company cars
67 Put in bold type
68 Dinosaur DNA preserver
69 Catcher known for his malapropisms
74 Wounded Knee loc.
75 Sicily's highest point
76 Dirty bed?
78 It's drawn from a vein
79 Reddi-___
80 "Mr. Basketball" Holman
81 Pinafore letters

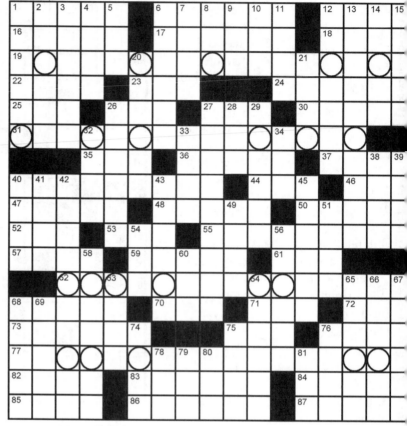

AFTER THE FALL   by Jim Page
An off-the-wall theme from a veteran wordsmith.

ACROSS

1 Beetle larva
5 Manet's "___ at the Folies-Bergère"
9 Down the road
14 Prince Louis' grandmother
15 Popular DVRs
17 Exhilarating
18 Dish named after 46/50 Across?
20 "The Sopranos" restaurateur
21 Roman goddess of fruit
22 Mighty mount
24 Viking quaff
25 Online food-ordering co.
26 Hermione Granger's Patronus
28 Passive protests
30 Improve on
31 All-clear signal after the fall?
33 Ultimatum word
34 Piedmont bubbly
35 "Mighty ___ a Rose"
38 Ski spot near Santa Fe
41 Healing sign
44 Star over Paris
46 Off-the-wall character? (with 50-A)
49 Copacabana city
50 See 46 Across
51 Muse of astronomy
52 Coastal eagles
54 Goddess with a horned crown
55 Rock group Steely ___
56 Source of pollen
58 Wear well
61 What 46/50 Across experienced?
64 Smog alert stat
67 Thusly
69 Sorrel in "Adam Bede"
70 Tiebreaker
71 The Travers, e.g.
72 Fibula neighbor
74 Time-honored sayings
76 One voice
78 How 46/50 Across failed to land?
80 Request of Mr. Bojangles
81 Coco contemporary
82 Winery sights
83 Furlongs in a mile
84 Petite poodles
85 Café sign

DOWN

1 Male "arm candy"
2 Ames Brothers classic
3 Reverse
4 Bird in a hayloft
5 Cell energizer
6 Jacqueline in "September"
7 "___ santé!"
8 Womanizer
9 "Gotcha!"
10 Molasses cookie
11 Shirley in "Goldfinger"
12 "Hasta la vista"
13 Changed locks?
14 Home ___
16 Hogwarts homework
19 Pledges
23 Lost on purpose
27 Draws
29 Verdi aria
32 He passed Ruth in 1974
33 SportsCenter channel
35 Gloss targets
36 Prefix for meter
37 "Superwoman" singer Alicia
38 Lead-balloon noise
39 Surrounding glow
40 OPEC member
42 Brookie basket
43 Go public with
45 Fail to name
47 Sabbath contribution
48 Most quick to the helm
53 Piggy bank feature
57 Plaza Hotel girl
59 Play the role of
60 Free fall
61 Rough draft
62 Religion of Tokyo
63 "Death of a Naturalist" poet
64 Silvery white
65 Waiting lines
66 NYPD ranks
67 Oahu veranda
68 Short-handed NHL act
71 Insolent
73 "Pikes Peak or ___!"
75 Sarah McLachlan song
77 So far
79 "You got it!"

THEMELESS by Theresa Yves

In India, 21 Across is known as the dog flower.

ACROSS

1 Rug rat
8 Bon mot
17 Garden-variety
18 At bottom
19 Fits
20 Tref
21 Flower with spiky blooms
23 Cleo of jazz
24 Songs for one voice
25 "Six Feet Under" vehicles
27 Fork over, with "up"
31 Melissa of "Wayward Pines"
32 Run off
33 Where some students study
35 CPU
40 "Lemon Tree" singer Lopez
41 Waikiki welcome
42 Cross one's fingers
43 "Grey's Anatomy" setting
47 Competes
48 More or less vertical, at sea
49 Mick or Keith
50 Heading for a splashdown
52 Grows up
54 "___ No Sunshine"
55 Balanchine step
56 Over and done
57 Physical endurance
61 1992 Nicholson biopic
63 Hermit
64 Michelin product
69 New York waterway
72 1970 World Series winners
73 Green land
74 "Black Magic Woman" band
75 America, abroad
76 "When Will ___ Again?" (1974 hit)

DOWN

1 Day planner features
2 Roasting place
3 Penn. neighbor
4 Discontinue
5 Finishes a flight
6 Easter event
7 Car dealer offerings
8 Lushes
9 A party to
10 Half score
11 Chiding sound
12 Fence off
13 Romero who played the Joker
14 "It's ___ Kiss" (1964 hit)
15 Public spectacle
16 Paris parents
22 Sticky stuff
25 Stir
26 Dana of "The Sting"
27 Still serving
28 C.S. Lewis kingdom
29 Comparatively hackneyed
30 "Ready Player One" author Cline
32 WWE star Lesnar
34 Augsburg article
35 Make one's case
36 "Zip it!"
37 State bordering Arizona
38 Thinks out loud
39 Measure again
41 Prevent, as danger
44 Greeted and seated
45 Toothpaste in "Grease"
46 Erhard's self-help org.
51 Punk, e.g.
52 Partners in crime
53 To the extent that
55 Seal group
57 "George Washington ___ here"
58 Temple text
59 Licorice-flavored plant
60 Track events
61 Forces to go
62 Dress shape
64 Go bananas
65 Haul around
66 "Now ___ me down . . ."
67 Gambling city
68 Jacob tricked him
70 Astral altar
71 D.C. team member

THEMELESS by Theresa Yves

13 Down comes from a Cantonese word meaning "swallowing clouds."

CROSS

1 Where to hop, to Dr. Seuss
6 Award for Cameron Diaz
0 Binge-watcher
6 Hidalgo "Hi!"
8 Emulate the Gregorians
9 Sponsor's spiel
0 Spectator areas
1 Last pt. of SASE
2 Wave makers
3 BB propellant
4 Do doilies
5 Shriner sword
7 Salad toppers
9 Some trig ratios
0 Like burdensome toil
1 It may be swelled
2 1950 film noir classic
3 Five faculties
5 "Better Call Saul" network
8 Woes
1 Mall constituent
2 Like Mr. Clean
4 Got under the skin of
6 Tallow ingredient
7 Small stream
9 Food shortages
1 Kissing in the park, e.g.
2 Laundry headaches
4 Board game piece
5 Oohs' partners
7 Like strawberries in the spring
9 Lines of clothing
3 Added to the scrapbook

64 Element named after dynamite's inventor
65 Conduit bend
66 Spill catcher
67 Grapevine item
68 Golf major
69 Cottonwoods
71 Beaver, to Wally
73 Like some fingerprints
74 Prime property location
75 Garbo and Bergman
76 Roach, for one
77 Speeding bills

DOWN

1 Dwell on
2 Shade
3 Like hipbones
4 Monogamous partner count
5 Bulletin board messages
6 "Three stripes" sportswear co.
7 Bottle size
8 Raincoats or computers
9 Fire residue
10 Mystical experiences
11 Butts in
12 Hellenic H
13 Chinese menu favorite
14 At risk
15 Musical marks
17 Cuspidor
23 Horror film director Aster

26 Author Rita ___ Brown
27 Enter on all fours
28 Adds color
30 John in "The Big Lebowski"
32 "You wish!"
34 Stiff bristle
35 Basics
36 Emergency declaration
37 Something to start over with
39 Flag thrower, at times
40 State rep.
43 Franklin, religiously
45 Detroit suburb
48 Patella

50 Swerve to the side
53 Cruel bunch
56 "Low Bridge" mule
58 Janet, to Tito
59 Front-line action
60 Gas thief's tool
61 City on the Willamette
62 Common sense
63 Sounds the bells
64 Art studio subjects
67 Pilaf ingredient
70 Club staffed by GOs
71 Keystone figure
72 Prefix for annual

236 CROSSING BOUNDARIES by Fred Piscop
Pick up a 63 Across and start solving!

ACROSS

1 Not as ruddy
6 Peach discards
10 Subway wall art
15 Like a gymnast
16 Where Margaret Mead studied
17 Cause to chuckle
18 Digital clock punctuation
19 Pageant crown
20 Meaner than mean
21 Reptile depicted in hieroglyphics*
24 W.C. Fields persona
25 Catches sight of
26 Archie, to Meghan Markle
27 Fiery emotion
28 NHL tiebreakers
30 "Not to mention . . ."
31 Early word for baby
33 College URL ender
34 Bridge installer's deg.
35 Galileo's hometown
38 Loaf pair
41 As opposed to
43 "The Thinker" sculptor
44 Demonic doings
45 Complete, as a comic strip
46 Palette selection
47 Former Intel CEO
48 Tag sale proviso
49 Unprecedented
50 River of the Carolinas
51 Sparrow's home
52 Was shy, in a way
53 Tailor's border
54 Tool set
55 Diner fare that's "slung"
57 HOV lane vehicle
58 Chef's vessel
59 Interest fig.
61 Nearly forever
63 Puzzle-solving aid
65 Portfolio holding, for short
66 What countries referenced in clue* answers span
71 Lo-cal food phrase
73 Bouquet tosser
74 First Lady after Hillary
75 Campaigner's blunder
76 Successful dieter
77 Invite for coffee
78 Fashionista's concern
79 Still-life vessel
80 Cries buckets

DOWN

1 Rate measured by a Fitbit
2 Really excited
3 Easter bloom
4 Bonds on the run
5 Airbnb payments
6 Showing anguish
7 Apples since 1998
8 Snowblower name
9 Former Volvo rivals
10 Procrastinator's reply
11 Thurman of "The Producers"
12 Stoli, e.g.*
13 Tycoon on the Titanic
14 MacArthur return site
16 Used bibs' features
22 Apple tablets
23 Winged Godzilla foe
28 Danish seaport
29 Hard, chewy candy*
32 PGA's John ___ Classic
33 Perrier competitor
34 Press for payment
35 Propelled, as a punt
36 Worshiped one
37 Title for Elton John
39 Enter headlong
40 Wintry downfall
42 Slangy sib
43 Act the nomad
46 Female walrus
47 Citrine, for one
49 "Ain't gonna happen"
50 Joe in "Home Alone"
53 Game pursuer
56 Living room piece
57 Toot
58 "I beg of you . . ."
59 Worrisome engine noises
60 Zagreb native
62 Unreactive, like neon
63 Grace under pressure
64 Acquired family member
67 Cornfield pest
68 Microwave, slangily
69 Travelocity booking
70 ___ serif (type style)
72 Buffalo Bills' old org.

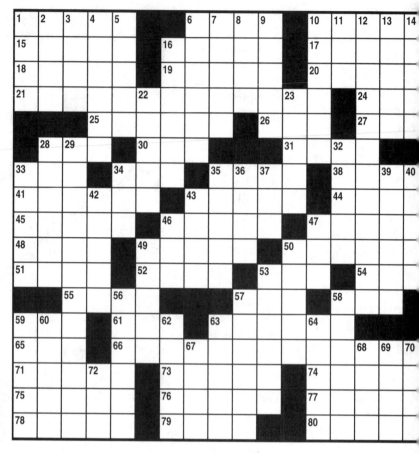

ACROSS

Bow of silents
Close, as a buddy
Calamari
A daughter of Lear
Seek forgiveness
Prevention measure?
Head off
Competed at Henley
Like pools on a beach
Trent Reznor's group
GoDaddy.com purchase
NJ clock setting
Part of a two-piece
Vientiane native
Gets the gist of
All cheered out
"Scram!"
Wide receiver's asset
"I wouldn't touch that with a ___!"
Puts to rest
Decks out
Be sociable
Siren's sound
Clod buster
New York swinger?
Surfing catch
"___ for Trespass": Grafton
"Honor Thy Father" author
Passe-partout
Place for a quarterback sneak
Most-preferred invitees
Surrealist Jean
63 Leave high and dry
65 Metro map point
68 MS. reviewers
71 Prefix for wife
72 Ruffman of "Avonlea"
75 Freight measure
76 Kennedy Era fitness challenge
80 Sans-serif typeface
82 Beantown hub
83 Haul to the station house
84 Backgammon piece
85 End of a Garbo line
86 Like the SEALS
87 Temporary tattoo dye
88 Retreads
89 "Camille" novelist

DOWN

1 Long-necked bird
2 Jeans label
3 Smiley or Smart
4 Like blue lobsters
5 Virus fighter
6 Wine rack on wheels, say
7 Tweeter's "Then again . . ."
8 Scattered seed
9 Tatum of "Paper Moon"
10 Targets of Trump tweets
11 They're often bombed
12 One the ___ vive
13 Not called for
14 Words of concern
15 Wooded valleys
23 Influential DC lobby
24 Access with a password
29 Additive sold at AutoZone
30 Become well
31 Anago, at a sushi restaurant
32 Either of two on a line
34 FWIW part
35 Made sure of
36 Without toppings
37 Beethoven's "Für ___"
39 Stir up, as trouble
40 Tramcar contents
41 Muscat resident
42 Walks the earth
43 Use elbow grease
45 Chinese dog breed
50 So last year
52 Join with a blowtorch
54 Paving crew need
55 Sib's nickname
57 Catered to base emotions
59 Kennel cry
60 PETA prefers them faux
64 Be out of sorts
65 Secret stockpile
66 Linz cake
67 Burger topper
69 C-sharp equivalent
70 Vodka brand, familiarly
72 1/60 dram
73 Curly-tailed dog
74 Biotech focus
76 Dog's annoyance
77 "Son of Frankenstein" role
78 Leonine locks
79 Streaming video service
81 Cape above Cod

THEMELESS by Harvey Estes
60 Across comes from the Italian word for "foothill."

ACROSS

1 Pen person
7 Army attack helicopter
12 Spit with vigor
16 Jane once of "Today"
17 Diarist Nin
18 Cinquefoil, e.g.
19 Positive aspect
20 Propeller heads
21 Underground type
22 Absolutely loathe
23 Part of the leg
24 Instant beginning
25 Granada greeting
27 In seventh heaven
29 Defensive success in baseball
33 Place for hardheaded presidents?
34 Light musical drama
35 Director Kazan
36 Some Noel decoration
37 Bridge makers
42 Bringing up the rear
43 Thought-provoking
44 Farm herder
49 Frankie Valli's voice
53 Style of gold chain
54 Not the real thing
55 They're tight-fisted
59 Not to mention
60 Turin's region
61 Fox of Remus tales
62 A lot, maybe
63 Worth keeping
65 Put folders back
70 ___ ex machina
71 Of greater concern
72 Skechers rival
73 Shore scavengers
74 Standing tall
75 Perch grabbers
76 McGwire's 1999 rival
77 Tranquil periods
78 So-so evaluation

DOWN

1 Starchy veggie
2 Good Hope, for one
3 Reddish brown
4 Former netman Nastase
5 Ersatz ghost costume
6 Canine
7 Over 200 Bach works
8 R.E.M.'s "The ___ Love"
9 Shaven and shorn
10 Deride
11 Booth, for one
12 Dr. Seuss character
13 Lickety-split
14 Cream-filled pastry
15 From what source
26 Concrete spreader
28 Pointer's word
29 Ducks and turkeys
30 "The Color Purple" star
31 Peewee or Della
32 Shipping case
38 Best example
39 Brief tussle
40 Grand name
41 Future fungus
45 Senior dance
46 Naive crusader
47 Start shooting
48 Hand signals
49 Thick-shelled nuts
50 Pt. of USA
51 Eggheads
52 Eyeballed
55 Dark suit
56 Chicago suburb
57 Recycled programs
58 Texas oil city
64 Anabaptists, for example
66 Occupy to capacity
67 Matinee figure
68 Hit the runway
69 Canadian gas brand

THEMELESS   by Harvey Estes
40 Down is also a 2017 film short about teen chauvinism.

CROSS

1 Enterprise Center, for one
6 Nudges
12 Harry Potter ID mark
16 Lounging slippers
17 Hugh on "Chance"
18 Set of standards
19 Misses
20 Not moving
21 Apple media player
22 Dame of South Bend?
23 Reacted to a scare
24 Kind of dream
25 Intermediate karate level
27 Part of SPCA
29 Desk site
30 Parade barrier
31 Plague bug
34 Ice dancer Torvill
35 Sea in "Waiting for the Sea"
36 Sesame seed paste
39 Got some shut-eye
44 Bumper dings
46 Esbat group
47 Temple reading
48 Lower, as prices
49 Come forward
51 Quote an authority
52 Subsided
54 This way
56 Big name in boxing
60 Streisand's "Funny Girl" role
62 11-year-old, e.g.
63 Canned fruit
67 "There ___ frigate like a book": Dickinson
68 Smitten one
70 Toothpaste brand
71 Bring crashing down
72 Baseball's "Mr. Tiger"
73 Vital carrier
74 Helm location
75 Kampala's country
76 Tricky problem
77 Midlothian miss
78 Basketball team, e.g.
79 Agent 99's partner

DOWN

1 In the midst of
2 Grapevine item
3 Glitterati
4 Bottom line
5 Green lights
6 On cloud nine
7 In recent days
8 Beyond well done
9 Blast-furnace input
10 Aphorism
11 Put in writing
12 General who defeated Hannibal
13 Jam locale, sometimes
14 Makes one's own
15 American all-nighter
26 Target of a practical joke
28 Treasure holder
30 Not so nutty
31 Buckos
32 Baseball's Hershiser
33 Water-to-wine town
34 Talked nonsense
37 Joint coverage?
38 Nice and cozy
40 Place for a pep talk
41 Buffalo's lake
42 Touches lightly
43 Telly's big telly role
45 Sex researcher Hite
50 Ivy League team
53 Disband
55 Polar coverings
56 Milky Way's shape
57 Andress in "The Blue Max"
58 Wish granters
59 Deals with guilt
60 Starr of old comics
61 Peruse anew
63 It may be fine
64 Vice follower
65 Aromatic compound
66 Pitch the first inning
69 Jones in "Mars Attacks!"

240

ON THE FARM   by Fred Piscop
55 Across was John Travolta's breakout role.

ACROSS

1 Ernest and Julio's winery
6 Burn with hot coffee
11 Leaders' positions
16 One way to think
17 Verboten
18 Blockhead
19 Upscale home furnishings chain
21 Formal decrees
22 All-inclusive
23 Parlor artwork, for short
25 Part of a tall cake
26 Takes a meeting with
27 UPS alternative
30 Mortar mate
32 Brownish-gray shade
34 Say "pretty please"
35 Letters on a Coppertone bottle
38 It may be marked by low inflation
45 Can't stomach
47 REO part
48 Sheriff Andy's fishing partner
49 Put to rest, as fears
50 M-1 or M-16
52 Pork cuts
53 Thomas who lampooned Tweed
54 Fireplace blackener
55 "Welcome Back, Kotter" Sweathog
56 Global warming factor
60 Responders with defib units
61 Torah holder
62 Like Neil Young's voice
64 California surfing spot
68 B-ball
70 "What a pity"
74 The Bard's stream
75 World Cup score
77 Arrange by category
79 Humidor item
81 Place for a Minuteman
84 Flared dress style
85 Elite squad
86 Broadcaster
87 Grew dimmer
88 "You're Sixteen" singer
89 Witherspoon of "Big Little Lies"

DOWN

1 Stares slack-jawed
2 Solo
3 Lenya of "Cabaret"
4 Medieval musician
5 Baltic Sea feeder
6 Messy digs
7 Vehicle that's hailed
8 Taper off
9 Dr. Seuss title creature
10 "___ mention it!"
11 Kept out of sight
12 Polishes before printing
13 Legally OK
14 "Psycho" setting
15 It may be blank or icy
20 Prove false
24 Glasses
28 Energy Star org.
29 Junior League member
31 Lead-in to centric or maniac
33 Grayish-white
34 Eliot's "Adam ___"
35 Street talk
36 Completely opposite
37 Answer in a simple quiz
39 Hay holders
40 Architectural add-on
41 Time when the sun is highest
42 Speak one's mind
43 1/60 dram
44 Assenting replies
46 Sharon of "Valley of the Dolls"
50 Knight's board neighbor
51 Debtor's letters
52 Kudrow of "The Boss Baby"
54 "Dunno" gesture
55 Worker for a feudal lord
57 Catch with the goods
58 Brian who produced U2
59 Break in continuity
63 Iconic TV canine
64 Big-beaked mimic
65 St. Teresa's home
66 Go online
67 Totally pointless
68 Nation of Hispaniola
69 Cohort of Kent and Lane
71 River of Tours
72 Where Van Gogh was prolific
73 Keep on file
76 Dorsey of "Selma"
78 Blacken on a grill
80 Cerise or cardinal
82 Yield to gravity
83 Texter's "Just sayin' . . ."

PENNY LANE   by Fred Piscop

In 1793 the penny was 100% copper. Today, it's 97.5% zinc and 2.5% copper.

CROSS

1 Castaway's signal
6 Mideast holy war
11 High-quality, as beef
16 Clark's partner in exploration
17 Launch an insurrection
18 NFL mascot Poe, e.g.
19 ___-jazz (Coltrane genre)
20 Freak out
21 Emmy or Edgar
22 You could get it for a penny once
25 Financially secure
26 Long, long time
27 Judge to be
28 Museum attraction
29 With ___ breath (anxiously)
32 Cherry variety
36 Read the UPC of
39 First zodiac sign
40 "Flip or Flop" concern
41 You could get it for a penny once
44 Star close to Venus?
45 "Heidi" peak
46 Itty-bitty
47 Seat seeker, briefly
48 Cleveland hoopster, briefly
49 Water park fixtures
51 You could play it for a penny once
55 Stuck in muck
56 Brownies group
57 ___-book exam
58 Taken in, in a way
59 Made macaroons, say
60 Played for a fool
62 iPhone image
64 Inning ender
65 "I figured so!"
68 You could get it for a penny, once
74 Ned who composed "Miss Julie"
75 Container with slats
76 Far from unwitting
77 Reader's download
78 Tin Pan ___
79 Committed to
80 Stop pedaling
81 Wins in a laugher
82 Gain popularity on Facebook

DOWN

1 Diamond defects
2 Flood-preventing barrier
3 Keep vigil for
4 Bathtub residue
5 "America's Mermaid" Williams
6 Kyoto's land
7 Birthplace of Bahaism
8 Like two of a dog's legs
9 "Think again, pal!"
10 Unscrambles a signal
11 Talk gibberish
12 Natural brown pigment
13 Lendl with 94 singles titles
14 "A ___ formality!"
15 Culminate
23 Young'un
24 Country legend Foley
28 Aesopian insect
29 Auto grille cover
30 Word before quotes or guitar
31 Chaough of "Mad Men"
33 Feature of Mars
34 Like a generic brand
35 Second Commandment word
36 Cramps, e.g.
37 Scottish dog
38 Shoot for the moon
39 The Red Baron, e.g.
40 Remove text
42 Blew away
43 Guitar innovator ___ Paul
44 Lawn-patching material
47 Gloppy fare
50 Inhabitants
51 Object of Indy's quest
52 Sushi roll garnish
53 Fish-and-chips fish
54 Pantheon member
56 Transporter of sulfuric acid
59 Respond to a bad call
60 Atlanta, to Delta
61 "It's about time!"
63 Orbiter with a nucleus
64 Toes the line
65 Quartz variety
66 HOMES lake
67 Add a rider to
68 Clown of renown
69 Prima donna's solo
70 Guthrie in "Roadside Prophets"
71 Bengay, e.g.
72 Sch. near the Rio Grande
73 Fancy pitcher
74 DVR button

242 THE EGG AND I*   by Emil Sappington
A theme explanation can be found at 48 Across.

ACROSS

1 Keep moist, in a way
6 Bundle of grain
11 Young lad, in Dublin
16 Drive forward
17 ___ loading (marathon prep)
18 Rose pest
19 Ripe target for pirates once*
21 Gaggle members
22 Gazelle group
23 Frizzed, as hair
24 Prohibition agent Eliot
25 Tram cargo
26 Analyze grammatically
27 Mount Olympus dwellers
29 Banned substance in MLB
30 Tina's role in "30 Rock"
31 Company store currency
34 Split-resistant wood
37 Soothsayer's deck
39 Suffix with gazillion
40 Lipton product
41 Was decked out in
44 "The Music Man" protagonist
46 "Hogwash!"
47 Like some odds, ironically
48 Varieties of these begin *clue answers
50 Breathe like a hot dog
51 Architect Maya ___
52 Fit for farming

53 Name on a check
54 Restroom, informally
55 Teen's interjection
56 Peace Nobelist Yitzhak
59 Hydrogen's atomic number
60 Scrooge's Christmas purchase
62 Chinese zodiac animal
63 Steven Tyler, to Liv
66 Meg of "The Women"
68 Out there
70 Second-largest bird
71 Watson of "Noah"
73 "Texas Tommy" dance move
75 Genesis shepherd
76 Embroidered ornament
78 Jerusalem prayer site*
80 Lamp dweller of lore
81 Water-loving mammal
82 Guitar-playing "Glee" character
83 Rob of "90210"
84 West Yorkshire city
85 One way to play

DOWN

1 Knight's neighbor
2 Unit of electrical current
3 Showed leniency toward
4 Work the bar

5 Nashville's ___ Young Band
6 Fast-paced piece
7 Gaza militant org.
8 Wipes clean
9 Irish Rose's love
10 Loving, as a memory
11 Groceries holder
12 Turn topsy-turvy
13 Platter at a wine bar*
14 Hershey candy
15 Homages in verse
20 Part of a flight
26 Drawing board creation
27 Some Little Leaguers
28 Pundit's piece, briefly
32 Nolan Ryan's spanned 27 years

33 Mob scene
35 Freetown coin
36 Non-glare finish
37 "Long" or "short" amount
38 Ancient capital of Egypt
41 "Anybody home?"
42 Like Audubon's art
43 Source of much U.S. coinage*
45 Pledge of Allegiance ending
48 Victim of Artemis
49 Deadly shark
50 One-star review
52 Bit of fish tank gunk
53 "That's a shame!"

57 Merry Men, notably
58 Dunkin' Donuts worker
61 Recyclable tech products
63 Kennedy–Nixon event
64 2009 Swank biopic
65 More like dishwater?
67 Skull and Bones member
69 Didn't dawdle
71 Upper hand
72 "The Simpsons" tavern
73 Illegally off base
74 Townshend of the Who
75 Off-course
77 "Of course!"
79 Catch red-handed

RANDOM DRAWINGS   by Harvey Estes
"Pie crust" is another anagram of 75 Across.

CROSS

1 Easy catch
5 Bloke
10 Humpty Dumpty's evil twin?
16 Come together as one
17 Verdi classic
18 Revisionist?
19 Charges for quarters
20 Play the lead
21 Cosa ___
22 Communion wine holders?
24 Hints for travelers?
26 Very plentiful
27 Aardvark entree
28 Carbon compound
31 Gamboling
35 Goofs up
40 Ancient Egyptian scrolls
42 Use a track
43 Initials at Calvary
44 Suffix with Samson
45 Lamentations follower
46 Gardens in the sands
49 Dry cherry seeds?
51 Large-scale corrosion?
53 Russian range
54 Rival of ancient Athens
56 Marie Antoinette's king
57 Standing in the military
58 Word on a door
59 Aft

61 Kind of statesman
63 Tiger type
65 "Ben-Hur" costumer designer
66 Vane dir.
68 King of Broadway?
70 Rooms at the cardiology clinic?
75 Drawings (and anagram of five answers)
79 Favorite hangouts
80 Dull discomfort
82 Lose ground
83 Enduring hits
84 Observed
85 Dig find
86 Works with meters
87 Moves crippled cars
88 Does nothing

DOWN

1 Jaguar engine sound?
2 "Tell me ___ haven't heard!"
3 Part of a peck
4 Plumb
5 Joe in "The Irishman"
6 Comics ghost
7 Website statistics
8 Toothpaste box letters
9 Hair line
10 Neighbor of Nigeria
11 Takes on
12 Frisbee, for one
13 Cry of shocked hurt
14 "Rango" director Verbinski
15 The "Fat" in "Fat Tuesday"
23 Florence art museum
25 Seafloor stinger
28 Food connoisseur
29 Musical sign
30 Divisor, e.g.
32 Annoying
33 ___ generis
34 Cage-fighting practice
36 Deceitful one
37 John Hancock, e.g.
38 Do a laundry chore
39 Chapel in the Apostolic Palace
41 Crunch units

46 Enumeration abbr.
47 Hosp. worker
48 "Bound for Glory" singer
50 Sommer of film
52 Slanted to the right
55 Stimpy's pal
60 Like faculty heads
62 News agency founder
63 Rouge or noir
64 Sigourney Weaver sci-fi film
67 "Urban Cowboy" heroine
69 Cheri in "Scary Movie"
70 Karate blow
71 ___ Verde Valley

72 Like some awakenings
73 Blue funk
74 Right on the map
75 "What a relief!"
76 Rock partner
77 Jean Stein bestseller
78 Min. parts
81 Corporate VIP

244 "I'LL BE AROUND" by Harvey Estes
A 1973 hit by the Spinners gave Harvey the idea for this theme.

ACROSS

1 Staff symbol
6 Snide expression
11 Peddles
16 Motrin competitor
17 River resident
18 Colorado River craft
19 Sarge's superior
20 Circumvent
21 "What ___ to do?"
22 The Parthenon was an example of this?
25 Obdurate
26 Ready
27 College football trophy
31 Plant pests
33 Serious encroachment
34 "No need to explain"
36 Bird of Arabian myth
39 Source of online conflict
40 Garden decorations
41 Affluent in Andalusia
42 Envelope material of stellar quality?
45 Like single malt Scotch
46 Comrade of Athos
47 On-ramp sign
48 Baseball manager Yost
49 Sleigh part
50 Jaguar filler
51 Richly deserve
52 Say another way
53 Slip away
56 Club for rural youth
58 Greek hero with physical discomforts?
64 Letter after eta
65 Like quiet colors
66 In the act
68 Abrasive cloth
69 "Prince Valiant" princess
70 From the keg
71 Rodeo equipment
72 House of Henry VIII
73 Breaks down

DOWN

1 Hoedown partner
2 Wooden-shoe sound
3 Fifth-century Pope
4 Like some twins
5 Suffer low self-esteem
6 "The Osbournes" mom
7 David in "Murder By Death"
8 Strong adhesive
9 Heroic saga
10 Harassed
11 Cast-iron cooker
12 Stands for things
13 City on the Saône
14 Jousting spear
15 Shooting type
23 Slightly
24 A little behind
27 Hired killer
28 Cause to see red
29 Worked on a board
30 Kind of geometry
31 Personal narrative
32 Checkout count
34 Little one
35 Lawrence's duet partner
36 Frida Kahlo's husband
37 American cat
38 Wicked light
40 With parsley, on menus
41 Grammy winner Bonnie
43 Hardy partner
44 Makeup item
49 They may be instant
50 Suspected lawbreaker
51 ___ d'hôtel
52 Boat blade
53 Mess participant
54 Airhead
55 Word from a bird
56 Meant to be
57 Bridge call, informally
59 Send out
60 Enterprise officer
61 Skye in "XOXO"
62 Nick's time
63 Break under strain
67 Location identifier, for short

THEMELESS by Harvey Estes

22 Across was awarded the Presidential Medal of Freedom in 1980.

ACROSS

1 Jabbing joint
6 For fear that
10 Gunmaker Colt
16 "Fahrenheit 11/9" director
17 Not taken in by
18 Recoil
19 Sgt. Pepper, for one
21 Naval standard
22 Yosemite photographer
23 Like 3-Down trees
24 At the ready
25 Declines participation
27 Fellas
28 "Wicked" actress Chenoweth
30 Miss Muffet's bugaboo
32 Denver university
35 Nova ___ (Halifax native)
38 Social gathering
42 Stuff to the gills
44 Flip out
45 Not novel
46 "Shut up!"
47 Not so bright
48 Desires
49 Clive of "Closer"
50 Long-eared pet
51 "24" time span
53 Prepare beans, in a way
55 Struck out
57 Ristorante order
62 Francis ___ Harte
64 Uses as a resource
67 Pony Express delivery
68 Varsity award
70 "In your dreams!"
72 Still serving
73 Car door opener, in a pinch
74 Fictional mastermind
75 Chisel feature
76 Explanation preceder
77 Snide looks
78 Like Marge Simpson's hair
79 Stands the test of time

DOWN

1 Protect from floods
2 Short-term wheels
3 Dwarf of a sort
4 Info for waiters
5 Drawing place
6 Dock work
7 Be over by
8 Holds back
9 Trunks of sculpture
10 Doubting Thomas
11 Pisa's river
12 Yule hangings
13 They merged with the Universalists
14 Did some 10/31 mischief
15 Allows to use
20 Less trying
26 Having a cow
29 Uses the fitting room
31 Sultry period
33 Eyewitness phrase
34 With more marbles
36 Cathedral nook
37 Veet, formerly
38 Tempo phrase
39 Humorist Lebowitz
40 Excellent condition
41 Then
43 Chicken stabber
46 Kitchen gadget
50 Secondary bank
52 Peel
54 Didn't go under
56 Enjoyed a ball
58 Blake of "Gunsmoke"
59 Bay of Bengal feeder
60 Most considerate
61 Gives a heads-up to
62 Doldrums
63 Military probe, briefly
65 Harrelson or Hayes
66 Edwin Booth's milieu
69 At least once
71 Flag down

246 THEMELESS   by Marie Langley
65 Across is the first Scandinavian woman to climb Mount Everest.

ACROSS

1 Excalibur part
5 Biotite
9 What Bobby Jones called a #2 wood
16 Where you won't find scabs
18 Pleasing sound
19 Chèvre source
20 Gatekeeper of jokes
21 Knights' game
22 Bakker's former org.
23 Janis Joplin biopic
24 More comfy
26 Editor's find
28 Loch of crosswords
29 Jerusalem server
30 Otoscope view
32 Blown away
34 Get-up-and-go
36 Levelheaded
38 Close one
39 Rowlands of "The Notebook"
40 Pitcher's success
41 Annual fact books
43 Ear part
47 Cooks in a hurry
48 Marveling at a lunar eclipse?
52 Hanukkah gift
55 Lex Luthor's lackey
56 Eggs in the lab
57 Went over the top
62 Wisconsin tribe
63 Helped with a line
64 The latest, once
65 Mountaineer Gammelgaard

66 Seneca tutored him
68 Those opposed
70 Workout wear
72 Having a predisposition for
74 Giant Mel
76 Automaker Citroën
77 Sat on a branch
78 Smiling runner-up
80 Decked out
81 Withdrawing
82 Dionysian women
83 Yoko's son
84 Bolts down

DOWN

1 Premonitions
2 Having debts
3 Wichita worker of song
4 Throat parts
5 NYC arena
6 Breakfast chain
7 Ulster supporter
8 With appropriateness
9 Gift
10 Naomi's daughter-in-law
11 Tack on
12 Tiger Khan
13 In a way
14 At bottom
15 Australia's largest lake
17 Where 3M is MMM
25 Platinum country album of 1988
27 "___ Loves Mambo"
31 Best effort
33 Dutch tree
35 Annie Oakley
37 Capri or Man

39 Stocky antelope
42 Prefix for choir
43 Book after Joel
44 Zip
45 Yay-or-nay event
46 Some tennis serves
49 "___ wish!"
50 Ironic probability
51 Surrealism predecessor
52 Pink Panther, for one
53 Prefix with skeleton
54 CRT successors
58 1968 hit by the Turtles
59 Scrolls site
60 Press
61 They may be just
63 Sandinista foe

67 Pine sap
69 Nirvana fans?
71 Goofy creator
72 Nana
73 Upset, with "off"
75 African hartebeest
79 Leonine home

247

NOVELTY WITHIN   by Tracy Bennett and Victor Fleming
The lyric below is from "Move On." ("Sunday in the Park With George.")

CROSS

1 Flying high
6 Like many a flapper's do
12 Latin friend?
18 Louisiana hero
19 Green, in a way
20 Take away a license
21 Before-surgery
22 "Bedtime for Bonzo" star
23 Preferred stock?
24 **Stephen Sondheim lyric: Part I**
26 Dove houses
27 Sore spot
28 Fifth-century Pope
30 Colorado resort town
33 Backsplash pieces
36 FiberCon rival
38 Rocks in a tavern
39 Corporate money mgr.
42 **Lyric: Part II**
46 Ransom of automotive history
48 Scorpion secretion
49 Primer numero
50 Sparks neighbor
51 Sell moonshine
53 Cherry parts
55 Carp in a pond
57 Toot
58 **Lyric: Part III**
61 Not hitched
65 ___ Schwarz
67 Go a practice round
68 Folder's craft
70 Green Nissan model
73 "Yowza!"
75 Fluff up, as hair
77 Albany canal

78 **Lyric: Part IV**
82 "The Marvelous ___ Maisel"
83 Back-to-school night org.
84 It flows into the Missouri
85 Become weatherworn
87 Final arbiter's authority
89 Chutzpah
92 Cassiterite, e.g.
96 1988 film fish
98 **Lyric: Part V**
101 Resort island of Florida
103 At an angle
104 Mork's language
105 Purdue's conference
106 Bening's "Bugsy" costar
107 Earthy flavor profile
108 Field sport stick
109 Size up
110 Of few words

DOWN

1 Horrify
2 "Bonanza" star Greene
3 Bends to the will of
4 Get there by walking
5 Passport vaccine
6 Inflammatory word in "Disco Inferno"
7 A hundred sawbucks
8 Cries from a donkey
9 Archie Bunker persona
10 Uniform decoration

11 TV room
12 Golden fleece ship
13 Butcher's tool
14 Brown, Penn et al.
15 Plot secretly
16 Island strings, informally
17 Address from a rev.
25 Moonstruck
26 Emoticon "eyes"
29 "The dog ate my homework," e.g.
31 Adam Smith's subj.
32 Nautilus captain
34 Plaintive poem
35 1 of 100 in D.C.
37 Out of control
39 Biofuel sources
40 Angel's dread
41 Effluvium
43 Fill the tank
44 Ape

45 Feature of 10 Down
47 Graf of tennis
52 "Aladdin" singer Salonga
54 Chucked
56 Yvette's "yes"
59 City on Lake Ontario
60 Deferential denial
62 Cordial
63 "Underground" director Kusturica
64 Buys the farm
66 Avian screechers
69 Cast another ballot
70 Botox targets
71 "Pushover" singer James
72 Jackie Gleason catchphrase
74 Michelle who wrote "Becoming"

76 Application blank info
79 Some Canadian coins
80 Causal links
81 Cut a scene
86 Huge, to Hugo
88 Adds gold to a mine
90 Majorca y Minorca
91 Act badly?
93 Heroic Schindler
94 Chews (out)
95 Counting-out word
97 "Hamlet" extra
99 Makes a pick
100 Curious George's creators
101 "Fresh Off the Boat" airer
102 Peace, in Moscow
103 Litigators' org.

ACROSS

1 Section of Algiers
7 Fight finishers
10 "Tiny Dancer" lyricist
16 On our field
17 Spanish port
19 Verdi opera
20 "For richer, for ___ . . ."
21 Spin-off sitcom of 1974
22 Climbing palm
23 **Start of a quip**
26 Pittsburgh Pirates' nickname
28 Oolong and souchong
29 Rose Murphy's love
30 Like black olives
33 Moment of realization?
34 Courage of "F Troop"
35 Tote-board data
37 Shrinking
38 Actress Portia de ___
40 England's FBI
42 Hydrogen's number
43 Queeg's ship
45 **Middle of quip**
49 Three after cue
50 Gives off
51 Adjust a skirt
52 Street events
56 "Newton's Apple" host Flatow
57 Part of FDIC
61 Olds model
62 Quiescent
65 Cry from a labor organizer
66 Not pos.
67 Picture border
69 Flight post
71 Stand-up standard
72 **Source of quip**
74 **Author of quip**
76 Manche capital
77 Eleatic School member
79 Chandler's "Duke of ___"
80 Pomegranate "jewel"
81 "Frasier" role
83 Duryea or Dorfman
85 Put on the tube
87 **End of quip**
95 First episode
96 Out-of-the-money horse
97 Like lemon juice
99 Graff of "Mr. Belvedere"
100 Speak well of
101 Balsam of "Mad Men"
102 Gillan in "Avengers: Endgame"
103 Memorable sayings
104 Scratch out a living
105 Banana oil, e.g.

DOWN

1 Zucchetto
2 Essandoh in "Hitch"
3 Display box
4 Spassky of chess
5 Iowa city
6 Regarding this matter
7 Hot dog brand
8 Glade target
9 It's usually a hit
10 Called
11 Oldest purebred horse
12 "___ den Linden"
13 Arquette in "Boyhood"
14 "___ pig's eye!"
15 "Solar Barque" author
17 Full of imagination
18 Rink machines
24 "Thanks, François!"
25 Large sea duck
26 "Blazing Saddles" sheriff
27 "Here comes trouble!"
31 Quarter-pint glass
32 "Smoke Gets in Your ___"
34 Sent quickly
36 Agenda
39 Instrument with a gulu
41 Downfall
42 Get hold of
44 Clio candidates
46 Diminutive
47 Camelot restroom sign?
48 Second word in Genesis
52 Hunger signs
53 On the ball
54 Sovereign
55 Outpouring
57 Not as much
58 Harshness
59 "Pong" creator
60 Within the rules
63 Whitaker's Oscar role
64 Chevy of the '70s
68 Ratso in "Midnight Cowboy"
70 Chinese leader Zhou ___
73 Kind of cookie
75 Mariachi shakers
78 Potemkin Mutiny site
79 Menu listing
82 More than not
84 Straddling
86 Spitting nails
87 Banjo player Fleck
88 Above, to Otto
89 ___ avis
90 Secluded valley
91 Dime novelist
92 Dresden duck
93 Hanukkah money
94 Sandusky lake
95 Hägar creator Browne
98 Place to buy a belt

98 Across is the first to manage World Series winners in both leagues.

ACROSS

1 Makes spiffy
7 Wimp
13 Part of a diamond
17 Armstrong's moniker
18 Ivy League town
19 "The Wizard of Oz" apple thrower
20 **Quote by 98 Across: Part 1**
22 Nickname for Nate Archibald
23 Horse of the Year (1960-64)
24 Burns and Allen, e.g.
25 "God willing"
27 Cockney perdition
28 Evil org. in "Get Smart"
30 Crucifix
31 ATM company
32 Like molasses in January
34 **Quote: Part 2**
39 Harvests alfalfa
41 1980s muscle car
42 Krusty Krab locale
43 Attaché attachments
46 Gives a lift
48 Bill
52 **Quote: Part 3**
54 Up for debate
57 "Heart of Dixie" st.
58 August 1 babies
59 Bath water?
60 Dirty digs
61 "___ Hour" (2017 film)
63 **Quote: Part 4**
67 "Absolutely, señor!"
68 Excessive pride
70 Soft-soaps
71 You stand to lose it

74 Sneak a look
75 Lowly chess piece
76 **Quote: Part 5**
81 Off-road wheels
85 Aberdeen turndown
86 "Wheel of Fortune" prize
87 "Are not!" rejoinder
89 In the know, old-style
90 What Bobby Jones called a #2 wood
92 Rapper's entourage
95 Golfer Calvin
97 "___ girl!"
98 **MLB manager with 2,194 wins**
101 Socks style
102 Meet officials
103 Added up
104 "Ol' Man River" composer
105 Be short with
106 Fixate on

DOWN

1 New Orleans pianist Crawford
2 Verdi opera set in Cyprus
3 Cardiology charts
4 "All ___ Up": Presley
5 Arlington school
6 Haughty
7 Judy, to Punch
8 Coup d'___
9 Conclusion starter
10 Letters after Sen. Shelby
11 Director's directive
12 Fuel guzzlers

13 URL start
14 Position properly
15 Stand-up guy
16 Famous stuffed donkey
17 Fagin's associate
21 Royals manager Ned
26 Dog of crosswords
29 Vast chasms
30 "The Feast of All Saints" author
33 One of the five W's
35 "___ and Stitch" (2002)
36 Qom's country
37 It may be cast
38 Puts the collar on
40 Like Simone Biles
43 Apple tablets
44 Head lama
45 Romanov rulers

46 The Coneheads, e.g.
47 Reliever's goal
49 Raleigh's rival
50 Other: Fr.
51 "Flowers for Algernon" author
53 Chris of "Law & Order"
55 F-14 fighters
56 Being pulled along
59 Patient replies?
62 A tad over two lbs.
63 German for "upper"
64 Footloose
65 Hawaiian talisman
66 Mandlíková of the court
69 "___ & Away": 5th Dimension
72 Stern areas

73 Pedants
75 Olive stuffer
76 Where cab fares ride
77 "Nausea" novelist
78 Less a mess
79 Cravat holder
80 Doug Hurley's org.
82 Doctoral work
83 Kills bills
84 Fork out
88 Astra and Corsa
91 Like lumber
92 Pre-op routine
93 Fried Cajun veggie
94 DOS part: Abbr.
96 Oilman Halliburton
99 Reddit Q&A
100 Smidgen

250 REBEL WITHOUT APPLAUSE by Harvey Estes
A side of an actor far away from the noise of praise.

ACROSS

1 "The Omega Man" star
7 Wide gulf
12 "Finally!"
18 Gotten by few
19 "We ___ please!"
20 Beer holder, maybe
21 Courtesy car
22 Uncomplaining
23 Car in "The Love Bug"
24 **Start of a quote from 30 Across**
27 "Sister Act" extras
28 Still in bed
29 A flat, e.g.
30 Dean in "Rebel Without a Cause"
31 Practice for a boxing match
35 Abu Dhabi is its cap.
36 Pass on
38 Red Monopoly pieces
40 Frau's abode
41 They attract
45 Navel variety
46 Legacy from mom or dad
48 Cardinal's cap
50 Wave feature
51 Billing unit, for some
52 Clamming spot
53 Nursery item
54 **More of quote**
58 Words of accusation
59 Vein filler
60 Writing style
61 Flunkies' responses
62 Spoils, perhaps
64 Manhattan nosh
65 Summit goals
66 Clowns wear big ones

67 ___ Duro Canyon State Park
68 Take turns
69 Professor's job insurance
71 Stars and Bars org.
73 Mireille on "Hanna"
74 **More of quote**
78 RR regulator of old
79 Madras mister
81 Goofing off
82 **End of quote**
88 Roland Garros sport
90 As good as it gets
91 Animal in a Beatles title
92 Galahad's mother
93 Slangy word of enthusiasm
94 Agony aunt's specialty
95 Dragon's blood et al.
96 Land in the lake
97 First supersonic human

DOWN

1 Super Bowl segment
2 Buck ending
3 Sarabi's brother-in-law
4 Zesty flavor
5 "There's ___ every crowd!"
6 On edge
7 Medieval helmet
8 Approach for a loan
9 Mine, to Maurice
10 Project
11 They make fun

12 Needing a whirlpool, perhaps
13 Ballerina's "pointe"
14 "Lethal Weapon 4" heroine
15 "River of Dreams" is one
16 Notre Dame's river
17 Lock in a salon
25 JFK posting
26 Caustic chemical
30 Day, in Dijon
31 Flabbergasted
32 Run up the score
33 Give evidence for
34 Puts out again
36 Untrue story
37 Move without effort
39 "Hey, why not?!"
40 Crook's take

42 Have fun
43 Ancient Italian
44 Spiked heel
46 Garden sticker
47 "Deadliest Catch" narrator Mike
48 Slanted surface
49 They're deep
52 Article of contention
55 Unpackaged
56 Ad image
57 Key blunder
63 "Wagon Train" wagon master
64 Lines at the grocery
67 "Tosca" composer
68 Train route
70 Palindromic diarist

71 Where to find wheels
72 "Billions" ntwk.
74 Carafe size
75 "Set Fire to the Rain" singer
76 Arm bones
77 Guardian spirits
79 Cabinet department
80 Grass unit
82 Makes do with
83 "Breakfast at Tiffany's" actress
84 Peace Nobelist Myrdal
85 Military lockup
86 "Time" cofounder
87 North Sea feeder
89 ___-Out Burger

ACROSS

1 Italian footwear brand
5 Wacky
12 Mystify
18 Made in reverse?
19 Stamp out
20 Musical key
21 Mythical avians
22 Goes ballistic
24 "Pépé le ___" (1937 French film)
25 So long, in Sonora
26 Once out, now in
27 Hibernians
29 Safari and Yukon
30 Pierre loc.
34 Roberto Duran's "Enough!"
35 Jazz vocalist Carmen
37 City on the Aar
38 American League team
40 Cross-promotion
41 Bison or yak
42 Standard & ___
43 John's song for Yoko
44 Heathrow listing
45 Neuter
46 Vital regions
47 Hypnotized state
48 Keyboard key
49 Marx Bros. comedy
51 Richard Branson's title
54 Camden Yards mascot
56 "All That Jazz" choreographer
57 Equine hybrid
58 Pugnacious
60 "Merrie Melodies" coyote
61 Oily compound
62 British medical journal
63 Writer's mark
64 Freshened a fern
65 Lead-off walk result
66 Societal customs
67 Like Catherine Zeta-Jones
68 Arctic bird
69 Cosmic times
70 Software trial run
73 "___ Frutti": Little Richard
75 Craft with no pilot
77 Off the premises
78 Yield time, in the Senate
82 Pack down
83 Like the Godhead
84 Optician's stock
85 "Anything ___?"
86 Rubbernecker
87 Takes umbrage
88 AC condenser base

DOWN

1 Atomic Age pioneer
2 "Every wall is ___": Emerson
3 Trap a boxer in the ring
4 Profuse apology
5 Caribbean cruise destination
6 Puts up with
7 Out
8 As well
9 What the picky pick
10 Blonde shade
11 Mr. Peabody's pal
12 Purple roots
13 Arab League bigwig
14 Serbia's first president
15 Cedar Falls college
16 Colin Hanks, to Tom
17 Centimeter dyne
23 Gospel singer Winans
28 "Sicko" targets
29 Texter's :)
31 Makes a bit crazy
32 Ballerina Tsygankova
33 Boat backbone
35 Plays charades
36 Official truce
37 Put up with
38 It abuts the bema
39 ___ up (absorbs)
40 "Velvet Fog" vocalist
41 Prop up
43 "___ Bully" (1965 hit)
44 Come to the fore
46 Usurp
47 Sports bar fixture
49 Age on the vine
50 Things to cast
52 Colleague of Jimmy and Bjorn
53 Amusing Foxx
55 Skilled storyteller
57 Stretches the facts
58 Meter mouth
59 Swagger stick
60 VFW part
61 Kedrova in "Torn Curtain"
63 Cypress or spruce
64 Fireballs
66 Dust speck
67 Assailed
69 The heavens
70 Oklahoma senator (1979–94)
71 Kafka hero Gregor
72 Easygoing sort
74 Ogden Publications magazine
75 Pulls off
76 Fifth line of seats
78 Dodge Viper ___
79 Subway line to Columbia U.
80 Itinerary word
81 Caustic cleaner

ACROSS

1 Air traveler's annoyance
6 Whiskey drink
10 Online gamer's annoyance
13 Apple debut of 2010
17 Gas brand relaunched in 2017
18 Shells, but not ziti
19 Source of milk
20 Hunter's garb, briefly
21 Popular UK takeaway food
23 Declare verboten
24 Son of Aphrodite
25 Former Eisenhower namesake at Augusta
26 Cover for a bad hair day
27 Kraft coating for chicken and pork
30 Musical sense
31 Infant's bodysuit
32 Animated Disney duo
38 Forced a checkmate
39 Food court enticement
43 Traffic report source
44 Like Santa's helpers
46 Farming students, familiarly
47 Favorite Van Gogh spot
48 Textile with a wavy pattern
49 Covert org. in "Argo"
50 One of the Indy 500's 200
51 Cold draft
52 Kitty feeder
53 Hauls in for booking
55 Frozen treat featuring 93 Across
60 Have coming
63 Goat's antithesis, in baseball
64 In command of
68 Pacific battle site, in brief
69 Roadhouse
70 Mantle's number
71 Comedian/banjoist Martin
72 Forward
74 Feeling blah
75 Like Serling tales
76 Lock of hair
77 Grand ___ (wine label words)
78 DJ Alan Freed's coinage
81 Eucalyptus munchers
83 Bit for Bowser
84 "Sweet Child O' Mine" band
88 108-card game
89 Don't catch
93 Nabisco bestseller
94 Carrier letters
95 Comfort food
98 Koko Head's island
99 Nectar gatherer
100 Eye like a lecher
101 Poker declaration
102 Go like a hummingbird
103 Big-eared brayer
104 Gym bag filler
105 Barbizon School painter

DOWN

1 Loony
2 Abu Dhabi leader
3 Diet successfully
4 Heat rub target
5 Over there, in verse
6 Where the simoom blows
7 Strike from a list
8 Diamond official
9 The NHL's Art ___ Trophy
10 Nation with a cedar on its flag
11 Greet the morning
12 DNA carriers
13 Cause of a 1912 disaster
14 Law firm worker, for short
15 Totally out of control
16 Rx measure
22 Neighbor of Niger
28 Mandel of "America's Got Talent"
29 Bridal Veil Falls locale
30 Mireille of "World War Z"
32 Chesapeake Bay catch
33 Luna Lovegood's Patronus
34 Like a loiterer
35 President after Fillmore
36 Téa of "Madam Secretary"
37 A-listers
40 Most Rembrandts
41 Much of a paleo diet
42 Nile Delta vipers
45 Not so clichéd
46 Suffix with gazillion
48 Supreme being
49 Leslie of "Gigi"
54 Drama queen
56 Roy who sang "It's Over"
57 Coffee table shape
58 "Not in this lifetime!"
59 Words to live by
60 Gossip that's "dished"
61 It has an ear and a mouth
62 Suffix for four
65 Beach of Florida
66 Like Batman's foes
67 Hose storage gadget
70 Dipsomaniac
71 Fired off
73 Invites to dinner
74 Tubas and trumpets
77 4:00 market events
79 Steelers RB James
80 McDonald's founder
82 Island off Venezuela
84 Make a bonehead move
85 Pechora's mountains
86 "M*A*S*H" soda brand
87 Unhealthful haze
88 The Daily Bruin's sch.
89 Radio City's style, informally
90 Caboose locale
91 Where the Storting sits
92 Clobber with snowballs
96 Scotch price factor
97 Sound from a 70 Down

"TIME" PERSONS OF THE YEAR*   by Fred Piscop
56 Across was nominated for the Nobel Peace Prize in 2019 and 2020.

ACROSS

1 Sat in sullen silence
8 Al who created Dogpatch
12 Title for Marie Tussaud
18 John Mortimer's barrister
19 Coloratura's highlight
20 Cause of fatigue
21 Chancellor of Germany (2015)*
23 Ford flops
24 Repair, as a raincoat
25 Guernsey or Sark
26 Tablelike formation
29 Place for a home theater
31 1999 Exxon merger partner
35 Not quite right
37 People Power Revolution figure (1986)*
42 Like Death Valley in summer
43 Bird's gullet
45 Beveled joints
46 Fish of fish sticks
47 H, on a fraternity house
48 Galley implement
49 Site of a famous bell tower
50 Feeder filler
51 Send another way
53 No great shakes
55 Some Little Leaguers
56 Climate activist (2019)*
60 Goes belly up
63 Don't catch
64 Some patches
68 Not between the uprights
69 Orchestral wind
71 Mere pittance
72 Ballpoint brand
73 Knot-tying words
74 Fitness center amenities
76 One of the Cartwrights
77 God's gift to man
78 Edward VIII's love (1936)*
81 Buddy in "Breakfast at Tiffany's"
83 Witness stand statements
84 Hairy Himalayan
85 Monthly expense, for some
86 Soft, holey shoe
89 Watch brand since 1875
93 Class for moms-to-be
96 Person of the Year publication
102 Iggy with the hit single "Fancy"
103 Sulfur attribute
104 Is mournful
105 Slower on the uptake
106 Bubble gum globs
107 Mack of early slapstick

DOWN

1 Lingerie item
2 Result of a stolen home?
3 Texter's "Holy cow!"
4 "Carmen" and "Elektra"
5 Name in pineapples
6 One way to the Holy Land
7 Moore of "Empire"
8 Nolan Ryan's spanned 27 years
9 "Noah" setting
10 Three Stooges missile
11 Good buddy
12 Follower of Fannie or Sallie
13 "Your point being . . . ?"
14 Arnaz and Ball's studio
15 Home of the ISU Cyclones
16 Grain grinder
17 Make less onerous
22 Fund, as a grant
26 Bill of HBO's "Real Time"
27 Act the ham
28 "Norwegian Wood" strings
30 Skater Naomi Nari ___
31 Something to second
32 Sacagawea coins
33 Theda of the silents
34 High stats for Mensans
36 Rubs clean
37 Shift-6 symbol
38 Closes, as a fly
39 Cake prettifier
40 Seasonal refrain
41 Kentucky Derby postings
44 Utility bill figure
50 ASL part
52 Get an eyeful of
53 Watch on Roku
54 "Just as I thought!"
55 Act the bellyacher
57 Hunky guy
58 Beast on old nickels
59 Bow-toting Greek god
60 Shorthand similar to "IMO"
61 Princess of opera
62 Teen magazine subject
65 Having a high BMI
66 Phileas Fogg portrayer
67 Potpourri quality
69 Brewery oven
70 Garden center buy
74 "Chandelier" singer
75 Bug-planting sort
76 Balderdash
79 Hometown folks
80 Cavalry blades
82 Full of chutzpah
86 Decked out
87 Reduce to rubble
88 Neighbor of Yemen
90 Can't keep up
91 "Puss in Boots" baddie
92 Far from humble
94 Ten-point Scrabble tile
95 It may be pierced or plugged
96 Skier's way up
97 Mrs. McKinley
98 Like Carnaby Street styles
99 "___ had it!"
100 Aerialist's safety gear
101 Body shop fig.

ACROSS

1 eBay submissions
5 Like leisure suits
10 Horse with a mottled coat
16 More than merely able
18 "Jelly Roll" of jazz
19 Portugal's locale
20 Sweet, tangy sauce*
22 Diviners' cards
23 Leftover pizza part, perhaps
24 Pedometer button
26 Fat in mincemeat recipes
27 Secured, as a tent
30 Old Deuteronomy's musical
32 Ran leisurely
34 Dow downturn
35 Rosebud's owner
36 Org. with probes
37 One-fifth of "Hamlet"
40 Bread crumb carrier
41 "A Star Is Born" song*
44 Underling's denial
46 LDS-owned school
47 Detective's clue
48 Crock-Pot part
49 Sudden outpouring
50 Wise old head
52 Hard to rattle
54 Olympic blade with a sensor
55 "And Still I Rise" poet Angelou
57 Fairy in "The Nutcracker"*
61 Untouchables leader
62 Without warranty
63 Enjoy a Harley, say
64 Chips go-with
66 Trash can insert
68 Former Egypt-Syria alliance
69 Raconteur's delivery
70 Locomotive part
73 Steer snagger
74 Friend of a wee septet*
77 Call to a flamenco dancer
78 Env. insertion
79 Drier than sec
81 Cosmetics "caller"
82 One with a burr
83 Totally flummoxed
85 Hyde Park carriage
86 Ducklings' fathers
88 "Slumdog Millionaire" city
90 Sourdough's filing
92 Communion plate
94 Evil intent
96 They're found in clue* answers
101 Made equal
102 Copies, informally
103 "The Venice of Japan"
104 Avoid court
105 Krupp family city
106 Hambletonian pace

DOWN

1 "Hogwash!"
2 Oath response
3 Home office site
4 Bits of dust
5 Contest mail-in, perhaps
6 Works at the Met
7 A-team member
8 Tender spots
9 Odds' partners
10 Agrees with
11 Lawyers' org.
12 In itself
13 Vain to the max*
14 Lo-cal, in ads
15 Team in some all-star games
17 Port of Phoenicia
18 Lambdas' followers
21 Horrible coffee, slangily
25 Spiral-horned antelope
27 Hefty hunk of bacon
28 Award for "Rent"
29 First Sherlock Holmes story*
31 "Life of Pi" director (with 65-D)
33 Bad reviews
35 Reeves in "Johnny Mnemonic"
36 Sam in "The Commuter"
38 Offers an example
39 Hammock holders
41 English cathedral city
42 Skein shapes
43 Emulate Jean Harlow at 16
45 Warms up the crowd
51 Welcome desert sights
52 Capital of 68 Across
53 Glen ___ Scotch
55 "Atlantic City" director Louis
56 Bhutanese, e.g.
58 Portrait on the fifty
59 Track star Bolt
60 Brewery grain
65 See 31 Down
67 Does pirate work
68 Favored cocktail
69 Emma of "Howards End"
71 Burn soother
72 Track action
75 Pregame routine
76 Huntington loc.
80 What a hairline may do
82 Least wacky
84 Make impure
85 Raking results
86 Skid row affliction
87 Towed-away auto, perhaps
88 Iowa college town
89 Was philanthropic
91 Part of the back 40
93 Vienna's land: Abbr.
95 "Fantasia" unit
97 Palindromic preposition
98 Matchbox toy
99 Win for Rocky
100 Parked it

"SPELL IT OUT" by Rob Gonsalves and Jennifer Lim

64 Across received a record forty-seven 5 Down during its run of 25 seasons.

CROSS

1 Mama's boys
5 "The River Sings" singer
9 Occasion to rent a tux
13 Swell, in '90s slang
17 "Desperate Housewives" divorcée
18 Beowulf's beverage
19 "D'oh!"
20 McEntire sitcom
21 (CVS) Pharmacy
25 Versailles agreement
26 Movie kid with a 666 birthmark
27 Overplay a scene
28 Grab bag: Abbr.
29 Word of denial
30 Ctrl+Y command
33 "Don't Be ___": Presley
36 (LG) Electronics
42 Bounce on the infield
43 Pickle-to-be, slangily
44 Piece of cake
45 Honolulu's ___ Wai Canal
46 "See you then!"
49 Lyric poem
51 Bit of choreography
52 Nursery need
53 Put down carpeting
54 No longer a couple
55 (SMART) Car
60 Family name at Tara
61 Bugs on a hill
62 Send forth
63 Melting clocks artist
64 #1 talk show for 24 consecutive seasons
66 Filled with happiness
70 Start to laugh?
71 Timbuktu's country
72 Not mine
73 Pasta ending
74 Navy (SEAL)
76 Canon setting
78 Lickety-split
80 "Man on the Moon" band
82 Ghostbuster Spengler
84 Forty-niner's stake
87 Virtuoso cellist
89 Tough nut to crack
94 (ZIP) code
97 Truant GI
98 Carefully eaten Japanese fish
99 Alphabet string
100 Bombard, as hail
101 Tear in despair
102 Igor, to Dr. Frankenstein
103 Puts down turf
104 Fabled Himalayan

DOWN

1 Splinter group
2 Skunk's defense
3 Sudoku square count
4 Bagel choice
5 Small-screen awards
6 Maiden name intro
7 After junk or stock
8 Go ahead
9 Organized society
10 Libertine
11 Carefree highway
12 Submissions to eds.
13 TV teasers
14 Villain vanquisher
15 Shill for
16 Shock, in a way
22 Gas or elec.
23 In a frenzy
24 Lingerie item
29 Brake neighbor
32 Ultimatum word
33 Tai ___
34 Go bad
35 FedEx alternative
37 It's picked in Kona
38 Crystal-filled rock
39 Mongolian invader
40 On the ball
41 Spellbound
43 Course after trig
47 "Pong" company
48 Facts and figures
49 Mork's second home
50 Photos
51 Petty quarrels
53 Dunham of "Girls"
54 Warts and all
55 Oil source
56 Half a Washington city
57 Bay Area county
58 Lead down the garden path
59 Dubai dignitary
60 Poems of praise
64 Crew equipment
65 Egg-laying mammal
66 Jon ___ Jovi
67 In shape
68 One, to Jose
69 Back talk
71 Home of the Heat
72 Goes on and on and on
75 Off the mark
76 Recover from a soaking
77 10th-century Pope
78 Calibri or Courier
79 Short-tempered
83 Canis, for wolves
84 Industry magnate
85 Rob of "9-1-1: Lone Star"
86 Soon, to the Bard
88 AAA and BBB, for two
89 Schoolyard retort
91 High spirits
92 Brewer's grain
93 In opposition
95 Juilliard degree
96 LAX posting

256 THEMELESS by Theresa Yves
84 Across may be used in connection with 80 Across.

ACROSS

1 Party people
10 Abandon neutrality
19 Realtor's come-on
20 History buff stuff
21 One in the minority
22 First atomic bomb town
23 "Make sure this gets done!"
24 Really smell
26 "Piece of cake!"
27 Corridors under curves
29 Purple shade
30 Not as expected
33 Formal ceremony
34 Mower brand
35 Start of school?
38 Prehistory novelist Jean
39 Coastal catch
40 Stew veggie
42 La leader
43 Dugout, for one
44 Sugarland songs
45 Not likely to work
46 Watering hole, perhaps
48 Artful dodges
49 Salami type
50 Story conclusion
51 Reduces the fare
52 ___-de-lis
53 Outdoor dining sites
54 Not all there
55 Went off
57 "Don't throw bouquets ___ . . ."
58 Hook-nosed Muppet
59 Rip-off
60 Dedicated lines
61 Initial capital
63 Kick out
64 Buster Brown's dog
65 East ender?
66 Top-of-the-line
67 Check
68 Got sick
69 FDR's park
70 Stay on top of
72 Multitude
75 Bowed instrument
76 "Oro y plata" state
80 Going over land
82 Oil for locks?
84 Seasickness tablet
85 Kind of school
86 Cancels a choice
87 Has

DOWN

1 "Star Wars: Episode I" racers
2 Ron Howard role
3 High-treason word
4 Set up for service
5 Evolution, to Darwin
6 Like White House columns
7 Ruthless
8 Sweet suffix
9 Notched
10 Hawthorne's were "twice-told"
11 Running wild
12 Jennifer Lien's "Voyager" role
13 Crossword smudges
14 Menlo Park's valley
15 Start of a boast
16 Not quite dry yet
17 Organic compound
18 Enc. with a ms.
25 Needle feature
28 Suffer from the heat
29 Frost and more
30 Swear words
31 Brain covering
32 College officer
34 Kilmer work
35 Cooking staple
36 Sharpness symbol
37 New Age singer
39 Motown music type
40 Beyond breezy
41 Censorship noise
43 Neck wraps
44 Caused by
47 Bobby Axelrod's trait
48 Fancy-schmancy
49 Down at the mouth
51 Gifted person
52 Campus brotherhood
53 Cosmetics holder
54 Metaphysical poet
55 GDP measures
56 Title document
58 Righteous rep
59 Homeland
62 Like some city races
63 Luggage carrier
64 Goes quietly into the night
67 Pal of Pooh
68 Em, for example
69 Blackjack phrase
70 Business records
71 Lyrics
72 Alan in "The Carpetbaggers"
73 Cork's country
74 Fat, in France
75 Blow off steam
77 Landers and others
78 "Good one!"
79 Wimbledon winners
81 London's Old ___
83 Red Cross system

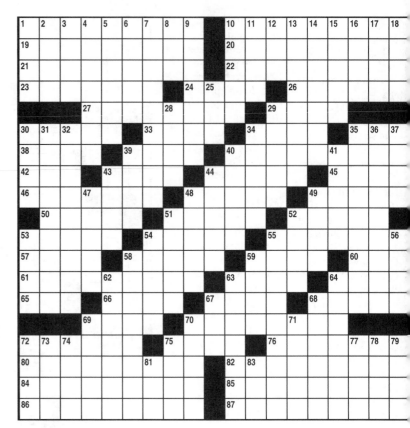

THEMELESS   by Theresa Yves

16 Down is also the title of a Joseph Heller novel.

ACROSS

1 "Like I said . . ."
11 New face
19 Flowerlike marine creature
20 Directly paired
21 Old military jackets, e.g.
22 Nicholas II and Alexandra
23 Central Honshu city
24 Cursive curlicue
25 ". . . who ___ heaven"
26 Skinny-___
27 Hosp. workers
29 Liberal arts maj.
30 Dulcet
31 Cosmetics holder
32 Téa of "Spanglish"
34 Slide show components
36 Kind of training
37 They're negatively charged
39 North African capital
40 Ballerina Fonteyn
41 Like gridlocked traffic
43 NY hrs.
44 Rich Italian dessert
45 Opera heroes, generally
47 Croat, e.g.
49 Alt.
50 Order of the Arrow org.
53 Gov. Reeves
54 Fires abruptly
56 HST successor
57 End the defense
59 Shed item
61 Baja bash
63 Occasionally
65 Finish'd
67 Family tree entry
71 Burnout cause
72 Chan portrayer Sidney
74 Conditioned reflex researcher
75 Missing till money
76 Blunder
78 "A Woman of No Importance" playwright
79 Till bills
80 Kinda
81 Mouse surface
83 Tender ender
84 From ___ Z
85 Succotash ingredients
86 Peter, in Puerto Rico
88 Corp. money handler
89 Calculated
91 Cochlear implant alternative
93 Patella
94 Made easier to bear
95 Herpetology study
96 Angels, e.g.

DOWN

1 "Not to mention . . ."
2 "Dead Man Walking" star
3 Unfounded suspicion
4 Coll. dorm staff
5 Obligation, in court
6 Parts of familles
7 Off-the-cuff stuff
8 Ask for
9 Sufficient, in Dogpatch
10 Some, on the Somme
11 Brown horses
12 Some govt. securities
13 Send, as payment
14 ___ all-time high
15 Prefix for profit or partisan
16 Absolutely dependable
17 Pictured
18 Considered individually
25 Is ready for
28 Sound from the sty
30 Tatooine orbited two
31 Marcel's menu
33 Narrow waterway
35 Takes to court
36 "Cheers" set
38 Counterparts to houses
40 Gets promoted
42 Fusses over
44 Tributes to the government
46 Stephen of "Breakfast on Pluto"
48 "Love Story" composer
50 The nitty-gritty
51 Establish an atmosphere
52 Johannes Kepler, notably
55 Pallet filling
58 Wedding cake features
60 Parrot perches
61 Lute ridge
62 Farrier's tool
64 Denver hrs.
66 Snow Queen of Arendelle
68 Ration out
69 Adjective or adverb
70 Ironic probability
72 Rancorous speeches
73 Takes off the books
76 Instant
77 San Diego team
80 Withhold release of
82 Ambition
85 Jiffy ___
86 Soccer great
87 "Come ___, the water's fine!"
90 Dash
91 Eggs Benedict ingredient
92 Practical joke

THEMELESS   by Harvey Estes
"Chinese gooseberry" is another term for 25 Across.

ACROSS

1 Parts of glasses
5 "The Children of the Poor" author
9 Belt maker's tools
13 Rip-off
17 Seasonal vaccine
19 Precipitated pellet
21 Feb. 2 celebrity
22 Moolah
23 Like UVC lights
25 Fuzzy fruit
26 Neg. opposite
27 Indent key
28 What Thoreau found on Walden Pond
31 Uncle Sam's dessert of choice?
36 Diving seabird
37 Dear friend?
41 2000 popular vote winner
42 Rush hour headache
45 Spoil, with "on"
46 Red Sox div.
49 Help out
50 Bernie Siegel and others
53 "Losing My Religion" band
54 Said a few choice words
56 Protected inventor
57 Military equipment
59 Canoe carryovers
60 Replace temporarily
61 Eye tinters
62 ACLU concern
64 Most discerning
65 Insurance grps.
66 Enjoy with gusto
68 Marx or Malden
69 1998 Susan Sarandon movie
72 Baum canine
73 Is out, in a way
76 Bird of the outback
77 Talk about seeing stars?
80 Come a little bit closer
83 Myrna of "The Jazz Singer"
84 Its HQ is the Pentagon

87 "Where Is the Life That Late ___?": Cole Porter
88 Enough to be considered
94 Like some track favorites
97 Female gangster?
98 Trojan War prophetess
99 Sightseeing group leader
100 Columnist Chase
101 Pt. of SSS
102 Ransom of automobiles
103 Tommy's gun

DOWN

1 Diana of "The Avengers"
2 About, in memos
3 "Dial ___ Murder" (1954)
4 Hit the low spots
5 Baggage porter
6 Cramp the style of
7 Company with a reptile logo
8 Long tales
9 Massage reactions
10 Oahu surfing spot
11 Poker raise max
12 Apply the brakes
13 ___ Thérèse, Quebec
14 Chicken pen
15 Part of AD
16 Hodgepodge
18 Amalgamate
20 Try to avoid a tag
24 Lolled around
29 Judy Garland's third husband
30 The last word
31 Petri dish medium
32 Involving dispute
33 Jumping the gun
34 Lush meadow
35 Corrective device
38 Behind
39 Verifies
40 Suffix for Congo
43 Explorer Tasman
44 Burns a bit
47 Public row
48 Puts down sod
51 Riverine mammal

52 Let out
55 Funny incidents
56 Lace with arsenic
58 Like a peer
59 Senior dance
60 Fifth Avenue retailer
61 Call into question
63 Go to market
65 Sphere start
67 Inc., in England
70 Chicken strips
71 "The Natural" novelist
74 ___ facie
75 Clip joints
78 Back teeth
79 Looking at
81 Darling girl
82 Bookstore category
84 Metric prefix
85 Humpty Dumpty's shape
86 PC place
89 Kind of box or chest
90 Like so

91 "I'll get around ___!"
92 Sourdough's strike
93 Site of a garden snake
95 Eavesdropping org.
96 Sun ___-sen

THEMELESS by Harvey Estes

When pluralized, 51 Across is a Booker T. & the M.G.'s song title.

ACROSS

1 Brand of sugar
10 Happy-go-lucky
19 Out of the blue
20 CPU
21 Like kissing disease
22 Vibrant sound quality
23 January song ender
24 Canvas covering
25 "Are we ___ off?"
26 They're big in Tibet
27 Antifur org.
28 Lighter fuel
30 Panoramic view
34 "Movie Home Companion" author
36 Hawks
41 Cornell University's home
43 More shifty
45 Blue moon, e.g.
46 Greenhorns
48 Trooper's device
50 Mocking birds
51 Scallion
53 Make lace
55 Early Briton
56 Without expression
57 Esteemed
59 "Hawaii Five-O" setting
61 Cold War proj.
62 Beast gave Belle a magic one
65 Smug smile
67 All fired up
69 Field the kickoff
70 Commandment breaker
72 Like brut to sec
74 Stubble-free
75 Like superstore shopping
77 Gold content analysis
79 "Empire" producer Chaiken
80 Some scouts seek it
82 Iditarod terminus
84 "Can ___ true?"
88 Least of the litter
89 Toaster waffle
90 Charitable giving
94 Join the family, in a way
96 Royal jester
98 "Exodus" director

99 Like white-collar crimes
100 "___ in the Night": Sinatra
101 Like Victoria in 1838

DOWN

1 Jacksonville team, to fans
2 One in your corner
3 Highlands family
4 Boy Wonder's creator
5 Florist letters
6 Auto club suggestion
7 Airing in the wee hours
8 Egyptian symbols
9 U. of Maryland athlete
10 Shot up
11 Don't exist
12 "You wish!"
13 Harsh critic
14 State rep.
15 Start of a country song
16 Annapolis inits.
17 Weatherbird
18 Makes angry
27 Al in "The Irishman"
28 Skater Boitano
29 Red rind contents
30 Tenn. neighbor
31 "Like ___ not"
32 Oxford job?
33 Alternate
35 Judy Jetson's brother
37 Special K, for one
38 Baseball "rope"
39 List-ending abbr.
40 Part of CBS
42 Millennia upon millennia
44 Turn in
47 Rudely sarcastic
49 Time off, briefly
52 Homer masterwork
54 Heavy volumes
57 Lone-eared hoppers
58 "Happy Days" boy
59 Trattoria "bone"
60 Notorious Idi

62 Stickup
63 Dutch ___
64 Magritte or Russo
66 Etta of old comics
68 Researcher's benefactors, e.g.
71 Like the '20s
73 Burmese river
76 Dramatic drop
78 Healthy snack
81 Register
83 Shape-shift
84 Naughty kids
85 Pucker-producing
86 Title in "Song of the South"
87 Satirist Bombeck
89 Behold, in old Rome
90 Ethnic coif
91 Usurer's offering
92 Tiny speck
93 Vehicle for winter fun
95 Chinese principle

97 A.L. East team, on scoreboards

260 THEMELESS by Harvey Estes

Marlowe and Shakespeare were the main developers of 38 Down.

ACROSS

1 Words to the bride
11 Dash for crossdressers?
19 Like some imaginations
20 Mr. Fix-It
21 Sketched out
22 In development
23 Letters of fashion
24 Huge racket
25 Propeller head
27 Tried to mislead
28 Córdoba cattleman
30 Cyberspace initials
31 Opponent of Caesar
34 Kept under wraps
35 Type of school for docs
37 Went out
42 Successful party people
45 Beach urchin
47 Heavy rains
48 Having a light touch
49 Item in a garage
50 Less wordy
51 Blue "Yellow Submarine" characters
52 Minimal tide
53 Flippable top
54 "No, not that!"
55 Signaled "thumbs up"
56 Name misspelled on a Graceland grave
58 Conclude from the facts
59 Broker's advice
62 Keyboard instrument
63 Fancy fur
64 When hell freezes over
65 Saunter on by
67 Managua miss
68 Cheri in "Scary Movie"
69 Aunt in "Bambi"
70 Generation separator
71 High-five sound
72 Canal site
74 Jellyfish appendage
78 Like vague answers
82 Very cold temperature
83 London facility
84 "Holy cow!"
87 Syracuse's county
89 "Give!" or "Take!"
92 Classroom corner wear
93 Breaks from shooting
94 Road menaces
95 Property valuation

DOWN

1 Kind of language
2 Preholiday nights
3 Succeed at pitching
4 Corn starter
5 Sykes of "Black-ish"
6 Strand at O'Hare, perhaps
7 Stops the flow of
8 Web page visit
9 Justified, as margins
10 Passover ritual
11 Stowe novel
12 Gun the motor
13 Speed skater Ohno
14 "Bohemian Rhapsody" cry
15 La ___ Gauche of Paris
16 Desiccated
17 Small coin
18 And so
26 It has a prominent bridge
28 Chuck Berry was an early one
29 Hers complement
30 Discombobulates
31 "___ la vie!"
32 Skin moisturizer
33 Disconnect
36 Missing nothing
38 Unrhymed poetry
39 Mascot for Cameron Crazies
40 "Do I dare to ___ peach?": Eliot
41 Steep slope
43 Prepared to drive
44 Make a blunder
45 Really hot
46 Some NFL linemen
48 Develop like a seed
51 Joseph Smith follower
54 Pitcher
55 Not taken in by
56 These slugs have shells
57 Dig like a pig
58 Setting for O'Neill's "Ile"
59 "Positively Entertaining" network
60 ___ good example
61 Pebble Beach hazard
64 Like some mountain guides
66 Gave way
67 Was in session
70 Garden decorations
73 Lickety-split
75 Kane of "All My Children"
76 Fruit centers
77 Lallygags
78 Drifts off
79 And higher, in cost
80 Fine-tune
81 Suffix with differ
82 Deletes electronically
84 End of a footrace
85 Hot spot
86 Left on the map
88 Needle-nosed fish
90 Mates of mas
91 "A Christmas Carol" tyke

THEMELESS by Marie Langley
44 Down is also another name for Elton John's "Border Song."

ACROSS

1 Looks after
8 Watering hole
15 "Star Wars" genre
20 Hightailed it
21 "So soon?"
22 One of us
23 Spent
24 Superficial shines
25 "Witches" author Jong
26 Restricted fare
27 Hottest
28 Formal ceremonies
29 Most severely inclined
31 Goes out in rummy
32 How some sci-fi aliens come
34 Error evidence
36 Blue tint
37 Like lifeguards
38 Ties another knot
42 Insurance grps.
43 Urban eyesore
44 ___ d'oeuvres
45 "Tangled" composer Menken
46 Big shots
47 Stuff to the gills
48 Nomadic tribe
49 Ornamental columns
52 Alden Ehrenreich role
53 Animation unit
54 Cooler
55 Stable parents
56 NYC planetarium
60 Aloof
61 Jazz section
62 Meadow Soprano's mom
63 Philatelist's collection
64 "Downton Abbey" valet John
65 Type of defense
66 Wide size
67 Long Island park
68 Women's businesswear
69 Throw money around
72 Sugar in "Some Like It Hot"
73 Prevailing style
74 Flying fisher
75 Throw the dice
76 Taking action
77 Turn sharply
78 Swears
80 Cable One, for one
81 Steamed
82 Native American food
84 Way out
86 Cruel marquis
87 Disaster rescue group
92 Planter's needs
93 Red Baron's fighter
96 Guam's islands
97 Davis of "King"
98 Gives bearings
99 Transistor part
100 Step part
101 Continuous
102 In a daze
103 Babe's nose
104 Heaven on earth
105 Pasta preference

DOWN

1 Pre-Lenin leaders
2 Ostentatious display
3 Nick of "Cape Fear"
4 Herd member
5 Bent over
6 Sawbucks
7 Name of a Forsyth file
8 Yard sale needs
9 Brisk tempos
10 Stand-ins
11 Varnish ingredients
12 Gardens amidst the sands
13 Lines of tribute
14 That certain something
15 Asian mountaineer
16 Madame with a Nobel
17 Copycat
18 One of twelve in a deck
19 Kind of
30 Vacation memento
33 Book before Deut.
35 Diamond foursome
36 Choral section

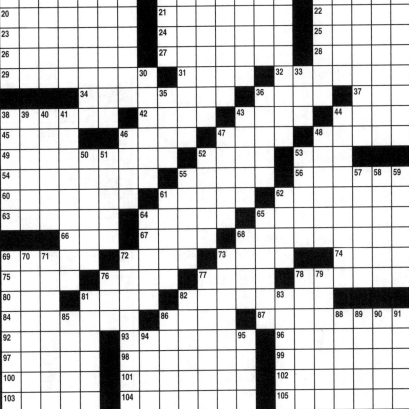

38 Kayaking hazard
39 Call forth
40 Lech of Solidarity
41 Putting into effect
43 Company division
44 "Cowabunga!"
46 Life jacket, for one
47 Bumps and bruises
48 A squid has three
50 Designed to fit
51 Present, for one
52 Las Vegas boxcars
53 "USA! USA!" is one
55 Debussy contemporary
57 Says no
58 Mrs. Robinson's daughter
59 City on the Loire
61 John, Paul, or George
62 Pedestrian staff
64 Twisted lock
65 El Prado's city
68 Cowper creation
69 Gift-wrapping aid
70 Copies from the clipboard
71 Strong joe
72 Patella
73 Scrapbook entries
76 URL suffix
77 Hindu philosophical system
78 Milky Way ingredient
79 Not yet tested
81 Advertising section
82 Light in the extreme
83 Galaxy S20 feature
85 "Goodbye, cheri!"
86 Drives for pleasure
88 Proof of car ownership
89 Stay home for supper
90 In regard to
91 Homer's honey
94 High-performance Camaro
95 Make out

ACROSS

1 Precious prefix
5 Large Matisse
10 Come clean about
15 Sci-fi fleet
19 Flamenco shouts
20 Demon of Hindu myth
21 Hanger-on
22 "Scarface" drug lord
23 "Fantasy" singer Nova
24 Sir, in Saharanpur
25 Tree with catkins
26 Jack in "The Cannonball Run"
27 Friend of Lucy Van Pelt
29 Duke Ellington classic
31 Hounds quarry, at times
32 Blanco and Branco
34 Shoots down, so to speak
35 Thrice: Rx
36 Starts a triathlon
38 Super
40 "A Delicate Balance" playwright
43 Denny of the Moody Blues
44 Plain in Spain
45 Pitt panther
48 Ratted
49 Lust after
50 Mortal
51 Luau song
52 Apteryx relative
53 Britt Reid alias
55 Eponym of Wednesday
56 Unwanted
58 Swaziland currency
59 Kidder in "Superman"
60 Completes a shoot
61 Caulking material
63 A lie-abed is a late one
64 Stick
66 Scottish salmon source
67 Scottish pony
70 Duplex deal
71 Oldest U.S. national park
74 Word in alumni newsletters
75 Cronies
76 Estranged wife of Jason
77 Flip remark?
78 One of the Ghostbusters
79 Horace work
80 They're struck in Buddhist temples
81 Old Alaskan capital
82 About
83 Parson's place
84 Suffuse with light
85 Relay segment
86 Lodger
89 Fill to the gills
90 Post products
94 Annual Hard Rock Stadium event
97 D.H. Lawrence novel
100 Insufficiency
101 Visit again
102 "The West Wing" creator Sorkin
103 Picasso's Maar
104 Medieval menial
105 Anesthetic of yore
106 Devoid of meaning
107 On any occasion
108 Concrete
109 "Deirdre" playwright
110 Kind of light show
111 Tear in two

DOWN

1 White Italian wine
2 Couturier Perry
3 French wine region
4 Unlinked
5 Dog's best friend
6 Manner
7 River to the Rhine
8 La Scala song
9 Minotaur's confines
10 Cottonwoods
11 Birthplace of Artemis
12 Beatles hit "Love ___"
13 Did in, Soprano-style
14 Prosperous
15 Comfortable with
16 Book leaf
17 Siouan tribe
18 Hera's birthplace
28 Sword with a fuller
30 Pixar clownfish
33 George Harrison's "___ Mine"
36 Goalie stats
37 Mozart's home, to Mozart
38 Pursued busily
39 Storm
40 Egyptian sun god
41 Togo's largest city
42 Largest animal
43 Wind-deposited loam
44 Kravitz in "The Hunger Games"
45 "Galloping Ghost" of football
46 It comes in sticks
47 "Ac-___-tchu-ate the Positive"
49 Brunch fare
50 Holy terror
51 Sponge mushroom
53 Optical driving hazard
54 Prefix meaning "straight"
55 Trifle away
57 Work code subject
59 Attitudes
61 Global extremes
62 Campus near Beverly Hills
63 Griffis in "Runaway Jury"
64 Gravy Train rival
65 Qumran's sea
66 Overhang
67 Investment
68 Strip lighting
69 Parking-lot souvenir?
71 Deep desires
72 Virginia deer
73 Third son of the first man
76 California peninsula
78 Cause
80 Bloods, for one
81 Warmed the bench
82 Flying prefix
83 Trophy spot
84 Haying machines
85 Not as plump
86 Shanghai's Jin Mao ___
87 Remove all traces
88 Mother's mother
89 Like Georgia Brown
90 "Macbeth" soothsayer
91 Too good for
92 Sophia in "Lady L"
93 Village green
95 ___ noire
96 Labor Dept. watchdog
98 "The English Patient" heroine
99 Historic times

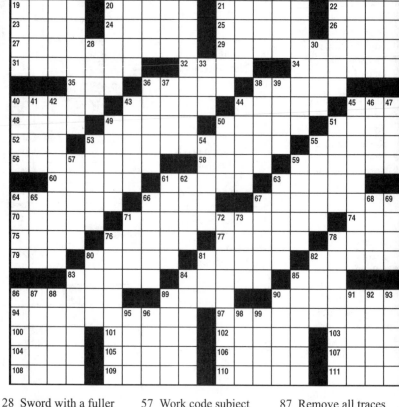

ACROSS

1 ESPN figure
5 Too refined for
10 Spain's ___ del Sol
15 Gumbo veggie
19 Starry bear
20 Chill out
21 DuPont's Fiber A, now
22 Word on a dime
23 Rabin's predecessor
24 Absinthe ingredient
25 Rain forest swing
26 Spork feature
27 "Mogambo" star*
29 "President of the Underground Railroad"*
31 Movie theaters
32 Franklin stove fuel
34 Box the compass
35 Preschooler
36 Fra Angelico, e.g.
38 "The Balcony" playwright
40 Product of stress
43 Vulgar
44 Former "SNL" announcer
45 Elly May Clampett's pa
48 Auctioneer's pronouncement
49 Early Scottish noble
50 Capital of Bulgaria
51 Feature of "Saw" films
52 Long in "Boiler Room"
53 "The Hills Beyond" novelist*
55 Conductor from Mumbai
56 No place special
58 Cod relative
59 Defeated on a mat
60 Avian perch
61 Christensen in "Traffic"
63 ___ de Toulouse-Lautrec
64 "The Naked and the Dead" author
66 Highway hazard
67 Noble Neapolitan
70 Talus locale
71 What answers to clues* are
74 Postal Creed word
75 Golf architect Jones

76 Fleur-___
77 Tour de France measure
78 Nestlé chocolate bar
79 Grain beard
80 De Gaulle's birthplace
81 Going rate?
82 Like a land baron
83 Singer Springfield
84 Flex and Focus
85 Shout at a Greek gala
86 Document proviso
89 Together
90 Called it quits
94 "C'est Si Bon" singer*
97 NBA MVP (2015, 2016)*
100 Yours, to Yves
101 Bob of "Full House"
102 "Wake Up" girl of song
103 Löwenbräu logo
104 Star-dotted
105 Cynewulf poem
106 Opposite of exeunt
107 Programmer's work
108 Cy Young stats
109 America's first saint
110 Pips
111 Vein pursuits

DOWN

1 Poisonous shrub
2 Pietro da Cortona fountain
3 Like sandalwood
4 Aimed at
5 Genesis landfall
6 Makes a concession
7 Lena in "Chocolat"
8 Spray container
9 Works out
10 Clothing item worn by Yogi Bear
11 Protruding window
12 Belarussian, e.g.
13 Braxton or Tennille
14 Tropical snake
15 Ensemble
16 It goes with steak
17 Angry encounter

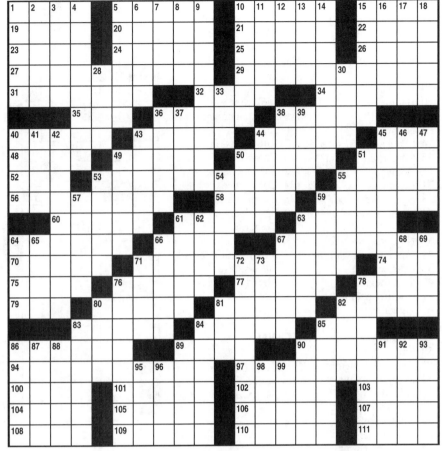

18 Catkin
28 Cupid
30 Cookie with its name on it
33 ___ in "Oscar"
36 Scaffolding
37 Genus of pond frogs
38 Social blunder
39 Canal in a Springsteen song
40 Where Jack Ryan taught history
41 Chop cut
42 "This Is the Night" singer*
43 To-do list item
44 Oktoberfest music
45 Winner of the longest Wimbledon match*
46 Deco legend
47 Like a zero-charged battery
49 Not our
50 Linger in the tub
51 Artist's niche

53 Number of toes a rhino has
54 Emulate a dervish
55 After-dinner candy
57 "The Time Machine" author
59 Slant-cut pasta
61 Like "The Walking Dead"
62 Early American cars
63 Stash away
64 Kate in "Transcendence"
65 With freshness
66 Flirt
67 Alludes to
68 Smarting
69 Teammate of Jeter
71 Boston cager, for short
72 Has a great effect on
73 Could really use
76 Pathologist's study
78 Mexican vacation site
80 Profuse

81 Fils, to a French student
82 Final Bible bk.
83 Border payments
84 Make round, in a way
85 Golden Rule pronoun
86 Discontinue
87 Parting word
88 Appetite stimulus
89 Shorthand user
90 Emulated George Smiley
91 Rank below abbot
92 Wear away, as rock
93 Units of force
95 Do-re-mi
96 "___ Around": Beach Boys
98 "American ___": Paul Simon
99 Sunrise locale, in Roma

TRAFFIC JAM by Gary Larson
115 Across comes from berries grown on vines like grapes.

ACROSS

1 Fix a button
6 Denali locale
12 Rosh Hashanah horn
18 Husband of Bathsheba
19 Bundle
20 Bar order
21 Close call*
23 Night lights
24 "Vatican Rag" singer
25 Center of Portland?*
28 Bother
31 Least bit
33 Shoemaker's tool
34 Arizona New-Age mecca*
35 NYC subway line
36 Caution sign warning
38 Opened wide
41 Math degree
42 Conflict-ending agreement*
46 Exhibiting toploftiness
50 Young salmon
51 Ducks or Penguins
53 Compulsory threats
57 Schindler of "Schindler's List"
59 Blink of an eye
60 PBS funder
62 HBO drama set in Utah
63 Place
65 Peripherals
67 Trail
68 Long of film
69 Yosemite range*
73 John Reid's epithet*
76 Lille buddy
77 Race part
78 Ruined
80 Full house sign
81 Like Lake Nasser
83 Go right
84 Shock partner
86 Features of green rooms
90 Terrier type
92 Traffic lights
95 R.E.M.'s "Letter Never ___"
96 Guide
98 Like the fax machine in 1966*
100 Grocery chain
103 Stirs up
105 Actor Mineo
106 Diminutive suffix
107 Slang term for a Muscovite
111 Much too explicit, in textspeak
112 Playboy Hugh's nickname
115 Steak au poivre ingredient
117 Rite of passage*
120 Chinese liquor
122 Subway fare
123 Conscience*
128 Bloomer and Earhart
129 Spritelike
130 Center of Disneyworld
131 Make a shuffleboard surface faster*
132 The Pharmacists frontman
133 Simple tune

DOWN

1 Bolt
2 Geologic time period
3 Paul McCartney, for one
4 Noblemen
5 "___ is coming with us?"
6 Mimicker
7 Eye surgery tool
8 African capital
9 Cousin of reggae
10 Set aside
11 Had oysters at a bar
12 House of worship
13 Catnip and lovage, e.g.
14 Gondolier's song opener
15 Electrical unit
16 Internet giant
17 Take offense at
20 Rear
22 Jill of "The Love Boat"
26 Barley beards
27 Arena shout
28 Safari sight
29 Parts
30 Utter
32 Viking crematory
37 Big name in newspaper publishing
39 Major Joppolo's post
40 Look-alike
43 Pileup
44 Exonerate
45 Nonprescription item
47 Thorny plants
48 They can't be choosers
49 Handbag monogram
52 College in Atherton, CA
54 Recital number
55 Sofia's "Descendants" role
56 Scorch
58 Schedule again
61 Not voiced
64 Linked
66 Krone spenders
69 Radio operators
70 Apple on a desk
71 "I Just Wanna Stop" singer Vannelli
72 Gets rid of
74 Just beginning
75 Lasso loop
79 Prepare for winter takeoff
82 "Newhart" production co.
85 Yalies
87 Sick and tired
88 Vantage point
89 Have the helm
91 Sit-and-soak sites
93 Talk effusively
94 Come to attention
97 "Coriolanus" setting
99 Sparkled
100 Sportscaster Cross
101 Gibson Chet Atkins SST, e.g.
102 Take for granted
104 Fortune
108 Trig functions
109 Aussie "bear"
110 "Living ___": Bon Jovi
113 Yahoo! service
114 Untrue
116 Miss Longstocking
118 Campus hangout
119 Lacquered metalware
121 Quatro y quatro
124 Mayberry address
125 Be in a cast
126 Juicer
127 Hog heaven

VACATION EXTRAS   by Pam Klawitter
95 Across first appeared in Barrie's novel "The Little White Bird."

ACROSS

1 Brings under control
6 Old map letters
10 Heath genus
15 Sawyer's pal
19 Screenshot
20 Biblical miracle spot
21 Hat worn by Phil Mickelson
22 Plays a part or parts of plays
23 Honeymoon hotspot rental?
26 Hit with a beam
27 Exxon in Canada
28 Aretha Franklin's label
29 "The court ___ the opinion . . ."
30 E! sister channel
31 Lacking face value
33 UPS rival
35 Oceans
37 RSA political party
40 U.S. symbol of freedom look-alike?
47 Overdid the all-you-can-eat buffet
49 About
50 Simon & Garfunkel hit
51 "Space Invaders" company
52 Aqua Velva rival
54 Copier issue
55 Pirate's cry
56 Curling wave hitting L.A.'s shore?
62 Sudoku fillers: Abbr.
63 Art critic Faure
64 Taco Bell parent
65 "The Hobbit" actor McKellen
66 Twitch
68 Hunt for Treasure Island's location?
76 Green prefix
77 Greek interjection
78 GI's furlough
79 "XXX's and ___": Yearwood
81 "Bad" cholesterol
84 Railway terminal vehicle?
90 Mars counterpart
92 Diffident
93 "That was close!"
94 Curly-tailed dog
95 "I've Gotta Crow" singer
98 Jared in "Dallas Buyers Club"
100 Produce freshener
101 Splash Mountain, for one?
105 Dedicated lines
106 Interstellar meas.
107 "National Enquirer" publisher
108 Hall's rock partner
110 One way out
112 Robert of "The Sopranos"
115 Word with holy or sheer
118 Genesis murderer
122 Morlock prey
123 Part of a midnight countdown party?
126 Cut back on the workout
127 Nightmarish film address
128 Unsightly fruit?
129 New wing, maybe
130 They're aged in oak
131 Say outright
132 Verb suffixes in Essex
133 Word on a maze

DOWN

1 Rake tooth
2 Suzy in "Twister"
3 Barnyard bleats
4 Urge a hen to lay?
5 Bikini Bottom locale
6 June bug's family
7 "On Language" columnist
8 Genetic strands
9 Pretzel topper
10 Type widths
11 Submit an updated tax form
12 Woes
13 "So long!" in Salerno
14 Hobby kit with a habitat
15 Sport in "My Side of the Mountain"
16 "Whew, ready to drop!"
17 Crash probers: Abbr.
18 Brief bit of time
24 Breakneck
25 ___-slipper (orchid)
32 Soapmaking acid
34 "Insecure" network
36 Debussy's "Air de ___"
37 Century plant
38 Type of motel
39 Head cases
41 "The Godfather" composer
42 Gillette razor name
43 Neeson of "Taken"
44 Petting zoo animal
45 Amazon speaker
46 WWE jumping cutters
48 Dolphin QB for 14 years
52 Snug as ___ in a rug
53 Disaster relief org.
54 Folk singer Mitchell
57 "Keep your ___ the ball!"
58 Try to swat
59 Corden's karaoke spot
60 Forever, poetically
61 Coastal stream
67 Dies like a frog?
69 Richmond campus
70 TriStar Pictures owner
71 Gobs' jobs
72 ___-dieu (kneeler)
73 "The Hunger Games" president
74 "___ ergo sum": Descartes
75 Razzed
80 Side drum
81 Friday's employer
82 Crowd in Cologne
83 Throws off the constraints
85 Caesar's "vidi"
86 "Rats!"
87 Airbnb listings: Abbr.
88 Holier-than-___
89 Ralph of "The Waltons"
91 Watches not meant for wrists
96 "Curious George" creator
97 They glitter like gold
98 Advanced legal deg.
99 Pares prose
100 British bishop's hat
102 Hardest to find
103 Team spirit
104 "Whale Rider" people
109 Barely enough
110 A few bucks
111 Nivea competitor
113 Bouncy melody
114 Costar of Daniel and Rupert
116 Prefix like iso-
117 They get walked on
119 "Frozen" princess
120 Bakery employee
121 Welcome call in a waiting room
124 Île ___ Marie
125 Court figures, briefly

266 SLOGANS by Katherine Omak
George C. Scott also refused to accept his 15 Down.

ACROSS

1 Stuff to the gills
5 Say "Tsk!" to
10 Thermos inventor James
15 Dept. of Labor agency
19 Gathering clouds, to some
20 Berlin river
21 Pueblo brick
22 Soup recipe direction
23 Classic KFC slogan
26 Links conveyance
27 Get grayer
28 "Aye" or "nay"
29 Where shots are put
30 Like a string bikini
32 No longer edible
34 Car window adornments
37 Swiss ___
38 Apple-tossing goddess
40 Trump slogan acronym
41 Fresh talk
42 Texter's bosom buddy
45 Classic UPS slogan
51 Thailand, until 1949
52 A nephew of Donald Duck
53 Many a godmother
54 Oscar winner Jannings
55 Manhattan trains of yore
56 McNamara's ensemble
57 Chaplain's nickname
59 Dog's acute sense
60 "Romeo and Juliet" finale
63 Renee Fleming solo
64 Place to graze
65 Classic GEICO slogan
73 Many English degs.
74 "Sorry to say . . ."
75 Feeler
76 Running back's attempt
79 Bacon unit
80 Poor, as excuses go
82 "Society's Child" singer Janis
83 Trendy smoothie flavor
84 Beaufort scale category
85 Enjoy the kiddie pool
86 Like par-five holes
87 Classic Lay's slogan
93 "___ bodkins!"
94 Show curiosity
95 Sandberg in Cooperstown
96 Stalag detainees
97 They're to be expected
99 Gave the thumbs-down
101 Mortar mate
105 Chairperson's plan
107 Goatee spot
108 1/640 square mile
110 "Frost/Nixon" director Howard
111 NHL's Art ___ Trophy
112 Classic Ajax slogan
117 Price to play
118 New Hampshire's "Elm City"
119 Lindsay of "Mean Girls"
120 Complexion woe
121 Worthy of a blue ribbon
122 Exodus feast
123 Botch up
124 Tailgate party drink

DOWN

1 To this point
2 Good buddy
3 Guiding belief
4 Chang's twin
5 Constantly recurring
6 "Don't come any closer!"
7 Like Wrigley Field's walls
8 Boxing Day mo.
9 Grand Teton grazer
10 Viking rule, in old England
11 Barely beats
12 "Awesome!" in a text
13 Blood-typing letters
14 Apparent change in a star's color
15 Award Brando refused
16 Ben E. King hit
17 "Java" trumpeter
18 Stylized to a fault
24 Chris of tennis fame
25 Adult insect
31 Mob bigwig
33 Locker room group
35 War zone reporter
36 Grant of "To Catch a Thief"
37 Lab-generated copy
39 Much of North Africa
43 Saran Wrap alternative
44 Out of room
45 Radio word after "Roger"
46 Cause of careless errors
47 Catholic school teacher
48 Gymnast Comaneci
49 When doubled, "Hungry Like a Wolf" band
50 Like "King Kong" in 2005
51 Atlas expanses
56 Super deals
57 Bel ___ (Italian cheese)
58 Limb that's figuratively twisted
59 Text message status
61 Silk or satin
62 Anthem beginning
64 Bowler's assignment
66 Easter lily
67 "A Quiet Place" killer
68 Wet/dry ___ (shop accessory)
69 Was mentioned
70 Chive cousin
71 Just plain silly
72 Cranberry sauce quality
76 Baja resort, for short
77 Passed with flying colors
78 Scenes of disorder
79 Flour holders
80 Grow darker
81 Modifying wd.
84 Riot squad gear
85 TSA agent's scanner
86 Result of a gridiron sack
88 High on the Mohs scale
89 Fitness guru
90 Looking over
91 "Elsa's Dream" singer
92 Middle schooler, perhaps
98 Beginning stage
99 Performed brilliantly
100 They're taken at trials
102 Split second
103 "SNL" creator Michaels
104 "Come on in"
105 Scheherazade, for one
106 No longer in town
107 Street ___ (urban rep)
109 2000 election dangler
113 Kickoff aid
114 Tree in Frost's "The Cocoon"
115 Financial yield fig.
116 Hair gel amount

BIGGEST LOSERS   by Fred Piscop
55 and 83 Across are "losers" on a first-name basis only.

CROSS

1 "Yu-Gi-Oh!" cartoon genre
6 Join the cast of
11 Diamond shape
15 Seemingly endless
19 Synonym maven
20 Prefix meaning "lizard"
21 Idina's "Frozen" role
22 "Harry Potter" librarian Pince
23 Clown shoes, e.g.
25 Maple syruping pail
27 Apocalypse quartet
28 Handyman's belt item
30 Lavatory sign
31 A Bobbsey twin
32 Paper to fill out
34 Streak in marble
35 Algae-fungi symbiosis
39 Lacking toppings
40 One with a will
44 Tunnel sound effect
45 Dashboard alert
48 Sci-fi transport
49 Big-toe woe
50 Camcorder button
51 In medias ___
52 Mattress name
54 Suffix with Marx or Lenin
55 Becky Thatcher's creator
59 Vampire killers
60 Places for brews
63 "Java" trumpeter Al
64 Instagram, to Facebook
65 "Indian head" coins of old
66 Sunlight and garlic, to vampires
67 Hero pilot played by Hanks
68 Stick fast
70 Shamu, for one
71 Puts emphasis on
74 Faces courageously
75 Horse player's buy
77 Bossy's breakfast
78 Made a fillet of
79 Sibling's nickname
80 "___ to believe . . ."
81 Ethanol source
82 Texters's "Unbelievable!"
83 "I Fall to Pieces" singer
88 Texan's tie
89 Stay dry, in a way
93 Bell tower sounds
94 Hung in there
96 Slangy prefix meaning "super"
97 Things to cure
98 Prefix meaning "egg"
99 "I pass," in poker
101 Packed off
103 Helium, e.g.
108 Declarer's bridge partner's cards
110 Sneaky blow
113 Inventor's spark
114 Kindle download, for short
115 How checks are endorsed
116 Nobelist President
117 Harvard rival, for short
118 Over-the-top anger
119 Org. that "tracks" Santa
120 Handled clumsily

DOWN

1 Bunker's nickname
2 Agnew's plea, briefly
3 Bronson's "House of Wax" role
4 Big Pharma products
5 Sweet-smelling hydrocarbon
6 Quaker in a forest
7 ___ Crunch cereal
8 Elect. day
9 Like some vbs.
10 Blowhole
11 Coin with a $ sign
12 Line to Ben Gurion
13 Nile viper
14 Canine contagion
15 Andean source of wool
16 Chests in synagogues
17 Hook's sidekick
18 Skin pic
24 Rial spender
26 BTU part
29 Name in luxury hotels
32 Churchgoers, collectively
33 Stable morsel
34 November honorees
35 On the up and up
36 Prefix meaning "twenty"
37 Mere pittance
38 On a roll
39 Places for seaside strolls
40 Not now?
41 Piece of cake, slangily
42 More than occasionally
43 Insult in jest
46 Perfume measures
47 Southern side dish
52 Past its "sell by" date, perhaps
53 Some British peers
55 Specks of dust
56 Choreographer Twyla
57 React to a pinch
58 Fields of expertise
59 Sudden burst of growth
61 Chaucerian tale teller
62 Traffic sign: NO RIGHT ___
66 Give a leg up to
67 Oktoberfest mug
68 Monastery honcho
69 Suffix with hippo
71 Weigh station vehicles
72 "Copperhead Road" singer
73 Council of clergy
75 Use a rotary phone
76 Cough drop brand
79 Sail support
81 Stephen Colbert's network
84 Roulette action
85 Gorbachev's successor
86 Ripken, Jr. in Cooperstown
87 Young eel
90 Abolitionist Harriet
91 Follow orders
92 Dog's restraint
95 Cook without oil, in a way
98 Without a break
99 Like some art class models
100 Sign of impending doom
101 Negotiations hang-up
102 Head start, e.g.
103 DIYer's furniture chain
104 Dixieland horn
105 Chew like a squirrel
106 Toon TNT seller
107 Herring's cousin
108 Vegetable tray condiment
109 Org. for Fauci
111 Game with Draw Two cards
112 EMT's expertise

ACROSS

1 Nonschool diploma
4 Prefix with med or law
7 Scotch whisky distillery founder of note
12 Surprise ending
17 Reactor fuel
19 Not easily ruffled
20 Stated with authority
21 Picks up on
22 Set of political goals*
24 Lenders' claims
25 Sponge features
26 Chinese noodle dish
27 Real estate unit
28 Called a stop to
30 Hoops player
31 Leaves in the bag?
34 Measure up*
36 "Pretty please?"
37 Rush job initials
38 Woodstock stage gear
39 The End of the Road World Tour event*
42 Mustachioed Soviet leader
45 Pooped out
47 Evenings, on marquees
48 Arthurian wizard
49 Use one's index finger
50 Meals for weevils
52 "CIA Diary" author
53 Police academy enrollee
54 Early computer language
55 Burrows who wrote "Can-Can"
58 Sources of hanging chads*
61 Poacher pursuer*
63 Workplace with props
64 Place for a dumpster
65 Like a chatterbox
66 Picked out of a lineup
67 "Skyfall" singer
68 Ends of the earth
69 Narrows gradually
71 Home of Hammett's falcon
73 Swimming pool part
74 Beepers on belts
75 Of superb quality*
78 Cantina munchie
79 Creole stew
80 Boxing champ's prize
81 Federal funding, of sorts*
87 Vintage automaker
88 Take in, as a stray
90 Tissue sample
91 Limburger quality
92 Be successful
94 Left Bank eateries
95 Name in English china
96 What's found at starts of clue* answers
99 Planets roughly
101 Unc's mate
102 Human frailty
103 Legalese conjunction
104 Candy man H.B.
105 Stinking to high heaven
106 Prefix with air or field
107 Skilled at trickery

DOWN

1 Penultimate race circuit
2 Beethoven's Symphony No. 3
3 Carbon-14 technicians
4 Insta postings
5 Wish undone
6 Defib unit users
7 More precious
8 Misspoke, say
9 Hoses down
10 Undefined quantity
11 Baseball challenge viewings
12 Snuffy Smith's child
13 Coffee shop convenience
14 "Beats me . . ."
15 Cold War-era inits.
16 Male Manx
18 Sudoku numbers
19 Informal "What if . . ."
20 Bar order, with "the"
23 Sudoku solver's skill
25 Tom Brady's ex-team
28 Herb in curry powder
29 Armchair QB's channel
30 Throw out, as a line
32 Places for studs
33 Well-suited
35 French Sudan, now
36 Diner freebie
37 Doesn't just sit
39 Gotham City reporter
40 Blowing softly, as a fan
41 Nabisco wafer brand
42 Smooth transition
43 16th-century council site
44 Baldwin who spoofs Trump
45 Like freshly laid lawn
46 Slapstick ammo
48 Shopping mall features
49 "Gay" city of song
50 Lays an egg
51 Follow to the letter
53 Poker player's declaration
54 Pole tossed by Scots
55 Abacus user
56 Pilsners and bocks
57 Comes to a grinding halt
59 Couldn't help but
60 Fully understandable
61 Wind speed category
62 Ready for plucking
65 Hammered instrument
67 Sporty Italian car, briefly
68 Ben & Jerry's quantity
69 In poor taste
70 All keyed up
71 Karaoke need
72 Pupil dilator
73 Cheerful ditty
74 Campaign-backing orgs.
75 Word on a gift tag
76 More or less
77 Stayed away from
78 Goes one better than
81 Closet door style
82 Lerner's Broadway partner
83 Lariat wielder
84 Is gaga about
85 "All bets are off!"
86 Coiffed like Rapunzel
88 Woman with an online list
89 Pill bottle datum
90 Benton of "Hee Haw"
93 Workers with antennae
94 Gambler's IOU
95 Slough off
96 Road repair material
97 Crayon characteristic
98 Nail site
99 Guy in a personal ad, for short
100 Honor society letter

SOLVE-A-PUZZLE by Jean Omay

In 1998, 39 Down was inducted into the National Toy Hall of Fame.

ACROSS

1 Peace talks goal
5 Criminal's handle, maybe
10 Barely enough
15 Underground workplace
19 Dept. of Labor division
20 Punch bowl go-with
21 Copy center supply
22 Scored 100 on
23 Arcade game with a mallet
25 Attendees for hire
27 Watchful ones
28 Load on board
29 Like a lace handkerchief
30 Altoids buys
31 ___ serif (type style)
32 They're above the abs
33 Most risqué
37 Vaper's buy
38 Kitten caboodles
42 A Musketeer
43 "The San Francisco Treat"
46 Driver's aid
47 A heavy metal
48 Mr. Hulot's creator
51 Gillespie's genre
52 Stab wound memento
53 Rapid eye blinking, e.g.
54 Flea-market items
58 "Sir" in colonial India
59 Don't hurry
62 Drinks with scones
63 Parish officials
64 Mimic's forte
65 "Person of Interest" hero
66 Pride Lands sounds
67 Straighten, in a way
69 Scavenger ___
70 One frequently on the charts
73 Propelled a punt
74 Ali's "Rumble in the Jungle" tactic
76 Holiday lead-in
77 Country club figures
78 Pfizer product
79 Woolly females
80 Break or brake
81 PC bailout key
82 Source of phone chuckles
87 Nut case
88 Repairs a stocking cap
90 Blood-related
91 Squirms
93 "Jimmy Crack Corn" singer
94 Hustler's ploy
95 Personal bearing
96 Martinsville Speedway org.
99 Slow as molasses
100 Some high voices
105 Merry Men minstrel
107 Popular carnival ride
108 Well-behaved
109 Divination deck
110 Disney mermaid
111 Florence's river
112 David Korins designs
113 Blissful spots
114 Winner at Gettysburg
115 Show grief

DOWN

1 Hanoi Hilton dwellers
2 Big Apple tennis venue
3 Charlie of whodunits
4 Social asset
5 "Thank U" singer Morissette
6 Sing the blues
7 Ones on pedestals
8 ". . . and ___ well!"
9 Catch, so to speak
10 Way out there
11 Ole Miss misses
12 Comic Meara
13 Fish tank accessory
14 Car-deal allowance
15 Poughkeepsie college
16 Desktop folder, e.g.
17 Colorful salamander
18 Guitar great Duane
24 Airborne boxes
26 Mescal and saguaro
28 Not of the clergy
31 Chem. or phys.
32 Sound heard at Trevi Fountain
33 "Nick of Time" singer Bonnie
34 Well-lit lobbies
35 Tightly packed
36 Electrolyte particle
37 Dane of "Grey's Anatomy"
39 Classic drawing toy
40 Show in syndication
41 Djokovic and Tesla, e.g.
44 Cause to feel shame
45 Winged elephant eater
48 Sporty Ford, briefly
49 Hawkeye Pierce's branch
50 No-win situation
52 Pelvic bones
55 Really enjoyed
56 Designer Geoffrey
57 Dreads sporter
58 King Mongkut's land
60 Pentathlon blades
61 Keep watch over
63 Does one's civic duty
65 Valerie Harper title role
66 Ready to harvest
67 Less desirable bunk
68 Viking-related
70 Partner of a reporter's five W's
71 Summon, as a memory
72 Many auctioned autos
74 Theological subj.
75 Celebrity chef Paula
78 December 25 service
80 Be in session
82 Living room piece
83 Say again
84 Hardcover covers
85 Thumbs-up
86 Kipling classic
87 Ligament
89 Early laptop batteries
91 Droopy, like lettuce
92 House flip
94 Lawgiver of Athens
95 Hawaiian racing canoe
96 Pesters nonstop
97 Potted succulent
98 Arcade machine opening
99 Peel a pippin
100 Forest ranger's worry
101 Easing of tensions
102 It's mounted on Wrangler tailgates
103 River of Normandy
104 Sty fare
106 Paul Sorvino, to Mira
107 Cap for Angus

270 MAKE IT COUNT   by Lee Taylor
24 Across is generally accepted to be a food hygiene myth.

ACROSS

1 Spanish explorer
7 Repeated a poem
14 Bones in the upper arm
20 Type of patch
21 Illustration
22 Tigon, for one
23 Prairie dog, e.g.
24 Guideline for dropped food?
26 Ball cheese
27 Pell-mell
29 Cobra killers
30 Consignment shop transactions
32 Grey of tea shops
35 Thor Heyerdahl craft
36 Henpecks
37 Sturdy carts
39 Alternatively
45 Fails miserably
49 Double-parking area?
51 Really bothered
52 "___-ching!"
54 Holiday drink
55 Margery Daw's board
56 Take along
57 Water power, for short
60 In addition
62 "Scream" actress Campbell
63 Roman footwear
65 Indicates
67 Made a defensive chess move
70 Septennial marriage issue
74 Chinese canine
78 Plastic wrap brand
79 SAT participant
84 Early presidential caucus state
85 And all that jazz
88 Arms and legs
90 Flora and fauna
91 Bakery basket fillers
94 Stationary runner
96 Card collection
97 Neural transmitters
98 Tri-light
102 Pooh-pooh
104 Burdened
105 Richard Bachman, for one
107 Sitar music
108 Haul
110 Fiddlehead
111 Sign Jeff Goldblum to play Mini-Me?
115 Setup wizard
121 Glide downhill
123 Low-carb diet
124 Censored item
127 Neptune, e.g.
129 Grabs some shut-eye
130 Wore away
131 Free from ropes
132 First of the litter
133 Winery visitors, at times
134 Rap retinues

DOWN

1 More desperate
2 Whittle away
3 Drinks with combo meals
4 Three Dog Night hit
5 Stone weight or 142.857 stones
6 Busy, busy, busy
7 Calls the shots
8 Left the stage
9 Lascaux paintings, e.g.
10 "___ Mine": Beatles
11 Festoons with Charmin
12 Grade sch.
13 Interior design
14 Mobiles, e.g.
15 Reverse
16 Spanish painter Joan
17 They come from the Land Down Under
18 Harsh breathing sound
19 Dots in la mer
25 Broadcasting
28 Per se
31 Desperate final effort
33 Like sushi fish
34 City on the Rhone
38 Aberdeen denizen
40 Freelancer's encl.
41 Nottingham river
42 Stand for a painter
43 Tequila plant
44 Like morning grass
45 Streisand's nickname
46 Senorita's "other"
47 "Count ___!"
48 Oregano relative
50 Anciently
53 Yemen port
58 Fish with "wings"
59 Hoopster Shaquille
61 Big mo. for pumpkin sales
64 Liberace's nickname
66 Bollywood costume
68 Do thespian's work
69 2000 Ricky Martin hit
71 Go head to head
72 Namath's last team
73 Sacked out
74 River deposits
75 Hullabaloo
76 Loving cup
77 Wrote a glowing review
80 "Washboard" muscles
81 Wrench or drill
82 Active European volcano
83 Not rocket science
86 Give it a shot
87 Where the conga was born
89 Enya's "___ in Africa"
92 Teleost fish
93 Superlatively super
95 ___ of Mexico
99 Ticket category
100 Tiger's concern
101 Checkout lines?
103 Stays awake until the kids are home
106 Annoying roommate
109 Insinuate
112 Auspices
113 "JFK" director
114 Lincoln in-laws
115 "Should that be the case"
116 Winning coach of Super Bowl XIV
117 Took to court
118 Hornbeam, for one
119 Zermatt mountains
120 Pee-wee's mail lady
122 Puts two and two together
125 Charing Cross Sta. traffic
126 English rebel Tyler
128 Rock producer Brian

The building at 59 Across became a UNESCO World Heritage Site in 2007.

ACROSS

1 Spill the beans
5 Capital on the Vistula
11 Hit hard, in cricket
17 Commode
19 On equal terms
20 Like golf gloves
22 Must
23 Setting
24 Knockout
25 Not a replica
27 Synonym books
28 They'll "never hurt me"
29 Cockney chickens
30 Trust fund recipient
31 Say thay
32 Bay of Fundy bore
34 NBAers' stats
36 Cooked in sugar
38 ___ wrestling
39 Hacienda room
41 Chaotic sequence
45 "Enquirer" couple
47 Motherese
50 Unworldly
51 Horse whisperer
53 Still-life vessel
54 It's a long story
58 Drescher of "The Nanny"
59 Opera house with concrete "shells"
60 Acts conceited
62 Wide receiver
64 Dressing table
66 Provoke dismay
68 Tennis racket accessory
72 Pump parts
74 Amtrak stops
79 Like a samara
80 Ski spot near Santa Fe
82 "The Black Cat" author
83 Stage-diving spot
84 Brought on
86 Whale shark's dinner
89 Hip-hop trio ___ Soul
90 The "K" in MLK, e.g.
94 Some products have "1,001"
96 Lehman Caves loc.
97 More than you can handle
98 Wassailer's song
100 Café cup
102 Secretive
105 Sprightly
106 Kind of answer
107 Run off with
109 Ceremonial cleansing
111 Somewhat surprising event
115 Less polished
116 Gout area
117 Particle size
118 One who has a second helping?
119 Chancellor Merkel
120 Bidding
121 Clandestine meetings
122 Yellowstone attraction
123 Hardens

DOWN

1 One killed Adonis
2 Zombies
3 Sour brew
4 Early
5 In fine fettle
6 Wading bird
7 Scopes out
8 Goes postal
9 Compatriot
10 Penultimate letter
11 Samurai code of honor
12 Temporary
13 Winter bugs
14 Noted screenwriting software
15 Weltschmerz
16 ___-tongue (wild vanilla)
17 Albeit, briefly
18 Voice quality
21 Dribble
26 Building stone
27 Be inclined
30 Bradley in "The Post"
32 Radiates
33 Singing cowboy Gene
35 Blarney Stone gift
36 "Iron Man" Ripken
37 Many, many moons
40 Temporarily inactive
41 Called
42 Life-or-death
43 Heidi Hansen's "dear" son
44 Tear apart
46 Sixty secs.
48 Mongolian tent
49 Salvers
52 Campbell in "Skyscraper"
55 Egyptian cobras
56 Transcript stat
57 Waiter's query before clearing
60 Ballpoint pen inventor
61 Where dos are done
63 "Spandau Phoenix" novelist
65 Teachers' org.
67 Cheat at hide-and-seek
68 "The BFG" author
69 Word after inter or et
70 "War of the Worlds" world
71 Hideous
73 October birthstone
75 Third degree
76 Hepburn-Tracy affair, e.g.
77 Mosaic pieces
78 Fend (off)
81 Like Thai cuisine
83 Ramadan faster
85 Roman god
87 "Well, ___-di-dah!"
88 Elect. day
91 Most meddlesome
92 They're not domestic
93 Gyrate
95 Narratives
98 City on the Loire
99 "Becket" star
101 Combat chopper
102 ATM insert
103 Approximately
104 Model builder, at times
106 Kind of savings bank
108 Hammock support
110 "___ means war!"
111 Dangerous job site
112 Raise
113 Red ink entry
114 Shady Tolkien creature?
116 Suitcase

272 OVERHEAD ITEMS   by Fran & Lou Sabin
They don't hand out trophies for the award at 118 Across.

ACROSS

1 Castle stronghold
5 Fitting
8 Charged
13 Argentine expanse
19 Part of TAE
20 Between phi and psi
21 Monsieur Zola
22 Old Line State bird
23 2003 Mike Myers role
26 Mint product
27 "Old MacDonald" sounds
28 This pen can't write
29 Set right
31 Artist Magritte
32 RDU guesstimates
35 Pineapple fiber
37 Oxygen-breathing organisms
39 2011 Amanda Seyfried film
43 Psychologist Bettelheim
44 Eight eights
45 Starz rival
46 Social no-nos
48 "Songland" network
51 Cactus bud
54 ___ Plains
58 Stand beside
59 Kobe drama
60 Masonry tool
62 Lip disservice
63 Olin in "The Reader"
64 Displayed contempt
65 Globetrot
67 ___ familias
68 Siren song
69 Heavy reading
70 Recommended daily intake
72 Point of view
75 Hot breakfast fare
76 Like the Sphinx
80 Casino game
81 "K-PAX" hero
83 Robert Burns poem
85 Rosary bead
86 Horse for Lawrence
87 Mirren in "Hobbs & Shaw"
88 Make certain of
89 Source of gluten
90 Boston Red Sox anthem
92 1958 Mideast alliance
94 NFL linemen
95 Benchmarks
97 Female heir to the throne
103 Boot stud
105 "Sesame Street" resident
106 Tweezer case
107 Awards for J.K. Rowling et al.
108 Org. against workplace discrimination
110 Son of Isaac
112 Massenet opera
116 More slender and lean
118 "Award" for striking out four times in a game
122 Annette's "Bikini Beach" role
123 Fat substitute
124 Mil. aide
125 Rat Pack name
126 Belgian seaport
127 Dates set for attacks
128 Patriotic org.
129 Hang out

DOWN

1 Green Hornet's driver
2 Large textbook market
3 Knotted
4 Lambeau Field gridder
5 "Do it!"
6 Part of PBK
7 Canterbury cans
8 Go over
9 "___ that!"
10 Fed. well-being watchdog
11 Public garden
12 Champagne head
13 Mighty big
14 "Exodus" freedom fighter
15 Millionth of a meter
16 Jemima Puddle-Duck's hat
17 Coeur d'___ Lake
18 Serbian tennis great
24 ___ spumante
25 It's out on a limb
30 Agnew called them "nattering"
33 Stick-to-it type
34 Close kin
36 49er great Ronnie
38 Autumn hue
39 Gets around
40 "Conspiracy of Fools" subject
41 Combine name
42 A-OK opposite
47 False god in Judges
49 Clavicle, for one
50 Burn a bit
52 "Willow Song" opera
53 Lash of westerns
55 Drumroll sounds
56 Diamond flaw
57 Nudist
61 Cecil ___ Mille
62 Grover's street
63 Hispanics
66 Open to bribery
67 Smooth-shelled nut
70 "___ Rheingold"
71 Come into
72 Way off yonder
73 Blue hue
74 SEAL's Army counterpart
75 Smart keys
77 Practice piece
78 "Curses!"
79 Comber's concern
81 Debuted
82 Go to the mat, slangily
84 And higher, cost-wise
86 Handle for a razor
87 "Mein ___" ("Cabaret" song)
91 Well-chilled
93 "People ___ Strange": Doors
96 Last-minute NFL kick
98 TV's "___ at a Time"
99 Makes broader
100 Ginza lighting
101 Feeling no pain
102 "Person to Person" poet
103 Folksy greeting
104 Awards given Sam Shepard
109 "___, Our Help in Ages Past"
111 Texts: Abbr.
113 It may be pressing
114 Like valedictories
115 "All gone!"
117 Poetic nightfall
119 Where kine dine
120 Mama bear, in Baja
121 Casablanca loc.

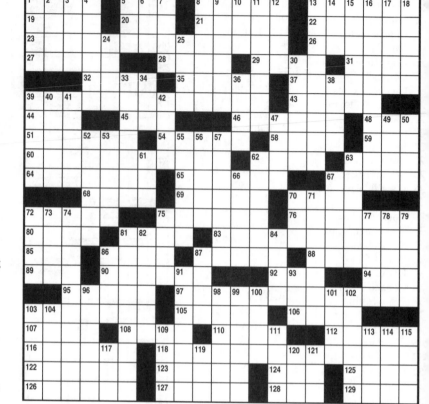

65 Across is the editor-in-chief of the fictional "Daily Bugle."

ACROSS

1 Flooded
6 Pentateuch writer
11 Chokes on jokes
15 Physical responses
18 DEA agent, in slang
19 In fine ___ (healthy)
20 Butt up against
21 Prefix with "slip" or "stop"
22 "Is this knockoff Rolex I bought accurate?"
24 Chief support
26 Rock artist?
27 Sleuth (out)
28 Caribou group
29 Dr. Seuss reptile
30 "What happened to the paint I had sitting out?"
34 Encl. for the editor
37 Zion Williamson's org.
38 "Three's Company" landlord
39 "Any idea when this mist will clear and we can fly out?"
48 Court plea, informally
49 Gist
50 Potentates of old
51 Throw out
55 Sharpness
57 "Chili today, hot ___"
59 Toys for ___
61 Conchita's cheer
62 Duel measures
64 Midori on ice
65 Marvel's J. ___ Jameson
66 Party in the UK
67 "Is it an attic or a second level?"
72 AHA course
74 "No ___": Beatles
75 Crest
76 1978 Elaine Paige role
78 Exceptionally creditworthy
79 Prunus spinosa
80 Paleontologist's find
83 Roulette bet
85 Welding shop sound
87 Righteous

89 A captain and a clownfish
91 Fashion brand with a rhino label
92 "Are you saying I have a split personality, Doc?"
96 Orgs.
99 Adversary
100 Prefix for factor
101 "Should I opt for a nip/tuck or a tummy tuck?"
107 Black key by B
112 Perfectly, with "to"
113 Word-of-mouth
114 Cape Cod, for one
117 What trainees are shown
119 "What's it like working on a farm now?"
121 Type of roof
122 Football feint
123 Ruins
124 Sounds of the wild
125 Long-eared equine
126 Balneotherapy sites
127 Environmentalist Adams
128 Pass over a flame

DOWN

1 Fidgety
2 MLB Hall-of-Famer Hoyt
3 Suit for Valiant
4 Pheromone
5 "Any another way?"
6 "Alice" diner
7 First Holy Roman Emperor
8 Artery implant
9 Plumbing connection
10 French chef's seasoning
11 Range
12 Make ashamed
13 Appearance
14 MTA stop
15 Pay what is due
16 All cheered out

17 "Man of Steel" director
19 Lantana loc.
23 "Let me explain"
25 Bamboo edibles
27 Hooks
31 Medicare Part A coverage: Abbr.
32 Amin's predecessor
33 Slugger's stat
35 Manuscript mark
36 Sicilian peak
39 "Concerto ___": Gershwin
40 Cager's target
41 San Francisco Bay island
42 Certify
43 Ground corn
44 Sister of Polyhymnia
45 John Deere UTV
46 Clubs for Rickie Fowler
47 Biltmore ___
52 Worcester ___
53 "The Book of ___" (2010)
54 Educator Du Bois
56 Pan-fries
58 State-run game
60 It's more than a push
63 Martyred Bishop of Formiae
65 "Call Me Maybe" singer
68 Parody
69 Siren, e.g.
70 Mubarak of Egypt
71 Metal fastener
72 Uber alternative
73 "Piedra de Sol" poet
77 "My Way" songwriter
80 Flabbergast
81 Film info site
82 Shake a tail
84 Inebriate
86 Smaller than small
88 Horrible
90 Salvaging tools
93 Colorado hrs.
94 "Family Guy" daughter
95 Wise counselors

96 Fictional sleuth Raisin
97 Van Halen's "___ is Love?"
98 TV-ratings week
102 Excite
103 City NE of Eureka
104 Desert springs
105 Drives
106 Concise
108 Red River delta city
109 Of Nordic stock
110 Corp. makeover
111 DVR button
115 Ground cover
116 "Queen Sugar" network
118 AM drinks
119 G&S princess
120 Freight weight

ALL THE RAGE   by Ted Williams
. . . but not in a fashion sense.

ACROSS

1 Drug raid
5 Phantom's milieu
10 Biblical dancer
16 Cupid's holding
19 Way off
20 Eats fashionably
21 Great admirer
22 Shirley's "Being There" role
23 The angry cleric was ___
26 Match the bet
27 Rock genre of Paramore
28 Terminer's law partner?
29 Building site
30 "Sober" singer
31 The angry sauna patron was ___
35 Western ski mecca
38 Little lad
39 Illusionist Jillette
40 Show of hands
41 Poet Laureate Kooser
42 Embrace fondly
45 Thumbs-up
46 Carry on
47 Way uphill
49 Until ___ notice
50 Lays down the lawn
51 Mulligrubs
52 Conceit
53 "Letters From ___ Jima" (2006)
54 "Watch out!"
57 NYC neighbor of Chinatown
58 It's a fact
60 Change a bill
61 Sprinkle with water
62 Half an umlaut
63 "Hey, pal!"
66 Hop of the Swing Era
67 The angry barber was ___
70 Coast condition
71 Kett of the comics
72 Will Smith, to Willow
73 Flora's counterpart
74 City in N France
75 Smudges
77 Crania
79 Klatch beverage
80 Shooter pellet
82 Booze or bread
83 Supporter of art
84 More than extra dry
85 Claimed but not proven

87 Raises one's hackles
88 Blind louver
89 What Tiger turned in 1996
92 Lone Ranger's horse
93 Half and half
94 Once ___ a time
95 Region
96 Greek island in the Aegean
97 "Laughing" scavenger
99 The angry clockmaker was ___
101 Metallica's "Nothing ___ Matters"
103 Legal matter
104 It may have a fork in it
106 Go bad
107 ___ a whit
108 The angry pool attendant ___
115 Akashi accessory
116 Toughen by heat
117 Tropical roots
118 Torres of Bon Jovi
119 NYSE watchdog
120 Like a Van Gogh night
121 Commencement
122 Frosty's makeup

DOWN

1 "Phooey!"
2 Spooky ship
3 Glossy cotton fabrics
4 President from Lamar
5 Like unmatched socks
6 Crusty dessert
7 In transit
8 Correct a typo
9 Arthur with three majors
10 Fluid-filled cyst
11 Hurly-burly
12 Lounged about
13 Acrylic fiber
14 Beyond Burger's lack
15 Foul up
16 The angry clone was ___

17 Dutch ___
18 Half a fortnight
24 Pierre or Louis, e.g.
25 Paleontology period
30 Hair line
31 Person of intelligence
32 Ball bearing item
33 Sidestep
34 Cynophobia fear
36 Part of a flight
37 Soul singer Sledge
38 Deck with a fool
42 Bandleader Xavier
43 Chain stitch
44 Shubert Alley sign
46 Verbose
47 After-shower need
48 The angry electrician ___
49 Soft-brimmed hat
50 Beach wear
51 Musical finale
54 Bundle of hay
55 Spew
56 The angry arms dealer ___
57 Highway curve
59 Raise the spirits
61 Not impartial
62 Man caves, often
64 Garage event
65 Leaves home?

68 Some are tall
69 Boat bottom
70 Influence
72 It's full of hot air
76 Impulses
77 Water source for Paris
78 Ms. Silkwood
79 Sourpuss
80 Ballet step
81 High priest of Shiloh
84 Voting group
86 Bacchanalian shout
88 U. of Richmond team
89 Essential nutrient
90 Ump's kin
91 Lummox
93 Raw bar item
94 Jazz fan, most likely
95 Takes on
97 Auburn dye
98 Rover's remark
100 Afore, of yore
101 First son of Seth
102 Place for a ring
103 Ripped
105 Bart's bus driver
108 Is in the past
109 Galley mover
110 Take the red-eye
111 Buck's belle
112 Part of i.e.
113 On-base club

114 Jones of Wall Street

CROSS

1 Narrow in outlook*
6 Equalizer setting
0 Adobe file format
3 Understaffed*
8 Tony Soprano's mother
9 Roll topper
0 Crayfish cookout
1 Tahitian skirt
2 "The Paper Chase" students
3 Papal cap
5 Source of play money?
6 Rx book
7 "Star Trek: TNG" empath
9 "I lack iniquity" speaker
0 Park in "Aquaman"
2 Street and seed
4 Where "karma" comes from
6 Mass. motto word
7 Studio tapes
8 Streisand's nickname
9 "¿Como esta ___?"
1 Aardvark digging area
3 Odometer increments
5 Singer Grande, familiarly
8 Like modern freezers*
1 Canal in a Springsteen song
2 Mahershala in "Moonlight"
3 Bk. after Proverbs
5 Baseball Hall-of-Famer Edd
6 100 yrs.
7 Mideast land
8 Corporate shark
9 NYC summer time
0 Coach's strategy
2 Tin-lead alloy
3 Ballpark figure
6 [extension]
7 Rockfish
0 Give a stemwinder
1 Superior hotel rating
3 West in "I'm No Angel"
4 Like some inspections
6 Trig ratio
7 Airport code for McCarran
8 Sonia in "The Rookie"
0 "Nobody ___ Better": Simon

81 Army bunk
82 Minimal
83 [extension]
84 Genetic chain
85 Win-win
87 Puts it away, away
89 Lake Nasser dam
90 Häagen-___
91 Godzilla, for one
94 Book before Romans
97 Deprive of energy
100 Westminster Kennel Club event
102 German artist Richter
104 Cannabis
105 Aquarius vessel
106 Suffix for morph
107 "___ It" (Red Skelton film)
108 From that point on
111 Betel palm
113 Brett in Super Bowl XXXI
114 Ceremonial act
115 James ___ Carter
116 Red October finder
117 [extension]
118 "___ on a tuffet . . ."
119 Put a lid on it
120 [extension]

DOWN

1 Does a swill job
2 [extension]
3 Disinclined
4 Hip-hop's ___ Kim
5 December, to January
6 Clowns
7 His, in Paris
8 Two shakes
9 Outgoing
10 "My Name Is Asher Lev" author
11 Morse "E"
12 What Eliza wanted to be
13 Getz or Musial
14 [extension]
15 John Bull's instrument
16 Country dances
17 Bridal veil material

20 Panhandles
24 "Frozen" prince
28 Take it easy
31 Where Rosa Parks refused to sit
33 Gather
34 Like a deer lick
35 Altercation
38 Phoenician galley
40 Steep slope
42 Goddess of witchcraft
43 Mexican masa dish
44 Brio
45 Local pol
46 "Pioneer Woman" Drummond
47 Neighbor of Leb.
48 [extension]
49 Furlong's forty
50 1997 Lemmon/Matthau film
54 Cannes film
57 Italian cuisine staple*
60 Imposing castle entrance
61 Tiptoe, in ballet
62 Makes frizzy
64 Bearded bloom

65 Morning prayers
67 Some are flying
68 UFC octagon
69 Took top billing*
71 Verizon bundle
72 Lowlife
74 Strange
75 Oui opposite
76 British biscuit
78 Kentucky*
79 Moreno and Hayworth
82 Mrs. Lovett's wares
86 Audrey of "Dallas"
88 "Boléro" instrument
89 Beached
90 Equine mothers
92 "Queen of the Jungle"
93 U.S. Navy jet
94 "It's ___" (Fields film)
95 Large evergreens*
96 Treasure stash
98 Bonnie Blue Butler's dad
99 "Billy Budd" captain
100 Resided
101 "___ the Champions": Queen
103 Poolside drinks

105 Oatmeal color
109 By way of
110 Lazy refusal
112 Biodegrade

IT'S A GUY THING   by Vernon Dungen
37 Down has been dubbed "The King of the Jukebox."

ACROSS

1 Curving billiards shot
6 Walk like a rooster
11 Hub near Paris
15 Sty fare
19 "Round up the ___ suspects"
20 Moleskin color
21 Bridges or Brummell
22 Club in a Manilow hit
23 "Wild and crazy guy" of comedy
25 "The Cable Guy" actor
27 Motorcycle add-on
28 Sired
30 Greys in "Dark Skies"
31 Part of a tall cake
33 Enticement on a hook
34 Concertgoer's keepsake
35 It may be vented in anger
39 Does a trucker's work
41 Tree-lined walkways
45 Treasure collection
46 "Jealous Guy" singer
48 Culinary phrase
49 Dirty old man
50 Hand over formally
51 Beehive State tribesman
52 Miss, in a way
53 "___ losing it?"
54 "The Fall Guy" actor
58 Without a sou
59 FBI files
62 Skedaddles
63 Showing anguish
64 Barista's servings, slangily
65 Shutterbug's request
66 "E" in the box score
67 BBQ joint appliance
69 Chanel of fashion
70 Salty tavern munchies
73 Jackrabbits
74 "My Guy" singer
76 Woman in an order
77 Bygone GM brand
78 Watering hole
79 Roger of "Cheers"
80 Prefix for allergenic
81 School support org.
82 "He's a Right Guy" composer
86 Filmmaker Pier ___ Pasolini
87 Sahara formation
90 Overgrown, as some walls
91 Defeated on the mat
92 Make a decision
93 Part of a process
94 One living near Loch Ness
96 Give the thumbs-up
99 Truth twister
100 Espresso coffee
105 Voice of Meg Griffin on "Family Guy"
107 "Nice guys finish last" speaker
111 Line on a list
112 Head-butting beasts
113 Think similarly
114 Semifrozen downpour
115 Moist, like grass
116 Site with a "can't sell" list
117 Sing "The Lonely Goatherd"
118 Lippy

DOWN

1 Rumple, as hair
2 Source of Italian bubbly
3 Dragged to court
4 "Ctrl-S" command
5 November winner
6 Weigh-in psych job
7 Black goo
8 Same old, same old
9 News org. since 1958
10 Pool game
11 ___ d'art (curio)
12 Tara of "Sharknado"
13 Criminal's flight
14 Cozumel's peninsula
15 Book copier of old
16 Handed-down tales
17 Accepting business
18 Forks over
24 Common street name
26 Degree holder, briefly
29 Levitator's command
32 Home of the Colossus
33 Bratwurst holder
34 Pucker-inducing fruit
35 Classic violin, briefly
36 Movie trailer, e.g.
37 "Five Guys Named Moe" composer
38 Apple of Adam's eye?
40 Subtle "Excuse me . . ."
41 Pangolin's meal
42 Writer who inspired "Guys & Dolls"
43 Hard to tell apart
44 Beyond appeased
46 Hecklers' sounds
47 Emergency room staffer
50 Sunny forecast
52 Heavenly hunter
55 USS Monitor's plates
56 Titillating, as gossip
57 At minimal power
58 Roseanne of "Roseanne"
60 Sushi bar libations
61 Currier's partner
63 Weightlifter's rep
65 Hiccups cure?
66 Conger catcher
67 Compares prices
68 Where Kinnie is drunk
70 Isn't colorfast
71 Database table row
72 Cafeteria hair net
74 Tom or stag
75 Russian-born deco designer
78 Shade of white
80 Seoul river
82 Ethnology focus
83 Pocket made of dough
84 Tracing paper, e.g.
85 Upholstery problem
86 Casino honcho
88 Lost in thought
89 Dip into coffee
91 Broke
93 Spacek of "Carrie"
95 Like de Sade
96 Mixed in with
97 Google find
98 Whole bunch
99 Succotash bean
101 Arthur Ashe's alma mater
102 "___ Leaving Home": Beatles
103 Pro shop bagful
104 Pseudo-stylish
106 Catch in the act
108 Prefix with centric or maniac
109 O'Hare's airport code
110 Low mark

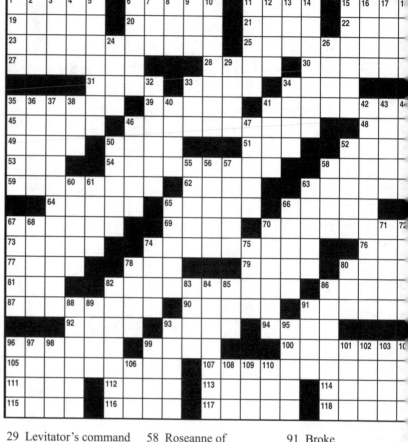

SPLIT P'S by Vernon Dungen

Before mace, 68 Across was the defensive weapon of choice for many women.

ACROSS

1 Use a Kindle
5 A creamy dressing
10 Gaza Strip group
15 Become wearisome
19 Model Macpherson
20 Weed B Gon company
21 Came to light
22 Berry in smoothies
23 Dippable munchie
25 Flint's Walrus, for one
27 Out, socially
28 Bridge measure
29 Gamboling goat-men
30 Depot postings, informally
32 Weed whacker
33 Trunk item
35 Got forty winks
38 Our feathered friends
41 Unwrap in a hurry
45 DuPont acrylic fiber
46 Model T starter
47 Boy detective of kid-lit
49 Passport datum
50 Install in office
51 Monotonous job
52 Stoker who created Dracula
53 Alamo rental
54 Election winners
55 Lobby, e.g.
59 Nanny's offspring
60 Dilapidated digs
62 Tip jar bills
63 In a snoopy way
65 Footnote term
67 Horrible coffee, slangily
68 Milliner's fastener
70 Evolved into
72 "What a pity!"
74 Walked wearily
77 Bitterly cold and damp
78 Cosmetic applied with a sponge
83 Sign of a sellout
84 Hit "send" prematurely, say
85 "Heaven forbid!"
86 Rifle-toting Oakley
87 Shellfish at a bake
88 Hit from Moe
90 Walk wearily

91 Chekov portrayer Yelchin
92 White ___ (random signal)
93 Prepare for printing
95 Hockey team line, e.g.
97 Admitted for free
98 Bits of dialogue
100 Grassy area
101 Don't stand erect
103 Sister of Blanche DuBois
106 Bumbling sort
108 Elections following elections
112 Home for city birds
114 Appliance with sockets
117 Gobs
118 Give birth, as a whale
119 First sign of the zodiac
120 Place for an icicle
121 Harper of "Breaking Bad"
122 Called a halt to
123 Past perfect, e.g.
124 Crock-Pot meal

DOWN

1 Forfeited wheels, briefly
2 Musk of SpaceX
3 Resort north of Provo
4 Area with poor reception
5 Supported a team
6 Flew like a javelin
7 Unspecified degree
8 Hellenic X
9 Oahu-to-Maui flight, e.g.
10 Come to pass
11 Solo often sung in Italian
12 Times to crow
13 Hard-rock center
14 Start a voyage
15 Attach, in a way

16 Like overworked muscles
17 Hibernation spot
18 Manlis in "Dick Tracy"
24 No longer up for grabs
26 Tombstone marshal
28 Relax in the tub
31 Bollywood garments
32 Vishnu worshiper
34 Excellent, slangily
35 Private's denial
36 Mineirinho, e.g.
37 Leftovers preserver
39 Many airport shuttles
40 Ridged fabric
42 Document in a shipment
43 iPhone folder contents
44 Socially inept
46 Party pancake
48 Home to cattails
51 Like a good egg
52 Bow to pressure
55 Fuss before a mirror

56 Shake out of slumber
57 Not factual
58 Annoying Web ad
61 Place-holding abbr.
64 Caesar of 1950s TV
66 Rambo-esque
67 Powerful shark
69 Had leftovers, say
70 French naval port
71 Before the deadline
73 Completes a flight
75 Clear from memory
76 Like an enclosed stadium
79 Nick of "Cape Fear"
80 Powerful ray
81 Kitty input
82 Macramé units
87 Cooked fruit concoctions
89 Air rifle ammo
90 Sinner's atonement
91 Felled in a forest
92 Factory whistle times
94 Cylindrical storehouse

96 Got hitched on the run
97 Salad or dessert, say
99 Call onto the carpet
102 Arbor Day plantings
103 Went "ptui"
104 Bathroom square
105 Divas' clashers
107 "From Russia With ___" (1963)
109 Place to rush, in college
110 Brubeck's "Take ___"
111 Gush lava
113 All-you-___-eat
114 Obedient puppy's reward
115 Underground resource
116 Top the field

278 WHAT POLLY WANTS by Scott Atkinson
What Polly wants can be found at 107 Across.

ACROSS

1 Strait bordering Sumatra
8 "You slay me!"
14 Rear muscles
20 Leave in the lurch
21 Sketcher's need
22 Disney duck
23 Hand-tightened fastener*
24 Carnival game prize*
26 All-Pro linebacker Junior
27 Beverage made with eggs
29 Israeli seaport
30 Unwillingly abroad
31 Depeche Mode's "___ Good"
33 Decompose
34 WW2 ally of the USA
35 "Empress of the Blues" Smith
38 "Woo-hoo, the weekend!"
40 Toll rd.
41 "Sonic Dash" game company
45 1993 Clint Eastwood film*
48 Hip-length boot
49 Lassoed
50 Justice Gorsuch
51 "Survivor" immunity tiki
52 Peptide acid
53 Attired
54 Belittle
55 Chess champion Mikhail
56 Playground retort
57 Word before trick or dance
58 Bull's warning
59 Spiritual advisor to 12 U.S. Presidents*
61 Battle souvenir
62 "Big" London landmark
63 Galena and bauxite
64 Label on tuna cans*
69 Post-grace instructions
71 AWOL pursuers
74 Islands off Portugal
75 Campaign pro
76 Use a Bounty
77 Visibly shaken
78 100%
79 Short-billed rail
80 Not quite shut
81 Hawaiian veranda
82 "___ we meet again"
83 Berlin song in "Young Frankenstein"*
86 Statistical midpoint
87 First name in spydom
88 Inventory: Abbr.
89 Recently
90 Junkyard dogs
91 "Up First" network
92 Jamaican folk music genre
94 Most avant-garde
98 Italian beloved
99 12 meses
100 Part of RFK: Abbr.
104 Kingston Trio classic*
107 What Polly wants (and a theme hint)
109 Person of Perth
110 1995 World Series winners
111 "The Russia House" author
112 Defend against criticism
113 Out like a light
114 Saw-edged

DOWN

1 Gaping holes
2 "___ Baby" ("Hair" song)
3 Turner in "Peyton Place"
4 Painfully conflicted
5 Cloudflare offering
6 One at a sidebar
7 "Star Trek" actor Yelchin
8 "___ So Shy": Pointer Sisters
9 Small blood vessel
10 Remove, as an old refrigerator
11 Comparably plump
12 Bulk
13 "Right you ___!"
14 Solidarity birthplace
15 Hermit
16 Linux rival
17 "Ashes to Ashes" author Hoag
18 Airline to Tel Aviv
19 Unscheduled
25 Put to rest a rumor
28 Approached
32 "My hands are ___"
34 Open a sleeping bag
35 Hiawatha's canoe wood
36 Name on a famous B-29
37 Ireland's patron, briefly
39 Suffix for polter or Zeit
40 Type of basin or wave
41 Identical to
42 "Dingbat" of '70s TV
43 Birthplace of Columbus
44 "___ in My Heart": Faith Hill
46 Connate
47 Conform
48 Rabbit colony
54 "Ladders to Fire" author Nin
56 "Get ___!" (Snap out of it!")
58 Maximilian in "Topkapi"
59 It makes oil boil
60 Dannon product
61 Ankle injury
62 Key of "The Star-Spangled Banner"
64 Factual tidbit
65 It's high in smoggy air
66 "Whole ___ Love": Led Zeppelin
67 Gargoyles
68 Left ventricle exit route
69 Karate schools
70 Rio beach of song
71 Craze
72 Oliver of "The West Wing"
73 Take by force
76 "Gidget" star
77 Train lounge
79 King Leonidas' land
81 Not right?
84 Better
85 Roasted one
87 Did the Iditarod
90 DeMille of Hollywood
91 Lacking a rich vocal tone
93 SASEs, e.g.
94 Twin in Genesis
95 Bra spec
96 "Gee willikers"
97 "Make ___!": Picard
98 Naval VIPs
101 Gumbo thickener
102 123 Sesame Street resident
103 Fairway obstacle
105 Cavalier org.?
106 Nile viper
108 Clue dir.

ACROSS

1 Crumples (up)
5 Univ. stat
8 Degrees in art hist.
12 Reduced, in a way
18 Burger King drink
19 Muscle car from Chevy
20 "What more ___ say?"
21 Jacket fastener
22 Cuban vehicle?
24 Space cadet
25 Vail activity
26 Most trivial
27 Disproves
29 Allowed
30 Laughing syllables
31 Earth's crust layer
33 Painfully (aware)
35 Wagering parlor
37 Most sturdy
40 Mountain lion
41 Winter Park loc.
44 Jingle writer
46 Averred
48 Like Évian
50 Whirlaway's jockey
51 Window shop, e.g.
52 Effluent to a treatment plant
53 "M*A*S*H" pop star?
54 "Who's there?" reply
56 New Age artist John
59 ___ Hall U.
60 English clink
61 Proper condition
63 P. Hearst's captors
64 Liberace's nickname
65 And so on
66 Ancient Irish capital
67 Karel Capek play
69 "O Patria Mia" singer
71 Toothpaste letters
74 Cringing exclamation
76 Hot season for French chefs?
78 Hershey rival
80 Dubya, once
81 "Without ___" (1988 Caine film)
83 Supermarket section
85 Aviary sound
86 Words to a betrayer
87 Delphic seer
89 Winter Olympics event
91 "Yes, that lady!"
93 Coney Island contest sponsor
95 Where Mark Twain is buried
96 Stick with a pouch
97 London landmark
98 Sushi fish
100 Relinquish
102 Bonus NHL periods
103 Selfish shout
105 Sweet-milk cheese
106 CIC advisors
108 Sgts. and cpls.
110 Tone deafness
112 Squash often fried
116 Pirate refrain
118 Fox News pundit Hannity
119 Most disgusting
120 Rival of 13 Down
121 Rikers Island river
122 "___ Day Has Come": Dion
123 AAA suggestions
124 Bone connectors
125 "I Wish" rapper ___-Lo
126 "Are we there ___?"
127 Previous owner of Matchbox

DOWN

1 Will-o'-the-___
2 Pang
3 Dessert with a menacing name
4 Perfect Sleeper maker
5 Connecticut governor (1975–80)
6 Passion Play role
7 Bill the Cat outburst
8 A train
9 Bomb a final, e.g.
10 Caper
11 Evaluate
12 Light wts.
13 Inventive friend of Mark Twain
14 Liked Lady Liberty's crown
15 ". . . baked in ___"
16 Make like a librarian
17 Unit of work
19 Social follower
23 Mug
27 Less distinct
28 Concert souvenir
32 Bear witness
34 Jimmy Eat World fans
35 Juice choice
36 Mailed fist, e.g.
38 Siberian sleigh
39 "Fifth Beatle" Sutcliffe
41 Group for the level-headed?
42 Danish toy company
43 Yemeni port
45 Word after fan or chain
47 Odd couple?
49 Bird sound
55 Slumberous
57 Online periodical of note
58 "The Lion" Selassie
62 "Let's get out of here!"
66 CBS franchise since 1993
68 La-Z-Boy bestseller
70 Portray
72 Abhor
73 Heavenly hues
75 Pained response
77 Alternative
79 Propped (up)
80 Uruguayan coin
81 Outstanding
82 "Smoking Gun" bluesman Robert
84 Fidgety
88 Ample, in text
90 Diplomatic off.
92 Marianas ___
94 Fit of ire
99 Surfaces
101 Lucky charm
103 LOOM member
104 QB's goal-line call, often
107 Father's Day gift
108 Plot twists
109 Whiskered area
111 Get the pot going
113 "Sesame Street" org., pre-2000
114 Tiny time period: Abbr.
115 "But thinking makes ___": Shak.
116 Survey choice
117 Switch ups?
119 Wray in "King Kong"

280

HONOR SOCIETY   by Cindy Wheeler
James Woods played 94 Across in a 1995 film.

ACROSS

1 Shell game
5 São ___, Brazil
10 Clubs for St. Andrews
15 Spring melt
19 Makarova's skirt
20 "Bear" novelist Marian
21 Talking bird
22 Charity begins here
23 Seed case
24 Screenwriter Ephron
25 "Love in the Dark" singer
26 Black and lustrous
27 "Steve Canyon" cartoonist*
29 President who was never elected*
31 Nurse's concern
32 ___-de-lance
33 By a crackling fire
34 Salem summer hrs.
35 Literary Bell
38 Pilsner holder
40 Like dad jokes
43 Done in
44 On the left, on deck
45 Monster.com listing
48 "Glee" actor Monteith
49 This and that
50 Saki, for one
51 Former Maltese currency
52 Place for a band
53 "Battlefield Earth" novelist*
55 Halley's discovery
56 St. John Lateran, for one
58 Major at Little Bighorn
59 Refrigerates
60 Keep tabs on
61 Does teamster work
63 "Cuchi-Cuchi" girl
64 Calm, cool, and collected
66 White House room
67 Bought it
70 Maine college town
71 Father of a real-life TV family*
74 Poetic preposition
75 Last Stuart queen

76 "___ and Whispers" (1972)
77 Ornamental quartz
78 Gaelic name for Scotland
79 Cooper's creation
80 Growing ___
81 "Hamlet" or "House"
82 "Stormy Weather" composer
83 Touch, say
84 Gettysburg general
85 Speedway area
86 Eye component
89 Rolling ___
90 Brings down to size?
94 White House Chief of Staff (1969–1973)*
97 Honor achieved by each clue* answer
100 Musk, for one
101 River through the French Alps
102 Many a Comic-Con costume
103 Occupation
104 Kevin's "Tin Cup" costar
105 American fur trader
106 Symphonic finale
107 "The Bird Cage" artist
108 Scott in the 1857 news
109 Caroling songs
110 Hiccup, e.g.
111 Lick and close

DOWN

1 "Forever" item
2 Papal court
3 Cocked, as a hat
4 Proliferate
5 Self-proclaimed polymath
6 Apropos of
7 Citrus hybrid
8 Son of Eric the Red
9 Elgar's "King ___"
10 Public personae
11 Golf cup not on the green
12 Nonpareil
13 Beyoncé's "Lion King" role

14 Homes for the homeless
15 1981 Lauren Bacall film
16 Drifters
17 Spiritless
18 Casper's witchy friend
28 Lose gracefully
30 Daring words
32 Five-spot
35 Gluck's "Paride ed ___"
36 Eyewinker
37 "In ___ of flowers . . ."
38 Veep between Hubert and Gerald
39 Grahame's terrible driver
40 No friend of unions
41 1/3 a 1970 war film
42 Apollo 11 commander*
43 Awe partner
44 Bean and Paton
45 Apollo 13 astronaut*
46 Turgenev's birth city

47 Cooperstown souvenirs
49 In a ___ (quickly)
50 Magwitch of "Great Expectations"
51 Chateaux river
53 Gaucho's turf
54 Caesar's last word
55 Link together
57 One of the Horae
59 Fineman of "SNL"
61 Does a hell week job
62 Sale advisory
63 Pelota basket
64 Pre-wash
65 Osprey's cousin
66 Online reading
67 What to put on Mame
68 Kathryn of "Law & Order: CI"
69 Big man on campus
71 Swiss watch company
72 Ancient capital of Japan
73 "Horrors!"

76 Alex Trebek, by birth
78 "A" and "the"
80 Fuzzy peach part
81 Bear lair
82 Vents
83 Entangled
84 UTEP team
85 Rising star
86 C-E-G, e.g.
87 Directive
88 Lake Geneva feeder
89 Verbal
90 Ski-Doo vehicles
91 Bête ___
92 Kinte of "Roots"
93 Danielle of romance
95 Montreal gas sign
96 Dispense justice
97 Mousketeer wear
98 On an angle
99 Governor Raimondo

ZODIAC FIGURES   by Brenda Cox
Billy Porter originated the role of 22 Across on Broadway.

CROSS

1 One objecting to a called strike
5 Cry from the trenches
9 Gripping tool
15 "___ Leaving Home": Beatles
19 Hairnet
20 Kind of symmetry
21 Viking of comics
22 "Kinky Boots" drag queen
23 Karachi language
24 Dorrit on "Lost"
25 Diva Hartig
26 Word of affirmation
27 Mascot of a Bronx university
29 "Property Brothers" brothers
31 Large wine bottles
32 Start to date?
34 City on Lake Erie
35 Victorian ___
36 Oscar Night VIP
38 Jazz trumpeter Butterfield
40 Hot stuff at ski resorts
43 Ant that can fly
44 Worked with Java
45 Me-time place
48 South American cape
49 Russian Tea Room order
50 Mishandled a pop-up
51 One kind of test
52 Iraqi "AP"
53 Event for Simone Biles
55 Sax legend, familiarly
56 "Of ___ and kings . . .": Carroll
58 "Curses!"
59 Throw cold water on
60 Ehrenreich in "Solo"
61 "Talk turkey," e.g.
63 Prove to be mistaken
64 Shock
66 Chihuahua choo-choo
67 Fit in
70 Peter Rabbit's sister
71 "Material Girl" album
74 "Yes, Yvette"
75 "Vogue" shelfmate
76 He's toast
77 Britt and Falco
78 Oldest peerage title
79 Bishop's bailiwick
80 Carrying
81 SMERSH figure
82 Panegyrize
83 Affixed with rubber cement
84 Place for a peck
85 Mlle. after the wedding
86 Houdini specialty
89 Chinwag
90 "___ of the Sorrows": Synge
94 Hog's portion
97 "Fatal Attraction" Oscar nominee
100 Jones in "American Virgin"
101 Edmonton center?
102 Apple headphones
103 "I am not what I am" speaker
104 "Honest to ___!"
105 Not for vegans
106 Demolish
107 Stockroom pallet
108 Interstate sign
109 New car of 1957
110 Manicurist's board
111 Make lighter

DOWN

1 Baseball blemish
2 "The Brady Bunch" mom
3 McDonald in "Beauty and the Beast"
4 Club
5 Procrastinator's word
6 Physicals, e.g.
7 Gucci rival
8 "___ Camera": Isherwood
9 Like exciting movie scenes
10 Pure as the driven snow
11 Pointed weapon
12 Exchange premium
13 Helm in "The Silencers"
14 Went on and on
15 Bit by bit
16 Virginia Tech student
17 Serengeti grazer
18 Final authority
28 Bat mitzvah dance
30 Spilled the beans
33 Cape Town negative
36 Alaska's Mount St. ___
37 "Buddenbrooks" author
38 Sacha Baron Cohen film
39 As above
40 Elegant and stylish
41 Chaplin of "Game of Thrones"
42 Tart jelly fruit
43 "Café Society" director
44 Mousse ingredient
45 Blame-bearer
46 Knotty ___
47 Yemeni city
49 Bialy relative
50 River of Aragón
51 Quark player Shimerman
53 In the worst way
54 Jennifer's "Ab Fab" role
55 Condor claw
57 Seen-it-all feeling
59 Fleur-___
61 Miffed
62 "The ___ Park": Mailer
63 Father, Biblically
64 Iowa college town
65 Gdansk native
66 Like pitchforks
67 Threshold
68 Schilling successor
69 Herb for salmon
71 Togo capital
72 Celeriac, for one
73 Nice thought
76 Grisly
78 One route to fitness
80 Chamonix peaks
81 "Found you!"
82 Kuwaiti royal
83 Large seabird
84 "Suburgatory" star Hines
85 Piddling
86 Save on wedding costs
87 Ovenware glass
88 Raccoon relative
89 "Zorba the Greek" setting
90 Scare off
91 Capital of Bangladesh
92 Denver university
93 Diminish by friction
95 Went in a hurry
96 "Oh, well"
98 "Divine Tree" of India
99 What a narthex leads to

282 THEMELESS by Harvey Estes

21 Across is also the name of a 19th-century Mississippi steamboat.

ACROSS

1 Major gains
11 Any Stephen King novel
21 Former New Orleans statue
22 Meeting apart
23 Greek ceremony
24 Folds into ridges
25 Furry companions
26 Victrolas
28 Auditioned for a musical
29 Moneymaking venture
30 Landlord's self-description
31 Crater feature
33 Spectacles
35 Scooter user
39 Wear down
40 Biblical garden
41 Gave the slip to
42 "Is that a fact!"
44 Soapbox toppers
49 Offers a mortgage
50 Shelley and Keats
52 Leading impressionist
53 Eeyore's outburst
54 Kind of model
55 "Gloria in Excelsis ___"
56 Pete Best was one
57 WarnerMedia parent
58 Elimination
61 Nothing new
62 Balloon gas
64 Detroit union
65 Ready already
66 Showbiz types
67 What escape artists do?
71 Sturgeon steerer
73 "Finally!"
74 Informer
75 Prefix for tubbies
76 Pope who confronted Attila
77 Standing rib
78 Suitable for watering
81 "Death Be Not Proud" poet
82 Beatles manager Brian
84 Running story
85 Financial
86 Court minutes
88 Put into piles
89 Off-shore lodgings
90 Bucks
94 "Hollywood Squares" square

95 Actor James ___ Jones
96 Mallet game
97 Loading area
99 Goodies
101 ___-Pei dog
105 Repeats
108 Then
110 Billet-doux
111 Was a sponge
112 Goes over the line
113 Filet mignon quality

DOWN

1 Get a handle on
2 Skye on the screen
3 Not much
4 Shrimping gear
5 Prefix with corn
6 Eschewed paper clips
7 Restraining rope
8 Prufrock's creator
9 Menial laborer
10 Mexican miss
11 Pen to flick
12 Mireille of "World War Z"
13 Remove barnacles
14 Storm-chasing targets
15 Like pants after a feast
16 Hosp. heart chart
17 Andean pack animal
18 Language of Livy
19 Major happening
20 Closes the defense
27 Bewitching beauty
30 Caesar's bad day
32 "China Syndrome" danger
34 Like some cookware
35 Peachy dessert
36 Too too
37 Long cigars
38 Swirling water
39 Oscar winner Marisa
42 Chowderhead
43 Stead
45 Warty croakers
46 Torn
47 Having a connection
48 Leave in the text
50 Dorm unit
51 Simple sack
54 Waken rudely
56 Held up
58 Beef with a bone
59 Most wacky
60 Moo goo ___ pan
63 Tiniest bit
65 Laundry load
66 Give a darn

67 "That makes me mad!"
68 Disneyland souvenirs
69 Chance to get a hit
70 Round sound
72 Nobel physicist Bohr
76 Got the bronze
78 Mass starters
79 Old English coin
80 Escadrille members
81 Clock feature
83 Summer refresher
85 On the block
87 Sporty neckwear
89 Enjoyed a soak
90 Like milk not worth tears
91 Glider's lack
92 Motrin competitor
93 Seedy areas?
95 Suffix with moth
98 It's taken in protest
100 To be, in Toulon
101 Country suffix
102 Raw leather
103 Iowa hub
104 John Reed biopic
106 Piz Bernina, e.g.
107 AARP members
109 Craggy hill

THEMELESS by Harvey Estes

In 1995, Nike distributed a braille poster with 8 Down on it.

ACROSS

1 Kitchen cloth
8 "We're in This Love Together" singer
15 Jazzy riffs
20 Part of RIP
21 Like leftovers
22 Raven's call
23 Hotel attendants
24 Level of achievement
25 Wipe over
26 Words before "off"
27 Arranged
29 Jazzy Brubeck
31 Bright night light
32 Fermented drink
34 Sound in a studio
35 Without end
37 On top of, in poetry
39 Something extra
41 Carbon compound
42 Racket extension
43 1961 rival of Maris
46 Site of three rings
48 Transferred title
50 Samuel's judge
51 Plumed wader
53 Assault team
56 Some HS math
57 Like sherry
58 Chewed on a ring
60 Conveyance weight
64 Mideastern capital
66 Big name at Yalta
67 Pioneer copier company
68 Pitched well?
69 Pibb Xtra, for one
70 Pants leg feature
71 Official decree
72 Sunnyvale's valley
73 Judge's room
74 Rod attachment
75 Angela of "Waiting to Exhale"
76 Chop ___
77 Addams family cousin
78 Twists
80 French Revolution figure
81 Sultan suffix
82 Groundhog Day focus
85 Desert bloomers
88 Emulated Ogden Nash

90 Dawber of "Mork and Mindy"
91 Tip
94 Auditioners' quests
95 Part of a geisha's garb
96 It's got you covered
99 Staff members
101 Icicle locale, often
105 Cathedral nook
106 Similar things
107 On the back
109 "First Knight" actor
110 Airborne toys
112 Like the Pride Lands
114 "The Russia House" author
116 Ocular outflow
117 Leads on
118 Celeb status
119 Select from the menu
120 Lab personnel
121 "Top Hat" star

DOWN

1 Performed so-so
2 Combined
3 "Airplane!" or "Hot Shots!"
4 "All Creatures Great and Small" vet
5 St. Louis NFLer
6 Peerless pitchers
7 Salami type
8 Slogan next to the Swoosh
9 Prelude to a deal
10 Computer report
11 Dump denizen
12 Chopin exercise
13 Make fizzy
14 Hit-or-miss
15 Blu-ray forerunner
16 NBA venue
17 Walked the runway
18 One out early
19 Rock's Lynyrd ___
28 Caused some friction
30 Undercut
33 Brushed up on, in Eton

36 NY Met or LA Dodger
38 Marley music
40 Hot button
43 More substantial
44 President of Chile (1970–73)
45 Lingerie item
47 George C. Scott role
49 Regard
52 Stimpy's bud
54 Stack acronym
55 Vixen's home
58 Clears away the clutter
59 Make it legal
61 Oil-rich peninsula
62 Floral cake garnish
63 Brought to bear
65 "Father of Geometry"
66 Cardinal of Henry VIII
67 CT-scanner part
69 Spanish ayes
70 Inferior, slangily
72 Laura ___ Giacomo

73 Mean mongrel
75 Shady recesses
76 Teases with backtalk
79 Function
80 Sleep Number product
82 Address
83 In better spirits
84 Historic slave ship
86 Bergen in "Gandhi"
87 Bing Crosby, for one
89 Honeymoon falls
92 Good-luck charm
93 Creed of Christians
97 Caterpillar rival
98 Bar orders
100 Latin music
102 "La Traviata" composer
103 Mistake
104 "Let's talk" note
108 Repeated services
111 Ga., once
113 Lead-in for wit or pick

115 Minerva McGonagall's Patronus

284 ELS IN THE LOOP   by James Connolly
We're not talking about Chicago here.

ACROSS

1 Jiggly garnish
6 Antiquing "cheater"
10 Home of Iowa State
14 City on the Arno
18 Good-for-nothing
19 LPGA golfer Hataoka
20 It doesn't pay, it's said
21 Friends of Tarzan
22 Not abridged
24 Upper-right keyboard key
26 "Praise the Lord!"
27 Nouveau ___
29 Sumptuous spreads
30 Texter's "r"
31 Jakob Dylan's mother
32 Sharp-as-a-marble sort
34 Batista's overthrower
38 Fairway position on a slope
40 Ides exclamation
44 Organic part of soil
45 ___-Columbian Era
46 Serta rival
47 Quinella or exacta
48 "La La Land" song
49 Presidential emblem
50 Like Clark Kent
52 Gas station adjunct, perhaps
53 Kilmer who played Moses
54 Ogden Nash beast
58 Really turn off
60 Building add-on
61 Brinker of kid-lit
62 All-inclusive
63 Harder to believe, as tales go
64 Participates in a riot
66 In push-up position
67 Cornerman's throw-in
68 BoSox division
70 Gawk at
71 Pitchfork point
72 Upper left keyboard key
75 Some parlor pieces
77 Admired by many
79 "I knew it!"
80 Brady's former team, for short
81 Monopoly pair
83 Some Ivy League alums
84 Petri dish stuff
85 Wall-E's love
86 Loafer bottoms
89 Source of Roku revenue
90 Sea froth
91 Squishy ball
93 Genre of Van Gogh's "Sunflowers"
95 Most pickable
96 One of the Coens
98 Greasy-spoon sign
99 "THAT guy!"
100 Lack of vitality
103 Painted Desert flora
105 Gets the job done
110 Protection from telemarketers
112 Gamer's difficulty setting
114 Up to no good
115 Loads with cargo
116 Royal address
117 Place to play or fight
118 Carry on, as war
119 Innovation's basis
120 Pop the top from
121 Country's Travis

DOWN

1 Letter before Bravo
2 Motown genre
3 Propel a rickshaw
4 Maroon's confines
5 Places for wines
6 "Tomorrow" musical
7 Enthusiastic, plus
8 Body shop fig.
9 Full of team spirit
10 Gothic window feature
11 Enos of "Good Omens"
12 Angsty music genre
13 Arms-length photo
14 Wine taster's asset
15 Wall St. debuts
16 Schismatic group
17 Seeks a price of
20 Beginner's piano exercise
23 Irish pound's replacement
25 "Seinfeld" uncle
28 Pupil's place
31 Hogwarts lesson
33 Handy sort, informally
34 Vichyssoise garnish
35 Ear-related
36 One of three in Utah?
37 Vintner's barrel
38 Russian range
39 Class for moms-to-be
41 Organization for little hitters
42 Short and sweet
43 Give voice to
45 Doers of tedious work
49 Smacked hard
51 Camphor et al.
52 Stubborn equine
54 Things pointed at
55 Egg size
56 Reefy island
57 Nickel-copper alloy
59 Handled roughly
65 Part of GORP
66 Former secretary of state Colin
67 Hawaiian carvings
68 Trembling tree
69 Take a hike
71 Part of São Paulo
73 Pillow prettifiers
74 Editor's "add this"
76 Proud woman, in slang
78 Toronto skaters, for short
82 Be synchronous
84 Google Photos, e.g.
87 Sends to the Hill
88 Blind crosspiece
90 Much the same
92 Pen or sow
93 "Want me to?"
94 Retort to "Ain't!"
95 Lunar valley
97 "Open ___ late"
99 Trojan War beauty
100 From square one
101 Long-running PBS series
102 Vape shop buy
104 On the briny
105 Foreboding disaster
106 Gown designer Wang
107 Unlike this clue
108 Tear to pieces
109 Do away with
111 Young Scot
113 Currency of Laos

METER MEASURES by Fred Piscop
Nurses will know the answer to 83 Across.

ACROSS

1 Male voice
5 Really ticked off
10 Home to a small part of Egypt
14 Fancy jug
18 Seacrest's cohost
19 Command to a junkyard dog
20 Bartlett or Bosc
21 Part of NAFTA
22 What an ammeter measures
25 Frequent Andrew Wyeth subject
26 Frequent Andrew Wyeth subject
27 Line up a shot
28 Worker at an oyster bar
30 County of Northern Ireland
31 Desktop gadget
35 Sparkling wine spot
36 Schooner filler
38 Nintendo system since 2006
39 Rank above viscount
41 Bravo parent
44 Sea-___ (WA airport)
47 What a hydrometer measures
51 Toothpaste type
52 Prefix with tourism
53 Bear viewed with a telescope
54 French wine valley
55 "Hairspray" heroine Turnblad
56 Gunslinging pal of Holliday
58 Spout off
59 Energizer mascot
60 Toilet tissue layers
61 Mosque towers
63 Mauritian birds of yore
64 Sumptuous spreads
65 Backspace over, say
66 Sides in an age-old "battle"
67 Assert as fact
68 "Get lost!"
70 Blasted with pepper spray
71 Grand Canyon discoverer
74 Parolee, e.g.
75 Bicuspid neighbor
76 Soak up the sun
77 Son of Seth
78 Like cotton candy
79 Immunizing fluid
80 Rotten reviews
81 Rank for Potter or Klink: Abbr.
82 Regatta implement
83 What a sphygmomanometer measures
87 Moody music genre
88 Network with VJs
89 Propels a dory
90 Country's ___ Young Band
91 EGOT winner Brooks
92 An original sinner
94 Earth, wind, or fire
98 Selena's music style
103 As yet
106 Munched on
107 Attached, like some patches
109 Loudspeaker output
110 What a pyrometer measures
114 The Jetsons' son
115 Breaker of a mental block
116 Make impure
117 Pataky of "The Fate of the Furious"
118 Critter on road signs
119 Poet's early hours
120 Makes ecstatic
121 Pipe feature

DOWN

1 French naval port
2 Alvin of choreography
3 Harpoon
4 Vanzetti's trial partner
5 Shekel spender
6 Reformer Jacob
7 Bank holdings: Abbr.
8 Private eye, slangily
9 Avian source of oil
10 Earth Day month
11 Terse note from the boss
12 Fleming who created Le Chiffre
13 Word with graphic or lively
14 Not hunched over
15 What a pedometer measures
16 Defeat by a hair
17 Keister
21 Like so, informally
23 Key-related
24 BART part
29 Bret who created Poker Flat
32 Surprise ending
33 "O Patria Mia" singer
34 Frankincense and amber, for two
37 Regard as identical
40 Far from stuffy
42 "John Brown's Body" poet
43 Reunion group
44 Come down hard
45 Trendy smoothie flavor
46 What a keratometer measures
48 Buffet table vessels
49 Slipped past
50 Toddler taboos
55 Morgan le Fay's sister
57 Dolly of Dollywood
58 Take five
59 Square-muzzled dog
60 Chihuahua cash
62 Drought ender
63 Pull up stakes quickly
64 Pay, with "over"
66 Toast word
67 Animal that plays dead
68 Broom of twigs
69 American in Paris, perhaps
70 Down in the dumps
71 Supermarket shelf array
72 Destine for failure
73 Nobel Peace Center city
75 Cat's utterance
76 Companion of 14 Across
79 Replay effect
80 Mononymous soccer great
83 V.S.O.P. spirit
84 Held a follow-up session
85 Snappy comebacks
86 Tennis player Dementieva
93 Kickstarter contributor
95 Brewpub option
96 "Mission: Impossible" hero
97 Deflected basketball score
99 Ballet leaps
100 Not for minors
101 Icelandic speakers
102 Wee hour, briefly
103 Played for a sap
104 Either of two extremes
105 Fanciful notion
108 Rip violently
111 Altar assent
112 Romulans, to Kirk
113 Daisy ___ Yokum

UNFORGETTABLE QUOTES . . . by Victor Fleming
. . . from forgettable films.

ACROSS

1 Beethoven's "Archduke ___"
5 Salzburg setting
9 Guesstimations
14 C neighbor
19 Frolicsome play
20 Hide from a bear
21 Confused struggle
22 Root of statesmanship
23 Caen cleric
24 Lute-shaped fruit
25 Like some cousins
27 Hoffman line from "The Dieter"?
30 Appropriate
31 Plowing harness
32 Snarky laugh
33 Chafe
34 What's more
36 Takes home
38 Aweather antonym
40 Grp. in 1960s protests
43 Pindaric ode stanza
47 To the full extent
50 Fin Tutuola portrayer
51 Garland line from "The Wizard of Alaska"?
55 Canyon area
56 Apt rhyme for Mork
57 Relievers' stats
58 Like some flights
59 Sarkeesian or Baker
62 Beta carotene source
64 "Rooster Cogburn" prequel
66 Brass and bronze
68 Boone or Bradley
70 Place for an eye test: Abbr.
71 Eminem's "___ the Coffin"
75 Merchant
78 Hammer locale
80 Party line
81 Judge
84 King of early comics
86 Grumpy housemate
88 Picayune point
89 Guinness line from "Slapstick Wars"?
94 Sea whip's home
95 Soap segment
96 Watches on a Roku TV
97 Some 12-Step grp. members
98 Auto with a four-ring logo
100 Cast out
102 What a sniggler snares
103 Key near Ctrl
104 Nittany Lions school
107 Miles away
109 Start of Ethiopia's capital
113 Nicholson line from "A Few Good Dentists"?
119 Digital audio service
120 "Up Where We Belong" is one
121 Post-larva stage
122 "___ say more?"
123 ". . . and everything ___ place"
124 ATP rival org.
125 Mushroom color
126 Apparel
127 "Hogwash!"
128 Clingstone stones
129 Atomic number 10

DOWN

1 Cafeteria items
2 Bomb squad machine
3 Suffuse
4 Jim Croce song
5 Med. visit
6 Cautious
7 Go into overtime
8 Gershwin's "___ the Band"
9 Air pollutant
10 A dime, to a dollar
11 Aluminum giant
12 Oktoberfest hangout
13 Arid
14 Like an ingenue
15 Congregation
16 "___ Free or Die" (NH motto)
17 "Beg pardon"
18 Arrogance in the 'hood
26 Falco of "Nurse Jackie"
28 Form a secret union
29 Annoy
35 Extremely
37 Set out
39 Dishonest
40 Aberdeen resident
41 Floor model
42 "Watch your ___!"
43 Super Bowl IV coach
44 What once was yours?
45 Fork over
46 Prof. Higgins, to Eliza
48 Virtual greeting
49 Begin again
50 Doing hard time
52 Rain forest denizen
53 "Hee Haw" radio station
54 Digital dinosaur
60 Import duty
61 Queen of the Misty Isles
63 Zambia neighbor
65 Avoid
67 Quip ending
69 Hatcher and Garr
72 Chanteuse Lotte
73 "I'm all ears," e.g.
74 Brother of Boreas
76 Curved
77 Caramel candies
79 Spreadsheet lines
81 Big name in razors
82 Perlman in "Ted & Venus"
83 Spell-offs
85 Boyhood bud
87 Allude to
90 Revelation
91 Reinforced
92 Halloween choice
93 Reserved
98 "Your House" singer Morissette
99 Magazine founder Eric
101 Tall African tribe
103 Acetic and nitric
105 "11.22.63" heroine
106 Agreement
108 "Frankly, my dear . . ." speaker
110 "Irma la ___" (1963)
111 App designer, e.g.
112 Snowboarder Palmer
113 "___ Cassius has a lean . . ."
114 Nonesuch
115 Fonda's bee picture role
116 Svelte
117 Medicate
118 Touchdown guesses

TWISTABLE TREAT   by Katherine Omak
. . . and that treat can be found at 116 Across.

CROSS

- SoFi Stadium team
- Cornish of "Jack Ryan"
- Horseshoe ___
- Big date for a teen
- Drooling pooch of comics
- Like Kansas in August
- Prove helpful to
- Like a soft persimmon
- Dessert for Bugs?*
- State dessert of Florida*
- Like a one-celled organism
- Dog-summoner's word
- Treat like a pet
- "Over my dead body!"
- Taro dish
- Roués
- Lower in dignity
- Spiral-horned antelopes
- Surgically removes
- Give the slip to
- DVR button
- Like Clark Kent
- Plenty angry
- Larry the Stooge
- Thick liqueurs
- Guitar man Paul
- Bronze-hued
- "I'm ___ loss"
- Fountain treat*
- Woody Herman's "___ Autumn"
- Beer hall vessel
- "Amscray!"
- Drop in rank
- For no profit
- Cryptology org.
- Muscular woe
- Taper off
- Sparkling wine, familiarly
- Goes ape, to Bart Simpson
- Surrealist Jean
- Ghirardelli product*
- "That's it!"
- Maj.'s superior
- Above, to bards
- Mark up, as a score

88 Negotiations hang-up
89 Take a blue pencil to
91 Walk like a rooster
93 Coffee shop stack
94 Composer Previn
95 Embedded below the surface of
97 Down in the dumps
99 Was too sweet
100 Compote fruits
102 Scuba diver's supply
103 Soda insert
105 Fixed part of a motor
108 Fence support
110 "Moonstruck" and "Groundhog Day"
114 Martini option*
116 Clue* answers have been varieties of this
119 Lake-effect snow lake
120 Hotel in "Barton Fink"
121 "The Chosen" author Chaim
122 Aswan Dam's river
123 Dog food brand
124 John Jasper's nephew Edwin
125 Quid pro quo deals
126 Undulating swimmers

DOWN

1 Jay-Z's ___-Fella Records
2 Eden refugee
3 Surrealist Joan
4 Suitor's song
5 On the roster
6 Game with wooden balls
7 Intimate apparel
8 Calligrapher's fluid
9 Glass prosthetic
10 Forged licenses et al.
11 State firmly
12 Wedding cake tier
13 Diminutive, in rap names
14 Smooth raincoat
15 De-wrinkles
16 Features of some trendy jeans
17 Jax's friend on "Sons of Anarchy"
18 Come face to face
24 Like bariatric surgery patients
26 "The Simpsons" tavern
28 Sweetie pie
31 Find new tenants for
32 Name on a check
34 Rebuttal to "Am not!"
35 Trim a steak
36 Ms. Perón
37 Dessert in a boat*
39 Souvlaki meat
40 Bacteria-fighting drug
42 Carnival confection*
43 Blue eyes or red hair
44 Know intuitively
46 Cattle pokers
48 Clobbers with snowballs
51 Cinco de Mayo beer
52 Word after jam or bull
56 Did a motocross
57 Smart TV brand
58 Price for a plug
59 Say "Nyah nyah!" to
62 Gold units: Abbr.
65 Farrow of "Zelig"
67 One accepting a bet
68 Unspecified degree
70 Sinatra's "___ Life"
71 Loafer's lack
72 Wear away gradually
74 Rugby restart
76 Midwest hub
77 Fought a war
80 Whirlybird part
81 Lemon or lime, e.g.
82 Escalator maker
83 Fills with freight
88 Icy treat
90 Walks lightly
91 Played on the A-team
92 Raised a glass to
94 1836 siege site
96 Like a bright 81 Down
98 Slower, in mus.
99 Onion soup holders
101 Veep who resigned
104 Brownie group
105 Transport for Nanook
106 Giga- times 1,000
107 Surrounded by
109 Peace Prize city
111 Muskogee resident of song
112 Grain grinder
113 Gets the gist of
115 Card game for two
116 Special ___ (SEAL missions)
117 Propel a trireme
118 H, to Athenians

288

107 Across is also the title of a Bruce Springsteen song.

ACROSS

1 Tribute
9 Potter's biology professor
15 Meat-and-potatoes
20 Detached
21 Antony's friend
22 Met performance
23 Need not rush
25 Hoodwinked
26 Activist Brockovich
27 With reverence
28 Prompt
29 Danish Modern, e.g.
31 Very revealing photo
32 Female robot in "Ex Machina"
34 Mine, to Marcel
35 Black keys
39 Thompson of the NBA
40 Dilbert, e.g.
41 Now
45 Head honcho
47 Maiden name preceder
48 Beauty lovers
49 "Runaway" singer Shannon
50 Ill-suited
52 Official orders
53 Hedge shrubs
55 Terrific time
58 Hrs. in California
59 "Hey, you there"
60 Barrio resident
61 "Place de l'Opera" artist
62 Eponymous Lauder perfume
64 Sea lane
67 Bed
68 German industrial locale
69 Barely make
70 Clock numeral
72 B&O et al.
73 Cadiz country
75 Concise summary
76 Like plainchants
78 Mock playfully
80 "___ too shabby"
81 Fiendish
82 Accepted ones
84 Strongly recommended
86 Every three or four days
87 Handle difficulties
89 Put in the overhead
90 Moat locales
91 Robbie Knievel's dad
92 Lithium-___ battery
93 Motel employee
94 Try to avoid a tag
99 Grew into
101 Groomed to personal specs
105 Has the stage
106 Dress shape
107 God's gift to Abraham
110 Showy bloomers, for short
111 Funny Phyllis
112 "___ in My Mind"
113 Taco topping
114 Track records
115 Alluded to

DOWN

1 Yearned
2 Nun influenced by St. Francis
3 Kind of duty
4 Bridge bid, briefly
5 Turned on
6 Kind of rock
7 Title for Judi Dench
8 Atlas abbr.
9 Absolutely clean
10 Farfalle and farfel
11 Email option
12 Anthem exultation
13 Egypt and Syr., once
14 Three, in Torino
15 Tree trunk
16 Hypothetical primate
17 Sandstone or shale
18 Birmingham resource
19 Voltaire satire
24 Deadly agents
28 Jersey material
30 Turn into something else
32 Climber's challenge
33 "Domine, quo ___?": Peter
36 Red veggies
37 Some Mozart works
38 Naysayers' words
39 Caffeine source
41 Interferes
42 "Fore!"
43 Part of a Dana Carvey line
44 Norm: Abbr.
45 Long and tiresome
46 Shoot the breeze
49 Home of Lions and Tigers
51 Courtroom entry
53 House style
54 Fall to pieces
56 Related to the chest
57 Without excess verbiage
60 Hardly used at all
63 Buffalo's lake
65 Hurricane pronoun, at times
66 Like some dancers
67 Den mother
71 Blown away
74 Catch forty winks
75 Italian sauce
76 Cry from a crib
77 Overtime creator
79 "Wake Up" girl of song
81 Rare
82 Swelling packs
83 "The Mist" is one
85 Dearie
86 Frigate crew
88 African herd
90 In twos
93 Baseball bat wood
95 French textile city
96 "Let me repeat . . ."
97 Ritchie Valens classic
98 Conclude by
100 Astral table
101 Prefix with commuter
102 Rolling in it
103 Morales of "My Family"
104 Bruce in "The Cowboys"
107 QB successes
108 Beatnik's "aware"
109 Ellipsis element

THEMELESS by Theresa Yves
84 Across is 282 feet below sea level.

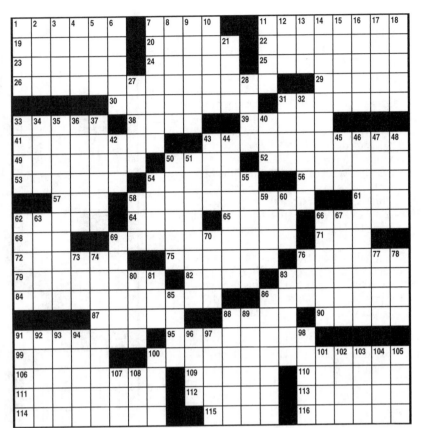

ACROSS

1 It's attractive on the fridge
7 Capone pursuer
11 Water coolers
19 From the beginning
20 "Weird Al" Jackson song parody
22 Neighbors of Egyptians
23 Laugh line, e.g.
24 Persona non ___
25 Cut short
26 Question asked of a limbo dancer?
29 Took the plunge
30 Chomp on
31 Wash-and-wear
33 Track competitor
38 Laura of "Recount"
39 Spoken
41 On a pedestal
43 Male-dominated subordination
49 Thickness measurer
50 Old-time teacher
52 Dawn
53 Chewed the scenery
54 Traffic cones
55 Rolex ___ Perpetual
57 Legal matters
58 How some temps are hired
61 Organic suffix
62 Terrific time
64 Cadet's org.
65 Side dish with fish
66 'Noles' rivals
68 Unpaved-road hazard
69 Organized data groups
71 Honeydew eater
72 Pertaining to orbs
75 Minor mission
76 Swamp
79 Terrier type
82 Some X's, in a game
83 Busybody
84 Badwater Basin locale
86 Actor in the Boxing Hall of Fame
87 Snap course
88 Soft spread
90 "Ghost Hunters" network
91 "A Rake's Progress" painter
95 Senior citizens' concern
99 Ease off
100 Making petty distinctions
106 Clinker
109 Andrew Lloyd Webber's title
110 Sydney citizen, informally
111 Fundraising show
112 In isolation
113 Had a vision
114 Sized up
115 Neighbor of Nor.
116 Satisfies a thirst

DOWN

1 Sonic speed
2 Curly do
3 Shot up
4 Elise in "Hustle & Flow"
5 Old U.S. gas brand
6 "Supernatural" network
7 Brought to nought
8 Bread source
9 "___ Alive": Bee Gees
10 Suppress a story
11 Analogy phrase
12 Mean mongrel
13 End of many a URL
14 Hat in the ring
15 Open a medicine bottle
16 Male Amish feature
17 Aromatic compound
18 In sorry shape
21 Strung tightly
27 Halloween drink
28 Grown-up kid
31 Explorer of Nickelodeon
32 Speaks at length
33 "The Vampire Lestat" author
34 Orlando's servant
35 Operatic soprano
36 High and mighties
37 Most ready for plucking
40 Sportscaster Berman
42 London Zoo character?
43 Debate list
44 Blocked rememberer
45 Guitar master Paul
46 Dogged in the pursuit of
47 Public spectacle
48 Parts of famlies
50 South Carolina beach
51 Menu option
54 Lap lovers place
55 Places of art
58 To's partner
59 Hourglass sight
60 Injection reactions, maybe
62 Sweeping
63 Tennis star Safarova
66 Cooking oil kind
67 Luanda's nation
69 Three-piece suit accessory
70 Airline seat part
73 Badminton do-over
74 Support group
76 Aunt in "Bambi"
77 Advance
78 At liberty
80 Lid hair
81 Tarzan portrayer
83 Unsmiling
85 Street fixture
86 Like some glass
88 Indy service area
89 Stage beginning
91 Start of an Arnoldism
92 Woodwind section
93 Grenoble guys
94 Words in a Kilmer simile
96 Isle near Corsica
97 Features of old phones
98 "Holy crow!"
100 Fax function
101 Be a pitcher
102 Cruising
103 "Out of Africa" author Dinesen
104 Frosty covering
105 Some volleyball hits
107 Sounds of surprise
108 Lower digit

LAUGHING ALL THE WAY   by Elizabeth C. Gorski
The career of 115 Across spanned more than 75 years.

ACROSS

1 Evil Disney lion
5 Sarah McLachlan single
9 Sprint
13 On the job
19 "Let's go!"
21 Jai ___
22 Bronx college
23 1957 comedy starring 115 Across
25 Kazan in "Beaches"
26 Aloof
27 More wacky
29 Nat King Cole song written by 115 Across
30 ___ good example
31 Ballpark fig.
33 Last: Abbr.
34 Experts
36 "___ Troyens": Berlioz
38 Online crafts site
40 1952 comedy-drama starring 115 Across
45 Diva's pride
48 "Diana" singer
49 Gaelic
50 Tuscan "Ta-ta!"
51 **Beginning of a quote by 115 Across**
55 Sister of Zsa Zsa
56 Needle target
57 These whoppers are hard to swallow
58 Bird from a green egg
59 Handmade, as cigars
60 Curved letter
61 James in "Elf"
62 Bausch's business partner
64 HBO sitcom starring Robert Wuhl
65 Shack
66 **Middle of quote**
69 New Jersey cape
70 Strive (toward)
73 Uppity one
74 Stagger
76 Quirky
79 In a lather
80 Chemical suffix
81 Tolstoy's Karenina
82 Fencing blade
83 Zodiac borders
84 **End of quote**
87 Sgt. Snorkel's dog
88 Personal appearance
90 Span. ladies
91 Brilliance
92 1928 silent film starring 115 Across
94 "Take ___ leave it!"
95 Scarf for Mae West
96 Dog of detective fiction
97 Marseille Mrs.
98 Bus. alias
100 Treaty
104 Comic persona made famous by 115 Across
107 Reporter's need
111 Shakespeare tragedy
113 Sluggish state
115 "The Gold Rush" star
117 Dense
118 Ex-Yankee Martinez
119 "Great job!"
120 Composed
121 Being broadcast
122 "A Room of ___ Own"
123 Subpar grades

DOWN

1 Bunches
2 Journalist Roberts
3 Love-in-___ (flower)
4 Vacation expense, perhaps
5 Flared skirts
6 Verboten acts
7 Hostel
8 On in years
9 Thin insect
10 Soaring
11 Delhi wedding dress
12 Scouting outing
13 100%
14 Prickly-leafed plant
15 In a fanciful manner
16 Hotel chain
17 Banister
18 Patella site
20 Radwanska of tennis
24 C Wisconsin city
28 Dodge trucks
32 "___ a Dance": Rodgers & Hart
35 Terrific end?
37 "Yipes!"
39 Fight stoppages
40 Peanut, for one
41 Anger
42 Lopez/Affleck film
43 Where the Styx flows
44 Pond hoppers
45 Faucets brand
46 Texter's "Then again . . ."
47 Big-ticket ___
48 Kate Dillon on "Billions"
52 Euphoric
53 Change a tag
54 Out of control
55 Parable message
59 "Castor et Pollux" composer
61 Restores to health
63 Scene of fowl play?
65 Seahorse genus
67 Rings on a pizza
68 Like some 45s
70 Fancy neckwear
71 Snowbird's winter home
72 Wallpaper adhesive
75 Slaughter of baseball
76 Autobahn auto
77 Crème ___ crème
78 Nimble
81 Roundish do
82 Sci-fi getaway vehicle
84 Pot-au-___
85 Of bones
86 Rock's ___ Speedwagon
88 "The A-Team" actor
89 Optimist's credo
93 Countrified "What if . . ."
94 Ad-libbed comedy style
95 Soaks in the tub
97 Signified
99 Italian bowling game
101 "Kate & ___"
102 "Crazy" singer Patsy
103 Ice bucket utensil
104 Sporty car roof
105 Prefix with call or cop
106 Intro studio class
108 Word form for "eight"
109 Slender
110 Football coach Babers
112 Witchy woman
114 Visibly embarrassed
116 Aachen article

THEMELESS by Harvey Estes
The clue at 62 Across may require a little extra thought.

ACROSS

1 Crass character
5 Large influx
10 Blowout victory
14 Puts a wave in
19 Take bounding steps
20 Winter of "Modern Family"
21 Carbon compound
22 Cybercommerce
23 Decision makers
26 Soup seasoning
27 Jamboree group
28 Moonshine
29 Tonsil's neighbor
31 Drove obliquely
33 Re or so
34 Cursive curlicue
35 Put up with
39 Three R's supporter
41 Synagogue scroll
43 "Drawing Hands" lithographer
46 Eleventh hour
49 Grapevine item
51 Need to pay the piper
52 R.E.M.'s "The ___ Love"
53 Put in piles, say
55 Drama in Kyoto
56 Ran easily
58 Knocked on the noggin
60 "The Burden of Proof" author
62 Frugivore's concern
64 Bit of bling
65 Darling dog
66 Vital carrier
67 Many mos.
68 1990 Spike Lee film
72 Cartesian conclusion
75 Port on the Seine
76 Words before delighted
77 Plan of action
79 Opposed successfully
82 Devoted groups
84 Bird in a Paul Simon song title
85 Peter of Herman's Hermits
86 Get-up-and-go
88 Alternative to publish
90 Market corrections
91 Burmese leader of the 1950s
92 "Let me repeat . . ."
94 Start out
96 Bill passer?
99 Projector load
101 Waver's syllable
102 James Taylor's "___ Fool to Care"
103 Fairway chunk
105 Type of board or joint
107 Start of trip or trek
109 Source of riboflavin
111 Platter players
113 Cantina creation
117 Caught a bug
118 Dental school final?
122 MacMahon in "Babbitt"
123 "Brothers & Sisters" matriarch
124 Safari sighting
125 Prefix for potent
126 Grace word
127 Ancient German
128 "Tootsie" Oscar winner
129 Monument Valley elevation

DOWN

1 Luncheonette order
2 Laser light show sounds
3 Crude cartel
4 Debtor's car, maybe
5 Took care of
6 Puts forward
7 Go public with
8 John of New Age music
9 John of "Tommy"
10 China syndrome cause
11 Like a fugitive
12 Wild bunch
13 Guilty and more
14 Bernadette in "The Jerk"
15 Kind of cuisine
16 Silver lining
17 "Rent" heroine
18 "Citizen Kane" prop
24 Better
25 Least bit of concern
30 "The Yearling" creature
32 Ethan Allen, religiously
35 Stuck-up
36 Musically challenged organ
37 Indian et al.
38 Giving the green light to
40 Check entry
42 Without scruples
44 Ovine females
45 Shades of remorse
47 Gradual disappearance
48 Veering off
50 Buckeye State sch.
54 Molded muscles
56 "Come on!"
57 "Leaving ___ Jet Plane"
59 "Freaky Deaky" author Leonard
61 Sings like a bird
63 Annoyingly didactic
69 Sounds of a jam
70 Evoke good feelings about
71 Sell up the river
72 Gandhi who wrote "My Truth"
73 Makes one's own
74 Mason in "The Cheap Detective"
75 Japanese "King Lear" film
78 Give a grant
79 Threaded metal fastener
80 Make more effective
81 "Trust me!"
83 Farmscape sights
87 Graph that shows slices
89 Cutting grooves
92 Sporty Camaro
93 Mononymous radio personality
95 Solid, in a phrase
97 Tablecloths and such
98 Gets around
100 Long sentence
104 Flip-flop feature
106 Monitor dot
108 "Biography" network
109 Sad-sounding auto
110 Aspirin unit
112 Hacienda room
114 Submolecule
115 Twist, sometimes
116 Many, many moons
119 Pal of Pooh
120 "Whew!"
121 Long on the screen

292

CUSTOMIZED THEME by Harvey Estes
A made-to-order challenge for solvers young and old.

ACROSS

1 Coen brothers film
6 Dry as dust
10 Dummy
14 Cadet's negative
19 Book flap bit
20 One who fears foreigners
22 "Ready or not, here ___!"
23 "Enough kid stuff!"
25 Passport feature
26 Sean in "The Goonies"
27 It's just for show
28 Exercise aid
30 Two-toned snack
31 Snake sound
33 "Fancy" singer McEntire
35 Toe-___ (catchy tunes)
37 Avoiding, as an issue
42 Packed tight
45 French 101, e.g.
46 They're higher up in a tree
48 Tempest-swept
50 Porter's "Anything ___"
51 Like Homo sapiens
53 Nike logo
54 River bend
56 Amazon business
58 Gibson Chet Atkins ___
59 Heavy reading
63 Unwelcome obligation
65 New York Harbor island
67 Some book sizes
70 Casino table competition
75 Ties
76 Give birth to
77 NY Met, for one
78 At the end of the line
79 Essandoh of "Vinyl"
82 Cranial cavity
84 Plants in a dry place
87 Bounces off
90 Artful dodges
92 Fan noise
93 Impacted molar, perhaps

98 Get joe ready
100 Base command
101 Fiddled around
103 Circle statistic
104 On the throne
106 Head set?
108 Part of TGIF
109 Sporty Camaro
110 Finesse
113 Unthinking repetition
115 ___ Aquarius
119 Gutter site
121 Completely
125 Moves briskly
126 "As far as yours truly is concerned . . ."
127 Time on the job
128 Flirt with
129 Blue Triangle org.
130 Scratch a dele
131 Absolutely must

DOWN

1 Comey's former org.
2 Coloratura Gluck
3 Daily grinds
4 Poetic cavern
5 Group that needs reeds
6 Rose of rock
7 Foxx who played Sanford
8 Figure out
9 Ill-fated
10 Controversial preservative
11 Sounds of envy
12 Solemn column
13 Overwhelmed
14 "___ for Noose": Grafton
15 Detroit Red Wings mascot
16 Eagles, at times
17 Engage completely
18 Laid back
21 Deep-space vehicles
24 Type of inspection
29 Peace accords
32 Nap noise
34 They make pantry raids
36 Pal of Piglet
37 Palm starch

38 Fort in "Goldfinger"
39 Cold appliances of old
40 Like a ring in one's ear
41 Grimm girl
43 Pen mothers
44 Asteroid in "Ender's Game"
47 Injure with water
49 Type of skill
52 Scrabble pieces
55 Wimpy type
57 Progresses unevenly
59 What zebras aren't
60 Ulster, for one
61 Calendar abbr.
62 Abbr. on a business sign
64 Moo ___ pork
66 Flight part
68 "New Day" network
69 Soft rock
70 ___ Aviv
71 Spacewalk, for short

72 Dizzying creative work
73 Come clean
74 Brand-new
80 Blow the whistle
81 Novel of the South Seas
83 Letter enhancement
85 Shopping bag
86 Elbe tributary
87 ___ Nostra
88 Catkin
89 Ocular woe
91 Bug on a pyramid
93 Least trustful
94 Go over again
95 Spanish guitarist
96 Christmas gifts of song
97 Like a satisfying meal
99 "It just hit me!"
102 Hangs down
105 Atlantic City candy
107 Mar. 17 honoree

111 Dawn sound
112 Celtic neck ring
114 Versailles verb
116 Jazz singer James
117 2011 Jay-Z/Kanye West song
118 Typesetter's option
120 Uey from NNW
122 Octagon sport
123 Baseball great Mel
124 "Customized" letters

293 THEMELESS   by Harvey Estes

5 Down is also the oldest state capital in the United States.

ACROSS

1 Sage of the East
7 Promised Land
13 Calamity Jane, e.g.
20 Beat to the tape
21 Facilitate
22 Banned
23 Familiarize
24 Stand-up guys
26 Fritter away the hours
28 Senator's constituency
29 Kind of sausage
30 Met highlights
32 8th Greek letter
34 Naive (with 114-A)
40 Grape arbors
46 ___ up and up
47 Greek epic
50 Public image
51 Sons of, in Hebrew
52 Sound system component
56 St. Lawrence U. team
57 Alpine capital
58 Prophet
60 Social worker's load
61 Livy's "Lo!"
62 Hampton ___
63 Set aside
64 Thursday's eponym
65 Aachen article
66 ___ sci major
67 Some hosp. rooms
69 Platoon leaders: Abbr.
71 Pump part
73 Lot measurement
76 "The Subject Was ___" (1968)
78 Mongkut's monarchy
79 Pack carriers
80 Thumb
82 "Peculiar" prefix
83 Bacon strip
85 Drained of color
86 Patton namesake
87 Originates
89 Crackerjack
90 Private pupil
91 Fireplugs
93 Small store owners
97 Holds
100 Precipitates
101 Helen's "Pay It Forward" character
106 Emulated Elsie
109 Dilapidated places
114 See 34 Across
117 Lisbon's peninsula
118 "The American Language" author
119 Perfect place
120 Food preserver
121 Diner sign
122 Tough questions
123 "Bewitched" mother

DOWN

1 Part of a lasso
2 Vital glow
3 Mayberry detainee
4 Very, in Verdun
5 Highest state capital
6 Missing nothing
7 Some flakes
8 Request to Sajak
9 Badgers
10 Share a border
11 "___ Once You Love Her"
12 Opposite of o'er
13 "What's the ___?"
14 Puts on a pedestal
15 Weight-loss pill
16 Mark of omission
17 Painter Schiele
18 Sign of disinterest
19 Fashion maven Klensch
25 Projector part
27 Big number, slangily
31 In need of laundering
33 Dance noisily
34 Subcontracted (with "out")
35 Superfluous
36 Thwarted by fate
37 Amish pronoun
38 Darts
39 Colonial flute
41 Lots
42 Piston great Thomas
43 Bring together
44 Scott Joplin rag (with "The")
45 Smart stuff
48 Has a bug
49 Oscar ___ Hoya
52 High-profile hairdo
53 Long green
54 Rolling grassland
55 Go back to
59 Draw back
66 Old money of Spain
68 Like some eBay items
70 Camel pack
72 "The Merry Widow" composer
74 Jazz singer James
75 Biting, as wit
76 Fiennes of "The English Patient"
77 Bombastic speaker
78 Exercise for the abs
79 St. Louis landmark
81 Some tools for the garden
84 Verdict deliverer, e.g.
88 Canadian map abbr.
90 Nuclear restraint accord
92 Interstate rumbler
94 Some winter wear
95 Motors in Seoul
96 Dangle a carrot
98 Finish off, as operations
99 ___ voce
101 "Don't look ___ that way!"
102 Saturn satellite
103 Gave temporarily
104 Emulate Dürer
105 Zap in the kitchen
107 Deity of desire
108 Make a fool of
110 Rip to bits
111 Pitti Palace river
112 Waterfront sight
113 Tegan's duet partner
115 U-turn from SSW
116 IRS head

The temple complex at 40 Across is the world's largest religious monument.

ACROSS

1 Provide gratis
5 Trooper's device
10 Bit of fire
15 Fancy-schmancy
19 Flatfoot's lack
20 Orchestrate
21 Imam's book
22 Like a doily
23 Affluent, in Acapulco
24 Speak boastfully of
25 Knocker's reply
26 PDQ, politely
27 Plunders suckers?
30 Cold-blooded one
32 Poker reminder
33 Part of Picard's name
34 Unlucky one at love?
36 Piggy's title
40 Angkor Wat locale
42 Atmosphere
46 Seraglio
47 Saw
52 Canine tracker's document?
54 Fare for streetcars?
56 "The Last Tycoon" director Kazan
57 Attack from concealment
60 Overtime creator
61 Gardner of mystery
62 Low points
64 Civil rights concern
66 Narrow escape
69 Long E's, in Greek
72 African Plains grazer
73 French infinitive
74 Victorian prime minister
78 Proscribed act
80 Poem parts
85 Arctic shelter
86 Uey from WSW
88 Nocturnal lizard of Tennessee
91 Autobahn sight
92 Winnie's hopes?
96 About a quart on the rocks?
98 Sound system
99 Bond girl Roberts
102 "Jaws" star
103 Like Shylock
105 Mozart opera title starter

106 Ancient Greek waterway?
110 Fla. airport
112 "Frasier" character
117 Heavy coats
118 Knocks the decision?
122 Darling dog
123 Ganges country
126 Totally ridiculous
127 Can't stomach
128 ". . . like ___ not!"
129 Brings home
130 "On the Beach" author Shute
131 Therapist's response
132 Sinks below the horizon
133 Helped the economy
134 Backspace over
135 BOLO target

DOWN

1 Film producer Ponti
2 Stars with a belt
3 Enterprise doctor
4 Part of a driver's license
5 Please answer, briefly
6 Antioxidant berry
7 Astronaut Hurley
8 Synthetic fiber brand
9 Alter a photo
10 Hits the slopes
11 Poker prize
12 "___ Poetica": Horace
13 Push a bill through
14 Under-the-table flirtation
15 "Beetle Bailey" brain
16 Desert pit stop
17 Minimum wage
18 Bouncing off the walls
28 Poison oak, for one
29 Nonprofit sports org.
31 Blood part
34 Germany's first president
35 Saône tributary
37 Lickety-split
38 Rip-off
39 Balkan native
41 "I pity the fool" speaker
42 Flabbergasted

43 CIA infiltrator
44 Radar screen flash
45 "___ first you don't . . ."
48 "The Colossus" is one
49 Calvary letters
50 Sushi seafood
51 Isn't a natural
53 Rubber ducky's pond
55 Come together
58 Communicate manually
59 Capital on the Red River
63 "Isn't ___ bit like . . .": Beatles
65 Vocalized
67 Video game parlors
68 "The Smythes" creator Irvin
70 Helm location
71 "Tony Rome" star
74 Short dreams?
75 "___ a Name": Croce
76 Tart plum
77 German industrial locale

79 Yvette's yes
81 Inexperienced one
82 Odette's wear
83 Lofty lines
84 Dated letter opener
87 Online letters
89 "High Voltage" band
90 Caligula's nephew
93 Two in the hand
94 First Communion gifts
95 Cone starter
97 Narrative enhancement
100 Johnny of "The Rebel"
101 Ill-considered
104 Open, as a change purse
106 Pueblo builders
107 Make heady
108 "Lead ___ into temptation . . ."
109 Castor and Pollux
111 Mary Tyler Moore's costar
113 "Like, no problem, man"

114 Let
115 Word on some maze
116 Pricey
118 Over and done
119 Applet language
120 United, to Ionesco
121 Mark of omission
124 Anthony's "Black-ish" role
125 Lodging place

295 ORDINATION   by Fred Piscop
57 Across is usually clued in a musical sense.

CROSS

1 May–December romance feature
7 Bouncer's concern
13 Bonkers
20 Consisting of three
21 Where the Nile begins
22 Ear-shaped shellfish
23 Starting lineup member
25 Audited a course
26 Request
27 Gets value from
29 Coin with a shield
30 Suffix with theater or concert
31 Diner sandwich, briefly
32 "One of ___ days, Alice . . ."
36 Photoshop company
40 Punch-in-the-gut reaction
41 Enjoy a Harley
42 Yin/yang principle
45 New burst of energy
49 Undeveloped countries
52 Eager volunteer's words
53 Vocalizes vehemently
54 Type again
55 Pinochle maneuver
56 It may result in a commission
57 Mexican stop sign word
58 Newcastle river
59 Giraffe features
60 Manicotti kin
62 "Any day now . . ."
63 Ramshackle digs
65 When most Hail Marys are thrown
68 Eminent scholar
71 Beat the pants off
72 "The Praise of Folly" author
76 Any of twelve of our teeth
77 Sub captain's command
78 Arab League dignitary
79 Device for an Apple Pencil
81 Roswell sightings, briefly
82 Sharp-witted
84 Right on the nose
85 Popular fish fillet
86 Double-date tagalong
88 Remote viewing, for one
90 Cocoa butter, e.g.
91 Euro-Asian range
92 Muscle below a delt
93 Sneaker bottom's pattern
94 "Gypsy" composer
95 St. Anthony's cross
96 "You Are My Destiny" singer
99 Plumlike fruit
102 Essen's region
104 Exactly right
108 Like an ode
112 Cloud nine
115 Issue forth
116 Walk like a show horse
117 Unstable
118 Wiped off the computer
119 Having good placement
120 Verdi opera set in Cyprus

DOWN

1 Explosives-regulating org.
2 Tennis lesson topic
3 County Kerry's land
4 Umbrella-inverting wind
5 Type of COVID-19 test
6 Ristorante sauce
7 Public outburst
8 Opposed to, in dialect
9 Dodge City loc.
10 Consume
11 That is
12 Have the chutzpah
13 Many English degs.
14 Lawyers' org.
15 D.C. ballplayer
16 Guest of the Mad Hatter
17 It's worse than half a loaf
18 In a bit, to bards
19 Snail-mailed
24 Super Bowl impossibility
28 Walk off the job
31 Physiques, informally
33 Put on staff
34 Drainage effect
35 Work on a seam
36 Seller's disclaimer
37 Model plane add-on
38 City W of Daytona Beach
39 Doggy bag treats
40 Word after catch or latch
42 Reznor of Nine Inch Nails
43 Kegler's spot
44 Pari-mutuel postings
46 Fire-breathing beast
47 Thumbelina's cradle shell
48 Lay to rest
49 Theatrical routine.
50 Dye in temporary tattoos
51 Neighbor of Yemen
58 Lumberjack's cap
59 "The War of the Worlds" world
61 Worship from ___
62 Sandbox toy
63 To the letter
64 Locale of a Dickens cricket
66 Played out
67 Big name in real estate
68 Vergara of "Modern Family"
69 Like a drone in operation
70 Seemingly boundless
73 Tight-fisted sort
74 Slightly ahead
75 Piquant topping for tacos
76 Fail to catch
77 Hamilton or Burr, notably
78 Cloverleaf feature
80 Scout's good work
82 Off-course
83 Jackie of action movies
84 Hirsute brother of Jacob
87 "Survivor" dwelling
89 Eye impolitely
92 Moths-to-be
94 Sardine net
95 "Done!"
96 Started a pot
97 Unspecified degree
98 Artist Frida
99 Hillside ride
100 Tick-borne disease
101 Like pills, but not injections
103 American Tour de France team (2004)
104 Without repeat
105 Kaplan who played Kotter
106 Satanic doings
107 Bluffer's giveaway
109 Jazz club habitue
110 Enjoyed a spread
111 Called the shots
113 Drew Brees target
114 Opposite of paleo

NO LITTLE GREEN MEN   by Peter Wentz
An alternate title can be found at 126 Across.

ACROSS

1 Cry from one having an identity crisis
7 Not really meaning it
14 British potato chips
20 Offshoots of ventricles
21 Grows up
22 One of the "Top Gun" crew
23 S&L account summary with zero transactions?
25 "You and Me" singer Jackson
26 Lake rental
27 Show some enthusiasm
28 Works up a sweat
30 Kenyan runner Keino
31 "Look for yourself!"
33 Chant for the Dream Team
35 On board
36 Some Morse taps
37 Parasite adept at two-way travel?
42 Houston-based scandal of 2001
44 Bit of livestock feed
45 "___ Did It Again": Spears
46 Not masc. or fem.
48 Like some gaming WiFi routers
51 Melville's great white hunter?
53 Good name for a herding dog
55 Many a future actuary
57 Dwindle
60 Pertaining to the ear
62 A little less than a football field
63 Blue Nile source
64 Altarpiece
66 Rolls-___ Wraith
68 XXVI × IV
69 Long Island campus
72 Just pathetic
74 Avon rival
76 Prefix for light
77 French upper house
80 Submarine captain's order
83 Fish with no pelvic fins
85 River of water parks
86 Magic power
87 Pullover rainwear
91 Masked man's cry
93 Hard drinkers
95 Reputation stain
96 Copier refills
97 Remini in "Second Act"
100 Super Bowl prizes
103 Not hitting the pitch
104 Grind grinders
106 One who's really into pancakes?
109 Palm Beach city, informally
111 Yokohama "yes"
113 Billy's baby
114 Use a dough hook
115 Childcare writer LeShan
116 "Capeesh?"
118 Smithy
121 Shogun's spy
124 Space cloud
126 Ufology topic/TITLE
129 Became part of
130 Paint the town red
131 Miller in "Stardust"
132 Some navels
133 "___ fits all"
134 First arrival

DOWN

1 NYC talk-radio station
2 Honduras hello
3 Sumatran ape
4 When a nautical day begins
5 Gets by
6 2020 SpaceX destination
7 Wet nurse of India
8 2017 Indy 500 winner
9 Went to a luncheon
10 Doesn't bother to test the water
11 Argentite, e.g.
12 "The Garden of England"
13 Put an end to, legally
14 Ask a koi a question?
15 Sea inlets
16 First Big Apple subway
17 Flat tool for a Blazer?
18 ___ Forward Day (April 28)
19 Goes on a rampage
24 Pipsqueaks
29 Unbridled anger
32 Theater for DDE
34 It leads a run in pinochle
36 "Goodbye, Mr. Chips" Oscar winner
37 Loud outburst
38 Punchbowl Crater's island
39 "___ the Sheriff": Clapton
40 Respect born from duty
41 Kal Penn role
43 "Murmur" band
47 Sandwich that crunches
49 Michigan city
50 Southern partner of biscuits
52 Lunch favorites
54 Instagram postings
56 Sign by a free sample
58 Table scraps
59 Leaders in the Wi-Fi sector?
61 It might be yawning
65 China Clipper airline
67 It preludes a conclusion
69 Bikini Atoll event
70 Learn directly from
71 Woodsy H&R Block branch?
73 Doubles teams
75 Strong inclinations
78 Color of el cielo
79 Easygoing sort
81 Singer from Iceland
82 It recurs in novels
84 Elaborate aria
88 State of bliss
89 Sulking mood
90 "Carmina Burana" composer
92 Malayan isthmus
94 Unclogged a drain
98 Genesis vessel
99 Cow girls?
101 "America Says" network
102 It can help you make a letter
105 Tricorne
107 Yahweh, by another name
108 Set a trap
109 1974 dog film
110 "___ Melancholy": Keats
112 Stage after pupa
116 Unabashed happiness
117 Carolina campus
119 Give the Bronx cheer
120 Brief farewell
122 Favreau and Stewart
123 Advanced bio. course
125 Two less than tri-
127 Runway hazard
128 Customary practice

ACROSS

1 Explorer Heyerdahl
5 Ersatz chocolate
10 On the up-and-up
15 Now!
19 Like black olives
20 Leeward Antilles isle
21 Aviator Balbo
22 Prefix for trooper
23 Solar disk
24 Zenith's opposite
25 Made a pitch
26 Added bonus
27 Mexican brew*
29 Dream poker hand*
31 Greene's "___ with My Aunt"
32 Pub quaffs
34 "Queen of Soul" Franklin
35 Obstinate animal
36 Lone Star river
38 Whets
40 Puts a lid on it
43 Heavenly whale
44 Paris newspaper (with "Le")
45 Trigram on an LP
48 Skye in "XOXO"
49 Echo or Cyllene, e.g.
50 "Them" novelist
51 Ward of "House"
52 Tel Aviv suburb
53 Brando's drama coach*
55 Interoffice notes
56 Employs a da Vinci robot
58 Oman currency
59 Nabokov novel
60 Star in Orion's foot
61 Kitchen gadget
63 "The Age of Bronze" sculptor
64 Mason, for one
66 Science-fiction award
67 Expressed disinterest
70 "Das Boot" vessel
71 They're found in clue* answers
74 Japan's Big Board: Abbr.
75 Nippy
76 Thompson in "Rain"
77 Transport
78 One slew Adonis
79 "The Spanish Tragedy" dramatist
80 Quirky
81 "Did you get the flowers ___?"
82 First head of the USSR
83 Silicon Valley college
84 Use a dough hook
85 It might have an electric organ
86 Peace out
89 Home to Chang and Eng
90 Constitution section
94 He was Proximo in "Gladiator"*
97 "1984" dictator*
100 Bank of Paris
101 Mecca religion
102 Vaquero's range
103 Means ___ end
104 Irving's "___ of the Circus"
105 Andrew Lloyd Webber musical
106 "___ Gantry" (1960)
107 Virna in "Arabella"
108 Groks
109 Coffee stirrer
110 Forward thinkers?
111 "Symphony in Black" artist

DOWN

1 Housing development
2 ___-miss (erratic)
3 Covent Garden staging
4 Refurbish
5 Martian markings
6 Show horses
7 Uncouth
8 "Village Voice" award
9 Plymouth muscle car
10 British bottle sizes
11 Societal standards
12 Cartoonist Larson
13 One of Athena's names
14 Southern Scotland
15 Barrel fruits
16 Port ___ cheese
17 Coldplay's "___ of Blood to the Head"
18 Ottoman VIP
28 Suffix for dark
30 Gratis
33 Part of LAPD
36 Does some KP work
37 Collective abbr.
38 Purchase for Baltic Avenue
39 Doozy
40 Hay holder
41 Barrel part
42 "Southbound" singer Carrie*
43 Angling basket
44 Cheekbone
45 Noted painter of cowboys*
46 Frame-up job
47 Tortilla dough
49 Mink cousin
50 Jim Davis character
51 Manfred's MLB predecessor
53 "Full House" star
54 Exemplar of straightness
55 ___ operandi
57 Qatar currency
59 "Casablanca" actor
61 Valentine's Day figure
62 Pointed arch
63 Bonnie Blue's dad
64 The Irish have it
65 "If I Were ___": Beyoncé
66 Prefix for electric
67 "___ by Me": Ben E. King
68 Morales of "NYPD Blue"
69 Laura in "Wild"
71 Pheasant feature
72 Takes after
73 Intestinal divisions
76 Watches
78 Disparage
80 "You ___ saying . . ."
81 Concert suffix
82 Mother of Artemis
83 Connoisseurs
84 Nicole in "Lion"
85 Box-score entries
86 Hip-hop head wrap
87 "Somewhere in Time" heroine
88 Spin on one foot
89 "From ___ shining . . ."
90 Tiny Yokum's brother
91 Loft group
92 LCD component
93 Heisman winner Davis
95 "Answer, please"
96 "Call Me by Your Name" youth
98 "Winnie ___ Pu"
99 Kind of fish or bird

298 STATE LAWS   by John M. Samson
Fortunately, many of these outrageous laws are not enforced.

ACROSS

1 Kid sounds
5 Lab sounds
10 Come (from)
15 Let off steam
19 Hendrix hairstyle
20 Avalor princess
21 Synonym master
22 Pal of Garfield
23 Moose order
24 The Doctor, for one
25 007 actor
26 Grocery store staples
27 In Maine, it's illegal to advertise on ___
29 In Virginia, it's illegal to go trick-or-treating ___
31 Hollywood hopeful
32 Lays down the lawn
34 South Pole's latitude
35 Big time
36 Crustacean claw
38 Arouses
40 Brassy sound
43 "___ Rain's a-Gonna Fall"
44 Ralph of "The Waltons"
45 NASCAR sponsor
48 Bonkers
49 Shrovetide pancakes
50 "Sons of Anarchy" actress Sagal
51 Bell the cat
52 Eugene O'Neill play
53 In Alabama, it's illegal to drive while ___
55 "Macbeth" director Welles
56 Running of the bulls city
58 Require
59 Kuwaiti's neighbors
60 Cheer up
61 Stood toe-to-toe
63 Total mess
64 Nashville team
66 Tweety's home
67 Banana relative
70 Change a charter
71 In Florida, it's illegal to wear a military uniform while ___
74 Chinese menu general
75 Trunk "donut"
76 Photographer Simpson
77 Lose ground, in a way
78 Healing sign
79 "___ questions?"
80 Like soy sauce
81 Deep-felt
82 Collarless jacket
83 Frère de la mère
84 Norman and LeMond
85 Prostate test
86 Max Perkins, e.g.
89 "Oh, dear!"
90 Omen
94 In Connecticut, all pickles ___
97 In Kansas, ___ of tires is prohibited
100 Prefix for prop
101 Like tiger moms
102 Sporting wings
103 Dorsey of "Queen Sugar"
104 Once again
105 Bird in the finch family
106 Deer stomach
107 Nerve network
108 Harper Lee's "Go ___ Watchman"
109 Poem with couplets
110 Candles may represent them
111 Once, once

DOWN

1 Soda-shop orders
2 "Come, Watson, the game's ___ !"
3 It excites a sense
4 In New Mexico, it's illegal to dance around a ___
5 Licked
6 Divvy out
7 Smarty Jones' control
8 Arthroscopy area
9 Like Helvetica
10 Royal Navy foe of 1588
11 Places for gardens
12 "___ a Woman": Ray Charles
13 Desertlike
14 Forever and a day
15 Birds in "Trees"
16 Truism
17 Elie Wiesel book
18 In a peeved mood
28 Gin flavorer
30 Leinster locale
33 GOP member
36 Slow boat destination
37 Bridge holding
38 Wanting no more
39 Laced up
40 Spot in the control tower
41 Granola of "Opus"
42 In New Hampshire, it's illegal to picnic in ___
43 Sixties dress style
44 Walked in water
45 In Washington, it's illegal to hunt ___
46 Enterprise empath
47 Bar mitzvah gifts
49 Record blemishes
50 Swiss abstractionist
51 Keg beer
53 In need of zip
54 "___ jolly swagman . . ."
55 Sumatran ape
57 Memphis Belle, for one
59 Devoid of logic
61 Brice of Follies
62 Ottoman pooh-bah
63 Playground sight
64 "Peace out!"
65 "Heaven, ___ heaven . . ."
66 Bistro menu
67 Storylines
68 Bavarian river
69 Chef Matsuhisa
71 Election report
72 Indispensable
73 Merck product
76 College stick sport
78 Vacation spot
80 Name-dropper
81 Macaw genus
82 Billionth of a min.
83 Ontario hub
84 Headly on "Monk"
85 Dolls up
86 Peel and Thompson
87 Bounty hunter Chapman
88 Ocean oasis
89 Astringent
90 Finch in "Network"
91 One eying a target
92 Tiny stingers
93 Everglades bird
95 Baylor rival
96 Claudius I's successor
98 Lead
99 "The Jungle Book" water buffalo

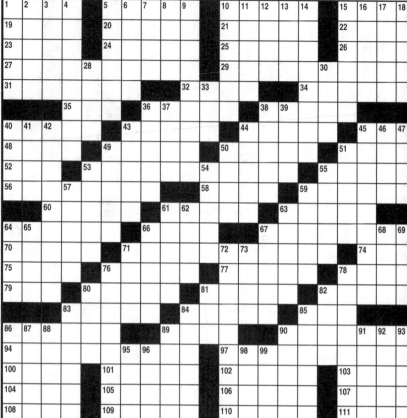

BANDLEADERS* by Elizabeth C. Gorski
43 Across has its origin with the Pilgrims in Plymouth Colony.

CROSS

1 Encounter a banana peel
5 Home row keyboard letters
9 "___ that's your game!"
13 High roller's advice
19 Not prerecorded
20 Drywall
22 Tack on
23 "Superstore" star*
25 Somersaulting dive
26 Intense, as a love affair
27 Valedictorian's grade
29 Bonn pronoun
30 Computer chip giant
31 First lady before Jackie
33 Origami bird
35 Tax prep pros
38 Ne'er-do-well
41 Edges up to
43 Traditional New England dish*
49 Gulf War missile
52 Leaves the amateur ranks
53 Reactions to puppies
54 Make ___ of (jot down)
56 Buckeyes' sch.
57 Bikini half
58 Hotsy-___
60 Puma and Jaguar, e.g.
62 Capital of Honduras?
63 "Nick of Time" singer Bonnie
65 Perspire
66 Sources of online help
69 CBS medical drama*
73 Online crafts market
74 Less than 90 degrees
76 "I remember now!"
77 "He's ___ the world!"
79 Inexpensive dried fruits?
82 "Fawlty Towers" wife
83 Six-pack muscles
86 Sock part
87 Feel
88 ___ Vicente
90 Unflappable
92 Emilio and Charlie, to Martin
94 T.S. Eliot poem*
97 Jazzman Peterson
99 ___-Wreck
100 Fine spray
101 1994 trade pact
103 Lake Nasser's dam
106 Refrain starters
110 Rm. coolers
111 Finnish tech giant
113 Quesadilla
118 Nova ___ lox
120 Cogitation process*
123 Absent-minded student?
124 Escapade
125 Laugh-a-minute
126 Elis
127 Despot
128 Carolina college
129 Ltr. add-ins

DOWN

1 Type of hockey shot
2 Peru capital
3 Oscar winner in "The Big Country"
4 Doesn't give up
5 Yachting neckwear
6 Alan Ladd western
7 "The Three-Cornered Hat" composer
8 Hexameter's six
9 Famed Bruin #4
10 Tool of cultivation
11 "Vamoose!"
12 Animal discovered in 1900
13 Pasta sauce brand
14 Mississippi River source
15 Sporty Subaru
16 Nickname of Gale Sayers*
17 Strand during a blizzard
18 French hens count in song
21 Italian for 18 Down
24 "There's no ___ team!"
28 "Give Peace a Chance" singer
31 Rx bottle contents
32 Securities trader, for short
34 $200 Monopoly props.
35 Bygone NYC punk club
36 "___ Richard's Almanack"
37 Cruising the Baltic
39 Thumbs-up
40 Attach a patch
42 Cornerstone letters
44 Sailing dinghy
45 Campus midshipmen's org.
46 Bungle
47 View from the Moon
48 Henry Gray's area
50 "___ directed"
51 Singer Springfield
55 Starfleet Academy grad
59 Japanese massage
60 Book jacket briefs
61 "Don't be ___ blanket!"
62 "The Thin Man" dog
63 Beams
64 Number on a birthday cake
66 Trivia quiz fodder
67 Sneeze sound
68 Aretha Franklin sobriquet*
70 Gaiety
71 "Blue Ribbon" beer
72 Mary's sister on "Downton Abbey"
75 Graphics file extension
78 Medicinal plant
80 "___ Vu": Warwick
81 Parka
82 Fireplace residue
83 Antioxidant berry
84 Satchels
85 Cut in a skirt
88 Spotted
89 Objectivist Rand
91 Childish
93 2005 Prince hit
95 An FDR agency
96 Momentous
98 Pooch
101 Horribly mean
102 Ghana's capital
104 Occupy, as a desk
105 Voting districts
107 Chic again
108 Pale as a ghost
109 Zodiac cat
112 Feedbag fill
113 Anderson Cooper's channel
114 Table d'___
115 Opposite of "fer"
116 Van/___/Straw
117 Mel and Ed of baseball
119 ___ chi
121 "Selma" director DuVernay
122 Suffix with cash

300   THEATER IN THE ROUND   by Elizabeth C. Gorski
An award-winning challenger from a crossword legend.

ACROSS

1 Hair tangle
6 Talking point?
10 Use a library
14 Fairway hazard
18 When Macbeth murders Duncan
19 Start of Idaho's motto
20 "I Am Not My Hair" singer
21 Make angry
22 Impressive to the max
25 City on the Red Sea
27 Diane's "Godfather" role
28 Hex
29 "Our message needs to get out!"
31 Ship's safety rope
32 100 yrs.
33 Carefree existence
34 Humorist Silverstein
37 Keyboard virtuosi?
40 Envelope abbr.
41 Oklahoma tribe
44 DVR brand
45 Pine products
46 Group that plays the mating game
49 O. Henry plot twists
51 West African coins
53 Billy Blanks workout system
54 Pants measure
55 Fabric leftovers
57 "Frozen" Olaf's carrot
58 "Blue Bloods" actor Cariou
59 Observed
61 Italian wine region
62 "Are not!" retort
65 Long prison stretch
68 Song from "The Lion King" (and a theme hint)
73 Love of Hercules
74 Totals
78 Rock rabbit
79 Faux ___ (blunder)
80 Heroic tale
83 Disavows
86 Serve your country
88 Office copier brand
90 "The Seven Year Itch" star
91 Access with a password
92 Shallow
95 Arrive, as fog
97 Swerve
98 Air show locale
99 Ohio or Hudson: Abbr.
100 Wall paneling
102 Whirlpool
103 Rescue vessel
105 Wide shoe widths
106 Feral fauna
109 Lettuce dish
113 Arm bones
114 Sound file
117 Service holders in the service
118 Inflatable jackets
121 "Downton Abbey" countess
122 1998 French Open winner
123 Take a chance
124 "Swell!"
125 Country star Loretta
126 Gray's subj.
127 "___ Will": Backstreet Boys
128 Throat infection

DOWN

1 Virologist Jonas
2 March Madness gp.
3 "Give it ___!"
4 Oil-drilling structure
5 "The Sound of Music" teenager
6 Diplomatic thaws
7 Judd and Tisdale
8 Biased type: Abbr.
9 Junior
10 Engrossed
11 Notched like a leaf
12 Stealth home
13 Can't stomach
14 Fact-based
15 Rap's Flo ___
16 Winged
17 Await judgment
23 School in Troy, NY
24 As we get older, we learn from them
26 Most timid
30 Tolkien tree creature
31 Like enduring friendships
32 Movie theater
34 Cezanne's "The Basket of Apples," e.g.
35 New staffers
36 Wimbledon champ Goolagong
38 Heap
39 Picturesque
41 Nondairy spread
42 Vats
43 Bassoon's kin
45 Mend shoes, in a way
47 DDE predecessor
48 Portage vessel
50 "___ die for!" ("I love this!")
52 Jazz cornetist Adderley
55 GOP org.
56 Delhi wedding dress
60 Cabinet dept.
63 Nancy of "The Division"
64 Word on the street?
66 "Excalibur" star Williamson
67 Bars, legally
69 Online ID nos.
70 Editorialized
71 Observed Lent
72 Biography
75 Coffee vessel
76 What Mickey Rooney experienced eight times
77 Sherbet servings
80 Historic periods
81 Flamingo's color
82 Ugh-inducing
84 Suffix for morph
85 Snitch
87 Anna Kendrick HBO series
89 Tea type
91 Skating commentator Tara
93 Historical museum display
94 Taxpayer's crime
96 Sue Grafton's "L"
101 "Isn't ___ bit like you and me?"
103 The adult mayfly's is about a day
104 "Delta Dawn" singer Tucker
107 Seaport of New Guinea
108 Bruce and Laura of film
109 Half of DCC
110 "Hi, sailor!"
111 Deserve
112 Exam for an aspiring atty.
113 Michael of "Ugly Betty"
114 Partner of wash
115 Museo display
116 Brandy-bottle letters
119 Snoop
120 VFW member

FOREWORD

1. son(JA W.S). Gilbert
2. memoran(DUM BO)re
3. ti(PSY CHO)se
4. me(AL I EN)joyed
5. intro(VERT I GO)aded
6. ida(HO OK)lahoma
7. c(ROC KY)oto
8. bra(G AND HI)light
9. cu(BA BE)aring
10. go(NE TWO RK)os
11. div(A MADE US)hers

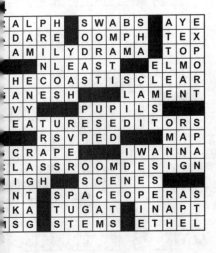

2

3

5

6

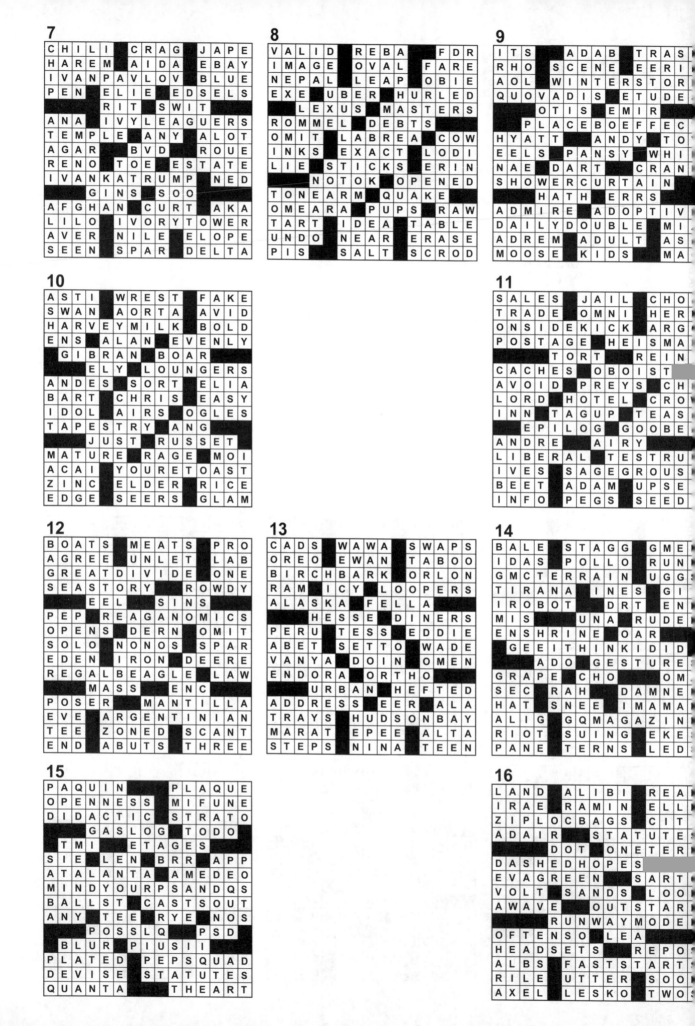

7

```
C H I L I   C R A G   J A P E
H A R E M   A I D A   E B A Y
I V A N P A V L O V   B L U E
P E N   E L I E   E D S E L S
    R I T   S W I T
A N A   I V Y L E A G U E R S
T E M P L E   A N Y   A L O T
A G A R   B V D   R O U E
R E N O   T O E   E S T A T E
I V A N K A T R U M P   N E D
    G I N S   S O O
A F G H A N   C U R T   A K A
L I L O   I V O R Y T O W E R
A V E R   N I L E   E L O P E
S E E N   S P A R   D E L T A
```

8

```
V A L I D   R E B A     F D R
I M A G E   O V A L   F A R E
N E P A L   L E A P   O B I E
E X E   U B E R   H U R L E D
  L E X U S   M A S T E R S
R O M M E L   D E B T S
O M I T   L A B R E A   C O W
I N K S   E X A C T   L O D I
L I E   S T I C K S   E R I N
  N O T O K   O P E N E D
T O N E A R M   Q U A K E
O M E A R A   P U P S   R A W
T A R T   I D E A   T A B L E
U N D O   N E A R   E R A S E
P I S   S A L T   S C R O D
```

9

```
I T S   A D A B   T R A S
R H O   S C E N E   E E R I
A O L   W I N T E R S T O R
Q U O V A D I S   E T U D E
  O T I S   E M I R
  P L A C E B O E F F E C
H Y A T T   A N D Y   T O
E E L S   P A N S Y   W H I
N A E   D A R T   C R A N
S H O W E R C U R T A I N
  H A T H   E R R S
A D M I R E   A D O P T I V
D A I L Y D O U B L E   M I
A D R E M   A D U L T   A S
M O O S E   K I D S   M A
```

10

```
A S T I   W R E S T   F A K E
S W A N   A O R T A   A V I D
H A R V E Y M I L K   B O L D
E N S   A L A N   E V E N L Y
  G I B R A N   B O A R
  E L Y   L O U N G E R S
A N D E S   S O R T   E L I A
B A R T   C H R I S   E A S Y
I D O L   A I R S   O G L E S
T A P E S T R Y   A N G
  J U S T   R U S S E T
M A T U R E   R A G E   M O I
A C A I   Y O U R E T O A S T
Z I N C   E L D E R   R I C E
E D G E   S E E R S   G L A M
```

11

```
S A L E S   J A I L   C H O
T R A D E   O M N I   H E R
O N S I D E K I C K   A R G
P O S T A G E   H E I S M A
  T O R T   R E I N
C A C H E S   O B O I S T
A V O I D   P R E Y S   C H
L O R D   H O T E L   C R O
I N N   T A G U P   T E A S
  E P I L O G   G O O B E
A N D R E   A I R Y
L I B E R A L   T E S T R U
I V E S   S A G E G R O U S
B E E T   A D A M   U P S E
I N F O   P E G S   S E E D
```

12

```
B O A T S   M E A T S   P R O
A G R E E   U N L E T   L A B
G R E A T D I V I D E   O N E
S E A S T O R Y   R O W D Y
  E E L   S I N S
P E P   R E A G A N O M I C S
O P E N S   D E R N   O M I T
S O L O   N O N O S   S P A R
E D E N   I R O N   D E E R E
R E G A L B E A G L E   L A W
  M A S S   E N C
P O S E R   M A N T I L L A
E V E   A R G E N T I N I A N
T E E   Z O N E D   S C A N T
E N D   A B U T S   T H R E E
```

13

```
C A D S   W A W A   S W A P S
O R E O   E W A N   T A B O O
B I R C H B A R K   O R L O N
R A M   I C Y   L O O P E R S
A L A S K A   F E L L A
  H E S S E   D I N E R S
P E R U   T E S S   E D D I E
A B E T   S E T T O   W A D E
V A N Y A   D O I N   O M E N
E N D O R A   O R T H O
  U R B A N   H E F T E D
A D D R E S S   E E R   A L A
T R A Y S   H U D S O N B A Y
M A R A T   E P E E   A L T A
S T E P S   N I N A   T E E N
```

14

```
B A L E   S T A G G   G M E
I D A S   P O L L O   R U N
G M C T E R R A I N   U G G S
T I R A N A   I N E S   G I
I R O B O T   D R T   E N
M I S   U N A   R U D E
E N S H R I N E   O A R
  G E E I T H I N K I D I D
  A D O   G E S T U R E
G R A P E   C H O   O M
S E C   R A H   D A M N E
H A T   S N E E   I M A M A
A L I G   G Q M A G A Z I N
R I O T   S U I N G   E K E
P A N E   T E R N S   L E D
```

15

```
P A Q U I N     P L A Q U E
O P E N N E S S   M I F U N E
D I D A C T I C   S T R A T O
  G A S L O G   T O D O
  T M I   E T A G E S
S I E   L E N   B R R   A P P
A T A L A N T A   A M E D E O
M I N D Y O U R P S A N D Q S
B A L L S T   C A S T S O U T
A N Y   T E E   R Y E   N O S
  P O S S L Q   P S D
  B L U R   P I U S I I
P L A T E D   P E P S Q U A D
D E V I S E   S T A T U T E S
Q U A N T A   T H E A R T
```

16

```
L A N D   A L I B I   R E A
I R A E   R A M I N   E L L
Z I P L O C B A G S   C I T
A D A I R   S T A T U T E S
  D O T   O N E T E R
D A S H E D H O P E S
E V A G R E E N   S A R T
V O L T   S A N D S   L O O
A W A V E   O U T S T A R
  R U N W A Y M O D E
O F T E N S O   L E A
H E A D S E T S   R E P O
A L B S   F A S T S T A R T
R I L E   U T T E R   S O O
A X E L   L E S K O   T W O
```

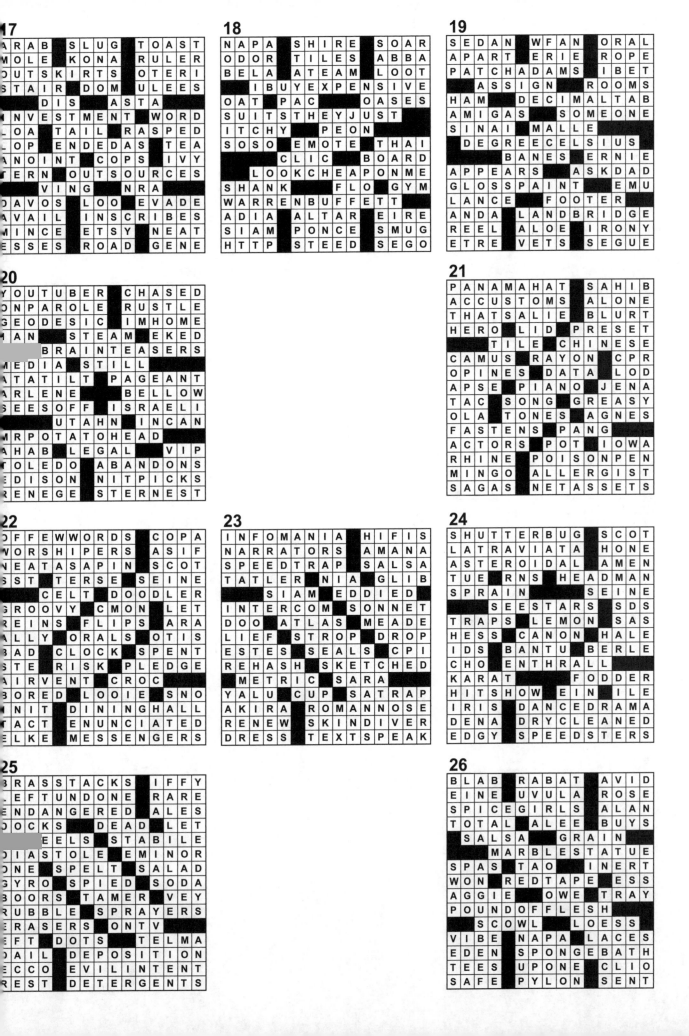

17

```
ARAB  SLUG   TOAST
MOLE  KONA   RULER
OUTSKIRTS    OTERI
STAIR DOM    ULEES
      DIS  ASTA
INVESTMENT   WORD
LOA   TAIL   RASPED
LOP   ENDEDAS  TEA
ANOINT COPS    IVY
TERN  OUTSOURCES
      VING   NRA
DAVOS LOO    EVADE
AVAIL INSCRIBES
MINCE ETSY   NEAT
ESSES ROAD   GENE
```

18

```
NAPA  SHIRE   SOAR
ODOR  TILES   ABBA
BELA  ATEAM   LOOT
   IBUYEXPENSIVE
OAT  PAC    OASES
SUITSTHEYJUST
ITCHY      PEON
SOSO  EMOTE  THAI
     CLIC  BOARD
   LOOKCHEAPONME
SHANK    FLO  GYM
WARRENBUFFETT
ADIA  ALTAR  EIRE
SIAM  PONCE  SMUG
HTTP  STEED  SEGO
```

19

```
SEDAN  WFAN   ORAL
APART  ERIE   ROPE
PATCHADAMS    IBET
   ASSIGN   ROOMS
HAM   DECIMALTAB
AMIGAS    SOMEONE
SINAI MALLE
   DEGREECELSIUS
       BANES  ERNIE
APPEARS    ASKDAD
GLOSSPAINT    EMU
LANCE     FOOTER
ANDA  LANDBRIDGE
REEL  ALOE   IRONY
ETRE  VETS   SEGUE
```

20

```
YOUTUBER    CHASED
ONPAROLE    RUSTLE
GEODESIC    IMHOME
MAN   STEAM   EKED
   BRAINTEASERS
MEDIA STILL
ATATILT     PAGEANT
ARLENE      BELLOW
SEESOFF     ISRAELI
     UTAHN   INCAN
   MRPOTATOHEAD
AHAB  LEGAL    VIP
TOLEDO   ABANDONS
EDISON   NITPICKS
RENEGE   STERNEST
```

21

```
PANAMAHAT   SAHIB
ACCUSTOMS   ALONE
THATSALIE   BLURT
HERO  LID   PRESET
      TILE  CHINESE
CAMUS RAYON   CPR
OPINES DATA   LOD
APSE  PIANO  JENA
TAC   SONG  GREASY
OLA   TONES  AGNES
FASTENS    PANG
ACTORS  POT   IOWA
RHINE  POISONPEN
MINGO  ALLERGIST
SAGAS  NETASSETS
```

22

```
OFFEWWORDS   COPA
WORSHIPERS   ASIF
NEATASAPIN   SCOT
SST   TERSE  SEINE
     CELT   DOODLER
GROOVY CMON   LET
REINS  FLIPS  ARA
ALLY  ORALS  OTIS
BAD   CLOCK  SPENT
STE   RISK  PLEDGE
AIRVENT    CROC
BORED  LOOIE  SNO
NIT   DININGHALL
TACT  ENUNCIATED
ELKE  MESSENGERS
```

23

```
INFOMANIA   HIFIS
NARRATORS   AMANA
SPEEDTRAP   SALSA
TATLER  NIA  GLIB
    SIAM   EDDIED
INTERCOM   SONNET
DOO   ATLAS  MEADE
LIEF  STROP  DROP
ESTES  SEALS  CPI
REHASH  SKETCHED
METRIC    SARA
YALU  CUP   SATRAP
AKIRA  ROMANNOSE
RENEW  SKINDIVER
DRESS  TEXTSPEAK
```

24

```
SHUTTERBUG   SCOT
LATRAVIATA   HONE
ASTEROIDAL   AMEN
TUE   RNS  HEADMAN
SPRAIN      SEINE
    SEESTARS  SDS
TRAPS  LEMON  SAS
HESS  CANON  HALE
IDS   BANTU  BERLE
CHO   ENTHRALL
KARAT      FODDER
HITSHOW EIN   ILE
IRIS  DANCEDRAMA
DENA  DRYCLEANED
EDGY  SPEEDSTERS
```

25

```
BRASSTACKS   IFFY
LEFTUNDONE   RARE
ENDANGERED   ALES
DOCKS  DEAD   LET
     EELS  STABILE
DIASTOLE   EMINOR
ONE   SPELT  SALAD
GYRO  SPIED  SODA
BOORS  TAMER  VEY
RUBBLE  SPRAYERS
ERASERS    ONTV
EFT   DOTS  TELMA
JAIL  DEPOSITION
ECCO  EVILINTENT
REST  DETERGENTS
```

26

```
BLAB  RABAT   AVID
EINE  UVULA   ROSE
SPICEGIRLS   ALAN
TOTAL ALEE   BUYS
   SALSA   GRAIN
   MARBLESTATUE
SPAS  TAO    INERT
WON   REDTAPE  ESS
AGGIE   OWE   TRAY
POUNDOFFLESH
   SCOWL    LOESS
VIBE  NAPA  LACES
EDEN  SPONGEBATH
TEES  UPONE  CLIO
SAFE  PYLON  SENT
```

27

```
C A R B S . . G O D . . S T R A Y
A L A R M . S A V E S . W E I R D
M A R I A . C R E M E . O A S E S
. B E E R B A R R E L P O L K A .
D A B . T E N . S A L I N E . . .
A M I D S T . S E N S E . O O P S
D A T A . A W E . . . I N G O T .
. . M A R G A R I T A V I L L E .
A H A . B E R T . F U M E . E L M
T E Q U I L A S U N R I S E . . .
V A U N T . . . S O N . A B O Y .
S P A S . I N P U T . D E R I V E
. . T A R T A R . L O X . Z E N .
. W H I S K E Y I N T H E J A R .
B E A C H . S T O O D . R E R U N
L A T K E . T O U R S . T E R S E
T R E S S . . N S A . . S P E E D
```

28

```
M I F F . . S C A N S . R I P
A T R A . A M P S U P . A T E
J U I C E D A L I M E . Z E N
S P E E D E R S . E C Z E M A
. . . D E A L T . E R T E . .
D E B A T E S . H A R D W A Y
E R A S E . . H U L A . A D A
P I C T . C L O D S . P S A T
T K O . D R A T . K A T I E .
H A N K I E S . B A N T E R S
. . A S A S . I S A I D . . .
G O B A C K . P R I C E T A G
A D O . O I L E D A K N I F E
Z O O . R E G A I N . T M A N
A R K . D R A K E . . S E R E
```

29

```
N A R C . O S H A . F L A G S
I T O O . U T E S . A E R I E
C R O S S T A L K . S T E N T
H I S T O R Y I S T H E . . .
E A T . R A S . A I M S A T .
. E D E N . A T M O . T R U .
B O R O N . S C I E N C E O F
A S T I . R A T E D . L E S T
W H A T N E V E R . P A L E S
L E I . A C E D . P I N G . .
S A L I V A . U A E . U S F .
. . H A P P E N S T W I C E .
S T R O H . T I C T A C T O E
Z E P P O . A R L O . T A R P
A R I E S . S E E R . U R N S
```

30

```
. D O G T A G S . P R O M O
. I V O R I E S . H O V E L
. M A T E R N I T Y W A R D
A P R O N . D A L . L I L T
C L I . C B S . M U D . T I E
M E A T H E A D . M A V E N S
E D N A . A L E C . R I D E S
. . T A M E R L A N E . . .
D E W A R . M A U L . W I N G
A S H R A M . T E A M S T E R
I K E . B A T . D S T . A M A
S I R S . M O D . H O L E Y
. M E T A M O R P H O S I S
. O B A M A . A R E O L A E
. S Y B I L . T E N D O N S
```

31

```
D A W N . S U I T S . C A S T
E L I A . E S S E N . P I T H
B A S K E T C A S E . A R E A
A B E E T . G A L A S . M A N
S A D D A M . C A K E W A L K
E M U . L A S . Y E A S T .
R A P A . I P O D . D I S H
. . S A L A D D A Y S . . .
S U N Y . Y E A H . T U M S
A L E A D . Y A W . N A P
F L Y W H E E L . B E L U G A
R E S . S E X E D . L O S E R
U R S A . P U N C H D R U N K
I N E S . E D D I E . N A T L
T O S S . R E S I N . A L A E
```

32

```
R A M B O . E S S E S . S T P
S N A I L . M A T E Y . T R A
A N K L E B I T E R S . J A R
. . E G G O N . P O T L U C K
M D S E . H E M A . . I D E A
O A F . A R M T W I S T E R S
C R O W D . V A P O R . . .
S A R A L E E . Y O D E L E D
. . L I M A S . A S I D E .
B A C K B U R N E R S . N A P
E L H I . L O D E . L I M P
E C O N O M Y . I D I O M .
P O R . H E A D B A N G E R S
E V E . M O G U L . C A N E A
R E S . S W E D E . A N T E D
```

33

```
L O W S . A G E S . D R A M S
Y O R E . L U C A . I A M S O
C H I M N E Y C L E A N E R S
R E T I E . L E V A R . S P O
A D E . R P I . O R I G . .
. R A T I N G S P E R I O D
. . I S N E R . . S A D I E
S T U N . T R I T T . H O L E
E A R T H . E R I C A . . .
W I N S E V E R Y G A M E .
. O R E L . T E M . A B C
I R E . B R I T H . E S T E E
T I D I E S T H E F L O O R S
S P O O R . E A S E . D U E T
A S C O T . S T E W . A T T A
```

34

```
M A G E . M A N A G E . D A M
A R O N . A T O N E R . E L I
K I T T Y C O R N E R . C P L
E G O . E E L . . . D E A D
W A S P S . L A S T P L A C E
A T E E . . S A B E R S A V
R O A L D . N I N A S . E S S
. . L E M O N D R O P . . .
A C T . S I S I S . S L A T E
S H A R K F I N . E L A L
H A N D S F R E E . T B I R D
R I G A . . D I S . S H E
A T E . K I C K S T A R T E R
M E N . A R M I E S . K E E L
S A T . Y E A R L Y . O R L Y
```

35

```
C U M I N . A L C O A . B U T
A N O D E . B A R D S . R N H
R A R E S P E C I E S . A L I
S I N . S O A K S . A V O N
A R I A . M R S P E A C O C K
L E N S E S . . S L E E K S
E D G A R . H A I T I . D S O
. . P A P E R S A C K . . .
E B B . S I X T H . I O W A N
C L A R E T . M A N A N A
O U T E R S P A C E . A S T I
C E R N . S P O R T . O I L
I T O . S P A R E C H A N G E
D I P . S A L O N . A L T E R
E T E . H Y M N S . N E O N S
```

36

```
G O A T . I T S A . A C T E D
U R S A . S H A M . S H E A R
M A I N T H E M E . S E R T A
S L A K E . S O N G . W R A P
. . . S T E A D Y S T A T E
F I E S T A . . M E H . . .
E S A U . B O N E . L E A S H
M I C R O S O F T O F F I C E
A S H E N . F L A P . A D A M
. . W E E . . A S T E R S
L U C I L L E B A L L . . .
A N O N . S N U B . A I S L E
S C A N T . D E E P W A T E R
E L S E S . I N T O . G O N G
R E T R O . T A S E . O P T S
```

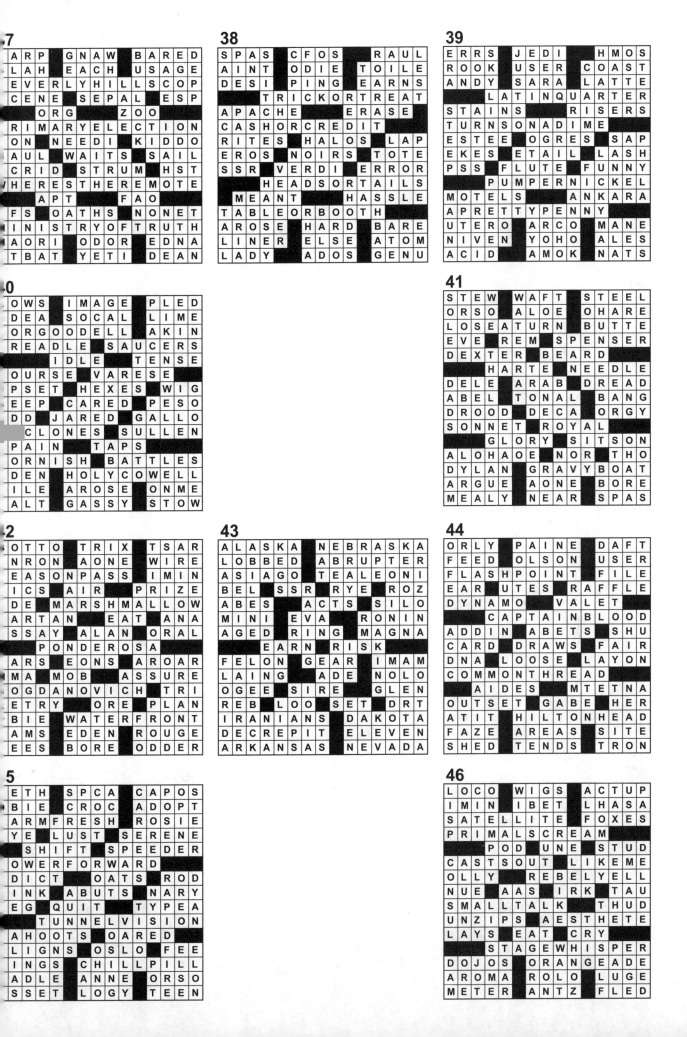

37

A	R	P		G	N	A	W			B	A	R	E	D
L	A	H		E	A	C	H			U	S	A	G	E
E	V	E	R	L	Y	H	I	L	L	S	C	O	P	
C	E	N	E			S	E	P	A	L		E	S	P
			O	R	G			Z	O	O				
R	I	M	A	R	Y	E	L	E	C	T	I	O	N	
O	N		N	E	E	D	I			K	I	D	D	O
A	U	L		W	A	I	T	S			S	A	I	L
C	R	I	D		S	T	R	U	M			H	S	T
H	E	R	E	S	T	H	E	R	E	M	O	T	E	
		A	P	T				F	A	O				
F	S		O	A	T	H	S			N	O	N	E	T
I	N	I	S	T	R	Y	O	F	T	R	U	T	H	
A	O	R	I		O	D	O	R			E	D	N	A
T	B	A	T		Y	E	T	I			D	E	A	N

38

S	P	A	S		C	F	O	S			R	A	U	L
A	I	N	T		O	D	I	E		T	O	I	L	E
D	E	S	I		P	I	N	G		E	A	R	N	S
			T	R	I	C	K	O	R	T	R	E	A	T
A	P	A	C	H	E			E	R	A	S	E		
C	A	S	H	O	R	C	R	E	D	I	T			
R	I	T	E	S		H	A	L	O	S		L	A	P
E	R	O	S		N	O	I	R	S		T	O	T	E
S	S	R		V	E	R	D	I		E	R	R	O	R
			H	E	A	D	S	O	R	T	A	I	L	S
	M	E	A	N	T			H	A	S	S	L	E	
T	A	B	L	E	O	R	B	O	O	T	H			
A	R	O	S	E		H	A	R	D		B	A	R	E
L	I	N	E	R		E	L	S	E		A	T	O	M
L	A	D	Y		A	D	O	S			G	E	N	U

39

E	R	R	S		J	E	D	I			H	M	O	S
R	O	O	K		U	S	E	R		C	O	A	S	T
A	N	D	Y		S	A	R	A		L	A	T	T	E
			L	A	T	I	N	Q	U	A	R	T	E	R
S	T	A	I	N	S			R	I	S	E	R	S	
T	U	R	N	S	O	N	A	D	I	M	E			
E	S	T	E	E		O	G	R	E	S		S	A	P
E	K	E	S		E	T	A	I	L		L	A	S	H
P	S	S		F	L	U	T	E		F	U	N	N	Y
			P	U	M	P	E	R	N	I	C	K	E	L
M	O	T	E	L	S			A	N	K	A	R	A	
A	P	R	E	T	T	Y	P	E	N	N	Y			
U	T	E	R	O		A	R	C	O		M	A	N	E
N	I	V	E	N		Y	O	H	O		A	L	E	S
A	C	I	D		A	M	O	K			N	A	T	S

40

O	W	S		I	M	A	G	E			P	L	E	D
D	E	A		S	O	C	A	L			L	I	M	E
O	R	G	O	O	D	E	L	L			A	K	I	N
R	E	A	D	L	E		S	A	U	C	E	R	S	
			I	D	L	E			T	E	N	S	E	
O	U	R	S	E		V	A	R	E	S	E			
P	S	E	T		H	E	X	E	S			W	I	G
E	E	P		C	A	R	E	D			P	E	S	O
D	D		J	A	R	E	D			G	A	L	L	O
		C	L	O	N	E	S		S	U	L	L	E	N
P	A	I	N				T	A	P	S				
O	R	N	I	S	H		B	A	T	T	L	E	S	
D	E	N		H	O	L	Y	C	O	W	E	L	L	
I	L	E		A	R	O	S	E			O	N	M	E
A	L	T		G	A	S	S	Y			S	T	O	W

41

S	T	E	W		W	A	F	T			S	T	E	E	L
O	R	S	O		A	L	O	E			O	H	A	R	E
L	O	S	E	A	T	U	R	N			B	U	T	T	E
E	V	E		R	E	M		S	P	E	N	S	E	R	
D	E	X	T	E	R		B	E	A	R	D				
			H	A	R	T	E		N	E	E	D	L	E	
D	E	L	E		A	R	A	B			D	R	E	A	D
A	B	E	L		T	O	N	A	L			B	A	N	G
D	R	O	O	D		D	E	C	A			O	R	G	Y
S	O	N	N	E	T		R	O	Y	A	L				
			G	L	O	R	Y		S	I	T	S	O	N	
A	L	O	H	A	O	E		N	O	R		T	H	O	
D	Y	L	A	N		G	R	A	V	Y	B	O	A	T	
A	R	G	U	E		A	O	N	E			B	O	R	E
M	E	A	L	Y		N	E	A	R			S	P	A	S

42

O	T	T	O		T	R	I	X			T	S	A	R
N	R	O	N		A	O	N	E			W	I	R	E
E	A	S	O	N	P	A	S	S			I	M	I	N
I	C	S		A	I	R			P	R	I	Z	E	
D	E		M	A	R	S	H	M	A	L	L	O	W	
A	R	T	A	N			E	A	T		A	N	A	
S	S	A	Y		A	L	A	N			O	R	A	L
		P	O	N	D	E	R	O	S	A				
A	R	S		E	O	N	S		A	R	O	A	R	
M	A		M	O	B			A	S	S	U	R	E	
O	G	D	A	N	O	V	I	C	H			T	R	I
E	T	R	Y		O	R	E			P	L	A	N	
B	I	E		W	A	T	E	R	F	R	O	N	T	
A	M	S		E	D	E	N			R	O	U	G	E
E	E	S		B	O	R	E			O	D	D	E	R

43

A	L	A	S	K	A		N	E	B	R	A	S	K	A
L	O	B	B	E	D		A	B	R	U	P	T	E	R
A	S	I	A	G	O		T	E	A	L	E	O	N	I
B	E	L		S	S	R		R	Y	E		R	O	Z
A	B	E	S			A	C	T	S		S	I	L	O
M	I	N	I		E	V	A			R	O	N	I	N
A	G	E	D		R	I	N	G		M	A	G	N	A
			E	A	R	N		R	I	S	K			
F	E	L	O	N		G	E	A	R		I	M	A	M
L	A	I	N	G			A	D	E		N	O	L	O
O	G	E	E		S	I	R	E			G	L	E	N
R	E	B		L	O	O		S	E	T		D	R	T
I	R	A	N	I	A	N	S		D	A	K	O	T	A
D	E	C	R	E	P	I	T		E	L	E	V	E	N
A	R	K	A	N	S	A	S		N	E	V	A	D	A

44

O	R	L	Y		P	A	I	N	E			D	A	F	T
F	E	E	D		O	L	S	O	N			U	S	E	R
F	L	A	S	H	P	O	I	N	T			F	I	L	E
E	A	R		U	T	E	S			R	A	F	F	L	E
D	Y	N	A	M	O			V	A	L	E	T			
			C	A	P	T	A	I	N	B	L	O	O	D	
A	D	D	I	N		A	B	E	T	S		S	H	U	
C	A	R	D		D	R	A	W	S			F	A	I	R
D	N	A		L	O	O	S	E			L	A	Y	O	N
C	O	M	M	O	N	T	H	R	E	A	D				
		A	I	D	E	S			M	T	E	T	N	A	
O	U	T	S	E	T		G	A	B	E		H	E	R	
A	T	I	T		H	I	L	T	O	N	H	E	A	D	
F	A	Z	E		A	R	E	A	S			S	I	T	E
S	H	E	D		T	E	N	D	S			T	R	O	N

45

E	T	H		S	P	C	A			C	A	P	O	S
B	I	E		C	R	O	C			A	D	O	P	T
A	R	M	F	R	E	S	H			R	O	S	I	E
Y	E		L	U	S	T			S	E	R	E	N	E
	S	H	I	F	T			S	P	E	E	D	E	R
O	W	E	R	F	O	R	W	A	R	D				
D	I	C	T			O	A	T	S			R	O	D
I	N	K		A	B	U	T	S			N	A	R	Y
E	G		Q	U	I	T			T	Y	P	E	A	
	T	U	N	N	E	L	V	I	S	I	O	N		
A	H	O	O	T	S		O	A	R	E	D			
L	I	G	N	S		O	S	L	O			F	E	E
I	N	G	S		C	H	I	L	L	P	I	L	L	
A	D	L	E		A	N	N	E			O	R	S	O
S	S	E	T		L	O	G	Y			T	E	E	N

46

L	O	C	O		W	I	G	S			A	C	T	U	P
I	M	I	N		I	B	E	T			L	H	A	S	A
S	A	T	E	L	L	I	T	E			F	O	X	E	S
P	R	I	M	A	L	S	C	R	E	A	M				
			P	O	D		U	N	E			S	T	U	D
C	A	S	T	S	O	U	T			L	I	K	E	M	E
O	L	L	Y			R	E	B	E	L	Y	E	L	L	
N	U	E		A	A	S		I	R	K		T	A	U	
S	M	A	L	L	T	A	L	K			T	H	U	D	
U	N	Z	I	P	S		A	E	S	T	H	E	T	E	
L	A	Y	S		E	A	T			C	R	Y			
			S	T	A	G	E	W	H	I	S	P	E	R	
D	O	J	O	S		O	R	A	N	G	E	A	D	E	
A	R	O	M	A		R	O	L	O			L	U	G	E
M	E	T	E	R		A	N	T	Z			F	L	E	D

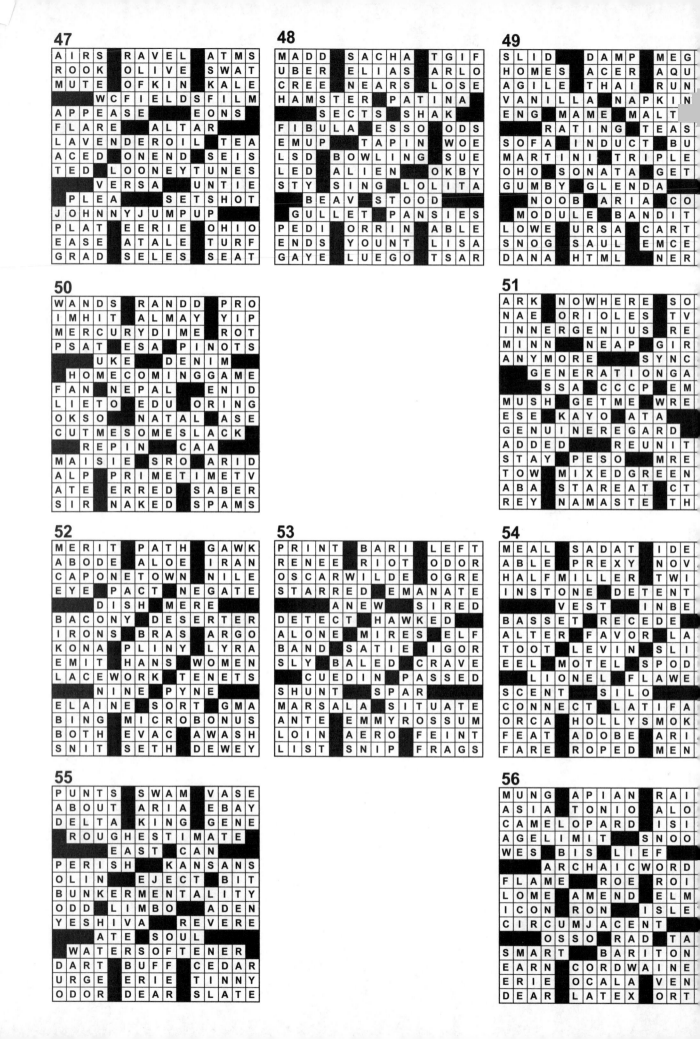

57

```
HALO  ARAB  SKEWS
SIN   MALL  UNLIT
FILL  ONTO  BILLY
 FYOURDOGISFAT
   OKAY    SEE
ACKAL LEST   MBA
OBOES PERU  SOON
OURENOTGETTING
UTS   OPTS  YARDS
TH   AMES  SLIEST
    RCS   AVER
 ENOUGHEXERCISE
QUASI AXIL  ADAY
RAIT  SPOT  SOLE
ONNY  HOME  ELKS
```

58

```
THAW  STOOD  SWAB
OATH  POUCH  PAVE
FRIO  ONTHE  ALIT
UPTONOGOODS  KAT
    PILAF  EBONY
ASSETS   CTSCAN
DINER  CHAI  GARB
ADO  ONRAMPS  ITO
MEWL  BORE  ACRES
   BINACA  VLASIC
SALVO    COAST
ALI  SHOTGLASSES
BING  UTERI  ELLE
LADE  SORES  YALE
ESSO  HESSE  EWAN
```

59

```
DEARSIRS  MCBEAL
ALLFORIT  SLANGY
SKISLOPE  SATORI
HOG   BETS  NIKON
 NYLONSTOCKING
   OATS   AMYS
ALARM  SIN    MIA
BASEBALLDIAMOND
ETS   NAY  GAINS
    ETTU  SMUG
 CAMPAIGNTRAIL
ABOIL  HOYT   EDD
PAUPER  BROADWAY
ESSENE  LOADLINE
SEENTO  ENDORSED
```

60

```
WORE  SPEC  BASS
AARON ALTO  URAL
SWEETCREAM  CITI
HAS  ROAD  MAKEIT
   LASH  TOPPLES
DUPONT  SANER
AFOOT MACE  IPAD
OOS  SAVER  VANE
SLE  TROT  SANTA
   CARLY  FATTEN
SOMALIA   MOVE
PLANED DATA  GAS
ODIN  EYECONTACT
RINO  NEMO  NAURU
KEEN  TWIN  ARLEN
```

61

```
CARDS  SPAT  SLAG
ONEAL  PAGE  PERU
DONLEMONEXTRACT
ANTIWAR   THESES
     TESS  REEDY
ADIDAS  TUTU
LOCAL  SOLE  SEAS
FIONAAPPLEWATCH
ANNE  COPY  AMATI
    PARE  ODESSA
WAVER  TREX
IRISES  TERSEST
MISSPEACHNECTAR
PETA  ERIE  DANCE
SLAY  DEAR  STAKE
```

62

```
AB   PODS  WAGED
BED  ALOE  ESSES
OLO  LANE  APART
BULLSEYERASH
STALK    SNEAKER
   AIOLI  ALLEGE
BOARDROOM   TARA
NS  SEAWAYS  NEC
TTS   DARTMOUTH
KARATS  SEDAN
POUSES   LANAI
 THROWPILLOWS
OMEI  DIET  OPAL
ASTER ARTE  GERE
BUNDT SEAM   SET
```

63

```
RAMS  OGRES  ALBA
OBIT  FLESH  DAUB
MAMA  FIFTYFIFTY
ETICKETS   LOFTS
   CIRC  TRUSSES
EQUALSHARES
GUSTO  LEAH   OPS
GINO  BOOED  ISEE
ODA  POGO  ETHEL
 HALFANDHALF
GRANITE   BANE
REGAL   ISRAELIS
EVENSTEVEN  WIRE
TUNA  OMANI  ETON
APTS  PUNTA  DENT
```

64

```
ROAD  THUS  STRAP
AXLE  OOZE  AROMA
JILLSTEIN   HELEN
ADELE    AWAKENS
HEY  TOASTER
  DOUBLEBARREL
ERRANTLY   NAIVE
WEIR  SEDGE  ICES
ESTEE  OILINESS
STAINEDGLASS
   DORSALS   FAD
ARIZONA    USAGE
SOBER  POWDERKEG
AMISS  EPEE  TINA
PASTE  STEW  ARTS
```

65

```
EAR   SPUN  PLUM
UTO   HONED ROBE
ROD   AROSE OWES
SOMEONE   TATTERS
   OMG    ETHER
DRS  WHOSAHEADOF
RAW  AKA   SMELL
ADO  HISTIME  CLI
MORAY  ONO   KIN
ANDBEHINDON  SET
  DUNES    DOG
AVATARS   HISRENT
RANT  BUTTE  ALOE
MICE  SEEMS  FLUX
SLED  DELT   TENT
```

66

```
VIVA  ALLSO  GMEN
EDIT  REACH  ROXY
TOOTHFAIRY  EWES
OLLIE  FREELANCE
 SALAD     WAIT
   APRILSHOWERS
GEM  SOSO  NAVAL
OPAL  PURER  RICE
NEWER  ASIA   LED
GERMANEXPORT
    MIEN   TOAST
ENDINATIE  MINES
COIN  RINGGALAXY
HUNG  BROOM  ERAS
ONES  YENTA  DENT
```

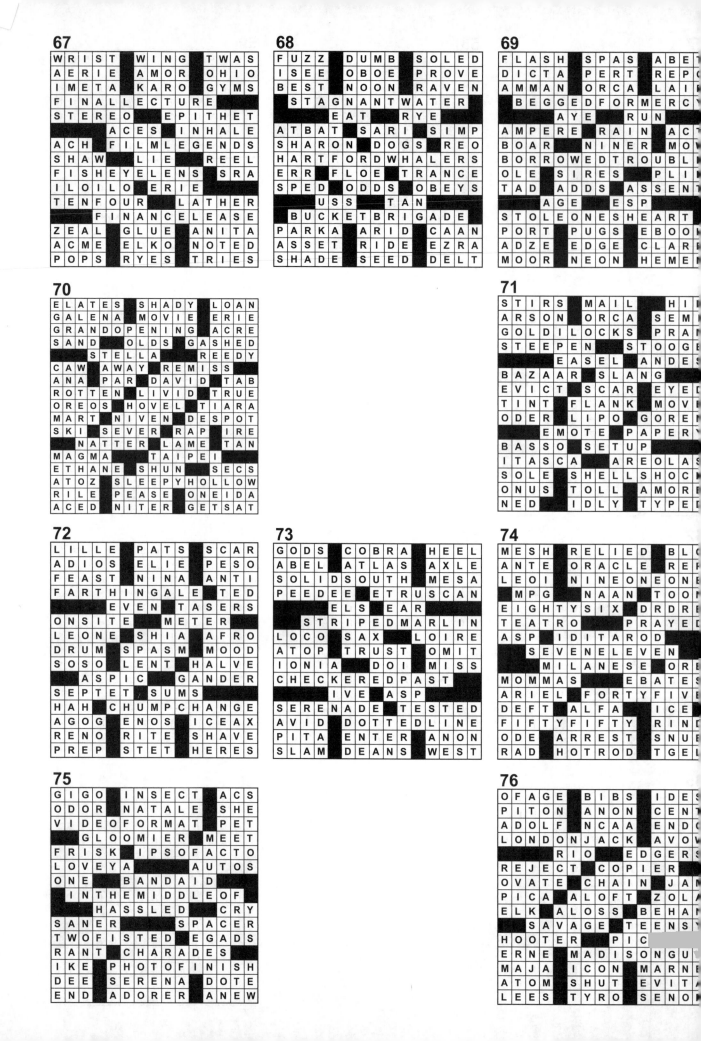

67

W	R	I	S	T		W	I	N	G		T	W	A	S
A	E	R	I	E		A	M	O	R		O	H	I	O
I	M	E	T	A		K	A	R	O		G	Y	M	S
F	I	N	A	L	L	E	C	T	U	R	E			
S	T	E	R	E	O				E	P	I	T	H	E	T
			A	C	E	S		I	N	H	A	L	E
A	C	H		F	I	L	M	L	E	G	E	N	D	S
S	H	A	W		L	I	E		R	E	E	L
F	I	S	H	E	Y	E	L	E	N	S		S	R	A
I	L	O	I	L	O		E	R	I	E
T	E	N	F	O	U	R		L	A	T	H	E	R
		F	I	N	A	N	C	E	L	E	A	S	E
Z	E	A	L		G	L	U	E		A	N	I	T	A
A	C	M	E		E	L	K	O		N	O	T	E	D
P	O	P	S		R	Y	E	S		T	R	I	E	S

68

F	U	Z	Z		D	U	M	B		S	O	L	E	D
I	S	E	E		O	B	O	E		P	R	O	V	E
B	E	S	T		N	O	O	N		R	A	V	E	N
	S	T	A	G	N	A	N	T	W	A	T	E	R
			E	A	T		R	Y	E
A	T	B	A	T		S	A	R	I		S	I	M	P
S	H	A	R	O	N		D	O	G	S		R	E	O
H	A	R	T	F	O	R	D	W	H	A	L	E	R	S
E	R	R		F	L	O	E		T	R	A	N	C	E
S	P	E	D		O	D	D	S		O	B	E	Y	S
		U	S	S		T	A	N
	B	U	C	K	E	T	B	R	I	G	A	D	E
P	A	R	K	A		A	R	I	D		C	A	A	N
A	S	S	E	T		R	I	D	E		E	Z	R	A
S	H	A	D	E		S	E	E	D		D	E	L	T

69

F	L	A	S	H		S	P	A	S		A	B	E
D	I	C	T	A		P	E	R	T		R	E	P
A	M	M	A	N		O	R	C	A		L	A	I
	B	E	G	G	E	D	F	O	R	M	E	R	C
			A	Y	E		R	U	N
A	M	P	E	R	E		R	A	I	N		A	C	T
B	O	A	R		N	I	N	E	R		M	O
B	O	R	R	O	W	E	D	T	R	O	U	B	L
O	L	E		S	I	R	E	S		P	L	I
T	A	D		A	D	D	S		A	S	S	E	N	T
	A	G	E		E	S	P
S	T	O	L	E	O	N	E	S	H	E	A	R	T
P	O	R	T		P	U	G	S		E	B	O	O
A	D	Z	E		E	D	G	E		C	L	A	R
M	O	O	R		N	E	O	N		H	E	M	E

70

E	L	A	T	E	S		S	H	A	D	Y		L	O	A	N
G	A	L	E	N	A		M	O	V	I	E		E	R	I	E
G	R	A	N	D	O	P	E	N	I	N	G		A	C	R	E
S	A	N	D		O	L	D	S		G	A	S	H	E	D
		S	T	E	L	L	A		R	E	E	D	Y
C	A	W		A	W	A	Y		R	E	M	I	S	S
A	N	A		P	A	R		D	A	V	I	D		T	A	B
R	O	T	T	E	N		L	I	V	I	D		T	R	U	E
O	R	E	O	S		H	O	V	E	L		T	I	A	R	A
M	A	R	T		N	I	V	E	N		D	E	S	P	O	T
S	K	I		S	E	V	E	R		R	A	P		I	R	E
	N	A	T	T	E	R		L	A	M	E		T	A	N
M	A	G	M	A			T	A	I	P	E	I
E	T	H	A	N	E		S	H	U	N		S	E	C	S
A	T	O	Z		S	L	E	E	P	Y	H	O	L	L	O	W
R	I	L	E		P	E	A	S	E		O	N	E	I	D	A
A	C	E	D		N	I	T	E	R		G	E	T	S	A	T

71

S	T	I	R	S		M	A	I	L		H	I
A	R	S	O	N		O	R	C	A		S	E	M
G	O	L	D	I	L	O	C	K	S		P	R	A	N
S	T	E	E	P	E	N		S	T	O	O	G	E
			E	A	S	E	L		A	N	D	E	S
B	A	Z	A	A	R		S	L	A	N	G
E	V	I	C	T		S	C	A	R		E	Y	E	D
T	I	N	T		F	L	A	N	K		M	O	V
O	D	E	R		L	I	P	O		G	O	R	E	N
		E	M	O	T	E		P	A	P	E	R	Y
B	A	S	S	O		S	E	T	U	P
I	T	A	S	C	A		A	R	E	O	L	A	S
S	O	L	E		S	H	E	L	L	S	H	O	C
O	N	U	S		T	O	L	L		A	M	O	R	E
N	E	D		I	D	L	Y		T	Y	P	E

72

L	I	L	L	E		P	A	T	S		S	C	A	R
A	D	I	O	S		E	L	I	E		P	E	S	O
F	E	A	S	T		N	I	N	A		A	N	T	I
F	A	R	T	H	I	N	G	A	L	E		T	E	D
			E	V	E	N		T	A	S	E	R	S
O	N	S	I	T	E		M	E	T	E	R
L	E	O	N	E		S	H	I	A		A	F	R	O
D	R	U	M		S	P	A	S	M		M	O	O	D
S	O	S	O		L	E	N	T		H	A	L	V	E
	A	S	P	I	C		G	A	N	D	E	R
S	E	P	T	E	T		S	U	M	S
H	A	H		C	H	U	M	P	C	H	A	N	G	E
A	G	O	G		E	N	O	S		I	C	E	A	X
R	E	N	O		R	I	T	E		S	H	A	V	E
P	R	E	P		S	T	E	T		H	E	R	E	S

73

G	O	D	S		C	O	B	R	A		H	E	E	L
A	B	E	L		A	T	L	A	S		A	X	L	E
S	O	L	I	D	S	O	U	T	H		M	E	S	A
P	E	E	D	E	E		E	T	R	U	S	C	A	N
			E	L	S		E	A	R
	S	T	R	I	P	E	D	M	A	R	L	I	N
L	O	C	O		S	A	X		L	O	I	R	E
A	T	O	P		T	R	U	S	T		O	M	I	T
I	O	N	I	A		D	O	I		M	I	S	S
C	H	E	C	K	E	R	E	D	P	A	S	T
		I	V	E		A	S	P
S	E	R	E	N	A	D	E		T	E	S	T	E	D
A	V	I	D		D	O	T	T	E	D	L	I	N	E
P	I	T	A		E	N	T	E	R		A	N	O	N
S	L	A	M		D	E	A	N	S		W	E	S	T

74

M	E	S	H		R	E	L	I	E	D		B	L
A	N	T	E		O	R	A	C	L	E		R	E
L	E	O	I		N	I	N	E	O	N	E	O	N	E
	M	P	G		N	A	A	N		T	O	O	N
E	I	G	H	T	Y	S	I	X		D	R	D	R	E
T	E	A	T	R	O		P	R	A	Y	E	D
A	S	P		I	D	I	T	A	R	O	D
	S	E	V	E	N	E	L	E	V	E	N
	M	I	L	A	N	E	S	E		O	R
M	O	M	M	A	S		E	B	A	T	E	S
A	R	I	E	L		F	O	R	T	Y	F	I	V	E
D	E	F	T		A	L	F	A		I	C	E
F	I	F	T	Y	F	I	F	T	Y		R	I	N
O	D	E		A	R	R	E	S	T		S	N	U
R	A	D		H	O	T	R	O	D		T	G	E	L

75

G	I	G	O		I	N	S	E	C	T		A	C	S
O	D	O	R		N	A	T	A	L	E		S	H	E
V	I	D	E	O	F	O	R	M	A	T		P	E	T
	G	L	O	O	M	I	E	R		M	E	E	T
F	R	I	S	K		I	P	S	O	F	A	C	T	O
L	O	V	E	Y	A		A	U	T	O	S
O	N	E		B	A	N	D	A	I	D
	I	N	T	H	E	M	I	D	D	L	E	O	F
		H	A	S	S	L	E	D		C	R	Y
S	A	N	E	R		S	P	A	C	E	R
T	W	O	F	I	S	T	E	D		E	G	A	D	S
R	A	N	T		C	H	A	R	A	D	E	S
I	K	E		P	H	O	T	O	F	I	N	I	S	H
D	E	E		S	E	R	E	N	A		D	O	T	E
E	N	D		A	D	O	R	E	R		A	N	E	W

76

O	F	A	G	E		B	I	B	S		I	D	E
P	I	T	O	N		A	N	O	N		C	E	N
A	D	O	L	F		N	C	A	A		E	N	D	O
L	O	N	D	O	N	J	A	C	K		A	V	O	W
			R	I	O		E	D	G	E	R	S
R	E	J	E	C	T		C	O	P	I	E	R
O	V	A	T	E		C	H	A	I	N		J	A
P	I	C	A		A	L	O	F	T		Z	O	L
E	L	K		A	L	O	S	S		B	E	H	A
	S	A	V	A	G	E		T	E	E	N	S
H	O	O	T	E	R		P	I	C
E	R	N	E		M	A	D	I	S	O	N	G	U
M	A	J	A		I	C	O	N		M	A	R	N	E
A	T	O	M		S	H	U	T		E	V	I	T	A
L	E	E	S		T	Y	R	O		S	E	N	O

77

```
?OLID  ALAS  BOWS
RACE   DART  EDIT
SNER   ASEA  IDLE
ODDINGHAM   REDA
      VEE  POURED
HALET      SHEATH
INED   STADT   OAR
STO   SUAVE  JUNE
SI    BERNE  MANTA
MAILED     GIRDER
LATTE        AIL
ADE   CUDDLEFISH
NDA   TRIO  AUDIO
KES   ODOR  GRIMM
YRE   RUNE  ELOPE
```

78

```
BOMB   IRISH   DBA
EWER  CACHE  CRAN
GETAMOVEON  HONG
   VENISON   OPAL
BOSOM      ALPINE
IRA   OATHS  OCTAD
ZIGS   CHALLAH
GETTHELEADOUT
   EVERTED   PROS
STUPA  ESKER  NGO
PARODY      ESSAY
ALAN   EPISODE
RONI  LOSENOTIME
TNUT   PSALM  OREM
ASS    STYLE  NEXT
```

79

```
JARS  SCRAM  HERB
OREO  TAIGA  OVER
GRANNYKNOT  MESA
 SPOILED  TWENTY
    FLU    SHUE
SHAG  SISTERCITY
COLOR  DHOWS   GHI
ASIDE   YUP  TULIP
RES   VALLI  SNORE
FATHERLAND   CODS
   ARTS    EEL
MINUTE   ACTRESS
ADEN  MOTHERSHIP
TEXT  INNER  AILS
HATS  STOWS  MALI
```

80

```
ABLA   EPICS  MIT
URAL   RABAT  EVA
ROSSINCOME   RAN
AW  ABET  EALING
ESETAS    ARMED
  BIRTHDAYGIFT
ENEAS  EIS   AAH
UANN   WAN  RONDO
RT    TED  CENSER
OURTHESTATE
  ROWED  WRIGGLY
EADER  LOON   LOA
LL   LAPOFLUXURY
LL   VIVRE  ELENA
AY   ENTER  SIDES
```

81

```
JUKED   BOAR  TWIT
ALIVE   ALVA  SINE
INDIANHEAD  ELSE
 ASTRO  ASIS   LEN
  ATLANTICCITY
ARR   HIS     IRS
SEEP   MES  SOIREE
PACIFICPRINCESS
SPINET  YUL   KEPT
  ROT    HIC   DYE
 ARCTICCIRCLE
BIL   DRED  OINKS
ALIE  OCEANFRONT
SEND  NIAS  FOLIO
EDGY  ELLA  SNAPE
```

82

```
ROTA   AMMAN  UMPS
AHU   TESLA  NOAH
STAGEMAGIC  WORE
SHRUB    RERAISED
   RIGS   NENE
RISKROSS   SLOPE
AC   EURO  HIDDEN
NIT  FERMI   YARD
IEOFF   TUTU   WOE
NROL   TACOSTAND
   KALE   KNEE
LCAPONE     RECAP
ORN   PASTASHELL
DEA  ENSOR   ELLE
EEP   STONE  ELSA
```

83

```
EMITS   SAGA  LETS
GARRY   ICON  ELAN
OCEAN   GEST  ALIA
  LOANSHARKING
ARMANI     COASTS
  LOLLYGAGGING
ACLAM  BALD  EBBS
RHE   SALES   ORT
MESA  UCLA  STRIA
  LOCKSMITHING
SHTICK     IRISES
  LONGDIVISION
INON   TACO  KAPPA
METE   USES  EIDER
EYED   PESO  DRANK
```

84

```
BARRACUDA   TOSCA
ALIENATED   ACORN
RELAYRACE   MELON
NEEDTO  OED   LAPS
   YOLK  RECORD
CROMWELL   ARTFUL
LAVIN  EARLY   LSU
APEX   PIPES  HATS
ISR   LINEN  BERET
RETAIL  LAMASERY
  SHILOH   LILI
ISEE   TED  NOTONE
TITLE  LAMINATED
TOOLS  PRIMETIME
ONPOP  SETEYESON
```

85

```
EACH   SHOOTBACK
ALLAY  PEACEABLE
RILKE  YESTERDAY
MIENS   DEADSURE
IGDATA  SNO   LED
NA   SUMS    EFS
ATE   BOTH  FORCE
TOM   SNEAK  SIAM
ERIF   GERE  ANNO
  RAF   REBA   TOT
NE   TOR  MANKINI
ORNCRIB    BIONIC
IVEAGAIN    MATZO
ARISTOTLE   ALIEN
ENTSTAKE    LANDS
```

86

```
LALALAND   TOXINS
OILCOLOR   AVENUE
WEARABLE   PANAMA
ELMO   ATA  ELAPSE
SLASH  EMIRS   AKA
TOSSES  ENS  SNUG
   RANDB   SKILL
MARCONI   UPCYCLE
ALOIS    CEDAR
GLUT   PEC  HANGAR
ITT   CARLA  MEESE
CHIMES  ILL  CALC
AENEAS   PLUMTREE
CREASE   SATIATES
TESTED   EYEDROPS
```

87

A	T	P	E	A	C	E		H	O	T	B	E	D	S
R	O	O	T	E	R	S		O	V	E	R	S	A	W
L	I	N	A	G	E	S		M	A	R	I	A	N	A
O	L	D	T	I	M	E	R	E	L	I	G	I	O	N
				S	E	N	O	R	S					
O	D	I	E			C	P	U		G	R	A	S	S
S	E	R	V	I	C	E	E	N	T	R	A	N	C	E
S	L	E	I	G	H				S	A	N	D	A	L
I	T	S	T	O	O	D	E	E	P	F	O	R	M	E
E	A	T	A	T		E	T	V			N	A	P	S
				O	P	T	I	C	S					
M	I	S	S	F	I	R	E	C	R	A	C	K	E	R
E	S	T	E	L	L	E		T	O	R	O	N	T	O
G	O	A	T	E	E	S		E	N	A	M	O	R	S
A	N	T	H	E	R	S		D	E	N	O	T	E	S

88

A	R	F		S	C	A	L	D		O	P	A	R	T
L	O	U		O	L	L	I	E		R	A	D	I	O
E	S	L		F	A	L	S	E	A	R	R	E	S	T
C	E	L	L	A	R		T	R	U		A	L	E	E
		B	O	R	I	S		E	R	A	S	E	R	S
A	C	L	U		S	K	I		A	G	O			
S	T	A	T	E	S	I	D	E		A	L	B	O	M
I	R	S		F	A	R	E	A	S	T		R	U	E
A	L	T	A	R		T	A	S	T	E	L	E	S	S
		R	E	M		S	E	A		O	A	T	H	
B	A	T	S	M	A	N		S	N	A	C	K		
A	C	R	E		T	I	C		D	R	I	F	T	S
F	R	E	N	C	H	T	O	A	S	T		A	I	L
T	I	E	I	N		E	L	L	I	S		S	K	A
A	D	D	O	N		R	A	I	N	Y		T	I	P

89

I	P	A	D		N	A	P	A	L	M		A	P	
S	L	U	E		S	L	I	D	E	R		G	I	
N	O	T	S		C	O	N	D	O	I	N	A	S	
T	W	O	A	M		E	S	A	I		O	T	A	
	S	P	L	A	T			L	I	S	T	E	N	
W	H	A	T	S	H	A	P		I	N	G			
O	A	R		S	E	G	A			L	O	C	H	
M	R	T		N	O	V	A	K			H	E		
B	E	S	T	S		E	M	I	R		I	R		
		A	U	S	T	R	A	L	I	A	N	O		
S	P	I	N	N	E	R			N	I	C	A	D	
T	I	N	G		N	A	I	L		S	E	W	O	
	E	L	O	P	E	C	R	U	Z		T	A	T	
E	T	A		I	C	E	A	G	E		A	R	U	
R	A	W		E	A	R	N	E	D		L	E	S	

89 pen/ink rebus

90

P	O	L	E	S		E	D	I	T		A	S	P	S
C	H	E	E	P		D	O	S	E		S	P	A	T
S	M	O	K	I	N	G	G	U	N		S	O	R	E
				R	U	E	S		S	H	E	R	E	E
G	A	M	B	I	T	S		S	P	O	T	T	E	D
A	L	E	R	T	S		Q	U	E	A	S	Y		
S	O	D	A	S		C	U	R	E	R		S	T	U
U	N	I	T		C	H	I	L	D		S	P	A	S
P	E	C		B	O	O	T	Y		N	O	I	C	E
	I	C	A	N	S	O		J	U	I	C	E	R	
P	E	N	A	N	C	E		H	A	M	L	E	T	S
E	M	E	R	G	E		Z	O	N	E				
E	C	H	O		P	R	I	M	E	R	C	O	A	T
P	E	A	L		T	O	T	E		A	P	A	C	E
S	E	T	S		S	T	I	R		L	O	F	T	Y

91

B	U	G		R	O	T	O	R		C	A	S	T	
E	G	O		E	X	I	L	E		U	L	T	R	
A	L	E		H	A	R	D	B	A	R	G	A	I	
M	I	S	S	I	L	E	S		L	E	A	K	E	
			C	R	I	S		S	O	D		E	S	
A	D	O	R	E	S		S	H	O	O	T			
S	I	D	E	D		S	T	I	F	F	W	I	N	
I	D	E	A		A	E	R			O	D	I		
F	I	R	M	O	F	F	E	R		S	T	O	L	
			S	U	R	E	R		C	O	O	L	E	
M	E	T		T	A	R		S	H	U	N			
A	R	I	S	E	N		O	M	A	R	E	P	P	
C	O	M	P	A	C	T	D	I	S	C		A	L	
A	D	O	U	T		N	O	L	T	E		V	A	
W	E	N	D	S		T	R	E	E	S		E	Y	

92

S	A	C		M	E	S	A	S		T	A	P	I	R
I	L	L		I	L	L	B	E		E	R	A	S	E
A	L	I	E	N	L	I	F	E		A	I	S	L	E
M	A	P	L	E		M	A	M	B	A		T	A	L
E	G	A	L		C	Y	B	E	R	C	R	I	M	E
S	E	R	A	P	H			A	T	O	M	I	C	
E	S	T		D	O	L	L	S			S	E	C	T
		S	Q	U	E	A	K	T	O	Y				
E	W	O	K		A	D	I	E	U		W	O	E	
M	I	L	E	R	S			A	T	T	I	C	A	
B	I	D	D	I	N	G	W	A	R		A	N	T	S
A	M	P		N	O	A	H	S		B	E	G	A	T
S	O	R	O	S		P	U	P	P	Y	L	O	V	E
S	T	O	R	E		E	M	C	E	E		L	I	N
Y	E	S	E	S		S	P	A	N	S		D	A	D

93

G	A	F	F		S	K	E	E		C	O	O	P	T
E	L	L	A		T	A	T	A		A	B	N	E	R
R	O	U	N	D	A	B	O	U	T	R	O	U	T	E
M	E	X		A	T	O	N		I	R	I	S	E	S
			S	N	U	B		L	E	I	S			
M	A	G	P	I	E		M	A	D	E	T	I	M	E
A	F	R	O	S		O	A	T	Y		N	O	T	
M	O	U	T	H	O	F	T	H	E	S	O	U	T	H
B	U	N		M	A	Z	E		U	N	I	T	E	
A	L	T	E	R	E	G	O		E	D	I	T	O	R
		D	A	R	E		T	R	O	T				
I	M	H	U	R	T		M	A	R	K		G	A	S
S	P	E	C	I	A	L	S	H	O	U	T	O	U	T
M	A	N	E	T		I	G	O	R		A	N	T	E
S	A	S	S	Y		U	T	E	S		M	E	O	W

94

G	R	I	D	S		C	A	L	M		F	A	C	
M	O	O	R	E		A	L	O	U		A	L	E	X
S	O	N	I	A		S	P	I	N		M	I	D	
	F	A	L	S	E	P	O	S	I	T	I	V	E	S
		L	I	M	E				A	L	E	R	T	
F	A	K	E	C	U	R	R	E	N	C	Y			
O	Z	A	R	K		E	R	N	O		L	G	A	
R	U	T	S		S	T	A	G	E		T	E	E	N
E	L	Y		S	L	E	D		A	W	A	R		
		P	H	O	N	Y	B	A	L	O	N	E		
A	D	I	E	U		E	L	A	T					
M	O	C	K	T	U	R	T	L	E	S	O	U	P	
B	R	I	O		N	O	R	A		K	O	R	E	A
L	A	N	E		I	B	E	T		A	N	G	E	L
E	G	G	S		T	O	K	E		N	E	E	L	Y

95

B	R	A	C	E		S	O	F	T	C		N	A	P
A	A	R	O	N		S	A	R	A	H		O	D	E
T	H	I	R	D	S	T	R	I	K	E		N	O	W
			G	A	P	S		S	E	E	D	E	R	S
M	O	B	I	L	E		S	E	R	R	A	T	E	
E	V	A		L	E	F	T		S	U	M	O		
N	A	N	S		D	O	R	A		P	A	S	T	A
S	L	A	W		S	E	E	K	S		G	P	A	S
A	S	N	A	P		S	A	I	L		E	A	R	S
		A	N	A	S		K	N	O	T		R	T	E
	U	S	E	R	I	D	S		G	O	W	E	S	T
A	T	P	E	A	C	E		G	A	T	E			
B	E	L		D	I	A	G	O	N	A	L	L	E	Y
U	N	I		E	L	L	E	R		L	L	A	N	O
T	N	T		S	Y	S	O	P		S	S	G	T	S

96

S	O	S	O		S	E	R	G	E		R	A	S	P
O	V	E	R		T	R	U	E	R		E	L	M	O
D	U	M	B	W	A	I	T	E	R		G	L	O	W
A	M	I		I	C	E	S		D	E	E	R	E	
		N	I	G	H			S	P	I	N	N	E	R
C	L	O	T	H	E	S	V	A	L	E	T			
R	E	L	I	T		M	I	D	A	S		W	O	V
O	N	E	S		T	O	X	I	N		K	A	N	E
W	A	S		B	I	K	E	S		S	E	L	M	
		S	I	L	E	N	T	B	U	T	L	E		
S	P	O	T	T	E	D		E	G	O	S			
C	L	A	R	E		A	U	R	A		P	H		
R	A	K	E		R	U	B	B	E	R	M	A	I	D
U	T	E	S		I	N	L	E	T		A	C	R	E
M	E	N	S		B	O	E	R	S		T	E	E	S

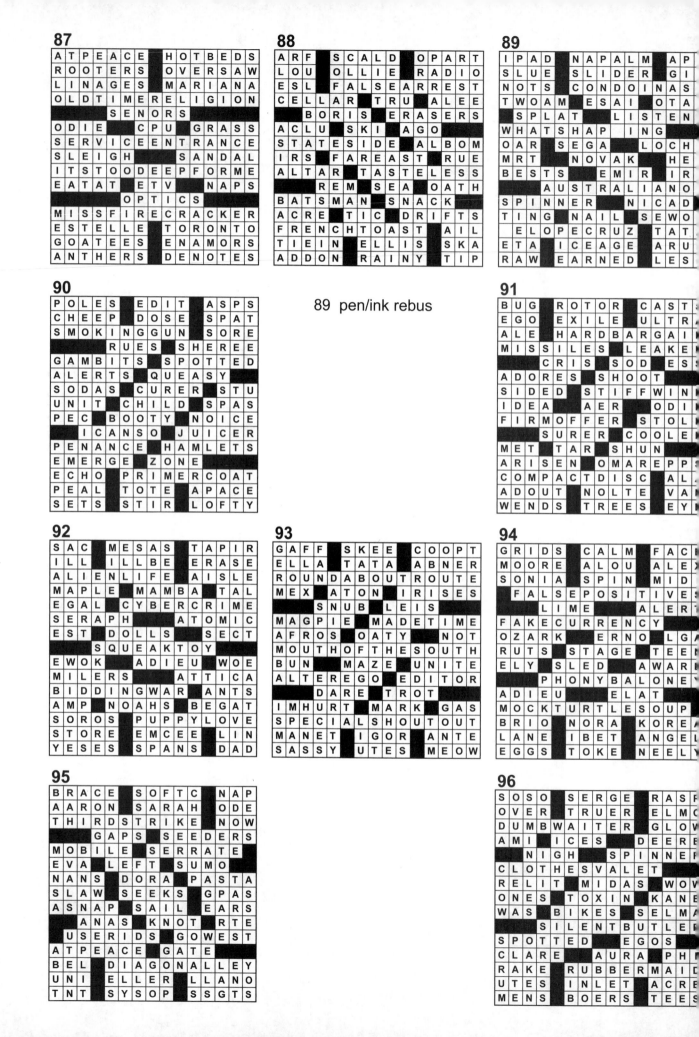

97

```
P A S T A   C A B O   S A S H
A L I A S   E B A Y   E L M O
S P A R K P L U G S   E L O N
T O M   S I L T   T O D A T E
      G O G O   R E A C H E D
S A V E U S   P A R K A
A V E R T   L A C E   T I L E
W O R M   F I N E R   A R I D
S N O W   I V E S   S L A V E
      A P R I L   C H O S E N
S K I R T E D   D R A G
N O N F A T   B O O P   C T A
U R S A   R O O T C E L L A R
B E E R   A N N E   L E A S T
S A T E   P E N D   Y A N K S
```

98

```
P A L E R   T O U R   N A D A
O R A T E   A C R E   E M A G
P O T A T O C H I P   V O T E
U S E   R U E S   R E E K E D
P E R F E C T   L I A R
      A A H   R E S T S T O P
E L E C T   S E G A   A R G O
T A R T   S T E A L   Y O L O
C R O C   T A L L   A D D E R
H A S H T A G S   A L I
      E O N S   R U L E S O N
S P I C E D   S A L T   T W O
H O N K   F A T S D O M I N O
O N C E   O B I T   L I N E N
T E A R   R A R A   D O E R S
```

99

```
A B R A   A S T R O   B A S H
T I E D   S T R A P   A D I A
T O G O   P O I N T B L A N K
I N E R T   P C T   A I M E E
L I N E B A C K E R S
A C T   A B O   D A I R I E S
      B R Y C E   I C I N G S
A G E R   S K E I N   S A G E
R E A I R S   K N O C K
K E R O U A C   H U H   A B S
      P L A N E T I C K E T
A L G A E   N O R   C H I N A
S P A C E C A D E T   A T I T
A G U E   A D A N O   R A G E
P A L S   B A T T Y   S S N S
```

100

```
L E T O   B R U T   R A C E R
A M I D   R O S E   E L A T E
M I N D G A M E S   M O R A L
A L G E R I A   S P I N D L Y
S E E R E D   O N E S
      A S S   H I D   H O T
C O M E T   O R E S   B A N E
O B E Y   P L U M E   O R C A
M O T E   R A G A   T O P E R
B E E   F I R   N S W
      R O I D   T E A B A G
T E M P L E S   S U R N A M E
A V A I L   P A L M P I L O T
S E I N E   A T O P   S E N T
E N D E D   N E T S   E D G Y
```

101

```
B E D S   K E P I   P O L E D
I C O N   I V E S   E M O T E
T R O O P W I T H D R A W A L
S U R R E A L   A T R E S T
      T A N   M A T
A A H   T I R E B A L A N C E
S L O E   S E G A   A C O R N
P A S T E   C A T   D I V E D
I M E A N   I T E M   D E M O
C O A L D E P O S I T   L E W
      L E N   L I V
E V E R T S   S I L E S I A
G E N E R A L I N T E R E S T
G R O P E   A C A I   D E E M
S A S S Y   V E G A   I D E S
```

102

```
S O M A   E N A C T   S T A N
C H A N   D E L H I   L I M O
A N T I   G R E A T L A K E S
B O T T L E O F R E D W I N E
      R O D   M R S
B E M A N   I F S   F A R O
A L A   D O D O   E X O T I C
Y E L L O W S U B M A R I N E
O C T A N E   N O U N   L G A
U T A H   S T Y   A S T O N
      S S T   D D T
G R E E N T A M B O U R I N E
R E A L L Y C O O L   E D E N
A N T S   L E V E L   A L S O
J O S E   E Y E R S   M E T S
```

103

```
C H E F   L A S T S   L I E S
L O V E   A C T U P   I D E A
A P E R   O C A L A   G R O W
D E R M A T O G L Y P H I C S
      I S S U E   I T S
E G G   C E N   B O G
D R A M A   T O A D   S P I T
N O R E P E A T L E T T E R S
A G R A   A N O D   A E S O P
      C U T   E M U   O N S
      S P A   G A R N S
U N C O P Y R I G H T A B L E
T O R E   E A R L Y   L O A D
A M O S   O G L E D   V O T E
H E D Y   H E S S E   O M E N
```

104

```
W E L T   M E G A   P I Z Z A
A L O E   O R A L   A R I E L
R I S E   T I R O   R E P E L
P A S T T H E B U C K
      H O R   D R A P E R S
G O P   R A N T   E Y E L E T
A R I A S   A R T S   N A N A
M I S T O P P O R T U N I T Y
M O T O   H E M I   R E N E E
A L O N S O   P O N G   E D D
S E L E C T S   E E R
      H O R S T A R O U N D
A G A T E   T O O T   O V E R
M A X I M   A C R E   S E R A
O B E S E   S K I N   T A F T
```

105

```
S P S   A T B A T   A D A G E
H A L   L O R C A   T O N E R
A G O   T R I A L L A W Y E R
P A T H   U N I C O R N
E N M A S S E   O I L C A N
      A C E   S E W S   O L G A
C A C K L E   M O E   W O R M
O S H   L A G B O L T   S E E
A C I D   R O E   Y A L I E S
L O N I   L A R A   R A N
S T E L M O   G E O R G I A
      B O B A T E A   S T O P
Z O N E D E F E N S E   I T S
A D O R E   T A C E T   M A E
P E S T S   S T Y L E   E S S
```

106

```
A N A   A L C O A   S A T E S
L O X   P E A R L   T E R N E
G O L D E N L A B   A T I L T
I D R I S   N E A L   B I T
E L O N   E U G E N E L E V Y
R E S E L L S   T R I C E P
S S E   A L E X A   L A N E
      S P A R K S F L Y
H A N K   S E P I A   F A S
O N E I D A   E A T D I R T
M Y S T I C M I N T   E T T U
E M T   S T A G   S A T I N
D O L T S   F L I N T L O C K
I R E N E   I O N I A   A L A
N E S T S   A O K A Y   T E T
```

107

```
A S T I   F I B   C A S C A
L I O N C A G E   U B O L T S
P R O F L I N E   P O L I T E
    L A R O S A   M A M I E
S C R A P E R   D E B C A R D
G R I M   R E A L M   E X E S
T A P E S     N E M O
  B A D C R E D R A T I N G
    I O N S     C H E A P
C U S S   S T O A S   O A T H
B P L A Y E R   C H O P P E D
E L I T E   E S T A T E
R A V E L S   L O S I N G I T
S T E E L E   O U T C O A C H
  E R N S T   P T A   T R E E
```

108

```
I F N O T   L Y E   C U B A N
B R A V O   E E C   O N O N E
M O N E Y L I S T   Y E G G S
  M A R C O   M O O N D U S T
    D A W S   H E I S T S
M O T O R C Y C L I S T
I R E   S U P R A   S E W U P
S C A N   T H U D S   D A M E
S A R A H   O S I E R   G P S
  M O U N T E V E R E S T
I D L E S T   S E C O
M O L D T E S T   R O M A N
A W A R E   O U T E R M O S T
M E M O S   N B A   D E K E S
S L A P S   G A B   S L I C K
```

109

```
C U B A   L O B O   S T A L
I T E N   O P A L   C A N O
S H A G   T E N D   A R I S
C A M E R O N C H A M P
O N E L E S S   A M P   M B A
  T R A C   F I T S   P A U
    I R O N   T S H I R
  V I C T O R F L E M I N G
M I L I E U   R E L Y
O S L O   N C A A   R A G A
M A S   P D A   D O N T L I
  M A S T E R H A R O L
R O S E S   T R O G   E R I
A R I E S   L I L O   S I N
T A S T E   E K E D   T A G S
```

110

```
F O N T A I N E   C A L V I N
U N I O N M A N   E L O I S E
G U N F I G H T   D E C R E E
U S A U S A   R O E   A G E D
    E Y E U P   E L I
A C I D S   B S T A R   L A T
L O K I   M A T   O R N E R Y
P R E S S O N   I N S E A M S
H A C K I T   D O E   T R I O
A L L   D E P O T   A S P E N
  A C E   B L A I R
D I N O   U R L   N E B U L A
A S T R O S   O K C O R R A L
B L O N D E   P A U L A N K A
S E N S E D   S T R E S S E S
```

111

```
S H A G   A B E L   P A P A
A I D A   S A B E   L L A M A
S L A P   S E R A   A B N E
S T R I K E Z O N E S   T A
    N O N   T E T   O N E
C A U G H T L O O K I N G
U R N   L S S U   S C A R E D
B E S S   D T S   B A S
S A C H E M   O T T O   P T A
  R E L I E F P I T C H E
C S A   E M U   P I E
R U M   C I R C U S C A T C
O R B I T   E R S T   S H E A
S A L V E   K A N E   E A S T
S T E E D   A G A R   S I T E
```

112

```
C L A M   B R I M   C A S E Y
L I R A   A O N E   A F I R E
A M O R   R O D S   S T R A W
N E W Y O R K Y A N K E E S
    A R E S     E E R
A B A S E D   M E A T   P T A
S O F T C   K E N T   S L A T
B R O O K L Y N D O D G E R S
I G O R   A L S O   E R A S E
G E L   B R E A   S T A D I A
    S E C   C H E F
  P I T C H E D P E R F E C T
R O M E O   L I L I   I S E E
A L A R M   S A U L   T A L E
P E N N E   E L S A   O U T S
```

113

```
G A L O P   C I T Y   B E S S
O L I V E   A C H E   A L T O
A D L E R   S E R A   N C A R
P E T R U C H I O   A D A G E
E R S T   F E N   U S O P E N
    H O W   A G E L I N E
  S A G E S   A S H   E T A S
P I P E R   E D U   T R A M S
E L O N   I R E   S H O N E
D E S E R V E   B E E
E N T R E E   M E N   W A L T
S T O A T   R O A D T O R I O
T E L L   T A U S   H O I S T
A R I L   I N S T   A D E L E
L A C Y   O D E S   I S L E S
```

114

```
C H O P   F I V E S E N S E S
R E N O   A T A S T R E T C H
A R E O   C H I L I S A U C E
W E A R   E E L   E A R N E
L A T E S T   S S T
S N A R E   A S I   Z O R B A
P D T   T A I P E I   T A U T
A N I M A L M A G N E T I S
C O M E   I S W E A R   S H O
E W E R S   A N S   I T E M S
    P U T   S K Y M A
I N A R U T   A S E   R O S
R O B E R T E L E E   A N T
E V E N T E M P E R   N E E
S A L E S R O O M S   T Y R
```

115

```
I R A N G A T E   S H R I F T
M I N I A T U R E P O O D L E
E M O T I O N A L A P P E A L
T E N S E N E S S   P E A R L
    T E D     F E S S E S
M A R V Y     L I E D
E S A I   I D E N T I F I E S
A T T O R N E Y G E N E R A L
D I S L O C A T E D   T O R A
    S U R E     M A N L Y
R A F T E R     E C O
A L E R T   C Y C L A M E N S
P O L I T I C A L A N I M A L
I N O N E S S P A R E T I M E
D E N I S E   S T A R T L E D
```

116

```
A D A S   P D A S   E G G S
L I M N   C L U M P   G R O W
B O O O O O O O O O O O O O O
  R O P E   S N O W   O D O
P R E P A R E   K E L V I N
R A T S   C U S   E E E S
A D T   D I R T   L E G
M O O O O O O O O O O O O O O
  J A N   O W L S   R O N
O C T A   D E L   A D Z E
R A R I N G   N I N N I E S
A J I   S L I M   P A I N
T O O O O O O O O O O M A N Y
E L L E   S W A M P   A R S E
D E E D   S A N A   L Y F
```

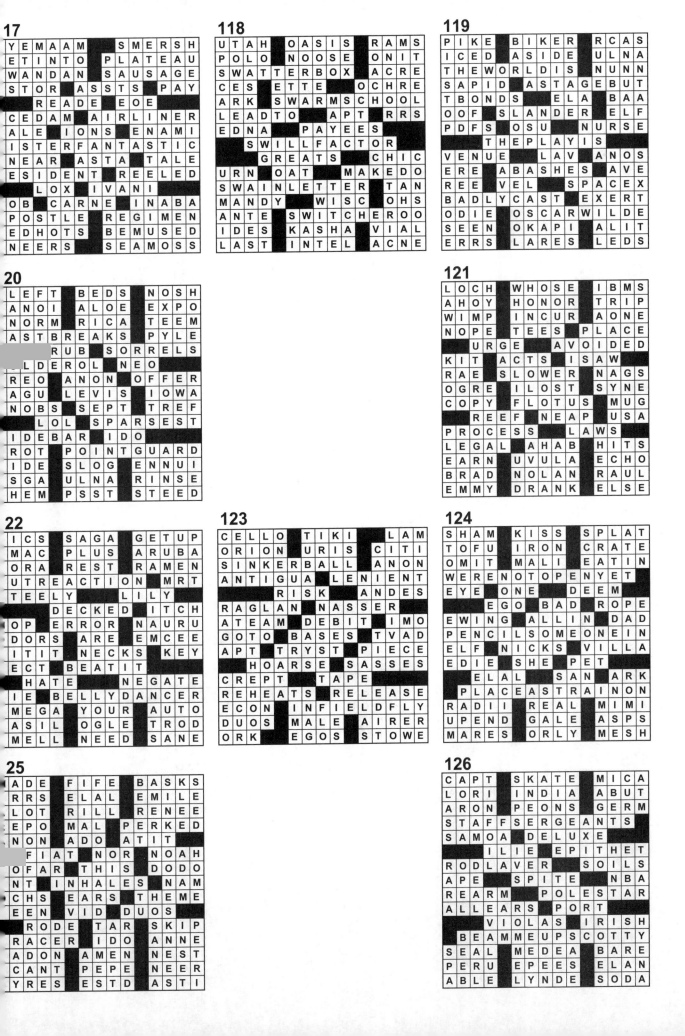

17

```
Y E M A A M   S M E R S H
E T I N T O   P L A T E A U
W A N D A N   S A U S A G E
S T O R   A S S T S   P A Y
    R E A D E     E O E
C E D A M   A I R L I N E R
A L E   I O N S   E N A M I
I S T E R F A N T A S T I C
N E A R   A S T A   T A L E
E S I D E N T   R E E L E D
    L O X   I V A N I
O B   C A R N E   I N A B A
P O S T L E   R E G I M E N
E D H O T S   B E M U S E D
N E E R S   S E A M O S S
```

118

```
U T A H   O A S I S   R A M S
P O L O   N O O S E   O N I T
S W A T T E R B O X   A C R E
C E S   E T T E   O C H R E
A R K   S W A R M S C H O O L
L E A D T O   A P T   R R S
E D N A   P A Y E E S
    S W I L L F A C T O R
    G R E A T S   C H I C
U R N   O A T   M A K E D O
S W A I N L E T T E R   T A N
M A N D Y   W I S C   O H S
A N T E   S W I T C H E R O O
I D E S   K A S H A   V I A L
L A S T   I N T E L   A C N E
```

119

```
P I K E   B I K E R   R C A S
I C E D   A S I D E   U L N A
T H E W O R L D I S   N U N N
S A P I D   A S T A G E B U T
T B O N D S   E L A   B A A
O O F   S L A N D E R   E L F
P D F S   O S U   N U R S E
    T H E P L A Y I S
V E N U E   L A V   A N O S
E R E   A B A S H E S   A V E
R E E   V E L   S P A C E X
B A D L Y C A S T   E X E R T
O D I E   O S C A R W I L D E
S E E N   O K A P I   A L I T
E R R S   L A R E S   L E D S
```

20

```
L E F T   B E D S   N O S H
A N O I   A L O E   E X P O
N O R M   R I C A   T E E M
A S T B R E A K S   P Y L E
    R U B   S O R R E L S
L D E R O L   N E O
R E O   A N O N   O F F E R
A G U   L E V I S   I O W A
N O B S   S E P T   T R E F
    L O L   S P A R S E S T
I D E B A R   I D O
R O T   P O I N T G U A R D
I D E   S L O G   E N N U I
S G A   U L N A   R I N S E
H E M   P S S T   S T E E D
```

121

```
L O C H   W H O S E   I B M S
A H O Y   H O N O R   T R I P
W I M P   I N C U R   A O N E
N O P E   T E E S   P L A C E
    U R G E   A V O I D E D
K I T   A C T S   I S A W
R A E   S L O W E R   N A G S
O G R E   I L O S T   S Y N E
C O P Y   F L O T U S   M U G
    R E E F   N E A P   U S A
P R O C E S S   L A W S
L E G A L   A H A B   H I T S
E A R N   U V U L A   E C H O
B R A D   N O L A N   R A U L
E M M Y   D R A N K   E L S E
```

22

```
I C S   S A G A   G E T U P
M A C   P L U S   A R U B A
O R A   R E S T   R A M E N
U T R E A C T I O N   M R T
T E E L Y     L I L Y
    D E C K E D   I T C H
O P   E R R O R   N A U R U
D O R S   A R E   E M C E E
I T I T   N E C K S   K E Y
E C T   B E A T I T
  H A T E   N E G A T E
I E   B E L L Y D A N C E R
M E G A   Y O U R   A U T O
A S I L   O G L E   T R O D
M E L L   N E E D   S A N E
```

123

```
C E L L O   T I K I   L A M
O R I O N   U R I S   C I T I
S I N K E R B A L L   A N O N
A N T I G U A   L E N I E N T
    R I S K   A N D E S
R A G L A N   N A S S E R
A T E A M   D E B I T   I M O
G O T O   B A S E S   T V A D
A P T   T R Y S T   P I E C E
    H O A R S E   S A S S E S
C R E P T   T A P E
R E H E A T S   R E L E A S E
E C O N   I N F I E L D F L Y
D U O S   M A L E   A I R E R
O R K   E G O S   S T O W E
```

124

```
S H A M   K I S S   S P L A T
T O F U   I R O N   C R A T E
O M I T   M A L I   E A T I N
W E R E N O T O P E N Y E T
E Y E   O N E   D E E M
    E G O   B A D   R O P E
E W I N G   A L L I N   D A D
P E N C I L S O M E O N E I N
E L F   N I C K S   V I L L A
E D I E   S H E   P E T
    E L A L   S A N   A R K
  P L A C E A S T R A I N O N
R A D I I   R E A L   M I M I
U P E N D   G A L E   A S P S
M A R E S   O R L Y   M E S H
```

25

```
A D E   F I F E   B A S K S
R R S   E L A L   E M I L E
L O T   R I L L   R E N E E
E P O   M A L   P E R K E D
N O N   A D O   A T I T
  F I A T   N O R   N O A H
O F A R   T H I S   D O D O
N T   I N H A L E S   N A M
C H S   E A R S   T H E M E
E E N   V I D   D U O S
  R O D E   T A R   S K I P
R A C E R   I D O   A N N E
A D O N   A M E N   N E S T
C A N T   P E P E   N E E R
Y R E S   E S T D   A S T I
```

126

```
C A P T   S K A T E   M I C A
L O R I   I N D I A   A B U T
A R O N   P E O N S   G E R M
S T A F F S E R G E A N T S
S A M O A   D E L U X E
    I L I E   E P I T H E T
R O D L A V E R   S O I L S
A P E   S P I T E   N B A
R E A R M   P O L E S T A R
A L L E A R S   P O R T
    V I O L A S   I R I S H
  B E A M M E U P S C O T T Y
S E A L   M E D E A   B A R E
P E R U   E P E E S   E L A N
A B L E   L Y N D E   S O D A
```

127

```
B I B L E . F O A L . P R I M
A L L O Y . O M N I . R E N O
H E A V E . C A T V . E S A I
. T H E F O U R S E A S O N S
. . S U D S . . U S E N E T
N I C O L E . C A P I T A .
O L I N . . S A N T A . N O R
B I G G I R L S D O N T C R Y
S E A . B O A T S . . H E S A
. R E S U M E . G O E S O N
K I S M E T . . T O R A
A N T O N I O V I V A L D I
P L O T . N A I L . T A I N T
P A R E . E T T E . O M E G A
A W E D . S H A D . R O D E O
```

128

```
M A R A T . S P A . S C A M S
A L E N E . N A S . R O D I N
B E A N S T A L K . S M I L E
E X P O S U R E . . B E A R
L A S T . B L O O D H O U N D
. A P E . . B O Y S .
A N I T A . S L I D E . E S A
P E T E R C O T T O N T A I L
T E T . T R U S S . A O R T A
. A L O T . . D S L .
C H E V Y C H A S E . L A C S
R A V I . . D E C A F T E A
A R E A S . B A C K T R A C K
V E N T I . A G T . A E R I E
E S T E R . Y E S . N E I L S
```

129

```
A M I S S . S L I P . M A A
R I G I D . L O N I . G L U
C A A N C O U R S E . M A D
. . B A R R E T T E . M I
B E W A R E . N A A N N O O
A L A D D I N . . S T A D I
G I N . D A I S . E V E N
. S A A B S T O R Y .
L A B O R . S H U N . P D
I N D I A N . D E T R O I
B A A L B O N D . S I E G
E L L . S T O O L I E S
L O T S . A A M E E T I N G
E G O S . T H E N . A D I E
D Y N E . E S S O . C E N S
```

130

```
C O P E D . B L O B . T O U R
A R O A R . E I R E . A C N E
T B I R D . S C A N . S O U P
. . P R E S E N T T E N S E
W O R S E N . G O A . N U N
I R E . D O P E . T R E A T
G O F I G U R E . P E A R L S
. . C A R D S H A R P .
C A P O T E . T O Y S T O R Y
O V E N S . T O T O . A Y E
P I T . B T W . F L A R E S
P A R T Y H O P E F U L .
O T O E . A B E T . S C I F I
L O C A . W I N S . T O N E R
A R K S . S T A Y . S A K E S
```

131

```
P A P A Y A . A M A L G A M
A N I M A L . R A M P A G E
S H O P P I N G C E N T E R
. E N E S C O . E S S E N C
S U E D . I D S . . D E
T S E . F A S T F O R W A R
B E R L E . Y A L I E .
D R S E U S S . B E L L L A
. . I D S A Y . E L I D
S P L A S H G U A R D . G A
E L O . . L I E . O H M
R E C A S T S . D A U N T S
. B A S K E T B A L L T E A
. E T H I C A L . M E A S L
. S E E T H R U . S E P T E
```

132

```
B A C H . Z O R R O . O P T S
O S L O . O S I E R . N E A T
T H A T D O E S I T . M A M A
H Y M I E . E N E M Y S P Y
. . T O O L . . G E O
M L L E . W I T H A T W I S T
A H E M . N O R A . E N V O I
N A H . A S T O U N D . A B M
I S A A C . T U N E . K N E E
C A R G O H A T C H . E A R S
. . I R E . H I D E .
L A S T N A M E . U N C L E
A L K A . P A S S T H E H A T
I B E T . E L S I E . S E C T
C A G E . D E E R E . T R E E
```

133

```
A B B A . A H M E D . S T A R
T A L L . P Y G M Y . P O L E
T R E E . A B S T E M I O U S
I N S . B R R . D O R E M I
C O S M E T I C S . L E A N S
U N M E T . D U P L E . S A T
S E E N T O . S C I . T Y E S
. . D E M I T A S S E .
R C T S . A P O . A E R A T E
E A R . A N O D E . A R S O N
G R I L L . D Y N A M I T E D
A R M I E S . I T S . A T M
T I M E C H A N G E . C I A O
T E E N . M I A M I . E R G S
A D D S . O R G A N . L E S T
```

134

```
R I C E . T U F T S . D U K
I M O K . A L O H A . E R I
B A S E . I C E E S . C A S
. M I D D L E S C H O O L S
. B E E R . W I R Y .
B A N Y A N . . M A S A L
A R E . T D S . O I L . M A
S M I T H . M I T . B R O W
K Y L E . P U N T A . I S N
. . D I A G N O S I S .
D I X O N . . P L E A T
S A N . N E M E S E S . R B
H I G H E R E D U C A T I O
A L O E . A N G S T . W A N
M Y T H . S Y S . . O L E
```

135

```
R A J A . B E A C H . T B S P
U B E R . M O S E Y . H U L A
M O S C O W M A L E . E G A D
B U S H E S . R E N E W S .
A T E I N . T U B A L I B R E
. . V O C A L S . C R U E L
T A P E . A G E . S I E N N A
B R O . J R S . Q E D . N A T
A N K L E S . S U E . P Y L E
L I E O N . A N I M A L .
L E M O N C R O P . M U L T I
. O N A U T O . L A S E R S
J O N I . F U Z Z Y N O V E L
U R G E . F R E O N . N O N E
T K O S . S O R E N . E N D S
```

136

```
C H A T . F A D S . B A S E S
L A V A . A B U T . O C T A L
O N E S . T O N E . S O O T Y
C O R K S C R E W C U R L S
K I T . P A T . A N N E
. . S I T . A M P . S N O R
A S T I N . A C C R A . C U E
S P I R A L S T A I R C A S E
P E D . L E T O N . C A R T S
S C A N . A I R . M A P .
. L O A N . S A D . P E A
. T W I S T I N T H E W I N D
B E A S T . R I A L . I N T O
R A V E R . A C R E . S T E P
A R E S O . S E E R . H A R T
```

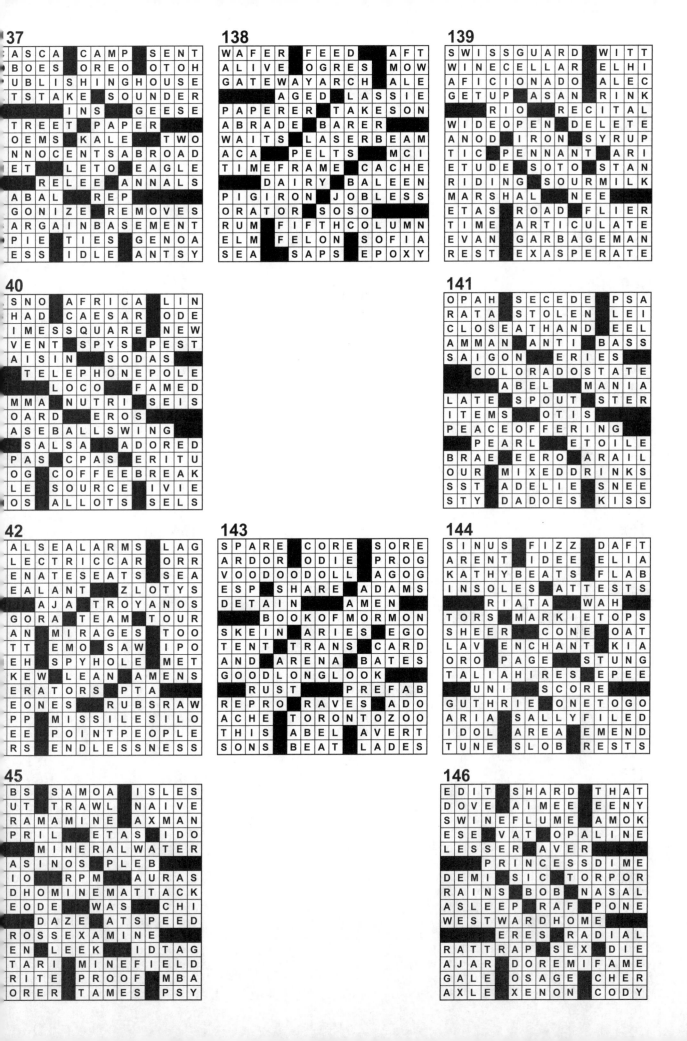

37

```
A S C A   C A M P   S E N T
B O E S   O R E O   O T O H
U B L I S H I N G H O U S E
T S T A K E   S O U N D E R
        I N S     G E E S E
T R E E T   P A P E R
O E M S   K A L E     T W O
N N O C E N T S A B R O A D
E T   L E T O     E A G L E
    R E L E E   A N N A L S
A B A L     R E P
G O N I Z E   R E M O V E S
A R G A I N B A S E M E N T
P I E   T I E S   G E N O A
E S S   I D L E   A N T S Y
```

138

```
W A F E R   F E E D     A F T
A L I V E   O G R E S   M O W
G A T E W A Y A R C H   A L E
        A G E D   L A S S I E
P A P E R E R   T A K E S O N
A B R A D E   B A R E R
W A I T S   L A S E R B E A M
A C A   P E L T S     M C I
T I M E F R A M E   C A C H E
    D A I R Y   B A L E E N
P I G I R O N   J O B L E S S
O R A T O R   S O S O
R U M   F I F T H C O L U M N
E L M   F E L O N   S O F I A
S E A   S A P S   E P O X Y
```

139

```
S W I S S G U A R D   W I T T
W I N E C E L L A R   E L H I
A F I C I O N A D O   A L E C
G E T U P   A S A N   R I N K
        R I O   R E C I T A L
W I D E O P E N   D E L E T E
A N O D   I R O N   S Y R U P
T I C   P E N N A N T   A R I
E T U D E   S O T O   S T A N
R I D I N G   S O U R M I L K
M A R S H A L     N E E
E T A S   R O A D   F L I E R
T I M E   A R T I C U L A T E
E V A N   G A R B A G E M A N
R E S T   E X A S P E R A T E
```

40

```
S N O   A F R I C A   L I N
H A D   C A E S A R   O D E
I M E S S Q U A R E   N E W
V E N T   S P Y S   P E S T
A I S I N   S O D A S
  T E L E P H O N E P O L E
      L O C O   F A M E D
M M A   N U T R I   S E I S
O A R D   E R O S
A S E B A L L S W I N G
  S A L S A   A D O R E D
P A S   C P A S   E R I T U
O G   C O F F E E B R E A K
L E   S O U R C E   I V I E
O S   A L L O T S   S E L S
```

141

```
O P A H   S E C E D E   P S A
R A T A   S T O L E N   L E I
C L O S E A T H A N D   E E L
A M M A N   A N T I   B A S S
S A I G O N   E R I E S
    C O L O R A D O S T A T E
        A B E L   M A N I A
L A T E   S P O U T   S T E R
I T E M S     O T I S
P E A C E O F F E R I N G
    P E A R L     E T O I L E
B R A E   E E R O   A R A I L
O U R   M I X E D D R I N K S
S S T   A D E L I E   S N E E
S T Y   D A D O E S   K I S S
```

42

```
A L S E A L A R M S   L A G
L E C T R I C C A R   O R R
E N A T E S E A T S   S E A
E A L A N T   Z L O T Y S
    A J A   T R O Y A N O S
G O R A   T E A M   T O U R
A N   M I R A G E S   T O O
T T   E M O   S A W   I P O
E H   S P Y H O L E   M E T
K E W   L E A N   A M E N S
E R A T O R S   P T A
E O N E S   R U B S R A W
P P   M I S S I L E S I L O
E E   P O I N T P E O P L E
R S   E N D L E S S N E S S
```

143

```
S P A R E   C O R E   S O R E
A R D O R   O D I E   P R O G
V O O D O O D O L L   A G O G
E S P   S H A R E   A D A M S
D E T A I N     A M E N
    B O O K O F M O R M O N
S K E I N   A R I E S   E G O
T E N T   T R A N S   C A R D
A N D   A R E N A   B A T E S
G O O D L O N G L O O K
    R U S T     P R E F A B
R E P R O   R A V E S   A D O
A C H E   T O R O N T O Z O O
T H I S   A B E L   A V E R T
S O N S   B E A T   L A D E S
```

144

```
S I N U S   F I Z Z   D A F T
A R E N T   I D E E   E L I A
K A T H Y B E A T S   F L A B
I N S O L E S   A T T E S T S
      R I A T A     W A H
T O R S   M A R K I E T O P S
S H E E R   C O N E   O A T
L A V   E N C H A N T   K I A
O R O   P A G E   S T U N G
T A L I A H I R E S   E P E E
    U N I   S C O R E
G U T H R I E   O N E T O G O
A R I A   S A L L Y F I L E D
I D O L   A R E A   E M E N D
T U N E   S L O B   R E S T S
```

45

```
B S   S A M O A   I S L E S
U T   T R A W L   N A I V E
R A M A M I N E   A X M A N
P R I L   E T A S   I D O
    M I N E R A L W A T E R
A S I N O S   P L E B
I O   R P M   A U R A S
D H O M I N E M A T T A C K
E O D E   W A S   C H I
    D A Z E   A T S P E E D
R O S S E X A M I N E
E N   L E E K   I D T A G
T A R I   M I N E F I E L D
R I T E   P R O O F   M B A
O R E R   T A M E S   P S Y
```

146

```
E D I T   S H A R D   T H A T
D O V E   A I M E E   E E N Y
S W I N E F L U M E   A M O K
E S E   V A T   O P A L I N E
L E S S E R   A V E R
    P R I N C E S S D I M E
D E M I   S I C   T O R P O R
R A I N S   B O B   N A S A L
A S L E E P   R A F   P O N E
W E S T W A R D H O M E
    E R E S   R A D I A L
R A T T R A P   S E X   D I E
A J A R   D O R E M I F A M E
G A L E   O S A G E   C H E R
A X L E   X E N O N   C O D Y
```

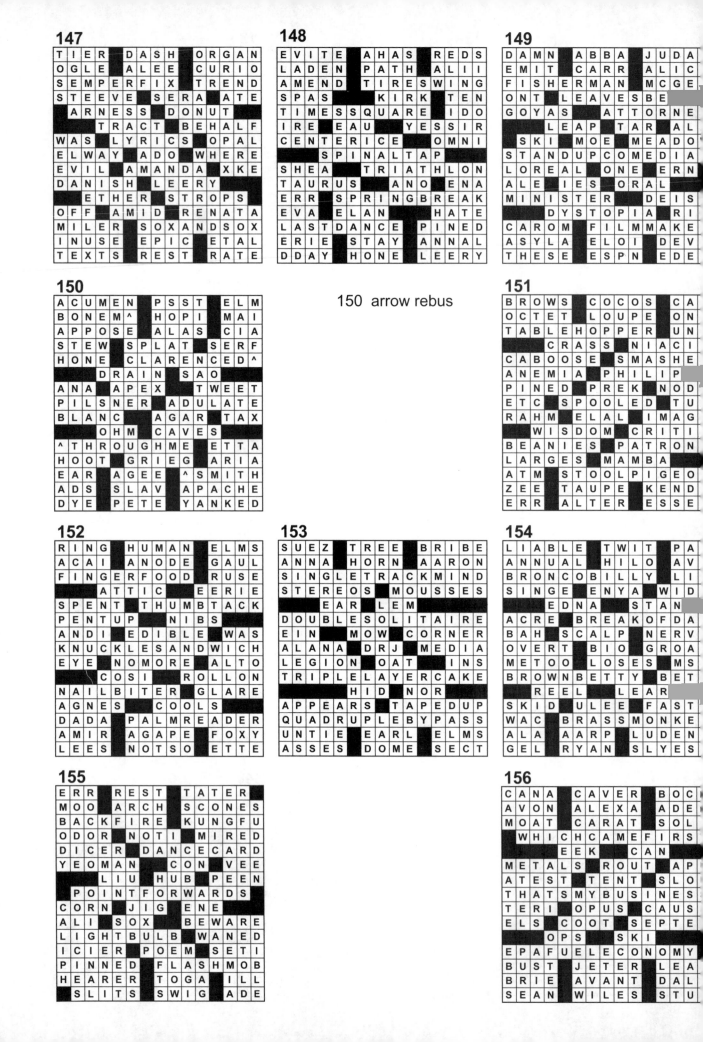

147

T	I	E	R		D	A	S	H		O	R	G	A	N
O	G	L	E		A	L	E	E		C	U	R	I	O
S	E	M	P	E	R	F	I	X		T	R	E	N	D
S	T	E	E	V	E		S	E	R	A		A	T	E
	A	R	N	E	S	S		D	O	N	U	T		
			T	R	A	C	T		B	E	H	A	L	F
W	A	S		L	Y	R	I	C	S		O	P	A	L
E	L	W	A	Y		A	D	O		W	H	E	R	E
E	V	I	L		A	M	A	N	D	A		X	K	E
D	A	N	I	S	H		L	E	E	R	Y			
		E	T	H	E	R		S	T	R	O	P	S	
O	F	F		A	M	I	D		R	E	N	A	T	A
M	I	L	E	R		S	O	X	A	N	D	S	O	X
I	N	U	S	E		E	P	I	C		E	T	A	L
T	E	X	T	S		R	E	S	T		R	A	T	E

148

E	V	I	T	E		A	H	A	S		R	E	D	S
L	A	D	E	N		P	A	T	H		A	L	I	I
A	M	E	N	D		T	I	R	E	S	W	I	N	G
S	P	A	S			K	I	R	K		T	E	N	
T	I	M	E	S	S	Q	U	A	R	E		I	D	O
I	R	E		E	A	U		Y	E	S	S	I	R	
C	E	N	T	E	R	I	C	E		O	M	N	I	
			S	P	I	N	A	L	T	A	P			
S	H	E	A		T	R	I	A	T	H	L	O	N	
T	A	U	R	U	S		A	N	O		E	N	A	
E	R	R		S	P	R	I	N	G	B	R	E	A	K
E	V	A		E	L	A	N		H	A	T	E		
L	A	S	T	D	A	N	C	E		P	I	N	E	D
E	R	I	E		S	T	A	Y		A	N	N	A	L
D	D	A	Y		H	O	N	E		L	E	E	R	Y

149

D	A	M	N		A	B	B	A		J	U	D	A	
E	M	I	T		C	A	R	R		A	L	I	C	
F	I	S	H	E	R	M	A	N		M	C	G	E	
O	N	T		L	E	A	V	E	S	B	E			
G	O	Y	A	S		A	T	T	O	R	N	E		
	L	E	A	P		T	A	R		A	L			
S	K	I		M	O	E		M	E	A	D	O		
S	T	A	N	D	U	P	C	O	M	E	D	I	A	
L	O	R	E	A	L		O	N	E		E	R	N	
A	L	E		I	E	S		O	R	A	L			
M	I	N	I	S	T	E	R		D	E	I	S		
	D	Y	S	T	O	P	I	A		R	I			
C	A	R	O	M		F	I	L	M	M	A	K	E	
A	S	Y	L	A		E	L	O	I		D	E	V	
T	H	E	S	E		E	S	P	N		E	D	E	

150

A	C	U	M	E	N		P	S	S	T		E	L	M
B	O	N	E	M	^		H	O	P	I		M	A	I
A	P	P	O	S	E		A	L	A	S		C	I	A
S	T	E	W		S	P	L	A	T		S	E	R	F
H	O	N	E		C	L	A	R	E	N	C	E	D	^
			D	R	A	I	N		S	A	O			
A	N	A		A	P	E	X		T	W	E	E	T	
P	I	L	S	N	E	R		A	D	U	L	A	T	E
B	L	A	N	C		A	G	A	R		T	A	X	
		O	H	M		C	A	V	E	S				
^	T	H	R	O	U	G	H	M	E		E	T	T	A
H	O	O	T		G	R	I	E	G		A	R	I	A
E	A	R		A	G	E	E		^	S	M	I	T	H
A	D	S		S	L	A	V		A	P	A	C	H	E
D	Y	E		P	E	T	E		Y	A	N	K	E	D

150 arrow rebus

151

B	R	O	W	S		C	O	C	O	S		C	A
O	C	T	E	T		L	O	U	P	E		O	N
T	A	B	L	E	H	O	P	P	E	R		U	N
			C	R	A	S	S		N	I	A	C	I
C	A	B	O	O	S	E		S	M	A	S	H	E
A	N	E	M	I	A		P	H	I	L	I	P	
P	I	N	E	D		P	R	E	K		N	O	D
E	T	C		S	P	O	O	L	E	D		T	U
R	A	H	M		E	L	A	L		I	M	A	G
	W	I	S	D	O	M		C	R	I	T	I	
B	E	A	N	I	E	S		P	A	T	R	O	N
L	A	R	G	E	S		M	A	M	B	A		
A	T	M		S	T	O	O	L	P	I	G	E	O
Z	E	E		T	A	U	P	E		K	E	N	D
E	R	R		A	L	T	E	R		E	S	S	E

152

R	I	N	G		H	U	M	A	N		E	L	M	S
A	C	A	I		A	N	O	D	E		G	A	U	L
F	I	N	G	E	R	F	O	O	D		R	U	S	E
			A	T	T	I	C		E	E	R	I	E	
S	P	E	N	T		T	H	U	M	B	T	A	C	K
P	E	N	T	U	P		N	I	B	S				
A	N	D	I		E	D	I	B	L	E		W	A	S
K	N	U	C	K	L	E	S	A	N	D	W	I	C	H
E	Y	E		N	O	M	O	R	E		A	L	T	O
			C	O	S	I		R	O	L	L	O	N	
N	A	I	L	B	I	T	E	R		G	L	A	R	E
A	G	N	E	S		C	O	O	L	S				
D	A	D	A		P	A	L	M	R	E	A	D	E	R
A	M	I	R		A	G	A	P	E		F	O	X	Y
L	E	E	S		N	O	T	S	O		E	T	T	E

153

S	U	E	Z		T	R	E	E		B	R	I	B	E
A	N	N	A		H	O	R	N		A	A	R	O	N
S	I	N	G	L	E	T	R	A	C	K	M	I	N	D
S	T	E	R	E	O	S		M	O	U	S	S	E	S
			E	A	R		L	E	M					
D	O	U	B	L	E	S	O	L	I	T	A	I	R	E
E	I	N		M	O	W		C	O	R	N	E	R	
A	L	A	N	A		D	R	J		M	E	D	I	A
L	E	G	I	O	N		O	A	T		I	N	S	
T	R	I	P	L	E	L	A	Y	E	R	C	A	K	E
			H	I	D		N	O	R					
A	P	P	E	A	R	S		T	A	P	E	D	U	P
Q	U	A	D	R	U	P	L	E	B	Y	P	A	S	S
U	N	T	I	E		E	A	R	L		E	L	M	S
A	S	S	E	S		D	O	M	E		S	E	C	T

154

L	I	A	B	L	E		T	W	I	T		P	A
A	N	N	U	A	L		H	I	L	O		A	V
B	R	O	N	C	O	B	I	L	L	Y		L	I
S	I	N	G	E		E	N	Y	A		W	I	D
			E	D	N	A		S	T	A	N		
A	C	R	E		B	R	E	A	K	O	F	D	A
B	A	H		S	C	A	L	P		N	E	R	V
O	V	E	R	T		B	I	O		G	R	O	A
M	E	T	O	O		L	O	S	E	S		M	S
B	R	O	W	N	B	E	T	T	Y		B	E	T
	R	E	E	L		L	E	A	R				
S	K	I	D		U	L	E	E		F	A	S	T
W	A	C		B	R	A	S	S	M	O	N	K	E
A	L	A		A	A	R	P		L	U	D	E	N
G	E	L		R	Y	A	N		S	L	Y	E	S

155

E	R	R		R	E	S	T		T	A	T	E	R	
M	O	O		A	R	C	H		S	C	O	N	E	S
B	A	C	K	F	I	R	E		K	U	N	G	F	U
O	D	O	R		N	O	T	I		M	I	R	E	D
D	I	C	E	R		D	A	N	C	E	C	A	R	D
Y	E	O	M	A	N		C	O	N		V	E	E	
		L	I	U		H	U	B		P	E	E	N	
	P	O	I	N	T	F	O	R	W	A	R	D	S	
C	O	R	N		J	I	G		E	N	E			
A	L	I		S	O	X		B	E	W	A	R	E	
L	I	G	H	T	B	U	L	B		W	A	N	E	D
I	C	I	E	R		P	O	E	M		S	E	T	I
P	I	N	N	E	D		F	L	A	S	H	M	O	B
H	E	A	R	E	R		T	O	G	A		I	L	L
	S	L	I	T	S		S	W	I	G		A	D	E

156

C	A	N	A		C	A	V	E	R		B	O	C
A	V	O	N		A	L	E	X	A		A	D	E
M	O	A	T		C	A	R	A	T		S	O	L
	W	H	I	C	H	C	A	M	E	F	I	R	S
			E	E	K		C	A	N				
M	E	T	A	L	S		R	O	U	T		A	P
A	T	E	S	T		T	E	N	T		S	L	O
T	H	A	T	S	M	Y	B	U	S	I	N	E	S
T	E	R	I		O	P	U	S		C	A	U	S
E	L	S		C	O	O	T		S	E	P	T	E
			O	P	S		S	K	I				
E	P	A	F	U	E	L	E	C	O	N	O	M	Y
B	U	S	T		J	E	T	E	R		L	E	A
B	R	I	E		A	V	A	N	T		D	A	L
S	E	A	N		W	I	L	E	S		S	T	U

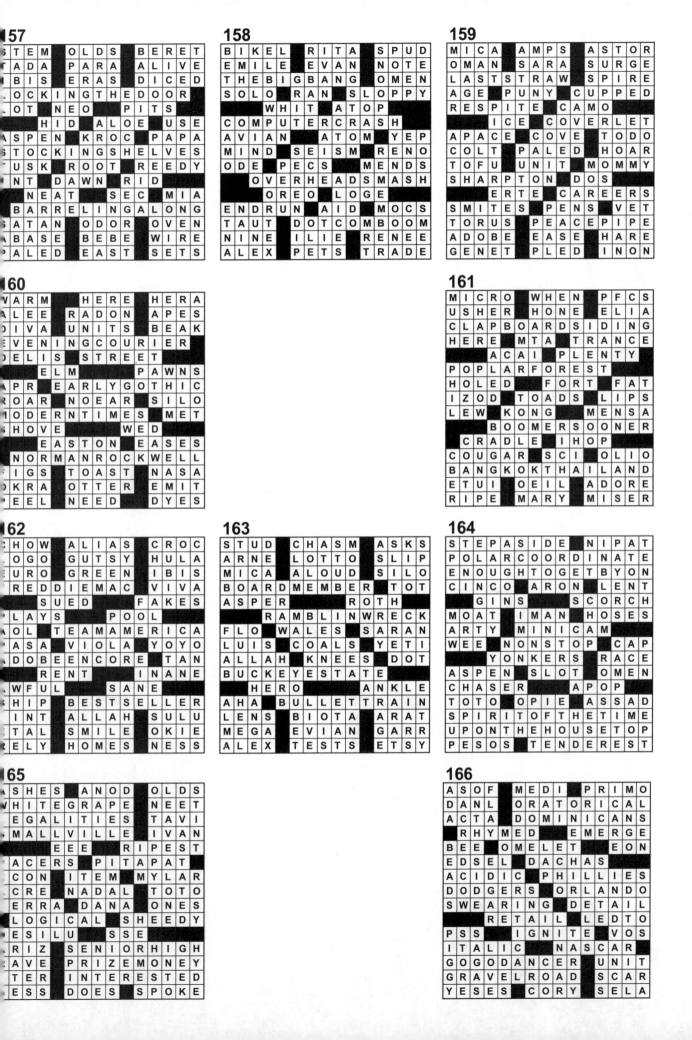

157

```
STEM OLDS  BERET
ADA  PARA  ALIVE
BIS  ERAS  DICED
OCKINGTHEDOOR
OT NEO    PITS
   HID ALOE  USE
ASPEN KROC  PAPA
STOCKINGSHELVES
USK ROOT   REEDY
NT  DAWN    RID
  NEAT SEC  MIA
BARRELINGALONG
ATAN ODOR  OVEN
ABASE BEBE WIRE
ALED  EAST  SETS
```

158

```
BIKEL  RITA   SPUD
EMILE  EVAN   NOTE
THEBIGBANG    OMEN
SOLO  RAN   SLOPPY
     WHIT  ATOP
COMPUTERCRASH
AVIAN     ATOM  YEP
MIND  SEISM   RENO
ODE   PECS   MENDS
   OVERHEADSMASH
     OREO  LOGE
ENDRUN  AID   MOCS
TAUT  DOTCOMBOOM
NINE  ILIE   RENEE
ALEX  PETS   TRADE
```

159

```
MICA AMPS   ASTOR
OMAN SARA   SURGE
LASTSTRAW   SPIRE
AGE  PUNY  CUPPED
RESPITE     CAMO
    ICE  COVERLET
APACE COVE   TODO
COLT  PALED  HOAR
TOFU  UNIT  MOMMY
SHARPTON     DOS
    ERTE  CAREERS
SMITES  PENS   VET
TORUS  PEACEPIPE
ADOBE EASE   HARE
GENET PLED   INON
```

160

```
WARM   HERE   HERA
ALEE  RADON   APES
DIVA  UNITS   BEAK
EVENINGCOURIER
DELIS  STREET
   ELM     PAWNS
APR  EARLYGOTHIC
ROAR  NOEAR  SILO
MODERNTIMES   MET
HOVE      WED
   EASTON   EASES
NORMANROCKWELL
IGS  TOAST   NASA
KRA  OTTER   EMIT
EEL  NEED    DYES
```

161

```
MICRO  WHEN   PFCS
USHER  HONE   ELIA
CLAPBOARDSIDING
HERE  MTA   TRANCE
    ACAI   PLENTY
POPLARFOREST
HOLED    FORT   FAT
IZOD  TOADS   LIPS
LEW   KONG   MENSA
   BOOMERSOONER
  CRADLE   IHOP
COUGAR  SCI   OLIO
BANGKOKTHAILAND
ETUI   OEIL  ADORE
RIPE   MARY  MISER
```

162

```
HOW  ALIAS   CROC
OGO  GUTSY   HULA
URO  GREEN   IBIS
REDDIEMAC    VIVA
  SUED     FAKES
LAYS      POOL
OL  TEAMAMERICA
ASA  VIOLA   YOYO
DOBEENCORE    TAN
  RENT     INANE
WFUL     SANE
HIP  BESTSELLER
INT  ALLAH   SULU
TAL  SMILE   OKIE
ELY  HOMES   NESS
```

163

```
STUD  CHASM   ASKS
ARNE  LOTTO   SLIP
MICA  ALOUD   SILO
BOARDMEMBER   TOT
ASPER      ROTH
   RAMBLINWRECK
FLO  WALES  SARAN
LUIS  COALS  YETI
ALLAH  KNEES  DOT
BUCKEYESTATE
   HERO     ANKLE
AHA  BULLETTRAIN
LENS  BIOTA  ARAT
MEGA  EVIAN  GARR
ALEX  TESTS  ETSY
```

164

```
STEPASIDE    NIPAT
POLARCOORDINATE
ENOUGHTOGETBYON
CINCO  ARON   LENT
   GINS    SCORCH
MOAT  IMAN  HOSES
ARTY  MINICAM
WEE  NONSTOP   CAP
   YONKERS   RACE
ASPEN  SLOT   OMEN
CHASER     APOP
TOTO  OPIE   ASSAD
SPIRITOFTHETIME
UPONTHEHOUSETOP
PESOS  TENDEREST
```

165

```
ASHES  ANOD   OLDS
WHITEGRAPE    NEET
EGALITIES     TAVI
MALLVILLE     IVAN
   EEE    RIPEST
ACERS   PITAPAT
CON  ITEM   MYLAR
CRE  NADAL   TOTO
ERRA  DANA   ONES
LOGICAL    SHEEDY
ESILU     SSE
RIZ  SENIORHIGH
AVE  PRIZEMONEY
TER  INTERESTED
ESS  DOES   SPOKE
```

166

```
ASOF  MEDI   PRIMO
DANL  ORATORICAL
ACTA  DOMINICANS
  RHYMED    EMERGE
BEE  OMELET    EON
EDSEL    DACHAS
ACIDIC   PHILLIES
DODGERS   ORLANDO
SWEARING   DETAIL
   RETAIL    LEDTO
PSS   IGNITE   VOS
ITALIC    NASCAR
GOGODANCER   UNIT
GRAVELROAD   SCAR
YESES  CORY   SELA
```

167

A	P	P	E	A	R	T	O	B	E	■	C	A	N	T
B	E	E	R	B	A	R	R	E	L	■	A	F	A	R
B	E	S	O	C	I	A	B	L	E	■	E	T	T	A
A	R	T	S	■	S	U	S	A	N	■	N	E	I	N
■	■	■	R	O	M	■	Y	O	U	■	R	V	S	■
S	A	N	T	A	N	A	■	E	R	R	A	T	I	C
O	N	E	N	E	S	S	■	D	E	N	T	A	T	E
A	T	W	O	■	■	■	■	■	■	I	S	I	N	■
P	A	S	T	U	R	E	■	S	M	E	L	T	E	D
F	R	E	E	M	A	N	■	H	O	S	T	E	S	S
L	C	D	■	A	D	D	■	O	C	T	■	■	■	■
A	T	I	P	■	O	Z	A	R	K	■	N	E	E	D
K	I	T	E	■	■	M	O	N	T	E	C	A	R	L	O
E	C	O	N	■	E	N	T	E	R	P	R	I	S	E
S	A	R	A	■	S	E	E	R	S	U	C	K	E	R

168

S	A	A	B	■	R	O	M	P	■	R	A	P	T
A	X	L	E	■	R	U	P	E	E	■	A	V	E	R
P	E	A	T	■	O	N	E	A	T	■	T	A	K	E
■	■	■	B	A	D	C	O	N	N	E	C	T	I	O	N
T	S	A	■	E	O	N	S	■	R	O	L	L	E	D
H	O	M	E	E	C	■	■	E	I	N	E	■	■	■
R	A	I	L	R	O	A	D	T	I	E	■	O	V	A
O	V	A	L	■	B	I	N	■	■	A	L	A	N
B	E	N	■	S	A	U	S	A	G	E	L	I	N	K
■	■	S	P	I	T	■	A	L	E	V	E	L	■	■
A	N	S	W	E	R	■	H	A	R	M	■	E	S	E
M	U	N	I	C	I	P	A	L	B	O	N	D
B	E	A	R	■	E	A	S	E	L	■	O	R	A	L
E	V	I	L	■	S	C	O	R	E	■	G	A	G	A
R	E	L	Y	■	T	E	N	T	■	O	B	E	Y

169

L	A	S	■	S	A	I	D	■	R	S	V	P	S
A	D	E	S	■	I	R	M	A	■	O	V	E	R	T
H	I	L	L	■	G	O	A	T	■	S	E	T	U
R	O	M	A	N	N	U	M	E	R	A	L
■	S	A	M	O	A	N	■	A	N	T	O	N
■	M	I	L	D	M	A	N	N	E	R	E
P	A	C	E	R	■	E	R	T	E	■	L	E
O	L	O	R	■	N	I	L	E	S	■	N	O	D
L	O	O	■	H	E	R	O	■	D	E	N	Y
O	N	E	W	O	M	A	N	S	H	O	W
S	E	D	A	T	E	■	H	A	W	A	I	I
■	T	R	A	V	E	L	I	N	G	M	A
B	A	S	S	O	■	O	D	O	R	■	E	S	M
B	R	O	O	D	■	O	N	C	D	■	R	E	B
S	T	U	N	S	■	M	A	K	O	■	T	S

170

S	O	R	R	O	W	S	■	C	C	S	■	S	E	T
P	R	I	O	R	T	O	■	O	O	P	■	O	V	A
E	S	C	O	B	A	R	■	M	O	R	A	N	I	S
W	O	E	S	■	■	T	A	B	L	E	S	A	L	T
■	■	T	A	S	E	R	■	E	S	T	E	E
E	N	T	E	R	P	R	I	S	E	■	E	A	R	S
R	O	A	D	I	E	■	D	A	M	N	S
A	D	D	■	S	A	D	■	G	P	A	■	M	A	T
■	H	E	R	O	S	■	A	D	R	A	T	E
O	G	L	E	■	S	H	I	F	T	Y	E	Y	E	D
R	A	I	M	I	■	L	O	H	A	N
A	L	T	A	R	C	A	L	L	■	E	V	I	L
L	L	A	N	E	R	O	■	K	E	Y	W	E	S	T
B	U	N	■	N	U	N	■	S	W	E	E	N	E	Y
S	P	Y	■	E	X	E	■	Y	E	A	R	N	E	R

171

P	U	T	O	N	■	G	I	F	■	F	R	E	U
I	V	A	N	A	■	E	R	S	■	L	E	I	L	A
Q	U	I	T	E	A	L	O	T	■	U	T	T	E
U	L	N	A	■	I	T	N	O	■	T	E	H	E
E	A	T	R	A	W	■	P	O	I	S	E
■	I	W	A	N	T	■	M	E	T	R	I
T	A	B	O	O	■	E	A	S	E	■	S	O	D	A
E	C	O	■	L	O	W	R	E	N	T	■	N	O
S	A	W	S	■	A	T	O	N	■	Y	I	E	L	D
S	I	L	E	N	T	■	T	T	O	P	S
■	E	R	A	S	E	■	W	E	L	C	H	S
B	A	G	G	Y	■	M	A	T	E	■	A	L	A
R	E	G	I	S	■	B	I	R	D	S	N	E	S	T
A	R	E	N	A	■	E	R	A	■	E	D	A	T
D	O	D	G	Y	■	D	S	M	■	E	S	T	E	S

172

B	I	T	■	T	A	N	G	O	■	I	N	F	O
A	N	O	■	A	V	I	A	N	■	M	E	A	N	T
I	L	L	■	S	E	T	D	E	S	I	G	N	E	R
K	O	D	A	K	■	I	A	N	■	C	O	O
A	V	O	N	■	W	I	E	L	D	■	B	O	N	O
L	E	F	T	W	I	N	G	■	D	E	T	R	O	P
■	■	R	I	C	O	■	M	O	A	N	S
■	T	H	O	U	G	H	T	B	U	B	B	L	E
S	H	O	R	N	■	I	A	T	E
N	E	W	A	G	E	■	S	H	E	D	R	O	O	F
I	T	L	L	■	M	I	T	T	S	■	A	R	A	L
F	E	E	■	T	M	C	■	S	P	Y	F	I
F	E	D	C	H	A	I	R	M	A	N	■	X	I	N
S	N	A	R	E	■	N	A	O	M	I	■	E	S	C
■	S	T	U	N	■	G	E	T	I	T	■	S	H	H

173

P	O	P	S	■	H	A	T	S	■	T	R	U	T	H
I	D	E	A	■	A	T	O	P	■	R	E	T	R	O
T	I	N	Y	■	B	O	G	O	■	E	A	Z	Y	E
A	N	A	H	E	I	M	A	N	G	E	L
■	L	I	S	T	■	G	A	B	■	S	W	A
P	A	T	■	T	A	B	L	E	S	O	C	C	E	R
A	M	Y	S	■	T	I	E	■	P	A	R	E	N	T
W	O	K	E	■	O	D	E	■	A	N	T	I
S	U	I	T	U	P	■	U	C	F	■	P	I	T	S
A	R	C	H	S	U	P	P	O	R	T	■	C	O	T
T	S	K	■	B	R	A	■	Y	A	R	D
■	C	H	A	N	G	E	C	O	U	R	S	E
L	E	F	O	U	■	T	O	G	O	■	M	I	L	O
P	L	A	N	B	■	E	R	G	O	■	O	V	E	N
S	I	X	E	S	■	D	E	S	K	■	R	E	D	S

174

A	C	H	E	■	A	R	T	Y	■	A	T	A	C
M	O	O	N	■	C	O	R	E	■	G	E	N	O	A
I	P	O	D	■	H	O	O	T	E	N	A	N	N	Y
R	E	V	I	V	I	F	Y	■	P	O	S	I	E	S
■	E	V	I	L	■	P	O	M	P	E	Y
U	N	R	E	A	L	■	P	A	S	E	O
P	A	D	■	L	E	G	I	T	■	N	O	H	I	T
A	L	A	R	■	S	A	L	E	M	■	N	O	S
T	A	M	E	R	■	M	A	R	I	S	■	O	L
■	M	O	P	E	R	■	C	H	A	F	E	S
■	S	N	I	P	E	R	■	R	O	M	P
C	L	O	N	E	D	■	E	S	O	T	E	R	I	C
H	O	O	D	W	I	N	K	E	D	■	L	I	S	A
A	P	N	E	A	■	H	E	R	O	■	I	N	N	S
W	E	E	D	Y	■	L	S	A	T	■	A	T	T	A

175

U	F	O	S	■	C	A	M	E	■	C	A	L	F
C	A	L	L	S	■	A	P	E	X	■	O	R	A	L
L	I	L	A	C	■	P	U	N	C	H	L	I	N	E
A	R	A	P	A	H	O	■	R	E	T	A	K	E
■	■	S	P	I	N	S	T	E	R
S	T	A	T	U	S	■	E	A	T	■	M	U	D
P	U	P	I	L	S	■	C	R	E	A	K	I	L	Y
A	B	A	C	A	■	N	E	E	■	V	I	N	C	A
M	A	R	K	E	T	E	D	■	S	I	C	C	E	D
S	S	T	■	E	V	E	■	P	O	K	E	R	S
■	■	C	H	A	S	T	E	N	S
T	R	O	U	P	E	■	E	D	I	T	O	R	S
H	I	T	P	A	R	A	D	E	■	C	A	B	A	L
A	L	T	O	■	A	V	O	N	■	S	N	O	R	E
N	E	O	N	■	N	E	T	S	■	D	E	E	D

173 main obstacle crash

176

S	I	A	M	■	G	E	S	S	O	■	A	V	E
I	N	C	A	■	O	R	K	A	N	■	W	A	S	H
T	H	U	M	B	D	R	I	V	E	■	E	N	S	E
S	A	M	B	A	S	■	E	S	A	■	Q	E	D
B	L	E	A	T	■	I	N	D	E	X	F	U	N	D
Y	E	N	■	T	A	T	I	■	C	E	L	I	C	A
■	D	E	M	A	N	D	■	U	S	E	R
■	M	I	D	D	L	E	E	A	R	T	H
S	L	I	M	■	Y	I	P	P	E	E
H	E	S	A	I	D	■	S	O	P	S	■	O	S	U
R	I	N	G	L	I	G	H	T	■	A	R	S	O	N
I	S	O	■	E	A	U	■	C	L	A	M	P	S
M	U	M	S	■	L	I	T	T	L	E	J	O	H
P	R	E	P	■	E	L	I	Z	A	■	A	S	I
S	E	R	A	■	R	E	N	E	W	■	H	E	A	R

177

```
P E   G E S S O     S E R R A
I S   U L C E R     A M O U R
N P U T F I L E     C O U N T
E A T S   F L O U R   L A T
O N E   K I S S M E K A T E
I O P I C     A D I D A S
L L   D A U B S     D E B T
    B A R G R A P H S
A D E     H A N O I   E L I
L I E R S     S E P T I C
T S T O O L A T E   E A V E
O T   S W A T H   C A G E D
O U B T   S W I P E L E F T
N R Y E   S A N E R   R O E
A B E R   O R G A N   E R A
```

178

```
F L A S H E S     P A W N E D
R E C L U S E   M A C H O N E
E S C O R T S   A T T E N D S
D O U B L E   A C H I L L E S
R T S     S O L E   M I M E
I H A D A   R I S E S   F I R
C O L D F E E T   D E F E C T
    A L E S     A N N E
L I B Y A N   G L A S S J A W
E V A   T Y P E D   E T U D E
T O Y A     E N O S     N E B
I R O N F I S T   P L A I N S
T I N I E S T   C O A L P I T
B E E T L E S   C O N V E N E
E S T A T E     C L E A R E R
```

179

```
H U S H   P A I R S     I T E M
I N T O   U S N O T   N A L A
G R A S P T H E M E A N I N G
H E R E A T   Z E P P E L I N
H A W   L Y E     P R O N E
A D A G E   R I C H E   R O T
T Y R E   U N S O U N D
    S E I Z E T H E D A Y
    K N I S H E S   M U L E
M G M   A S T E R   R E L A X
A R I E S     E S O   E S T
R I N S E O U T   T S E T S E
C L U T C H S I T U A T I O N
E L I E   I N C A N   O D E D
L E T S   O A S I S   N E S S
```

180

```
D A M   T H A R   C O L B Y
A V E   H O L E   O B O E S
R E A   R O D E   R I V A L
I R D S O F A F E T T E R
N S E C T   S E E   S A P
G E   A T A D   E X P E R T
  I N L A I D   L A M A
L E T T E R J A C K E T S
I B E   P O L A N D
V E R S O   N Y S E   S H U
E N   E W E   T E L L O N
W E T T E R B A L L O O N S
I Z E T   A U T O   D U C T
R E N E   S L O T   E C H O
E R S E   E L M S   S H O P
```

181

```
F L E W   I B I S   R A J A H
L U S H   K E M P   B L U M E
E X P O S E D P O S I T I O N
D E N S E   S A U L   C N N
    E X I T S T R A T E G Y
A T V   T W A S   S P A
N A A N   O N E S   O L D E R
E X P O U N D   E X P O R T S
W I E S T   S C A M   N O T V
    I N S   A T A D   Z A P
E X P R E S S B U S E S
L A O   G A R R   K O A L A
E X P E R T W I T N E S S E S
N I E T O   I D L E   A T O P
A S S A Y   N E E D   D O N S
```

182

```
O B I N   J U R O R   W O K
N A N E   A R E N A   A B E
U R K E Y B A C O N   L O G
S K S   A B L Y   I D L E S
  M I T E   C O N D O
I C E B E R G L E T T U C E
C R A M S   R E D O   T A D
A I R   C O D   S L I D
R T   A F R O   W A T E R Y
E I R L O O M T O M A T O
  C A G E S   O K A Y
W I P E   S I D E   A L A S
I Z   B L T S A N D W I C H
D E   R A I N Y   S A S H A
E D   A B E T S   T Y P E D
```

183

```
S U M A C   M E R G E   B A G
O N A I R   U T U R N   R H O
D I A M O N D H E A D   O A R
A T M   Q E D   S N E A K B Y
    S U R E R   D A L E
    T H E F R O G P R I N C E
S C O O T   Y E A S   D A D
K A Y O   C L A M S   A O N E
E M S   P O O L   E D W I N
W O O D R O W W I L S O N
    L E E K   E M I T S
B A D N E W S   E A U   I R S
E L I   M A K E A R A C K E T
T O E   P R I E S   R E E V E
H E R   T E S T Y   Y E A S T
```

184

```
E G G S   N A R C   S E D G E
R U L E   E T T U   U N A R M
A L O T   P E E P I N G T O M
S P O T L E S S   T H I E V E
  M E A N T   M E A N D E R
D R Y R O T   F O R T E
R U G   H A L T   S E D A N
A B U T   E N A T E   R A L E
B E S E T   I R O N   P T A
  M O R S E   T E A P O T
C R A P P I E   V I N C E
H E R E I N   A I R S T R I P
A V E R A G E J O E   I D O L
O U T E R   B A L L   N A T O
S E E D Y   B R A Y   G N A T
```

185

```
O C H S   E T T A   D O V E
V A D E   N A A N   E D I T
A Y T R A D I N G   T E S H
  V A L E N S   S A U T E
  P A R T Y A N I M A L
R A D E S   C E L
O R E   P A I N E   A I R
L I V E K I T T E R I D G E
E S   M E T E S   G A L A
  S I R   P E A P O D
I G H T F O O T E D   T O Y
S H E S   A D R O I T
L O E   G R E E N B A C K S
E S T   P E T S   L O U I S
S T S   A D O S   E S T A R
```

186

```
E L S A   S O T T O   N O P E
J E L L   U R B A N   E B A Y
E G A L   G E S T E   S O R E
C R Y S T A L P A L A C E
T E E T E R S     W A S T E
S E D A N   E D S E L F O R D
    R E D   W A R   E L O I
B U S   T U B E T O P   O U T
O R T S   L I E   S U B
S N O W G L O B E   T E A M S
C S P O T   N E U T R O N
    P R O J E C T A P O L L O
G A L E   A L E R T   N E A R
A R A B   M A D E A   I N R E
S K Y Y   S L E E T   T E S S
```

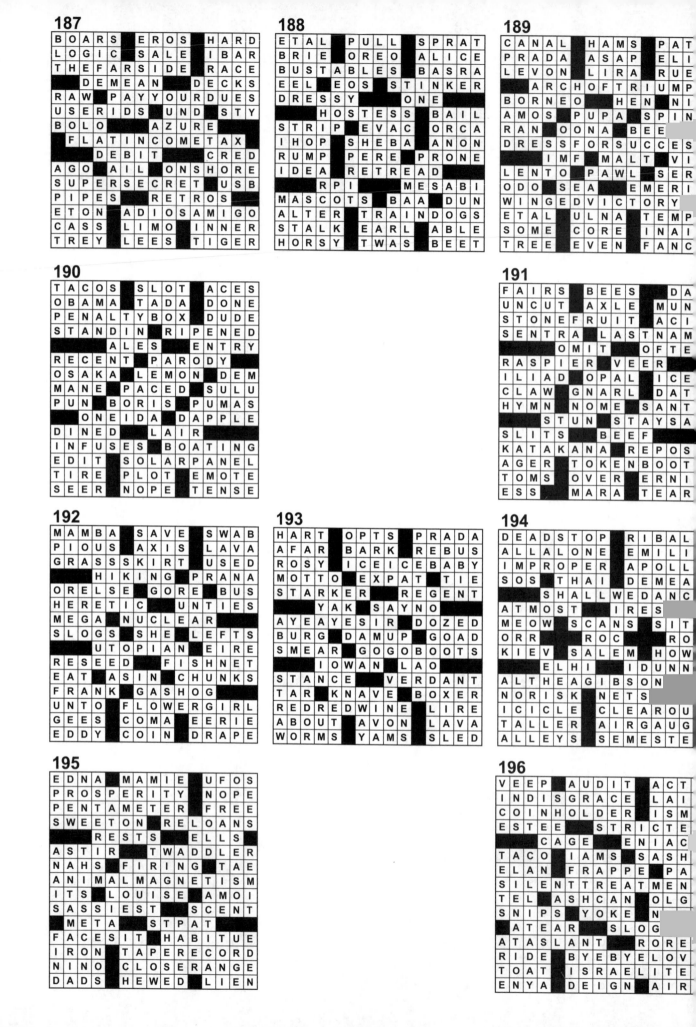

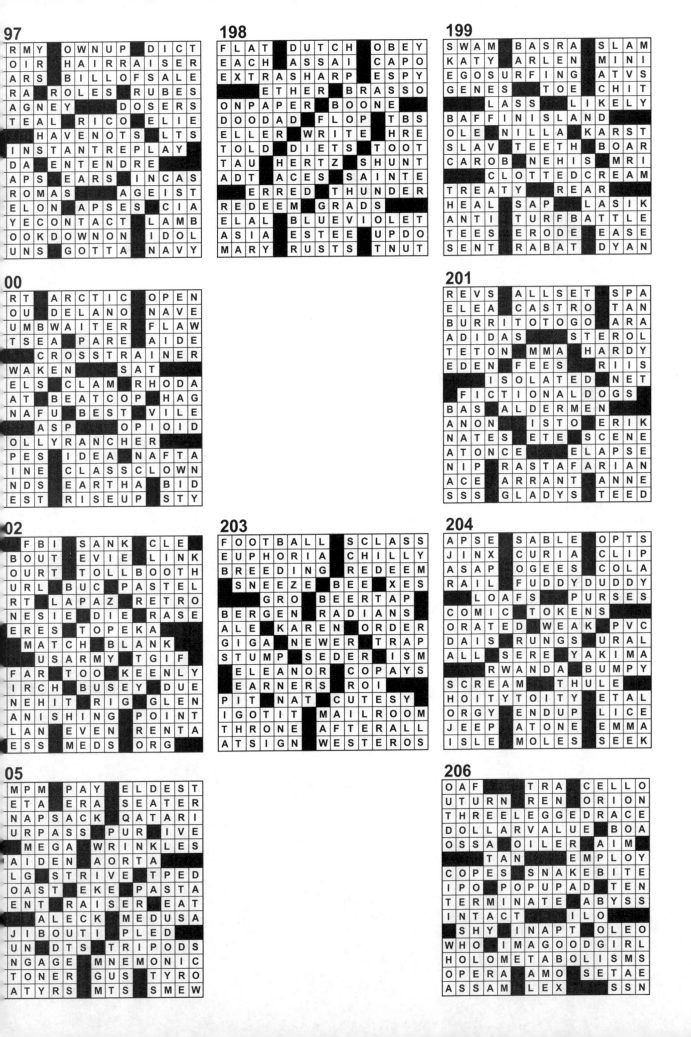

197

```
R M Y . O W N U P . D I C T
O I R . H A I R R A I S E R
A R S . B I L L O F S A L E
R A . R O L E S . R U B E S
A G N E Y . . D O S E R S
T E A L . R I C O . E L I E
. . H A V E N O T S . L T S
. I N S T A N T R E P L A Y
D A . E N T E N D R E . .
A P S . E A R S . I N C A S
R O M A S . . A G E I S T
E L O N . A P S E S . C I A
Y E C O N T A C T . L A M B
O O K D O W N O N . I D O L
U N S . G O T T A . N A V Y
```

198

```
F L A T . D U T C H . O B E Y
E A C H . A S S A I . C A P O
E X T R A S H A R P . E S P Y
. . . E T H E R . B R A S S O
O N P A P E R . B O O N E .
D O O D A D . F L O P . T B S
E L L E R . W R I T E . H R E
T O L D . D I E T S . T O O T
T A U . H E R T Z . S H U N T
A D T . A C E S . S A I N T E
. E R R E D . T H U N D E R
R E D E E M . G R A D S . .
E L A L . B L U E V I O L E T
A S I A . E S T E E . U P D O
M A R Y . R U S T S . T N U T
```

199

```
S W A M . B A S R A . S L A M
K A T Y . A R L E N . M I N I
E G O S U R F I N G . A T V S
G E N E S . T O E . C H I T
. . L A S S . L I K E L Y
B A F F I N I S L A N D . .
O L E . N I L L A . K A R S T
S L A V . T E E T H . B O A R
C A R O B . N E H I S . M R I
. C L O T T E D C R E A M
T R E A T Y . R E A R . .
H E A L . S A P . L A S I K
A N T I . T U R F B A T T L E
T E E S . E R O D E . E A S E
S E N T . R A B A T . D Y A N
```

200

```
R T . A R C T I C . O P E N
O U . D E L A N O . N A V E
U M B W A I T E R . F L A W
T S E A . P A R E . A I D E
. C R O S S T R A I N E R
W A K E N . . S A T . .
E L S . C L A M . R H O D A
A T . B E A T C O P . H A G
N A F U . B E S T . V I L E
. A S P . . O P I O I D
O L L Y R A N C H E R . .
P E S . I D E A . N A F T A
I N E . C L A S S C L O W N
N D S . E A R T H A . B I D
E S T . R I S E U P . S T Y
```

201

```
R E V S . A L L S E T . S P A
E L E A . C A S T R O . T A N
B U R R I T O T O G O . A R A
A D I D A S . . S T E R O L
T E T O N . M M A . H A R D Y
E D E N . F E E S . R I I S
. . I S O L A T E D . N E T
. F I C T I O N A L D O G S
B A S . A L D E R M E N . .
A N O N . I S T O . E R I K
N A T E S . E T E . S C E N E
A T O N C E . . E L A P S E
N I P . R A S T A F A R I A N
A C E . A R R A N T . A N N E
S S S . G L A D Y S . T E E D
```

202

```
. F B I . S A N K . C L E
B O U T . E V I E . L I N K
O U R T . T O L L B O O T H
U R L . B U C . P A S T E L
R T . L A P A Z . R E T R O
N E S I E . D I E . R A S E
E R E S . T O P E K A . .
. M A T C H . B L A N K .
. . U S A R M Y . T G I F
F A R . T O O . K E E N L Y
I R C H . B U S E Y . D U E
N E H I T . R I G . G L E N
A N I S H I N G . P O I N T
L A N . E V E N . R E N T A
E S S . M E D S . O R G
```

203

```
F O O T B A L L . S C L A S S
E U P H O R I A . C H I L L Y
B R E E D I N G . R E D E E M
. S N E E Z E . B E E . X E S
. . G R O . B E E R T A P
B E R G E N . R A D I A N S
A L E . K A R E N . O R D E R
G I G A . N E W E R . T R A P
S T U M P . S E D E R . I S M
. E L E A N O R . C O P A Y S
. E A R N E R S . R O I .
P I T . N A T . C U T E S Y
I G O T I T . M A I L R O O M
T H R O N E . A F T E R A L L
A T S I G N . W E S T E R O S
```

204

```
A P S E . S A B L E . O P T S
J I N X . C U R I A . C L I P
A S A P . O G E E S . C O L A
R A I L . F U D D Y D U D D Y
. L O A F S . P U R S E S
C O M I C . T O K E N S . .
O R A T E D . W E A K . P V C
D A I S . R U N G S . U R A L
A L L . S E R E . Y A K I M A
. R W A N D A . B U M P Y
S C R E A M . T H U L E .
H O I T Y T O I T Y . E T A L
O R G Y . E N D U P . L I C E
J E E P . A T O N E . E M M A
I S L E . M O L E S . S E E K
```

205

```
M P M . P A Y . E L D E S T
E T A . E R A . S E A T E R
N A P S A C K . Q A T A R I
U R P A S S . P U R . I V E
. M E G A . W R I N K L E S
A I D E N . A O R T A . .
L G . S T R I V E . T P E D
O A S T . E K E . P A S T A
E N T . R A I S E R . E A T
. A L E C K . M E D U S A
J I B O U T I . P L E D .
U N . D T S . T R I P O D S
N G A G E . M N E M O N I C
T O N E R . G U S . T Y R O
A T Y R S . M T S . S M E W
```

206

```
O A F . T R A . C E L L O
U T U R N . R E N . O R I O N
T H R E E L E G G E D R A C E
D O L L A R V A L U E . B O A
O S S A . O I L E R . A I M
. . T A N . E M P L O Y
C O P E S . S N A K E B I T E
I P O . P O P U P A D . T E N
T E R M I N A T E . A B Y S S
I N T A C T . I L O .
. S H Y . I N A P T . O L E O
W H O . I M A G O O D G I R L
H O L O M E T A B O L I S M S
O P E R A . A M O . S E T A E
A S S A M . L E X . S S N
```

207

```
D S T _ H A R D _ H E A P S
E P A _ A T R I P _ E R N I E
M E T _ H O R S E T R A D E R
I C E D A M _ T R U E _ S R I
S I R E S _ D A F T _ M O R E
E A T S _ S I N E _ T I N E S
C L O C K W A T C H E R _ _ _
_ S T R A I G H T A R R O W _
_ _ I A M N O T A R O B O T
A S S E T _ O R E S _ R E N E
D A I S _ A S I N _ H E D D A
A L E _ A R I Z _ T I D I E S
P O S T I T N O T E S _ E R E
T O T A L _ G N A T S _ N E T
S N A G S _ S U E Y _ T D S
```

208

```
E P I C F A I L _ S H A W L S
F E R R I G N O _ P O P E Y E
T A K E B E T S _ I R O N I C
_ _ W E R E E V E N _ T N T
R I C E R _ R O I L _ T A G S
A D A D _ K N U T _ B O P
M E N _ T E E T O T A L E R S
B A D S O R T _ C A L L O U T
O L Y M P I C G O L D _ V I E
_ C O S _ H E R E _ F E N N
S L O G _ G A E L _ S O R G O
A L A _ R E T W E E T S _ _
B A T M A N _ H O A R S E L Y
E M E R G E _ I N T U I T E D
R A D I U S _ Z E S T L E S S
```

209

```
O L D S _ P O O R _ J U L Y
P E A T _ A R G O _ A P I A
E N F O R C E R S _ G A B L
D O T O A T _ E T A _ H E I
_ _ G I S T _ E N T E R E
S H I E D _ H A R D H A T
H U N S _ M O P _ R I D I N
A L T _ C O R P S E S _ N I
D A R E R S _ L A W _ L E N
_ O N E S E E D _ E A S E
N A V I D A D _ E B B S _
A P E S _ D I P _ R A S C A
D A R L A _ B R A I N I A C
A C T E D _ L O N G _ E L L
_ E S S O _ E D Y S _ S M U
```

210

```
T A N G O _ P A S T _ S P A T
A C O R N _ O N L Y _ C A S H
C R U I S E S T O P _ A R I A
T E N P I N S _ B E E R C A N
_ _ G O E S _ _ S C E N E
F I F T H S _ P R O P E L _
U N L I T _ B R A W N _ P A M
E C O N _ M A I N E _ P O L O
L A W _ H A T E D _ A S S E T
_ E P O C H S _ S N I T C H
S T R E W _ _ T A T A _ _
T O P P L E S _ C E L E S T E
E R O S _ B E A U T Y S P O T
A S T I _ R A F T _ S A U N A
L O S S _ O N C E _ T U N E S
```

211

```
C A S C A _ W R E S T _ A S
A L T A R _ A U G E R _ C I
P O I N T O F N O R E T U R
P E R T _ I F S _ F E A R E
_ _ B A L L O T _ N A N
M O S E S _ E N S I G N _
U S E _ P B S _ P R A I S E
T H E D I E _ _ I S C A S
T A P E R E D _ E S T _ U S
_ R E B O R N _ O R L O
C L A M _ _ M E D I N A _
A U D I O S _ W O O _ V A P
C R O S S T H E R U B I C O
A I R _ L A U D S _ A N T E
O D E _ O B E S E _ R E S T
```

212

```
M A W R _ S M A L L _ K E N T
O M O O _ S A N A A _ I B I S
N O R T H W I N D S _ L A N A
A R N I E _ D E S T R O Y E R
_ _ N A P _ _ L U G _ _
_ M I L I T A R Y B R A S S
R T E _ S T O V E _ Y A C H T
A U T O _ S P E C S _ M E A L
S T U N K _ P R U N E _ R H O
P U P P E T S T R I N G S _
_ _ A L I _ _ P D A _ _
S H A R P E D G E _ E R N I E
P E T A _ B R A K E D R U M S
A R I D _ A N G E L _ E D I T
M O T E _ R O S S I _ T E N D
```

213

```
A S S A M _ R U T H _ R S V P
C H I L I _ A S I A _ H A I R
D E F I N I T E A R T I C L E
C A T _ E V E R _ D O N K E Y
_ _ P R O D _ O H I O _ _
L A T E A R R I V A L _ H O B
O R A L L Y _ N E T _ B I L E
F I S T S _ M E N _ M E N S A
T A T S _ S A P _ C O L D E R
S L Y _ S K A T E A R O U N D
_ _ S H I M _ D R A W _ _
I M G O O D _ A W A Y _ O A K
C O N F E D E R A T E A R M Y
E T A T _ E M I R _ E X C E L
D E W Y _ D U A D _ L E A S E
```

214

```
S A Y A H _ I S L E _ T W A
O S A G E _ O L A V _ O I N
F A R A N D W I D E _ E D N
A P E S _ E A T E N _ T O U
_ _ S A L _ _ S H O W M
I N S I D E A N D O U T _
T O W _ T O S I R _ M O O C
C L A M _ N O V A S _ E N Z
H O B O S _ N E W E R _ C A
_ H E R E A N D T H E R _
F A J I T A _ _ A S I _
A L E C _ T R A C K _ N E M
S O D A _ H I G H A N D L O
T H I N _ E C R U _ B E L L
S A S S _ R E A M _ C R E E
```

215

```
F O G H O R N _ _ V A S T E R
I N R E V I E W _ O R I O L E
T E R R E N C E _ I M D O W N
_ _ A R D E N T L Y _ K A T
S P I L T _ S T O A _ L A Y S
T O D D _ A S T O _ H U H
A P B _ I D I O T B O X E S
B U R S T A T T H E S E A M S
_ P A N A M A H A T S _ D O H
_ _ C O L _ T E N S _ A E R O
K N E W _ R E D D _ E R R E D
A I L _ H E D O N I S M _ _
P L E X U S _ _ G A S T A N K S
P E T I T E _ S I L E N C E S
A S S I S T _ _ L E S I O N S
```

216

```
D R A T _ M E S O _ T R A D
R E B A _ A P A R _ H O M E
I C B M _ C A N T _ I B S E
P A R A C H U T E T R O O P S
S P E L E O L O G I S T _ _
_ _ V E R N E _ A R T I C L
S R I _ F E T A _ E S C R O
H E A T _ S A G _ S O L
O U T I E S _ S A S E _ P A S
O P E N S U P _ M U T E D _
_ _ S T E A M E R T R U N
T H O M A S J E F F E R S O
H A B I T _ A S I A _ A T W
E L I T E _ M A S C _ N E A
M O T H S _ A S H E _ D R Y
```

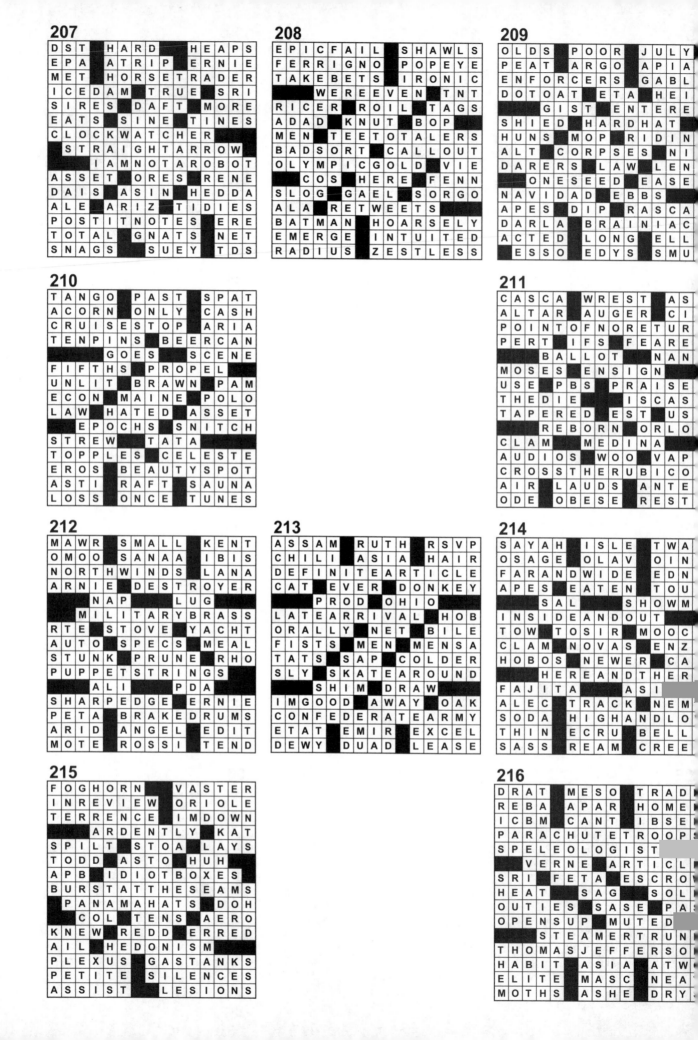

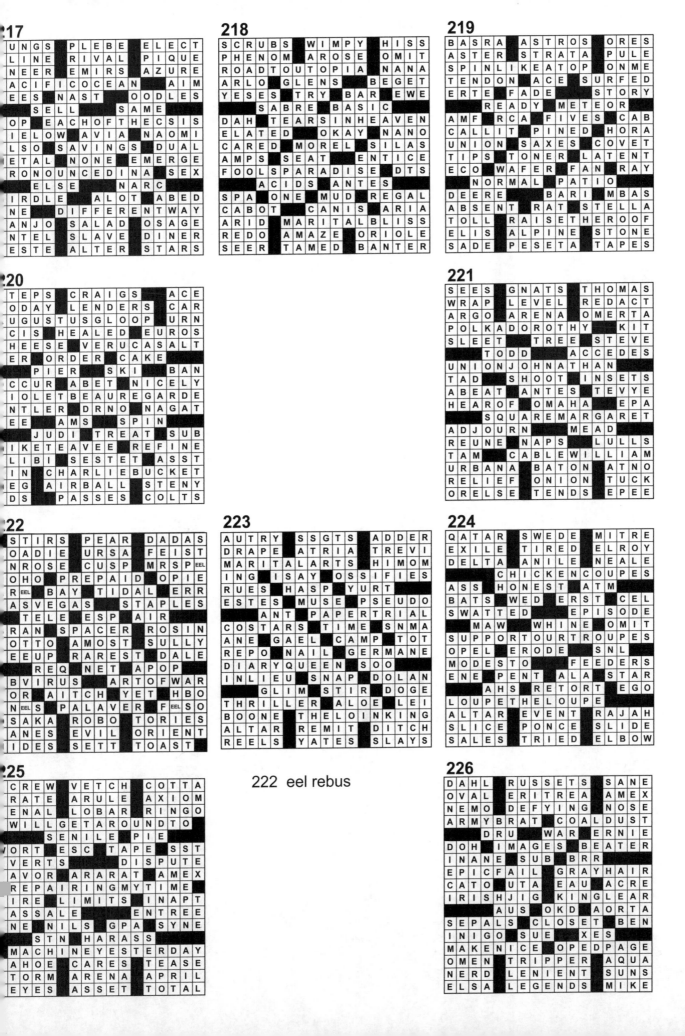

217

```
UNGS . PLEBE . ELECT
LINE . RIVAL . PIQUE
NEER . EMIRS . AZURE
ACIFICOCEAN . . AIM
EES . NAST . OODLES
. SELL . . SAME . .
OP . EACHOFTHECSIS
IELOW . AVIA . NAOMI
LSO . SAVINGS . DUAL
ETAL . NONE . EMERGE
RONOUNCEDINA . SEX
. ELSE . . NARC . .
IRDLE . ALOT . ABED
NE . DIFFERENTWAY
ANJO . SALAD . OSAGE
NTEL . SLAVE . DINER
ESTE . ALTER . STARS
```

218

```
SCRUBS . WIMPY . HISS
PHENOM . AROSE . OMIT
ROADTOUTOPIA . NANA
ARLO . GLENS . BEGET
YESES . TRY . BAR . EWE
. SABRE . BASIC .
DAH . TEARSINHEAVEN
ELATED . OKAY . NANO
CARED . MOREL . SILAS
AMPS . SEAT . ENTICE
FOOLSPARADISE . DTS
. ACIDS . ANTES .
SPA . ONE . MUD . REGAL
CABOT . CANIS . ARIA
ARID . MARITALBLISS
REDO . AMAZE . ORIOLE
SEER . TAMED . BANTER
```

219

```
BASRA . ASTROS . ORES
ASTER . STRATA . PULE
SPINLIKEATOP . ONME
TENDON . ACE . SURFED
ERTE . FADE . . STORY
. READY . METEOR
AMF . RCA . FIVES . CAB
CALLIT . PINED . HORA
UNION . SAXES . COVET
TIPS . TONER . LATENT
ECO . WAFER . FAN . RAY
. NORMAL . PATIO
DEERE . BARI . MBAS
ABSENT . RAT . STELLA
TOLL . RAISETHEROOF
ELIS . ALPINE . STONE
SADE . PESETA . TAPES
```

220

```
TEPS . CRAIGS . ACE
ODAY . LENDERS . CAR
UGUSTUSGLOOP . URN
CIS . HEALED . EUROS
HEESE . VERUCASALT
ER . ORDER . CAKE
. PIER . SKI . BAN
CCUR . ABET . NICELY
IOLETBEAUREGARDE
NTLER . DRNO . NAGAT
EE . AMS . SPIN
. JUDI . TREAT . SUB
IKETEAVEE . REFINE
LIBI . SESTET . ASST
IN . CHARLIEBUCKET
EG . AIRBALL . STENY
DS . PASSES . COLTS
```

221

```
SEES . GNATS . THOMAS
WRAP . LEVEL . REDACT
ARGO . ARENA . OMERTA
POLKADOROTHY . KIT
SLEET . TREE . STEVE
. TODD . ACCEDES
UNIONJOHNATHAN
TAD . SHOOT . INSETS
ABEAT . ANTES . TEVYE
HEAROF . OMAHA . EPA
. SQUAREMARGARET
ADJOURN . MEAD
REUNE . NAPS . LULLS
TAM . CABLEWILLIAM
URBANA . BATON . ATNO
RELIEF . ONION . TUCK
ORELSE . TENDS . EPEE
```

222

```
STIRS . PEAR . DADAS
OADIE . URSA . FEIST
NROSE . CUSP . MRSP[EEL]
OHO . PREPAID . OPIE
R[EEL] . BAY . TIDAL . ERR
ASVEGAS . STAPLES
TELE . ESP . AIR
RAN . SPACER . ROSIN
OTTO . AMOST . SULLY
EEUP . RAREST . DALE
. REQ . NET . APOP
BVIRUS . ARTOFWAR
OR . AITCH . YET . HBO
N[EEL]S . PALAVER . F[EEL]SO
SAKA . ROBO . TORIES
ANES . EVIL . ORIENT
IDES . SETT . TOAST
```

223

```
AUTRY . SSGTS . ADDER
DRAPE . ATRIA . TREVI
MARITALARTS . HIMOM
ING . ISAY . OSSIFIES
RUES . HASP . YURT
ESTES . MUSE . PSEUDO
. ANT . PAPERTRIAL
COSTARS . TIME . SNMA
ANE . GAEL . CAMP . TOT
REPO . NAIL . GERMANE
DIARYQUEEN . SOO
INLIEU . SNAP . DOLAN
. GLIM . STIR . DOGE
THRILLER . ALOE . LEI
BOONE . THELOINKING
ALTAR . REMIT . DITCH
REELS . YATES . SLAYS
```

224

```
QATAR . SWEDE . MITRE
EXILE . TIRED . ELROY
DELTA . ANILE . NEALE
. CHICKENCOUPES
ASS . HONEST . ATM
BATS . WED . ERST . CEL
SWATTED . EPISODE
MAW . WHINE . OMIT
SUPPORTOURTROUPES
OPEL . ERODE . SNL
MODESTO . FEEDERS
ENE . PENT . ALA . STAR
AHS . RETORT . EGO
LOUPETHELOUPE
ALTAR . EVENT . RAJAH
SLICE . PONCE . SLIDE
SALES . TRIED . ELBOW
```

225

```
CREW . VETCH . COTTA
RATE . ARULE . AXIOM
ENAL . LOBAR . RINGO
WILLGETAROUNDTO
. SENILE . PIE
VORT . ESC . TAPE . SST
VERTS . DISPUTE
AVOR . ARARAT . AMEX
REPAIRINGMYTIME
IRE . LIMITS . INAPT
ASSALE . ENTREE
NE . NILS . GPA . SYNE
. STN . HARASS
MACHINEYESTERDAY
AHOE . CARES . TEASE
TORM . ARENA . APRIL
EYES . ASSET . TOTAL
```

222 eel rebus

226

```
DAHL . RUSSETS . SANE
OVAL . ERITREA . AMEX
NEMO . DEFYING . NOSE
ARMYBRAT . COALDUST
. DRU . WAR . ERNIE
DOH . IMAGES . BEATER
INANE . SUB . BRR
EPICFAIL . GRAYHAIR
CATO . UTA . EAU . ACRE
IRISHJIG . KINGLEAR
. AUS . OKD . AORTA
SEPALS . CLOSET . BEN
INIGO . SUE . XES
MAKENICE . OPEDPAGE
OMEN . TRIPPER . AQUA
NERD . LENIENT . SUNS
ELSA . LEGENDS . MIKE
```

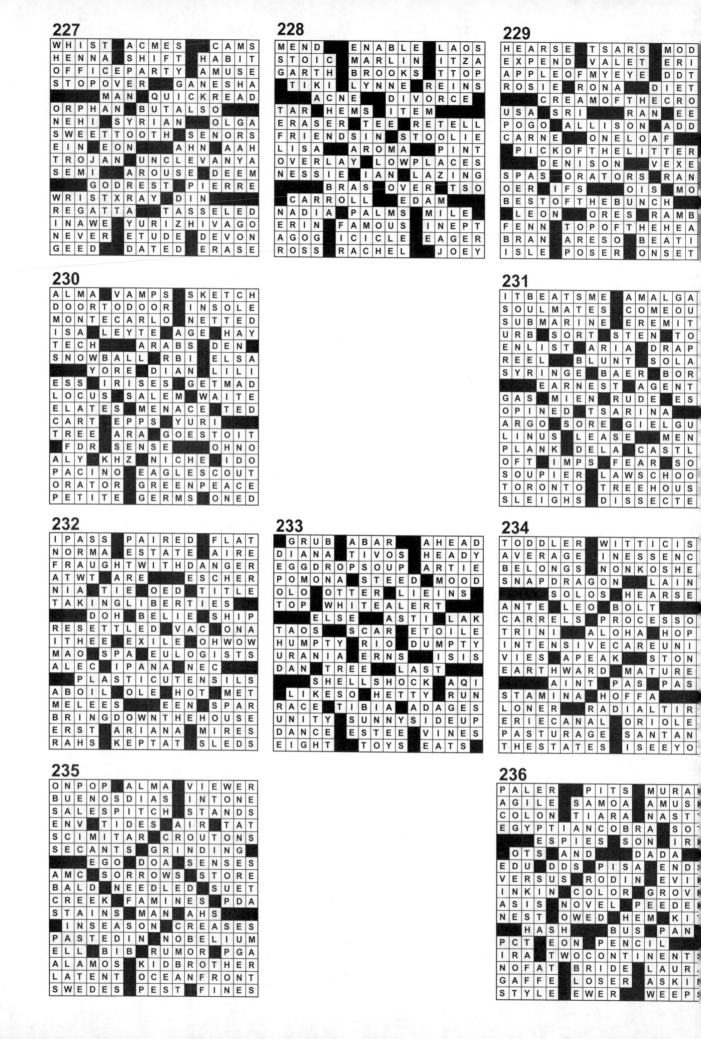

227

W	H	I	S	T	■	A	C	M	E	S	■	■	C	A	M	S
H	E	N	N	A	■	■	S	H	I	F	T	■	H	A	B	I	T
O	F	F	I	C	E	P	A	R	T	Y	■	A	M	U	S	E
S	T	O	P	O	V	E	R	■	■	G	A	N	E	S	H	A
■	■	■	M	A	N	■	Q	U	I	C	K	R	E	A	D
O	R	P	H	A	N	■	■	B	U	T	A	L	S	O
N	E	H	I	■	S	Y	R	I	A	N	■	■	O	L	G	A
S	W	E	E	T	T	O	O	T	H	■	S	E	N	O	R	S
E	I	N	■	E	O	N	■	■	A	H	N	■	A	A	H
T	R	O	J	A	N	■	U	N	C	L	E	V	A	N	Y	A
S	E	M	I	■	A	R	O	U	S	E	■	D	E	E	M
■	■	G	O	D	R	E	S	T	■	P	I	E	R	R	E
W	R	I	S	T	X	R	A	Y	■	D	I	N
R	E	G	A	T	T	A	■	■	T	A	S	S	E	L	E	D
I	N	A	W	E	■	Y	U	R	I	Z	H	I	V	A	G	O
N	E	V	E	R	■	E	T	U	D	E	■	D	E	V	O	N
G	E	E	D	■	■	D	A	T	E	D	■	E	R	A	S	E

228

M	E	N	D	■	E	N	A	B	L	E	■	L	A	O	S
S	T	O	I	C	■	M	A	R	L	I	N	■	I	T	Z	A
G	A	R	T	H	■	B	R	O	O	K	S	■	T	T	O	P
■	T	I	K	I	■	L	Y	N	N	E	■	R	E	I	N	S
■	■	A	C	N	E	■	D	I	V	O	R	C	E
T	A	R	■	H	E	M	S	■	I	T	E	M
E	R	A	S	E	R	■	T	E	E	■	R	E	T	E	L	L
F	R	I	E	N	D	S	I	N	■	S	T	O	O	L	I	E
L	I	S	A	■	A	R	O	M	A	■	P	I	N	T
O	V	E	R	L	A	Y	■	L	O	W	P	L	A	C	E	S
N	E	S	S	I	E	■	I	A	N	■	L	A	Z	I	N	G
■	■	B	R	A	S	■	O	V	E	R	■	T	S	O
C	A	R	R	O	L	L	■	E	D	A	M
N	A	D	I	A	■	P	A	L	M	S	■	M	I	L	E
E	R	I	N	■	F	A	M	O	U	S	■	I	N	E	P	T
A	G	O	G	■	I	C	I	C	L	E	■	E	A	G	E	R
R	O	S	S	■	R	A	C	H	E	L	■	J	O	E	Y

229

H	E	A	R	S	E	■	T	S	A	R	S	■	M	O	D
E	X	P	E	N	D	■	V	A	L	E	T	■	E	R	I
A	P	P	L	E	O	F	M	Y	E	Y	E	■	D	D	T
R	O	S	I	E	■	R	O	N	A	■	D	I	E	T
■	■	■	C	R	E	A	M	O	F	T	H	E	C	R	O
U	S	A	■	S	R	I	■	■	R	A	N	■	E	E
P	O	G	O	■	A	L	L	I	S	O	N	■	A	D	D
C	A	R	N	E	■	■	O	N	E	L	O	A	F
■	P	I	C	K	O	F	T	H	E	L	I	T	T	E	R
■	■	D	E	N	I	S	O	N	■	■	V	E	X	E
S	P	A	S	■	O	R	A	T	O	R	S	■	R	A	N
O	E	R	■	I	F	S	■	■	O	I	S	■	M	O
B	E	S	T	O	F	T	H	E	B	U	N	C	H
■	L	E	O	N	■	O	R	E	S	■	R	A	M	B
F	E	N	N	■	T	O	P	O	F	T	H	E	H	E	A
B	R	A	N	■	A	R	E	S	O	■	B	E	A	T	I
I	S	L	E	■	P	O	S	E	R	■	O	N	S	E	T

230

A	L	M	A	■	V	A	M	P	S	■	S	K	E	T	C	H
D	O	O	R	T	O	D	O	O	R	■	I	N	S	O	L	E
M	O	N	T	E	C	A	R	L	O	■	N	E	T	T	E	D
I	S	A	■	L	E	Y	T	E	■	A	G	E	■	H	A	Y
T	E	C	H	■	■	A	R	A	B	S	■	D	E	N
S	N	O	W	B	A	L	L	■	R	B	I	■	E	L	S	A
■	■	Y	O	R	E	■	D	I	A	N	■	L	I	L	I
E	S	S	■	I	R	I	S	E	S	■	G	E	T	M	A	D
L	O	C	U	S	■	S	A	L	E	M	■	W	A	I	T	E
E	L	A	T	E	S	■	M	E	N	A	C	E	■	T	E	D
C	A	R	T	■	E	P	P	S	■	Y	U	R	I
T	R	E	E	■	A	R	A	■	G	O	E	S	T	O	I	T
■	F	D	R	■	S	E	N	S	E	■	■	O	H	N	O
A	L	Y	■	K	H	Z	■	N	I	C	H	E	■	I	D	O
P	A	C	I	N	O	■	E	A	G	L	E	S	C	O	U	T
O	R	A	T	O	R	■	G	R	E	E	N	P	E	A	C	E
P	E	T	I	T	E	■	G	E	R	M	S	■	O	N	E	D

231

I	T	B	E	A	T	S	M	E	■	A	M	A	L	G	A
S	O	U	L	M	A	T	E	S	■	C	O	M	E	O	U
S	U	B	M	A	R	I	N	E	■	E	R	E	M	I	T
U	R	B	■	S	O	R	T	■	S	T	E	N	■	T	O
E	N	L	I	S	T	■	A	R	I	A	■	D	R	A	P
R	E	E	L	■	■	B	L	U	N	T	■	S	O	L	A
S	Y	R	I	N	G	E	■	B	A	E	R	■	B	O	R
■	■	■	E	A	R	N	E	S	T	■	A	G	E	N	T
G	A	S	■	M	I	E	N	■	R	U	D	E	■	E	S
O	P	I	N	E	D	■	T	S	A	R	I	N	A
A	R	G	O	■	S	O	R	E	■	G	I	E	L	G	U
L	I	N	U	S	■	L	E	A	S	E	■	■	M	E	N
P	L	A	N	K	■	D	E	L	A	■	C	A	S	T	L
O	F	T	■	I	M	P	S	■	F	E	A	R	■	S	O
S	O	U	P	I	E	R	■	L	A	W	S	C	H	O	O
T	O	R	O	N	T	O	■	T	R	E	E	H	O	U	S
S	L	E	I	G	H	S	■	D	I	S	S	E	C	T	E

232

I	P	A	S	S	■	P	A	I	R	E	D	■	F	L	A	T
N	O	R	M	A	■	E	S	T	A	T	E	■	A	I	R	E
F	R	A	U	G	H	T	W	I	T	H	D	A	N	G	E	R
A	T	W	T	■	A	R	E	■	■	E	S	C	H	E	R
N	I	A	■	T	I	E	■	O	E	D	■	T	I	T	L	E
T	A	K	I	N	G	L	I	B	E	R	T	I	E	S
■	■	D	O	H	■	B	E	L	I	E	■	S	H	I	P
R	E	S	E	T	T	L	E	D	■	V	A	C	■	O	N	A
I	T	H	E	E	■	E	X	I	L	E	■	O	H	W	O	W
M	A	O	■	S	P	A	■	E	U	L	O	G	I	S	T	S
A	L	E	C	■	I	P	A	N	A	■	N	E	C
■	P	L	A	S	T	I	C	U	T	E	N	S	I	L	S
A	B	O	I	L	■	O	L	E	■	H	O	T	■	M	E	T
M	E	L	E	E	S	■	■	E	E	N	■	S	P	A	R
B	R	I	N	G	D	O	W	N	T	H	E	H	O	U	S	E
E	R	S	T	■	A	R	I	A	N	A	■	M	I	R	E	S
R	A	H	S	■	K	E	P	T	A	T	■	S	L	E	D	S

233

■	G	R	U	B	■	A	B	A	R	■	■	A	H	E	A	D
D	I	A	N	A	■	T	I	V	O	S	■	H	E	A	D	Y
E	G	G	D	R	O	P	S	O	U	P	■	A	R	T	I	E
P	O	M	O	N	A	■	S	T	E	E	D	■	M	O	O	D
O	L	O	■	O	T	T	E	R	■	L	I	E	I	N	S
T	O	P	■	W	H	I	T	E	A	L	E	R	T
■	■	E	L	S	E	■	■	A	S	T	I	■	L	A	K
T	A	O	S	■	S	C	A	R	■	E	T	O	I	L	E
H	U	M	P	T	Y	■	R	I	O	■	D	U	M	P	T	Y
U	R	A	N	I	A	■	E	R	N	S	■	■	I	S	I	S
D	A	N	■	T	R	E	E	■	■	L	A	S	T
■	■	S	H	E	L	L	S	H	O	C	K	■	A	Q	I
L	I	K	E	S	O	■	■	E	T	T	Y	■	R	U	N
R	A	C	E	■	T	I	B	I	A	■	A	D	A	G	E	S
U	N	I	T	Y	■	S	U	N	N	Y	S	I	D	E	U	P
D	A	N	C	E	■	E	S	T	E	E	■	V	I	N	E	S
E	I	G	H	T	■	■	T	O	Y	S	■	E	A	T	S

234

T	O	D	D	L	E	R	■	W	I	T	T	I	C	I	S
A	V	E	R	A	G	E	■	I	N	E	S	S	E	N	C
B	E	L	O	N	G	S	■	N	O	N	K	O	S	H	E
S	N	A	P	D	R	A	G	O	N	■	■	L	A	I	N
■	■	■	S	O	L	O	S	■	■	H	E	A	R	S	E
A	N	T	E	■	L	E	O	■	B	O	L	T
C	A	R	R	E	L	S	■	P	R	O	C	E	S	S	O
T	R	I	N	I	■	■	A	L	O	H	A	■	H	O	P
I	N	T	E	N	S	I	V	E	C	A	R	E	U	N	I
V	I	E	S	■	A	P	E	A	K	■	■	S	T	O	N
E	A	R	T	H	W	A	R	D	■	M	A	T	U	R	E
■	■	■	A	I	N	T	■	P	A	S	■	P	A	S
S	T	A	M	I	N	A	■	H	O	F	F	A
L	O	N	E	R	■	■	R	A	D	I	A	L	T	I	R
E	R	I	E	C	A	N	A	L	■	O	R	I	O	L	E
P	A	S	T	U	R	A	G	E	■	S	A	N	T	A	N
T	H	E	S	T	A	T	E	S	■	I	S	E	E	Y	O

235

O	N	P	O	P	■	A	L	M	A	■	V	I	E	W	E	R
B	U	E	N	O	S	D	I	A	S	■	I	N	T	O	N	E
S	A	L	E	S	P	I	T	C	H	■	S	T	A	N	D	S
E	N	V	■	T	I	D	E	S	■	A	I	R	■	T	A	T
S	C	I	M	I	T	A	R	■	C	R	O	U	T	O	N	S
S	E	C	A	N	T	S	■	G	R	I	N	D	I	N	G
■	■	■	E	G	O	■	D	O	A	■	S	E	N	S	E	S
A	M	C	■	S	O	R	R	O	W	S	■	S	T	O	R	E
B	A	L	D	■	N	E	E	D	L	E	D	■	S	U	E	T
C	R	E	E	K	■	F	A	M	I	N	E	S	■	P	D	A
S	T	A	I	N	S	■	M	A	N	■	A	H	S
■	I	N	S	E	A	S	O	N	■	C	R	E	A	S	E	S
P	A	S	T	E	D	I	N	■	N	O	B	E	L	I	U	M
E	L	L	■	B	I	B	■	R	U	M	O	R	■	P	G	A
A	L	A	M	O	S	■	K	I	D	B	R	O	T	H	E	R
L	A	T	E	N	T	■	O	C	E	A	N	F	R	O	N	T
S	W	E	D	E	S	■	■	P	E	S	T	■	F	I	N	E	S

236

P	A	L	E	R	■	■	P	I	T	S	■	M	U	R	A
A	G	I	L	E	■	S	A	M	O	A	■	A	M	U	S
C	O	L	O	N	■	T	I	A	R	A	■	N	A	S	T
E	G	Y	P	T	I	A	N	C	O	B	R	A	■	S	O
■	■	■	E	S	P	I	E	S	■	S	O	N	■	I	R
■	O	T	S	■	A	N	D	■	■	D	A	D	A
E	D	U	■	D	D	S	■	P	I	S	A	■	E	N	D	S
V	E	R	S	U	S	■	R	O	D	I	N	■	E	V	I
I	N	K	I	N	■	C	O	L	O	R	■	G	R	O	V
A	S	I	S	■	N	O	V	E	L	■	P	E	E	D	E
N	E	S	T	■	O	W	E	D	■	H	E	M	■	K	I	T
■	■	H	A	S	H	■	■	B	U	S	■	P	A	N
P	C	T	■	E	O	N	■	P	E	N	C	I	L
I	R	A	■	T	W	O	C	O	N	T	I	N	E	N	T	S
N	O	F	A	T	■	B	R	I	D	E	■	L	A	U	R
G	A	F	F	E	■	L	O	S	E	R	■	A	S	K	I
S	T	Y	L	E	■	E	W	E	R	■	W	E	E	P	S

7

```
ARA  BOSOM  SQUID
GAN  ATONE  OUNCE
ERT  ROWED  TIDAL
NEINCHNAILS   URL
T  BRA  LAO  SEES
 HOARSE   GIT
EED  TENFOOTPOLE
LAYS  ADORNS  MIX
IL  HOE  MET  WAVE
S  TALESE  OPENER
EYARDLINE   ALIST
ARP    STRAND
OP  EDS  MID  MAG
N  FIFTYMILEHIKE
IAL  LOGAN  RUNIN
ONE  ALONE  ELITE
NNA  TIRES  DUMAS
```

238

```
SCRIBE  COBRA  SPEW
PAULEY  ANAIS  ARCH
UPSIDE  NERDS  MOLE
DETEST  TIBIA  INAN
    HOLA  ECSTATIC
FORCEOUT  RUSHMORE
OPERETTA  ELIA
WREATHES  DENTISTS
LAST        DEEP
SHEEPDOG  FALSETTO
    ROPE  IMITATOR
SCROOGES  LETALONE
PIEDMONT  BRER
ACRE  OFUSE  REFILE
DEUS  DIRER  ADIDAS
ERNS  ERECT  TALONS
SOSA  RESTS  ITLLDO
```

239

```
ARENA  ELBOWS  SCAR
MULES  LAURIE  CODE
OMITS  ATREST  IPOD
NOTRE  TENSED  PIPE
GREENBELT  SOCIETY
   STUDY  SAWHORSE
LOCUST   JAYNE
ARAL  TAHINI  SLEPT
DENTS  COVEN  TORAH
SLASH  EMERGE  CITE
   EBBED   LIKESO
SUGARRAY   BRICE
PRETEEN  PRESERVES
ISNO  ADORER  CREST
RUIN  KALINE  AORTA
ALEE  UGANDA  POSER
LASS  PENTAD  SMART
```

0

```
LLO  SCALD  HELMS
OUD  TABOO  IDIOT
TTERYBARN   DICTA
TIRE   TATS   TIER
ES  FEDEX  PESTLE
 TAUPE    BEG
 STABLEECONOMY
ATHE   OLDS   OPIE
LAY  RIFLE  LOINS
ST  SOOT  VINNIE
EENHOUSEGAS   EMS
ARK    NASAL
LIBU  HOOPS  ALAS
ON  GOAL  ASSORT
GAR  MISSILESILO
INE  ATEAM  AIRER
NED  RINGO  REESE
```

241

```
FLARE  JIHAD  PRIME
LEWIS  ARISE  RAVEN
AVANT  PANIC  AWARD
WEIGHTANDFORTUNE
SET  EON    DEEM
   ART  BATED  BING
SCAN  ARIES  DECOR
POSTALCARD  SERENA
ALP  WEE   POL  CAV
SLIDES  ARCADEGAME
MIRED  TROOP  OPEN
SEEN  BAKED  HAD
   ICON   OUT  AHA
 BAZOOKABUBBLEGUM
ROREM  CRATE  AWARE
EZINE  ALLEY  SETON
COAST  ROMPS  TREND
```

2

```
STE  SHEAF  BUCKO
PEL  CARBO  APHID
ANISHMAIN   GEESE
RD  TEASED   NESS
E  PARSE    GODS
D  LIZ  SCRIP  ELM
 TAROT  AIRE  TEA
DON   HAROLD  ROT
EN  OMELETS  PANT
N  ARABLE  PAYEE
V  LIKE  RABIN
E  GOOSE  RAT  DAD
RYAN  WACKY  EMU
MA  APACHE  ABEL
ILY  WESTERNWALL
NIE  OTTER  ARTIE
TES  LEEDS  BYEAR
```

243

```
POPUP  CHAP  BADEGG
UNITE  AIDA  EDITOR
RENTS  STAR  NOSTRA
RITECUPS  TRIPCUES
    RIFE   ANT
ENOL  FRISKY  SLIPS
PAPYRI  RUN   INRI
ITE  EZEKIEL  OASES
CUREPITS  EPICRUST
URALS  CORINTH  ROI
RANK   MEN  ASTERN
ELDER  BENGAL  ERTE
    ESE   LION
CPRSUITE  PICTURES
HAUNTS  ACHE  ERODE
OLDIES  SEEN  RELIC
POETRY  TOWS  IDLES
```

244

```
GCLEF  SNEER  SELLS
ALEVE  HIPPO  KAYAK
LOOIE  AVOID  ISONE
 PILLAREXCELLENCE
   STONY   ALLSET
HEISMAN   MITES
INROAD  IGETIT  ROC
TROLL  GNOMES  RICA
MANILLAFROMHEAVEN
AGED  ARAMIS  YIELD
NED  RUNNER  PETROL
 MERIT   RESTATE
ESCAPE   FOURH
ACHILLESANDPAINS
THETA  MUTED  DOING
EMERY  ILENE  ONTAP
ROPES  TUDOR  WEEPS
```

5

```
BOW  LEST  SAMUEL
ORE  ONTO  CRINGE
NDLEADER  ENSIGN
SELADAMS  POTTED
AR  SITSOUT  LADS
ISTIN   SPIDER
 REGIS  SCOTIAN
FAIR  SATE  GOAPE
ITE  CANIT  DENSE
NTS  OWEN  BASSET
EHOUR  REFRY
FANNED  LASAGNA
ET  DRAWSON  MAIL
TTER  NOTACHANCE
TIVE  COATHANGER
LMES  EDGE  IDEST
EERS  DYED  LASTS
```

246

```
HILT  MICA  BRASSIE
UNIONSHOP  EUPHONY
NANNYGOAT  STPETER
CHESS  PTL  THEROSE
HOMIER  TYPO  NESS
ELAL  EAR  AWED  PEP
SENSIBLE  PAL  GENA
   SALE  ALMANACS
ANVIL      NUKES
MOONEYED  GELT
OTIS  OVA  EXCEEDED
SAC  CUED  MOD  LENE
NERO  NAYS  SWEATS
GIVENTO  OTT  ANDRE
ROOSTED  GOODLOSER
ATTIRED  INRETREAT
MAENADS  SEAN  EATS
```

247

| A L O F T | B O B B E D | A M I C U S |

ALOFT BOBBED AMICUS
POBOY UNRIPE REVOKE
PREOP REAGAN GAINER
ANYTHINGYOU COTES
LESION STLEO ASPEN
TILES EXLAX ICE
CFO DOLETITCOMEFROM
OLDS VENOM UNO RENO
BOOTLEG PITS KOI
SPREE YOUTHEN UNWED
FAO SPAR ORIGAMI
LEAF WOW TEASE ERIE
ITWILLBENEWGIVE MRS
PTA OSAGE ERODE
SAYSO MOXIE TINORE
WANDA USMORETOSEE
AMELIA ASLOPE ORKAN
BIGTEN BEATTY UMAMI
CROSSE ASSESS TERSE

248

CASBAH KOS TAUPIN
ATHOME CADIZ ERNANI
POORER RHODA RATTAN
WISEMENREMEMBER
BUCS TEAS ABIE RIPE
AHA FORT ODDS COY
ROSSI CID ONE CAINE
THEIRWIVESBIRTHDAYS
TEE EMITS HEM
PARADES IRA FEDERAL
ALERO PASSIVE UNITE
NEG FRAME NEWEL GAG
GRAFFITI GENEMORA
STLO ZENO EARL ARIL
ROZ DAN AIR
BUTFORGETTHEIRAGE
DEBUT ALSORAN ACERB
ILENE RESPECT TALIA
KAREN ANA EKE ESTER

249

DOESUP WETRAG HO
SATCHMO ITHACA TR
IVEGOTMYFAULTS TI
KELSO POETS IHOPE
ELL KAOS ROOD N
SLOW BUTLIVINGINT
HAYS IROC SEA
IDTAGS ELATES BE
PASTISNTONE ATISS
ALA LEOS AVON
DARKEST OFTHEMTHE
SISI HUBRIS COAX
LAP PEEK PAWN
ISNOFUTUREINIT AT
NAE TRIP AMSO H
BRASSIE POSSE PEE
ATTA SPARKYANDERS
CREW TIMERS TALLI
KERN SNAPAT OBSES

250

HESTON CHASM ATLAST
ARCANE AIMTO COOLER
LOANER STOIC HERBIE
FORGIVEQUICKLY NUNS
NOTUP KEY JAMES
SPAR UAE FOREGO
HOTELS HAUS LURES
OUTIE TRAIT BIRETTA
CREST HOUR BED CRIB
KISSSLOWLYLOVETRULY
ETTU ORE TONE YESES
DOTESON BAGEL PACTS
NOSES PALO ROTATE
TENURE CSA ENOS
LAUGH ICC SAHIB
IDLE UNCONTROLLABLY
TENNIS IDEAL WALRUS
ELAINE NEATO ADVICE
RESINS ISLET YEAGER

251

FABI BANANAS BEMU
EDAM ABOLISH EMIN
ROCS HITSTHECEILI
MOKO ADIOS RETRO
IRISHMEN GMCS SD
NOMAS MCRAE BER
ASTROS TIEIN BOVI
POORS WOMAN ARRIV
SPAY CORES TRANCE
ESC ROOMSERVICE S
ORIOLE FOSSE MU
SCRAPPY WILEE LIP
LANCET CARET MIST
ONEON MORES WELSH
TERN EONS BETATE
TUTTI DRONE AW
GIVETHEFLOORTO TA
TRIUNE EYEWEAR EL
STARER RESENTS SL

252

DELAY SOUR LAG IPAD
AMOCO AMMO EWE CAMO
FISHNCHIPS BAN EROS
TREE HAT SHAKENBAKE
EAR ONESIE
CHIPNDALE WON AROMA
RADIO ELFIN AGGIES
ARLES MOIRE CIA LAP
BEER ANTE ARRESTS
COOKIESNCREAM
DESERVE HERO OVER
IWO BAR SEVEN STEVE
REMAIL BORED EERIE
TRESS CRU ROCKNROLL
KOALAS ORT
GUNSNROSES UNO DROP
OREO USS MACNCHEESE
OAHU BEE OGLE ICALL
FLIT ASS GEAR COROT

253

BROODED CAPP MADAME
RUMPOLE ARIA ANEMIA
ANGELAMERKEL EDSELS
RELINE ISLE
MESA DEN MOBIL
AMISS CORAZONAQUINO
HOT CRAW MITERS COD
ETA OAR PISA SEED
REROUTE SOSO GIRLS
GRETATHUNBERG
FAILS DROP IRONONS
WIDE OBOE SOU BIC
IDO SAUNAS HOSS EVE
WALLISSIMPSON EBSEN
OATHS YAK RENT
CROC BULOVA
LAMAZE TIMEMAGAZINE
AZALEA ODOR GRIEVES
DENSER WADS SENNETT

254

BIDS PASSE DAPP
ADEPT MORTON IBER
HONEYMUSTARD TARO
CRUST RESET SU
STAKED CATS LOPED
LOSS KANE NASA A
ANT EVERGREEN NOS
BYU LEAD LID SPA
DOYEN COOL EP
MAYA SUGARPLUM NE
ASIS RIDE SALSA
LINER UAR TALE
LASSO SNOWWHITE
ENC BRUT AVON SC
ATSEA PRAM DRAK
AGRA CLAIM PATEN
MALICE CLUESUSPEC
EVENED REPROS OSA
SETTLE ESSEN TR

255

SONS ENYA PROM PHAT
EDIE MEAD OOPS REBA
CONSUMERVALUESTORES
TREATY DAMIEN EMOTE
MISC NOT REDO
CRUEL LUCKYGOLDSTAR
HOP CUKE EASY ALA
ITSADATE EPODE STEP
TALC LAID APART
SWATCHMERCEDESART
OHARA ANTS EMIT
DALI OPRAH BLISSFUL
ELL MALI YOUR INI
SEAAIRANDLAND FSTOP
FAST REM EGON
CLAIM YOYOMA ENIGMA
ZONEIMPROVEMENTPLAN
AWOL FUGU RSTU PELT
REND ASST SODS YETI

256

POLITICOS TAKESID
OPENHOUSE AMERICA
DISSENTER LOSALAM
SEETOIT REEK SIMP
ARCHWAYS PUCE
ODDLY RITE TORO P
AUEL SOLE GREENBE
TRA BOAT DUETS LA
HANGOUT RUSES GEN
MORAL DIETS FLEU
CAFES DOTTY ERUPT
ATME GONZO SCAM P
SEEDMONEY BOOT TI
ERN AONE REIN AIL
HYDE FOLLOWUP
LEGION VIOL MONTA
AIRTRAVEL HAIRTON
DRAMAMINE OBEDIEN
DESELECTS POSSESS

257

```
S PROMISED   STRANGER
EA ANEMONE   ONETOONE
AR SURPLUS   ROMANOVS
NA SERIF ARTIN DIP
PNS SOC SWEET CASE
EONI VISUALS BASIC
NIONS TUNIS MARGOT
NARLED EST TORTONI
 TENORS SLAV ELEV
SA TATE AXES DDE
EST TEAR FIESTA
TTIMES OER SURNAME
TRESS TOLER PAVLOV
HORT MISSTEP WILDE
ENS SORTA PAD LOIN
TO LIMAS PEDRO CFO
OMPUTED HEARINGAID
NEEBONE ALLEVIATED
ERPENTS MESSENGERS
```

258

```
RIMS RIIS AWLS SCAM
INFLUENZA HAILSTONE
GROUNDHOG SIMOLEONS
GERMICIDAL KIWI POS
    TAB SOLITUDE
APPLEPIE AUK PENPAL
GORE TRAFFIC DOTE
ALEAST ABET HOLISTS
REM CURSED PATENTEE
MATERIEL PORTAGES
SITINFOR IRISES RTS
ACUTEST HMOS RELISH
KARL STEPMOM TOTO
SLEEPS EMU NAMEDROP
  DRAWNIGH LOY
DOD ILED NOTALITTLE
EVENMONEY WOMANHOOD
CASSANDRA TOURGUIDE
ILKA SYST OLDS STEN
```

259

```
JACKFROST SANSSOUCI
ALLATONCE PROCESSOR
GLANDULAR RESONANCE
SYNE TARP ONOR YAKS
    PETA BUTANE
VISTA EBERT PEDDLES
ITHACA SLIER RARITY
ROOKIES RADAR MYNAS
GREENONION TAT CELT
  STONILY HONORED
OAHU SDI HANDMIRROR
SMIRK EAGER RECEIVE
SINNER DRIER SHAVEN
ONESTOP ASSAY ILENE
  TALENT NOME
ITBE RUNT EGGO ALMS
MARRYINTO COURTFOOL
PREMINGER CORPORATE
STRANGERS ENTHRONED
```

260

```
ESTWISHES DRAGRACE
VERACTIVE REPAIRER
ELINEATED EVOLVING
SL DIN NERD LIEDTO
  RANCHERO AOL
ATO HID MED EBBED
LECTEES SANDDOLLAR
OAKERS GENTLE AUTO
ERSER MEANIES NEAP
LID HORRORS OKD
RON SURMISE INVEST
OOG ERMINE NOTEVER
OSEYALONG SENORITA
TERI ENA GAP SLAP
  EAR TENTACLE
OHELP ZERO LOO WOW
NONDAGA IMPERATIVE
UNCECAP CEASEFIRES
PEEDERS ASSESSMENT
```

261

```
TENDSTO TAPROOM SCIFI
SCOOTED ALREADY HUMAN
ALLGONE GLOSSES ERICA
RATIONS SEXIEST RITES
STEEPEST GINS INPEACE
  ERASURES AQUA TAN
REWEDS HMOS SLUM HORS
ALAN VIPS SATE HORDE
PILASTERS SOLO CEL
ICECHEST SIRES HAYDEN
DISTANT SAXES CARMELA
STAMPS BATES MANTOMAN
EEE RIIS PANTSSUIT
SPEND KANE MODE ERNE
CAST ONIT VEER CUSSES
ISP IRED PEMMICAN
STRANGE SADE DARTTEAM
SEEDS BIPLANE MARIANA
OSSIE ORIENTS EMITTER
RISER NONSTOP REELING
SNOUT ECSTASY ALDENTE
```

262

```
EMI MURAL ADMIT UFOS
LES ASURA LEECH SOSA
LDO SAHIB ALDER ELAM
IOLETGRAY MOODINDIGO
SCAPEE RIOS VETOES
TER SWIMS PRIMO
LBEE LAINE LLANO ROC
OLD COVET BEING MELE
MU GREENHORNET WODEN
EEDLESS RAND MARGOT
WRAPS PUTTY RISER
DHERE LOCH SHETLAND
EASE YELLOWSTONE NEE
ALS MEDEA HEADS EGON
DE GONGS SITKA ANENT
  MANSE BATHE LEG
ENANT SATE CEREALS
RANGEBOWL THERAINBOW
ANT RESEE AARON DORA
SNE ETHER INANE EVER
EAL YEATS LASER REND
```

263

```
STAT ABOVE COSTA OKRA
URSA RELAX ORLON UNUM
MEIR ANISE LIANA TINE
AVAGARDNER LEVICOFFIN
CINEMAS COAL ORIENT
  TOT FRIAR GENET
ULCER CRASS PARDO JED
SOLD THANE SOFIA GORE
NIA THOMASWOLFE MEHTA
ANYWHERE HAKE PINNED
  AERIE ERIKA HENRI
MAILER DEER CONTESSA
ANKLE CAROLINIANS NOR
REES DELIS METRE AERO
AWN LILLE SPEED ACRED
  DUSTY FORDS OPA
CLAUSE SANE STOPPED
EARTHAKITT STEPHCURRY
ATOI SAGET SUSIE LION
SEME ELENE ENTER CODE
ERAS SETON SEEDS ORES
```

264

```
RESEW ALASKA SHOFAR
URIAH PACKET THESAME
NARROWESCAPE AURORAS
  LEHRER TRAILBLAZER
HASSLE RAP AWL SEDONA
IRT SLO YAWNED NTH
PEACEACCORD SNOBBY
PARR NHLTEAM DURESSES
OSKAR SEC NEA BIGLOVE
 SET ADDONS LAG NIA
HIGHSIERRA LONERANGER
AMI LEG UNDONE SRO
MANMADE GEE AWE SOFAS
SCOTTISH SIGNALS SENT
  MENTOR CUTTINGEDGE
IGA STOKES SAL ULE
RUSSKI TMI HEF PEPPER
VISIONQUEST MAOTAI
TUNASUB MORALCOMPASS
AMELIAS ELFISH EPCOT
RESAND TEDLEO DITTY
```

265

```
AMES SSRS ERICA FINN
MAGE CANA MELIN ACTS
IAGARAFALLSFLAT LASE
SSO ARISTA ISOF CNBC
  NOPAR DHL ALOT
NC LIBERTYBELLRINGER
ORGED ORSO IAMAROCK
TARI AFTA JAM YOHO
ENICEBEACHCOMBER NOS
LIE YUM IAN TIC
LASVEGASSTRIPSEARCH
ECO OPA RNR OOOS
DL UNIONSTATIONWAGON
RES SHY PHEW AKITA
ETERPAN LETO MISTER
ISNEYWORLDSUMMIT ODE
  LTYR AMI OATES
OOR ILER TERROR CAIN
LOI TIMESSQUAREDANCE
ASE ELMST UGLI ANNEX
YES STATE ISES START
```

266

```
SATE CHIDE DEWAR OSHA
OMEN HAVEL ADOBE STIR
FINGERLICKINGOOD CART
AGE VOTE MEET SCANTY
ROTTEN DECALS CHARD
  ERIS MAGA LIP BFF
WHATCANBROWNDOFORYOU
SIAM HUEY AUNT EMIL
ELS BAND PADRE SMELL
ACTFOUR ARIA LEA
SOEASYACAVEMANCANDOIT
  BAS ALAS ANTENNA
CARRY SLICE LAME IAN
ACAI GALE WADE LONG
BETCHACANTEATJUSTONE
ODS ASK RYNE POWS
NORMS SAIDNO PESTLE
AGENDA CHIN ACRE RON
ROSS STRONGERTHANDIRT
ANTE KEENE LOHAN ACNE
BEST SEDER MISDO BEER
```

267

```
ANIME  ACTIN  PEAR  VAST
ROGET  SAURO  ELSA  IRMA
CLODHOPPERS  SAPBUCKET
HORSEMEN  TOOL  INUSE
NAN  FORM  VEIN
LICHEN  PLAIN  TESTATOR
ECHO  IDIOTLIGHT  UFO
GOUT  REC  RES  SERTA
ISM  MARKTWAIN  STAKES
TAPROOMS  HIRT  PARENT
CENTS  BANES  SULLY
ADHERE  ORCA  STRESSES
BRAVES  DOPESHEET  HAY
BONED  SIS  AMI  CORN
OMG  PATSYCLINE  BOLO
TEETOTAL  PEALS  LASTED
UBER  ILLS  OVI
NOBET  SENT  INERTGAS
DUMMYHAND  SUCKERPUNCH
IDEA  EMAG  INPEN  OBAMA
PENN  RAGE  NORAD  PAWED
```

268

```
GED  PRE  DEWAR  TWIST
URANIUM  SERENE  SAIDSO
NOTICES  PARTYPLATFORM
LIENS  PORES  LOMEIN
ACRE  CEASED  CAGER  TEA
PASSMUSTER  MAYI  ASAP
AMPS  KISSCONCERT
STALIN  SPENT  NITES
MERLIN  POINT  BOLLS
AGEE  CADET  COBOL  ABE
PUNCHCARDS  GAMEWARDEN
SET  ALLEY  GABBY  IDED
ADELE  POLES  TAPERS
MALTA  LINER  PAGERS
FITFORAKING  TACO
OKRA  BELT  BLOCKGRANT
REO  ADOPT  BIOPSY  ODOR
PANOUT  CAFES  SPODE
THINGSTOTHROW  SPHERES
AUNTIE  FOIBLE  WHEREAS
REESE  FETID  MID  SLY
```

269

```
PACT  ALIAS  SCANT  MI
OSHA  LADLE  TONER  AC
WHACKAMOLE  RENTACRO
SENTINELS  LADE  DAIN
TINS  SANS  PECS
RACIEST  ECIG  LITTE
ATHOS  RICEARONI
IRON  TATI  BOP  SC
TIC  BRICABRAC  SAH
TAKETIME  TEAS  VICA
APERY  REESE  ROARS
UNBEND  HUNT  HITMAK
POLED  ROPEADOPE  E
PROS  MED  EWES  T
ESC  DIALAJOKE  SIC
REKNITS  AKIN  WRITH
IVES  SCAM  MIEN
NASCAR  POKY  FALSETT
ALLANADALE  TILTAWHI
GOOD  TAROT  ARIEL  AR
SETS  EDENS  MEADE  WE
```

270

```
DESOTO  RECITED  HUMERI
IRONON  EXAMPLE  ANIMAL
RODENT  FIVESECONDRULE
EDAM  HASTE  MONGOOSES
RESALES  EARL  RAI
NAGS  DRAYS  INSTEAD
BOMBSOUT  TWOCARGARAGE
ATEAT  CHA  NOG  SEESAW
BRING  HYDRO  TOO  NEVE
SANDAL  MEANS  CASTLED
SEVENYEARITCH
SHARPEI  SARAN  TESTEE
IOWA  ETC  LIMBS  BIOTA
LOAVES  RUG  SET  AXONS
THREEWAYBULB  DOWNPLAY
SADDLED  ALIAS  RAGA
LUG  FERN  MISCAST
INSTALLER  COAST  KETO
FOURLETTERWORD  SEAGOD
SLEEPS  ABRADED  UNBIND
OLDEST  TASTERS  POSSES
```

271

```
BLAB  WARSAW  BIFFE
TOILET  EVENLY  UNLIN
HAVETO  LOCALE  STUNN
ORIGINALCOPY  THESAU
NAMES  ENS  HEIR  LIS
EAGRE  HGTS  CANDIED
MUD  SALA  RANDOMORDE
ITEM  BABYTALK  NAI
TRAINER  URN  SAGA  FRA
SYDNEY  BRAGS  SPLITE
VANITY  APPALL
DAMPENER  SOLES  DEPO
ALAR  TAOS  POE  MOSHP
HIRED  PLANKTON  DEL
LASTINITIAL  USES  N
TOOMUCH  NOEL  TASS
CAGY  SPRY  PAT  ELOPE
ABLUTION  MINORMIRACL
ROUGHER  BIGTOE  MICRO
DUELIST  ANGELA  BEHES
TRYSTS  GEYSER  SETS
```

272

```
KEEP  APT  RANAT  PAMPAS
ALVA  CHI  EMILE  ORIOLE
THECATINTHEHAT  NICKEL
OINKS  SWAN  MEND  RENE
ETAS  ISTLE  AEROBES
REDRIDINGHOOD  BRUNO
ONE  HBO  TABOOS  NBC
AREOLE  GREAT  ABUT  NOH
MORTARBOARD  SASS  LENA
SNEERED  TRAVEL  PATER
LURE  TOMES  DIET
ANGLE  FARINA  ANCIENT
FARO  PROT  TAMOSHANTER
AVE  ARAB  HELEN  ENSURE
RYE  TESSIE  UAR  DTS
NORMS  CROWNPRINCESS
HOBNAIL  ERNIE  ETUI
OBES  EEOC  EDOM  MANON
WIRIER  GOLDENSOMBRERO
DEEDEE  OLEAN  GSO  DEAN
OSTEND  DDAYS  SAR  IDLE
```

273

```
AWASH  MOSES  GAGS  AHS
NARCO  FETTLE  ABUT  NON
TIMEWILLTELL  MAINSTAY
STONEMASON  SUSS  HERD
YERTLE  ITSONTHEHOUSE
SASE  NBA  ROPER
IHAVENTTHEFOGGIEST
NOLO  TENOR  TSARS  SPEW
FOCUS  TAMALE  TOTS  OLE
PACES  ITO  JONAH  LIB
THATSANOTHERSTORY
CPR  REPLY  TOP  EVITA
AAA  SLOE  FOSSIL  EVENS
BZZT  MORAL  NEMOS  ECKO
IMOFTWOMINDSONTHAT
ASSNS  FOE  BENE
GOWITHYOURGUT  ASHARP
ATEE  ORAL  RESORTAREA
THEROPES  ITGROWSONYOU
HIP  JUKE  DOESIN  ROARS
ASS  SPAS  ANSEL  SINGE
```

274

```
BUST  OPERA  SALOME  BC
AFAR  DINES  ADORER  EV
HOTUNDERTHECOLLAR  SE
EMO  OYER  LOT  PIN
STEAMEDUP  ASPEN  TAD
PENN  VOTE  TED  CARES
YES  WAGE  TBAR  FURTHE
SODS  COLIC  EGO  IV
BEWARE  BOWERY  DATUM
AMEND  BEDEW  DOT  PSS
LINDY  INALATHER  CLEA
ETTA  DAD  FAUNA  LILL
BLURS  SKULLS  COFFE
PEA  RYE  EASEL  BRUT
ALLEGED  IRES  SLAT  PR
SILVER  ONE  UPON  ARE
IOS  HYENA  TICKEDOF
ELSE  RES  ROAD  ROT
NOT  WENTOFFTHEDEEPEN
OBI  ANNEAL  TAROS  TIC
SEC  STARRY  ONSET  SNO
```

275

```
SMALL  BASS  PDF  SHORT
LIVIA  OLEO  BOIL  PAREU
ONELS  ZUCCHETTO  ANGEL
PDR  TROI  IAGO  RANDALL
SESAMES  SANSKRIT  ENSE
DEMOS  BABS  USTED
ANTHILL  TENTHS  ARI
FROST  ERIE  ALI  ECCLES
ROUSH  CEN  OMAN  RAIDER
EDT  GAMEPLAN  TERNE
ESTIMATE  OIL  SEAPERCH
ORATE  FIVESTAR  MAE
ONSITE  SINE  LAS  BRAGA
DOESIT  COT  MERE  LINED
DNA  NOLOSE  EATSOUT
ASWAN  DAZS  BEAST
ACTS  ENERVATE  DOGSHOW
GERHARD  HEMP  EWER  EME
IDOOD  EVERSINCE  ARECA
FAVRE  RITE  EARL  SONAR
TREES  SAT  SHUT  STATE
```

276

```
MASSE  STRUT  ORLY  SLO
USUAL  TAUPE  BEAU  COP
STEVEMARTIN  JIMCARRE
SIDECAR  BRED  ALIEN
TIER  BAIT  STUB
SPLEEN  HAULS  ALAMEDA
TROVE  JOHNLENNON  AL
ROUE  CEDE  UTE  OMI
AMI  LEEMAJORS  BROK
DOSSIERS  RUNS  PAINE
JAVAS  SMILE  ERROR
SMOKER  COCO  BEERNUT
HARES  MARYWELLS  NU
OLDS  BAR  REES  HYP
PTA  COLEPORTER  PAOL
SANDDUNE  IVIED  PINNE
RULE  STEP  SCOT
ASSENT  LIAR  ROBUST
MILAKUNIS  LEODUROCHE
ITEM  RAMS  AGREE  SLEE
DEWY  EBAY  YODEL  SASS
```

Crossword Answer Grids

277
```
EAD RANCH HAMAS PALL
LE ORTHO AROSE ACAI
TATOCHIP PIRATESHIP
ADATE SPAN SATYRS
SKEDS HOE SPARE
APPED AVIANS RIPOPEN
RLON CRANK EMIL NAME
EAT GRIND BRAM CAR
NS PRESSUREGROUP KID
ATTRAP ONES NOSILY
IBIDEM MUD HATPIN
ECAME ALAS TRUDGED
AW PANCAKEMAKEUP SRO
RR OHNO ANNIE CLAM
AP PLOD ANTON NOISE
PESET SEXTET COMPED
LINES LEA STOOP
ELLA CLOD RUNOFFS
GEONCOOP POWERSTRIP
OT CALVE ARIES EAVE
SS ENDED TENSE STEW
```

278
```
MALACCA HAHAHA GLUTEI
ABANDON ERASER DONALD
WINGNUT STUFFEDANIMAL
SEAU NOG ELAT INEXILE
ITSNO ROT USSR
BESSIE TGIF TNPK SEGA
INTHELINEOFFIRE WADER
ROPED NEIL IDOL AMINO
CLAD ABASE TAL ARETOO
HAT SNORT BILLYGRAHAM
SCAR BEN ORES
DOLPHINSAFE DIGIN MPS
AZORES POL SOPUP PALE
TOTAL SORA AJAR LANAI
UNTIL PUTTINONTHERITZ
MEAN MATA MDSE OFLATE
CURS NPR MENTO
EDGIEST CARA ANO ROBT
SCOTCHANDSODA CRACKER
AUSSIE BRAVES LECARRE
UPHOLD ASLEEP SERRATE
```

279
```
WADS GPA BFAS ONSALE
ICEE IROC CANI ZIPPER
SHARKTANK DITZ SKIING
PETTIEST BELIES OKED
HAS SIAL ACUTELY
OTB STOUTEST PUMA FLA
RHYMER STATED BOTTLED
ARCARO PERUSE SEWAGE
NEHI ITISI TESH SETON
GAOL KILTER SLA LEE
ETC TARA RUR AIDA ADA
OOH ETE NESTLE PREZ
ACLUE DELI CHEEP ETTU
ORACLE SLALOM ITSHER
NATHANS ELMIRA CROSSE
EYE TUNA ABNEGATE OTS
MEFIRST EDAM NSC
NCOS TINEAR ZUCCHINI
YOHOHO SEAN FILTHIEST
EDISON EAST ANEW RTES
SINEWS SKEE YET TYCO
```

280
```
CAM PAULO IRONS THAW
JTU ENGEL MYNAH HOME
RIL DELIA ADELE EBON
LTCANIFF GERALDFORD
ATIENT FER TOASTY
PDT ELLIS STEIN
TALE SLAIN APORT JOB
DRY THESE ALIAS LIRA
RM LRONHUBBARD COMET
ASILICA RENO CHILLS
TRACK HAULS CHARO
ERENE EAST BELIEVED
RONO OZZIENELSON ERE
NNE CRIES AGATE ALBA
EG PAINS DRAMA ARLEN
SENSE MEADE PIT
ORNEA PIN SHRINKS
RHALDEMAN EAGLESCOUT
DOR ISERE ALIEN LINE
ENE ASTOR RONDO ERTE
RED NOELS SPASM SEAL
```

281
```
SCAB MEDIC CLAMP SHES
CAUL AXIAL HAGAR LOLA
URDU NAOMI ANITA OKAY
FORDHAMRAM SCOTTTWINS
FLAGONS ANTE TOLEDO
ERA EMCEE BILLY
COCOA ALATE CODED SPA
HORN BLINI ERRED ACID
INA BALANCEBEAM TRANE
CABBAGES DRAT DAMPEN
ALDEN IDIOM BELIE
APPALL TREN BELONGED
MOPSY LIKEAVIRGIN OUI
ELLE GONER EDIES EARL
SEE ARMED AGENT EXTOL
GLUED CHEEK MME
ESCAPE CHAT DEIRDRE
LIONSSHARE ANNEARCHER
OLAN OILER BEATS IAGO
PETE MEATY LEVEL SKID
EXIT EDSEL EMERY EASE
```

282
```
ANTSTEPS BESTSELLER
OBERTELEE INCONCLAVE
NITIATION CORRUGATES
ETS PHONOS SANG MINT
ILET RIM PAGEANTS
OPEDER TIRE EDEN
VADED DOTELL ORATORS
ENDS ROMANTICS MONET
RAY ROLE DEO BEATLE
TT ROOTINGOUT OLDHAT
HELIUM UAW PRESET
ELEBS GETINABIND FIN
TLAST RAT TELE LEOI
OAST IRRIGABLE DONNE
PSTEIN SERIAL FISCAL
ACTA SORT BOATELS
MACKERS TAC EARL
OLO DOCK TREATS SHAR
TERATIONS ATTHATTIME
OVELETTER FREELOADED
RESPASSES TENDERNESS
```

283
```
DISHRAG JARREAU VAMPS
INPEACE UNEATEN CROAK
DOORMEN STATURE REDRY
ONOR SORTED DAVE NEON
KEFIR AUDIO ETERNALLY
OER BONUS ENOL EER
MANTLE BIGTOP DEEDED
ELI EGRET RAIDERS
ALG AGED TEETHED TARE
TEHERAN WINSTON XEROX
INTUNE SODAPOP CREASE
EDICT SILICON CHAMBER
REEL BASSETT SUEY ITT
IRONIES MARAT ATE
SHADOW YUCCAS PUNNED
PAM LEAN PARTS OBI
EPIDERMIS NOTES EAVES
APSE SUCH DORSAL GERE
KITES LEONINE LECARRE
TEARS ENTICES STARDOM
ORDER TESTERS ASTAIRE
```

284
```
ASPIC AGER AMES PISA
LOUSE NASA CRIME APES
FULLLENGTH SCROLLLOCK
ALLELUIA RICHE FEASTS
ARE SARA IDIOT
CASTRO UPHILLLIE ETTU
HUMUS PRE SEALY BET
IRAN SEAL MEEK MART
VAL TWOLLLAMA REPULSE
ELL HANS ATOZ TALLER
LOOTS PRONE TOWEL
ALEAST OGLE TINE ESC
SETTEES WELLLIKED AHA
PATS DICE ELIS AGAR
EVE SOLES ADS SPUME
NERF STILLLIFE RIPEST
ETHAN EATS HIM
ANEMIA CACTI DELIVERS
NOCALLLIST SKILLLEVEL
EVIL LADES SIRE ARENA
WAGE IDEA OPEN RANDY
```

285
```
ASS IRATE ASIA EWER
IPA SICEM PEAR TRADE
LECTRICCURRENT HELGA
EACOAST AIM SHUCKER
YRONE STAPLER ASTI
ALE WII EARL NBC
AC LIQUIDDENSITY GEL
CO URSA LOIRE EDNA
ARP RANT BUNNY PLIES
INARETS DODOS FEASTS
ERASE SEXES POSIT
EATIT MACED CORONADO
XCON MOLAR BASK ENOS
PUN SERUM PANS COL
AR BLOODPRESSURE EMO
TV ROWS ELI MEL
ADAM ELEMENT TEJANO
PTONOW ATE IRONEDON
OUND HIGHTEMPERATURE
LROY IDEA TAINT ELSA
EER MORN SENDS STEM
```

286
```
TRIO ALPS STABS DFLAT
ROMP PELT MELEE ELIHU
ABBE PEAR ONCEREMOVED
YOURETRYINGTOREDUCEME
STEAL YOKE HAH IRK
TOO NETS ALEE SDS
STROPHE UTTERLY ICET
THERESNOPLACELIKENOME
RIM ORK ERAS NONSTOP
ANITA YAM TRUEGRIT
METALS PAT DMV NAILIN
RETAILER EAR CREDO
ARBITER AROO DOC NIT
THEFARCEWILLBEWITHYOU
REEF EPISODE STREAMS
AAS AUDI SPEW EEL
ALT PSU AFAR ADDIS
YOUCANTHANDLETHETOOTH
ONLINERADIO DUET PUPA
NEEDI INITS USTA ECRU
DRESS MYEYE PITS NEON
```

287

```
RAMS ABBIE FALLS PROM
ODIE CORNY AVAIL RIPE
CARROTCAKE KEYLIMEPIE
AMOEBIC HERE COSSET
    NEVER POI RAKES
DEBASE ELANDS RESECTS
EVADE PLAY SUPER SORE
FINE CREMES LES TAN
ATA ROOTBEERFLOAT TIS
TANKARD SCAT DEMOTE
ATCOST NSA STRAIN
LESSEN ASTI HASACOW
ARP DARKCHOCOLATE AHA
COL OER NOTATE SNAG
EDIT STRUT LIDS ANDRE
SETINTO MOROSE CLOYED
    PEARS AIR STRAW
STATOR POST ROMCOMS
LEMONTWIST OREOCOOKIE
ERIE EARLE POTOK NILE
DADS DROOD SWAPS EELS
```

288

```
ACCOLADE SPROUT BASIC
CLINICAL CAESAR OPERA
HAVETIMETOSPARE LEDON
ERIN DEVOUTLY REMIND
DECOR XRAY AVA AMOI
   EBONIES KLAY NERD
THISSECOND TOPDOG NEE
AESTHETES DEL INAPT
MANDATES CEDARS BLAST
PDT PST LATINO ERTE
ESTEE SHIPROUTE LAYER
RUHR EKEOUT XII RRS
SPAIN PRECIS MONOTONE
TEASE NOT SATANICAL
INS PUSHED SEMIWEEKLY
COPE STOW PALACES
EVEL ION MAID SLIDE
BECAME TAILORED ISON
ALINE THEPROMISEDLAND
GLADS DILLER CAROLINA
SALSA SPEEDS HINTEDAT
```

289

```
MAGNET NESS ICECUB
AFRESH EATIT SUDANE
CREASE GRATA TRUNCA
HOWLOWCANYOUGO DAR
    BITEINTO DRIPD
RACER DERN ALOUD
IDOLIZED PATERNALI
CALIPER MARM NASCEN
EMOTED PYLONS OYST
RES FORASEASON
BLAST ROTC SLAW CAN
RUT COLLATIONS ANT
OCULAR ERRAND ENGU
AIREDALE TACS SNOOP
DEATHVALLEY STALLO
    EASYA PATE
HOGARTH MEDICARE
ABATE SPLITTINGHAI
SOURNOTE BARON AUSS
TELETHON ALONE DREA
ASSESSED SWED SLAK
```

290

```
SCAR ADIA DASH ATWORK
COMEALONG ALAI LEHMAN
AKINGINNEWYORK LAINIE
DISTANT DAFFIER SMILE
SETA EST ULT ACES
   LES ETSY LIMELIGHT
VOICE ANKA ERSE CIAO
ITTAKESCOURAGE MAGDA
GOER LIES EMU ROLLED
OHM CAAN LOMB ARLISS
   HUT TOMAKEA MAY
ASPIRE SNOB REEL ODD
SOAPED INE ANNA EPEE
CUSPS FOOLOFYOURSELF
OTTO MIEN SRAS ECLAT
THECIRCUS ITOR BOA
ASTA MME DBA PACT
TRAMP NOTEPAD OTHELLO
TORPOR CHARLIECHAPLIN
OBTUSE TINO NICEGOING
POISED ONTV ONES DEES
```

291

```
BOOR SPATE ROMP PER
LOPE ARIEL ENOL ETA
THEPOWERSTHATBE THY
SCOUTS HOOCH ADENO
   TOED NOTE SERIF
STOOD NEA TORA ESCHE
NICKOFTIME RUMOR OV
ONEI ASSORT NOH LOPE
BEANED TUROW RIPENES
BANGLE NANA AORTA
YRS MOBETTERBLUES IA
   ROUEN IDBE AGEN
THWARTED CULTS CONDO
NOONE PEP PERISH DIF
UNU ISAID SALLYFORT
TELLER REEL YOO IWAS
   DIVOT CLIP STAR
SPINACH HIFIS TAMALE
AILED ORALEXAMINATIO
ALINE NORA ELAND OMN
BLESS GOTH LANGE MES
```

292

```
FARGO ARID BOOB NOSIR
BLURB XENOPHOBE ICOME
IMTOOOLDFORTHIS STAMP
ASTIN DEMO STEP OREO
   SSS REBA TAPPERS
SKIRTING DENSE COURSE
ANCESTORS STORMTOSSED
GOES ERECT SWOOSH
OXBOW ETAIL SST TOME
ONUS ELLIS OCTAVOS
TEXASHOLDEMTOURNAMENT
EVENSUP SPAWN NLER
LAST ATO SINUS CACTI
   CAROMS RUSES BOOS
WISDOMTOOTH PERCOLATE
ATEASE TOYED DIAMETER
REGNANT EARS FRI
IROC TACT ROTE AGEOF
EAVES FROMTOPTOBOTTOM
STIRS FORMYPART STINT
TEASE YWCA STET HASTO
```

293

```
LAOTSE CANAAN DEADEYE
OUTRAN ENABLE ILLEGAL
ORIENT REGULARFELLOWS
PASSTIME STATE VIENNA
   ARIAS THETA
JUSTFELLOFF LATTICES
ONTHE ILIAD PERSONA
BNAI AMPLIFIER SAINTS
BERN FORETELLER CASES
ECCE ROADS SAVE THOR
DER POLI ICUS LTS
SOLE AREA ROSES SIAM
ASSES HITCHARIDE IDIO
RASHER ETIOLATED TANK
CREATES ADEPT TUTEE
HYDRANTS SHOPKEEPERS
   DEEMS RAINS
ARLENE MOOED RATTRAPS
THETURNIPTRUCK IBERIA
MENCKEN UTOPIA CANNER
EATHERE POSERS ENDORA
```

294

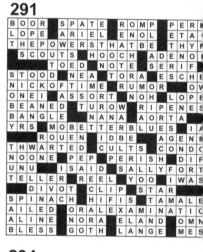

```
COMP RADAR SPARK POS
ARCH SCORE KORAN LAC
RICO VAUNT ITSME ASA
LOOTSPIGEONS REPTIL
ONYOU LUC EROSLOSE
   MISS CAMBODIA
AMBIANCE HAREM ESPIE
WOLFCHART TRAMSMONE
ELIA AMBUSH TIE ERL
DEPTHS BIAS NEARMIS
   ETAS GNU ETRE
DISRAELI NONO CANTO
IGLU ENE IGUANA AUD
POOHDREAMS ICEDLITE
STEREO TANYA DREYFUS
   USURIOUS COSI
ZEUSCANAL MIA NILE
ULSTERS PANSJUDGMEN
NANA INDIA INANE HAT
ITOR EARNS NEVIL ISE
SETS SPENT ERASE PER
```

295

```
AGEGAP FAKEID BANANAS
TRIUNE UGANDA ABALONE
FIRSTSTRINGER SATINON
PETITION USES CENT
   GOER BLT THESE
ADOBE OOF RIDE TAO
SECONDWIND THIRDWORLD
ICAN RANTS REKEY MELD
SALE ALTO TYNE MANES
LASAGNE SOON SHANTY
   FOURTHQUARTER
SAVANT ROUT ERASMUS
MOLAR DIVE EMIR IPAD
UFOS ACUTE EXACT SOLE
FIFTHWHEEL SIXTHSENSE
FAT URAL LAT TREAD
   STYNE TAU ANKA
SLOE RUHR ONTARGET
LYRICAL SEVENTHHEAVEN
EMANATE PRANCE LABILE
DELETED SEEDED OTELLO
```

296

```
WHOAMI ASAJOKE CRISP
AORTAS MATURES AIRMA
BLANKSTATEMENT LATOY
CANOE WHOOP TOILS KI
   GOSEE USA PRO DIT
ROUNDTRIPTICK ENRON
OAT OOPSI NEUT TENGI
AHAB SHEP MATHMAJO
RUNLOW OTIC ACRE TAN
   TRIPTYCH ROYCE CI
HOFSTRA SAD MARYKA
TWI SENAT SUBMERGE
EELS LAZY MOJO PONCH
STICKEMUP SOTS SLU
TONERS LEAH RINGSOF
GNASH BREAKFASTBUF
BOCA HAI KID KNEAD
EDA GETME FORGE NINJ
NEBULA ALIENABDUCTIO
JOINED GOCRAZY SIENN
INNIES ONESIZE ELDES
```

298

MAAS BARKS ARISE RANT
AFRO ELENA ROGET ODIE
LOOM ALIEN MOORE BAGS
TOMBSTONES AFTEREIGHT
STARLET SODS NINETY
EON CHELA STIRS
BLARE AHARD WAITE STP
LOCO BLINI KATEY DARE
ILE BLINDFOLDED ORSON
PAMPLONA NEED IRAQIS
ELATE FACED SNAFU
TITANS CAGE PLANTAIN
AMEND PANHANDLING TSO
TIRE LORNA ERODE SCAB
ANY SALTY ACUTE NEHRU
ONCLE GREGS PSA
EDITOR ALAS PRESAGE
MUSTBOUNCE SCREECHING
MALA STERN ALATE OMAR
ANEW SERIN RUMEN RETE
SETA EPODE YEARS ERST

299

SLIP ASDF OHSO RISKIT
LIVE SHEETROCK ATTACH
AMERICAFERRERA GAINER
PASSIONATE APLUS SIE
INTEL MAMIE CRANE
CPAS LOSER NEARS
BOSTONBAKEDBEANS SCUD
GOESPRO AWS ANOTE OSU
BRA TOTSY BRANDNAMES
AITCH RAITT SWEAT
FAQS CHICAGOHOPE ETSY
ACUTE AHYES MADAT
CHEAPDATES SYBIL ABS
TOE SENSE SAO STOICAL
SONS JOURNEYOFTHEMAGI
OSCAR RENTA MIST
NAFTA ASWAN TRALA
ACS NOKIA CHEESETACO
SCOTIA TRAINOFTHOUGHT
TRUANT ADVENTURE RIOT
YALIES TSAR ELON ENCS

(Leftmost grid)

R CAROB LEGAL ASAP
E ARUBA ITALO PARA
N NADIR THREW PLUS
ONABEER ROYALFLUSH
VELS ALES ARETHA
ASS PECOS HONES
TS CETUS MONDE RPM
E OREAD OATES SELA
STELLAADLER MEMOS
RATES RIAL LOLITA
IGEL CORER RODIN
YER HUGO SHRUGGED
AT TYPEWRITERS TSE
L SADIE ELATE BOAR
WEIRD ISENT LENIN
MENLO KNEAD EEL
ART SIAM ARTICLE
VERREED BIGBROTHER
E ISLAM LLANO TOAN
N EVITA ELMER LISI
S SPOON SEERS ERTE

300

SNARL DAIS READ TRAP
ACTII ESTO ARIE RILE
LARGERTHAN* PORTSUDAN
KAY SPELL LETSBEHEARD
LINE CEN EASY
SHEL TYPISTS STE OTO
TIVO RESINS CHESSCLUB
IRONIES LEONES TAEBO
LENGTH REMNANTS NOSE
LEN SEEN ASTI AMSO
SENTENCE CIRCLEOF
IOLE SUMS PIKA PAS
EPIC RETRACTS ENLIST
RICOH MONROE LOGONTO
ANKLEDEEP ROLLIN VEER
SKY RIV SHIPLAP EDDY
BOAT EES WILD
CAESARSALAD ULNAE WAV
CHAPLAINS *PRESERVERS
CORA MOYA RISK NEATO
LYNN ANAT YESI STREP

* = LIFE

THE MEGA SER

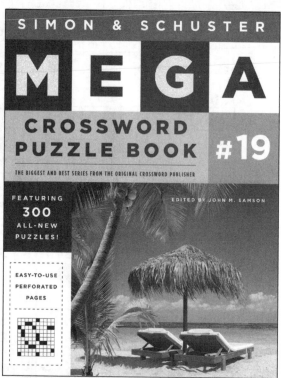

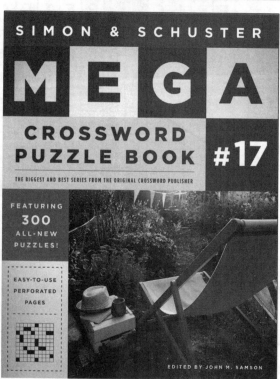